### MILLER

# GOVERNMENTAL
# GAAP
## PRACTICE
## MANUAL

A Guide to GASB 34

**LARRY P. BAILEY, Ph.D., CPA**

**ASPEN LAW & BUSINESS**
A Division of Aspen Publishers, Inc.
New York    Gaithersburg

This publication is designed to provide accurate and authoritative information in regard to the subject matter covered. It is sold with the understanding that the publisher is not engaged in rendering legal, accounting, or other professional services. If legal advice or other professional assistance is required, the services of a competent professional person should be sought.
—From a *Declaration of Principles* jointly adopted by a Committee of the American Bar Association and a Committee of Publishers and Associations

Copyright © 2002 by Aspen Law & Business
A Division of Aspen Publishers, Inc.
*A Wolters Kluwer Company*
*www.aspenpublishers.com*

All rights reserved. No part of this publication may be reproduced or transmitted in any form or by any means, electronic or mechanical, including photocopy, recording, or any information storage and retrieval system, without permission in writing from the publisher. Requests for permission to make copies of any part of this publication should be mailed to:

> Permissions
> Aspen Law & Business
> 1185 Avenue of the Americas
> New York, NY 10036
> (212) 597-0200

Printed in the United States of America

ISBN 0-73-552867-5

# About Aspen Law & Business

Aspen Law & Business is a leading publisher of authoritative treatises, practice manuals, services, and journals for attorneys, corporate and bank directors, accountants, auditors, environmental compliance professionals, financial and tax advisors, and other business professionals. Our mission is to provide practical solution-based how-to information keyed to the latest original pronouncements, as well as the latest legislative, judicial, and regulatory developments.

We offer publications in the areas of accounting and auditing; antitrust; banking and finance; bankruptcy; business and commercial law; construction law; corporate law; criminal law; environmental compliance; government and administrative law; health law; insurance law; intellectual property; international law; legal practice and litigation; matrimonial and family law; pensions, benefits, and labor; real estate law; securities; and taxation.

Other Aspen Law and Business products treating accounting and auditing issues include:

    Accounting Irregularities and Financial Fraud
    Audit Committees: A Guide for Directors, Management, and
       Consultants
    Construction Accounting Deskbook
    CPA's Guide to Developing Effective Business Plans
    CPA's Guide to Effective Engagement Letters
    CPA's Guide to e-Business
    European Accounting Guide
    Federal Government Contractor's Manual
    How to Manage Your Accounting Practice
    Medical Practice Management Handbook
    Miller Audit Procedures
    Miller Compilations and Reviews
    Miller GAAP Financial Statement Disclosures Manual
    Miller GAAP Guide
    Miller GAAP Practice Manual
    Miller GAAS Guide
    Miller GAAs Practice Manual
    Miller Governmental GAAP Guide
    Miller International Accounting Standards Guide
    Miller Local Government Audits
    Miller Not-for-Profit Organization Audits
    Miller Not-for-Profit Reporting
    Miller Single Audits
    Professional's Guide to Value Pricing

ASPEN LAW & BUSINESS
A Division of Aspen Publishers, Inc.
A Wolters Kluwer Company
*www.aspenpublishers.com*

## SUBSCRIPTION NOTICE

This Aspen Law & Business product is updated on a periodic basis with supplements to reflect important changes in the subject matter. If you purchased this product directly from Aspen Law & Business, we have already recorded your subscription for the update service.

If, however, you purchased this product from a bookstore and wish to receive future updates and revised or related volumes billed separately with a 30-day examination review, please contact our Customer Service Department at 1-800-234-1660, or send your name, company name (if applicable), address, and the title of the product to:

**ASPEN LAW & BUSINESS**
**A Division of Aspen Publishers, Inc.**
**7201 McKinney Circle**
**Frederick, MD 21704**

# Contents

*Preface*     vii
*About the Author*     xi

## Part I: Introduction

Chapter 1: Overview     1-1

## Part II: Governmental Funds

Chapter 2: The General Fund     2-1
Chapter 3: Special Revenue Funds     3-1
Chapter 4: Capital Projects Funds     4-1
Chapter 5: Debt Service Funds     5-1
Chapter 6: Permanent Funds     6-1

## Part III: Proprietary Funds

Chapter 7: Enterprise Funds     7-1
Chapter 8: Internal Service Funds     8-1

## Part IV: Fiduciary Funds

Chapter 9: Pension Trust Funds     9-1
Chapter 10: Private-Purpose Trust Funds     10-1
Chapter 11: Agency Funds     11-1

## Part V: The Consolidation and Conversion Process

Chapter 12: Developing Information for Fund Financial Statements     12-1
Chapter 13: Developing Information for Government-Wide Financial Statements     13-1

## Part VI: The Financial Statements and Related Disclosures

Chapter 14: Basic Financial Statements     14-1
Chapter 15: Management's Discussion and Analysis, Notes and Other Required Supplementary Information and Notes     15-1

*Appendix: GASB 34*     **APP-1**
*Accounting Resources on the Web*     **WEB-1**
*Index*     **IND-1**

# Preface

Over the next few years governmental accounting will change significantly because of the issuance of GASB Statement 34 (Basic Financial Statements—and Management's Discussion and Analysis—for State and Local Governments). In its desire to establish accounting and reporting standards that will make governmental financial reports more relevant to users, the GASB has chosen to establish two sets of financial statements. Fund financial statements focus on individually significant funds, while government-wide financial statements attempt to provide insight into the overall financial position and activities of the governmental reporting entity.

The dual presentation approach adopted by the GASB adds a significant degree of complexity to an already challenging financial reporting model. While GASB-34 introduces a variety of challenges to both those who prepare and read governmental financial statements, the major implementation problem facing those who prepare governmental financial statements is the development of an approach that seamlessly produces the two distinct financial statements.

Most governmental entities are expected to solve this problem by maintaining their accounting systems on a modified accrual basis, which will be the basis for preparing the fund financial statements, and then using a worksheet approach to convert from the modified accrual basis to the accrual basis in order to prepare government-wide financial statements. The purpose of this book is to demonstrate in a detailed manner how a governmental entity can implement the complex standards established by GASB-34 through a worksheet approach.

## The Structure of This Book

The fundamental issue for understanding how to implement the standards established by GASB-34 is the development of a clear understanding of the relationship between the modified accrual basis of accounting (as used at the fund financial statement level for governmental funds) and the accrual basis of accounting (as used at the government-wide financial statement level for governmental activities and business-type activities). The first chapter of the *Governmental GAAP Practice Manual: A Guide to GASB 34* provides a detailed analysis of the interrelationship of the two bases of accounting. There are innumerable transactions that governmental entities experience that first have to be recorded on the modified accrual basis (for presentation in the fund financial statements) and then converted to the accrual basis (for presentation in the government-wide financial statements). Included in Chapter 1 is a comprehensive checklist of transactions and events that typically will require a worksheet conversion entry. An understanding of these entries will provide a governmental accountant with a basis for analyzing unique and complex transactions and then converting their initial recording on the modified accrual basis to the accrual basis.

Starting in Chapter 2 is a comprehensive illustration that continues through the remaining chapters of the book. For governmental funds, a variety of transactions are illustrated and journalized in Chapters 2 through 6, which result in a year-end trial balance for each individual fund based on the modified accrual basis of accounting. In Chapter 12 these trial balances are used as the basis for developing the information needed to prepare the fund financial statements. Chapter 13 illustrates the worksheet methodology for converting the information related to governmental funds (modified accrual basis) to information that is needed for the governmental activities column of the government-wide financial statements (accrual basis of accounting). Throughout the book, transactions are labeled with ID numbers so readers can refer from finanical statements back to worksheet and journal entries.

A similar approach is used for proprietary funds (Chapters 7 and 8) and fiduciary funds (Chapters 9 through 11): Illustrative entries are developed for each of the funds and the resulting trial balances become the basis for preparing fund financial statements (Chapter 12) and the business-type activities column of the government-wide financial statements (Chapter 13).

In Chapter 14 the basic financial statements are prepared based on the information developed in Chapters 12 and 13. Finally, Chapter 15 uses the information developed in previous chapters to present management's discussion and analysis, notes, and other required supplementary information as mandated by GASB-34.

## How to Use This Text

This text is structured so that it may be used in a number of ways. For a thorough understanding of how to implement the standards established by GASB-34 the reader can read the entire text beginning with the first chapter and ending with the final chapter. This approach is helpful to governmental accountants who must decide how to modify their existing accounting procedures in order to comply with the standards established by GASB-34. The sequential reading of all of the chapters also serves as an excellent professional development course for new accounting professionals who have been hired by a governmental entity and need to be fully immersed in governmental financial reporting.

The text can also be read with an emphasis on a single chapter. Furthermore, a cluster of chapters can be read depending on the needs of the reader. Throughout the book, transactions are labeled with ID numbers so readers can refer from finanical statements back to worksheet and journal entries. For example, for a governmental accountant interested in understanding how the accounts related to Internal Service Funds are to be integrated into both the fund financial statements and the government-wide financial statements, a careful study of Chapter 8 ("Internal Service Funds") will provide a complete foundation for understanding this fund's role in governmental financial reporting. A reader concerned with understanding the basis for the conversion from the modified accrual basis to the accrual basis will find a thorough reading of Chapter 1 ("Overview") to be an excellent foundation for understanding the issue. A reader confused about how specific governmental funds are tweaked in order to create the governmental activities column of the government-wide financial statement will find in the section on governmental funds (Chapters 2 through 6) and Chapter 13 ("Developing Information for Government-Wide Financial Statements") a clear explanation of the interrelationship of accounts in governmental funds and amounts reported in the government-wide financial statements.

The emphasis of the *Governmental GAAP Practice Manual* is on the financial statement preparation process. That is, the specific accounting transactions are straightforward—and there is a strategy to avoid getting bogged down in GASB standards that are complex in and of themselves. Once the conversion process, as clearly described in this text, is understood, more complicated accounting and reporting issues can easily be handled by referring to the GASB standards discussed in this text's companion work, the *Miller Governmental GAAP Guide*. Using the two books, it is our desire to provide governmental accountants with a highly effective and efficient approach that can help them in their day-to-day responsibilities.

## Acknowledgments

The writing of this book was made possible by the efforts of a number of dedicated people. Mark Fried, Tony Powell, and many others at Aspen Publishers provided the much-needed editorial support that makes any professional book an accurate and readable work.

Although the individuals mentioned above played an important role in the preparation of the *Miller Governmental GAAP Practice Manual: A Guide to GASB 34*, any errors or omissions are the responsibility of the author. We will update this book in a timely manner as governmental accounting continues to evolve. If you have suggestions that may improve the quality of the material, please send them to the publisher.

*Larry P. Bailey*
Lawrenceville, New Jersey

## Dedication

Dedicated to Ashlie Lauren, Keli Kristen, Genevieve Alexis, Kaitlyn Sarah, and Dan Paige.

# About the Author

Larry P. Bailey is a Professor of Accounting at Rider University, in Lawrenceville, New Jersey, where he teaches auditing and financial accounting. Dr. Bailey earned a B.S. degree in business from Concord College and a Master's and Ph.D. from the University of Pennsylvania. He is a Certified Public Accountant (Virginia) and has worked in public accounting (Arthur Young & Company), in government (intern for the State of New Jersey), and as an educational consultant.

Professor Bailey is a member of the American Institute of Certified Public Accountants and the American Accounting Association. His research interests include auditing and governmental financial reporting, and he has published numerous articles in such journals as *Management Accountant, CPA Journal,* and *Governmental Accountants Journal.* He is also the author of various pamphlets and books, including the *Miller GAAS Guide* and the *Miller Governmental GAAP Guide,* as well as the *Miller Governmental GAAP Update Service.*

# PART I.
# INTRODUCTION

# CHAPTER 1
# OVERVIEW

## CONTENTS

| | |
|---|---|
| Introduction | 1-3 |
|     Implementation Issue | 1-5 |
|     Modified Accrual Basis of Accounting | 1-6 |
|     Accrual Basis of Accounting | 1-8 |
|     Fund Financial Statements | 1-8 |
|         Governmental Funds (Emphasizing Major Funds) | 1-8 |
|         Proprietary Funds | 1-8 |
|         Fiduciary Funds and Similar Component Units Funds | 1-9 |
|     Government-Wide Financial Statements | 1-9 |
|     Methodology Used to Convert from Modified Accrual to Accrual Basis | 1-11 |
| Worksheet Conversion Entry Checklist | 1-12 |
|     Long-Term Debt and Related Transactions | 1-12 |
|     Capital Assets and Related Transactions | 1-13 |
|     Noncurrent Monetary Assets | 1-13 |
|     Operating and Other Transactions | 1-13 |
|     Reclassification Entries | 1-13 |
| Analysis for Year Ended June 30, 20X1 | 1-14 |
|     Issuance of Debt | 1-14 |
|     Issuance of Long-Term Debt—Previous Year's Balances | 1-15 |
|     Debt Service Transactions | 1-15 |
|         Interest Paid During the Year | 1-16 |
|         Principal Repaid During the Year | 1-16 |
|         Amortization of Discount/Premium | 1-17 |
|     Deep-Discount Debt | 1-18 |
|     Zero-Coupon Bonds | 1-18 |
|     Discount Bonds (Less than 20%) | 1-19 |
|     Advance Refundings of Debt | 1-21 |
|     Early Extinguishments of Debt (Nonrefunding) | 1-22 |
|     Capital Expenditures—Current Period Transactions | 1-23 |

| | |
|---|---|
| Capital Assets—Previous Year's Balances | **1-24** |
| Capital Leases—Current Period Transactions | **1-25** |
| Capital Leases—Previous Year's Balances | **1-26** |
| Leasehold Improvements | **1-28** |
| Gains and Losses to Capital Asset Dispositions | **1-28** |
| Nonmonetary Exchanges (Trade-Ins) | **1-29** |
|    Exchange of Dissimilar Capital Assets | **1-29** |
|    Exchange of Similar Capital Assets with a Loss | **1-30** |
|    Exchange of Similar Capital Assets with a Gain (No Boot Involved) | **1-31** |
|    Exchange of Similar Capital Assets with a Gain (Boot Involved) | **1-32** |
| Donations of Capital Assets from Outside Parties | **1-33** |
| Donations of Capital Assets to Outside Parties | **1-34** |
| Gains and Losses Related to Capital Asset Dispositions | **1-34** |
| Involuntary Conversions of Capital Assets | **1-35** |
| Maintenance and Preservation Costs | **1-36** |
| Changes in Accounting Principles | **1-37** |
| Changes in Accounting Estimates | **1-39** |
| Long-Term Noninterest Bearing Notes Receivable | **1-40** |
| Lease Payments Receivable | **1-41** |
|    Sales-Type Lease | **1-41** |
|    Direct Financing Lease | **1-43** |
| Accrual of Expenses—Current Period Transactions | **1-44** |
| Accrual of Expenses—Previous Year's Balances | **1-45** |
| Accrual of Revenues—Current Period Transactions | **1-46** |
| Accrual of Revenues—Previous Year's Balances | **1-47** |
| Extraordinary Items | **1-48** |
| Special Items | **1-49** |
| Merging Internal Service Funds | **1-49** |
| Eliminations of Transfers and the Identification of Internal Balances | **1-52** |
|    Interfund Loans (Reciprocal Interfund Activity) | **1-52** |
|    Interfund Service Provided and Used (Reciprocal Interfund Activity) | **1-53** |
|    Interfund Transfers (Nonreciprocal Interfund Activity) | **1-53** |
|    Interfund Reimbursements (Nonreciprocal Interfund Activity) | **1-54** |
| Terminology and Format | **1-55** |

| | |
|---|---:|
| Governmental Funds Financial Statements | **1-55** |
| Government-Wide Financial Statements | **1-56** |
| Effective Dates | **1-58** |
| Comprehensive Illustration | **1-59** |
| Governmental Funds | **1-59** |
| Proprietary Funds | **1-60** |
| Fiduciary Funds | **1-61** |

## INTRODUCTION

In June 1999, GASB-34 (Basic Financial Statements—and Management's Discussion and Analysis—for State and Local Governments) was issued to address various deficiencies of governmental financial reporting. GASB-34 requires that a governmental entity present in its general purpose external financial statements both fund financial statements and government-wide financial statements.

The purpose of the new reporting model is, in part, to make current governmental financial reporting more consistent with the fundamental concepts adopted in GASB Concept Statement No. 1 (GASB: CS-1) (Objectives of Financial Reporting). GASB: CS-1 identifies the following primary user groups of governmental financial reports:

- Citizens of the governmental entity
- Direct representatives of the citizens (legislatures and oversight bodies)
- Investors, creditors, and others involved in the lending process

GASB: CS-1 identifies accountability as the paramount objective of financial reporting by state and local governments. Accountability is based on the transfer of responsibility for resources or actions from the citizenry to another party, such as the management of a governmental entity. Financial reporting should communicate adequate information to user groups to enable them to assess the performance of those parties empowered to act in the place of the citizenry.

The assessment of accountability is fulfilled in part when financial reporting enables user groups to determine to what extent current-period expenditures are financed by current-period revenues. This reporting objective is based on the concept of interperiod equity, which argues that the citizenry, as a group, that benefits from an expenditure should pay for the expenditure. For this reason, financial reporting should provide a basis for determining whether, during a budgetary period, (1) a surplus was created (a benefit to the future citizenry), (2) a deficit was incurred (a burden to the future citizenry), (3) a surplus from a previous budgetary period was used to finance current expenditures (a benefit to the current citizenry), (4) a deficit from a previous budgetary period was satisfied with current revenues (a burden to the current citizenry), or (5) current, and only current, expenditures were financed by using current and only current revenues (a balanced budget).

Financial reporting by a state or local government should provide a basis for user groups to determine whether (1) the governmental entity obtained and used resources consistent with the legally adopted budget and (2) finance-related legal and contractual requirements have been met. A budget reflects a myriad of public policies adopted by a legislative body and generally has the force of law as its basis for authority. The legally adopted budget is an important document in establishing and assessing the accountability of those responsible for the management of a governmental entity. While finance-related legal and contractual requirements are not as fundamental as the legally adopted budget, they nonetheless provide a basis for accountability, and financial reporting should demonstrate that this accountability either has or has not been achieved with respect to the requirements.

The basis of accounting and measurement focus are fundamental to providing a financial reporting model that can help user groups to determine whether a governmental entity has demonstrated fiscal accountability. Currently, fund financial statements are based on modified accrual accounting concepts and the flow of current financial resources. Generally, current governmental accounting standards interpret the flow of current financial resources applied on a modified accrual basis to mean that revenues, and the resulting assets, are accrued at the end of the year only if the revenues are earned and the receivables are expected to be collected in time to pay for liabilities in existence at the end of the period. Expenditures and the related liabilities are accrued when they are expected to be paid out of revenues recognized during the current period.

The standards established by GASB-34 apply to external financial reports prepared by state and local governments. The standards focus on general-purpose governments that are prepared by states, cities, counties, towns, and villages.

> ▶ **NEW STANDARD:** Public colleges and universities must follow the guidance established by GASB-35 (Basic Financial Statements—and Management's Discussion and Analysis—for Public Colleges and Universities). GASB-35 requires that, in general, public colleges and universities use the same accounting and financial reporting standards that will be used by all other governmental entities once the standards established by GASB-34 become effective. Specifically, public colleges and universities that issue separate financial reports should observe the guidance established in GASB-34 for special-purpose governmental entities (paragraphs 134–138).

The *Miller Governmental GAAP Practice Manual* is created in a sequential fashion so that the reader can start from Chapter 2 and follow how a typical governmental entity can create its financial statements based on the requirements of GASB-34. However, readers can also focus on a particular topic, read that material, and then follow the remaining chapters that result in the preparation of the financial statements. For example, if a reader is interested in how the information accounted for in Internal Service Funds is presented in a governmental entity's financial statements, he or she can start with Chapter 8 (Internal Service Funds), then go to Chapter 12 (Developing Information for Fund Financial Statements), then proceed to Chapter 13 (Developing Information for Government-Wide Financial Statements), and finally end with a reading of Chapter 14 (Basic Financial Statements).

## Implementation Issue

The major implementation problem facing those who prepare governmental financial statements based on the standards established by GASB-34 is the development of system procedures that facilitate the presentation of the two levels of financial statements. Most governmental entities are expected to solve this problem by maintaining their accounting systems on a modified accrual basis or (budgetary/statutory basis), which will be the basis for preparing the fund financial statements, and then use a worksheet approach to convert from the modified accrual basis to the accrual basis in order to prepare the government-wide financial statements. The purpose of this book is to demonstrate in a detailed manner how a governmental entity can implement the standards established by GASB-34.

One of the unique aspects of GASB-34 was the creation of two levels of reporting: fund financial statements and government-wide financial statements. Fund-based financial statements must be included in a governmental entity's financial report in order to demonstrate that restrictions imposed by statutes, regulations, or contracts have been followed. These financial statements have a short-term emphasis and generally measure and account for cash and "other assets that can easily be converted to cash." However, unlike current governmental financial reporting standards, GASB-34 requires that fund reporting be restricted to a governmental entity's General Fund, *major funds* (individual presentation), and *nonmajor funds* (aggregated presentation). Fund financial statements are based on a flow of current financial resources applied on a modified accrual basis.

Government-wide financial statements were established by GASB-34 in order to provide a basis for determining (1) the extent to which current services provided by an entity were financed with current revenues and (2) the degree to which a governmental entity's financial position has changed during the fiscal year. In order to achieve these objectives, government-wide financial statements include a statement of net assets and a statement of activities. Government-wide financial statements are based on a flow of all economic resources applied on the accrual basis of accounting. The flow of economic resources refers to all assets available to the governmental unit for the purpose of providing goods and services to the public. When the flow of economic resources and the accrual basis of accounting are combined, they provide the foundation for generally accepted accounting principles used by business enterprises in that essentially all assets and liabilities, both current and long-term, are reported in the government-wide financial statements.

## Modified Accrual Basis of Accounting

The modified accrual basis of accounting uses both cash and accrual concepts. Revenues are recorded when they are both measurable and available to finance current expenditures of the government. Revenue is considered available when it is collectible during the current period, or the actual collection will occur either during the current period or after the end of the period but in time to pay current year expenditures and liabilities.

Governmental funds generally record a liability when it is expected that the liability will be paid from revenues recognized during the current period. For many years accountants have criticized the definitions of governmental revenues/assets and expenditures/liabilities because the definitions are based on circular reasoning. That is, revenue can only be accrued at the end of a period if the revenue will be collected in time to pay accrued liabilities; however, liabilities can be accrued at year-end only when they are paid from revenues recognized during the current period. Those definitions do very little to facilitate the understanding of when accruals should be recognized in fund financial statements. These definitions have been interpreted by many practitioners to mean that accruals can be made only when the related cash flow is collected or paid "shortly" after the end of the fiscal accounting period.

■ **CONTINUING STANDARD:** GASBI-6 was issued in March 2000 in order to address some of these issues. The GASB describes the Interpretation as exactly that—an interpretation. The Interpretation is not an attempt to change the standards that are the basis for the preparation of fund financial statements, but rather its purpose is "to improve the comparability, consistency and objectivity of financial reporting in governmental fund financial statements by providing a common, internally consistent interpretation of standards affecting the recognition of certain fund liability and expenditures, in areas where practice differences have occurred or could occur."

The GASBI-6 Interpretation addresses what is meant by "shortly" in the context of the accrual of liabilities related to future expenditures. Liabilities that will be paid with current financial resources should be presented as a fund liability, while liabilities that have been incurred but that will not be paid with current financial resources should be considered "general long-term liabilities." General long-term liabilities are presented in the government-wide financial statements (statement of net assets) and not a fund statement.

The basic guidance for determining when a governmental fund should accrue an expenditure/liability is found in NCGA-1, paragraph 70, which states that "most expenditures and transfers out are measurable and should be recorded when the related liability is incurred." GASBI-6 expands on this general guidance by noting the following (paragraph 12):

> Governmental fund liabilities and expenditures that should be accrued include liabilities that, once incurred, normally are paid in a timely manner and in full from current financial resources—for example, salaries, professional services, supplies, utilities, and travel.

These transactions give rise to fund liabilities that are considered mature liabilities because they are "normally due and payable in full when incurred." However, GASBI-6 points out that there are several significant exceptions to this general guidance established in NCGA-1. Specifically, NCGA-1 states that "unmatured long-term indebtedness" should not be reported as a fund liability (except for debts that are related to proprietary and trust funds). Unmatured long-term indebtedness is defined as "the portion of general long-term indebtedness that is not yet due for payment," and it includes debts such as the following (paragraphs 9, 10, and 11):

1. Formal debt agreements such as bonds and notes
2. Liabilities not "normally expected to be liquidated with expendable available financial resources"
3. Other commitments that are not current liabilities properly recorded in governmental funds

GASBI-6 points out that the three specified categories listed above are exceptions to the general rule that a liability is recorded as a fund liability and "in the absence of an explicit requirement to do otherwise, a government should accrue a governmental fund liability and expenditure in the period in which the government incurs the liability" (paragraph 12).

■ **CONTINUING STANDARD:** The basis of accounting used to prepare financial statements for governmental funds

(General Fund, Special Revenue Funds, Capital Projects Funds, Debt Service Funds, and Permanent Funds) continues to be the modified accrual basis of accounting as defined in NCGA-1 (GASB-34, par. 79).

## Accrual Basis of Accounting

The accrual basis of accounting is used by commercial enterprises to prepare their financial statements. Generally, under this accounting basis, revenues are recognized when earned and expenses are recorded when incurred for activities related to exchange and exchange-like activities. In addition, long-lived assets (such as buildings and equipment) are capitalized and depreciated over their estimated economic lives, and long-term debt is reported as an obligation of the entity.

Unlike commercial enterprises, much of the revenue received by governments is not based on an exchange or exchange-like transaction (the selling of a product or service and receiving something of approximate equal value), but rather arises from the entity's taxing powers or as grants from other governmental entities or individuals (nonexchange transactions). Nonexchange transactions are accounted for based on the standards established by GASB-33 (Accounting and Financial Reporting for Nonexchange Transactions).

The accrual basis of accounting is used to prepare government-wide financial statements.

## Fund Financial Statements

GASB-34 identifies the following as fund types that are to be used to record a governmental entity's activities during an accounting period (GASB-34, par. 63).

*Governmental Funds (Emphasizing Major Funds)*

- General Fund
- Special Revenue Funds
- Capital Projects Funds
- Debt Service Funds
- Permanent Funds

*Proprietary Funds*

- Enterprise Funds (emphasizing major funds)
- Internal Service Funds

*Fiduciary Funds and Similar Component Units Funds*

- Pension (and other employee benefit) Trust Funds
- Investment Trust Funds
- Private-Purpose Trust Funds
- Agency Funds

> ▶ **NEW STANDARD:** Two new fund types, namely Permanent Fund and Private-Purpose Trust Funds, are defined by GASB-34. Permanent Funds are to be used to report resources that are legally restricted to the extent that only earnings and no principal (corpus) may be used for purposes that support the reporting government's programs (i.e., for the benefit of the public). For example, a fund established to maintain a city park in perpetuity but only through the earnings of the fund is an example of a Permanent Fund. Permanent Funds are similar to the no longer used Nonexpendable Trust Funds. Private-Purpose Trust Funds are to be used to account for trust arrangements under which principal and income benefit individuals, private organizations, and other governments and that are not accounted for in other fiduciary funds (Pension Trust Funds, Investment Trust Funds, and Agency Funds) (GASB-34, par. 65).

> ▶ **NEW STANDARD:** A significant change in the focus of reporting governmental funds and proprietary funds is that major funds are reported for these funds; however, combined financial statements for fund types do not have to be presented.

## Government-Wide Financial Statements

The focus of government-wide financial statements is on the overall financial position and activities of the government as a whole. These financial statements are constructed around the concept of a primary government as defined by GASB-14 (The Financial Reporting Entity) and therefore encompass the primary government and its component units except for fiduciary funds of the primary government and component units that are fiduciary in nature. Financial statements of fiduciary funds are not presented in the government-wide financial statements but are included in the fund financial statements (GASB-34, par. 13).

GASB-34 requires that government-wide financial statements be formatted following these guidelines (GASB-34, pars. 14 and 15):

- Separate rows and columns should be used to distinguish between the primary government's governmental activities and business-like activities

- A total column should be used for the primary government
- Separate rows and columns should distinguish between the total primary government (governmental activities plus business-like activities) and its discretely presented component units
- A total column may be used for the reporting entity (primary government and discretely presented component units), but this is optional
- A total column may be used for prior-year information, but this is optional

Governmental activities should be accounted for and reported based on all applicable GASB pronouncements, NCGA pronouncements, and the following pronouncements issued on or before November 30, 1989, unless they conflict with GASB or NCGA pronouncements (GASB-34, par. 17):

- Financial Accounting Standards Board (FASB) Statements and Interpretations
- Accounting Principles Board (APB) Opinions
- Accounting Research Bulletins (ARBs) of the Committee on Accounting Procedure

> ▶ **NEW STANDARD:** In the past, pronouncements of the FASB, the APB, and the Committee on Accounting Procedures have not, for the most part, been applied to information presented in governmental funds. The GASB decided that government-wide financial statements must be prepared by applying these pronouncements issued on or before November 30, 1989 (unless they conflict with GASB pronouncements) on a retroactive basis (with exceptions discussed in paragraph 146 of GASB-34). Pronouncements issued by the FASB after November 30, 1989 do not have to be followed in the preparation of financial statements for governmental activities in the government-wide financial statements.

Business-type activities must follow either Alternative 1 or Alternative 2 as described in GASB-20 (Accounting and Financial Reporting for Proprietary Funds and Other Governmental Entities that Use Proprietary Fund Accounting). Under Alternative 1, governmental entities using proprietary fund accounting must follow (1) all GASB pronouncements and (2) FASB Statements and Interpretations, APB Opinions, and Accounting Research Bulletins (ARBs) issued on or before November 30, 1989 except those that conflict with a GASB pronouncement. Under Alternative 2, governmental entities using proprietary fund accounting must follow (1) all GASB pronouncements and (2) all FASB Statements and Interpretations, APB Opinions, and ARBs no matter when issued except those that conflict with a GASB pronouncement. Unlike Alternative 1, Alternative 2 has no cutoff date for determining the applicability of FASB pronouncements.

## Methodology Used to Convert from Modified Accrual to Accrual Basis

The remainder of the chapters of this book are based on a comprehensive example that begins at the transaction point and ends with the preparation of the basic financial statements and selected disclosures. For governmental funds, a variety of transactions are illustrated and journalized in Chapters 2 through 6, which results in a year-end trial balance for each individual fund based on the modified accrual basis of accounting.

In Chapter 12, these trial balances are used as the basis for developing the information needed to prepare the fund financial statements.

> **OBSERVATION:** The transactions illustrated in these chapters are routine. There is no attempt to illustrate every type of transaction that could be processed through a particular fund. The emphasis throughout this book is the conversion process and not a comprehensive analysis of GASB pronouncements. A discussion of all GASB pronouncements can be found in the *Miller Governmental GAAP Guide*.

Chapter 13 illustrates a worksheet methodology for converting the information related to governmental funds (modified accrual basis) to information that is needed for the governmental activities column of the government-wide financial statements (accrual basis of accounting).

A similar approach is used for proprietary funds (Chapters 7 and 8) and fiduciary funds (Chapters 9 through 11) in that illustrative entries are developed for each of the funds and the resulting trial balances become the basis for preparing fund financial statements (Chapter 12) and the business-type activities column of the government-wide financial statements (Chapter 13). However, the specific process for developing the information for proprietary funds and fiduciary funds is somewhat different from that used for governmental funds. Proprietary funds are reported on an accrual basis, thus there is no need to develop a worksheet approach that converts from the modified accrual to the accrual basis of accounting, but there is a need to merge certain balances related to Internal Service Funds in order to present business-type activities in a manner required by GASB-34. Also, fiduciary fund information is presented only in the fund financial statements. GASB-34 prohibits the presentation of the information in the government-wide financial statements.

In Chapter 14, the basic financial statements as required by GASB-34 are prepared based on the information created in Chapters 12 and 13. Finally, Chapter 15, using the information illustrated in previous chapters, presents management's discussion and analysis, notes, and other required supplementary information mandated by GASB-34. Chapter 15 does not illustrate all of the disclosures required by governmental GAAP, just those discussed in GASB-34.

## WORKSHEET CONVERSION ENTRY CHECKLIST

Perhaps the major implementation problem facing those who prepare governmental financial statements based on the standards established by GASB-34 is the development of procedures that facilitate the presentation of the two levels of financial statements. As noted earlier, most governmental entities are expected to solve this problem by maintaining their accounting systems on a modified accrual basis or budgetary/statutory basis, which will be the basis for preparing the fund financial statements, and then using a worksheet approach to convert from the modified accrual basis to the accrual basis in order to prepare the government-wide financial statements. That approach is illustrated throughout this book.

There are innumerable transactions that a governmental entity could experience that would first have to be recorded on the modified accrual basis (for presentation in the fund financial statements) and then converted to the accrual basis (for presentation in the governmental activities column of the government-wide financial statements). The following checklist has been developed to identify and illustrate typical transactions that will require a worksheet conversion entry. An understanding of these entries will provide a governmental accountant with the basis to analyze transactions that are uncommon and properly convert their initial recording on the modified accrual basis to the accrual basis.

The components of the worksheet conversion entry checklist are as follows.

### Long-Term Debt and Related Transactions

- ❏ Issuance of long-term debt—current transactions
- ❏ Issuance of long-term debt—previous year's balances
- ❏ Debt service transactions
- ❏ Deep discount debt
- ❏ Zero-coupon bonds
- ❏ Discount bonds (less than 20%)
- ❏ Advance refundings of debt
- ❏ Early extinguishments of debt (nonrefunding)

## Capital Assets and Related Transactions

- Capital expenditures—current period transactions
- Capital assets—previous year's balances
- Capital leases—current period transactions
- Capital leases—previous year's balances
- Leasehold improvements
- Gains/losses related to capital asset dispositions
- Nonmonetary exchanges (trade-ins)
- Donations of capital assets from outside parties (nonexchange transaction)
- Donations of capital asset to outside parties
- Gains and losses related to capital asset dispositions
- Involuntary conversions of capital assets
- Maintenance and preservation costs
- Changes in accounting principles
- Changes in accounting estimates

## Noncurrent Monetary Assets

- Long-term non-interest-bearing notes receivable
- Lease payments receivable

## Operating and Other Transactions

- Accrual of expenses—current period transactions
- Accrual of expenses—previous year's balances
- Accrual of revenues—current period transactions
- Accrual of revenues—previous year's balances
- Extraordinary items
- Special items

## Reclassification Entries

- Merging Internal Service Funds
- Eliminations of transfers and the identification of internal balances
- Terminology and format

> **OBSERVATION:** The emphasis of the discussion in this chapter is on governmental funds (General Fund, Special Revenue Funds,

Capital Projects Funds, Debt Service Funds, and Permanent Funds) rather than proprietary funds because the presentation basis for proprietary funds is accrual accounting. Also, fiduciary funds are not discussed in this chapter, because these funds are presented in the fund financial statements but are not incorporated into the government-wide financial statements.

## ANALYSIS OF YEAR ENDED JUNE 30, 20X1

The following analysis assumes, unless otherwise stated, that the worksheet conversion entry is made for the year ended June 30, 20X1.

### Issuance of Debt

Generally, liabilities that do not consume current financial resources of a governmental fund are not reported at the fund financial statement level. For example, the proceeds from the issuance of debt are recorded as an other financing source in a governmental fund rather than as a fund liability. On the other hand, in the government-wide financial statements, the debt must be presented as a liability related to governmental activities. To illustrate the conversion process required to convert from the modified accrual basis of accounting to the accrual basis, assume that 5%, 10-year general obligation bonds with a maturity value of $1,000,000 are sold on September 1, 20X0 at a price ($975,878) to yield 6%. The following entry is made to record the issuance of the debt in a governmental fund (modified accrual basis):

| | | |
|---|---:|---:|
| Cash | 957,878 | |
| Discount on long-term debt issued (other uses of financial resources) | 42,122 | |
| Long-term debt issued (other sources of financial resources) | | 1,000,000 |

In the governmental fund financial statements, the issuance of the debt is presented on the statement of revenues, expenditures, and changes in fund balances as an other financing source, but the amount is not presented in the balance sheet at the fund statement level. In order to convert the transaction from a modified accrual basis to an accrual basis, the following conversion worksheet entry is made at the end of the year:

| | | |
|---|---:|---:|
| Long-term debt issued (other sources of financial resources) | 1,000,000 | |
| Discount on long-term debt issued (other uses of financial resources) | | 42,122 |
| Bonds payable | | 957,878 |

**OBSERVATION:** The above entry records the net proceeds as bonds payable. It is also acceptable to create a separate discount account (contra liability account) and record the maturity value of the debt in a separate account for the government-wide financial statements.

The effect of the worksheet entry is to report the transaction as a long-term general obligation in the government-wide financial statements (governmental activities column).

## Issuance of Long-Term Debt—Previous Year's Balances

In addition to current year debt transactions, the previous year's balance of long-term debt outstanding must be considered. These amounts do not appear on the current year-end trial balance for governmental funds, but they must appear on the government-wide financial statements because they are obligations of the governmental entity. The worksheet conversion entry reduces the beginning "net asset" balance. For example, assume that a governmental entity had bonds payable outstanding at the end of the previous year of $45,000,000 (originally issued at par). The following worksheet entry is made to establish the beginning balances related to the governmental activities column in the statement of net assets:

| | | |
|---|---|---|
| Net assets | 45,500,000 | |
|     Bonds payable | | 45,000,000 |

**NOTE:** The beginning balance of the "Net Assets" account is based on the beginning balance for the governmental entity's "Fund Balance" account. The Fund Balance amount is adjusted through the worksheet entries in order to convert it from a modified accrual amount (Fund Balance) to an accrual amount (Net Assets).

It should be noted that the worksheet entry must be based on the amortized balance of the debt. That is, if the bonds were issued at a discount or premium, an amortization schedule must be made in order to determine the amount of the book value of the debt outstanding as of the end of the previous year.

## Debt Service Transactions

NCGA-1 points out that most expenditures are measurable and should be recorded when the related fund liability is incurred. One of several exceptions to this generalization is the treatment of interest and principal payments for general long-term indebtedness. Interest and principal on long-term debt are not recorded as expenditures as they accrue, but rather when they become due and payable. However, for the government-wide financial statements, debt service payments are reflected as reductions to outstanding debt (principal repayments) and interest expense. Debt service transactions that should be considered include the following:

- Interest paid during the year
- Principal repaid during the year
- Amortization of discount/premium

*Interest Paid During the Year*

The amount of interest expenditure recorded during the year will seldom be equal to the accrual-based interest expense that must be reflected in the government-wide financial statements. For example, assume that a governmental entity had the following general obligation bonds outstanding as of the end of the previous year and issued $7,000,000 on April 1, 20X1. All of the bonds were originally issued at par:

| Maturing Value | Stated Interest Rate | Interest Payment Date | Interest Expenditures (Modified Accrual) | Interest Expense (Accrual) |
|---|---|---|---|---|
| $20,000,000 | 5% | March 1 | $1,000,000 | $1,000,000 |
| 15,000,000 | 6% | August 1 | 900,000 | 900,000 |
| 10,000,000 | 5.5% | December 1 | 550,000 | 550,000 |
| 7,000,000 | 5% | April 1 | -0- | 87,500 |
| Total | | | $2,450,000 | $2,537,500 |

In order to record the additional interest expense for the year ended June 30, 20X1, the following worksheet entry is made:

Interest expense/expenditure ($2,537,500 –
$2,450,000)                                              87,500
    Interest payable                                                87,500

*Principal Repaid During the Year*

If long-term debt has been repaid during the year, the principal repayment is recorded as an expenditure in the fund financial statements, and a worksheet conversion entry is necessary to convert the principal payment from an expenditure to a reduction of the governmental entity's general debt. For example, if a $10,000,000 general obligation bonds matures during the year, its retirement is recorded in a governmental fund as follows:

| | | |
|---|---|---|
| Expenditures—principal | 10,000,000 | |
| Cash | | 10,000,000 |

In order to convert this transaction to an accrual basis, the following worksheet conversion entry is made:

| | | |
|---|---|---|
| Bonds payable | 10,000,0000 | |
| Expenditures—principal | | 10,000,000 |

*Amortization of Discount/Premium*

When a governmental entity issues debt at a discount or premium, the discount/premium is ignored in recording interest expenditures in a governmental fund; however, the discount/premium must be amortized annually in order to report interest on an accrual basis in the government-wide financial statements. For example, the following bond amortization schedule would be prepared for the $1,000,000 bonds that were issued at a discount in the previous section (Issuance of Debt):

| Date | Cash | 6% Interest | Amortization | Book Value |
|---|---|---|---|---|
| 9/1/X0 | | | | $957,878 |
| 9/1/X1 | $50,000 | $ 57,473 | $7,473 | $965,351 |
| 9/1/X2 | 50,000 | 57,921 | 7,921 | 973,272 |
| 9/1/X3 | 50,000 | 58,396 | 8,396 | 981,668 |
| 9/1/X4 | 50,000 | 58,900 | 8,900 | 990,568 |
| 9/1/X5 | 50,000 | 59,432 | 9,432 | 1,000,000 |
| Total | | $292,122 | $42,122 | |

Based on the above amortization schedule, no interest would be recorded during the fiscal year ended June 30, 20X1. However, in order to convert the transaction to an accrual basis, the following worksheet entry is made:

| | | |
|---|---|---|
| Interest expense/expenditure ($57,473 × 10/12) | 47,894 | |
| Interest payable ($50,000 × 10/12) | | 41,667 |
| Bonds payable | | 6,227 |

The credit to the account "Bonds Payable" represents the amortization of the discount for the partial year. If a separate discount is created, the credit would be to the discount account.

## Deep-Discount Debt

Governmental activities should be accounted for and reported based on all applicable GASB pronouncements, NCGA pronouncements, and the following pronouncements issued on or before November 30, 1989, unless they conflict with GASB or NCGA pronouncements (GASB-34, par. 17):

- Financial Accounting Standards Board (FASB) Statements and Interpretations
- Accounting Principles Board (APB) Opinions
- Accounting Research Bulletins (ARBs) of the Committee on Accounting Procedure

Generally, a governmental entity must apply the FASBs, APBs, and ARBs on a retroactive basis; however, the GASB did provide exceptions to this requirement. One of those exceptions applies to debt discounts and premiums. The standards established by APB Opinion 12 (Omnibus Opinion—1967) and APB Opinion 27 (Interest on Receivables and Payables) require that discounts and premiums related to debt (and receivables) be amortized as part of interest expense (and income). The GASB states that the standards established by these two APB Opinions may be applied on a prospective basis; that is, the standards apply only to debt issuances that occur on or after the effective date of GASB-34 (GASB-34, par. 146).

However, the discount/premium amortization exception does not apply to deep-discount or zero-coupon debt. GASB-34 defines zero-coupon debt as debt that is "originally sold at far below par value and pays no interest until it matures," and deep-discount debt is defined as "debt that is sold at a discount of 20 percent or more from its face or par value at the time it is issued."

## Zero-Coupon Bonds

To illustrate discount/premium amoritization exception, assume that a governmental entity issued zero-coupon bonds three years ago (6/30/W7) that have a maturity value of $1,000,000. The bonds were sold at a yield of 6% and the following amortization schedule applies to the debt:

| Date | Cash | 6% Interest | Amortization | Book Value |
|---|---|---|---|---|
| 6/30/W7 | | | | $747,260 |
| 6/30/W8 | 0 | $44,836 | $44,836 | 792,096 |
| 6/30/W9 | 0 | 47,526 | 47,526 | 839,621 |

| Date | Cash | 6%<br>Interest | Amortization | Book Value |
|------|------|----------------|--------------|------------|
| 6/30/X0 | 0 | 50,377 | 50,377 | 889,999 |
| 6/30/X1 | 0 | 53,400 | 53,400 | 943,399 |
| 6/30/X2 | 0 | 56,601 | 56,601 | 1,000,000 |
|         |   | $252,740 | $252,740 |            |

As of the year ended June 30, 20X1, there has only been one entry in the governmental fund, and that was for the receipt of the proceeds. However, in order to convert the information from a modified accrual to an accrual basis, the following worksheet conversion entry is made as of June 30, 20X1:

| | | |
|---|---|---|
| Interest expense/expenditure (see amortization schedule) | 53,400 | |
| Net assets | 889,999 | |
| Bonds payable | | 943,399 |

When the bonds mature on June 30, 20X2, the governmental fund will report an expenditure of $1,000,000 ($747,260 principal payment + $252,740 interest). In order to convert that transaction from a modified accrual to an accrual basis, the following worksheet conversion entry is made as of June 30, 20X2:

| | | |
|---|---|---|
| Interest expense/expenditure (see amortization schedule) | 56,601 | |
| Net assets | 943,399 | |
| Bonds payable | | 1,000,000 |
| | | |
| Bonds payable | 1,000,000 | |
| Interest expense/expenditure | | 252,740 |
| Expenditures—principal | | 747,260 |

**NOTE:** The first worksheet conversion entry accrues interest for the year and the second entry reduces the debt to zero. These entries are shown separately for illustrative purposes, but they may be combined in practice.

## Discount Bonds (Less than 20%)

As noted earlier, for bonds with a discount of less than 20% that were issued prior to the governmental entity's adoption of GASB-34, there is no requirement to take the discount amortization into consideration to determine interest expense on the government-wide financial statements. (However, amortization will apply to all bonds issued at a discount after the adoption of GASB-34.) For example, assume that the example described earlier is changed to assume that the bonds were issued on June 30, 20W7 (before the adoption of GASB-34 by the entity). The amortization schedule for the debt is reproduced as follows with the new dates:

| Date | 6% Cash | Interest | Amortization | Book Value |
|---|---|---|---|---|
| 6/30/W7 | | | | $957,878 |
| 6/30/W8 | $50,000 | $ 57,473 | $7,473 | 965,351 |
| 6/30/W9 | 50,000 | 57,921 | 7,921 | 973,272 |
| 6/30/X0 | 50,000 | 58,396 | 8,396 | 981,668 |
| 6/30/X1 | 50,000 | 58,900 | 8,900 | 990,568 |
| 6/30/X2 | 50,000 | 59,432 | 9,432 | 1,000,000 |
| Total | | $292,122 | $42,122 | |

There is no requirement to amortize the discount, because it amounts to only 4.2% ($42,122/$1,000,000). If the assumption continues that GASB-34 standards had not been adopted in 20W7 when the bonds were issued, the amount of interest expenditure recorded in the governmental fund for the year ended June 30, 20X1 would be $50,000. There would be no requirement to reflect the discount amortization (interest expense) on the government-wide financial statements; however, a worksheet conversion entry would be made as of June 30, 20X1 to record the original proceeds of the debt as follows:

| | | |
|---|---|---|
| Net assets | 957,878 | |
|   Bonds payable | | 957,878 |

**NOTE:** The amount of the debt presented on the government-wide financial statements does not change from the initial issuance proceeds because the discount is not amortized.

When the debt is retired on 6/30/X2, expenditures of $1,050,000 ($1,000,000 principal payment + $50,000 interest) will be recorded in the appropriate governmental fund and the following worksheet conversion entries will be made to convert the information from a modified accrual basis to an accrual basis:

| | | |
|---|---|---|
| Net assets | 957,878 | |
|   Bonds payable | | 957,878 |
| Bonds payable | 957,878 | |
| Interest expense/expenditure (the total amount of discount) | 42,122 | |
|   Expenditures—principal | | 1,000,000 |

The amount of interest expense reflected on the government-wide financial statements must include the discount because it was not accrued for in previous years.

> **NOTE:** If the amount of interest expense is materially distorted in the year the bonds are retired, the nature of the distortion should be explained in a note to the financial statements.

## Advance Refundings of Debt

An advance refunding of debt occurs when a governmental entity issues new debt and uses the proceeds to retire currently existing debt. In the fund financial statements, the advance refunding is reported as an other financing source/use transaction; however, in the government-wide financial statements, the transaction must be converted to an accrual-based presentation. That is, the old debt is removed and the new debt is established. In addition, the difference between the book value of the old debt and its reacquisition price is reported on the government-wide financial statements as a decrease (contra liability) or increase (valuation account) to the book value of the new debt issued to finance the advance refunding. Subsequently, the difference (deferral) is amortized over the original remaining life of the old debt or the life of the new debt, whichever is less.

For example, assume that the following amortization schedule represents bonds outstanding as of July 1, 20X0:

| Date | 6% Cash | Interest | Amortization | Book Value |
|---|---|---|---|---|
| 6/30/W7 | | | | $957,878 |
| 6/30/W8 | $50,000 | $ 57,473 | $7,473 | 965,351 |
| 6/30/W9 | 50,000 | 57,921 | 7,921 | 973,272 |
| 6/30/X0 | 50,000 | 58,396 | 8,396 | 981,668 |
| 6/30/X1 | 50,000 | 58,900 | 8,900 | 990,568 |
| 6/30/X2 | 50,000 | 59,432 | 9,432 | 1,000,000 |
| Total | | $292,122 | $42,122 | |

On July 1, 20X0, the governmental entity decides to take advantage of lower interest rates and issues new debt at par that has a maturity value of $1,100,000 and a maturity date of 5 years. In order to retire the old debt, the governmental entity must pay (based on the terms of the original bond agreement) existing bondholders $1,100,000.

The following entries are made in the appropriate governmental fund to issue the new debt and retire the old debt:

| | | |
|---|---|---|
| Cash | 1,100,000 | |
|     Other financing source—bonds issued | | 1,100,000 |
| | | |
| Other financing use—payment to refunded debt escrow agent | 1,100,000 | |
|     Cash | | 1,100,000 |

In order to convert the transaction from a modified accrual basis to an accrual basis for presentation in the government-wide financial statements, the following worksheet conversion entry is made at the end of the fiscal year ended June 30, 20X1:

| | | |
|---|---|---|
| Other financing source—bonds issued | 1,100,000 | |
|     Bonds payable (new debt) | | 1,100,000 |
| | | |
| Bonds payable (old debt) | 981,668 | |
| Deferred loss on early retirement of debt | 118,332 | |
|     Other financing use—payment to refund debt escrow agent | | 1,100,000 |

> **NOTE:** The entry above assumes that the governmental entity made a worksheet conversion entry that reflected all of the debt outstanding at the beginning of the year, including the debt retired during the year.

The "deferred loss on early retirement of debt" is presented in the government-wide financial statements as an offset to the new debt and is amortized over two years (which is remaining life of the old debt at retirement because its life is less than the 5-year life of the newly issued debt). For this reason, the following conversion worksheet entry is made as of June 30, 20X1 to record the amortization:

| | | |
|---|---|---|
| Interest expense ($118,332/2 years) | 59,166 | |
|     Deferred loss on early retirement of debt | | 59,166 |

## Early Extinguishments of Debt (Nonrefunding)

In some instances, a governmental entity retires debt early and uses internal resources as the basis for repayment of the debt rather than proceeds from the issuance of new debt (nonrefunding). Under this strategy, an expenditure (rather than an other financing use account) is used to record the transaction in the appropriate governmental fund; however, in the government-wide financial statements, the transaction must be converted to an accrual basis by removing the debt and recording an extraordinary gain or loss.

To illustrate an early extinguishment of debt that does not involve refunding, assume that a governmental entity retires debt that has a book value of $981,668 for a reacquisition price of $1,100,000. The following entry is made in the governmental fund that finances the retirement:

| | | |
|---|---|---|
| Expenditures—principal | 1,100,000 | |
| Cash | | 1,100,000 |

At the end of the year, the following worksheet conversion entry is made to report the early retirement on an accrual basis in the government-wide financial statements:

| | | |
|---|---|---|
| Bonds payable | 981,668 | |
| Extraordinary loss on early retirement of debt | 118,332 | |
| Expenditures—principal | | 1,100,000 |

## Capital Expenditures—Current Period Transactions

When capital assets are acquired by a governmental entity, payments related to acquisitions are recorded as expenditures at the fund statement level. However, in order to convert the fund financial statement information from a modified accrual basis to an accrual basis for the preparation of the government-wide financial statements, the expenditure is capitalized and any related depreciation expense is reported.

To illustrate the conversion of capital expenditures to an accrual basis, assume that on July 1, 20X0 a governmental entity constructed a building at a cost of $5,000,000. The estimated useful life of the building is 25 years with no residual value. The construction cost of the building would be recorded in the appropriate governmental fund as follows:

| | | |
|---|---|---|
| Expenditures—capital outlays | 5,000,000 | |
| Cash | | 5,000,000 |

In order to report the capital assets illustrated in this example in the government-wide financial statement as required by GASB-34, the following worksheet conversion entry is made:

| | | |
|---|---|---|
| Buildings | 5,000,000 | |
| Expenditures—capital outlays | | 5,000,000 |

In this example, the depreciation expense on the building is assumed to be related to general government expenses for purposes of classification on the statement of activities. In order to reflect depreciation expense, the following worksheet conversion entry is made:

| | | |
|---|---|---|
| Expenses—general government ($5,000,000/25 years) | 200,000 | |
|     Accumulated depreciation—building | | 200,000 |

> ▶ **NEW STANDARD:** GASB-34 requires a governmental entity to report all of its capital assets in the statement of net assets, based on their original historical cost plus ancillary charges such as transportation, installation, and site preparation costs. Capital assets include such items as (1) land and land improvements, (2) buildings and building improvements, (3) vehicles, (4) infrastructure assets, and (5) works of art, historical treasures, and other, similar assets. Capital assets should be presented in the statement of net assets at historical cost less accumulated depreciation. A single amount (net of accumulated depreciation) may be presented on the face of the financial statement, in which case accumulated depreciation and the major categories of capital assets (land, buildings, equipment, infrastructure, etc.) must be reported in a note (GASB-34, pars. 18–22).

## Capital Assets—Previous Year's Balances

In addition to current year transactions, previous years' transactions are analyzed to determine how permanent balances (statement accounts) that appeared on last year's accrual-based financial statements affect the current year's government-wide financial statements. As shown earlier, worksheet conversion entries arising from this analysis are made through the beginning balance of net assets.

For example, assume that a governmental entity had the following capital assets at the beginning of the year:

| | Cost | Accumulated Depreciation |
|---|---|---|
| Land | $100,000,000 | — |
| Buildings (60% depreciated) | 400,000,000 | $240,000,000 |
| Equipment (70% depreciated) | 200,000,000 | 140,000,000 |
| Total | $700,000,000 | $380,000,000 |

Based on the above analysis, the following worksheet conversion entry would be made to establish the beginning balances related to the governmental activities column in the statement of net assets:

| | | |
|---|---|---|
| Land | 100,000,000 | |
| Buildings | 400,000,000 | |

| | |
|---|---|
| Equipment | 200,000,000 |
| Accumulated deprecation—buildings | 240,000,000 |
| Accumulated deprecation—equipment | 140,000,000 |
| Net assets | 320,000,000 |

## Capital Leases—Current Period Transactions

Rather than purchase a capital asset directly from a vendor, a governmental entity may lease the item. If the agreement is considered a capitalized lease as defined in NCGA-5 (Accounting and Financial Reporting Principles for Lease Agreements of State and Local Governments) and FAS-13 (Accounting for Leases), the transaction is accounted for in the appropriate governmental fund as both an issuance of debt and a capital expenditure (both of which were discussed in previous sections). Thus, in order to convert the fund financial statements from a modified accrual basis to an accrual basis for the preparation of the government-wide financial statements, the expenditure must be capitalized, any related depreciation expense must be recorded, and the debt must be recognized along with the accrual of any related interest expense.

To illustrate the capitalization of a lease, assume a governmental entity leases office equipment that has an economic life of 5 years and no residual value. Lease payments of $50,000 are to be made in five annual installments beginning on July 1, 20X0. The governmental entity's incremental borrowing rate is 10%. The capitalized value of the lease is $208,493 ($50,000 × 4.16986) and the following amortization schedule applies to the agreement. (The equipment is part of general government overhead costs.)

| Date | Cash | 10% Interest | Amortization | Book Value |
|---|---|---|---|---|
| 7/1/X0 | | | | 208,493 |
| 7/1/X0 | 50,000 | — | 50,000 | 158,493 |
| 7/1/X1 | 50,000 | 15,849 | 34,151 | 124,342 |
| 7/1/X2 | 50,000 | 12,434 | 37,566 | 86,776 |
| 7/1/X3 | 50,000 | 8,678 | 41,322 | 45,454 |
| 7/1/X4 | 50,000 | 4,546 | 45,454 | 0 |

The execution of the lease would be recorded in the governmental by making the following entry:

| | | |
|---|---|---|
| Expenditures—general government | 208,493 | |
|    Other financing sources— | | |
|       Capitalized leases | | 208,493 |

| | | |
|---|---|---|
| Expenditures—general government | 50,000 | |
| Cash | | 50,000 |

In the governmental fund financial statements, the issuance of the debt component of the lease is presented on the statement of revenues, expenditures, and changes in fund balances as an other financing source, but the amount is not presented in the balance sheet as a liability at the fund statement level. Likewise, the capital expenditure component of the lease is presented as an expenditure. In order to convert the transaction from a modified accrual basis to an accrual basis, the following worksheet conversion entries are prepared:

| | | |
|---|---|---|
| Other financing sources—capitalized leases | 208,493 | |
|    Expenditures—general government | | 208,493 |
|    (To reverse other financing source and expenditure) | | |
| Equipment—capitalized leases | 208,493 | |
|    Lease obligation payable—due within one year | | 208,493 |
|    (To record capital asset and related obligation) | | |
| Lease obligation payable | 50,000 | |
|    Expenditures—general government | | 50,000 |
|    (To record initial payment as a reduction to the lease obligation rather than an expenditure) | | |
| Expenses—general government | 41,699 | |
|    Accumulated depreciation—capitalized leases | | 41,699 |
|    ($208,493/5 years) | | |
|    (To record depreciation on the capital lease) | | |
| Interest expenses | 15,849 | |
|    Interest payable (amount due on 7/1/X1 per amortization schedule) | | 15,849 |
|    (To accrue interest on the lease obligation for the year) | | |

## Capital Leases—Previous Year's Balances

In addition to capital lease agreements executed in the current year, the governmental entity must also consider those signed in previous years. The lease payments in the current period are accounted for as expenditures in the appropriate governmental fund, but at the end of the year, worksheet conversion entries are made to (1) recognize the obligation and the capital asset at the beginning of the year, (2) reduce the obligation by payments made during the current year (net of interest expense), and (3) record depreciation on the capital lease.

For example, assume that a governmental entity made a $20,000 payment during the current year (fiscal year ended June 30, 20X1) based on a lease agreement signed on June 30, 20X9. The amortization schedule for the lease agreement is as follows:

| Date | Cash | 8% Interest | Amortization | Book Value |
|---|---|---|---|---|
| 6/30/W9 | | | | 99,854 |
| 6/30/W9 | 20,000 | — | 20,000 | 79,854 |
| 6/30/X0 | 20,000 | 6,388 | 13,612 | 66,242 |
| 6/30/X1 | 20,000 | 5,299 | 14,701 | 51,541 |
| 6/30/X2 | 20,000 | 4,123 | 15,877 | 35,664 |
| 6/30/X3 | 20,000 | 2,853 | 17,147 | 18,517 |
| 6/30/X4 | 20,000 | 1,483 | 18,517 | 0 |

The current lease payment is recorded in the appropriate governmental fund during the June 30, 20X1 year as follows assuming the equipment was used for general government purposes:

| | | |
|---|---|---|
| Expenditures—general government | 14,701 | |
| Expenditures—interest | 5,299 | |
| Cash | | 20,000 |

In order to convert this payment from a modified accrual basis to an accrual basis, the following worksheet conversion entries are made at the end of the year assuming the capital lease was 20% depreciated as of the beginning of the year:

| | | |
|---|---|---|
| Leased capital assets | 99,854 | |
| Net assets | | 79,883 |
| Accumulated depreciation ($99,854 × 20%) | | 19,971 |

(To record the book value of the capital lease as of the beginning of the year)

| | | |
|---|---|---|
| Net assets | 66,242 | |
| Lease obligations payable | | 66,242 |

(To record obligation as of the beginning of the year)

| | | |
|---|---|---|
| Lease obligations payable | 14,701 | |
| Expenditures—general government | | 14,701 |

(To record the lease payment as a reduction to the principal obligation) (note that the interest recorded for the year is the same under the modified and accrual methods)

| | | |
|---|---|---|
| Expenses—general government | 19,971 | |
|    Accumulated depreciation—capital leases | | 19,971 |
|    (To record depreciation on the capital lease) | | |

## Leasehold Improvements

When a lessee makes improvements to a capital asset, the expenditure should be reported as a capital leasehold improvement and depreciated over the remaining life of the lease or the life of the improvement, whichever is less. Leasehold improvements are recorded in the appropriate governmental fund as expenditures, but at the end of the year the transaction must be converted to an accrual basis by capitalizing the improvement and recognizing the related depreciation.

For example, assume that on the first day of the current year a governmental entity makes a $500,000 improvement to a building it is leasing. The improvement is expected to have an economic life of about 12 years but the remaining life of the lease is 10 years. The improvement cost would be recorded in the appropriate governmental fund as follows:

| | | |
|---|---|---|
| Expenditures—general government | 500,000 | |
|    Cash | | 500,000 |

In order to convert the transaction to an accrual basis, the following worksheet conversion entry would be made at the end of the year:

| | | |
|---|---|---|
| Leasehold improvements | 500,000 | |
|    Expenditures—general government | | 500,000 |
| | | |
| Expenses—general government ($500,000/10 years) | 50,000 | |
|    Accumulated depreciation—leasehold improvements | | 50,000 |

## Gains and Losses Related to Capital Asset Dispositions

When a governmental entity sells or abandons capital assets, any proceeds from the disposition are recorded in a governmental fund as either miscellaneous revenue, an other source of financial resources, or a special item based on professional judgment. At the end of the year, the transaction is converted to an accrual basis, with any related gain or loss reflected in the government-wide financial statements. For example, assume that land and a building that had been used as a fire station are sold for $400,000. The land and building's original cost were $50,000 and $700,000, respectively. The building is 70% depreciated.

The following entry is made to record the transaction in the governmental fund that received the proceeds from the disposition:

| | | |
|---|---|---|
| Cash | 400,000 | |
|     Miscellaneous revenue | | 400,000 |

The following worksheet conversion entry is made at the end of the year:

| | | |
|---|---|---|
| Accumulated depreciation ($700,000 × 70%) | 490,000 | |
| Miscellaneous revenue | 400,000 | |
|     Land | | 50,000 |
|     Building | | 700,000 |
|     Gain on sale of capital assets | | 140,000 |

> **NOTE:** The gain on the sale of capital assets may be reported as a program revenue for the public safety program (fire protection) or it could be argued that the amount should be related to general government programs. It is also possible that the gain could be reported as a special item; however, it is unlikely that the gain would be considered extraordinary, because most governmental entities sell or abandon many of their capital assets at some point in time. In any case, professional judgment must be used to classify the gain on the governmental entity's government-wide financial statements.

## Nonmonetary Exchanges (Trade-Ins)

A governmental entity may trade in a variety of capital assets as partial payment for new capital assets. The accounting for nonmonetary exchanges of capital assets, which is based on APB Opinion 29 (Accounting for Nonmonetary Transactions), is classified as follows:

- Exchange of dissimilar capital assets
- Exchange of similar capital assets with a loss
- Exchange of similar capital assets with a gain (no boot involved)
- Exchange of similar capital assets with a gain (boot involved)

### Exchange of Dissimilar Capital Assets

When dissimilar capital assets are exchanged in a nonmonetary transaction, any gain or loss related to the transaction is reflected in the government-wide financial statements. The gain or loss is determined by comparing the fair value of the exchange (either the fair value of the asset received or the fair value of the asset given up—theoretically they should be the same) with the book value of the asset(s) given up.

For example, assume that on the first day of the current year a governmental entity exchanges a used vehicle that had an original cost of $40,000 and is 60% depreciated for machinery. The fair value of the vehicle is $20,000. The gain or loss on the exchange is determined as follows:

| | | |
|---|---|---|
| Fair value of exchange | | $20,000 |
| Book value of asset given up: | | |
| Cost | $40,000 | |
| Accumulated depreciation ($40,000 × 60%) | 24,000 | 16,000 |
| Gain on nonmonetary exchange | | $4,000 |

The nonmonetary exchange is not recorded in a governmental fund, because it does not involve current financial resources; however, the following worksheet conversion entry is made to reflect the exchange in the government-wide financial statements at the end of the year:

| | | |
|---|---|---|
| Machinery | 20,000 | |
| Accumulated depreciation—vehicles | 24,000 | |
| Vehicles | | 40,000 |
| Gain on exchange of capital assets | | 4,000 |

Professional judgment must be used to determine whether the gain on the exchange of a capital asset is reported as a special item or as program revenue. Special items are discussed later in this chapter.

*Exchange of Similar Capital Assets with a Loss*

When similar capital assets are exchanged in a nonmonetary transaction, any loss related to the transaction is reflected in the government-wide financial statements. For example, assume that a governmental entity exchanges equipment with an original cost of $40,000 and 60% depreciated for similar equipment. The transferred equipment has a fair value of $14,000. The loss on the exchange is determined as follows:

| | | |
|---|---|---|
| Fair value of exchange | | $14,000 |
| Book value of asset given up: | | |
| Cost | $40,000 | |
| Accumulated depreciation ($40,000 × 60%) | 24,000 | 16,000 |
| Loss on nonmonetary exchange | | $2,000 |

The nonmonetary exchange is not recorded in a governmental fund, because it does not involve current financial resources; however, the following worksheet conversion entry is made to reflect the exchange in the government-wide financial statements:

| | | |
|---|---|---|
| Machinery | 14,000 | |
| Accumulated depreciation—vehicles | 24,000 | |
| Loss on exchange of capital assets | 2,000 | |
| Vehicles | | 40,000 |

For financial reporting purposes, the loss would be classified as either a program expense or a special item. The management of the governmental entity must make that determination.

*Exchange of Similar Capital Assets with a Gain (No Boot Involved)*

When similar capital assets are exchanged in a nonmonetary transaction and there is no boot involved, any gain related to the transaction is deferred. Boot is defined as cash or some other monetary asset (such as a notes receivable). For example, consider the previous illustration but assume that the value of the asset transferred asset is $19,000. The gain on the exchange is determined as follows:

| | | |
|---|---|---|
| Fair value of exchange | | $19,000 |
| Book value of asset given up: | | |
| Cost | $40,000 | |
| Accumulated depreciation ($40,000 × 60%) | 24,000 | 16,000 |
| Gain on nonmonetary exchange | | $3,000 |

The nonmonetary exchange is not recorded in a governmental fund, because it does not involve current financial resources; however, the following worksheet conversion entry is made to reflect the exchange in the government-wide financial statements:

| | | |
|---|---|---|
| Machinery | 16,000 | |
| Accumulated depreciation—vehicles | 24,000 | |
| Vehicles | | 40,000 |

It should be noted that the newly acquired machinery is not recorded at fair value ($19,000), because the $3,000 gain is not reflected in the government-wide financial statements. In effect, the gain is indirectly recognized in the government-wide financial statements because depreciation expense will be understated by $3,000 over the life of the asset.

## Exchange of Similar Capital Assets with a Gain (Boot Involved)

When similar capital assets are exchanged in a nonmonetary transaction and boot is involved, no gain is recognized if the governmental entity does not receive boot. If boot is received, then a portion of the gain is recognized.

To illustrate the payment of boot, assume that a governmental entity exchanges equipment with an original cost of $70,000 that is 40% depreciated for similar equipment. The fair value of the asset received is $60,000 and the governmental entity pays boot (cash) of $10,000 to the other party. The gain on the exchange is determined as follows:

| | | |
|---|---|---|
| Fair value of exchange | | $60,000 |
| Book value of asset given up: | | |
|   Cost | $70,000 | |
|   Accumulated depreciation ($70,000 × 40%) | 28,000 | |
| | 42,000 | |
|   Cash | 10,000 | 52,000 |
| Gain on nonmonetary exchange | | $8,000 |

The following entry is made in a governmental fund to record the exchange because current financial resources are expended (assuming the machinery is related to general governmental services):

| | | |
|---|---|---|
| Expenditures—general government | 10,000 | |
|   Cash | | 10,000 |

At the end of the year, the following worksheet conversion entry is made to report the nonmonetary exchange on an accrual basis in the government-wide financial statements:

| | | |
|---|---|---|
| Equipment (new) | 52,000 | |
| Accumulated depreciation | 28,000 | |
|   Equipment (old) | | 70,000 |
|   Expenditures—general government | | 10,000 |

To illustrate the receipt of boot, assume that a governmental entity exchanges equipment with an original cost of $70,000 that is 40% depreciated for similar equipment. The fair value of the equipment received is $60,000 and the governmental entity also receives boot (cash) of $10,000 from the other party. The gain on the exchange is determined as follows:

| | | |
|---|---|---|
| Fair value of exchange ($60,000 + $10,000) | | $70,000 |
| Book value of asset given up: | | |
|   Cost | $70,000 | |
|   Accumulated depreciation ($70,000 × 40%) | 28,000 | 42,000 |
| Gain on nonmonetary exchange | | $28,000 |

The following entry is made in the governmental fund that receives the boot:

| | | |
|---|---|---|
| Cash | 10,000 | |
| Miscellaneous revenues | | 10,000 |

In some instances a special item would be recorded rather than miscellaneous revenue. Special items are discussed below.

At the end of the year a worksheet conversion entry is made to report the nonmonetary exchange on an accrual basis in the government-wide financial statements. Although the gain is $28,000, APB Opinion 29 requires that the following formula be used to determine the portion of the gain that can be recognized:

$$\frac{\text{Boot}}{\text{Fair Value of Exchange}} \times \text{Gain} = \text{Recognized Gain}$$

$$\frac{10,000}{70,000} \times 28,000 = 4,000 \text{ (recognized gain)}$$

The gain determined above is recognized in the following year-end worksheet conversion entry:

| | | |
|---|---|---|
| Miscellaneous revenue | 10,000 | |
| Equipment (new) | 36,000 | |
| Accumulated depreciation | 28,000 | |
| Equipment (old) | | 70,000 |
| Gain on exchange of capital assets | | 4,000 |

As discussed earlier, the gain—based on professional judgment—would be classified as either program revenue or a special item in the government-wide financial statements.

## Donations of Capital Assets From Outside Parties

When a governmental entity receives as a donation a capital asset, the receipt is not recorded in a governmental fund, because current financial resources are not involved; however, the transaction must be reflected in the government-wide financial statements based on the fair value of the donated property (GASB-34, par. 18).

To illustrate this concept, assume that an individual donates land ($1,000,000) and a building ($3,500,000) to a governmental entity. The property is to be used as a health center in a disadvantaged neighborhood. As stated above, the transaction is not recorded in a governmental fund, but the following worksheet conversion entry is made at the end of the year:

| | | |
|---|---|---|
| Land | 1,000,000 | |
| Building | 3,500,000 | |
|   Program revenues—capital grants and contributions | | 4,500,000 |

> **NOTE:** The donation is recorded as program revenues; however, it could be recorded as an extraordinary item if it is both infrequent and nonoperating.

The building would be depreciated over its estimated economic life.

## Donations of Capital Assets to Outside Parties

A governmental entity may donate capital assets to an external party. Again, because the transaction does not involve current financial resources, it is not recorded in a governmental fund. At the end of the year, a worksheet conversion entry must be made to reflect the transaction in the government-wide financial statements, based on the fair value of the donated property.

For example, assume that a state gives land and a building to a municipality to be used as a drug rehabilitation center. The land and building's original cost were $400,000 and $900,000, respectively. The building is 80% depreciated and the total fair value of the property at the donation date is $90,000. The following worksheet conversion entry is be made by the state at the end of the year:

| | | |
|---|---|---|
| Expenses—health and welfare | 90,000 | |
| Extraordinary loss on donation of capital assets | 490,000 | |
| Accumulated depreciation ($900,000 × 80%) | 720,000 | |
|   Land | | 400,000 |
|   Building | | 900,000 |

Professional judgment would be used to determine whether the difference between the fair value of the asset donated and its book value should be recorded as an extraordinary loss. If the two criteria (infrequent and nonoperating) are not satisfied, then the difference could be reported as (1) a program expense for health and welfare or perhaps as a general government expense or (2) a special item.

## Gains and Losses Related to Capital Asset Dispositions

When a governmental entity sells or abandons capital assets, proceeds from the disposition are recorded in the appropriate governmental fund as either miscellaneous revenue, an other source of financial resources, or a special item based on professional judgment. At the end of the year, the transaction is converted to an accrual basis with any related gain or loss reflected in the government-wide financial statements. For example, assume that land and a building that had been used as fire station is sold for $400,000. The land and building's original cost were $50,000 and $700,000, respectively. The building is 70% depreciated. The following entry is made to record the transaction in the governmental fund that received the proceeds from the disposition:

| | | |
|---|---|---|
| Cash | 400,000 | |
|     Miscellaneous revenue | | 400,000 |

The following worksheet conversion entry is made at the end of the year:

| | | |
|---|---|---|
| Accumulated depreciation ($700,000 × 70%) | 490,000 | |
| Miscellaneous revenue | 400,000 | |
|     Land | | 50,000 |
|     Building | | 700,000 |
|     Gain on sale of capital assets | | 140,000 |

The gain on sale of the capital asset may be reported as a program revenue for public safety program (fire protection) or it could be argued that the amount should be related to general government programs. It is also possible that the gain could be reported as a special item; however, it is unlikely that the gain would be considered extraordinary, because most governmental entities sell or abandon many of their capital assets at some point in time. In any case, professional judgment must be used to classify the gain on the governmental entity's government-wide financial statements.

### Involuntary Conversions of Capital Assets

A governmental entity may be involved in an involuntary conversion whereby an asset is destroyed, but because the asset is necessary to the governmental entity's operating activities, it is then replaced. The involuntary conversion is recorded in a governmental fund only when cash (or a claim that meets the definition of availability) is received. FASB Interpretation 30 (Accounting for Involuntary Conversions of Nonmonetary Assets to Monetary Assets) requires that any gain or loss related to the conversion of nonmonetary assets to monetary assets be recognized.

To illustrate this concept, assume that fire destroys a governmental entity's administrative building. The original cost of the building was $4,000,000 and is 40% depreciated. The governmental entity has fire insurance on the property and receives $3,000,000 from the insurance provider. The governmental entity constructs a new building at a cost of $5,200,000. The following entries are made to record the involuntary conversion in the appropriate governmental funds:

| | | |
|---|---|---|
| Cash | 3,000,000 | |
|    Extraordinary item—proceeds from fire insurance policy | | 3,000,000 |
|    (To record the fire insurance proceeds) | | |
| | | |
| Expenditures—capital outlays | 5,200,000 | |
|    Cash | | 5,200,000 |
|    (To record the construction of a new building) | | |

At the end of the year, the following worksheet conversion entry is made to reflect the involuntary conversion in the government-wide financial statements:

| | | |
|---|---|---|
| Extraordinary item—proceeds from fire insurance | 3,000,000 | |
| Accumulated depreciation ($4,000,000 × 40%) | 1,600,000 | |
|    Building | | 4,000,000 |
|    Extraordinary gain—involuntary conversion of capital assets | | 600,000 |
|    (To remove the capital assets destroyed and to record an extraordinary gain on the involuntary conversion) | | |
| | | |
| Buildings | 5,200,000 | |
|    Expenditures—capital outlays | | 5,200,000 |
|    (To reclassify capital expenditures) | | |

## Maintenance and Preservation Costs

Maintenance costs are normal costs that allow a capital asset to be used in a normal manner over its originally expected economic life. Preservation costs are defined in the GASB's "Guide to Implementation of GASB Statement 34 on Basic Financial Statements—and Management's Discussion and Analysis—for State and Local Governments" as costs "that extend the useful life of an asset beyond its original estimated useful life, but do not increase the capacity or efficiency of the asset" (Question 58).

Maintenance costs and preservation costs are reported as expenditures in a governmental fund, but in the government-wide financial statements maintenance costs are expensed and preservation costs are capitalized. To illustrate the accounting for these costs, assume that a governmental entity incurs maintenance cost of $100,000 and preservation costs (related to a building) of $250,000. The building is used for general government services.

The costs are recorded in the appropriate governmental fund by making the following entry:

| | | |
|---|---|---|
| Expenditures—general government | 350,000 | |
| Cash | | 350,000 |

At the end of the year, the following worksheet conversion entry is made to reflect the transaction in the government-wide financial statements:

| | | |
|---|---|---|
| Buildings | 250,000 | |
| Expenditures—general government | | 250,000 |

## Changes in Accounting Principles

When a governmental entity changes an accounting principle, the effect of the change is not reported in the entity's operating statement but instead is displayed as an adjustment to the beginning balance of its fund net asset account in the government-wide financial statements. (Generally, a change in an accounting principle will not be shown in a governmental fund, because there is no effect on current financial resources.)

The amount of the adjustment is the difference between (1) the actual beginning balance in the net asset account and (2) the assumed beginning balance in the net asset account, assuming that the new accounting principle had always been used by the governmental entity. The analysis of the difference between the two amounts always focuses on the balances at the beginning of the year in which the change is made no matter when the actual decision to make the change is made (GASB-34, par. 309).

To illustrate a change in an accounting principle, assume that a governmental entity changes its method of computing depreciation for the year ended June 30, 20X1 from an accelerated method to the straight-line method. The following balances apply to the beginning of the fiscal year:

| | Actual Balance—<br>Accelerated<br>Method | Recomputed Balance—<br>Straight-Line<br>Method |
|---|---|---|
| Accumulated depreciation as of July 1, 20X0 | $12,400,000 | $9,200,000 |

The change in the method of computing depreciation expense does not affect any governmental fund, but the following worksheet entry is made at the end of the year to reflect the change in the government-wide financial statements:

| | | |
|---|---|---|
| Accumulated depreciation ($12,400,000 − $9,200,000) | 3,200,000 | |
|     Cumulative effect of a change in an accounting principle | | 3,200,000 |

The cumulative effect from the change is presented at the bottom of the statement of activities in the governmental activities column as follows (except for the cumulative effect amount, all other amounts are assumed):

| | Governmental Activities |
|---|---|
| Change in net assets | $7,000,000 |
| Net assets—beginning balance before restatement | 450,000,000 |
| Add: Cumulative effect of a change in an accounting principle (See Note X) | 3,200,000 |
| Net assets—beginning balance after restatement | 453,200,000 |
| Net assets—ending balance | $460,200,000 |

If the government-wide financial statements are presented on a comparative basis, the previous year's financial statements are restated to reflect the change in the method used to compute depreciation expense in order to satisfy the consistency standard.

> ▶ **NEW STANDARD:** In general, the accounting for a change in an accounting principle is based on the standards established by APB Opinion 20 (Accounting Changes) with an exception. APB-20 general solution is to require that the effects from changes in accounting principles be presented on a commercial enterprise's income statement (with some exceptions) and therefore affects the computation of net income. However, GASB-34 requires that the effects be presented as an adjustment to the beginning balance of net assets rather than as the change in net assets (the equivalent of net income for a commercial enterprise). The GASB states that "the exception taken to the requirements of Opinion 20 is appropriate because it was intended to avoid the manipulation of 'earnings per share' by commercial enterprises" and there is no equivalent EPS number for a governmental entity.

## Changes in Accounting Estimates

A change in an accounting estimate is accounted for in a prospective manner. That is, a change in estimate does not require a cumulative effect adjustment similar to the one described in the previous section. For governmental fund financial statements the change in an accounting estimate may result in an adjustment to a balance sheet account (usually an asset) so that the account will reflect an amount that is compatible with the flow of current financial resources concept. For example, if a governmental entity believes that the estimated amount of uncollectible accounts related to property taxes receivable is understated, the new estimated percentage is reflected in the current financial statements by decreasing revenue and increasing the allowance account.

In government-wide financial statements a variety of assets and liabilities may be affected by changes in accounting estimates. For example, the life of a capital asset may change, the amount of an asset's residual value may change, or the estimated liability related to compensated absences may decrease or increase.

While all changes in accounting estimates are treated on a prospective basis, the effect of a change is dependent on the related asset or liability. For example, if it is estimated that for the last three years the provision for compensated absences has been understated by about 1% for each year, the total understatement for the three-year period (3%) is charged to the expense and related obligation. On the other hand, if the life of a depreciable asset has changed, the change is folded into the government-wide financial statements by taking the undepreciated cost (net of estimated residual value) and depreciating that amount over the remaining life of the property. To illustrate, assume a governmental entity purchased a building for $22,000,000 (with a residual value of $2,000,000) and an estimated economic life of 40 years. The asset is depreciated for 5 years and then it is estimated that the remaining life of the building is only 20 years. In the sixth year, the depreciating expense for each of the next 15 years is recomputed as follows:

| | |
|---|---:|
| Original cost of building | $22,000,000 |
| Less: estimated residual value | (2,000,000) |
| Depreciable cost | 20,000,000 |
| Depreciation for 5 years ($20,000,000 × 5/40 years) | 2,500,000 |
| Remaining depreciable cost at the beginning of the 6th year | 17,500,000 |
| New depreciation rate (1/20 years) | × 5% |
| Annual depreciation expense for years 6 through 25 | $875,000 |

Because accounting changes do not require a cumulative effects adjustment, there is no worksheet conversion entry to be made in order to convert the modified accrual financial statements to an accrual basis.

> **NOTE:** The change in the estimated economic life of a depreciable asset does not result in an adjustment to the fund financial statements, because it does not change the estimated value of a current financial resource.

## Long-Term Noninterest Bearing Notes Receivable

A governmental entity may enter into a transaction that involves the receipt of a long-term noninterest note receivable. The receipt of the note would not be reported in a governmental fund's statement of revenues, expenditures, and change in fund balance, because the transaction does not represent current financial resources. The transaction may or may not affect the entity's balance sheet, depending on the accounting method used. That is, the governmental entity could either not record a receivable or record a receivable but simultaneously establish a fund balance reserve. Either method is acceptable.

In the government-wide financial statements, the notes must be recorded after imputing interest as required by APB Opinion 21. The discount rate used to impute interest should be based on the credit risk related to the other party to the note.

To illustrate the accounting for a long-term noninterest bearing note receivable, assume that on July 1, 20X0 a governmental entity sells land to the county for $5,000,000. The original cost of the land is $2,000,000. The county signs a three-year, non interest bearing note. Based on the credit rating of the county, its incremental borrowing rate is estimated to be 6%. The present value of the note is $4,198,100 ($5,000,000 x .83962) and the following amortization schedule relates to the note:

| Date | Cash | 6% Interest | Amortization | Book Value |
|---|---|---|---|---|
| 7/1/X0 | | | | 4,198,100 |
| 6/30/X1 | 0 | 251,886 | 251,886 | 4,449,986 |
| 6/30/X2 | 0 | 266,999 | 266,999 | 4,716,985 |
| 6/20/X3 | 0 | 283,015 | 283,015 | 5,000,000 |

Using the second accounting alternative described above (recording the note and a reserve), the governmental entity makes the following entry in the governmental fund that will eventually receive the proceeds from the sale of the land:

| | | |
|---|---|---|
| Long-term notes receivable | 4,198,100 | |
|     Fund balance—reserved for long-term notes | | 4,198,100 |

At June 30, 20X1, the following worksheet conversion entry is made to restate the transaction on an accrual basis:

| | | |
|---|---|---|
| Fund balance—reserved for long-term notes receivable | 4,198,100 | |
|     Land | | 2,000,000 |
|     Gain on sale of land | | 2,198,100 |
| (To record the sale of the land and remove the fund balance reservation) | | |
| Long-term notes receivable | 251,886 | |
|     Interest revenue (see amortization schedule) | | 251,886 |
| (To accrue interest on the noninterest bearing note) | | |

▶ **NEW STANDARD:** The standards established by APB Opinion 21 do not have to be applied on a retroactive basis. They need only be applied to receivables and payables that originate during the year in which the standards established by GASB-34 are implemented by a governmental entity (GASB-34, par.146).

## Lease Payments Receivable

A governmental entity may lease property to another party that creates an in-substance sale that must be accounted for based on the standards established by NCGA-5 and FAS-13. The specific accounting for the lessor (governmental entity) depends upon whether the lease is a sales-type lease or a direct financing lease. When the governmental entity (lessor) is involved in an in-substance sale of property and the sales price is greater than the book value of the asset leased to the other party (lessee), the sales-type lease method must be used. If the governmental entity is simply functioning as a financing entity, the direct financing lease method is used.

*Sales-Type Lease*

In order to illustrate the accounting for sales-type lease, assume that a governmental entity leases used heavy-duty equipment to the county government. The equipment originally cost $1,000,000 and is 65% depreciated. The estimated fair value of the equipment is $431,213 and has a remaining estimated economic life of 5 years. The property was leased to the county on July 1, 20X0, and five annual payments of $100,000 (beginning on July 1, 20X0) are to be made by the county government. The lease payments are based on an 8% interest rate (implicit interest rate) and the amortization schedule for the lease agreement is as follows:

| Date | Cash | 8% Interest | Amortization | Book Value |
|---|---|---|---|---|
| 7/1/X0 | | | | 431,213 |
| 7/1/X0 | 100,000 | — | — | 331,213 |
| 7/1/X1 | 100,000 | 26,497 | 73,503 | 257,710 |
| 7/1/X2 | 100,000 | 20,617 | 79,383 | 178,327 |
| 7/1/X3 | 100,000 | 14,266 | 85,734 | 92,593 |
| 7/1/X4 | 100,000 | 7,407 | 92,593 | -0- |

The following entry is made in the appropriate governmental fund to record the lease transaction on July 1, 20X0:

| | | |
|---|---|---|
| Cash | 100,000 | |
| Long-term lease payments receivable | 331,213 | |
|    Other financing sources—disposition of capital asset | | 100,000 |
|    Fund balance reserved for long-term lease payments | | 331,213 |

**NOTE:** It would also be acceptable to record only the $100,000 cash flow.

At the end of the fiscal year, the following worksheet conversion entries are made to reflect the lease transaction in the government-wide financial statement on an accrual basis:

| | | |
|---|---|---|
| Fund balance reserved for long-term lease payments | 331,213 | |
| Other financing sources—disposition of capital asset | 100,000 | |
| Accumulated depreciation—equipment | 650,000 | |
|    Equipment | | 1,000,000 |
|    Gain on disposition of capital assets | | 81,213 |
| (To reflect the sales-type lease on an accrual basis) | | |
| | | |
| Interest receivable (see amortization schedule) | 26,497 | |
|    Interest revenue | | 26,497 |
| (To accrue interest earned during the year) | | |

## Direct Financing Lease

In a direct financing lease, the lessor (the governmental entity) does not have a gain or loss on the in-substance sale of property but simply acts as a financing agent in the agreement. To illustrate this approach, assume that the governmental entity in the above example decides to finance the purchase of the heavy-duty equipment for the county government. The purchase is made from a vendor, the governmental entity pays the vendor the fair value of the property ($431,213), and it then leases the property to the county government based on the lease terms described for a sales-type lease.

The direct financing lease would be recorded in the appropriate governmental fund at the date the lease is executed by making the following entry:

| | | |
|---|---:|---:|
| Other financing uses—execution of lease agreement | 431,213 | |
| Long-term lease payments receivable | 331,213 | |
| Cash (payment to vendor) | | 431,213 |
| Fund balance reserved for long-term lease payments | | 331,213 |
| (To record lease agreement) | | |
| | | |
| Cash (receipt from county government) | 100,000 | |
| Other financing sources—receipt of lease payments | | 100,000 |
| (To record initial lease receipt) | | |

At the end of the fiscal year, the following worksheet conversion entries are made to reflect the lease transaction in the government-wide financial statement on an accrual basis:

| | | |
|---|---:|---:|
| Fund balance reserved for long-term lease payments | 331,213 | |
| Other financing sources—receipt of lease payments | 100,000 | |
| Other financing uses—execution of lease agreement | | 431,213 |
| (To reflect the direct financing lease on an accrual basis) | | |
| | | |
| Interest receivable | 26,497 | |
| Interest revenue | | 26,497 |
| (To accrue interest earned during the year) | | |

## Accrual of Expenses—Current Period Transactions

The basic guidance for determining when a governmental fund should accrue an expenditure/liability is found in NCGA-1, paragraph 70, which states that "most expenditures and transfers out are measurable and should be recorded when the related liability is incurred." GASBI-6 (Recognition and Measurement of Certain Liabilities and Expenditures in Governmental Fund Financial Statements) expands on this general guidance by noting the following:

> Governmental fund liabilities and expenditures that should be accrued include liabilities that, once incurred, normally are paid in a timely manner and in full from current financial resources—for example, salaries, professional services, supplies, utilities, and travel.

These transactions give rise to fund liabilities that are considered mature liabilities because they are "normally due and payable in full when incurred."

Although NCGA-1 implies that a fund liability should be recorded when the obligation is incurred, one of the most important concepts that forms the basis for preparing the financial statements of a governmental fund is that liabilities are recorded only when they are normally expected to be liquidated with expendable available financial resources. As described in GASBI-6, this exception to the broad accrual assumption is based on the same guidance established for formal debt agreements as described in a previous section. That is, "governments, in general, are normally expected to liquidate liabilities with expendable available financial resources to the extent that the liabilities mature (come due for payment) each period." In order to apply this broad generalization to current practice, GASBI-6 notes that "a series of specific accrual modifications have been established pertaining to the reporting of certain forms of long-term indebtedness." Two of the exceptions deal with operating expenditures, namely debts that arise from compensated absences policies, and claims and judgments. For these two operating expenditures, only the portion of the estimated future payments that will use expendable available financial resources should be reported as a current expenditure on the operating statement and fund liability on the balance sheet. However, if these liabilities meet the general conditions of a contingency (probable incurrence and subject to a reasonable estimation), they must be accrued for the government-wide financial statements.

To illustrate this approach, assume that a governmental entity's legal department evaluates several claims from third parties related to the police department activities and has made the following analysis:

|  | Amount of Claim | Reasonable Estimate of Eventual Payment |
| --- | --- | --- |
| Claim #1 | $12,000,000 | $1,900,000 |
| Claim #2 | 5,000,000 | 800,000 |
| Claim #3 | 4,000,000 | 200,000 |
| Claim #4 | 2,000,000 | 100,000 |
| Total | $23,000,000 | $3,000,000 |

The legal staff of the governmental entity determines it is probable that all of the claims will have to be paid, but the estimate of the loss is about $3,000,000; however, the staff believes that these payments will not be made until sometime during the next budgetary period at the earliest.

FAS-5 (Accounting for Contingencies) requires that a loss contingency be accrued if it is subject to reasonable estimation and it is probable that a liability was incurred (or an asset was impaired). This event represents a loss contingency of $3,000,000, but because the loss will not use current expendable financial resources, the estimated losses are not reported in a governmental fund. However, at the end of the fiscal year, the following worksheet conversion entry is made to reflect the loss contingencies in the government-wide financial statements:

| | | |
|---|---|---|
| Expenses—public safety | 3,000,000 | |
|     Claims payable | | 3,000,000 |

## Accrual of Expenses—Previous Year's Balances

When operating expenses are reflected in the government-wide financial statements because of a worksheet conversion entry, care must be taken so that the expense is not reported twice if the item is reported in a governmental fund as an expenditure in the following year. For example, assume that Claims #3 and #4 discussed in the previous section are settled during the next year for $900,000 (the fiscal year ended June 30, 20X2). In addition, at the end of the fiscal year, the following analysis is made by the legal department:

|  | Amount of Claim | Reasonable Estimate of Eventual Payments |
| --- | --- | --- |
| Claim #1 | $12,000,000 | $1,900,000 |
| Claim #2 | 5,000,000 | 800,000 |
| Claim #5 | 6,000,000 | 300,000 |
| Claim #6 | 2,400,000 | 250,000 |
| Total | $25,400,000 | $3,250,000 |

The actual claims paid would be recorded in the appropriate governmental fund as follows:

| | | |
|---|---|---|
| Expenditures—public safety | 900,000 | |
|     Cash | | 900,000 |

The following worksheet conversion entry is made at the end of 20X2 to present the claims obligation on the statement of net assets at an accrual amount:

| | | |
|---|---|---|
| Expenses—public safety | 1,150,000 | |
| Net assets (beginning balance) | 3,000,000 | |
|     Expenditures—public safety | | 900,000 |
|     Claims payable | | 3,250,000 |

**NOTE:** The debit to net assets assumes that the beginning point in the worksheet is the governmental fund's balance, which does not have the $3,000,000 accrual from the last period.

## Accrual of Revenues—Current Period Transactions

GASB-33 (Accounting and Financial Reporting for Nonexchange Transactions) provides accounting and reporting standards for the following four categories of nonexchange transactions:

1. Derived tax revenues
2. Imposed nonexchange revenues
3. Government-mandated nonexchange transactions
4. Voluntary nonexchange transactions

The standards established by GASB-33 retain fundamental criteria for revenue recognition that applies to the modified accrual basis of accounting, namely, that revenue is to be recorded when it is both available and measurable. NCGA-1 defines available as "collectible within the current period or soon enough thereafter to be used to pay liabilities of the current period." Revenue is measurable when it is subject to reasonable estimation.

In preparing government-wide financial statements, the same standards established by GASB-33 should be used to determine when revenue related to nonexchange transactions should be recognized except that the availability criterion does not have to be satisfied. Thus, nonexchange transactions need to be analyzed at the end of the accounting period to identify those that require a worksheet adjustment to convert from the modified accrual to the accrual basis of accounting.

To illustrate the accrual of operating revenue, assume that at June 30, 20X1 a municipality has property taxes receivable (net) of $3,000,000 of which $2,600,000 is considered available as defined by NCGA-1 and satisfies the criteria established by GASB-33 for imposed nonexchange revenues. Assuming the municipality has already recorded property taxes at the full levied amount (net of estimated write-offs), the following entry is made in the appropriate governmental fund:

| | | |
|---|---|---|
| General revenues—property taxes | 400,000 | |
| Property taxes receivable ($3,000,000 − $2,600,000) | | 400,000 |

However, at the end of the period, a worksheet conversion entry is made for the $400,000 as follows, because the availability criterion does not have to be satisfied in order to reflect revenue in the government-wide financial statements:

| | | |
|---|---|---|
| Property taxes receivable ($3,000,000 − $2,600,000) | 400,000 | |
| General revenues—property taxes | | 400,000 |

## Accrual of Revenues—Previous Year's Balances

When operating revenues are reflected in the government-wide financial statements because of a worksheet conversion entry, care must be taken so that the revenue is not reported twice if the item is reported in a governmental fund as revenue in the following year. For example, in the previous illustration, the property taxes that were reflected in the government-wide financial statements as of June 30, 20X1 will be collected during the following accounting period and recorded as revenue in the appropriate governmental fund under the modified accrual basis of accounting. This fact must be taken into consideration when property tax revenue is accrued as of June 30, 20X2.

To illustrate, assume that as of June 20, 20X2 the municipality has property taxes receivable (net) of $3,400,000 of which $3,100,000 is considered available. The municipality makes the following entry in the appropriate governmental fund:

| | | |
|---|---|---|
| General revenues—property taxes | 300,000 | |
| Property taxes receivable ($3,400,000 − $3,100,000) | | 300,000 |

In addition, the following worksheet conversion entry is made to recognize the $300,000 as revenue during the current period (20X2) reported on the accrual basis of accounting but net of the accrual ($400,000) that was made during the previous year (20X1):

| | | |
|---|---|---|
| Property taxes receivable | 300,000 | |
| General revenues—property taxes | 100,000 | |
|    Net assets (beginning balance) | | 400,000 |

## Extraordinary Items

GASB-34 incorporates the definition of extraordinary items (unusual in nature and infrequent in occurrence) as provided in APB Opinion No. 30 (Reporting the Results of Operations—Reporting the Effects of Disposal of a Segment of a Business, and Extraordinary, Unusual and Infrequently Occurring Events and Transactions) into the preparation of both governmental fund and government-wide financial statements; however, extraordinary items are reported in a governmental fund only if the item increases or decreases current financial resources during the year. When an event or transaction is reported as extraordinary in both sets of financial statements, the amounts are generally not the same, because in the fund financial statements only the amount that affects current financial resources is reported and in the government-wide financial statements the amount of the gain or loss determined on an accrual basis is reported (GASB-34, par. 55).

To illustrate the accounting for an extraordinary item, assume that a governmental entity had several pieces of road equipment destroyed by a flash flood. The equipment had an original cost of $3,400,000 and was 20% depreciated. The equipment was fully insured, which resulted in proceeds of $2,500,000. The extraordinary item is reflected in the governmental fund that receives the insurance proceeds by making the following entry:

| | | |
|---|---|---|
| Cash | 2,500,000 | |
|    Extraordinary item—proceeds from casualty loss | | 2,500,000 |

To convert the extraordinary item from a modified accrual basis to an accrual basis for presentation in the government-wide financial statements, the following worksheet conversion entry is made:

| | | |
|---|---|---|
| Extraordinary item—proceeds from casualty loss | 2,500,000 | |
| Accumulated depreciation ($3,400,000 × 20%) | 680,000 | |
| Extraordinary loss—flood damage | 220,000 | |
|    Equipment | | 3,400,000 |

> **NOTE:** As shown above, it is possible to have an extraordinary item that is a credit on the modified accrual basis and have an extraordinary loss on the accrual basis or vice versa.

## Special Items

Unlike APB Opinion 30, the GASB identifies a new classification, "special items," which are described as "significant transactions or other events within the control of management that are either unusual in nature or infrequent in occurrence" but not both. Special items are reported separately and before extraordinary items. If a significant transaction or other event occurs but is not within the control of management and that item is either unusual or infrequent, the item is not reported as a special item, but the nature of the item must be described in a note to the financial statements (GASB-34, par. 56).

Special items may be reported in both a governmental fund and the government-wide financial statements; however, like extraordinary items, they are reported in a governmental fund only if the item increases or decreases current financial resources during the year.

To illustrate the accounting for a special item, assume that the management of a governmental entity decides to sell vacant land (with a historical cost basis of $200,000) to a commercial developer for $130,000 (its estimated fair value). The governmental entity has several vacant lots and over the past several years has sold the property to encourage development in the downtown area. The management believes the sales are unusual in nature (that is, nonoperating), but since they are frequent they are not considered extraordinary. The special item would be reflected in the appropriate governmental fund by making the following entry:

| | | |
|---|---|---|
| Cash | 130,000 | |
| Special item—proceeds from sale of land | | 130,000 |

To convert the special item from a modified accrual basis to an accrual basis for presentation in the government-wide financial statements, the following worksheet conversion entry is made:

| | | |
|---|---|---|
| Special item—proceeds from sale of land | 130,000 | |
| Special item—loss on sale of land | 70,000 | |
| Land | | 200,000 |

## Merging Internal Service Funds

GASB-34 introduced a number of changes to the governmental financial reporting model. In the past, Internal Service Funds were an integral part of the financial reporting model, and although GASB-34 continues with this type of proprietary fund, the nature of how Internal Service Funds are reported in the new model is significantly different.

The financial statements of all Internal Service Funds are combined into a single column and are presented to the right of the

**1-50** *Introduction*

Enterprise Funds. Thus, the major fund reporting concept established by GASB-34 does not apply to Internal Service Funds.

At the government-wide reporting level, Internal Service Funds and similar activities are eliminated to avoid doubling-up expenses and revenues in preparing the government activities column of the statement of activities. The effect of this approach is to adjust activities in an Internal Service Fund to a break-even balance. That is, if the Internal Service Fund had a "net profit" for the year there should be a pro rata reduction in the charges made to the funds that used the Internal Service Fund's services for the year. Likewise, a net loss would require a pro rata adjustment that would increase the charges made to the various participating funds. After making these eliminations, any residual balances related to the Internal Service Fund's assets, liabilities, and net assets are generally reported in the governmental activities column in the statement of net assets.

To illustrate the merging of an Internal Service Fund's accounts in the government-wide financial statements, assume that the following pre-closing trial balances for governmental funds exist at the end of a governmental entity's fiscal year:

Pre-Closing Trial Balance For Government Activities

|                     | Dr.    | Cr.    |
|---------------------|--------|--------|
| Assets              | 16,000 |        |
| Liabilities         |        | 6,000  |
| Program revenues    |        | 39,000 |
| Program A expenses  | 10,000 |        |
| Program B expenses  | 20,000 |        |
| Interest expense    | 4,000  |        |
| Investment income   |        | 1,000  |
| Net assets          |        | 4,000  |
| Totals              | 50,000 | 50,000 |

**NOTE:** These amounts include all governmental funds (General Fund, Special Revenue Funds, Capital Projects Funds, Debt Service Funds, and Permanent Funds) adjusted from a modified accrual basis (as presented in the fund-level financial statements) to an accrual basis (which is the basis required in the government-wide financial statements).

Pre-Closing Trial Balance For Government Activities

|             | Dr.   | Cr.   |
|-------------|-------|-------|
| Assets      | 4,000 |       |
| Liabilities |       | 2,000 |

|  | Dr. | Cr. |
|---|---|---|
| Revenues |  | 5,000 |
| Expenses | 4,500 |  |
| Net assets |  | 1,500 |
| Totals | 8,500 | 8,500 |

**NOTE:** The Internal Service Fund balances are reported on an accrual basis at the fund financial statement level.

The activities accounted for in the Internal Service Fund resulted in a "net profit" of $500 ($5,000 - $4,500), which means that the operating expenses listed in the pre-closing trial balance of government activities are overstated by $500. In order to merge the residual amounts of the Internal Service Fund into the government-activities column of the reporting entity, the following worksheet adjustments are made:

|  | Pre-Closing Trial Balance For Government Activities |  | Eliminations Based on Internal Service Residual Balances |  | Pre-Closing Trial Balance For Government Activities Including Internal Service Residual Balances |  |
|---|---|---|---|---|---|---|
|  | Dr. | Cr. | Dr. | Cr. | Dr. | Cr. |
| Assets | 16,000 | — | 4,000 | — | 20,000 | — |
| Liabilities | — | 6,000 | — | 2,000 | — | 8,000 |
| Program revenues | — | 39,000 | — | — | — | 39,000 |
| Program A expenses | 10,000 | — | — | 300 | 9,700 | — |
| Program B expenses | 20,000 | — | — | 200 | 19,800 | — |
| Interest expense | 4,000 | — | — | — | 4,000 | — |
| Investment income | — | 1,000 | — | — | — | 1,000 |
| Net assets | — | 4,000 | — | 1,500 | — | 5,500 |
|  | 50,000 | 50,000 | 4,000 | 4,000 | 53,500 | 53,500 |

**NOTE:** It is assumed that during the year the Internal Service Fund's activities were provided to Program A (60%) and Program B (40%), which were reported in governmental funds.

Once the governmental activities have been adjusted to include residual values (including assets, liabilities, net assets, and operating activities), the statement of net assets and statement of activities must be formatted to reflect the standards established by GASB-34.

The government-wide financial statements are divided into governmental activities and business-type activities. Generally, as illustrated above, the activities conducted by an Internal Service Fund are related to governmental activities and, therefore, the residual amounts of the Internal Service Fund are merged with other governmental funds and presented in the governmental activities column of the government-wide financial statements. However, the activities of an Internal Service Fund must be analyzed to determine whether they are governmental or business-type in nature or both. If the activities are business-type in nature the residual amounts must be merged with the business-type activities in the government-wide financial statements. In addition, the operating accounts (depreciation expenses, investment income, etc.) reported by the Internal Service Fund must be analyzed to determine whether they should be used to compute the "net profit or loss" that is the basis for allocation to the governmental or business-type activities. These issues are discussed in Chapter 8 ("Internal Service Funds").

## Eliminations of Transfers and the Identification of Internal Balances

GASB-34 classifies transfers within and among governmental funds, proprietary funds, and fiduciary funds as follows (GASB-34, par. 112):

- Reciprocal interfund activity
  — Interfund loans
  — Interfund services provided and used
- Nonreciprocal interfund activity
  — Interfund transfers
  — Interfund reimbursements

*Interfund Loans (Reciprocal Interfund Activity)*

Loans that are expected to be repaid are to be reported as interfund receivables by the lender fund and interfund payables by the borrower fund and are not eliminated at the fund financial statement level.

At the government-wide financial statement level, interfund loans are eliminated if the loan is between governmental funds. For example, a loan between the General Fund and a Special Revenue Fund is eliminated. However, a loan between a governmental fund and an Enterprise Fund is not eliminated but is reclassified as an *internal balance*. Internal balances are reported on the face of the statement of net assets in both the governmental activities column and the business-type activities column; however, the amounts will equal and are offset when the total column for the primary government is prepared.

For example, if there was a $1,000,000 loan from the General Fund to an Enterprise Fund, the following worksheet conversion entry would be made to prepare government-wide financial statements:

| Due to General Fund | 1,000,000 | |
| Internal balance | | 1,000,000 |
| | | |
| Internal balance | 1,000,000 | |
| Due from Enterprise Fund | | 1,000,000 |

The first entry is made on the worksheet that combines all governmental funds (converting from modified accrual to accrual) and the second entry is made on the worksheet that combines all Enterprise Funds for the preparation of the government-wide financial statements.

*Interfund Service Provided and Used (Reciprocal Interfund Activity)*

Interfund receivables/payables may arise from an operating activity (that is, the sale of goods and services) between funds rather than in the form of a loan arrangement. If the interfund operating activity is recorded at an amount that approximates the fair value of the goods or services exchanged, the provider/seller fund records the activity as revenue and the user/purchaser fund records an expenditure/expense. These nominal accounts are not eliminated at the fund financial statement level. Likewise, any unpaid balance at the end of the period is reported as an interfund receivable/payable at the fund financial statement level.

At the government-wide financial statement level, interfund receivables and payables between a governmental fund and an Enterprise Fund are eliminated through the use of an internal balance account as explained in the previous section. However, the revenue and expense related to the transaction are not eliminated at the government-wide financial statement level.

> **NOTE:** If the interfund activity is between two governmental funds, the activity and resulting balances are accounted for in a manner similar to the approach discussed earlier for Internal Service Funds if the amounts are material.

*Interfund Transfers (Nonreciprocal Interfund Activity)*

Interfund transfers are a type of nonreciprocal transaction that represents interfund activities whereby the two parties to the event do not receive equivalent cash, goods, or services. Governmental funds report transfers of this nature as other financing uses and other financial sources. Transfers and the related amounts that are due to other funds and due from other funds are not eliminated at the fund financial statement level.

At the government-wide financial statement level, transfers within the governmental fund group and the related amounts due to other funds and due from other funds are eliminated. For example, assume that the total transfers from the General Fund to a Capital Projects Funds were $250,000 but only $200,000 had been transferred at the end of the year. The following worksheet conversion entries are made in order to prepare the government-wide financial statements:

| | | |
|---|---|---|
| Transfers in—from General Fund | 250,000 | |
|     Transfers out—to Capital Projects Fund | | 250,000 |
| | | |
| Due to Capital Projects Fund | 50,000 | |
|     Due from General Fund | | 50,000 |

If the transfer is between a governmental fund and an Enterprise Fund, the transfers are not eliminated and any residual due to/due from amount outstanding at the end of the year is reclassified as an internal balance (described earlier).

*Interfund Reimbursements (Nonreciprocal Interfund Activity)*

A fund may incur an expenditure or expense that will subsequently be reimbursed by another fund. Reimbursements are reported only once, in the governmental fund that is eventually responsible for the item. There are no eliminations at either the fund financial statement level; however, if a governmental fund reimburses an Enterprise Fund (or vice versa) and there is an amount due to/due from that is outstanding at the end of the year, that amount would be reclassified as an internal balance.

For example, assume that the General Fund paid $100,000 of expenses for an Enterprise Fund and at the end of the year only $80,000 of the payment had been reimbursed. During the year, the two funds make the following entries to record the transactions:

**General Fund**

| | | |
|---|---|---|
|     Due from Enterprise Fund | 100,000 | |
|         Cash | | 100,000 |
| | | |
|     Cash | 80,000 | |
|         Due from Enterprise Fund | | 80,000 |

**Enterprise Fund**

| | | |
|---|---|---|
|     Expense | 100,000 | |
|         Due to General Fund | | 100,000 |

| | | |
|---|---|---|
| Due to General Fund | 80,000 | |
| Cash | | 80,000 |

At the fund financial statement level, there would be no eliminations; however, at the government-wide financial statement level, the following worksheet conversion entry is made:

| | | |
|---|---|---|
| Internal balance | 20,000 | |
|    Due from Enterprise Fund | | 20,000 |
| | | |
| Due to General Fund | 20,000 | |
|    Internal balance | | 20,000 |

The first entry is made on the worksheet that combines all governmental funds (converting from modified accrual to accrual basis) for presentation of balances in the governmental activities column of the government-wide financial statements and the second entry is made on the worksheet that combines all Enterprise Funds for the preparation of the business-type activities column on the government-wide financial statements.

## TERMINOLOGY AND FORMAT

### Governmental Funds Financial Statements

A governmental fund's balance sheet is prepared using the "balance sheet format," in which assets equal liabilities plus fund balances. The balance sheet reports the governmental entity's current financial resources and the claims to those resources for each major governmental fund and for the nonmajor funds. A total column is used to combine all of the major funds and nonmajor funds (GASB-34, par. 83).

> ■ **CONTINUING STANDARD:** Although the focus of presenting governmental funds has changed from a fund-type orientation to a major/nonmajor fund format, the balance sheet is essentially prepared in the same manner as previously required by NCGA-1.

The balance-sheet-format operating statement for governmental funds measures the flow of current financial resources and therefore essentially follows the current standards used to prepare governmental financial statements. The operating statement has columns for each major fund, one for all (combined) nonmajor funds, and a total column, as illustrated in the following (GASB-34, par. 86):

|  | General Fund | Major Fund #1 | Nonmajor Funds | Total |
|---|---|---|---|---|
| Revenues (detailed) | $XXX | $XXX | $XXX | $XXX |
| Expenditures (detailed) | XXX | XXX | XXX | XXX |
| Excess (deficiency) of revenues over (under) expenditures | XXX | XXX | XXX | XXX |
| Other financing sources and uses, including transfers (detailed) | XXX | XXX | XXX | XXX |
| Special and extraordinary items (detailed) | XXX | XXX | XXX | XXX |
| Net change in fund balance | XXX | XXX | XXX | XXX |
| Fund balances—beginning of period | XXX | XXX | XXX | XXX |
| Fund balances—end of period | $XXX | $XXX | $XXX | $XXX |

▶ **NEW STANDARD:** NCGA-1 illustrates three distinct formats that can be used to prepare the statement of revenues, expenditures, and changes in fund balances for governmental funds; however, GASB-34 mandates that the above format be observed (GASB-34, par. 86).

## Government-Wide Financial Statements

GASB-34 *recommends* that the statement of net assets be formatted so that the net asset amount of the reporting entity is formed by subtracting total liabilities from total assets. The category "net assets" as recommended would replace the "fund equity" section currently used by governmental entities (GASB-34, par. 30).

In addition, the following broad guidelines are to be followed in the preparation of the statement of net assets:

- Assets and liabilities are presented in the statement of net assets based on their relative liquidity.
- Capital assets (net of depreciation) are presented based on their original historical cost (including capitalized interest costs, if applicable) plus ancillary charges such as transportation, installation, and site preparation costs (capital assets include infrastructure assets).
- Three components of net assets, namely (1) invested in capital assets, net of related debt, (2) restricted net assets, and (3) unrestricted net assets are presented

The format for the government-wide statement of activities is significantly different from any operating statement currently used in governmental financial reporting. The focus of the statement of activities is on the *net cost* of various activities provided by the governmental entity. The statement begins with a column that identifies the cost of each governmental activity. Another column identifies the revenues that are specifically related to the classified governmental activities. The difference between the expenses and revenues related to specific activities computes the net cost or benefits of the activities, which "identifies the extent to which each function of the government draws from the general revenues of the government or is self-financing through fees and intergovernmental aid" (GASB-34, pars. 38–40)

GASB-34 identifies the following as specific classifications that are to be used to prepare the statement of activities:

- Program Revenues
  — Charges for services
  — Operating grants and contributions
  — Capital grants and contributions
- General revenues
- Contributions to Permanent Funds
- Special Items
- Extraordinary Items
- Transfers

In addition, the following broad guidelines are to be followed in the preparation of the statement of activities:

- Expenses are presented by major function (at a minimum, each functional program should include direct expenses).
- Depreciation expense is reported as a direct expense of the specific functional categories if the related capital asset can be identified with the functional category.
- Depreciation expense related to capital assets that are not identified with a particular functional category may be presented as a separate line item.
- Interest expense on general long-term debt is generally considered an indirect expense and is not to be allocated as a direct expense to specific functional categories but instead is presented as a single line item.

**OBSERVATION:** GASB-34 does not require infrastructure assets that are part of a network or subsystem of a network (referred to as eligible infrastructure assets) to be depreciated under certain conditions. This method is referred to as the "modified approach." If the modified approach is used, the implementation issues have far more to do with engineering concepts than financial reporting. The *Miller Governmental GAAP Practice Manual* assumes that the governmental entity depreciates all of its infrastructure assets.

As stated above, the format of the statement of activities is significantly different from other operating statements and is not compatible with the conventional accounting spreadsheet structure. In the *Miller Governmental GAAP Practice Manual*, the conventional spreadsheet structure is used (because of its convenience and simplicity) and the completed worksheet is then reformatted to create a statement of activities consistent with the standards established by GASB-34.

## EFFECTIVE DATES

The GASB encourages the early implementation of the standards established by GASB-34. As explained below, the effective date for implementing the standards varies depending upon the size of the governmental entity. If a governmental entity elects implementation of the standards for periods beginning before June 15, 2000, it must also simultaneously implement the standards established by GASB-33. Also, when an early implementation strategy is adopted, all of the primary government's component units must implement the standards early (GASB-34, par. 142).

The required implementation date depends on a governmental entity's total annual revenues in the first fiscal year ending after June 15, 1999. Total annual revenues for this purpose includes all revenues of the primary government's governmental and enterprise funds but does not include other financing sources and extraordinary gains. The following schedule identifies the required implementation date for a particular governmental entity (GASB-34, par. 143):

| The Amount of the Primary Government's Annual Revenues | The Required Implementation Date for the Standards Is |
|---|---|
| Equal to or greater than $100 million (Phase 1 Government) | For periods beginning after June 15, 2001 |
| Between $10 million and $100 million (Phase 2 Government) | For periods beginning after June 15, 2002 |
| Less than $10 million (Phase 3 Government) | For periods beginning after June 15, 2003 |

**OBSERVATION:** A special-purpose government that is involved solely in fiduciary activities should use total annual additions (not revenues) to determine its implementation date.

A governmental entity's component units must implement the standards no later than the same year as the primary government regardless of each component unit's total revenues.

In order to implement the standards established by GASB-34, a governmental entity must treat adjustments to its governmental, proprietary, and fiduciary funds as prior period adjustments with appropriate restatement of all periods presented on a comparative basis. If it is not practical to restate all previous periods, the adjustment should be made to the beginning fund balance or fund net assets for the earlier period restated. Under this circumstance, the earlier restated period would be the current period. For the first period restated due to the implementation of the standards, the financial statements should disclose the nature of the restatement and its effect (GASB-34, par. 144).

## COMPREHENSIVE ILLUSTRATION

The remainder of this book is structured around a comprehensive illustration based on the fictional City of Centerville, which has the following funds.

### Governmental Funds

- The General Fund
- Special Revenue Funds
  - *Center City Special Services District*—This fund provides special services, such as street maintenance, street cleaning, and similar services to approximately six square blocks of the business district. Businesses in this area pay a special service fee for these services.
  - *Local Fuel Tax Fund*—This fund receives a share of the fuel taxes collected by the state government. The fuel tax receipts are to be used to maintain and repair the City's streets and highways.
- Capital Projects Funds
  - *Easely Street Bridge Project*—This fund accounts for the construction of a bridge that will relieve traffic congestion between the downtown district and the east end of Centerville.
  - *Bland Street Drainage Project*—This fund accounts for construction work to mitigate flooding problems on one of the City's major thoroughfares.

- *West End Recreation Center Project*—This fund accounts for construction activities related to a recreational facility for pre-teen and teenage students.
- Debt Funds
    - *Senior Citizens' Center Bonds*—This fund is used to service serial bonds ($10,000,000) that were issued to build the Centerville Senior Citizens' Center.
    - *Easely Street Bridge Bonds*—This fund is used to service two bonds instruments ($2,000,000 and $10,000,000) that partially finance the construction of a new bridge.
    - *Bland Street Drainage Bonds*—This fund is used to service serial bonds ($4,900,000) that were issued to finance the Bland Street drainage project.
    - *West End Recreation Center Bonds*—This fund is used to service bonds ($3,000,000) that were issued to finance the construction of the recreation center.
- Permanent Funds
    - *City Cemetery Fund*—This fund accounts for a public cemetery that was endowed by contributions from interested individuals. Only the investment earnings from the permanent endowment can be used to preserve and maintain the cemetery.

## Proprietary Funds

- Enterprise Funds
    - *Centerville Toll Bridge*—The toll bridge was constructed several years ago and provides access across the Centerville River from the downtown area to a primarily residential section of the city.
    - *Centerville Utilities Authority*—This Authority provides sewer services to the citizens, businesses, and other institutions of the City.
    - *Centerville Parking Authority*—This Authority owns and manages parking garages and lots in downtown Centerville.
    - *Centerville Municipal Airport*—This regional airport serves the City and several smaller communities in three adjacent counties.
- Internal Service Funds
    - *Communications and Technology Support Center*—This fund provides a variety of communication and computer support services to all of the City's governmental and proprietary funds.

— *Fleet Management Unit*—This fund provides a motor pool to all of the City's governmental funds and to some other governmental units that are not part of the City's reporting entity. The unit provides no services to Enterprise Funds.
— *Special Services Support Center*—This fund provides support services exclusively for the Centerville Municipal Airport.

## Fiduciary Funds

- Pension Trust Funds
  — *City of Centerville Pension Trust Fund*—The City's defined benefits pension agreement is administered by the State Public Employees Retirement Fund (SPERF) and is reported by the City in this trust fund.
- Private-Purpose Trust Funds
  — *Scholarship Trust Fund*—This fund accounts for an endowment arrangement whereby needy students are assisted with their higher education expenditures.
- Agency Funds
  — *Community Support Fund*—This fund is used to distribute certain state grants to various not-for-profit organizations.

# PART II.
# GOVERNMENTAL FUNDS

# CHAPTER 2
# THE GENERAL FUND

## CONTENTS

| | |
|---|---|
| Nature of General Funds | 2-2 |
| Measurement Focus and Basis of Accounting | 2-2 |
|     Revenue Recognition | 2-2 |
|     Expenditure Recognition | 2-4 |
|     Other Financing Uses and Sources | 2-5 |
|     Interfund Billings and Activities | 2-5 |
|     Reimbursements | 2-6 |
|     Fund Balance Reservations | 2-6 |
| Financial Reporting at Fund Level | 2-6 |
| Financial Reporting at Government-Wide Level | 2-7 |
| Illustrative Transactions | 2-8 |
| Fund Financial Statements | **2-31** |
| Converting to Government-Wide Financial Statements | **2-33** |
|     Current Transactions | 2-34 |
|         Capital Lease (Worksheet Entries JE02..51A and JE02.51B) | 2-34 |
|         Unrestricted Operating Grant (Worksheet Entry JE02.52) | 2-36 |
|         Capital Assets Acquired (Worksheet Entries JE02.53A, JE02.53B, JE02.53D, and JE02.53C) | 2-37 |
|         Capital Assets Sold (Worksheet Entry JE02.54) | 2-38 |
|         Depreciation Expense (Worksheet Entry JE02.55) | 2-39 |
|         Extraordinary Item (Worksheet Entry JE02.56) | 2-40 |
|         Accrual for Claims/Assessments and Compensated Absences (Worksheet Entries JE02.57A, JE02.57B, and JE02.57C) | 2-40 |
|         Property Tax Revenue Accrual (Worksheet Entry JE02.58) | 2-42 |
|         Program Revenue Accruals (Worksheet Entry JE02.59) | 2-43 |
|     Beginning of Year Balances | **2-44** |
|         Capital Assets (Worksheet Entry JE02.60) | **2-44** |
|         Long-Term Debt (Worksheet Entry JE02.61) | **2-45** |

| | |
|---|---|
| Compensated Absences and Claims/Judgements (Worksheet Entry JE02.62) | 2-45 |
| Appendix 2A: Worksheet for Summarizing Current Transactions and Adjustments—Modified Accrual Basis | 2-48 |
| Appendix 2B: General Fund—Statement of Revenues, Expenditures, and Changes in Fund Balances and Balance Sheet | 2-58 |
| Appendix 2C: Worksheet to Convert from Modified Accrual Basis to Accrual Basis | 2-61 |
| Appendix 2D: General Fund—Adjusted Trial Balance | 2-65 |

## NATURE OF GENERAL FUNDS

An entity's General Fund is used to account for a governmental unit's current operations by recording inflows and outflows of financial resources. Current inflows are typically from revenue sources such as property taxes, income taxes, sales taxes, fines, and penalties. Current outflows are generally related to the unit's provision for various governmental services such as health and welfare, streets, public safety, and general governmental administration. Every state or local government must have a General Fund.

■ **CONTINUING STANDARD:** The definition of the General Fund continues to be based on the description established by NCGA-1 (Governmental Accounting and Financial Reporting Principles).

## MEASUREMENT FOCUS AND BASIS OF ACCOUNTING

The modified accrual basis and flow of current financial resources are used to prepare the financial statements of a General Fund. The flow of current financial resources applied on a modified accrual basis is a narrow interpretation of what constitutes revenues, expenditures, assets, and liabilities of a governmental entity.

### Revenue Recognition

Most governmental entities are involved in a number of nonexchange and exchange (and exchange-like) transactions. What distinguishes a nonexchange transaction from an exchange transaction is that in a nonexchange transaction a government "either gives value (benefit) to another party without directly receiving equal value in exchange or receives value (benefit) from another party without directly giving equal value in exchange" (GASB-33, par. 7).

In a nonexchange transaction two parties are the provider of the resources and the receiver of the resources. A state or local government could be either the provider or the receiver of the resources in a nonexchange transaction. GASB-33 (Accounting and Financial Reporting for Nonexchange Transactions) provides accounting and reporting standards for the following four categories of nonexchange transactions:

1. Derived tax revenues
2. Imposed nonexchange revenues
3. Government-mandated nonexchange transactions
4. Voluntary nonexchange transactions

In general, revenue related to a nonexchange transaction should be recognized when the revenue is both measurable and available. Measurable means that the expected asset flow is subject to reasonable estimation, while available means that the resources are realizable within the current accounting period, or shortly after the end of the period but in time to pay liabilities of the current accounting period.

> **NEW STANDARD:** In practice, the period of collectibility has generally ranged from thirty days to as much as a year. GASB-38 (Certain Financial Statement Note Disclosures) does not attempt to define the availability criterion in a more restricted manner, but it does require a governmental entity to specifically disclose what period of time is used to implement the standard. For example, the disclosure requirement could be met by simply stating "the city considers receivables collected within sixty days after year-end to be available and recognizes them as revenues of the current year."

When a governmental entity is involved in an exchange transaction, the revenue is recognized when it is earned, assuming that the timing of the receipt of the resources satisfies the availability criterion.

> **OBSERVATION:** For a discussion of revenue recognition criteria, see the chapter titled "Revenue—Nonexchange and Exchange Transactions" of the *Miller Governmental GAAP Guide*.

> **NEW STANDARD:** The detail guidance established by GASB-33 applies to both fund financial statements and government-wide financial statements except that revenues do not have to be *available* to accrue revenue for government-wide financial statements.

## Expenditure Recognition

NCGA-1, paragraph 70, states that "most expenditures and transfers out are measurable and should be recorded when the related liability is incurred." GASBI-6 (Recognition and Measurement of Certain Liabilities and Expenditures in Governmental Fund Financial Statements) expands on this general guidance by noting the following:

> Governmental fund liabilities and expenditures that should be accrued include liabilities that, once incurred, normally are paid in a timely manner and in full from current financial resources—for example, salaries, professional services, supplies, utilities, and travel [GASBI-6, par. 12].

These transactions give rise to fund liabilities that are considered mature liabilities because they are "normally due and payable in full when incurred." However, GASBI-6 points out that there are several significant exceptions to the general guidance established in NCGA-1. Specifically, NCGA-1 states that "unmatured long-term indebtedness" should not be reported as a fund liability (except for debts that are related to proprietary and trust funds). Unmatured long-term indebtedness is defined as "the portion of general long-term indebtedness that is not yet due for payment," and includes debts such as the following (NCGA-1, pars. 9–11):

- Formal debt agreements such as bonds and notes
- Liabilities not "normally expected to be liquidated with expendable available financial resources"
- Other commitments that are not current liabilities properly recorded in governmental funds

GASBI-6 points out that the three specified categories listed above are exceptions to the general rule that a liability is recorded as a fund liability and "in the absence of an explicit requirement to do otherwise, a government should accrue a governmental fund liability and expenditure in the period in which the government incurs the liability" (GASBI-6, par. 12).

> **OBSERVATION:** For a discussion of expenditure/liabilities recognition criteria, see the chapter titled "Liabilities" of the *Miller Governmental GAAP Guide*.

> ■ **CONTINUING STANDARD:** The accounting for expenditures/liabilities continues to be recorded based on the standards established by GASBI-6 (Recognition and Measurement of Certain Liabilities and Expenditures in Governmental Fund Financial Statements).

## Other Financing Uses and Sources

A General Fund may be involved in transactions that reduce or increase current financial resources but because of the nature of the transactions the items are not identified as revenues or expenditures. Examples of these transactions include the proceeds from the sale of debt, payments to bond refunding escrow agents, proceeds from the sale of capital assets (if considered immaterial amounts, they may be reported as miscellaneous revenue), and transfers (discussed below). Other financing sources and uses should be reported on the General Fund's statement of revenues, expenditures, and changes in fund balances after the excess (deficiency) of revenues over expenditures.

## Interfund Billings and Activities

Interfund transfers represent interfund activities whereby the two parties to the transaction do not receive equivalent cash, goods, or services. A General Fund should report transfers of this nature in their activity statements as other financing uses (Transfers Out) and other financial sources of funds (Transfers In). Any resulting balances at the end of the accounting period should be reported as amounts due to and due from other funds.

> ▶ **NEW STANDARD:** Based on the standards established by GASB-34, there is no differentiation between the operating transfers and residual equity transfers that now exist. There are simply only transfers. No transfers can be reported as adjustments to a fund's beginning equity balance as previously allowed (GASB-34, par. 112).

Loans among funds should be reported as interfund receivables by the lender fund and interfund payables by the borrower fund. That is, the proceeds from interfund loans should not be reported as *other financing sources or uses* in the General Fund's operating statement. If a loan or a portion of a loan is not expected to be repaid *within a reasonable time*, the interfund receivable/payable should be reduced by the amount not expected to be repaid, and that amount should be reported as an interfund transfer by both funds that are a party to the transfer.

Interfund receivables/payables may arise from an operating activity (that is, the sale of goods and services) between funds rather than in the form of a loan arrangement. If the interfund operating activity is recorded at an amount that approximates the fair value of the goods or services exchanged, the provider/seller fund should record the activity as revenue and the user/purchaser fund should record an expenditure/expense. Any unpaid balance at the end of the period should be reported as an interfund receivable/payable in the General Fund.

▶ **NEW STANDARD:** "Interfund services provided and used" replaces the previous term "quasi-external transactions." However, except for changes in terminology, GASB-34 does not change the essential manner by which reciprocal interfund activity is reported [GASB-34, par. 112a(2)].

## Reimbursements

The General Fund may incur an expenditure that will subsequently be reimbursed by another fund. Reimbursements should be recorded only once in order to avoid double counting the item and should be presented as an expenditure of the fund that is responsible for the payment [GASB-34, par. 112b(2)].

## Fund Balance Reservations

In general, a General Fund reports in its balance sheet resources that are available to fund the following year's budget. When assets are reported that are not available for this purpose, the fund balance should be reserved. Examples of these reservations include reserves for inventories, prepayments, and encumbrances.

## FINANCIAL REPORTING AT FUND LEVEL

The balances and activities of the General Fund are presented in the following financial statements at the fund financial statement level:

- Balance Sheet
- Statement of Revenues, Expenditures, and Changes in Fund Balances

■ **CONTINUING STANDARD:** Transactions and accounts recorded in the General Fund continue to be based on standards established by various NCGA/GASB Statements and Interpretations that were outstanding before the issuance of GASB-34.

These two fund financial statements include all of the governmental funds (General Fund, Special Revenue Funds, Capital Projects Funds, Debt Service Fund, and Permanent Funds). A governmental entity should present the financial statements of its governmental and proprietary fund, but the basis for reporting these funds is not by fund type but rather by major funds (GASB-34, par. 74).

▶ **NEW STANDARD:** A significant change in the focus of reporting governmental funds and proprietary funds is that major funds are reported for these fund types; however, combined financial statements for fund types are not reported (GASB-34, par. 75).

A fund is considered a major fund if both of the following criteria are satisfied (GASB-34, pars. 75 and 76):

- Total assets, liabilities, revenues, or expenditures/expenses of the governmental (enterprise) fund are equal to or greater than 10 percent of the corresponding element total (assets, liability, and so forth) for all funds that are considered governmental funds (enterprise funds).
- The same element that met the 10 percent criteria above is at least 5 percent of the corresponding element total for all governmental and enterprise funds combined.

The General Fund is always considered a major fund and therefore must be presented in a separate column.

▶ **NEW STANDARD:** GASB-34 requires that a budgetary comparison schedule be prepared for the General Fund. This schedule is discussed in Chapter 15 ("MD&A, Notes, and Other RSI Required Supplementary Information") (GASB-34, par. 70).

## FINANCIAL REPORTING AT GOVERNMENT-WIDE LEVEL

The fund-based financial statements as described above are included in a governmental entity's financial report in order to demonstrate that restrictions imposed by statutes, regulations, or contracts have been followed. These financial statements have a short-term emphasis and generally measure and account for cash and "other assets that can easily be converted to cash."

On the other hand, government-wide financial statements were established by GASB-34 in order to provide a basis for determining (1) the extent to which current services provided by the entity were financed with current revenues and (2) the degree to which a governmental entity's financial position has changed during the fiscal year. In order to achieve these objectives, government-wide financial statements include a statement of net assets and a statement of activities. Government-wide financial statements are based on a flow of all economic resources applied on the accrual basis of accounting. The flow of economic resources refers to all assets available to the governmental unit for the purpose of providing goods and services to the public. When the flow of economic resources and the accrual basis of accounting are combined, they provide the foundation for generally accepted accounting principles used by business enterprises in that essentially all assets and liabilities, both current and long-term, are reported in the government-wide financial statements.

The government-wide financial statements include a statement of net assets and a statement of activities with columns for governmental activities and business-type activities. For the most part, balances presented for governmental funds are converted from the modified accrual basis to the accrual basis of accounting and reported in the governmental activities column. Enterprise Funds are presented as business-type activities.

Perhaps the major implementation problem facing those who prepare governmental financial statements based on the standards established by GASB-34 is the development of system procedures that facilitate the presentation of the two levels of financial statements. Most governmental entities are expected to solve this problem by maintaining its accounting systems on a modified accrual basis or (budgetary/statutory basis), which will be the basis for preparing the fund financial statements, and then using a worksheet approach to convert from the modified accrual basis to the accrual basis in order to prepare the government-wide financial statements. This approach is adopted in this text.

For the most part, this approach requires that the General Fund's ending trial balance (which is on a modified accrual basis) be adjusted to reflect accrual balances; however, when a governmental entity has Internal Service Funds these latter funds must be merged into a governmental fund. Internal Service Funds and similar activities should be eliminated to avoid doubling-up expenses and revenues in preparing the government activities column of the statement of activities. The effect of this approach is to adjust activities in an Internal Service Fund to a break-even balance. That is, if the Internal Service Fund had a "net profit" for the year, there should be a pro rata reduction in the charges made to the funds that used the Internal Service Fund's services for the year. Likewise, a net loss requires a pro rata adjustment that increases the charges made to the various participating funds. After making these eliminations, any residual balances related to the Internal Service Fund's assets, liabilities, and net assets should generally be reported in the governmental activities column in the statement of net assets.

## ILLUSTRATIVE TRANSACTIONS

In order to illustrate accounting and financial reporting standards that should be observed for the General Fund, assume that the City of Centerville had the following trial balance for the fund at July 1, 20X0:

## The General Fund 2-9

| Accounts | Trial Balance Debits | Trial Balance Credits |
|---|---:|---:|
| Cash | $ 15,200,000 | |
| Interest receivable | 20,000 | |
| Property taxes receivable | 1,400,000 | |
| Allowance for uncollectible property taxes | | $ 1,000,000 |
| Investments in marketable debt securities | 1,800,000 | |
| Investments in marketable equity securities | 4,000,000 | |
| Inventories | 12,000 | |
| Accounts payable | | 8,320,000 |
| Deferred revenue—property taxes | | 245,000 |
| Due to other funds—Internal Service Fund—Communications and Technology Support Center | | 70,000 |
| Due to other funds—Internal Service Fund—Fleet Management Unit | | 22,000 |
| Fund balance—reserved for inventories | | 12,000 |
| Fund balance—reserved for encumbrances | | 10,000 |
| Fund balance | | 12,753,000 |
| Totals | $22,432,000 | $22,432,000 |

This section presents illustrative transactions and entries for the General Fund during the fiscal year ended June 30, 20X1.

When it is not obvious how expenditures of the General Fund should be allocated, the following assumption is made:

| Governmental Activity | Allocation Assumption |
|---|---:|
| General government | 60% |
| Public safety | 20% |
| Streets | 10% |
| Recreation and parks | 5% |
| Health and welfare | 5% |
| Total | 100% |

■ **CONTINUING STANDARD:** GASB-34 generally did not change the manner of accounting for transactions that are recorded in the General Fund.

*Transaction JE02.01*—Accounts payable of $8,320,000 from the previous year were paid:

| Accounts | Debit | Credit |
|---|---|---|
| Accounts payable | 8,320,000 | |
| Cash | | 8,320,000 |

Also, the encumbrance ($10,000) from the previous year was reversed, vouchered (general government expenditures), and paid:

| Accounts | Debit | Credit |
|---|---|---|
| Fund balance—reserve for encumbrances | 10,000 | |
|    Fund balance | | 10,000 |
| | | |
| Encumbrances | 10,000 | |
|    Reserve for encumbrances | | 10,000 |
| | | |
| Expenditures—general government | 10,000 | |
|    Accounts payable | | 10,000 |
| | | |
| Accounts payable | 10,000 | |
|    Cash | | 10,000 |
| | | |
| Reserve for encumbrances | 10,000 | |
|    Encumbrances | | 10,000 |

**OBSERVATION:** Many General Funds journalize their budgets. Because budgetary entries are reversed at the end of the period and have no effect on a General Fund's statement of revenues, expenditures, and changes in fund balances, these entries are not illustrated in this example. For a discussion of journalizing budgetary information see the chapter titled "General and Special Revenue Funds" in the *Miller Governmental GAAP Guide*.

▶ **NEW STANDARD:** Paragraph 92 of NCGA-1 (Governmental Accounting and Financial Reporting Principles) requires that a governmental entity disclose the method used to account for encumbrances. When NCGA-1 was issued, governmental accounting standards with respect to encumbrances were in transition in that previously some governmental entities had treated encumbrances as expenditures and some had not. Current generally accepted accounting principles require that encumbrances not be reported as expenditure/liabilities, and for that reason GASB-38 (Certain Financial Statement Note Disclosures) eliminates the disclosure requirement established by NCGA-1, since there are no acceptable alternatives for the treatment of encumbrances.

*Transaction JE02.02*—Interest and investment income accrued at the end of the previous year was collected during the year:

| Accounts | Debit | Credit |
|---|---|---|
| Cash | 20,000 | |
|    Interest receivable | | 20,000 |

*Transaction JE02.03*—Property taxes receivable of $400,000 at the beginning of the year were collected and the balance ($1,000,000) was written off:

| Accounts | Debit | Credit |
|---|---|---|
| Cash | 400,000 | |
| Allowance for uncollectible property taxes | 1,000,000 | |
|    Property taxes receivable | | 1,400,000 |

*Transaction JE02.04*—The town levied property taxes of $100,000,000. It is expected that 10% of the amount levied will be uncollectible:

| Accounts | Debit | Credit |
|---|---|---|
| Property taxes receivable | 100,000,000 | |
|    General revenues—property taxes | | 90,000,000 |
|    Allowance for uncollectible property taxes | | 10,000,000 |

■ **CONTINUING STANDARD:** Nonexchange revenues (such as property taxes) continue to be recorded and the accounting continues to be performed based on the standards established by GASB-33 (Accounting and Financial Reporting for Nonexchange Transactions).

*Transaction JE02.05*—Property taxes collected in advance in the previous year are applied to current property tax billings:

| Accounts | Debit | Credit |
|---|---|---|
| Deferred revenue—property taxes | 245,000 | |
|    Property taxes receivable | | 245,000 |

**NOTE:** Some governmental entities use the deferred revenue account to report receivables that are not expected to be collected within a short period of time after the end of the year. This illustration uses deferred revenue only for cash received from property owners before the period in which the revenue can be recognized.

## 2-12 Governmental Funds

*Transaction JE02.06*—Property tax collections totaled $87,000,000:

| Accounts | Debit | Credit |
|---|---|---|
| Cash | 87,000,000 | |
|   Property taxes receivable | | 87,000,000 |

*Transaction JE02.07*—Common stock of $200,000 was purchased for the City's marketable equities portfolio:

| Accounts | Debit | Credit |
|---|---|---|
| Investments in marketable equity securities | 200,000 | |
|   Cash | | 200,000 |

*Transaction JE02.08*—The City leased office equipment that has an economic life of 5 years and no residual value. Lease payments of $100,000 are to be made in five annual installments beginning on August 1, 20X0. The City's incremental borrowing rate is 8%. The capitalized value of the lease is computed as follows.

$100,000 \times (n = 4; i = 8\%) \; 3.31213 =$    $331,213
First payment on first day of contract =    100,000
Total present value    $431,213

The following amortization schedule applies to the lease:

| Date | Cash | Interest | Amoritization | Book Value |
|---|---|---|---|---|
| 8/1/X0 | | | | $431,213 |
| 8/1/X0 | $100,000 | | | 331,213 |
| 8/1/X1 | 100,000 | $26,497 | $73,503 | 257,710 |
| 8/1/X2 | 100,000 | 20,617 | 79,383 | 178,327 |
| 8/1/X3 | 100,000 | 14,266 | 85,734 | 92,593 |
| 8/1/X4 | 100,000 | 7,407 | 92,593 | -0- |

The equipment is part of the general government overhead costs, and the lease transaction is recorded in the General Fund as follows:

| Accounts | Debit | Credit |
|---|---|---|
| Expenditures—general government | 431,213 | |
|   Other financing sources— capitalized leases | | 431,213 |
| Expenditures—general government | 100,000 | |
|   Cash | | 100,000 |

In addition, payments of $1,500,000 for capital lease agreements signed in a previous year totaled $1,500,000. The following amortization schedule applies to these items:

| Date | Cash | Interest | Amoritization | Book Value |
|---|---|---|---|---|
| 6/30/W9 | | | | $7,818,540 |
| 6/30/W9 | $1,500,000 | | | 6,318,540 |
| 6/30/X0 | 1,500,000 | $379,112 | $1,120,888 | 5,197,652 |
| 6/30/X1 | 1,500,000 | 311,859 | 1,188,141 | 4,009,512 |
| 6/30/X2 | 1,500,000 | 240,571 | 1,259,429 | 2,750,082 |
| 6/30/X3 | 1,500,000 | 165,005 | 1,334,995 | 1,415,087 |
| 6/30/X4 | 1,500,000 | 84,913 [R] | 1,415,087 | -0- |

The equipment is used for various governmental activities, and the lease payment is recorded as follows:

| Accounts | Debit | Credit |
|---|---|---|
| Expenditures—general government ($1,188,141 × 60%) | 712,885 | |
| Expenditures—public safety ($1,188,141 × 20%) | 237,628 | |
| Expenditures—streets ($1,188,141 × 10%) | 118,814 | |
| Expenditures—recreation and parks ($1,188,141 × 5%) | 59,407 | |
| Expenditures—health and welfare ($1,188,141 × 5%) | 59,407 | |
| Expenditures—interest | 311,859 | |
| Cash | | 1,500,000 |

■ **CONTINUING STANDARD:** The accounting for capital leases continues to be performed based on the standards established by NCGA-5 (Accounting and Financial Reporting Principles for Lease Agreements of State and Local Governments).

*Transaction JE02.09*—The state government approved unrestricted operating grants for various localities for the fiscal year ended June 30, 20X1. The City's share of the grant is $24,000,000, to be paid in four equal installments. The last installment ($6,000,000) does not meet the definition of "available" resources, but the terms of the grant satisfy the accrual standards as established by GASB-33 (Accounting and

Financial Reporting for Nonexchange Transactions) and is therefore reported as revenue in the government-wide financial statements:

| Accounts | Debit | Credit |
|---|---|---|
| Intergovernmental grants receivable | 18,000,000 | |
| General revenues—unrestricted grants | | 18,000,000 |

> ▶ **NEW STANDARD:** The availability criterion requires that resources only be recorded as revenue if those resources are expected to be collected or otherwise realized in time to pay liabilities reported in the governmental fund at the end of the accounting period. In practice, the period of collectibility has generally ranged from thirty days to as much as a year. GASB-38 (Certain Financial Statement Note Disclosures) does not attempt to define the availability criterion in a more restricted manner, but it does require a governmental entity to specifically disclose what period of time is used to implement the standard. For example, the disclosure requirement could be met by simply stating "the city considers receivables collected within sixty days after year-end to be available and recognizes them as revenues of the current year" (GASB-38, par. 7).

*Transaction JE02.10*—A purchase order for $50,000 for office supplies is signed:

| Accounts | Debit | Credit |
|---|---|---|
| Encumbrances | 50,000 | |
| Reserve for encumbrances | | 50,000 |

*Transaction JE02.11*—The supplies ordered in Transaction JE02.10 are received. All supplies are used for general governmental purposes. The consumption method is used to account for supplies:

| Accounts | Debit | Credit |
|---|---|---|
| Reserve for encumbrances | 50,000 | |
| Encumbrances | | 50,000 |
| | | |
| Inventories | 50,000 | |
| Accounts payable | | 50,000 |

> ■ **CONTINUING STANDARD:** Based on the standards established by NCGA-1 (Governmental Accounting and Financial Reporting Principles) either the consumption

method or the purchase method may be used to account for inventories/supplies at the fund financial statement level; however, the consumption method must be used to prepare the government-wide financial statements.

***Transaction JE02.12***—The liability arising from the supplies received in Transaction JE02.11 is paid:

| Accounts | Debit | Credit |
|---|---|---|
| Accounts payable | 50,000 | |
| Cash | | 50,000 |

***Transaction JE02.13***—The City received dividends of $40,000 from investments held in marketable equity securities:

| Accounts | Debit | Credit |
|---|---|---|
| Cash | 40,000 | |
| Interest and investment income | | 40,000 |

***Transaction JE02.14***—An investment in the marketable equities securities portfolio was sold for $550,000. Its carrying value was $500,000:

| Accounts | Debit | Credit |
|---|---|---|
| Cash | 550,000 | |
| Investment in marketable equity securities | | 500,000 |
| Change in fair value of investments (revenue) | | 50,000 |

■ **CONTINUING STANDARD:** The accounting for investments continues to be based on the standards established by GASB-31 (Accounting and Financial Reporting for Certain Investments and for External Investment Pools).

***Transaction JE02.15***—An operating grant of $2,000,000 was received from the state to be used to promote recreational activities:

| Accounts | Debit | Credit |
|---|---|---|
| Cash | 2,000,000 | |
| Program revenues—operating grants (recreation and parks) | | 2,000,000 |

***Transaction JE02.16***—On November 1, a purchase order for $900,000 for various vehicles for the following governmental programs was signed (the vehicles have estimated useful lives of 3 years and no residual values):

| | |
|---|---|
| General government | $100,000 |
| Police activities | 300,000 |
| Streets department | 400,000 |
| Parks department | 100,000 |
| Total payments | $900,000 |

| Accounts | Debit | Credit |
|---|---|---|
| Encumbrances | 900,000 | |
|    Reserve for encumbrances | | 900,000 |

*Transaction JE02.17*—On December 1, the vehicles ordered in the previous transaction were received:

| Accounts | Debit | Credit |
|---|---|---|
| Reserve for encumbrances | 900,000 | |
|    Encumbrances | | 900,000 |
| Expenditures—general government | 100,000 | |
| Expenditures—public safety | 300,000 | |
| Expenditures—streets | 400,000 | |
| Expenditures—recreation and parks | 100,000 | |
|    Accounts payable | | 900,000 |

*Transaction JE02.18*—On December 15, the vendor was paid for the vehicles received on December 1:

| Accounts | Debit | Credit |
|---|---|---|
| Accounts payable | 900,000 | |
|    Cash | | 900,000 |

*Transaction JE02.19*—On December 31, the City purchased $500,000 of investments for the City's debt securities portfolio:

| Accounts | Debit | Credit |
|---|---|---|
| Investments in debt securities | 500,000 | |
|    Cash | | 500,000 |

*Transaction JE02.20*—The City received three of the four installments ($18,000,000) of the state operating grant accrued in a previous transaction:

| Accounts | Debit | Credit |
|---|---|---|
| Cash | 18,000,000 | |
|    Intergovernmental grants receivable | | 18,000,000 |

*Transaction JE02.21*—During the year the City had the following capital asset transactions.

The following capital assets were sold:

|  | Original Cost | Accumulated Depreciation | Proceeds | Loss on Sale of Asset |
|---|---|---|---|---|
| Buildings (related to general administrative activities) | $7,000,000 | $2,000,000 | $4,500,000 | $500,000 |
| Equipment (related to general administrative activities) | 1,400,000 | 1,000,000 | 200,000 | 200,000 |
| Vehicles (related to public safety activities | 3,200,000 | 3,000,000 | 100,000 | 100,000 |
| Total | $11,600,000 | $6,000,000 | $4,800,000 | $800,000 |

The dispositions are recorded as follows:

| Accounts | Debit | Credit |
|---|---|---|
| Cash | 4,800,000 | |
|     Miscellaneous revenue | | 4,800,000 |

■ **CONTINUING STANDARD:** Based on the standards established by NCGA-1 (Governmental Accounting and Financial Reporting Principles) the disposition of a capital asset is only recorded to the extent that cash (or near cash) is received; however, a gain or loss on the disposition must be recorded in order to prepare the government-wide financial statements. (Alternatively, the $900,000 could have been recorded as an other financing source.)

The following equipment was acquired for cash:

|  | Cost | Depreciation for Current Year |
|---|---|---|
| General government | $2,000,000 | $170,000 |
| Public safety | 1,300,000 | 110,000 |
| Streets | 700,000 | 95,000 |
| Recreation and parks | 500,000 | 40,000 |
| Health and welfare | 200,000 | 22,000 |
| Total | $4,700,000 | $437,000 |

The authorization, voucher, and payment of the expenditures are recorded as follows:

| Accounts | Debit | Credit |
|---|---|---|
| Encumbrances | 4,700,000 | |
|     Reserve for encumbrances | | 4,700,000 |

| Accounts | Debit | Credit |
|---|---|---|
| Reserve for encumbrances | 4,700,000 | |
|     Encumbrances | | 4,700,000 |
| | | |
| Expenditures—general government | 2,000,000 | |
| Expenditures—public safety | 1,300,000 | |
| Expenditures—streets | 700,000 | |
| Expenditures—recreation and parks | 500,000 | |
| Expenditures—health and welfare | 200,000 | |
|     Accounts payable | | 4,700,000 |
| | | |
| Accounts payable | 4,700,000 | |
|     Cash | | 4,700,000 |

In addition, the state gave the City several acres of land for development as a system of parks. The land has an estimated appraisal value of $20,000,000, and this type of gift from the state is considered unusual and nonoperating (an extraordinary item).

No entry is made for the land received as a gift from the state because it does not represent expendable financial resources. The land will be reported in the government-wide financial statements as an extraordinary item.

> ▶ **NEW STANDARD:** GASB-34 establishes two new categories for governmental fund operating statements and for government-wide financial statements, namely extraordinary items and special items. GASB-34 incorporates the definition of "extraordinary items" (unusual in nature and infrequent in occurrence) as provided in APB Opinion No. 30 (Reporting the Results of Operations—Reporting the Effects of Disposal of a Segment of a Business, and Extraordinary, Unusual and Infrequently Occurring Events and Transactions) (GASB-34, par. 55). Unlike APB-30, the GASB identifies a new classification, "special items," which are described as "significant transactions or other events within the control of management that are either unusual in nature or infrequent in occurrence." Special items should be reported separately and before extraordinary items. If a significant transaction or other event occurs but is not within the control of management and that item is either unusual or

infrequent, the item is not reported as a special item, but the nature of the item must be described in a note to the financial statements (GASB-34, par. 56).

***Transaction JE02.22***—The City received a contribution of $50,000 from a corporation to support the City's obesity awareness program:

| Accounts | Debit | Credit |
| --- | --- | --- |
| Cash | 50,000 | |
|   Program revenues—operating contributions (health and welfare) | | 50,000 |

***Transaction JE02.23***—The City received a capital grant of $500,000 from the state for the purchase of police vehicles:

| Accounts | Debit | Credit |
| --- | --- | --- |
| Cash | 500,000 | |
|   Program revenues—capital grants (public safety) | | 500,000 |

***Transaction JE02.24***—The City signed a purchase order for the acquisition of $520,000 of police vehicles:

| Accounts | Debit | Credit |
| --- | --- | --- |
| Encumbrances | 520,000 | |
|   Reserve for encumbrances | | 520,000 |

***Transaction JE02.25***—The City received dividends of $30,000 from investments held in marketable equity securities:

| Accounts | Debit | Credit |
| --- | --- | --- |
| Cash | 30,000 | |
|   Interest and investment income | | 30,000 |

***Transaction JE02.26***—On May 1, the City received the police vehicles ordered in a previous transaction. The vehicles have an estimated economic life of three years and have nominal residual values:

| Accounts | Debit | Credit |
| --- | --- | --- |
| Reserve for encumbrances | 520,000 | |
|   Encumbrances | | 520,000 |
| | | |
| Expenditures—public safety | 520,000 | |
|   Accounts payable | | 520,000 |

## 2-20 Governmental Funds

***Transaction JE02.27***—The City paid the invoice for the police vehicles received on May 1. The purchase was financed from the capital grant received on March 1 ($500,000) and from general resources:

| Accounts | Debit | Credit |
|---|---|---|
| Accounts payable | 520,000 | |
|     Cash | | 520,000 |

***Transaction JE02.28***—The City received $300,000 of property tax receipts that apply to the next fiscal year:

| Accounts | Debit | Credit |
|---|---|---|
| Cash | 300,000 | |
|     Deferred revenues—property taxes | | 300,000 |

***Transaction JE02.29***—The City signed a purchase order for $25,000 for office supplies:

| Accounts | Debit | Credit |
|---|---|---|
| Encumbrances | 25,000 | |
|     Reserve for encumbrances | | 25,000 |

***Transaction JE02.30***—During the fiscal year the following cash payments were made for the following expenditures:

| | |
|---|---|
| General government | $20,000,000 |
| Public safety | 12,000,000 |
| Streets | 9,000,000 |
| Recreation and parks | 5,000,000 |
| Health and welfare | 7,000,000 |
| Education (payment to school district—a component unit) | 32,000,000 |
| Total payments | $85,000,000 |

| Accounts | Debit | Credit |
|---|---|---|
| Expenditures—general government | 20,000,000 | |
| Expenditures—public safety | 12,000,000 | |
| Expenditures—streets | 9,000,000 | |
| Expenditures—recreation and parks | 5,000,000 | |
| Expenditures—health and welfare | 7,000,000 | |
| Expenditures—education (component unit) | 32,000,000 | |
|     Cash | | 85,000,000 |

The General Fund  2-21

- **CONTINUING STANDARD:** Based on the standards established by GASBI-6 (Recognition and Measurement of Certain Liabilities and Expenditures in Governmental Fund Financial Statements) expenditures should continue to be recorded on an accrual basis except with respect to the expenditures identified in the Interpretation.

- **CONTINUING STANDARD:** Expenditures presented in the statement of revenues, expenditures, and changes in fund balances should continue to be classified consistent with the standards discussed in NCGA-1 (par. 110 and pars. 111–116).

*Transaction JE02.31*—During the fiscal year the following cash receipts were received:

| | |
|---|---:|
| Charges for events held by Parks Department | $125,000 |
| Fines related to police activities | 200,000 |
| Fees charged by Streets Department | 150,000 |
| Licenses and permits collected by the various governmental agencies (receipts are related to general government activities) | 50,000 |
| Total collections | $525,000 |

| Accounts | Debit | Credit |
|---|---:|---:|
| Cash | 525,000 | |
| Program revenues—charges for services (recreation and parks) | | 125,000 |
| Program revenues—charges for services (public safety) | | 200,000 |
| Program revenues—charges for services (streets) | | 150,000 |
| Program revenues—charges for services (general government) | | 50,000 |

*Transaction JE02.32*—Franchise taxes collected during the year amounted to $1,300,000:

| Accounts | Debit | Credit |
|---|---:|---:|
| Cash | 1,300,000 | |
| General revenues—franchise taxes | | 1,300,000 |

■ **CONTINUING STANDARD:** The accounting for non-exchange revenues (such as franchise taxes) continues to be performed based on the standards established by GASB-33 (Accounting and Financial Reporting for Nonexchange Transactions).

***Transaction JE02.33***—During the year contributions of $7,000,000 were made to the City of Centerville Public Employee Retirement Fund:

| Accounts | Debit | Credit |
|---|---|---|
| Expenditures—general government ($7,000,000 × 60%) | 4,200,000 | |
| Expenditures—public safety ($7,000,000 × 20%) | 1,400,000 | |
| Expenditures—streets ($7,000,000 × 10%) | 700,000 | |
| Expenditures—recreation and parks ($7,000,000 × 5%) | 350,000 | |
| Expenditures—health and welfare ($7,000,000 × 5%) | 350,000 | |
| Cash | | 7,000,000 |

■ **CONTINUING STANDARD:** The accounting for pension expenditures continues to be performed based on the standards established by GASB-27 (Accounting for Pensions by State and Local Governmental Employers).

***Transaction JE02.34 (Adjustment)***—The investments in the marketable equity securities portfolio had a net increase in fair value of $240,000 at the end of the year:

| Accounts | Debit | Credit |
|---|---|---|
| Investments in marketable equity securities | 240,000 | |
| Change in fair value of investments (revenue) | | 240,000 |

***Transaction JE02.35 (Adjustment***—The investments in the debt securities portfolio had a net decrease in fair value of $150,000 at the end of the year:

| Accounts | Debit | Credit |
|---|---|---|
| Change in fair value of investments (revenue) | 150,000 | |
| Investments in debt securities | | 150,000 |

***Transaction JE02.36 (Adjustment)***—The City's Legal Department notes that a $5,000,000 claim was raised during the year by an individual based on alleged personal and property damages caused by a police vehicle. It is believed that it is *probable* that the claim will have to be paid but the estimate of the loss is about $300,000. It is also believed that the claim will be settled during the latter part of next year. This claim represents a loss contingency of $300,000, but since the loss will not use current expendable financial resources it is not accrued in the General Fund. The amount will be reported in the governmental activities column of the government-wide financial statements, as shown later in the chapter.

Estimated claims and judgments of $2,000,000 were outstanding as of the beginning of the year and two of the claims (related to public safety activities) were settled for $400,000. The payment is recorded as follows:

| Accounts | Debit | Credit |
|---|---|---|
| Expenditures—public safety | 400,000 | |
| Cash | | 400,000 |

The balance of the estimated unsettled claims at the beginning of the year ($1,600,000) is expected to be settled during the next two to five years.

■ **CONTINUING STANDARD:** The accounting for loss contingencies (such as claims and judgments) continues to be performed based on the standards established by NCGA-4 (Accounting and Financial Reporting Principles for Claims and Judgments and Compensated Absences).

*Transaction JE02.37 (Adjustment)*—Compensated absences paid during the year totaled $60,000 and were included in Transaction JE02.30. Compensated absences earned by employees during the year amounted to $220,000. The $220,000 amount will not use current expendable financial resources, so it is not reflected in the fund financial statements. (As illustrated later, the $220,000 will be reported in the government-wide financial statements.)

*Transaction JE02.38 (Adjustment)*—Property taxes receivable from specific residents of $9,000,000 is identified as uncollectible:

| Accounts | Debit | Credit |
|---|---|---|
| Allowance for uncollectible property taxes | 9,000,000 | |
| Property taxes receivable | | 9,000,000 |

*Transaction JE02.39 (Adjustment)*—After additional analysis the allowance for uncollectible accounts is increased by $1,000,000. This is a change in an accounting estimate:

## 2-24 Governmental Funds

| Accounts | Debit | Credit |
|---|---|---|
| General revenues—property taxes | 1,000,000 | |
|    Allowance for uncollectible property taxes | | 1,000,000 |

**Transaction JE02.40 (Adjustment)**—It is expected that the remaining balance of property taxes receivable (net of the allowance) will be collected during the next fiscal year. Approximately 70% of that amount will not be collected in time to pay existing liabilities, thus not satisfying the availability criterion:

| Accounts | Debit | Credit |
|---|---|---|
| General revenues—property taxes ($2,000,000 × 70%) | 1,400,000 | |
|    Property taxes receivable | | 1,400,000 |

| | PT Receivable | U/Accts | Allowance Revenue |
|---|---|---|---|
| Beginning balance | $1,400,000 | $1,000,000 | — |
| Collections and write-offs | (1,400,000) | (1,000,000) | — |
| Application of deferred taxes received in the previous year | (245,000) | — | — |
| Amounts recognized at levy date | $100,000,000 | 10,000,000 | $90,000,000 |
| Receivables collected | (44,000,000) | — | — |
| Receivables collected | (43,000,000) | — | — |
| Specific write-offs | (9,000,000) | (9,000,000) | — |
| Change in estimate | — | 1,000,000 | (1,000,000) |
| Balances—accrual basis | 3,755,000 | 2,000,000 | 89,000,000 |
| Receivables estimated to be collected in the next fiscal year but not in time to pay existing liabilities ($2,000,000 × 70%) | (1,400,000) | — | (1,400,000) |
| Balance—modified accrual basis | $2,355,000 | $2,000,000 | $87,600,000 |

**Transaction JE02.41 (Adjustment)**—The City uses the consumption method to account for supplies. At the end of the year, $17,000 of inventories was on hand. The amount of supplies consumed during the year was $45,000 ($12,000 + $50,000 - $17,000):

The General Fund 2-25

| Accounts | Debit | Credit |
|---|---|---|
| Expenditures—general government ($45,000 × 60%) | 27,000 | |
| Expenditures—public safety ($45,000 × 20%) | 9,000 | |
| Expenditures—streets ($45,000 × 10%) | 4,500 | |
| Expenditures—recreation and parks ($45,000 × 5%) | 2,250 | |
| Expenditures—health and welfare ($45,000 × 5%) | 2,250 | |
| Inventories | | 45,000 |
| | | |
| Fund balance | 5,000 | |
| Fund balance—reserved for inventories | | 5,000 |

*Transaction JE02.42 (Adjustment)*—The following charges, fees, and permits apply to activities that occurred during the current fiscal year, but approximately 60% will be collected in time to pay existing liabilities:

| | |
|---|---|
| Charges for events held by Parks Department | $10,0000 |
| Fines related to police activities | 2,000 |
| Fees charged by public health activities | 4,000 |
| Licenses and permits collected by the various governmental agencies (receipts are related to general government activities) | 5,000 |
| Total collections | $21,000 |

| Accounts | Debit | Credit |
|---|---|---|
| Other receivables ($21,000 × 60%) | 12,600 | |
| Program revenues—charges for services (recreation and parks) ($10,000 × 60%) | | 6,000 |
| Program revenues—charges for services (public safety) ($2,000 × 60%) | | 1,200 |
| Program revenues—charges for services (health and welfare) ($4,000 × 60%) | | 2,400 |
| Program revenues—charges for services (general government) ($5,000 × 60%) | | 3,000 |

## 2-26 Governmental Funds

***Transaction JE02.43 (Adjustment)***—The encumbrance ($25,000) incurred on June 25th is outstanding at the end of the year, but the City intends to honor the encumbrance and reappropriate funds to pay for the commitment in the next fiscal year (see Transaction JE02.29):

| Accounts | Debit | Credit |
|---|---|---|
| Reserve for encumbrances | 25,000 | |
|     Encumbrances | | 25,000 |
| | | |
| Fund balance | 25,000 | |
|     Fund balance—reserve for encumbrances | | 25,000 |

***Transaction JE02.44 (Adjustment)***—The following expenditures are recognized at the end of the year based on the modified accrual basis of accounting:

| | |
|---|---|
| General government | $600,000 |
| Public safety | 30,000 |
| Streets | 20,000 |
| Recreation and parks | 10,000 |
| Health and welfare | 5,000 |
| Total | $665,000 |

| Accounts | Debit | Credit |
|---|---|---|
| Expenditures—general government | 600,000 | |
| Expenditures—public safety | 30,000 | |
| Expenditures—streets | 20,000 | |
| Expenditures—recreation and parks | 10,000 | |
| Expenditures—health and welfare | 5,000 | |
|     Accounts payable | | 665,000 |

***Transaction JE02.45 (Adjustment)***—Interest and investment income of $23,000 is accrued at the end of the year:

| Accounts | Debit | Credit |
|---|---|---|
| Interest receivables | 23,000 | |
|     Interest and investment revenue | | 23,000 |

***Transaction JE02.46***—The following transfers were made to various funds during the year:

| | |
|---|---|
| Special Revenue Fund—Center City Special Services Fund | $ 75,000 |
| Capital Projects Fund—Easely Street Bridge | 1,000,000 |
| Capital Projects Fund—Bland Street Drainage Project | 600,000 |
| Capital Projects Fund—West End Recreation Center Project | 300,000 |
| Debt Service Fund—Senior Citizens' Center Bonds | 1,300,000 |
| Debt Service Fund—Easely Street Bridge Bonds | 220,000 |
| Debt Service Fund—Bland Street Drainage Bonds | 1,100,000 |
| Debt Service Fund—West End Recreation Center Bonds | 700,000 |
| Internal Service Fund—Communications and Technology Support Center | 40,000 |
| Enterprise Fund—Centerville Toll Bridge | 50,000 |
| Enterprise Fund—Centerville Parking Authority | 90,000 |
| Total | $5,475,000 |

| Accounts | Debit | Credit |
|---|---|---|
| Transfers out—Special Revenue Fund—Center City Special Services Fund | 75,000 | |
| Transfers out—Capital Projects Fund—Easely Street Bridge | 1,000,000 | |
| Transfers out—Capital Projects Fund—Bland Street Drainage Project | 600,000 | |
| Transfers out—Capital Projects Fund—West End Recreation Center Project | 300,000 | |
| Transfers out—Debt Service Fund—Senior Citizens' Center Bonds | 1,300,000 | |
| Transfers out—Debt Service Fund—Easely Street Bridge Bonds | 220,000 | |
| Transfers out—Debt Service Fund—Bland Street Drainage Bonds | 1,100,000 | |
| Transfers out—Debt Service Fund—West End Recreation Center Bonds | 700,000 | |
| Transfers out—Internal Service Fund—Communications and Technology Support Center | 40,000 | |
| Transfers out—Enterprise Fund—Centerville Toll Bridge | 50,000 | |
| Transfers out—Enterprise Fund—Centerville Parking Authority | 90,000 | |
|     Cash | | 5,475,000 |

▶ **NEW STANDARD:** Various interfund transfers occur within most governmental reporting entities. GASB-38 (Certain Financial Statement Note Disclosures) requires certain disclosures for both interfund balances outstanding at the end of the year and transfers made during the year.

***Transaction JE02.47***—A transfer of $50,000 from an Internal Service Fund (Fleet Management Unit) was received by the General Fund:

| Accounts | Debit | Credit |
| --- | --- | --- |
| Cash | 50,000 | |
|    Transfers in—Internal Service Fund— Fleet Management Unit | | 50,000 |

***Transaction JE02.48***—During the year, the Communications and Technology Support Center (an Internal Service Fund) billed the General Fund $4,500,000 for services performed. The General Fund made payments of $4,400,000:

| Accounts | Debit | Credit |
| --- | --- | --- |
| Expenditures—general government ($4,500,000 × 60%) | 2,700,000 | |
| Expenditures—public safety ($4,500,000 × 20%) | 900,000 | |
| Expenditures—streets ($4,500,000 × 10%) | 450,000 | |
| Expenditures—recreation and parks ($4,500,000 × 5%) | 225,000 | |
| Expenditures—health and welfare ($4,500,000 × 5%) | 225,000 | |
|    Cash | | 4,400,000 |
|    Due to other funds—Internal Service Fund—Communications and Technology Support Center | | 100,000 |

***Transaction JE02.49***—During the year, the Fleet Management Unit (an Internal Service Fund) billed the General Fund $4,700,000 for services performed. The General Fund made payments of $4,650,000 during the year:

| Accounts | Debit | Credit |
| --- | --- | --- |
| Expenditures—general government ($4,700,000 × 60%) | 2,820,000 | |
| Expenditures—public safety ($4,700,000 × 20%) | 940,000 | |
| Expenditures—streets ($4,700,000 × 10%) | 470,000 | |

| Accounts | Debit | Credit |
|---|---|---|
| Expenditures—recreation and parks ($4,700,000 × 5%) | 235,000 | |
| Expenditures—health and welfare ($4,700,000 × 5%) | 235,000 | |
| Cash | | 4,650,000 |
| Due to other funds—Internal Service Fund—Fleet Management Unit | | 50,000 |

***Transaction JE02.50***—During the year the following Enterprise Funds made loans to the General Fund:

| | |
|---|---|
| Centerville Utilities Authority | $2,000,000 |
| Centerville Municipal Airport | 400,000 |
| Total | $2,400,000 |

| Accounts | Debit | Credit |
|---|---|---|
| Cash | 2,400,000 | |
| Due to other funds—Enterprise Fund—Centerville Utilities Authority | | 2,000,000 |
| Due to other funds—Enterprise Fund—Centerville Municipal Airport | | 400,000 |

After the transactions for the year are posted the year-end trial balance (June 30, 20X1) for the City's General Fund appears as follows:

| Accounts | Adjusted Trial Balance Debits | Credits |
|---|---|---|
| Cash | $ 9,440,000 | |
| Interest receivable | 23,000 | |
| Property taxes receivable | 2,355,000 | |
| Allowance for uncollectible property taxes | | $ 2,000,000 |
| Other receivables | 12,600 | |
| Investments in marketable debt securities | 2,150,000 | |
| Investments in marketable equity securities | 3,940,000 | |
| Inventories | 17,000 | |
| Accounts payable | | 665,000 |
| Deferred revenue—property taxes | | 300,000 |
| Due to other funds—Internal Service Fund—Communications and Technology Support Center | | 170,000 |
| Due to other funds—Internal Service Fund—Fleet Management Unit | | 72,000 |

## 2-30 Governmental Funds

| Accounts | Adjusted Trial Balance Debits | Adjusted Trial Balance Credits |
|---|---:|---:|
| Due to other funds—Enterprise Fund—Centerville Utilities Authority | | 2,000,000 |
| Due to other funds—Enterprise Fund—Centerville Municipal Airport | | 400,000 |
| Fund balance—reserved for inventories | | 17,000 |
| Fund balance—reserved for encumbrances | | 25,000 |
| Fund balance | | 12,733,000 |
| Program revenues—charges for services (general government) | | 53,000 |
| Program revenues—operating grants (recreation and parks) | | 2,000,000 |
| Program revenues—charges for services (recreation and parks) | | 131,000 |
| Program revenues—charges for services (health and welfare) | | 2,400 |
| Program revenues—operating contributions (health and welfare) | | 50,000 |
| Program revenues—charges for services (health and welfare) | | 150,000 |
| Program revenues—capital grants (public safety) | | 500,000 |
| Program revenues—charges for services (public safety) | | 201,200 |
| General revenues—property taxes | | 87,600,000 |
| General revenues—franchise taxes | | 1,300,000 |
| General revenues—unrestricted grants | | 18,000,000 |
| Miscellaneous revenue | | 4,800,000 |
| Interest and investment revenue | | 93,000 |
| Change in fair value of investments | | 140,000 |
| Expenditures—general government | 33,701,098 | |
| Expenditures—public safety | 18,036,628 | |
| Expenditures—streets | 11,863,314 | |
| Expenditures—recreation and parks | 6,481,657 | |
| Expenditures—health and welfare | 8,076,657 | |
| Expenditures—interest | 311,859 | |
| Expenditures—education (component unit) | 32,000,000 | |
| Other financing sources—capitalized leases | | 431,213 |
| Transfers in—Internal Service Fund—Fleet Management Unit | | 50,000 |

|  | Adjusted Trial Balance | |
| Accounts | Debits | Credits |
| Transfers out—Special Revenue Fund—Center City Special Services Fund | 75,000 | |
| Transfers out—Capital Projects Fund—EaselyStreet Bridge | 1,000,000 | |
| Transfers out—Capital Projects Fund—Bland Street Drainage Project | 600,000 | |
| Transfers out—Capital Projects Fund—West End Recreation Center Project | 300,000 | |
| Transfers out—Debt Service Fund—Senior Citizens' Center Bonds | 1,300,000 | |
| Transfers out—Debt Service Fund—Easely Street Bridge Bonds Bridge Bonds | 220,000 | |
| Transfers out—Debt Service Fund—Bland Street Drainage Bonds | 1,100,000 | |
| Transfers out—Debt Service Fund—West End Recreation Center Bonds | 700,000 | |
| Transfers out—Internal Service Fund—Communications and Technology Support Center | 40,000 | |
| Transfers out—Enterprise Fund—Centerville Toll Bridge | 50,000 | |
| Transfers out—Enterprise Fund—Centerville Parking Authority | 90,000 | |
| Totals | $133,883,813 | $133,883,813 |

The worksheet that summarizes the foregoing journal entries for the General Fund for the year-end trial balance (on a modified accrual basis) is presented in Appendix 2A.

## FUND FINANCIAL STATEMENTS

At the fund financial statement level, a governmental fund must prepare a statement of revenues, expenditures, and changes in fund balances and a balance sheet. Based on the adjusted trial balances created above, the following financial statements reflect the balances and activities of the General Fund (Appendix 2-B).

> ▶ **NEW STANDARD:** NCGA-1 illustrates three distinct formats that can be used to prepare the statement of revenues, expenditures, and changes in fund balances for governmental funds; however, GASB-34 eliminates two of the options and only the format illustrated below can now be used (GASB-34, par. 86).

■ **CONTINUING STANDARD:** The formatting of the balance sheet at the fund financial statement level was not changed by GASB-34.

## General Fund
## Statement of Revenues, Expenditures, and Changes in Fund Balances
### June 30, 20X1

| | |
|---|---:|
| **REVENUES** | |
| Property taxes | $ 87,600,000 |
| Franchise taxes | 1,300,000 |
| Intergovernmental grants | 20,500,000 |
| Charges for services | 537,600 |
| Contributions | 50,000 |
| Interest and investment revenue | 93,000 |
| Miscellaneous revenue | 4,800,000 |
| Change in fair value of investments | 140,000 |
| Total revenues | 115,020,600 |
| **EXPENDITURES** | |
| Current: | |
|   General government | 33,701,098 |
|   Public safety | 18,036,628 |
|   Streets | 11,863,314 |
|   Recreation and parks | 6,481,657 |
|   Health and welfare | 8,076,657 |
|   Interest | 311,859 |
|   Education (component unit) | 32,000,000 |
| Total expenditures | 110,471,213 |
| Excess (deficiency) of revenues over expenditures | 4,549,387 |
| **OTHER FINANCING SOURCES (USES):** | |
| Execution of capital leases | 431,213 |
| Transfers in | 50,000 |
| Transfers out | (5,475,000) |
| Total other financing sources and uses | (4,993,787) |
| Net change in fund balances | (444,400) |
| Fund balances—beginning | 12,775,000 |
| Fund balances—ending | $12,330,600 |

**General Fund
Balance Sheet
June 30, 20X1**

| ASSETS | |
|---|---:|
| Cash | $ 9,440,000 |
| Property taxes receivable (net) | 355,000 |
| Other receivables | 35,600 |
| Investments | 6,090,000 |
| Inventories | 17,000 |
| Total assets | $15,937,600 |

| LIABILITIES AND FUND BALANCES | |
|---|---:|
| Liabilities: | |
|     Accounts payable | $ 665,000 |
|     Due to other funds | 2,642,000 |
|     Deferred revenue | 300,000 |
|     Total liabilities | 3,607,000 |
| FUND BALANCES | |
| Reserved for inventories | 17,000 |
| Reserved for encumbrances | 25,000 |
| Unreserved | 12,288,600 |
| Total fund balances | 12,330,600 |
| Total liabilities and fund balances | $15,937,600 |

The General Fund financial statements are not reported separately in the governmental entity's financial report, but they are used in Chapter 12 ("Developing Information for Fund Financial Statements").

## CONVERTING TO GOVERNMENT-WIDE FINANCIAL STATEMENTS

As noted earlier, government-wide financial statements are reported on the accrual basis of accounting. Generally, most governments will work from their governmental fund financial statements trial balances (which are on a modified accrual basis), and through the use of worksheet entries convert to accrual based financial statements. In order to convert the transactions that were recorded in the General Fund from a modified accrual basis to an accrual basis, the following worksheet entries are made.

▶ **NEW STANDARD:** GASB-34 introduces the concept of accrual based financial statements for governmental activities. For most governmental entities, the conversion of the General Fund from a modified accrual basis to an accrual basis will be an important part of developing government-wide financial statements. The focus of government-wide financial statements is on the overall financial position and activities of the government as a whole. These financial statements are constructed around the concept of a primary government as defined by GASB-14 (The Financial Reporting Entity) and therefore encompass the primary government and its component units except for fiduciary funds of the primary government and component units that are fiduciary in nature (GASB-34, par. 13).

## Current Transactions

Worksheet entries to convert from the modified accrual basis to the accrual basis are made for the following transactions that occurred during the year:

- Capital lease (Worksheet Entries JE02.51A and JE02.51B)
- Unrestricted operating grant (Worksheet Entry JE02.52)
- Capital assets acquired (Worksheet Entries JE02.53A, JE02.53B, JE02.53D, and JE02.53C)
- Capital assets sold (Worksheet Entry JE02.54)
- Depreciation expense (Worksheet Entry JE02.55)
- Extraordinary item (Worksheet Entry JE02.56)
- Accrual for claims/assessments and compensated absences (Worksheet Entry JE02.57A, JE02.57B, and JE02.57C)
- Property tax revenue accrual (Worksheet Entry JE02.58)
- Program revenue accruals (Worksheet Entry JE02.59)

*Capital Lease (Worksheet Entries JE02.51A and JE02.51B)*

Rather than purchase a capital asset directly from a vendor, a governmental entity may lease the item. If the agreement is considered a capitalized lease as defined in NCGA-5 (Accounting and Financial Reporting Principles for Lease Agreements of State and Local Governments), the transaction is accounted for in a governmental fund as both an issuance of debt and a capital expenditure. Thus, in order to convert the fund financial statements from a modified accrual basis to an accrual basis for the preparation of the government-wide financial statements, the expenditure must be capitalized, any related depreciation expense must be recorded, and the debt must be recognized along with the accrual of any related interest expense.

As shown in Transaction JE02.08, the City entered into a lease on August 1, 20X0. In order to convert from a modified accrual basis to an accrual basis, the following worksheet entries are made at the end of the year:

| | | |
|---|---|---|
| JE02.51A Other financing sources—capitalized leases | 431,213 | |
|     Expenditures—general government | | 431,213 |
|     (To reverse other financing source and expenditure) | | |
| Leased capital assets | 431,213 | |
|     Lease obligation payable | | 431,213 |
|     (To record capital asset and related obligation) | | |
| Lease obligation payable | 100,000 | |
|     Expenditures—general government | | 100,000 |
|     (To record initial payment as a reduction to the lease obligation rather than an expenditure) | | |
| Expenses—general government | 79,058 | |
|     Accumulated depreciation—leased capital assets | | 79,058 |
|     ($431,213 \times 1/5 \times 11/12$) | | |
|     (To record depreciation on the capital lease) | | |
| Interest expense | 24,290 | |
|     Interest payable ($26,497 \times 11/12$)—(see the original amortization schedule) | | 24,290 |
|     (To accrue interest on the lease obligation) | | |

**OBSERVATION:** If in the previous year interest expense was also accrued, the previous accrual would have to be omitted from the current year's statement of activities (debiting net assets and crediting interest expense) because the interest would have been recorded in the current year under the modified accrual basis of accounting. In this illustration it is assumed no accrual was made in the previous year.

Also in Transaction JE02.08, a $1,500,000 lease payment was made for capital leases executed in a previous year. In order to convert this payment from a modified accrual basis to an accrual basis, the following worksheet entries are made at the end of the year:

| | | | |
|---|---|---|---|
| JE02.51B | Lease obligation payable (see the original amortization schedule) | 1,188,141 | |
| | Expenditures—general government | | 712,885 |
| | Expenditures—public safety | | 237,628 |
| | Expenditures—streets | | 118,814 |
| | Expenditures—recreation and parks | | 59,407 |
| | Expenditures—health and welfare | | 59,407 |
| | (To record lease payments as a reduction to the principal obligation and an increase to interest expense rather than as an expenditure) | | |

## Unrestricted Operating Grant (Worksheet Entry JE02.52)

GASB-33 (Accounting and Financial Reporting for Nonexchange Transactions) establishes revenue recognition criteria for nonexchange transactions, including operating grants (voluntary nonexchange transactions). As noted in Transaction JE02.09, the fourth installment ($6,000,000) of the unrestricted operating grant is not recorded as revenue under the modified accrual basis but is considered revenue under the accrual basis of accounting. Thus, the following worksheet entry is made:

| | Accounts | Debit | Credit |
|---|---|---|---|
| JE02.52 | Intergovernmental grants receivable | 6,000,000 | |
| | General revenues— unrestricted grants | | 6,000,000 |
| | (To accrue grant revenue that was not subject to accrual under the modified accrual method) | | |

> **OBSERVATION:** If in the previous year grant revenue was also accrued, the previous accrual would have to be omitted from the current year's statement of activities (by debiting revenue and crediting net assets) because it would have been recorded in the current year under the modified accrual basis of accounting. In this illustration it is assumed no accrual was made in the previous year.

## Capital Assets Acquired (Worksheet Entries JE02.53A, JE02.53B, JE02.53D, and JE02.53C)

When capital assets are acquired by a governmental entity, payments related to acquisitions are recorded as expenditures at the fund statement level. However, in order to convert the fund financial statements from a modified accrual basis to an accrual basis for the preparation of the government-wide financial statements, the expenditure must be capitalized and any related depreciation expense must be recorded. Based on an analysis of Transactions JE02.17, JE02.21, and JE02.26, the following worksheet entries are made.

**Analysis of vehicles purchased on December 1, 20X0 (Transaction JE02.17)**

| | | | |
|---|---|---|---|
| JE02.53A | Vehicles | 900,000 | |
| | Expenditures—general government | | 100,000 |
| | Expenditures—public safety | | 300,000 |
| | Expenditures—streets | | 400,000 |
| | Expenditures—recreation and parks | | 100,000 |
| | (To capitalize payments for capital assets that were accounted for as expenditures) | | |
| JE02.53B | Expenses—general government ($175,000 × 1/9) | 19,445 | |
| | Expenses—public safety ($175,000 × 3/9) | 58,333 | |
| | Expenses—streets ($175,000 × 4/9) | 77,778 | |
| | Expenses—recreation and parks ($175,000 × 1/9) | 19,444 | |
| | Accumulated depreciation—vehicles ($900,000 × 1/3 × 7/12) | | 175,000 |
| | (To record depreciation expense) | | |

**Analysis of equipment purchased (Transaction JE02.21)**

| | | | |
|---|---|---|---|
| JE02.53D | Equipment | 4,700,000 | |
| | Expenditures—general government | | 2,000,000 |
| | Expenditures—public safety | | 1,300,000 |
| | Expenditures—streets | | 700,000 |
| | Expenditures—recreation and parks | | 500,000 |
| | Expenditures—health and welfare | | 200,000 |
| | (To capitalize payments for capital assets that were accounted for as expenditures) | | |

|  |  |  |
|---|---|---|
| Expenses—general government (See details of Transaction JE02.21) | 170,000 | |
| Expenses—public safety | 110,000 | |
| Expenses—streets | 95,000 | |
| Expenses—recreation and parks | 40,000 | |
| Expenses—health and welfare | 22,000 | |
| Accumulated depreciation—equipment | | 437,000 |
| (To record depreciation expense) | | |

**Analysis of vehicles purchased on May 1, 20X1 (Transaction JE02.26)**

|  |  |  |  |
|---|---|---|---|
| JE02.53C | Vehicles | 520,000 | |
| | Expenditures—public safety | | 520,000 |
| | (To capitalize payments for capital assets that were accounted for as expenditures) | | |
| | Expenses—public safety | 28,889 | |
| | Accumulated depreciation—vehicles ($520,000 × 1/3 × 2/12) | | 28,889 |
| | (To record depreciation expense) | | |

*Capital Assets Sold (Worksheet Entry JE02.54)*

As described in Transaction JE02.21, the City sold a variety of capital assets during the year. Under the modified accrual basis only the cash proceeds ($4,800,000) are recorded as miscellaneous revenue. In order to convert to the accrual basis, the following worksheet entry is made:

|  |  |  |  |
|---|---|---|---|
| JE02.54 | Accumulated depreciation—buildings | 2,000,000 | |
| | Accumulated depreciation—equipment | 1,000,000 | |
| | Accumulated depreciation—vehicles | 3,000,000 | |
| | Miscellaneous revenue | 4,800,000 | |
| | Expenses—general government (loss on sale of assets) ($500,000 + $200,000) | 700,000 | |

| | | |
|---|---:|---:|
| Expenses—public safety (loss on sale of assets) | 100,000 | |
| Buildings | | 7,000,000 |
| Equipment | | 1,400,000 |
| Vehicles | | 3,200,000 |
| (To remove the net book value and record the related gain/loss on the sale of capital assets for the year) | | |

*Depreciation Expense (Worksheet Entry JE02.55)*

In addition, to the depreciation expense recorded in the previous worksheet entries, depreciation expense on capital assets acquired in previous years was as follows:

| | |
|---|---:|
| Buildings | $ 8,000,000 |
| Equipment | 1,500,000 |
| Vehicles | 22,000,000 |
| Leased capital assets | 1,200,000 |
| Infrastructure assets | 700,000 |
| Total | $33,400,000 |

**NOTE:** All of the depreciation related to infrastructure assets is allocated to streets activities.

In order to record depreciation expense in the government-wide financial statements, the following entry is made:

| JE02.55 | | |
|---|---|---:|
| | Expenses—general government ($32,700,000 × 60%) | 19,620,000 |
| | Expenses—public safety ($32,700,000 × 20%) | 6,540,000 |
| | Expenses—streets ($32,700,000 × 10%) + $700,000 | 3,970,000 |
| | Expenses—recreation and parks ($32,700,000 × 5%) | 1,635,000 |
| | Expenses—health and welfare ($32,700,000 × 5%) | 1,635,000 |

|   |   |   |
|---|---|---|
| Accumulated depreciation—buildings | | 8,000,000 |
| Accumulated depreciation—equipment | | 1,500,000 |
| Accumulated depreciation—vehicles | | 22,000,000 |
| Accumulated depreciation—leased capital assets | | 1,200,000 |
| Accumulated depreciation—infrastructure assets | | 700,000 |

(To record depreciation expense)

▶ **NEW STANDARD:** GASB-34 does not require that infrastructure assets that are part of a network or subsystem of a network (referred to as eligible infrastructure assets) be depreciated if certain conditions relating to the asset management system and the documentation of the condition level of the infrastructure are met. The illustration in this book assumes that the governmental entity depreciates all of its infrastructure assets (GASB-34, par. 23).

*Extraordinary Item (Worksheet Entry JE02.56)*

GASB-34 incorporates the definition of extraordinary items (unusual in nature and infrequent in occurrence) as provided in APB Opinion No. 30 (Reporting the Results of Operations—Reporting the Effects of Disposal of a Segment of a Business, and Extraordinary, Unusual and Infrequently Occurring Events and Transactions).

The donation of land to the City (Transaction JE02.21) by the state is considered by the City to be an extraordinary item and is recorded on the accrual basis as follows:

| JE02.56 | Land | 20,000,000 | |
|---|---|---|---|
| | Extraordinary item—donation of land by the state | | 20,000,000 |

(To record the receipt of land as an extraordinary item)

*Accrual for Claims/Assessments and Compensated Absences (Worksheet Entries JE02.57A, JE02.57B, and JE02.57C)*

The basic guidance for determining when a governmental fund should accrue an expenditure/liability is found in NCGA-1, paragraph 70, which states that "most expenditures and transfers out are measurable and should be recorded when the related liability is incurred." GASBI-6 (Recognition and Measurement of Certain Liabilities and Expenditures in Governmental Fund Financial Statements) expands on this general guidance by noting the following:

> Governmental fund liabilities and expenditures that should be accrued include liabilities that, once incurred, normally are paid in a timely manner and in full from current financial resources—for example, salaries, professional services, supplies, utilities, and travel.

These transactions give rise to fund liabilities that are considered mature liabilities because they are "normally due and payable in full when incurred."

■ **CONTINUING STANDARD:** Based on the standards established by GASBI-6 (Recognition and Measurement of Certain Liabilities and Expenditures in Governmental Fund Financial Statements) expenditures should continue to be recorded on an accrual basis except with respect to the expenditures identified in the Interpretation. Two of the exceptions identified in GASBI-6 are the accounting for compensated absences and loss contingencies.

As described in Transactions (Adjustments) JE02.36 and JE02.37, a claim of $300,000 and compensated absences of $220,000 must be accrued as follows:

**Analysis of legal claims**

| | | | |
|---|---|---|---|
| JE02.57A | Expenses—public safety | 300,000 | |
| | Claims payable | | 300,000 |
| | (To accrue claims expense at year end) | | |

**Analysis of compensated absences**

| | | |
|---|---|---|
| Expenses—general government (60% × $220,000) | 132,000 | |
| Expenses—public safety (20%) | 44,000 | |
| Expenses—streets (10%) | 22,000 | |
| Expenses—recreation and parks (5%) | 11,000 | |
| Expenses—health and welfare (5%) | 11,000 | |
| Compensated absences payable | | 220,000 |
| (To accrue compensated absences expense at year end) | | |

In addition, a claim of $400,000 was paid during the year (Transaction JE02.36) and charged to public safety expenditures. On an accrual basis that amount is charged to the claims payable account, not the expenditures account, as follows:

| Accounts | Debit | Credit |
|---|---|---|
| JE02.57B Claims payable | 400,000 | |
|     Expenditures—public safety | | 400,000 |

(To record payments of claims during the year as a reduction to the related obligation rather than as an expenditure)

Also, compensated absences of $60,000 were paid during the year (Transaction JE02.37) and charged to various activities. On an accrual basis, that amount is charged to the compensated absences payable account as follows:

| | | |
|---|---|---|
| E02.57C Compensated absences payable | 60,000 | |
|     Expenditures—general government ($60,000 × 60%) | | 36,000 |
|     Expenditures—public safety ($60,000 × 20%) | | 12,000 |
|     Expenditures—streets ($60,000 × 10%) | | 6,000 |
|     Expenditures—recreation and parks ($60,000 × 5%) | | 3,000 |
|     Expenditures—health and welfare ($60,000 × 5%) | | 3,000 |

(To record payments of compensated absences during the year as a reduction to the related obligation rather than as an expenditure)

*Property Tax Revenue Accrual (Worksheet Entry JE02.58)*

As noted in the analysis that supports Transaction JE02.40 (Adjustment), an additional amount ($1,400,000) of property taxes is earned based on accrual accounting. In order to record this amount the following worksheet entry is made:

| JE02.58 | Property taxes receivable | 1,400,000 | |
|---|---|---|---|
| | General revenues—property taxes | | 1,400,000 |
| | (To accrue property taxes that were not subject to accrual under the modified accrual basis) | | |

**OBSERVATION:** If in the previous year property tax revenue was also accrued, the previous year's accrual would have to be omitted from the current year's statement of activities (by debiting revenue and crediting net assets) because it would have been recorded in the current year under the modified accrual basis of accounting. In this illustration, for simplicity, it is assumed no accrual was made in the previous year.

*Program Revenue Accruals (Worksheet Entry JE02.59)*

As explained in Transaction JE02.42 (Adjustment), certain charges, fees, and permits were not accrued under the modified accrual basis of accounting. The following worksheet entry is needed to recognize those revenue items that should be accrued:

| JE02.59 | Other receivables ($21,000 × 40%) | 8,400 | |
|---|---|---|---|
| | Program revenues—charges for services (recreation and parks) ($10,000 × 40%) | | 4,000 |
| | Program revenues—charges for services (public safety) ($2,000 × 40%) | | 800 |
| | Program revenues—charges for services (health and welfare) ($4,000 × 40%) | | 1,600 |
| | Program revenues—charges for services (general government) ($5,000 × 40%) | | 2,000 |
| | (To accrue revenue related to service charges that were not subject to accrual under the modified accrual basis) | | |

**OBSERVATION:** If in the previous year program revenue was also accrued, the previous year's accrual would have to be omitted from the current year's statement of activities (by debiting revenue and crediting net assets) as explained above.

## Beginning of Year Balances

Worksheet entries to convert from the modified accrual basis to the accrual basis are made for the following accounts based on their beginning of the year balances:

- Capital assets (Worksheet Entry JE02.60)
- Long-term debt (Worksheet Entry JE02.61)
- Compensated absences and claims/judgements (Worksheet Entry JE02.62)

*Capital Assets (Worksheet Entry JE02.60)*

The following capital assets were held by the City at the beginning of the year:

|  | Cost | Accumulated Depreciation |
|---|---|---|
| Land and improvements | $105,000,000 |  |
| Construction in progress | 2,050,000 |  |
| Buildings | 220,000,000 | $75,000,000 |
| Equipment | 19,000,000 | 7,000,000 |
| Vehicles | 75,000,000 | 39,000,000 |
| Leased capital assets | 7,818,540 | 2,500,000 |
| Infrastructure assets | 20,000,000 | 12,000,000 |

To convert the fund financial statements to an accrual basis, the following worksheet entry is made:

| JE02.60 | Land and improvements | 105,000,000 |  |
|---|---|---|---|
|  | Construction in progress | 2,050,000 |  |
|  | Buildings | 220,000,000 |  |
|  | Equipment | 19,000,000 |  |
|  | Vehicles | 75,000,000 |  |
|  | Leased capital sssets | 7,818,540 |  |
|  | Infrastructure assets | 20,000,000 |  |
|  | Accumulated depreciation—buildings |  | 75,000,000 |
|  | Accumulated depreciation—equipment |  | 7,000,000 |
|  | Accumulated depreciation—vehicles |  | 39,000,000 |
|  | Accumulated depreciation—leased capital assets |  | 2,500,000 |

| | | |
|---|---:|---:|
| Accumulated depreciation—infrastructure assets | | 12,000,000 |
| Net assets | | 313,368,540 |
| (To record capital assets held at the beginning of the year) | | |

*Long-Term Debt (Worksheet Entry JE02.61)*

As shown in Transaction JE02.08, the City executed a capital lease in a previous year and the balance according to the amortization schedule at the beginning of the year is $5,197,652. To convert this lease to an accrual amount as of the beginning of the year, the following entry is made:

**JE02.61**

| | | |
|---|---:|---:|
| Net assets | 5,197,652 | |
| Lease obligations payable | | 5,197,652 |
| (To record a capital lease outstanding at the beginning of the year) | | |

> **OBSERVATION:** Other long-term liabilities as of the beginning of the year are accrued in Chapter 4 ("Capital Projects Funds") and Chapter 5 ("Debt Service Funds").

*Compensated Absences and Claims/Judgements (Worksheet Entry JE02.62)*

Liabilities not reported in the fund financial statements that were related to compensated absences and claims/judgements had beginning balances of $4,500,000 and $2,000,000, respectively. To convert the fund financial statements to an accrual basis for these liabilities the following worksheet entry is made:

| | | | |
|---|---|---:|---:|
| **JE02.62** | Net Assets | 6,500,000 | |
| | Compensated absences payable | | 4,500,000 |
| | Claims and judgements payable | | 2,000,000 |
| | (To record compensated absences and claims and judgements outstanding at the beginning of the year) | | |

After the foregoing worksheet entries are prepared, the adjusted trial balances (on an accrual basis) for the General Fund would appear as follows as of June 30, 20X1:

**2-46** *Governmental Funds*

|  | Adjusted Trial Balance |  |
|---|---|---|
| Accounts | Debits | Credits |
| Cash | $ 9,440,000 |  |
| Property taxes receivable (net) | 1,755,000 |  |
| Other receivables | 44,000 |  |
| Investments | 6,090,000 |  |
| Inventories | 17,000 |  |
| Intergovernmental grants receivable | 6,000,000 |  |
| Land and improvements | 125,000,000 |  |
| Construction in progress | 2,050,000 |  |
| Buildings | 213,000,000 |  |
| Equipment | 22,300,000 |  |
| Vehicles | 73,220,000 |  |
| Leased capital assets | 8,249,753 |  |
| Infrastructure assets | 20,000,000 |  |
| Accumulated depreciation—buildings |  | $ 81,000,000 |
| Accumulated depreciation—equipment |  | 7,937,000 |
| Accumulated depreciation—vehicles |  | 58,203,889 |
| Accumulated depreciation—leased capital assets |  | 3,779,058 |
| Accumulated depreciation—infrastructure assets |  | 12,700,000 |
| Accounts payable |  | 665,000 |
| Interest payable |  | 24,290 |
| Due to other funds |  | 2,642,000 |
| Deferred revenue |  | 300,000 |
| Claims payable |  | 1,900,000 |
| Compensated absences payable |  | 4,660,000 |
| Lease obligation payable |  | 4,340,724 |
| Fund balance/net assets |  | 314,445,888 |
| General revenue—property taxes |  | 89,000,000 |
| Franchise taxes |  | 1,300,000 |
| Intergovernmental grants—General revenues—unrestricted grants |  | 26,500,000 |
| Program revenues/charges for services (general government) |  | 55,000 |

|  | Adjusted Trial Balance | |
| --- | --- | --- |
| **Accounts** | **Debits** | **Credits** |
| Program revenues/charges for services (recreations and parks) |  | 135,000 |
| Program revenues/charges for services (public safety) |  | 202,000 |
| Program revenues/charges for services (health and welfare) |  | 4,000 |
| Program revenues/charges for services (streets) |  | 150,000 |
| Contributions |  | 50,000 |
| Interest and investment revenue |  | 93,000 |
| Miscellaneous revenue |  |  |
| Change in fair value of investments |  | 140,000 |
| General government expenditures/expenses | 51,041,503 |  |
| Public safety expenditures/expenses | 22,448,222 |  |
| Streets expenditures/expenses | 14,803,278 |  |
| Recreation and parks expenditures/expenses | 7,524,694 |  |
| Health and welfare expenditures/expenses | 9,482,250 |  |
| Interest expense | 336,149 |  |
| Education (component unit) | 32,000,000 |  |
| Extraordinary item—donation of land by the state |  | 20,000,000 |
| Execution of capital leases |  |  |
| Transfers in |  | 50,000 |
| Transfers out | 5,475,000 |  |
| Total | $630,276,849 | $630,276,849 |

The worksheet to convert from a modified accrual basis to an accrual basis is presented in Appendix 2C. (Appendix 2D is the adjusted trial balance for the General Fund.) This accrual based trial balance for the General Fund is used in Chapter 13 ("Developing Information for Government-Wide Financial Statements") in order to prepare the government-wide financial statements.

**2-48** *Governmental Funds*

## APPENDIX 2A
## WORKSHEET FOR SUMMARIZING CURRENT TRANSACTIONS AND ADJUSTMENTS—MODIFIED ACCRUAL BASIS

### WORKSHEET OF ENTRIES

| Accounts | Trial Balance Debits | Trial Balance Credits | | Adjustments Debits | | Adjustments Credits | Adjusted Trial Balance Debits | Adjusted Trial Balance Credits | Operating Statement Debits | Operating Statement Credits | Balance Sheet Debits | Balance Sheet Credits |
|---|---|---|---|---|---|---|---|---|---|---|---|---|
| Cash | 15,200,000 | — | JE02.02 | 20,000 | JE02.01 | 8,320,000 | 9,440,000 | — | — | — | 9,440,000 | — |
| | | — | JE02.03 | 400,000 | JE02.07 | 200,000 | — | — | — | — | — | — |
| | | — | JE02.06 | 87,000,000 | JE02.08 | 100,000 | — | — | — | — | — | — |
| | | — | JE02.13 | 40,000 | JE02.12 | 50,000 | — | — | — | — | — | — |
| | | — | JE02.14 | 550,000 | JE02.18 | 900,000 | — | — | — | — | — | — |
| | | — | JE02.15 | 2,000,000 | JE02.19 | 500,000 | — | — | — | — | — | — |
| | | — | JE02.22 | 50,000 | JE02.21 | 4,700,000 | — | — | — | — | — | — |
| | | — | JE02.23 | 500,000 | JE02.27 | 520,000 | — | — | — | — | — | — |
| | | — | JE02.25 | 30,000 | JE02.30 | 85,000,000 | — | — | — | — | — | — |
| | | — | JE02.28 | 300,000 | JE02.33 | 7,000,000 | — | — | — | — | — | — |
| | | — | JE02.31 | 525,000 | JE02.46 | 5,475,000 | — | — | — | — | — | — |
| | | — | JE02.32 | 1,300,000 | JE02.48 | 4,400,000 | — | — | — | — | — | — |
| | | — | JE02.47 | 50,000 | JE02.49 | 4,650,000 | — | — | — | — | — | — |
| | | — | JE02.50 | 2,400,000 | JE02.01 | 10,000 | — | — | — | — | — | — |
| | | — | JE02.20 | 18,000,000 | JE02.08 | 1,500,000 | — | — | — | — | — | — |
| | | — | JE02.21 | 4,800,000 | JE02.36 | 400,000 | — | — | — | — | — | — |
| | | — | JE02.45 | 23,000 | JE02.02 | 20,000 | — | — | — | — | — | — |
| Interest receivable | 20,000 | | | | | | 23,000 | — | — | — | 23,000 | — |

## The General Fund 2-49

### WORKSHEET OF ENTRIES (Continued)

| Accounts | Trial Balance Debits | Trial Balance Credits | Adjustments Debits | | Adjustments Credits | | Adjusted Trial Balance Debits | Adjusted Trial Balance Credits | Operating Statement Debits | Operating Statement Credits | Balance Sheet Debits | Balance Sheet Credits |
|---|---|---|---|---|---|---|---|---|---|---|---|---|
| Property taxes receivable | 1,400,000 | — | JE02.04 | 100,000,000 | JE02.03 | 1,400,000 | 2,355,000 | — | — | — | 2,355,000 | — |
|  |  |  |  |  | JE02.05 | 245,000 |  |  |  |  |  |  |
|  |  |  |  |  | JE02.06 | 87,000,000 |  |  |  |  |  |  |
|  |  |  |  |  | JE02.38 | 9,000,000 |  |  |  |  |  |  |
|  |  |  |  |  | JE02.40 | 1,400,000 |  |  |  |  |  |  |
| Allowance for uncollectible property taxes | — | 1,000,000 | JE02.03 | 1,000,000 | JE02.04 | 10,000,000 | — | 2,000,000 | — | — | — | 2,000,000 |
|  |  |  | JE02.38 | 9,000,000 | JE02.39 | 1,000,000 |  |  |  |  |  |  |
| Other receivables | — | — | JE02.42 | 12,600 |  | — | 12,600 | — | — | — | 12,600 | — |
| Intergovernmental grants receivable | — | — | JE02.09 | 18,000,000 | JE02.20 | 18,000,000 | 0 | — | — | — | 0 | — |
| Investments in marketable debt securities | 1,800,000 | — | JE02.19 | 500,000 | JE02.35 | 150,000 | 2,150,000 | — | — | — | 2,150,000 | — |
| Investments in marketable equity securities | 4,000,000 | — | JE02.07 | 200,000 | JE02.14 | 500,000 | 3,940,000 | — | — | — | 3,940,000 | — |
|  |  |  | JE02.34 | 240,000 |  |  |  |  |  |  |  |  |
| Inventories | 12,000 | — | JE02.11 | 50,000 | JE02.41 | 45,000 | 17,000 | — | — | — | 17,000 | — |
| Accounts payable | — | 8,320,000 | JE02.01 | 8,320,000 | JE02.11 | 50,000 | — | 665,000 | — | — | — | 665,000 |
|  |  |  | JE02.12 | 50,000 | JE02.17 | 900,000 |  |  |  |  |  |  |
|  |  |  | JE02.18 | 900,000 | JE02.26 | 520,000 |  |  |  |  |  |  |
|  |  |  | JE02.27 | 520,000 | JE02.44 | 665,000 |  |  |  |  |  |  |
|  |  |  | JE02.01 | 10,000 | JE02.01 | 10,000 |  |  |  |  |  |  |

## WORKSHEET OF ENTRIES (Continued)

| Accounts | Trial Balance Debits | Trial Balance Credits | Adjustments Debits | | Adjustments Credits | | Adjusted Trial Balance Debits | Adjusted Trial Balance Credits | Operating Statement Debits | Operating Statement Credits | Balance Sheet Debits | Balance Sheet Credits |
|---|---|---|---|---|---|---|---|---|---|---|---|---|
| Deferred revenue—property taxes | — | — | — | JE02.21 | 4,700,000 | JE02.21 | — | — | — | — | — | — |
| Due to other funds—Internal Service Fund—Communications and Technology Support Center | — | 245,000 | JE02.05 | 245,000 | 300,000 | JE02.28 | — | 300,000 | — | — | — | 300,000 |
| Due to other funds—Internal Service Fund—Fleet Management Unit | — | 70,000 | — | | 100,000 | JE02.48 | — | 170,000 | — | — | — | 170,000 |
| Due to other funds—Enterprise Fund—Centerville Utilities Authority | — | 22,000 | — | | 50,000 | JE02.49 | — | 72,000 | — | — | — | 72,000 |
| Due to other funds—Enterprise Fund—Centerville Municipal Airport | — | — | — | | 2,000,000 | JE02.50 | — | 2,000,000 | — | — | — | 2,000,000 |
| Reserve for encumbrances | — | — | — | JE02.50 | 400,000 | | — | 400,000 | — | — | — | 400,000 |
|  | — | — | 50,000 | JE02.11 | 50,000 | JE02.10 | 0 | — | — | — | — | — |
|  | — | — | 900,000 | JE02.17 | 900,000 | JE02.16 | — | — | — | — | — | — |
|  | — | — | 520,000 | JE02.26 | 520,000 | JE02.24 | — | — | — | — | — | — |
|  | — | — | 4,700,000 | JE02.21 | 25,000 | JE02.29 | — | — | — | — | — | — |
|  | — | — | 25,000 | JE02.43 | 10,000 | JE02.01 | — | — | — | — | — | — |
|  | — | — | 10,000 | JE02.01 | 4,700,000 | JE02.21 | — | — | — | — | — | — |
| Fund balance—reserved for inventories | — | 12,000 | — | | 5,000 | JE02.41 | — | 17,000 | — | — | — | 17,000 |
| Fund balance—reserved for encumbrances | — | 10,000 | JE02.01 | 10,000 | 25,000 | JE02.43 | — | 25,000 | — | — | — | 25,000 |

## The General Fund 2-51

### WORKSHEET OF ENTRIES (Continued)

| Accounts | Trial Balance Debits | Trial Balance Credits | Adjustments Debits | | Adjustments Credits | Adjusted Trial Balance Debits | Adjusted Trial Balance Credits | Operating Statement Debits | Operating Statement Credits | Balance Sheet Debits | Balance Sheet Credits |
|---|---|---|---|---|---|---|---|---|---|---|---|
| Fund balance | — | 12,753,000 | JE02.41 | 5,000 | 10,000 | — | 12,733,000 | — | — | — | 12,733,000 |
| | | | JE02.43 | 25,000 | — | | | | | | |
| Program revenues—charges for services (general government) | — | — | | — | JE02.31   50,000 | — | 53,000 | — | 53,000 | — | — |
| | | | | | JE02.42    3,000 | | | | | | |
| Program revenues—operating grants (Recreation and parks) | — | — | | — | JE02.15 2,000,000 | — | 2,000,000 | — | 2,000,000 | — | — |
| Program revenues—charges for services (recreation and parks) | — | — | | — | JE02.31  125,000 | — | 131,000 | — | 131,000 | — | — |
| | | | | | JE02.42    6,000 | | | | | | |
| Program revenues—charges for services (health and welfare) | — | — | | — | JE02.42    2,400 | — | 2,400 | — | 2,400 | — | — |
| Program revenues—operating contributions (Health and Welfare) | — | — | | — | JE02.22   50,000 | — | 50,000 | — | 50,000 | — | — |
| Program revenues—charges for services (streets) | — | — | | — | JE02.31  150,000 | — | 150,000 | — | 150,000 | — | — |
| Program revenues—capital grants (public safety) | — | — | | — | JE02.23  500,000 | — | 500,000 | — | 500,000 | — | — |
| Program revenues—charges for services (public safety) | — | — | | — | JE02.31  200,000 | — | 201,200 | — | 201,200 | — | — |

## 2-52 Governmental Funds

### WORKSHEET OF ENTRIES (Continued)

| Accounts | Trial Balance Debits | Trial Balance Credits | Adjustments Debits | | Adjustments Credits | | Adjusted Trial Balance Debits | Adjusted Trial Balance Credits | Operating Statement Debits | Operating Statement Credits | Balance Sheet Debits | Balance Sheet Credits |
|---|---|---|---|---|---|---|---|---|---|---|---|---|
| General revenues—property taxes | — | — | JE02.39 1,000,000 | JE02.40 1,400,000 | JE02.42 1,200 | JE02.04 90,000,000 | — | 87,600,000 | — | 87,600,000 | — | — |
| General revenues—franchise taxes | — | — | | — | JE02.32 | 1,300,000 | — | 1,300,000 | — | 1,300,000 | — | — |
| General revenues—unrestricted grants | — | — | | — | JE02.09 | 18,000,000 | — | 18,000,000 | — | 18,000,000 | — | — |
| Miscellaneous revenue | — | — | | — | JE02.21 | 4,800,000 | — | 4,800,000 | — | 4,800,000 | — | — |
| Interest and investment revenue | — | — | | — | JE02.13 JE02.25 JE02.45 | 40,000 30,000 23,000 | — | 93,000 | — | 93,000 | — | — |
| Change in fair value of investments | — | — | JE02.35 150,000 | | JE02.14 JE02.34 | 50,000 240,000 | — | 140,000 | — | 140,000 | — | — |
| Expenditures—general government | — | — | JE02.08 431,213 JE02.08 100,000 JE02.17 100,000 JE02.30 20,000,000 JE02.33 4,200,000 JE02.41 27,000 JE02.44 600,000 | | — — — — — — — | | 33,701,098 | — | 33,701,098 | — | — | — |

## The General Fund 2-53

**WORKSHEET OF ENTRIES** (Continued)

| Accounts | Trial Balance Debits | Trial Balance Credits | | Debits | Adjustments Credits | Adjusted Trial Balance Debits | Adjusted Trial Balance Credits | Operating Statement Debits | Operating Statement Credits | Balance Sheet Debits | Balance Sheet Credits |
|---|---|---|---|---|---|---|---|---|---|---|---|
| | — | — | JE02.48 | 2,700,000 | — | — | — | — | — | — | — |
| | — | — | JE02.49 | 2,820,000 | — | — | — | — | — | — | — |
| | — | — | JE02.01 | 10,000 | — | — | — | — | — | — | — |
| | — | — | JE02.21 | 2,000,000 | — | — | — | — | — | — | — |
| | — | — | JE02.08 | 712,885 | — | — | — | — | — | — | — |
| Expenditures—public safety | — | — | JE02.17 | 300,000 | — | 18,036,628 | — | 18,036,628 | — | — | — |
| | — | — | JE02.30 | 12,000,000 | — | — | — | — | — | — | — |
| | — | — | JE02.26 | 520,000 | — | — | — | — | — | — | — |
| | — | — | JE02.33 | 1,400,000 | — | — | — | — | — | — | — |
| | — | — | JE02.41 | 9,000 | — | — | — | — | — | — | — |
| | — | — | JE02.44 | 30,000 | — | — | — | — | — | — | — |
| | — | — | JE02.48 | 900,000 | — | — | — | — | — | — | — |
| | — | — | JE02.49 | 940,000 | — | — | — | — | — | — | — |
| | — | — | JE02.21 | 1,300,000 | — | — | — | — | — | — | — |
| | — | — | JE02.08 | 237,628 | — | — | — | — | — | — | — |
| | — | — | JE02.36 | 400,000 | — | — | — | — | — | — | — |
| Expenditures—streets | — | — | JE02.17 | 400,000 | — | 11,863,314 | — | 11,863,314 | — | — | — |
| | — | — | JE02.30 | 9,000,000 | — | — | — | — | — | — | — |
| | — | — | JE02.33 | 700,000 | — | — | — | — | — | — | — |
| | — | — | JE02.41 | 4,500 | — | — | — | — | — | — | — |
| | — | — | JE02.44 | 20,000 | — | — | — | — | — | — | — |
| | — | — | JE02.48 | 450,000 | — | — | — | — | — | — | — |
| | — | — | JE02.49 | 470,000 | — | — | — | — | — | — | — |

**2-54** *Governmental Funds*

## WORKSHEET OF ENTRIES (CONTINUED)

| Accounts | Trial Balance Debits | Trial Balance Credits | | Adjustments Debits | | Adjustments Credits | Adjusted Trial Balance Debits | Adjusted Trial Balance Credits | Operating Statement Debits | Operating Statement Credits | Balance Sheet Debits | Balance Sheet Credits |
|---|---|---|---|---|---|---|---|---|---|---|---|---|
| Expenditures— recreation and parks | — | — | JE02.21 | 700,000 | | — | 6,481,657 | — | 6,481,657 | — | — | — |
| | | | JE02.08 | 118,814 | | | | | | | | |
| | | | JE02.17 | 100,000 | | | | | | | | |
| | | | JE02.30 | 5,000,000 | | | | | | | | |
| | | | JE02.33 | 350,000 | | | | | | | | |
| | | | JE02.41 | 2,250 | | | | | | | | |
| | | | JE02.44 | 10,000 | | | | | | | | |
| | | | JE02.48 | 225,000 | | | | | | | | |
| | | | JE02.49 | 235,000 | | | | | | | | |
| | | | JE02.21 | 500,000 | | | | | | | | |
| | | | JE02.08 | 59,407 | | | | | | | | |
| Expenditures— health and welfare | — | — | JE02.30 | 7,000,000 | | — | 8,076,657 | — | 8,076,657 | — | — | — |
| | | | JE02.33 | 350,000 | | | | | | | | |
| | | | JE02.41 | 2,250 | | | | | | | | |
| | | | JE02.44 | 5,000 | | | | | | | | |
| | | | JE02.48 | 225,000 | | | | | | | | |
| | | | JE02.49 | 235,000 | | | | | | | | |
| | | | JE02.21 | 200,000 | | | | | | | | |
| | | | JE02.08 | 59,407 | | | | | | | | |
| Encumbrances | — | — | JE02.10 | 50,000 | JE02.11 | 50,000 | — | — | — | — | — | — |
| | | | JE02.16 | 900,000 | JE02.17 | 900,000 | | | | | | |
| | | — | JE02.24 | 520,000 | JE02.26 | 520,000 | | | | | | |

## WORKSHEET OF ENTRIES (Continued)

| Accounts | Trial Balance Debits | Trial Balance Credits | Adjustments Debits | | Adjustments Credits | | Adjusted Trial Balance Debits | Adjusted Trial Balance Credits | Operating Statement Debits | Operating Statement Credits | Balance Sheet Debits | Balance Sheet Credits |
|---|---|---|---|---|---|---|---|---|---|---|---|---|
| | — | — | JE02.29 | 25,000 | JE02.43 | 25,000 | — | — | — | — | — | — |
| | — | — | JE02.01 | 10,000 | JE02.01 | 10,000 | — | — | — | — | — | — |
| | — | — | JE02.21 | 4,700,000 | JE02.21 | 4,700,000 | — | — | — | — | — | — |
| Expenditures—interest | — | — | JE02.08 | 311,859 | | | 311,859 | — | 311,859 | — | — | — |
| Expenditures—education (component unit) | — | — | JE02.30 | 32,000,000 | | | 32,000,000 | — | 32,000,000 | — | — | — |
| Other financing sources—capitalized leases | — | — | | | JE02.08 | 431,213 | — | 431,213 | — | 431,213 | — | — |
| Transfers in—Internal Service Fund—Fleet Management Unit | — | — | | | JE02.47 | 50,000 | — | 50,000 | — | 50,000 | — | — |
| Transfers Out—Special Revenue Fund—Center City Special Services Fund | — | — | JE02.46 | 75,000 | | | 75,000 | — | 75,000 | — | — | — |
| Transfers Out—Capital Projects Fund—Easely Street Bridge | — | — | JE02.46 | 1,000,000 | | | 1,000,000 | — | 1,000,000 | — | — | — |
| Transfers Out—Capital Projects Fund—Bland Street Drainage Project | — | — | JE02.46 | 600,000 | | | 600,000 | — | 600,000 | — | — | — |

**2-56** *Governmental Funds*

## WORKSHEET OF ENTRIES (Continued)

| Accounts | Trial Balance Debits | Trial Balance Credits | | Adjustments Debits | Adjustments Credits | Adjusted Trial Balance Debits | Adjusted Trial Balance Credits | Operating Statement Debits | Operating Statement Credits | Balance Sheet Debits | Balance Sheet Credits |
|---|---|---|---|---|---|---|---|---|---|---|---|
| Transfers Out—Capital Projects Fund—West End Recreation Center Project | — | — | JE02.46 | 300,000 | — | 300,000 | — | 300,000 | — | — | — |
| Transfers Out—Debt Service Fund—Senior Citizens' Center Bonds | — | — | JE02.46 | 1,300,000 | — | 1,300,000 | — | 1,300,000 | — | — | — |
| Transfers Out—Debt Service Fund—Easely Street Bridge Bonds | — | — | JE02.46 | 220,000 | — | 220,000 | — | 220,000 | — | — | — |
| Transfers Out—Debt Service Fund—Bland Street Drainage Bonds | — | — | JE02.46 | 1,100,000 | — | 1,100,000 | — | 1,100,000 | — | — | — |
| Transfers Out—Debt Service Fund—West End Recreation Center Bonds | — | — | JE02.46 | 700,000 | — | 700,000 | — | 700,000 | — | — | — |
| Transfers Out—Internal Service Fund—Communications and Technology Support Center | — | — | JE02.46 | 40,000 | — | 40,000 | — | 40,000 | — | — | — |
| Transfers Out—Enterprise Fund—Centerville Toll Bridge | — | — | JE02.46 | 50,000 | — | 50,000 | — | 50,000 | — | — | — |

## The General Fund 2-57

**WORKSHEET OF ENTRIES** (Continued)

| Accounts | Trial Balance Debits | Trial Balance Credits | Adjustments Debits | Adjustments Credits | Adjusted Trial Balance Debits | Adjusted Trial Balance Credits | Operating Statement Debits | Operating Statement Credits | Balance Sheet Debits | Balance Sheet Credits |
|---|---|---|---|---|---|---|---|---|---|---|
| Transfers out— Enterprise Fund— Centerville Parking Authority | — | — | JE02.46 90,000 | — | 90,000 | — | 90,000 | — | — | — |
| Totals | 22,432,000 | 22,432,000 | 392,681,813 | 392,681,813 | 133,883,813 | 133,883,813 | 115,946,213 | 115,501,813 | 17,937,600 | 18,382,000 |
| Net increase (decrease) | | | | | | | (444,400) | | | (444,400) |
| | | | | | | | 115,501,813 | 115,501,813 | 17,937,600 | 17,937,600 |

# APPENDIX 2B: GENERAL FUND—STATEMENT OF REVENUES, EXPENDITURES, AND CHANGES IN FUND BALANCES, AND BALANCE SHEET

**WORKSHEET ENTRIES**

**General Fund**
Statement of Revenues, Expenditures, and Changes in Fund Balances
June 30, 20X1

| | |
|---|---:|
| **REVENUES** | |
| Property taxes | $ 87,600,000 |
| Franchise taxes | 1,300,000 |
| Intergovernmental grants | 20,500,000 |
| Charges for services | 537,600 |
| Contributions | 50,000 |
| Interest and investment revenue | 93,000 |
| Miscellaneous revenue | 4,800,000 |
| Change in fair value of investments | 140,000 |
| Total revenues | 115,020,600 |
| **EXPENDITURES** | |
| Current: | |
| General government | 33,701,098 |
| Public safety | 18,036,628 |
| Streets | 11,863,314 |
| Recreation and parks | 6,481,657 |
| Health and welfare | 8,076,657 |
| Interest | 311,859 |
| Education (component unit) | 32,000,000 |
| Total expenditures | 110,471,213 |
| Excess (deficiency) of revenues over expenditures | 4,549,387 |

## WORKSHEET ENTRIES (Continued)

**OTHER FINANCING SOURCES (USES):**

| | |
|---|---:|
| Execution of capital leases | 431,213 |
| Transfers in | 50,000 |
| Transfers out | -5,475,000 |
| Total other financing sources and uses | -4,993,787 |
| Net change in fund balances | -444,400 |
| Fund balances—beginning | 12,775,000 |
| Fund balances—ending | $12,330,600 |

### General Fund
### Balance Sheet
### June 30, 20X1

**ASSETS**

| | |
|---|---:|
| Cash | $ 9,440,000 |
| Property taxes receivable (net) | 355,000 |
| Other receivables | 35,600 |
| Investments | 6,090,000 |
| Inventories | 17,000 |
| Total assets | $15,937,600 |

**LIABILITIES AND FUND BALANCES**

Liabilities:

| | |
|---|---:|
| Accounts payable | $ 665,000 |
| Due to other funds | 2,642,000 |
| Deferred revenue | 300,000 |
| Total liabilities | 3,607,000 |

## WORKSHEET ENTRIES (Continued)

**FUND BALANCES**

| | |
|---|---:|
| Reserved for inventories | 17,000 |
| Reserved for encumbrances | 25,000 |
| Unreserved | 12,288,600 |
| Total fund balances | 12,330,600 |
| Total liabilities and fund balances | $15,937,600 |

# APPENDIX 2C: WORKSHEET TO CONVERT FROM MODIFIED ACCRUAL BASIS TO ACCRUAL BASIS

**WORKSHEET ENTRIES**

| Accounts | Modified Accrual Trial Balance Debits | Modified Accrual Trial Balance Credits | Adjustments Debits | | Adjustments Credits | | Accrual Trial Balance Debits | Accrual Trial Balance Credits |
|---|---|---|---|---|---|---|---|---|
| Cash | 9,440,000 | — | | | | | 9,440,000 | — |
| Property taxes receivable (net) | 355,000 | — | | | 1,400,000 | JE02.58 | — | 1,755,000 |
| Other receivables | 35,600 | — | 8,400 | JE02.59 | | | 44,000 | — |
| Investments | 6,090,000 | — | | | | | 6,090,000 | — |
| Inventories | 17,000 | — | | | | | 17,000 | — |
| Intergovernmental grants receivable | — | — | 6,000,000 | JE02.52 | | | 6,000,000 | — |
| Land and improvements | — | — | 20,000,000 | JE02.56 | | | 125,000,000 | — |
| | | | 105,000,000 | JE02.60 | | | | |
| Construction in progress | — | — | 2,050,000 | JE02.60 | | | 2,050,000 | — |
| Buildings | — | — | 220,000,000 | JE02.60 | 7,000,000 | JE02.54 | 213,000,000 | — |
| Equipment | — | — | 4,700,000 | JE02.53D | 1,400,000 | JE02.54 | 22,300,000 | — |
| | | | 19,000,000 | JE02.60 | | | | |
| Vehicles | — | — | 900,000 | JE02.53A | 3,200,000 | JE02.54 | 73,220,000 | — |
| | | | 520,000 | JE02.53C | | | | |
| | | | 75,000,000 | JE02.60 | | | | |
| Leased capital assets | — | — | 431,213 | JE02.51A | | | 8,249,753 | — |
| | | | 7,818,540 | JE02.60 | | | | |
| Infrastructure assets | — | — | 20,000,000 | JE02.60 | | | 20,000,000 | — |
| Accumulated depreciation—buildings | — | — | 2,000,000 | JE02.54 | 8,000,000 | JE02.55 | — | 81,000,000 |
| | | | 75,000,000 | JE02.60 | | | | |

## 2-62 Governmental Funds

### WORKSHEET ENTRIES (Continued)

| Accounts | Modified Accrual Trial Balance Debits | Modified Accrual Trial Balance Credits | Adjustments Debits | | Adjustments Credits | | Accrual Trial Balance Debits | Accrual Trial Balance Credits |
|---|---|---|---|---|---|---|---|---|
| Accumulated depreciation—equipment | — | — | JE02.54 | 1,000,000 | JE02.53D | 437,000 | — | 7,937,000 |
| | | | JE02.55 | 1,500,000 | | — | | |
| Accumulated depreciation—vehicles | — | — | JE02.54 | 3,000,000 | JE02.60 | 7,000,000 | — | 58,203,889 |
| | | | | | JE02.53B | 175,000 | | |
| | | | | | JE02.53C | 28,889 | | |
| | | | | | JE02.55 | 22,000,000 | | |
| | | | | | JE02.060 | 39,000,000 | | |
| Accumulated depreciation—leased capital assets | — | — | | | JE02.51A | 79,058 | — | 3,779,058 |
| | | | | | JE02.55 | 1,200,000 | | |
| | | | | | JE02.60 | 2,500,000 | | |
| Accumulated depreciation—infrastructure assets | — | — | | | JE02.55 | 700,000 | — | 12,700,000 |
| | | | | | JE02.60 | 12,000,000 | | |
| Accounts payable | — | 665,000 | | | | — | — | 665,000 |
| Interest payable | — | — | | | JE02.51A | 24,290 | — | 24,290 |
| Due to other funds | — | 2,642,000 | | | | — | — | 2,642,000 |
| Deferred revenue | — | 300,000 | | | | — | — | 300,000 |
| Claims payable | — | — | JE02.57B | 400,000 | JE02.57A | 300,000 | — | 1,900,000 |
| | | | | | JE02.62 | 2,000,000 | | |
| Compensated absences payable | — | — | JE02.57C | 60,000 | JE02.57A | 220,000 | — | 4,660,000 |
| | | | | | JE02.62 | 4,500,000 | | |
| Lease obligation payable | — | — | JE02.51A | 100,000 | JE02.51A | 431,213 | — | 4,340,724 |
| | | | JE02.51B | 1,188,141 | JE02.61 | 5,197,652 | | |
| Fund balance/net assets | — | 12,775,000 | JE02.61 | 5,197,652 | JE02.60 | 313,368,540 | — | 314,445,888 |
| | | | | | JE02.62 | 6,500,000 | | |
| General revenue—property taxes | — | 87,600,000 | | | JE02.58 | 1,400,000 | — | 89,000,000 |
| Franchise taxes | — | 1,300,000 | | | | — | — | 1,300,000 |

The General Fund   2-63

## WORKSHEET ENTRIES (Continued)

| Accounts | Modified Accrual Trial Balance Debits | Modified Accrual Trial Balance Credits | Adjustments Debits | | Adjustments Credits | | Accrual Trial Balance Debits | Accrual Trial Balance Credits |
|---|---|---|---|---|---|---|---|---|
| Intergovernmental grants—General revenues—unrestricted grants | — | 20,500,000 | — | | JE02.52 | 6,000,000 | — | 26,500,000 |
| Program revenues/charges for services (general government) | — | 53,000 | — | | JE02.59 | 2,000 | — | 55,000 |
| Program revenues/charges for services (recreations and parks) | — | 131,000 | — | | JE02.59 | 4,000 | — | 135,000 |
| Program revenues/charges for services (public safety) | — | 201,200 | — | | JE02.59 | 800 | — | 202,000 |
| Program revenues/charges for services (health and welfare) | — | 2,400 | — | | JE02.59 | 1,600 | — | 4,000 |
| Program revenues/charges for services (streets) | — | 150,000 | | | | | — | 150,000 |
| Contributions | — | 50,000 | | | | | — | 50,000 |
| Interest and investment revenue | — | 93,000 | | | | | — | 93,000 |
| Miscellaneous revenue | — | 4,800,000 | JE02.54 | 4,800,000 | | | — | — |
| Change in fair value of investments | — | 140,000 | | | | | — | 140,000 |
| General government expenditures/expenses | 33,701,098 | — | JE02.51A | 79,058 | JE02.51A | 431,213 | 51,041,503 | — |
| | | | JE02.53B | 19,445 | JE02.51A | 100,000 | | |
| | | | JE02.53D | 170,000 | JE02.51B | 712,885 | | |
| | | | JE02.54 | 700,000 | JE02.53A | 100,000 | | |
| | | | JE02.55 | 19,620,000 | JE02.53D | 2,000,000 | | |
| | | | JE02.57A | 132,000 | JE02.56C | 36,000 | | |
| Public safety expenditures/expenses | 18,036,628 | — | JE02.53B | 58,333 | JE02.51B | 237,628 | 22,448,222 | — |
| | | | JE02.53C | 28,889 | JE02.53A | 300,000 | | |
| | | | JE02.53D | 110,000 | JE02.53C | 520,000 | | |
| | | | JE02.54 | 100,000 | JE02.53D | 1,300,000 | | |
| | | | JE02.55 | 6,540,000 | JE02.57B | 400,000 | | |
| | | | JE02.57A | 300,000 | JE02.57C | 12,000 | | |
| | | | JE02.57A | 44,000 | | — | | |

## WORKSHEET ENTRIES (Continued)

| Accounts | Modified Accrual Trial Balance Debits | Modified Accrual Trial Balance Credits | Adjustments Debits | | Adjustments Credits | | Accrual Trial Balance Debits | Accrual Trial Balance Credits |
|---|---|---|---|---|---|---|---|---|
| Streets expenditures/expenses | 11,863,314 | — | JE02.53B | 77,778 | JE02.51B | 118,814 | 14,803,278 | — |
| | | | JE02.53D | 95,000 | JE02.53A | 400,000 | | |
| | | | JE02.55 | 3,970,000 | JE02.53D | 700,000 | | |
| | | | JE02.57A | 22,000 | JE02.57C | 6,000 | | |
| Recreation and parks expenditures/expenses | 6,481,657 | — | JE02.53B | 19,444 | JE02.51B | 59,407 | 7,524,694 | — |
| | | | JE02.53D | 40,000 | JE02.53A | 100,000 | | |
| | | | JE02.55 | 1,635,000 | JE02.53D | 500,000 | | |
| | | | JE02.57A | 11,000 | JE02.57C | 3,000 | | |
| Health and welfare expenditures/expenses | 8,076,657 | — | JE02.53D | 22,000 | JE02.51B | 59,407 | 9,482,250 | — |
| | | | JE02.55 | 1,635,000 | JE02.53D | 200,000 | | |
| | | | JE02.57A | 11,000 | JE02.57C | 3,000 | | |
| Interest expenditures/expense | 311,859 | — | JE02.51A | 24,290 | | — | 336,149 | — |
| Education (component unit) | 32,000,000 | — | | — | | — | 32,000,000 | — |
| Extraordinary item—donation of land by the state | — | — | | — | JE02.56 | 20,000,000 | — | 20,000,000 |
| Execution of capital leases | — | 431,213 | JE02.51A | 431,213 | | — | — | — |
| Transfers in | — | 50,000 | | — | | — | — | 50,000 |
| Transfers out | 5,475,000 | — | | — | | — | 5,475,000 | — |
| Total | 131,883,813 | 131,883,813 | | 542,969,396 | | 542,969,396 | 630,276,849 | 630,276,849 |

# APPENDIX 2D: GENERAL FUND—ADJUSTED TRIAL BALANCE

## WORKSHEET ENTRIES

| Accounts | Adjusted Trial Balance Debits | Credits |
|---|---|---|
| Cash | $ 9,440,000 | |
| Property taxes receivable (net) | 1,755,000 | |
| Other receivables | 44,000 | |
| Investments | 6,090,000 | |
| Inventories | 17,000 | |
| Intergovernmental grants receivable | 6,000,000 | |
| Land and improvements | 125,000,000 | |
| Construction in progress | 2,050,000 | |
| Buildings | 213,000,000 | |
| Equipment | 22,300,000 | |
| Vehicles | 73,220,000 | |
| Leased capital assets | 8,249,753 | |
| Infrastructure assets | 20,000,000 | |
| Accumulated depreciation—buildings | | $ 81,000,000 |
| Accumulated depreciation—equipment | | 7,937,000 |
| Accumulated depreciation—vehicles | | 58,203,889 |
| Accumulated depreciation—leased capital assets | | 3,779,058 |
| Accumulated depreciation—infrastructure assets | | 12,700,000 |

## WORKSHEET ENTRIES (Continued)

| Accounts | Adjusted Trial Balance Debits | Adjusted Trial Balance Credits |
|---|---|---|
| Accounts payable | | 665,000 |
| Interest payable | | 24,290 |
| Due to other funds | 300,000 | 2,642,000 |
| Claims payable | | 1,900,000 |
| Compensated absences payable | | 4,660,000 |
| Lease obligation payable | | 4,340,724 |
| Fund balance/net assets | | 314,445,888 |
| General revenue—property taxes | | 89,000,000 |
| Franchise taxes | | 1,300,000 |
| Intergovernmental grants—General revenues—unrestricted grants | | 26,500,000 |
| Program revenues/charges for services (general government) | | 55,000 |
| Program revenues/charges for services (recreations and parks) | | 135,000 |
| Program revenues/charges for services (public safety) | | 202,000 |
| Program revenues/charges for services (health and welfare) | | 4,000 |
| Program revenues/charges for services (streets) | | 150,000 |
| Contributions | | 50,000 |
| Interest and investment revenue | | 93,000 |
| Miscellaneous revenue | | |
| Change in fair value of investments | | 140,000 |
| General government expenditures/expenses | 51,041,503 | |
| Public safety expenditures/expenses | 22,448,222 | |

## WORKSHEET ENTRIES (Continued)

| Accounts | Adjusted Trial Balance Debits | Credits |
|---|---|---|
| Streets expenditures/expenses | 14,803,278 | |
| Recreation and parks expenditures/expenses | 7,524,694 | |
| Health and welfare expenditures/expenses | 9,482,250 | |
| Interest expense | 336,149 | |
| Education (component unit) | 32,000,000 | |
| Extraordinary item—donation of land by the state | | 20,000,000 |
| Execution of capital leases | | 50,000 |
| Transfers in | | |
| Transfers out | 5,475,000 | |
| Total | $630,276,849 | $630,276,849 |

# CHAPTER 3
# SPECIAL REVENUE FUNDS

## CONTENTS

| | |
|---|---|
| Nature of Special Revenue Funds | 3-1 |
| Measurement Focus and Basis of Accounting | 3-2 |
| Financial Reporting at Fund Level | 3-2 |
| Financial Reporting at Government-Wide Level | 3-3 |
| Illustrative Transactions | 3-3 |
|     Center City Special Services Fund | 3-3 |
|     Local Fuel Tax Fund | 3-7 |
| Fund Financial Statements | 3-9 |
| Converting to Government-Wide Financial Statements | 3-11 |
| Appendix 3A: Worksheet for Summarizing Current Transactions—Center City Special Services District Fund | 3-14 |
| Appendix 3B: Special Revenue Funds—Balance Sheet and Statement of Revenues, Expenditures, and Changes in Fund Balances | 3-16 |
| Appendix 3C: Worksheet for Summarizing Current Transactions—Local Fuel Tax Fund | 3-18 |
| Appendix 3D: Special Revenue Funds—Combined Adjusted Trial Balances | 3-19 |

## NATURE OF SPECIAL REVENUE FUNDS

NCGA-1 states that the purpose of a Special Revenue Fund is to account for the proceeds of specific revenue sources (other than for major capital projects) that are legally restricted to expenditures for specified purposes. For example, the following circumstances could be the basis for reporting activities in a Special Revenue Fund:

- Gasoline taxes are to be used only for road maintenance
- Lottery proceeds are to be used only for a drug prescription plan for elderly citizens

- Personal property taxes are to be used only for educational purposes

  ▶ **NEW STANDARD:** GASB-34 revised the fund structure for state and local governments. One of the changes was the elimination of Expendable Trust Funds, which previously had been used to account for resources for which both the principal and earnings could be expended. Resources that were previously accounted for in an Expendable Trust Fund are generally now reported in a Special Revenue Fund (GASB-34, par. 63).

GASB-24 (Accounting and Financial Reporting for Certain Grants and Other Financial Assistance) requires that a state government account for the distribution of food stamp benefits as revenue and expenditures in either a General Fund or a Special Revenue Fund (GASB-24, par. 6).

When a governmental entity has a component unit that is blended into its financial statements, the General Fund of the component unit must be reported as a Special Revenue Fund of the primary government (GASB-14, par. 54).

NCGA-1 makes the point that a Special Revenue Fund should be used only when it is legally mandated. In many instances, it may be possible to account for restricted resources directly in the General Fund if these restricted resources are used to support expenditures that are usually made from the General Fund.

## MEASUREMENT FOCUS AND BASIS OF ACCOUNTING

The modified accrual basis and flow of current financial resources are used to prepare the financial statements of Special Revenue Funds. The same accounting principles that are used to measure revenues, expenditures, assets, and liabilities of a General Fund are also used to account for those items in a Special Revenue Fund. These accounting principles are discussed in Chapter 2 ("The General Fund") and are not repeated here.

## FINANCIAL REPORTING AT FUND LEVEL

The balances and activities of Special Revenue Funds are presented in the following financial statements at the fund financial statement level:

- Balance Sheet
- Statement of Revenues, Expenditures, and Changes in Fund Balances

  ■ **CONTINUING STANDARD:** Transactions and accounts recorded in Special Revenue Funds continue to be based on standards established by various NCGA/GASB Statements and Interpretations that were outstanding before the issuance of GASB-34.

The two fund financial statements listed above include all of the governmental funds (General Fund, Special Revenue Funds, Capital Projects Funds, Debt Service Funds, and Permanent Funds), and these funds are reported based on the concept of a major fund as defined by GASB-34.

> ▶ **NEW STANDARD:** GASB-34 requires that a budgetary comparison schedule be prepared for each major Special Revenue Fund that has a legally adopted annual budget. This schedule is discussed in Chapter 15 ("MD&A, Notes and Other Required Supplementary Illustrations") in the context of the General Fund. For this illustration it is assumed that none of the Special Revenue Funds legally adopt an annual budget (GASB-34, par. 130).

## FINANCIAL REPORTING AT GOVERNMENT-WIDE LEVEL

The fund-based financial statements as described above are included in a governmental entity's financial report in order to demonstrate that restrictions imposed by statutes, regulations, or contracts have been followed. Balances in the fund financial statements are converted from a modified accrual basis to an accrual basis in order to create the basic information for the government-wide financial statements. For the most part this approach requires that all of the Special Revenue Funds combined ending trial balance (which is on a modified accrual basis) be adjusted to reflect accrual balances. This conversion is illustrated later in this chapter.

## ILLUSTRATIVE TRANSACTIONS

In order to illustrate accounting and financial reporting standards that should be observed for Special Revenue Funds, assume that the City of Centerville has the following Special Revenue Funds:

- Center City Special Services District
- Local Fuel Tax Fund

### Center City Special Services Fund

The Center City Special Services District (CCSSD) provides special services, such as street maintenance, street cleaning, and similar services to approximately six square blocks of the business district. Businesses in this area pay a special service fee that is approximately 5% of their property tax bill. The trial balance for this fund at the beginning of the fiscal year is as follows:

**3-4** *Governmental Funds*

|                                            | Trial Balance |          |
| ------------------------------------------ | ------------- | -------- |
| Accounts                                   | Debits        | Credits  |
| Cash                                       | $30,000       |          |
| Other receivables                          | 14,500        |          |
| Property taxes receivable                  | 50,000        |          |
| Allowance for uncollectible property taxes |               | $40,000  |
| Accounts payable                           |               | 26,000   |
| Deferred revenue—property taxes            |               | 12,000   |
| Fund balance                               |               | 16,500   |
| Totals                                     | $94,500       | $94,500  |

This section presents illustrative transactions and entries for the fund during the fiscal year ended June 30, 20X1.

■ **CONTINUING STANDARD:** GASB-34 generally did not change the manner of accounting for transactions that are recorded in a Special Revenue Fund.

*Transaction JE03.01*—Accounts payable and accrued expenses of $26,000 from the previous year were paid:

| Accounts         | Debit  | Credit |
| ---------------- | ------ | ------ |
| Accounts payable | 26,000 |        |
| Cash             |        | 26,000 |

*Transaction JE03.02*—Accrued interest receivable from the previous year was received:

| Accounts          | Debit  | Credit |
| ----------------- | ------ | ------ |
| Cash              | 14,500 |        |
| Other receivables |        | 14,500 |

*Transaction JE03.03*—Property taxes receivable of $10,000 at the beginning of the year were collected and the balance ($40,000) was written off:

| Accounts                                   | Debit  | Credit |
| ------------------------------------------ | ------ | ------ |
| Cash                                       | 10,000 |        |
| Allowance for uncollectible property taxes | 40,000 |        |
| Property taxes receivable                  |        | 50,000 |

*Transaction JE03.04*—The Center City Special Services District levied property taxes of $3,000,000. It is expected that 10% of the amount levied will be uncollectible:

| Accounts | Debit | Credit |
|---|---|---|
| Property taxes receivable | 3,000,000 | |
|    General revenues—property taxes | | 2,700,000 |
|    Allowance for uncollectible property taxes | | 300,000 |

> ▶ **NEW STANDARD:** All taxes are considered to be general revenues (for presentation on the statement of activities) even if they are restricted to a particular program or activity (GASB-34, par. 52).

> ■ **CONTINUING STANDARD:** The accounting for non-exchange revenues (such as property taxes) continues to be performed based on the standards established by GASB-33 (Accounting and Financial Reporting for Nonexchange Transactions).

*Transaction JE03.05*—Property taxes collected in the previous year are applied to current property tax billings:

| Accounts | Debit | Credit |
|---|---|---|
| Deferred revenue—property taxes | 12,000 | |
|    Property taxes receivable | | 12,000 |

> **NOTE:** Some governmental entities use the deferred revenue account to report receivables that are not expected to be collected within a short period of time after the end of the year. This illustration uses deferred revenue only for cash received from property owners before the period in which the revenue can be recognized.

*Transaction JE03.06*—Property tax collections totaled $2,610,000 for the year:

| Accounts | Debit | Credit |
|---|---|---|
| Cash | 2,610,000 | |
|    Property taxes receivable | | 2,610,000 |

*Transaction JE03.07*—The City received $10,000 of property tax receipts that apply to the next fiscal year:

| Accounts | Debit | Credit |
|---|---|---|
| Cash | 10,000 | |
|    Deferred revenues—property taxes | | 10,000 |

***Transaction JE03.08***—Property taxes receivable from specific business enterprises of $270,000 are identified as uncollectible:

| Accounts | Debit | Credit |
| --- | --- | --- |
| Allowance for uncollectible property taxes | 270,000 | |
| Property taxes receivable | | 270,000 |

***Transaction JE03.09***—After additional analysis the allowance for uncollectible accounts is increased by $30,000. This is an accounting change in estimate:

| Accounts | Debit | Credit |
| --- | --- | --- |
| General revenues—property taxes | 30,000 | |
| Allowance for uncollectible property taxes | | 30,000 |

***Transaction JE03.10***—Government expenditures of $2,750,000 were incurred, of which $2,700,000 was paid. Of the total expenditures, 20% are allocated to general government and 80% to street programs:

| Accounts | Debit | Credit |
| --- | --- | --- |
| Expenditures—general government ($2,750,000 × 20%) | 550,000 | |
| Expenditures—streets ($2,750,000 × 80%) | 2,200,000 | |
| Cash | | 2,700,000 |
| Accounts payable | | 50,000 |

■ **CONTINUING STANDARD:** Expenditures presented in the statement of revenues, expenditures, and changes in fund balances should continue to be classified consistent with the standards discussed in NCGA-1 (par. 110 and pars. 111–116).

***Transaction JE03.11***—The General Fund made a transfer of $75,000 to subsidize the activities of the Center City Special Services District:

| Accounts | Debit | Credit |
| --- | --- | --- |
| Cash | 75,000 | |
| Transfers in—General Fund | | 75,000 |

***Transaction JE03.12***—Interest and penalties of $18,000 were assessed during the year, of which $3,000 was collected. The balance is expected to be collected in time to pay current liabilities of the fund:

| Accounts | Debit | Credit |
|---|---|---|
| Cash | 3,000 | |
| Other receivables | 15,000 | |
| Miscellaneous revenue | | 18,000 |

After the transactions for the year are posted, the year-end trial balance (June 30, 20X1) for the Center City Special Services District appears as follows:

| | Adjusted Trial Balance | |
|---|---|---|
| Accounts | Debits | Credits |
| Cash | $ 26,500 | |
| Other receivables | 15,000 | |
| Property taxes receivable | 108,000 | |
| Allowance for uncollectible property taxes | | $ 60,000 |
| Accounts payable | | 50,000 |
| Deferred revenue—property taxes | | 10,000 |
| Fund balance | | 16,500 |
| General revenues—property taxes | | 2,670,000 |
| Miscellaneous revenue | | 18,000 |
| Expenditures—general government | 550,000 | |
| Expenditures—streets | 2,200,000 | |
| Transfers in—General Fund | | 75,000 |
| Totals | $2,899,500 | $2,899,500 |

The worksheet that summarizes the foregoing journal entries for the year-end trial balance is presented in Appendix 3A.

## Local Fuel Tax Fund

The Local Fuel Tax Fund (LFTF) receives a share of the fuel taxes collected by the state government. The fuel tax receipts are to be used to maintain and repair streets and highways. The trial balance for this fund at the beginning of the fiscal year is presented as follows:

| | Trial Balance | |
|---|---|---|
| Accounts | Debits | Credits |
| Cash | $25,000 | |
| Other receivables | 3,000 | |
| Accounts payable | | $15,000 |
| Fund balance | | 13,000 |
| Totals | $28,000 | $28,000 |

## 3-8 Governmental Funds

This section presents illustrative transactions and entries for the fund during the fiscal year ended June 30, 20X1.

*Transaction JE03.13*—Accounts payable of $15,000 from the previous year were paid:

| Accounts | Debit | Credit |
|---|---|---|
| Accounts payable | 15,000 | |
| Cash | | 15,000 |

*Transaction JE03.14*—Accrued interest receivable from the previous year was collected:

| Accounts | Debit | Credit |
|---|---|---|
| Cash | 3,000 | |
| Other receivables | | 3,000 |

*Transaction JE03.15*—During the year the state transferred $4,500,000 of motor fuel taxes to the City. The funds may be spent on either operating or capital expenditures:

| Accounts | Debit | Credit |
|---|---|---|
| Cash | 4,500,000 | |
| Program revenues—operating grants (streets) | | 4,500,000 |

*Transaction JE03.16*—Government expenditures of $4,200,000 were incurred, of which $4,175,000 were paid. Of the total expenditures, 5% are allocated to general government and 95% to streets programs:

| Accounts | Debit | Credit |
|---|---|---|
| Expenditures—general government ($4,200,000 × 5%) | 210,000 | |
| Expenditures—streets ($4,200,000 × 95%) | 3,990,000 | |
| Cash | | 4,175,000 |
| Accounts payable | | 25,000 |

*Transaction JE03.17*—Interest income of $6,000 was earned during the year, of which $4,000 was collected. The balance is expected to be collected in time to pay current liabilities of the fund:

| Accounts | Debit | Credit |
|---|---|---|
| Cash | 4,000 | |
| Other receivables | 2,000 | |
| Interest revenue | | 6,000 |

*Special Revenue Funds* 3-9

*Transaction JE03.18*—During the year, $100,000 was transferred to the Bland Street Drainage Project (Capital Projects Fund):

| Accounts | Debit | Credit |
|---|---|---|
| Transfers out—Capital Projects Fund (Bland Street Drainage) | 300,000 | |
| Cash | | 300,000 |

After the transactions for the year are posted, the year-end trial balance (June 30, 20X1) for the Local Fuel Tax Fund appears as follows:

| Accounts | Adjusted Trial Balance Debits | Credits |
|---|---|---|
| Cash | $ 42,000 | |
| Other receivables | 2,000 | |
| Accounts payable | | $ 25,000 |
| Fund balance | | 13,000 |
| Program revenues—operating grants (streets) | | 4,500,000 |
| Interest revenue | | 6,000 |
| Expenditures—general government | 210,000 | |
| Expenditures—streets | 3,990,000 | |
| Transfers out—Capital Projects Fund (Bland Street Drainage) | 300,000 | |
| Totals | $4,544,000 | $4,544,000 |

(See Appendix 3B.) The worksheet that summarizes the foregoing journal entries for the year-end trial balance is presented in Appendix 3C.

## FUND FINANCIAL STATEMENTS

At the fund financial statement level a governmental fund must prepare a statement of revenues, expenditures, and changes in fund balances and a balance sheet. Based on the adjusted trial balances created above, the following preliminary financial statements reflect the combined balances and activities of the two Special Revenue Funds. These financial statements are prepared to facilitate the preparation of the fund financial statements illustrated in Chapter 12 ("Developing Information for Fund Financial Statements").

▶ **NEW STANDARD:** NCGA-1 illustrates three distinct formats that can be used to prepare the statement of revenues, expenditures, and changes in fund balances for governmental funds; however,

GASB-34 eliminates two of the options and only the format illustrated below can now be used (GASB-34, par. 86).

■ **CONTINUING STANDARD:** The formatting of the balance sheet at the fund financial statement level was not changed by GASB-34.

### Special Revenue Funds
### Balance Sheet
### June 30, 20X1

|  | Center City Special Services Fund | Local Fuel Tax Fund | Total |
|---|---|---|---|
| **ASSETS** |  |  |  |
| Cash | $26,500 | $42,000 | $68,500 |
| Other receivables | 15,000 | 2,000 | 17,000 |
| Property taxes receivable (net) | 48,000 | — | — |
| Total assets | $89,500 | $44,000 | $133,500 |
| **LIABILITIES AND FUND BALANCES** |  |  |  |
| Liabilities: |  |  |  |
| Accounts payable | $50,000 | $25,000 | $75,000 |
| Deferred revenue—property taxes | 10,000 | — | 10,000 |
| Total liabilities | 60,000 | 25,000 | 85,000 |
| Fund balances: |  |  |  |
| Fund balance—reserved | 29,500 | 19,000 | 48,500 |
| Total liabilities and fund balances | $89,500 | $44,000 | $133,500 |

### Special Revenue Funds
### Statement of Revenues, Expenditures, and Changes in Fund Balances
### June 30, 20X1

|  | Center City Special Services Fund | Local Fuel Tax Fund | Total |
|---|---|---|---|
| **REVENUES** |  |  |  |
| Property taxes | $2,670,000 | — | $2,670,000 |
| Program revenues—operating grants (street) | — | $4,500,000 | 4,500,000 |

|  | Center City Special Services Fund | Local Fuel Tax Fund | Total |
|---|---|---|---|
| Interest | — | 6,000 | 6,000 |
| Miscellaneous | 18,000 |  | 18,000 |
| Total revenue | 2,688,000 | 4,506,000 | 7,194,000 |
| **EXPENDITURES** |  |  |  |
| General government | 550,000 | 210,000 | 760,000 |
| Streets | 2,200,000 | 3,990,000 | 6,190,000 |
| Total expenditures | 2,750,000 | 4,200,000 | 6,950,000 |
| Excess (deficiency) of revenues over expenditures | (62,000) | 306,000 | 244,000 |
| **OTHER FINANCING SOURCES (USES)** |  |  |  |
| Transfers in—General Fund | 75,000 | — | 75,000 |
| Transfers out—Capital Projects Fund (Bland Street Drainage) | — | (300,000) | (300,000) |
| Total other financing sources and uses | 75,000 | (300,000) | (225,000) |
| Net change in fund balances | 13,000 | 6,000 | 19,000 |
| Fund balances—beginning | 16,500 | 13,000 | 29,500 |
| Fund balances—ending | $29,500 | $19,000 | $48,500 |

The combined financial statements for the Special Revenue Funds are not reported separately in the governmental entity's financial report, but they are used later in Chapter 12 ("Developing Information for Fund Financial Statements").

# CONVERTING TO GOVERNMENT-WIDE FINANCIAL STATEMENTS

Government-wide financial statements are reported on the accrual basis of accounting. Generally most governments will work from their governmental fund financial statements (which are on a modified accrual basis) and through the use of worksheet entries convert to accrual based financial statements.

In order to illustrate the conversion of the Special Revenue Funds from a modified accrual to an accrual basis, it is assumed that both funds are due an operating grant from the state government and that the characteristics of the grants satisfy the revenue recognition criteria established by GASB-33 (Accounting and Financial Reporting for Nonexchange Transactions), except the resources will not be available to pay current expenditures of the funds.

If it is assumed that the Center City Special Services District is entitled to a $50,000 restricted operating state grant, the following entry is needed to convert the fund financial statements from a modified accrual basis to an accrual basis:

| JE03.19 | Intergovernmental grants receivable | 50,000 | |
|---|---|---|---|
| | Program revenues—operating grants (streets) | | 50,000 |
| | (To accrue grant revenue that was not subject to accrual under the modified accrual method) | | |

If it is assume that the Local Fuel Tax Fund is entitled to a $20,000 restricted operating state grant, the following entry is needed to convert the financial statements from a modified accrual basis to an accrual basis:

| JE03.20 | Intergovernmental grants receivable | 20,000 | |
|---|---|---|---|
| | Program revenues—operating grants (streets) | | 20,000 |
| | (To accrue grant revenue that was not subject to accrual under the modified accrual method) | | |

After these worksheet entries are prepared, the combined adjusted trial balances (on an accrual basis) for the Special Revenue Funds are as follows as of June 30, 20X1:

| | CCSSD | LFTF | Total |
|---|---|---|---|
| Cash | $ 26,500 | $ 42,000 | $ 68,500 |
| Other receivables | 15,000 | 2,000 | 17,000 |
| Property taxes receivable | 108,000 | — | 108,000 |
| Intergovernmental grants receivable | 50,000 | 20,000 | 70,000 |
| Allowance for uncollectible property taxes | (60,000) | — | (60,000) |
| Accounts payable | (50,000) | (25,000) | (75,000) |
| Deferred revenue— property taxes | (10,000) | — | (10,000) |

|  | CCSSD | LFTF | Total |
|---|---|---|---|
| Fund balance | (16,500) | (13,000) | (29,500) |
| General revenues—property taxes | (2,670,000) | — | (2,670,000) |
| Program revenues—operating grants | (50,000) | (4,520,000) | (4,570,000) |
| Miscellaneous revenues | (18,000) | — | (18,000) |
| Interest revenue | — | (6,000) | (6,000) |
| Expenditures—general government | 550,000 | 210,000 | 760,000 |
| Expenditures—streets | 2,200,000 | 3,990,000 | 6,190,000 |
| Transfers out—Capital Projects Fund (Bland Street Drainage) | — | 300,000 | 300,000 |
| Transfers in—General Fund | (75,000) | — | (75,000) |
| Totals | $ 0 | $ 0 | $ 0 |

These accrual based trial balances are used in Chapter 12 ("Developing Information for Government-Wide Financial Statements") in order to prepare the government-wide financial statements.

**3-14** Governmental Funds

## APPENDIX 3A
## WORKSHEET FOR SUMMARIZING CURRENT TRANSACTIONS—CENTER CITY SPECIAL SERVICES DISTRICT FUND

### WORKSHEET OF ENTRIES

| Accounts | Trial Balance Debits | Trial Balance Credits | Adjustments Debits | | Adjustments Credits | | Adjusted Trial Balance Debits | Adjusted Trial Balance Credits | Operating Statement Debits | Operating Statement Credits | Balance Sheet Debits | Balance Sheet Credits |
|---|---|---|---|---|---|---|---|---|---|---|---|---|
| Cash | 30,000 | — | 14,500 JE03.02 | 10,000 JE03.03 | 26,000 JE03.01 | 2,700,000 JE03.10 | 26,500 | — | — | — | 26,500 | — |
|  | — | — | 2,610,000 JE03.06 | | — | | — | — | — | — | — | — |
|  | — | — | 10,000 JE03.07 | | — | | — | — | — | — | — | — |
|  | — | — | 75,000 JE03.11 | | — | | — | — | — | — | — | — |
|  | — | — | 3,000 JE03.12 | | — | | — | — | — | — | — | — |
| Other receivables | 14,500 | — | 15,000 JE03.12 | | 14,500 JE03.02 | | 15,000 | — | — | — | 15,000 | — |
| Property taxes receivable | 50,000 | — | 3,000,000 JE03.04 | | 50,000 JE03.03 | | 108,000 | — | — | — | 108,000 | — |
|  | — | — | — JE03.05 | | 12,000 | | — | — | — | — | — | — |
|  | — | — | — JE03.06 | | 2,610,000 | | — | — | — | — | — | — |
|  | — | — | — JE03.08 | | 270,000 | | — | — | — | — | — | — |
| Allowance for uncollectible property taxes | — | 40,000 | 40,000 JE03.03 | | 300,000 JE03.04 | | — | 60,000 | — | — | — | 60,000 |
|  | — | — | 270,000 JE03.08 | | 30,000 JE03.09 | | — | — | — | — | — | — |
| Accounts payable | — | 26,000 | 26,000 JE03.01 | | 50,000 JE03.10 | | — | 50,000 | — | — | — | 50,000 |

## WORKSHEET OF ENTRIES (Continued)

| Accounts | Trial Balance Debits | Trial Balance Credits | Adjustments Debits | | Adjustments Credits | | Adjusted Trial Balance Debits | Adjusted Trial Balance Credits | Operating Statement Debits | Operating Statement Credits | Balance Sheet Debits | Balance Sheet Credits |
|---|---|---|---|---|---|---|---|---|---|---|---|---|
| Deferred revenue— property taxes | — | 12,000 | JE03.05 | 12,000 | JE03.07 | 10,000 | — | 10,000 | — | — | — | 10,000 |
| Fund balance | — | 16,500 | | — | | — | — | 16,500 | — | — | — | 16,500 |
| General revenues— property taxes | — | — | JE03.09 | 30,000 | JE03.04 | 2,700,000 | — | 2,670,000 | — | 2,670,000 | — | — |
| Miscellaneous revenue | — | — | | — | JE03.12 | 18,000 | — | 18,000 | — | 18,000 | — | — |
| Expenditures— general government | — | — | JE03.10 | 550,000 | | — | 550,000 | — | 550,000 | — | — | — |
| Expendiutres—streets | — | — | JE03.10 | 2,200,000 | | — | 2,200,000 | — | 2,200,000 | — | — | — |
| Transfers in— general fund | — | — | | — | JE03.11 | 75,000 | — | 75,000 | — | 75,000 | — | — |
| Totals | 94,500 | 94,500 | | 8,865,500 | | 8,865,500 | 2,899,500 | 2,899,500 | 2,750,000 | 2,763,000 | 149,500 | 136,500 |
| Net increase (decrease) | | | | | | | | | 13,000 | — | — | 13,000 |
| | | | | | | | | | 2,763,000 | 2,763,000 | 149,500 | 149,500 |

# APPENDIX 3B: SPECIAL REVENUE FUNDS—BALANCE SHEET AND STATEMENT OF REVENUES, EXPENDITURES, AND CHANGES IN FUND BALANCES

**WORKSHEET ENTRIES**

Special Revenue Funds
Balance Sheet
June 30, 20X1

|  | Center City Special Services Fund | Local Fuel Tax Fund | Total |
|---|---|---|---|
| **ASSETS** | | | |
| Cash | $26,500 | $42,000 | $68,500 |
| Other receivables | 15,000 | 2,000 | 17,000 |
| Property taxes receivable (net) | 48,000 | — | |
| Total assets | $89,500 | $44,000 | $133,500 |
| **LIABILITIES AND FUND BALANCES** | | | |
| Liabilities: | | | |
| Accounts payable | $50,000 | $25,000 | $75,000 |
| Deferred revenue—property taxes | 10,000 | — | 10,000 |
| Total liabilities | 60,000 | 25,000 | 85,000 |
| Fund balances: | | | |
| Fund balance—reserved | 29,500 | 19,000 | 48,500 |
| Total liabilities and fund balances | $89,500 | $44,000 | $133,500 |

## WORKSHEET ENTRIES (Continued)

### Special Revenue Funds
### Statement of Revenues, Expenditures, and Changes in Fund Balances
### June 30, 20X1

| | Center City Special Services Fund | Local Fuel Tax Fund | Total |
|---|---:|---:|---:|
| **REVENUES** | | | |
| Property taxes | $2,670,000 | — | $2,670,000 |
| Program revenues—operating grants (street) | — | $4,500,000 | 4,500,000 |
| Interest | — | 6,000 | 6,000 |
| Miscellaneous | 18,000 | | 18,000 |
| Total revenue | 2,688,000 | 4,506,000 | 7,194,000 |
| **EXPENDITURES** | | | |
| General government | 550,000 | 210,000 | 760,000 |
| Streets | 2,200,000 | 3,990,000 | 6,190,000 |
| Total expenditures | 2,750,000 | 4,200,000 | 6,950,000 |
| Excess (deficiency) of revenues over expenditures | (62,000) | 306,000 | 244,000 |
| **OTHER FINANCING SOURCES (USES)** | | | |
| Transfers in—General Fund | 75,000 | — | 75,000 |
| Transfers out—Capital Projects Fund (Bland Street Drainage) | — | (300,000) | (300,000) |
| Total other financing sources and uses | 75,000 | (300,000) | (225,000) |
| Net change in fund balances | 13,000 | 6,000 | 19,000 |
| Fund balances—beginning | 16,500 | 13,000 | 29,500 |
| Fund balances—ending | $29,500 | $19,000 | $48,500 |

**3-18** *Governmental Funds*

## APPENDIX 3C
## WORKSHEET FOR SUMMARIZING CURRENT TRANSACTIONS—LOCAL FUEL TAX FUND

### WORKSHEET OF ENTRIES

| Accounts | Trial Balance Debits | Trial Balance Credits | Adjustments Debits | | Adjustments Credits | | Adjusted Trial Balance Debits | Adjusted Trial Balance Credits | Operating Statement Debits | Operating Statement Credits | Balance Sheet Debits | Balance Sheet Credits |
|---|---|---|---|---|---|---|---|---|---|---|---|---|
| Cash | 25,000 | — | JE03.14 | 3,000 | JE03.13 | 15,000 | 42,000 | — | — | — | 42,000 | — |
| | | | JE03.15 | 4,500,000 | JE03.16 | 4,175,000 | | | | | | |
| | | | JE03.17 | 4,000 | JE03.18 | 300,000 | | | | | | |
| Other receivables | 3,000 | — | JE03.17 | 2,000 | JE03.14 | 3,000 | 2,000 | — | — | — | 2,000 | — |
| Accounts payable | — | 15,000 | JE03.13 | 15,000 | JE03.16 | 25,000 | — | 25,000 | — | — | — | 25,000 |
| Fund balance | — | 13,000 | — | | — | | — | 13,000 | — | — | — | 13,000 |
| Program revenues—operating grants (street) | — | — | — | | JE03.15 | 4,500,000 | — | 4,500,000 | — | 4,500,000 | — | — |
| Interest revenue | — | — | — | | JE03.17 | 6,000 | — | 6,000 | — | 6,000 | — | — |
| Expenditures—general government | — | — | JE03.16 | 210,000 | — | | 210,000 | — | 210,000 | — | — | — |
| Expenditures—streets | — | — | JE03.16 | 3,990,000 | — | | 3,990,000 | — | 3,990,000 | — | — | — |
| Transfers out—Capital Projects Fund (Bland Street Drainage) | — | — | JE03.18 | 300,000 | — | | 300,000 | — | 300,000 | — | — | — |
| Totals | 28,000 | 28,000 | | 9,024,000 | | 9,024,000 | 4,544,000 | 4,544,000 | 4,500,000 | 4,506,000 | 44,000 | 38,000 |
| Net increase (decrease) | | | | | | | | | 6,000 | | | 6,000 |
| | | | | | | | | | 4,506,000 | 4,506,000 | 44,000 | 44,000 |

## APPENDIX 3D: SPECIAL REVENUE FUNDS—COMBINED ADJUSTED TRIAL BALANCES

**WORKSHEET ENTRIES**

| | CCSSD | LFTF | Total |
|---|---|---|---|
| Cash | $ 26,500 | $ 42,000 | $ 68,500 |
| Other receivables | 15,000 | 2,000 | 17,000 |
| Property taxes receivable | 108,000 | — | 108,000 |
| Intergovernmental grants receivable | 50,000 | 20,000 | 70,000 |
| Allowance for uncollectible property taxes | (60,000) | — | (60,000) |
| Accounts payable | (50,000) | (25,000) | (75,000) |
| Deferred revenue—property taxes | (10,000) | — | (10,000) |
| Fund balance | (16,500) | (13,000) | (29,500) |
| General revenues—property taxes | (2,670,000) | — | (2,670,000) |
| Program revenues—operating grants | (50,000) | (4,520,000) | (4,570,000) |
| Miscellaneous revenues | (18,000) | — | (18,000) |
| Interest revenue | — | (6,000) | (6,000) |
| Expenditures—general government | 550,000 | 210,000 | 760,000 |
| Expenditures—streets | 2,200,000 | 3,990,000 | 6,190,000 |
| Transfers out—Capital Projects Fund (Bland Street Drainage) | — | 300,000 | 300,000 |
| Transfers in—General Fund | (75,000) | — | (75,000) |
| Totals | 0 | 0 | 0 |

# CHAPTER 4
# CAPITAL PROJECTS FUNDS

## CONTENTS

| | |
|---|---|
| Nature of Capital Projects Funds | 4-1 |
| Measurement Focus and Basis of Accounting | 4-2 |
| Financial Reporting at Fund Level | 4-3 |
| Financial Reporting at Government-Wide Level | 4-4 |
| Illustrative Transactions | 4-4 |
|    Easely Street Bridge Project | 4-5 |
|    Bland Street Drainage Project | 4-8 |
|    West End Recreation Center Project | 4-11 |
| Fund Financial Statements | 4-13 |
| Government-Wide Financial Statements | 4-15 |
|    Easely Street Bridge Project | 4-16 |
|    Bland Street Drainage Project | 4-16 |
|    West End Recreation Center Project | 4-17 |
| Appendix 4A: Worksheet for Summarizing Current Transactions—Easely Street Bridge Project | 4-19 |
| Appendix 4B: Worksheet for Summarizing Current Transactions—Bland Street Drainage Project | 4-21 |
| Appendix 4C: Worksheet for Summarizing Current Transactions—West End Recreation Center Capital Project | 4-23 |
| Appendix 4D: Capital Projects Funds—Balance Sheet and Statement of Revenues, Expenditures, and Changes in Fund Balances | 4-25 |
| Appendix 4E: Capital Projects Funds—Worksheet to Convert from Modified Accrual to Accrual Basis | 4-28 |
| Appendix 4F: Capital Projects Funds—Adjusted Trial Balances | 4-30 |

## NATURE OF CAPITAL PROJECTS FUNDS

A Capital Projects Fund is used to account for major capital expenditures, such as the construction of civic centers, libraries, and general administrative services buildings. The acquisition of other capital assets, such as machinery, furniture, and vehicles, is usually accounted for in the fund responsible for the financing of the expenditure. The purpose of a Capital Projects Fund, as defined by NCGA-1, is

> to account for financial resources to be used for the acquisition or construction of major capital facilities (other than those financed by proprietary funds or in trust funds for individuals, private organizations, or other governments). (Capital outlays financed from general obligation bonds proceeds should be accounted for through a Capital Projects Fund.)

A separate Capital Projects Fund is usually established when the acquisition or construction of a capital project extends beyond a single fiscal year and the financing sources are provided by more than one fund, or the capital asset is financed by specifically designated resources. Specifically designated resources may arise from the issuance of general governmental bonds, receipts of grants from other governmental units, designation of a portion of tax receipts, or a combination of these and other financing sources. A Capital Projects Fund is be used when mandated by law or stipulated by regulations or covenants related to the financing source. For control purposes, it also may be advantageous to use a separate Capital Projects Fund even though one is not legally required.

■ **CONTINUING STANDARD:** The definition of a Capital Projects Fund continues to be based on the description established by NCGA-1 (Governmental Accounting and Financial Reporting Principles).

## MEASUREMENT FOCUS AND BASIS OF ACCOUNTING

The modified accrual basis and flow of current financial resources are used to prepare the financial statements of a Capital Projects Fund. These concepts are discussed in Chapter 2 ("The General Fund").

As noted above, resources to finance the construction of a capital asset may come from a variety of sources. Grants (either government-mandated or voluntary nonexchange transactions) received from another government are reported as revenue when the standards established by GASB-33 (Accounting and Financial Reporting for Nonexchange Transactions) are satisfied. Proceeds from the issuance of debt are recorded as other financing sources when the proceeds are available to the governmental entity. Transfers from the General Fund or other intergovernmental transfers are reported in the entity's financial statements based on the guidance provided by GASB-34 (par. 112).

▶ **NEW STANDARD:** GASB-34 required that the *proceeds* from the sale of long-term debt be reported as an other financing source and that any related discount or premium, and/or debt issuance costs be separately reported. Taken literally, that cannot be accomplished, since the term *proceeds* generally means that any discount or premium and the related cost is netted against the face amount of the debt. GASB-37 (Basic Financial Statements—and Management's Discussion and Analysis—for State and Local Governments: Omnibus) points out that GASB-34 should have referred to the "face amount" of the debt and not to the proceeds. Under the clarified language, if debt with a face amount of $1,000,000 was issued for $1,050,000, the financial statements of the Capital Projects Fund would present two elements of the transactions, namely (1) long-term debt issued of $1,000,000 and (2) a premium on long-term debt issued of $50,000.

Generally the recording of expenditures of a Capital Projects Fund is limited to payments or commitments to pay contractors and payments of support services (usually classified as general government expenditures). Commitments (liabilities) to pay contractors should be recorded as expenditures of the current budgetary period if they are normally expected to be liquidated with expendable available financial resources as defined by GASBI-6 (Recognition and Measurement of Certain Liabilities and Expenditures in Governmental Fund Financial Statements).

In many instances, a Capital Projects Fund will have excess cash, which will be temporally invested. Temporary investments and the related revenue are reported in the fund's financial statements based on the guidance provided by GASB-31 (Accounting and Financial Reporting for Certain Investments and for External Investment Pools).

## FINANCIAL REPORTING AT FUND LEVEL

The balances and activities of Capital Projects Funds are presented in the following financial statements at the fund financial statement level:

- Balance Sheet
- Statement of Revenues, Expenditures, and Changes in Fund Balances

> ■ **CONTINUING STANDARD:** Transactions and accounts recorded in Capital Projects Funds continue to be based on standards established by various NCGA/GASB Statements and Interpretations that were outstanding before the issuance of GASB-34.

These two fund financial statements include all of the governmental funds (General Fund, Special Revenue Funds, Capital Projects Funds, Debt Service Funds, and Permanent Funds), and these funds are reported based on the concept of a major fund as defined by GASB-34.

> ▶ **NEW STANDARD:** A significant change in the focus of reporting governmental funds and proprietary funds is that major funds are reported for these funds; however, combined financial statements for fund types are not reported. Fund financial statements must present in a separate column a (major) fund that satisfied both of the following criteria: (1) total assets, liabilities, revenues, or expenditures/expenses of the governmental (enterprise) fund are equal to or greater than 10 percent of the corresponding total (assets, liabilities, and so forth) for all funds that are considered governmental funds (enterprise funds) and (2) total assets, liabilities, revenues, or expenditures/expenses of the governmental fund (enterprise fund) are equal to or greater than 5 percent of the corresponding total for all governmental and enterprise funds combined (GASB-34, pars. 74-76). In establishing these criteria, the GASB intended that a major fund arise when a particular element (assets for example) of a fund meets both the 10 percent threshold and the 5 percent threshold. Some preparers have read the requirement to mean that a major fund arises when one element (assets for example) satisfies the 10 percent threshold and another element (revenues, for example) satisfies the 5 percent threshold. GASB-37 amended GASB-34 to make clear the GASB's original intent: That is, a single element must satisfy both criteria.

## FINANCIAL REPORTING AT GOVERNMENT-WIDE LEVEL

The fund-based financial statements as described above are included in a governmental entity's financial report in order to demonstrate that restrictions imposed by statutes, regulations, or contracts have been followed. Balances in these fund financial statements are converted from a modified accrual basis to an accrual basis in order to create the basic information for the government-wide financial statements.

For the most part, this approach requires that all of the Capital Projects Funds' combined ending trial balances (which are on a modified accrual basis) be adjusted to reflect accrual balances. Briefly, this means that all capital expenditures for the current period are converted to a specific asset (building, infrastructure, etc.) and proceeds from the issuance of debt are converted from an other source of financial resources to long-term debt. This conversion is illustrated later in this chapter.

## ILLUSTRATIVE TRANSACTIONS

In order to illustrate accounting and financial reporting standards that are observed for Capital Projects Funds, assume that the City of Centerville has the following Capital Projects Funds:

- Easely Street Bridge Project
- Bland Street Drainage Project
- West End Recreation Center Project

## Easely Street Bridge Project

The Easely Street Bridge Project is being constructed to relieve traffic congestion between the downtown district and the east end of Centerville. Its trial balance for the beginning of the fiscal year is as follows:

| Accounts | Trial Balance Debits | Trial Balance Credits |
|---|---|---|
| Cash | $122,000 | |
| Temporary investments | 620,000 | |
| Accounts payable | | $26,000 |
| Fund balance | | 716,000 |
| Totals | $742,000 | $742,000 |

This section presents illustrative transactions and entries for the project during the fiscal year ended June 30, 20X1.

■ **CONTINUING STANDARD:** GASB-34 generally did not change the manner of accounting for transactions that are recorded in Capital Projects Funds.

*Transaction JE04.01*—Accounts payable of $26,000 from the previous year were paid:

| Accounts | Debit | Credit |
|---|---|---|
| Accounts payable | 26,000 | |
| Cash | | 26,000 |

*Transaction JE04.02*—During the year interest revenue of $30,000 was earned and received:

| Accounts | Debit | Credit |
|---|---|---|
| Cash | 30,000 | |
| Interest revenue | | 30,000 |

*Transaction JE04.03*—Capital expenditures of $11,100,000 were incurred and paid during the year:

| Accounts | Debit | Credit |
|---|---|---|
| Expenditures—capital outlays | 11,100,000 | |
| Cash | | 11,100,000 |

■ **CONTINUING STANDARD:** Based on the standards established by NCGA-1 (Governmental Accounting and Financial Reporting Principles), major expenditures for the acquisition or construction of capital projects continue to be reported in a Capital Projects Fund.

▶ **NEW STANDARD:** GASB-34 originally required that the cost of constructing a capital asset include certain interest costs as described in FAS-34 (Capitalization of Interest Cost). These costs would be part of the capital asset amount that is reported in the government-wide financial statements and would be the basis for computing depreciation expense. GASB-37 (Basic Financial Statements—and Management's Discussion and Analysis—for State and Local Governments: Omnibus) revises GASB-34 by stating that the cost basis of a capital assets does not include interest costs incurred during the construction of a capital asset related to governmental activities. The elimination of the provisions of FAS-34 does not apply to interest costs incurred by Enterprise Funds and, therefore, they are reported as business-type activities.

*Transaction JE04.04*—General government expenditures of $495,000 were incurred, of which $400,000 were paid:

| Accounts | Debit | Credit |
|---|---|---|
| Expenditures—general government | 495,000 | |
| Cash | | 400,000 |
| Accounts payable | | 95,000 |

■ **CONTINUING STANDARD:** Based on the standards established by GASBI-6 (Recognition and Measurement of Certain Liabilities and Expenditures in Governmental Fund Financial Statements), expenditures should continue to be recorded on an accrual basis except with respect to the expenditures identified in the Interpretation.

*Transaction JE04.05*—On October 1, 20X0, bonds with a maturity value of $10,000,000 were issued for $9,328,956. The bonds had a stated interest rate of 7% and were sold at an effective interest rate of 8%. Interest is paid annually:

| Accounts | Debit | Credit |
|---|---|---|
| Cash | 9,328,956 | |
| Discount on long-term debt issued (other uses of financial resources) | 671,044 | |
| Long-term debt issued (other sources of financial resources) | | 10,000,000 |

▶ **NEW STANDARD:** GASB-34 originally required that the *proceeds* from the sale of long-term debt be reported as an other financing source and that any related discount or premium, and/or debt issuance costs be separately reported. Taken literally, that cannot be accomplished since the term *proceeds* generally means that any discount or premium and the related cost is netted against the face amount of the debt. The GASB's Q&A Guide points out that GASB-34 should have referred to the "face amount" of the debt and not to the proceeds. GASB-37 (Basic Financial Statements—and Management's Discussion and Analysis—for State and Local Governments: Omnibus) amends GASB-34 by substituting the term "proceeds" with "face amount."

*Transaction JE04.06*—A capital grant of $1,250,000 was received from the state government:

| Accounts | Debit | Credit |
|---|---|---|
| Cash | 1,250,000 | |
| Program revenues—capital grants and contributions (streets) | | 1,250,000 |

*Transaction JE04.07*—Additional temporary investments of $75,000 were made during the year:

| Accounts | Debit | Credit |
|---|---|---|
| Temporary investments | 75,000 | |
| Cash | | 75,000 |

*Transaction JE04.08*—The General Fund made a transfer of $1,000,000 to help fund the project:

| Accounts | Debit | Credit |
|---|---|---|
| Cash | 1,000,000 | |
| Transfers in—general fund | | 1,000,000 |

After the transactions for the year are posted, the year-end trial balance (June 30, 20X1) for the Easely Street Bridge Capital Project appears as follows:

| Accounts | Adjusted Debits | Adjusted Trial Balance Credits |
|---|---|---|
| Cash | $ 129,956 | |
| Temporary investments | 695,000 | |
| Accounts payable | | $ 95,000 |
| Fund balance | | 716,000 |
| Program revenues—capital grants (street) | | 1,250,000 |
| Interest revenue | | 30,000 |
| Expenditures—capital outlays (streets) | 11,100,000 | |
| Expenditures—general government | 495,000 | |
| Long-term debt issued (other sources of financial resources) | | 10,000,000 |
| Discount on long-term debt issued (other uses of financial resources) | 671,044 | |
| Transfers in—general fund | | 1,000,000 |
| Totals | $13,091,000 | $3,091,000 |

The worksheet that summarizes the foregoing journal entries for the Easely Street Bridge Capital Project for the year-end trial balance is presented in Appendix 4A.

## Bland Street Drainage Project

The Bland Street Drainage Project is being constructed to mitigate flooding problems. Its trial balance for the beginning of the fiscal year is as follows:

| Accounts | Trial Balance Debits | Trial Balance Credits |
|---|---|---|
| Cash | $127,000 | |
| Temporary investments | 42,000 | |
| Accounts payable | | $ 33,000 |
| Fund balance | | 136,000 |
| Totals | $169,000 | $169,000 |

This section presents illustrative transactions and entries for the project during the fiscal year ended June 30, 20X1.

*Transaction JE04.09*—Accounts payable of $33,000 from the previous year were paid:

| Accounts | Debit | Credit |
|---|---|---|
| Accounts payable | 33,000 | |
| Cash | | 33,000 |

*Transaction JE04.10*—During the year, interest revenue of $4,000 was earned and received:

| Accounts | Debit | Credit |
|---|---|---|
| Cash | 4,000 | |
| Interest revenue | | 4,000 |

*Transaction JE04.11*—Capital expenditures of $1,500,000 were incurred and paid during the year:

| Accounts | Debit | Credit |
|---|---|---|
| Expenditures—capital outlays | 1,500,000 | |
| Cash | | 1,500,000 |

*Transaction JE04.12*—General government expenditures of $97,000 were incurred, of which $70,000 were paid:

| Accounts | Debit | Credit |
|---|---|---|
| Expenditures—general government | 97,000 | |
| Cash | | 70,000 |
| Accounts payable | | 27,000 |

*Transaction JE04.13*—A capital grant of $750,000 was received from the federal government:

| Accounts | Debit | Credit |
|---|---|---|
| Cash | 750,000 | |
| Program revenues—capital grants and contributions (streets) | | 750,000 |

*Transaction JE04.14*—Additional temporary investments of $20,000 were made during the year:

**4-10** *Governmental Funds*

| Accounts | Debit | Credit |
|---|---|---|
| Temporary investments | 20,000 | |
| Cash | | 20,000 |

*Transaction JE04.15*—The General Fund made a transfer of $600,000 to help fund the project:

| Accounts | Debit | Credit |
|---|---|---|
| Cash | 600,000 | |
| Transfers in—general fund | | 600,000 |

*Transaction JE04.16*—During the year, $100,000 was received from the Local Fuel Tax Fund (Special Revenues Fund):

| Accounts | Debit | Credit |
|---|---|---|
| Cash | 300,000 | |
| Transfers in—special revenue fund (local fuel tax fund) | | 300,000 |

After the transactions for the year are posted, the year-end trial balance (June 30, 20X1) for the Bland Street Drainage Project appears as follows:

| Accounts | Adjusted Trial Balance Debits | Credits |
|---|---|---|
| Cash | $ 158,000 | |
| Temporary investments | 62,000 | |
| Accounts payable | | $ 27,000 |
| Fund balance | | 136,000 |
| Program revenues—capital grants and contributions (street) | | 750,000 |
| Interest revenue | | 4,000 |
| Expenditures—capital outlays (streets) | 1,500,000 | |
| Expenditures—general government | 97,000 | |
| Transfers in—general fund | | 600,000 |
| Transfers in—special revenue fund (local fuel tax fund) | | 300,000 |
| Totals | $1,817,000 | $1,817,000 |

The worksheet that summarizes the foregoing journal entries for the Bland Street Drainage Capital Project for the year-end trial balance is presented in Appendix 4B.

## West End Recreation Center Project

Construction on the West End Recreation Center was started during the current year in order to provide recreational activities to pre-teen and teenage students. Prior to the current year, funds were accumulated in the fund before actual construction was begun. The West End Recreation Center Project Fund's trial balance for the beginning of the fiscal year is as follows:

|                        | Trial Balance |           |
|------------------------|---------------|-----------|
| Accounts               | Debits        | Credits   |
| Cash                   | $500,000      |           |
| Temporary investments  | 22,000        |           |
| Accounts payable       |               | $ 13,000  |
| Fund balance           |               | 509,000   |
| Totals                 | $522,000      | $522,000  |

*Transaction JE04.17*—Accounts payable of $13,000 from the previous year were paid:

| Accounts         | Debit  | Credit |
|------------------|--------|--------|
| Accounts payable | 13,000 |        |
| Cash             |        | 13,000 |

*Transaction JE04.18*—During the year interest revenue of $2,000 was earned and received:

| Accounts         | Debit | Credit |
|------------------|-------|--------|
| Cash             | 2,000 |        |
| Interest revenue |       | 2,000  |

*Transaction JE04.19*—Capital expenditures of $1,300,000 were incurred and paid during the year:

| Accounts                      | Debit     | Credit    |
|-------------------------------|-----------|-----------|
| Expenditures—capital outlays  | 1,300,000 |           |
| Cash                          |           | 1,300,000 |

*Transaction JE04.20*—General government expenditures of $25,000 were incurred, of which $20,000 were paid:

| Accounts                         | Debit  | Credit |
|----------------------------------|--------|--------|
| Expenditures—general government  | 25,000 |        |
| Cash                             |        | 20,000 |
| Accounts payable                 |        | 5,000  |

## 4-12 Governmental Funds

**Transaction JE04.21**—On December 31, 20X0, serial bonds of $3,000,000 were issued at par. The bonds mature at a rate of $500,000 every six months beginning on June 30, 20X1. Interest of 12% is due semiannually beginning on June 30, 20X1:

| Accounts | Debit | Credit |
|---|---|---|
| Cash | 3,000,000 | |
|    Long-term debt issued (other sources of financial resources) | | 3,000,000 |

**Transaction JE04.22**—A capital grant of $450,000 was received from the state government:

| Accounts | Debit | Credit |
|---|---|---|
| Cash | 450,000 | |
|    Program revenues—capital grants and contributions (recreation and parks) | | 450,000 |

**Transaction JE04.23**—Additional temporary investments of $2,900,000 were made during the year:

| Accounts | Debit | Credit |
|---|---|---|
| Temporary investments | 2,900,000 | |
|    Cash | | 2,900,000 |

**Transaction JE04.24**—The General Fund made a transfer of $300,000 to help fund the project:

| Accounts | Debit | Credit |
|---|---|---|
| Cash | 300,000 | |
|    Transfers in—general fund | | 300,000 |

After the transactions for the year are posted, the year-end trial balance (June 30, 20X1) for the West End Recreation Center Capital Project appears as follows:

| | Adjusted Trial Balance | |
|---|---|---|
| Accounts | Debits | Credits |
| Cash | $ 19,000 | |
| Temporary investments | 2,922,000 | |

|  | Adjusted Trial Balance | |
| --- | --- | --- |
| Accounts | Debits | Credits |
| Accounts payable |  | $ 5,000 |
| Fund balance |  | 509,000 |
| Program revenues—capital grants and contributions (recreation and parks) |  | 450,000 |
| Interest revenue |  | 2,000 |
| Expenditures—capital outlays (recreation and parks) | 1,300,000 |  |
| Expenditures—general government | 25,000 |  |
| Long-term debt issued |  | 3,000,000 |
| Transfers in—general fund |  | 300,000 |
| Totals | $4,266,000 | $4,266,000 |

The worksheet that summarizes the foregoing journal entries for the West End Recreation Center Capital Project for the year-end trial balance is presented in Appendix 4C.

## FUND FINANCIAL STATEMENTS

At the fund financial statement level, a governmental fund must prepare a statement of revenues, expenditures, and changes in fund balances and a balance sheet. Based on the adjusted trial balances created above, the following preliminary financial statements reflect the balances and activities of the three Capital Projects Funds. These financial statements are prepared to facilitate the preparation of the fund financial statements illustrated in Chapter 12 ("Developing Information For Fund Financial Statements"). (See Appendixes 4D and 4E.)

> ▶ **NEW STANDARD:** NCGA-1 illustrates three distinct formats that can be used to prepare the statement of revenues, expenditures, and changes in fund balances for governmental funds; however, GASB-34 eliminates two of the options, and only the format illustrated below can now be used (GASB-34, par. 86).

> ■ **CONTINUING STANDARD:** The formatting of the balance sheet at the fund financial statement level was not changed by GASB-34.

## Capital Projects Funds
## Balance Sheet
## June 30, 20X1

|  | Easely Street Bridge Project | Bland Street Drainage Project | West End Recreation Center Project | Total |
|---|---|---|---|---|
| **ASSETS** | | | | |
| Cash | $129,956 | $158,000 | $ 19,000 | $306,956 |
| Temporary investments | 695,000 | 62,000 | 2,922,000 | 3,679,000 |
| Total assets | $824,956 | $220,000 | $2,941,000 | $3,985,956 |
| **LIABILITIES AND FUND BALANCES** | | | | |
| Liabilities: | | | | |
| Accounts payable | $95,000 | $27,000 | $ 5,000 | $127,000 |
| Total liabilities | 95,000 | 27,000 | 5,000 | 127,000 |
| Fund balances: | | | | |
| Fund balance—reserved | 729,956 | 193,000 | 2,936,000 | 3,858,956 |
| Total liabilities and fund balances | $824,956 | $220,000 | $2,941,000 | $3,985,956 |

## Capital Projects Funds
## Statement of Revenues, Expenditures, and Changes in Fund Balances
## June 30, 20X1

|  | Easely Street Bridge Project | Bland Street Drainage Project | West End Recreation Center Project | Total |
|---|---|---|---|---|
| **REVENUES** | | | | |
| Program revenues—capital grants (street) | $1,250,000 | $750,000 | — | $2,000,000 |
| Program revenues—capital grants and contributions (recreation and parks) | — | — | $450,000 | 450,000 |
| Interest | 30,000 | 4,000 | 2,000 | 36,000 |
| Total revenue | 1,280,000 | 754,000 | 452,000 | 2,486,000 |

|  | Easely Street Bridge Project | Bland Street Drainage Project | West End Recreation Center Project | Total |
|---|---|---|---|---|
| **EXPENDITURES** | | | | |
| General government | 495,000 | 97,000 | 25,000 | 617,000 |
| Capital outlays | 11,100,000 | 1,500,000 | 1,300,000 | 13,900,000 |
| Total expenditures | 11,595,000 | 1,597,000 | 1,325,000 | 14,520,000 |
| Excess (deficiency) of revenues over expenditures | (10,315,000) | (843,000) | (873,000) | (12,030,000) |
| **OTHER FINANCING SOURCES (USES)** | | | | |
| Long-term debt issued | 10,000,000 | — | 3,000,000 | 13,000,000 |
| Discount on long-term debt issued | (671,044) | — | — | (671,044) |
| Transfers in | 1,000,000 | 900,000 | 300,000 | 2,200,000 |
| Total other financing sources and uses | 10,328,956 | 900,000 | 3,300,000 | 14,528,956 |
| Net change in fund balances | 13,956 | 57,000 | 2,427,000 | 2,498,956 |
| Fund balances—beginning | 716,000 | 136,000 | 509,000 | 1,361,000 |
| Fund balances—ending | $729,956 | $193,000 | $2,936,000 | $3,858,956 |

The combined financial statements for the Capital Projects Funds are not reported separately in the governmental entity's financial report, but they are used in Chapter 12 ("Developing Information for Fund Financial Statements").

## GOVERNMENT-WIDE FINANCIAL STATEMENTS

Government-wide financial statements are reported on the accrual basis of accounting. Generally, most governments will work from their governmental fund financial statements (which are on a modified accrual basis) and through the use of worksheet entries convert to accrual based financial statements.

In order to convert the transactions that were recorded in the Capital Projects Funds from a modified accrual basis to an accrual basis the following worksheet entries are made.

## Easely Street Bridge Project

The capital expenditure on the bridge is converted from an expenditure to a capital asset (infrastructure assets) by making the following worksheet entry:

| | Accounts | Debit | Credit |
|---|---|---|---|
| JE04.25 | Construction-in-progress | 11,100,000 | |
| | Expenditures—capital outlays | | 11,100,000 |

(To record the construction of a capital asset and reverse the recognition of the related expenditure

The issuance of debt is converted from net source of financial resources to a liability by making the following worksheet entry:

| | Accounts | Debit | Credit |
|---|---|---|---|
| JE04.26 | Long-term debt issued (other sources of financial resources) | 10,000,000 | |
| | Discount on long-term debt issued (other uses of financial resources) | | 671,044 |
| | Bonds payable | | 9,328,956 |

(To record the issuance of long-term debt and reverse the recognition of other sources of financial resources)

**OBSERVATION:** The conversion entry to accrue interest expense including the effects of the amortization of bond discount is made in Chapter 5 ("Debt Service Funds").

## Bland Street Drainage Project

The capital expenditure on the Bland Street drainage project is converted from an expenditure to a capital asset (infrastructure assets) by making the following worksheet entry:

| | Accounts | Debit | Credit |
|---|---|---|---|
| JE04.27 | Construction-in-progress | 1,500,000 | |
| | Expenditures—capital outlays | | 1,500,000 |
| | (To record the construction of a capital asset and reverse the recognition of the related expenditure) | | |

## West End Recreation Center Project

The capital expenditure on the recreation center is converted from an expenditure to a building (other capital assets) by making the following worksheet entry:

| | Accounts | Debit | Credit |
|---|---|---|---|
| JE04.28 | Construction-in-progress | 1,300,000 | |
| | Expenditures—capital outlays | | 1,300,000 |
| | (To record the construction of a capital asset and reverse the recognition of the related expenditure) | | |

The issuance of debt is converted from a source of financial resources to a liability by making the following worksheet entry:

| | Accounts | Debit | Credit |
|---|---|---|---|
| JE04.29 | Long-term debt issued (other sources of financial resources) | 3,000,000 | |
| | Bonds payable | | 3,000,000 |
| | (To record the issuance of long-term debt and reverse the recognition of other sources of financial resources) | | |

> **OBSERVATION:** The serial bonds in this example are due in $500,000 installments every six months. The long-term liabilities will be allocated between the amounts due within one year and beyond one year in Chapter 14 ("Basic Financial Statements").

After the foregoing entries are prepared, the adjusted trial balances (on an accrual basis) for the three Capital Projects Funds appear as follows as of June 30, 20X1 (see Appendix 4F):

## 4-18 Governmental Funds

### Adjusted Trial Balance

| Accounts | Easely Street Bridge Project Debits (Credits) | Bland Street Drainage Project Debits (Credits) | West End Recreation Center Project Debits (Credits) | Total Debits (Credits) |
|---|---|---|---|---|
| Cash | $ 129,956 | $ 158,000 | $ 19,000 | $ 306,956 |
| Temporary investments | 695,000 | 62,000 | 2,922,000 | 3,679,000 |
| Construction-in-progress | 11,100,000 | $1,500,000 | 1,300,000 | 13,900,000 |
| Accounts payable | (95,000) | (27,000) | (5,000) | (127,000) |
| Bonds payable | (9,328,956) | | (3,000,000) | (12,328,956) |
| Fund balance | (716,000) | (136,000) | (509,000) | (1,361,000) |
| Program revenues—capital grants (street) | (1,250,000) | (750,000) | — | (2,000,000) |
| Program revenues—capital grants and contributions (recreation and parks) | — | — | (450,000) | (450,000) |
| Interest revenue | (30,000) | (4,000) | (2,000) | (36,000) |
| Expenditures—general government | 495,000 | 97,000 | 25,000 | 617,000 |
| Transfers in | (1,000,000) | (900,000) | (300,000) | (2,200,000) |
| Totals | $ -0- | $ -0- | $ -0- | $ -0- |

This combined trial balance on the accrual basis is used in Chapter 13 ("Developing Information for Government-Wide Financial Statements").

## APPENDIX 4A
## WORKSHEET FOR SUMMARIZING CURRENT TRANSACTIONS—EASELY STREET BRIDGE PROJECT

Capital Projects Funds  4-19

### WORKSHEET ENTRIES

| Accounts | Trial Balance Debits | Trial Balance Credits | | Adjustments Debits | | Adjustments Credits | Adjusted Trial Balance Debits | Adjusted Trial Balance Credits | Operating Statement Debits | Operating Statement Credits | Balance Sheet Debits | Balance Sheet Credits |
|---|---|---|---|---|---|---|---|---|---|---|---|---|
| Cash | 122,000 | — | JE04.02 | 30,000 | JE04.01 | 26,000 | 129,956 | — | — | — | 129,956 | — |
| | | | JE04.05 | 9,328,956 | JE04.03 | 11,100,000 | | | | | | |
| | | | JE04.06 | 1,250,000 | JE04.04 | 400,000 | | | | | | |
| | | | JE04.08 | 1,000,000 | JE04.07 | 75,000 | | | | | | |
| Temporary investments | 620,000 | — | JE04.07 | 75,000 | | — | 695,000 | — | — | — | 695,000 | — |
| Accounts payable | — | 26,000 | JE04.01 | 26,000 | JE04.04 | 95,000 | — | 95,000 | — | — | — | 95,000 |
| Fund balance | — | 716,000 | | — | | — | — | 716,000 | — | — | — | 716,000 |
| Program revenues—capital grants and contributions (Street) | — | — | | — | JE04.06 | 1,250,000 | — | 1,250,000 | — | 1,250,000 | — | — |
| Interest revenue | — | — | | — | JE04.02 | 30,000 | — | 30,000 | — | 30,000 | — | — |
| Expenditures—capital outlays (streets) | — | — | JE04.03 | 11,100,000 | | — | 11,100,000 | — | 11,100,000 | — | — | — |
| Expenditures—general government | — | — | JE04.04 | 495,000 | | — | 495,000 | — | 495,000 | — | — | — |
| Long-term debt issued (other sources of financial resources) | — | — | | — | JE04.05 | 10,000,000 | — | 10,000,000 | — | 10,000,000 | — | — |

**4-20** *Governmental Funds*

## WORKSHEET ENTRIES (Continued)

| Accounts | Trial Balance Debits | Trial Balance Credits | Adjustments Debits | Adjustments Credits | Adjusted Trial Balance Debits | Adjusted Trial Balance Credits | Operating Statement Debits | Operating Statement Credits | Balance Sheet Debits | Balance Sheet Credits |
|---|---|---|---|---|---|---|---|---|---|---|
| Discount on long-term debt issued (other uses of financial resources) | — | — | JE04.05 671,044 | — | 671,044 | — | 671,044 | — | — | — |
| Transfers in—general fund | — | 742,000 | — | JE04.08 1,000,000 | — | 1,000,000 | — | 1,000,000 | — | — |
| Totals | 742,000 | 742,000 | 23,976,000 | 23,976,000 | 13,091,000 | 13,091,000 | 12,266,044 | 12,280,000 | 824,956 | 811,000 |
| Net increase (decrease) | | | | | | | 13,956 | — | — | 13,956 |
| | | | | | | | 12,280,000 | 12,280,000 | 824,956 | 824,956 |

## APPENDIX 4B
## WORKSHEET FOR SUMMARIZING CURRENT TRANSACTIONS—BLAND STREET DRAINAGE PROJECT

### WORKSHEET ENTRIES

| Accounts | Trial Balance Debits | Trial Balance Credits | | Adjustments Debits | | Adjustments Credits | Adjusted Trial Balance Debits | Adjusted Trial Balance Credits | Operating Statement Debits | Operating Statement Credits | Balance Sheet Debits | Balance Sheet Credits |
|---|---|---|---|---|---|---|---|---|---|---|---|---|
| Cash | 127,000 | — | JE04.10 | 4,000 | JE04.09 | 33,000 | 158,000 | — | — | — | 158,000 | — |
| | — | — | JE04.13 | 750,000 | JE04.11 | 1,500,000 | — | — | — | — | — | — |
| | — | — | JE04.15 | 600,000 | JE04.12 | 70,000 | — | — | — | — | — | — |
| | — | — | JE04.16 | 300,000 | JE04.14 | 20,000 | — | — | — | — | — | — |
| Temporary investments | 42,000 | — | JE04.14 | 20,000 | | — | 62,000 | — | — | — | 62,000 | — |
| Accounts payable | — | 33,000 | JE04.09 | 33,000 | JE04.12 | 27,000 | — | 27,000 | — | — | — | 27,000 |
| Fund balance | — | 136,000 | | — | | — | — | 136,000 | — | — | — | 136,000 |
| Program revenues—capital grants and contributions (street) | — | — | | — | JE04.13 | 750,000 | — | 750,000 | — | 750,000 | — | — |
| Interest revenue | — | — | | — | JE04.10 | 4,000 | — | 4,000 | — | 4,000 | — | — |
| Expenditures—capital outlays (streets) | — | — | JE04.11 | 1,500,000 | | — | 1,500,000 | — | 1,500,000 | — | — | — |
| Expenditures—general government | — | — | JE04.12 | 97,000 | | — | 97,000 | — | 97,000 | — | — | — |
| Transfers in—general fund | — | — | | — | JE04.15 | 600,000 | — | 600,000 | — | 600,000 | — | — |

**4-22** Governmental Funds

## WORKSHEET ENTRIES (Continued)

| Accounts | Trial Balance Debits | Trial Balance Credits | Adjustments Debits | Adjustments Credits | Adjusted Trial Balance Debits | Adjusted Trial Balance Credits | Operating Statement Debits | Operating Statement Credits | Balance Sheet Debits | Balance Sheet Credits |
|---|---|---|---|---|---|---|---|---|---|---|
| Transfers in—special revenue fund (local fuel tax fund) | — | 169,000 | — | JE04.16 300,000 | — | 300,000 | — | 300,000 | — | — |
| Totals | 169,000 | 169,000 | 3,304,000 | 3,304,000 | 1,817,000 | 1,817,000 | 1,597,000 | 1,654,000 | 220,000 | 163,000 |
| Net increase (decrease) | | | | | | | 57,000 | | | 57,000 |
| | | | | | | | 1,654,000 | 1,654,000 | 220,000 | 220,000 |

## APPENDIX 4C
## WORKSHEET FOR SUMMARIZING CURRENT TRANSACTIONS—WEST END RECREATION CENTER CAPITAL PROJECT

### WORKSHEET ENTRIES

| Accounts | Trial Balance Debits | Trial Balance Credits | Adjustments Debits | | Adjustments Credits | | Adjusted Trial Balance Debits | Adjusted Trial Balance Credits | Operating Statement Debits | Operating Statement Credits | Balance Sheet Debits | Balance Sheet Credits |
|---|---|---|---|---|---|---|---|---|---|---|---|---|
| Cash | 500,000 | — | JE04.18 | 2,000 | JE04.17 | 13,000 | 19,000 | — | — | — | 19,000 | — |
| | | | JE04.21 | 3,000,000 | JE04.19 | 1,300,000 | | | | | | |
| | | | JE04.22 | 450,000 | JE04.20 | 20,000 | | | | | | |
| | | | JE04.24 | 300,000 | JE04.23 | 2,900,000 | | | | | | |
| Temporary investments | 22,000 | — | JE04.23 | 2,900,000 | | — | 2,922,000 | — | — | — | 2,922,000 | — |
| Accounts payable | — | 13,000 | JE04.17 | 13,000 | JE04.20 | 5,000 | — | 5,000 | — | — | — | 5,000 |
| Fund balance | — | 509,000 | | — | | — | — | 509,000 | — | — | — | 509,000 |
| Program revenues—capital grants and contributions (recreation and parks) | — | — | | — | JE04.22 | 450,000 | — | 450,000 | — | 450,000 | — | — |
| Interest revenue | — | — | | — | JE04.18 | 2,000 | — | 2,000 | — | 2,000 | — | — |
| Expenditures—capital outlays (recreation and parks) | — | — | JE04.19 | 1,300,000 | | — | 1,300,000 | — | 1,300,000 | — | — | — |
| Expenditures—general government | — | — | JE04.20 | 25,000 | | — | 25,000 | — | 25,000 | — | — | — |

**4-24** *Governmental Funds*

## WORKSHEET ENTRIES (Continued)

| Accounts | Trial Balance Debits | Trial Balance Credits | Adjustments Debits | Adjustments | Adjustments Credits | Adjusted Trial Balance Debits | Adjusted Trial Balance Credits | Operating Statement Debits | Operating Statement Credits | Balance Sheet Debits | Balance Sheet Credits |
|---|---|---|---|---|---|---|---|---|---|---|---|
| Long-term debt issued | — | — | — | JE04.21 | 3,000,000 | — | 3,000,000 | — | 3,000,000 | — | — |
| Transfers in—general fund | — | — | — | JE04.24 | 300,000 | — | 300,000 | — | 300,000 | — | — |
| Totals | 522,000 | 522,000 | 7,990,000 | | 7,990,000 | 4,266,000 | 4,266,000 | 1,325,000 | 3,752,000 | 2,941,000 | 514,000 |
| Net increase (decrease) | | | | | | | | 2,427,000 | | | 2,427,000 |
| | | | | | | | | 3,752,000 | 3,752,000 | 2,941,000 | 2,941,000 |

## APPENDIX 4D: CAPITAL PROJECTS FUNDS—BALANCE SHEET AND STATEMENT OF REVENUES, EXPENDITURES, AND CHANGES IN FUND BALANCES

**WORKSHEET ENTRIES**

**Capital Projects Funds**
**Balance Sheet**
**June 30, 20X1**

| | Easely Street Bridge Project | Bland Street Drainage Project | West End Recreation Center Project | Total |
|---|---|---|---|---|
| **ASSETS** | | | | |
| Cash | $129,956 | $158,000 | $ 19,000 | $306,956 |
| Temporary investments | 695,000 | 62,000 | 2,922,000 | 3,679,000 |
| Total assets | $824,956 | $220,000 | $2,941,000 | $3,985,956 |
| **LIABILITIES AND FUND BALANCES** | | | | |
| Liabilities: | | | | |
| Accounts payable | $95,000 | $27,000 | $ 5,000 | $127,000 |
| Total liabilities | 95,000 | 27,000 | 5,000 | 127,000 |
| Fund balances: | | | | |
| Fund balance—reserved | 729,956 | 193,000 | 2,936,000 | 3,858,956 |
| Total liabilities and fund balances | $824,956 | $220,000 | $2,941,000 | $3,985,956 |

## WORKSHEET ENTRIES (Continued)

### Capital Projects Funds
### Statement of Revenues, Expenditures, and Changes in Fund Balances
### June 30, 20X1

| | Easely Street Bridge Project | Bland Street Drainage Project | West End Recreation Center Project | Total |
|---|---|---|---|---|
| **REVENUES** | | | | |
| Program revenues—capital grants (street) | $1,250,000 | $750,000 | — | $2,000,000 |
| Program revenues—capital grants and contributions (recreation and parks) | — | — | $450,000 | 450,000 |
| Interest | 30,000 | 4,000 | 2,000 | 36,000 |
| Total revenue | 1,280,000 | 754,000 | 452,000 | 2,486,000 |
| **EXPENDITURES** | | | | |
| General government | 495,000 | 97,000 | 25,000 | 617,000 |
| Capital outlays | 11,100,000 | 1,500,000 | 1,300,000 | 13,900,000 |
| Total expenditures | 11,595,000 | 1,597,000 | 1,325,000 | 14,520,000 |
| Excess (deficiency) of revenues over expenditures | (10,315,000) | (843,000) | (873,000) | (12,030,000) |
| **OTHER FINANCING SOURCES (USES)** | | | | |
| Long-term debt issued | 10,000,000 | — | 3,000,000 | 13,000,000 |
| Discount on long-term debt issued | (71,044) | — | — | (71,044) |

## WORKSHEET ENTRIES (Continued)

### Capital Projects Funds
### Statement of Revenues, Expenditures, and Changes in Fund Balances
### June 30, 20X1

|  | Easely Street Bridge Project | Bland Street Drainage Project | West End Recreation Center Project | Total |
|---|---|---|---|---|
| Transfers in | 1,000,000 | 900,000 | 300,000 | 2,200,000 |
| Total other financing sources and uses | 10,328,956 | 900,000 | 3,300,000 | 14,528,956 |
| Net change in fund balances | 13,956 | 57,000 | 2,427,000 | 2,498,956 |
| Fund balances—beginning | 716,000 | 136,000 | 509,000 | 1,361,000 |
| Fund balances—ending | $729,956 | $193,000 | $2,936,000 | $3,858,956 |

**4-28** Governmental Funds

## APPENDIX 4E: CAPITAL PROJECTS FUNDS—WORKSHEET TO CONVERT FROM MODIFIED ACCRUAL TO ACCRUAL BASIS

### WORKSHEET ENTRIES

| | Modified Accrual Basis | | Adjustments | | Accrual Basis |
|---|---|---|---|---|---|
| Cash | 306,956 | | | | 306,956 |
| Temporary investments | 3,679,000 | | | | 3,679,000 |
| Construction in progress | | JE04.25 | 11,100,000 | | 13,900,000 |
| | | JE04.27 | 1,500,000 | | |
| | | JE04.28 | 1,300,000 | | |
| Accounts payable | (127,000) | | | | (127,000) |
| Bonds payable | | JE04.26 | (9,328,956) | | (12,328,956) |
| | | JE04.29 | (3,000,000) | | |
| Fund balance—reserved | (1,361,000) | | | | (1,361,000) |
| Program revenues—capital grants (street) | (2,000,000) | | | | (2,000,000) |
| Program revenues—capital grants and contributions (recreation and parks) | (450,000) | | | | (450,000) |
| Interest | (36,000) | | | | (36,000) |
| General government | 617,000 | | | | 617,000 |
| Capital outlays | 13,900,000 | JE04.25 | (11,100,000) | | 0 |
| | | JE04.27 | (1,500,000) | | |
| | | JE04.28 | (1,300,000) | | |

## WORKSHEET ENTRIES (Continued)

| | Modified Accrual Basis | | Adjustments | Accrual Basis |
|---|---|---|---|---|
| Long-term debt issued | (13,000,000) | JE04.26 | 10,000,000 | 0 |
| | | JE04.29 | 3,000,000 | |
| Discount on long-term debt issued | 671,044 | | (671,044) | 0 |
| Transfers in | (2,200,000) | | | (2,200,000) |
| Total | 0 | | 0 | 0 |

# APPENDIX 4F: CAPITAL PROJECTS FUNDS—ADJUSTED TRIAL BALANCES

## WORKSHEET ENTRIES

### Adjusted Trial Balance

| Accounts | Easely Street Bridge Project Debits (Credits) | Bland Street Drainage Project Debits (Credits) | West End Recreation Center Project Debits (Credits) | Total Debits (Credits) |
|---|---|---|---|---|
| Cash | $ 129,956 | $ 158,000 | $ 19,000 | $ 306,956 |
| Temporary investments | 695,000 | 62,000 | 2,922,000 | 3,679,000 |
| Construction-in-progress | 11,100,000 | 1,500,000 | 1,300,000 | 13,900,000 |
| Accounts payable | (95,000) | (27,000) | (5,000) | (127,000) |
| Bonds payable | (9,328,956) | — | (3,000,000) | (12,328,956) |
| Fund balance | (716,000) | (136,000) | (509,000) | (1,361,000) |
| Program revenues—capital grants (street) | (1,250,000) | (750,000) | — | (2,000,000) |
| Program revenues—capital grants and contributions (recreation and parks) | — | — | (450,000) | (450,000) |
| Interest revenue | (30,000) | (4,000) | (2,000) | (36,000) |
| Expenditures—general government | 495,000 | 97,000 | 25,000 | 617,000 |
| Transfers in | (1,000,000) | (900,000) | (300,000) | (2,200,000) |
| Totals | $ -0- | $ -0- | $ -0- | $ -0- |

# CHAPTER 5
# DEBT SERVICE FUNDS

## CONTENTS

| | |
|---|---|
| Nature of Debt Service Funds | 5-2 |
| Measurement Focus and Basis of Accounting | 5-2 |
| Financial Reporting at Fund Level | 5-3 |
| Financial Reporting at Government-Wide Level | 5-4 |
| Illustrative Transactions | 5-4 |
|     Senior Citizens' Center Bonds | 5-4 |
|     Easely Street Bridge Bonds | 5-7 |
|     Bland Street Drainage Bonds | 5-8 |
|     West End Recreation Center Bonds | 5-10 |
| Fund Financial Statements | 5-12 |
| Converting to Government-Wide Financial Statements | 5-14 |
|     Debt Outstanding at the Beginning of the Year | 5-15 |
|     Senior Citizens' Center Bonds | 5-15 |
|     Easely Street Bridge Bonds | 5-16 |
|     Bland Street Drainage Bonds | 5-17 |
|     West End Recreation Center Bonds | 5-18 |
| Appendix 5A: Worksheet for Summarizing Current Transactions—Senior Citizens' Center Bonds | 5-20 |
| Appendix 5B: Worksheet for Summarizing Current Transactions—Easely Street Bridge Bonds | 5-21 |
| Appendix 5C: Worksheet for Summarizing Current Transactions—Bland Street Drainage Bonds | 5-22 |
| Appendix 5D: Worksheet for Summarizing Current Transactions—West End Recreation Center Bonds | 5-23 |
| Appendix 5E: Debt Service Funds—Balance Sheet and Statement of Revenues, Expenditures, and Changes in Fund Balances | 5-24 |
| Appendix 5F: Debt Service Funds—Worksheet to Convert from Modified Accrual to Accrual Basis | 5-26 |
| Appendix 5G: Debt Service Funds—Adjusted Trial Balances (Accrual Basis) | 5-28 |

## NATURE OF DEBT SERVICE FUNDS

A Debt Service Fund may be created to account for resources that will be used to service general long-term debt. General long-term debt includes noncurrent bonds and notes, as well as other noncurrent liabilities that might arise from capitalized lease agreements and other long-term liabilities not created by the issuance of a specific debt instrument.

The purpose of a Debt Service Fund, as defined by NCGA-1 is

> To account for the accumulation of resources for, and the payment of, general long-term debt principal and interest. (Debt Service Funds are required if they are legally mandated and/or if financial resources are being accumulated for principal and interest payments maturing in future years. The debt service transactions of a special assessment issue for which the government is not obligated in any manner should be reported in an Agency Fund rather than a Debt Service Fund to reflect the fact that the government's duties are limited to acting as an agent for the assessed property owners and the bondholders.)

> ■ **CONTINUING STANDARD:** The definition of Debt Service Funds continues to be based on the description established by NCGA-1 (Governmental Accounting and Financial Reporting Principles).

## MEASUREMENT FOCUS AND BASIS OF ACCOUNTING

The modified accrual basis and flow of current financial resources are used to prepare the financial statements of a Debt Service Fund. These concepts are discussed in Chapter 2 ("The General Fund").

The resources that flow into a Debt Service Fund may come from a variety of sources, including taxes specifically levied to service a particular debt issue, special assessments levied against certain property owners, transfers from other funds (usually the General Fund), any premium or accrued interest created when the related debt was issued, and any excess funds remaining in the related Capital Projects Fund when the capital asset is completed.

Taxes or special assessments levied specifically to service a particular debt issuance are recorded as revenue in the Debt Service Fund. Levies and assessments not specifically identified for the purpose of servicing a particular debt issuance are recorded as revenue in the fund that is responsible for the tax or assessment (usually the General Fund), and the eventual movement from that fund to the Debt Service Fund is reported as a transfer. Premiums, accrued interest, or excess funds remaining after construction received by the Debt Service Fund are also reported as transfers.

▶ **NEW STANDARD:** Prior to the issuance of GASB-34, transfers were identified as operating or residual equity transfers. GASB-34 eliminates these distinctions and all are referred to simply as transfers. Furthermore, no transfer can be reported as an adjustment to the beginning balance of the fund balance of a fund (GASB-34, par. 112).

Generally, the recording of expenditures of a Debt Service Fund is limited to payments servicing debt (both principal repayments and interest) and payments of support services (usually classified as general government expenditures). Interest and principal on long-term debt are not recorded as expenditures as they accrue, but rather when they become due and payable. For example, if a governmental entity issues a 30-year bond, the liability would not be reported as a fund liability until the debt is actually due and payable, which would be thirty years after issuance.

Current accounting standards provide for an exception to the basic concept that general long-term indebtedness is not reported as an expenditure until the amount becomes due and payable. When funds have been transferred to the Debt Service Fund during the fiscal year in anticipation of making debt service payments "shortly" after the end of the period, it is acceptable to accrue the related liability in the Debt Service Fund as an expenditure in the year the transfer is made.

▶ **NEW STANDARD:** Prior to the issuance of GASBI-6 (Recognition and Measurement of Certain Liabilities and Expenditures in Governmental Fund Financial Statements), there was a considerable amount of confusion about what is meant by "shortly." The Interpretation states that "shortly" means "early in the following year;" however, the period of time after the end of the year cannot be greater than one month (GASBI-6, pars. 9 and 13).

## FINANCIAL REPORTING AT FUND LEVEL

The balances and activities of Debt Service Funds are presented in the following financial statements at the fund financial statement level:

- Balance Sheet
- Statement of Revenues, Expenditures, and Changes in Fund Balances

    ■ **CONTINUING STANDARD:** Transactions and accounts recorded in Debt Service Funds continue to be based on standards established by various NCGA/GASB Statements and Interpretations that were outstanding before the issuance of GASB-34.

These two fund financial statements include all of the governmental funds (General Fund, Special Revenue Funds, Capital Projects Funds, Debt Service Funds, and Permanent Funds), and these funds are reported based on the concept of a major fund as defined by GASB-34.

## FINANCIAL REPORTING AT GOVERNMENT-WIDE LEVEL

The fund-based financial statements as described above are included in a governmental entity's financial report in order to demonstrate that restrictions imposed by statutes, regulations, or contracts have been followed. Balances in these fund financial statements are converted from a modified accrual basis to an accrual basis in order to create the basic information for the government-wide financial statements.

For the most part, this approach requires that all of the Debt Service Funds combined ending trial balances (which are on a modified accrual basis) be adjusted to reflect accrual balances. Briefly, this means that all debt outstanding at the end of the period must be reported as a liability and that interest (including the amortization of any discount or premium accounts) must be reported on an accrual basis. This conversion is illustrated later in this chapter.

## ILLUSTRATIVE TRANSACTIONS

In order to illustrate accounting and financial reporting standards that are observed for Debt Service Funds, assume that the City of Centerville has the following Debt Service Funds:

- Senior Citizens' Center Bonds
- Easely Street Bridge Bonds
- Bland Street Drainage Bonds
- West End Recreation Center Bonds

### Senior Citizens' Center Bonds

The Senior Citizens' Center Debt Service Fund is used to service serial bonds ($10,000,000) that were issued to build the Centerville Senior Citizens' Center. The fund's trial balance for the beginning of the fiscal year is as follows:

> ■ **CONTINUING STANDARD:** GASB-34 generally did not change the manner of accounting for transactions that are recorded in Debt Service Funds.

## Debt Service Funds 5-5

| Accounts | Trial Balance Debits | Credits |
|---|---|---|
| Cash | $14,000 | |
| Temporary investments | 5,000 | |
| Accounts payable | | $ 6,000 |
| Fund balance | | 13,000 |
| Totals | $19,000 | $19,000 |

This section presents illustrative transactions and entries for the fund during the fiscal year ended June 30, 20X1.

*Transaction JE05.01*—Accounts payable of $6,000 from the previous year were paid:

| Accounts | Debit | Credit |
|---|---|---|
| Accounts payable | 6,000 | |
| Cash | | 6,000 |

*Transaction JE05.02*—During the year interest revenue of $4,000 was earned and received:

| Accounts | Debit | Credit |
|---|---|---|
| Cash | 4,000 | |
| Interest revenue | | 4,000 |

*Transaction JE05.03*—During the year, $750,000 of the revenue bonds for the senior citizens' center were paid. In addition, $500,000 of interest was paid:

| Accounts | Debit | Credit |
|---|---|---|
| Expenditures—principal | 750,000 | |
| Expenditures—interest ($10,000,000 × 5%) | 500,000 | |
| Cash | | 1,250,000 |

■ **CONTINUING STANDARD:** Based on the standards established by GASBI-6 (Recognition and Measurement of Certain Liabilities and Expenditures in Governmental Fund Financial Statements), expenditures should continue to be recorded on an accrual basis except with respect to the expenditures identified in the Interpretation. One exception is that debt service payments are to be recorded when "due and payable."

*Transaction JE05.04*—General government expenditures of $9,000 were incurred, of which $7,000 was paid:

**5-6** *Governmental Funds*

| Accounts | Debit | Credit |
|---|---|---|
| Expenditures—general government | 9,000 | |
| Cash | | 7,000 |
| Accounts payable | | 2,000 |

*Transaction JE05.05*—Additional temporary investments of $15,000 were made during the year:

| Accounts | Debit | Credit |
|---|---|---|
| Temporary investments | 15,000 | |
| Cash | | 15,000 |

*Transaction JE05.06*—The General Fund made a transfer of $1,300,000 to service the debt and interest payments:

| Accounts | Debit | Credit |
|---|---|---|
| Cash | 1,300,000 | |
| Transfers in—General Fund | | 1,300,000 |

After the transactions for the year are posted, the year-end trial balance (June 30, 20X1) for the Senior Citizens' Center Bonds Debt Service Fund appears as follows:

| Accounts | Adjusted Trial Balance Debits | Credits |
|---|---|---|
| Cash | $ 40,000 | |
| Temporary investments | 20,000 | |
| Accounts payable | | $ 2,000 |
| Fund balance | | 13,000 |
| Interest revenue | | 4,000 |
| Expenditures—general government | 9,000 | |
| Expenditures—principal | 750,000 | |
| Expenditures—interest | 500,000 | |
| Transfers in—general fund | | 1,300,000 |
| Totals | $1,319,000 | $1,319,000 |

The worksheet that summarizes the foregoing journal entries for the Senior Citizens' Center Bonds Debt Service Fund for the year-end trial balance is presented in Appendix 5A.

## Easely Street Bridge Bonds

The Easely Street Bridge Debt Service Fund is used to service the two bond instruments ($2,000,000 and $10,000,000) that are partially financing the construction of the new bridge. Its trial balance for the beginning of the fiscal year is as follows:

|  | Trial Balance | |
| --- | --- | --- |
| Accounts | Debits | Credits |
| Cash | $25,000 | |
| Temporary investments | 12,000 | |
| Accounts payable | | $5,000 |
| Fund balance | | 32,000 |
| Totals | $37,000 | $37,000 |

This section presents illustrative transactions and entries for the fund during the fiscal year ended June 30, 20X1.

*Transaction JE05.07*—Accounts payable of $5,000 from the previous year were paid:

| Accounts | Debit | Credit |
| --- | --- | --- |
| Accounts payable | 5,000 | |
| Cash | | 5,000 |

*Transaction JE05.08*—During the year interest revenue of $1,000 was earned and received:

| Accounts | Debit | Credit |
| --- | --- | --- |
| Cash | 1,000 | |
| Interest revenue | | 1,000 |

*Transaction JE05.09*—During the year $200,000 of interest payments were made on the 10%, 5-year bonds that were issued to yield 9%:

| Accounts | Debit | Credit |
| --- | --- | --- |
| Expenditures—interest ($2,000,000 × 10%) | 200,000 | |
| Cash | | 200,000 |

*Transaction JE05.10*—General government expenditures of $11,000 were incurred, of which $8,000 was paid:

| Accounts | Debit | Credit |
|---|---|---|
| Expenditures—general government | 11,000 | |
|    Cash | | 8,000 |
|    Accounts payable | | 3,000 |

*Transaction JE05.11*—Additional temporary investments of $5,000 were made during the year:

| Accounts | Debit | Credit |
|---|---|---|
| Temporary investments | 5,000 | |
|    Cash | | 5,000 |

*Transaction JE05.12*—The General Fund made a transfer of $220,000 to service the debt and interest payments:

| Accounts | Debit | Credit |
|---|---|---|
| Cash | 220,000 | |
|    Transfers in—General Fund | | 220,000 |

After the transactions for the year are posted, the year-end trial balance (June 30, 20X1) for the Easely Street Bridge Debt Service Fund appears as follows:

| Accounts | Adjusted Trial Balance Debits | Credits |
|---|---|---|
| Cash | $ 28,000 | |
| Temporary investments | 17,000 | |
| Accounts payable | | $ 3,000 |
| Fund balance | | 32,000 |
| Interest revenue | | 1,000 |
| Expenditures—general government | 11,000 | |
| Expenditures—interest | 200,000 | |
| Transfers in—general fund | | 220,000 |
| Totals | $256,000 | $256,000 |

The worksheet that summarizes the foregoing journal entries for the Easely Street Bridge Debt Service Fund for the year-end trial balance is presented in Appendix 5B.

## Bland Street Drainage Bonds

The Bland Street Drainage Debt Service Fund is used to service the serial bonds ($4,900,000) that were issued to finance the project. Its trial balance for the beginning of the fiscal year is as follows:

|                      | Trial Balance |          |
|----------------------|---------------|----------|
| Accounts             | Debits        | Credits  |
| Cash                 | $15,000       |          |
| Temporary investments| 21,000        |          |
| Accounts payable     |               | $ 4,000  |
| Fund balance         |               | 32,000   |
| Totals               | $36,000       | $36,000  |

This section presents illustrative transactions and entries for the fund during the fiscal year ended June 30, 20X1.

*Transaction JE05.13*—Accounts payable of $4,000 from the previous year were paid:

| Accounts         | Debit | Credit |
|------------------|-------|--------|
| Accounts payable | 4,000 |        |
| Cash             |       | 4,000  |

*Transaction JE05.14*—During the year interest revenue of $3,000 was earned and received:

| Accounts         | Debit | Credit |
|------------------|-------|--------|
| Cash             | 3,000 |        |
| Interest revenue |       | 3,000  |

*Transaction JE05.15*—During the year, $700,000 of the serial bonds for the Bland Street Drainage Project Center were paid. In addition, $294,000 of interest was paid:

| Accounts                                  | Debit   | Credit  |
|-------------------------------------------|---------|---------|
| Expenditures—principal                    | 700,000 |         |
| Expenditures—interest ($4,900,000 × 6%)   | 294,000 |         |
| Cash                                      |         | 994,000 |

*Transaction JE05.16*—General government expenditures of $15,000 were incurred, of which $12,000 was paid:

| Accounts                       | Debit  | Credit |
|--------------------------------|--------|--------|
| Expenditures—general government| 15,000 |        |
| Cash                           |        | 12,000 |
| Accounts payable               |        | 3,000  |

*Transaction JE05.17*—Additional temporary investments of $3,000 were made during the year:

5-10  Governmental Funds

| Accounts | Debit | Credit |
|---|---|---|
| Temporary investments | 3,000 | |
| Cash | | 3,000 |

*Transaction JE05.18*—The General Fund made a transfer of $1,100,000 to service the debt and interest payments:

| Accounts | Debit | Credit |
|---|---|---|
| Cash | 1,100,000 | |
| Transfers in—General Fund | | 1,100,000 |

After the transactions for the year are posted, the year-end trial balance (June 30, 20X1) for the Bland Street Drainage Debt Service Fund appears as follows:

| Accounts | Adjusted Trial Balance Debits | Credits |
|---|---|---|
| Cash | $ 105,000 | |
| Temporary investments | 24,000 | |
| Accounts payable | | $ 3,000 |
| Fund balance | | 32,000 |
| Interest revenue | | 3,000 |
| Expenditures—general | 15,000 | |
| Expenditures—principal | 700,000 | |
| Expenditures—interest | 294,000 | |
| Transfers in—general fund | | 1,100,000 |
| Totals | $1,138,000 | $1,138,000 |

The worksheet that summarizes the foregoing journal entries for the Bland Street Drainage Debt Service Fund for the year-end trial balance is presented in Appendix 5C.

## West End Recreation Center Bonds

The West End Recreation Center Debt Service Fund is used to service the bonds ($3,000,000) that were issued to finance the project. The fund's trial balance for the beginning of the fiscal year is as follows:

| Accounts | Trial Balance Debits | Credits |
|---|---|---|
| Cash | $27,000 | |
| Temporary investments | 3,000 | |

## Debt Service Funds  5-11

| | | |
|---|---:|---:|
| Accounts payable | | $ 2,000 |
| Fund balance | | 28,000 |
| Totals | $30,000 | $30,000 |

This section presents illustrative transactions and entries for the fund during the fiscal year ended June 30, 20X1.

***Transaction JE05.19***—Accounts payable of $2,000 from the previous year were paid:

| Accounts | Debit | Credit |
|---|---:|---:|
| Accounts payables | 2,000 | |
| Cash | | 2,000 |

***Transaction JE05.20***—During the year, interest revenue of $1,000 was earned and received:

| Accounts | Debit | Credit |
|---|---:|---:|
| Cash | 1,000 | |
| Interest revenue | | 1,000 |

***Transaction JE05.21***—During the year, $500,000 of the serial bonds for the Bland Street Drainage Project Center were paid. In addition, $180,000 of interest was paid:

| Accounts | Debit | Credit |
|---|---:|---:|
| Expenditures—principal | 500,000 | |
| Expenditures—interest ($3,000,000 × 12% × 6/12) | 180,000 | |
| Cash | | 680,000 |

***Transaction JE05.22***—General government expenditures of $7,000 were incurred, of which $6,000 were paid:

| Accounts | Debit | Credit |
|---|---:|---:|
| Expenditures—general government | 7,000 | |
| Cash | | 6,000 |
| Accounts payable | | 1,000 |

***Transaction JE05.23***—Additional temporary investments of $3,000 were made during the year:

| Accounts | Debit | Credit |
|---|---:|---:|
| Temporary investments | 3,000 | |
| Cash | | 3,000 |

**Transaction JE05.24**—The General Fund made a transfer of $700,000 to service the debt and interest payments:

| Accounts | Debit | Credit |
|---|---|---|
| Cash | 700,000 | |
|     Transfers in—General Fund | | 700,000 |

After the transactions for the year are posted, the year-end trial balance (June 30, 20X1) for the West End Recreation Center Debt Service Fund appears as follows:

| Accounts | Adjusted Trial Balance Debits | Credits |
|---|---|---|
| Cash | $37,000 | |
| Temporary investments | 6,000 | |
| Accounts payable | | $ 1,000 |
| Fund balance | | 28,000 |
| Interest revenue | | 1,000 |
| Expenditures—general government | 7,000 | |
| Expenditures—principal | 500,000 | |
| Expenditures—interest | 180,000 | |
| Transfers in—general fund | | 700,000 |
| Totals | $730,000 | $730,000 |

The worksheet that summarizes the foregoing journal entries for the West End Recreation Center Debt Service Fund for the year-end trial balance is presented in Appendix 5D.

## FUND FINANCIAL STATEMENTS

At the fund financial statement level, a governmental fund prepares a statement of revenues, expenditures, and changes in fund balances and a balance sheet. Based on the adjusted trial balances created above, the following financial statements reflect the balances and activities of the Debt Service Funds. These financial statements are prepared to facilitate the preparation of the fund financial statements illustrated in Chapter 12 ("Developing Information For Fund Financial Statements"). (See Appendixes 5E and 5F.)

> ▶ **NEW STANDARD:** NCGA-1 illustrates three distinct formats that can be used to prepare the statement of revenues, expenditures, and changes in fund balances for governmental funds; however, GASB-34 eliminates two of the options, and

only the format illustrated below can now be used (GASB-34, par. 86).

■ **CONTINUING STANDARD:** The formatting of the balance sheet at the fund financial statement level was not changed by GASB-34.

### Debt Service Funds
### Balance Sheet
### June 30, 20X1

|  | Senior Citizens' Center Bonds | Easely Street Bridge Bonds | Bland Street Drainage Bonds | West End Recreation Center Bonds | Total |
|---|---|---|---|---|---|
| **ASSETS** | | | | | |
| Cash | $40,000 | $28,000 | $105,000 | $37,000 | $210,000 |
| Temporary investments | 20,000 | 17,000 | 24,000 | 6,000 | 67,000 |
| Total assets | $60,000 | $45,000 | $129,000 | $43,000 | $277,000 |
| **LIABILITIES AND FUND BALANCES** | | | | | |
| Liabilities: | | | | | |
| Accounts payable | $2,000 | $3,000 | $3,000 | $1,000 | $9,000 |
| Total liabilities | 2,000 | 3,000 | 3,000 | 1,000 | 9,000 |
| Fund balances: | | | | | |
| Fund balance—reserved | 58,000 | 42,000 | 126,000 | 42,000 | 268,000 |
| Total liabilities and fund balances | $60,000 | $45,000 | $129,000 | $43,000 | $277,000 |

### Debt Service Funds
### Statement of Revenues, Expenditures, and Changes in Fund Balances
### June 30, 20X1

|  | Senior Citizens' Center Bonds | Easely Street Bridge Bonds | Bland Street Drainage Bonds | West End Recreation Center Bonds | Total |
|---|---|---|---|---|---|
| **REVENUES** | | | | | |
| Interest | $ 4,000 | $ 1,000 | $ 3,000 | $ 1,000 | $ 9,000 |
| Total revenue | 4,000 | 1,000 | 3,000 | 1,000 | 9,000 |

|  | Senior Citizens' Center Bonds | Easely Street Bridge Bonds | Bland Street Drainage Bonds | West End Recreation Center Bonds | Total |
|---|---|---|---|---|---|
| **EXPENDITURES** | | | | | |
| General government | 9,000 | 11,000 | 15,000 | 7,000 | 42,000 |
| Principal | 750,000 | — | 700,000 | 500,000 | 1,950,000 |
| Interest | 500,000 | 200,000 | 294,000 | 180,000 | 1,174,000 |
| Total expenditures | 1,259,000 | 211,000 | 1,009,000 | 687,000 | 3,166,000 |
| Excess (deficiency) of revenues over expenditures | (1,255,000) | (210,000) | (1,006,000) | (686,000) | (3,157,000) |
| **OTHER FINANCING SOURCES (USES)** | | | | | |
| Transfers in | 1,300,000 | 220,000 | 1,100,000 | 700,000 | 3,320,000 |
| Total other financing sources and uses | 1,300,000 | 220,000 | 1,100,000 | 700,000 | 3,320,000 |
| Net change in fund balances | 45,000 | 10,000 | 94,000 | 14,000 | 163,000 |
| Fund balances—beginning | 13,000 | 32,000 | 32,000 | 28,000 | 105,000 |
| Fund balances—ending | $ 58,000 | $ 42,000 | $ 126,000 | $ 42,000 | $ 268,000 |

The combined financial statements for the Debt Service Funds are not reported separately in the governmental entity's financial report, but they are used in Chapter 12 ("Developing Information for Fund Financial Statements").

## CONVERTING TO GOVERNMENT-WIDE FINANCIAL STATEMENTS

Government-wide financial statements are reported on the accrual basis of accounting. Generally, most governments will work from their governmental fund financial statements (which are on a modified accrual basis) and through the use of worksheet entries convert to accrual based financial statements.

In order to convert the transactions that were recorded in the Debt Service Funds from a modified accrual basis to an accrual basis, the following worksheet entries are made.

## Debt Outstanding at the Beginning of the Year

The following balances of capital debt issues were outstanding at the beginning of the current year:

| | |
|---|---:|
| Revenue bonds—Senior Citizens' Center Bonds—5% serial bonds, interest is paid annually on June 30th | $10,000,000 |
| Easely Street Bridge Project—5-year bonds, 10% bonds, interest is paid annually on June 30th | 2,064,791 |
| Bland Street Drainage Project—6% serial bonds, interest is paid annually on June 30th | 4,900,000 |
| Total | $16,964,791 |

The following worksheet entry is made to record the debt outstanding at the beginning of the year, since it does not appear on the fund financial statements:

| | Accounts | Debit | Credit |
|---|---|---:|---:|
| JE05.25 | Fund balance—Senior Citizens' Center Bonds | 10,000,000 | |
| | Fund balance—Easely Street Bridge Bonds | 2,064,791 | |
| | Fund balance—Bland Street Drainage Bonds | 4,900,000 | |
| | Revenue bonds payable (Senior Citizens' Center Bonds) | | 10,000,000 |
| | Bonds payable (Easely Street Bridge Bonds) | | 2,064,791 |
| | Bonds payable (Bland Street Drainage Bonds) | | 4,900,000 |
| | (To record debt that was outstanding at the beginning of the year) | | |

## Senior Citizens' Center Bonds

The principal repayment of $750,000 through the Senior Citizens' Center Bond Fund is converted from an expenditure to a reduction of debt by making the following worksheet entry:

| | Accounts | Debit | Credit |
|---|---|---:|---:|
| JE05.26 | Revenue bonds payable | 750,000 | |
| | Expenditures—principal | | 750,000 |
| | (To record payments during the year as reductions to debt obligations rather than as expenditures) | | |

## Easely Street Bridge Bonds

The Easely Street Bridge Bond Fund has the following debt instruments outstanding:

- 10%, 5-year bonds that were issued to yield 9%.
- 7%, 8-year bonds that were issued to yield 8%

The 5-year bonds were issued on June 30, 20W9 and pay interest annually. The amortization schedule for the bonds is as follows:

| Date | Cash | Interest | Premium Amortization | Book Value |
| --- | --- | --- | --- | --- |
| 6/30/W9 | | | | $2,077,790 |
| 6/30/X0 | $200,000 | $187,001 | $12,999 | 2,064,791 |
| 6/30/X1 | 200,000 | 185,831 | 14,169 | 2,050,622 |
| 6/30/X2 | 200,000 | 184,556 | 15,444 | 2,035,178 |
| 6/30/X3 | 200,000 | 183,166 | 16,834 | 2,018,344 |
| 6/30/X4 | 200,000 | 181,656R | 18,344 | 2,000,000 |

R=rounding

On a modified accrual basis, the amount of interest expenditure recognized in the fund financial statements must be adjusted to include the amortization of the bond premium for the year, as shown in the following worksheet entry:

| | Accounts | Debit | Credit |
| --- | --- | --- | --- |
| JE05.27 | Bonds payable | 14,169 | |
| | Interest expense | | 14,169 |
| | (To record the amortization of bond premiums for the year) | | |

The 7-year bonds were issued on October 1, 20X0 and pay interest annually. The amortization schedule for the bonds is as follows:

| Date | Cash | Interest | Amortization | Book Value |
| --- | --- | --- | --- | --- |
| 10/1/X0 | | | | $9,328,956 |
| 10/1/X1 | $700,000 | $746,316 | $−46,316 | 9,375,272 |
| 10/1/X2 | 700,000 | 750,022 | −50,022 | 9,425,294 |

The bonds payment date is June 30th of each year, therefore, the cash expenditure for interest for the debt ($500,000) is equal to the interest expense on an accrual basis for the year and no adjustment is needed to convert interest to an accrual basis.

| Date | Cash | Interest | Amortization | Book Value |
|------|------|----------|--------------|------------|
| 10/1/X3 | 700,000 | 754,024 | −54,024 | 9,479,318 |
| 10/1/X4 | 700,000 | 758,345 | −58,345 | 9,537,663 |
| 10/1/X5 | 700,000 | 763,013 | −63,013 | 9,600,676 |
| 10/1/X6 | 700,000 | 768,054 | −68,054 | 9,668,730 |
| 10/1/X7 | 700,000 | 773,498 | −73,498 | 9,742,229 |
| 10/1/X8 | 700,000 | 779,378 | −79,378 | 9,821,607 |
| 10/1/X9 | 700,000 | 785,729 | −85,729 | 9,907,336 |
| 10/1/Y0 | 700,000 | 792,664$^R$ | −92,664 | 9,999,923 |

Because the 7-year bonds were issued during the current year and interest is not payable until October 1, 20X2, the following worksheet entry is made to report the interest on an accrual basis for the government-wide financial statements:

| | Accounts | Debit | Credit |
|---|---|---|---|
| JE05.28 | Interest expense ($746,316 × 9/12) | 559,737 | |
| | Interest payable ($700,000 × 9/12) | | 525,000 |
| | Bonds payable ($46,316 × 9/12) | | 34,737 |
| | (To accrue interest for the year) | | |

**OBSERVATION:** If in the previous year interest expenses were also accrued, the previous accrual would have to be omitted from the current year's statement of activities (debiting net assets and crediting interest expense) because the interest would have been recorded in the current year under the modified accrual basis of accounting. In this illustration, since the bonds were issued in the current year, there was no interest accrual at the end of the previous year.

## Bland Street Drainage Bonds

The principal repayment of $700,000 made through the Bland Street Drainage Bond Fund is converted from an expenditure to a reduction of debt by making the following worksheet entry:

| | Accounts | Debit | Credit |
|---|---|---|---|
| JE05.29 | Bonds payable | 700,000 | |
| | Expenditures—principal | | 700,000 |
| | (To record payments during the year as reductions to the debt obligation rather than as expenditures) | | |

The bonds' interest payment date is June 30th of each year, therefore the cash expenditure for interest for the debt ($294,000) is equal to the interest expense on an accrual basis for the year.

## West End Recreation Center Bonds

The principal repayment of $500,000 made through the West End Recreation Center Bond Fund is converted from an expenditure to a reduction of debt by making the following worksheet entry:

| | Accounts | Debit | Credit |
|---|---|---|---|
| JE05.30 | Bonds payable | 500,000 | |
| | Expenditures—principal | | 500,000 |
| | (To record payments during the year as reductions to the debt obligation rather than as expenditures) | | |

The bond interest payment date is June 30th of each year; therefore the cash expenditure for interest for the debt ($180,000) is equal to the interest expense on an accrual basis for the year.

After these entries are prepared, the adjusted trial balances (on an accrual basis) for the four funds would appear as follows as of June 30, 20X1 (see Appendix 5G):

| | Adjusted Trial Balance | | | | |
|---|---|---|---|---|---|
| | Senior Citizens' Center Bonds | Easely Street Bridge Bonds | Bland Street Drainage Bonds | West End Recreation Center Bonds | Totals |
| Accounts | Debits (Credits) | Debits (Credits) | Debits (Credits) | Debits (Credits) | Debits (Credits) |
| Cash | $40,000 | $28,000 | $105,000 | $37,000 | $210,000 |
| Temporary investments | 20,000 | 17,000 | 24,000 | 6,000 | 67,000 |
| Accounts payable | (2,000) | (3,000) | (3,000) | (1,000) | (9,000) |
| Interest payable | — | (525,000) | — | — | (525,000) |
| Revenue bonds payable | (9,250,000) | — | — | — | (9,250,000) |
| Bonds payable | — | (2,085,359) | (4,200,000) | 500,000 | (5,785,359) |

## Adjusted Trial Balance

| Accounts | Senior Citizens' Center Bonds Debits (Credits) | Easely Street Bridge Bonds Debits (Credits) | Bland Street Drainage Bonds Debits (Credits) | West End Recreation Center Bonds Debits (Credits) | Totals Debits (Credits) |
|---|---|---|---|---|---|
| Fund balance | 9,987,000 | 2,032,791 | 4,868,000 | (28,000) | 16,859,791 |
| Interest revenue | (4,000) | (1,000) | (3,000) | (1,000) | (9,000) |
| Expenditures—general government | 9,000 | 11,000 | 15,000 | 7,000 | 42,000 |
| Expenditures—interest | 500,000 | 745,568 | 294,000 | 180,000 | 1,719,568 |
| Transfers in | (1,300,000) | (220,000) | (1,100,000) | (700,000) | (3,320,000) |
| Totals | $ -0- | $ -0- | $ -0- | $ -0- | $ -0- |

**OBSERVATION:** The balance in the long-term liability account for the West End Recreation Center Bond Fund has a debit balance because the debt was issued during the current period and the long-term debt was recorded in a worksheet entry in Chapter 4 ("Capital Projects Funds"). These balances will be offset in Chapter 13 ("Developing Information for Government-Wide Financial Statements").

This combined trial balance on the accrual basis is used in Chapter 13 ("Developing Information for Government-Wide Financial Statements") in order to prepare the government-wide financial statements.

## APPENDIX 5A
## WORKSHEET FOR SUMMARIZING CURRENT TRANSACTIONS—SENIOR CITIZENS' CENTER BONDS

### WORKSHEET ENTRIES

| Accounts | Trial Balance Debits | Trial Balance Credits | Adjustments Debits | | Adjustments Credits | | Adjusted Trial Balance Debits | Adjusted Trial Balance Credits | Operating Statement Debits | Operating Statement Credits | Balance Sheet Debits | Balance Sheet Credits |
|---|---|---|---|---|---|---|---|---|---|---|---|---|
| Cash | 14,000 | — | 4,000 JE05.02 | | 6,000 JE05.01 | | 40,000 | — | — | — | 40,000 | — |
| | | | 1,300,000 JE05.06 | | 1,250,000 JE05.03 | | | | | | | |
| | | | | | 7,000 JE05.04 | | | | | | | |
| | | | | | 15,000 JE05.05 | | | | | | | |
| Temporary investments | 5,000 | — | 15,000 JE05.05 | | — | | 20,000 | — | — | — | 20,000 | — |
| Accounts payable | — | 6,000 | 6,000 JE05.01 | | 2,000 JE05.04 | | — | 2,000 | — | — | — | 2,000 |
| Fund balance | — | 13,000 | — | | — | | — | 13,000 | — | — | — | 13,000 |
| Interest revenue | — | — | — | | 4,000 JE05.02 | | — | 4,000 | — | 4,000 | — | — |
| Expenditures—general government | — | — | 9,000 JE05.04 | | — | | 9,000 | — | 9,000 | — | — | — |
| Expenditures—principal | — | — | 750,000 JE05.03 | | — | | 750,000 | — | 750,000 | — | — | — |
| Expenditures—interest | — | — | 500,000 JE05.03 | | — | | 500,000 | — | 500,000 | — | — | — |
| Transfers in—general fund | — | — | — | | 1,300,000 JE05.06 | | — | 1,300,000 | 1,300,000 | — | — | — |
| Totals | 19,000 | 19,000 | 2,584,000 | | 2,584,000 | | 1,319,000 | 1,319,000 | 1,259,000 | 1,304,000 | 60,000 | 15,000 |
| Net increase (decrease) | | | | | | | | | 45,000 | — | — | 45,000 |
| | | | | | | | | | 1,304,000 | 1,304,000 | 60,000 | 60,000 |

## APPENDIX 5B
## WORKSHEET FOR SUMMARIZING CURRENT TRANSACTIONS—EASELY STREET BRIDGE BONDS

### WORKSHEET ENTRIES

| Accounts | Trial Balance Debits | Trial Balance Credits | Adjustments Debits | | Adjustments Credits | | Adjusted Trial Balance Debits | Adjusted Trial Balance Credits | Operating Statement Debits | Operating Statement Credits | Balance Sheet Debits | Balance Sheet Credits |
|---|---|---|---|---|---|---|---|---|---|---|---|---|
| Cash | 25,000 | — | 1,000 | JE05.08 | 5,000 | JE05.07 | 28,000 | — | — | — | 28,000 | — |
| | — | — | 220,000 | JE05.12 | 200,000 | JE05.09 | — | — | — | — | — | — |
| | — | — | — | | 8,000 | JE05.10 | — | — | — | — | — | — |
| | — | — | — | | 5,000 | JE05.11 | — | — | — | — | — | — |
| Temporary investments | 12,000 | — | 5,000 | JE05.11 | — | | 17,000 | — | — | — | 17,000 | — |
| Accounts payable | — | 5,000 | 5,000 | JE05.07 | 3,000 | JE05.10 | — | 3,000 | — | — | — | 3,000 |
| Fund balance | — | 32,000 | — | | — | | — | 32,000 | — | — | — | 32,000 |
| Interest revenue | — | — | — | | 1,000 | JE05.08 | — | 1,000 | — | 1,000 | — | — |
| Expenditures—general government | — | — | 11,000 | JE05.10 | — | | 11,000 | — | 11,000 | — | — | — |
| Expenditures—interest | — | — | 200,000 | JE05.09 | — | | 200,000 | — | 200,000 | — | — | — |
| Transfers in— general fund | — | — | — | | 220,000 | JE05.12 | — | 220,000 | — | 220,000 | — | — |
| Totals | 37,000 | 37,000 | 442,000 | | 442,000 | | 256,000 | 256,000 | 211,000 | 221,000 | 45,000 | 35,000 |
| Net increase (decrease) | | | | | | | | | 10,000 | — | — | 10,000 |
| | | | | | | | | | 221,000 | 221,000 | 45,000 | 45,000 |

Debt Service Funds 5-21

## APPENDIX 5C
## WORKSHEET FOR SUMMARIZING CURRENT TRANSACTIONS—BLAND STREET DRAINAGE BONDS

### WORKSHEET ENTRIES

| Accounts | Trial Balance Debits | Trial Balance Credits | Adjustments Debits | | Adjustments Credits | | Adjusted Trial Balance Debits | Adjusted Trial Balance Credits | Operating Statement Debits | Operating Statement Credits | Balance Sheet Debits | Balance Sheet Credits |
|---|---|---|---|---|---|---|---|---|---|---|---|---|
| Cash | 15,000 | — | JE05.14 | 3,000 | JE05.13 | 4,000 | 105,000 | — | — | — | 105,000 | — |
|  |  |  | JE05.18 | 1,100,000 | JE05.15 | 994,000 |  |  |  |  |  |  |
|  |  |  |  |  | JE05.16 | 12,000 |  |  |  |  |  |  |
|  |  |  |  |  | JE05.17 | 3,000 |  |  |  |  |  |  |
| Temporary investments | 21,000 | — | JE05.17 | 3,000 | — |  | 24,000 | — | — | — | 24,000 | — |
| Accounts payable | — | 4,000 | JE05.13 | 4,000 | JE05.16 | 3,000 | — | 3,000 | — | — | — | 3,000 |
| Fund balance | — | 32,000 | — |  | — |  | — | 32,000 | — | — | — | 32,000 |
| Interest revenue | — | — | — |  | JE05.14 | 3,000 | — | 3,000 | — | 3,000 | — | — |
| Expendiutres—general | — | — | JE05.16 | 15,000 | — |  | 15,000 | — | 15,000 | — | — | — |
| Expenditures—principal | — | — | JE05.15 | 700,000 | — |  | 700,000 | — | 700,000 | — | — | — |
| Expenditures—interest | — | — | JE05.15 | 294,000 | — |  | 294,000 | — | 294,000 | — | — | — |
| Transfers in—general fund | — | — | — |  | JE05.18 | 1,100,000 | — | 1,100,000 | — | 1,100,000 | — | — |
| Totals | 36,000 | 36,000 |  | 2,119,000 |  | 2,119,000 | 1,138,000 | 1,138,000 | 1,009,000 | 1,103,000 | 129,000 | 35,000 |
| Net increase (decrease) |  |  |  |  |  |  |  |  | 94,000 | — | — | 94,000 |
|  |  |  |  |  |  |  |  |  | 1,103,000 | 1,103,000 | 129,000 | 129,000 |

## APPENDIX 5D
## WORKSHEET FOR SUMMARIZING CURRENT TRANSACTIONS— WEST END RECREATION CENTER BONDS

### WORKSHEET ENTRIES

| Accounts | Trial Balance Debits | Trial Balance Credits | | Adjustments Debits | | Adjustments Credits | Adjusted Trial Balance Debits | Adjusted Trial Balance Credits | Operating Statement Debits | Operating Statement Credits | Balance Sheet Debits | Balance Sheet Credits |
|---|---|---|---|---|---|---|---|---|---|---|---|---|
| Cash | 27,000 | — | JE05.20 | 1,000 | JE05.19 | 2,000 | 37,000 | — | — | — | 37,000 | — |
| | | | JE05.24 | 700,000 | JE05.21 | 680,000 | | | | | | |
| | | | | | JE05.22 | 6,000 | | | | | | |
| | | | | | JE05.23 | 3,000 | | | | | | |
| Temporary investments | 3,000 | — | JE05.23 | 3,000 | | — | 6,000 | — | — | — | 6,000 | — |
| Accounts payable | — | 2,000 | JE05.19 | 2,000 | JE05.22 | 1,000 | — | 1,000 | — | — | — | 1,000 |
| Fund balance | — | 28,000 | | — | | — | — | 28,000 | — | — | — | 28,000 |
| Interest revenue | — | — | | — | JE05.20 | 1,000 | — | 1,000 | — | 1,000 | — | — |
| Expenditures—general government | — | — | JE05.22 | 7,000 | | — | 7,000 | — | 7,000 | — | — | — |
| Expenditures—principal | — | — | JE05.21 | 500,000 | | — | 500,000 | — | 500,000 | — | — | — |
| Expendiutres—interest | — | — | JE05.21 | 180,000 | | — | 180,000 | — | 180,000 | — | — | — |
| Transfers in—general fund | — | — | | — | JE05.24 | 700,000 | — | 700,000 | — | 700,000 | — | — |
| Totals | 30,000 | 30,000 | | 1,393,000 | | 1,393,000 | 730,000 | 730,000 | 687,000 | 701,000 | 43,000 | 29,000 |
| Net increase (decrease) | | | | | | | | | 14,000 | | | 14,000 |
| | | | | | | | | | 701,000 | 701,000 | 43,000 | 43,000 |

# APPENDIX 5E: DEBT SERVICE FUNDS—BALANCE SHEET AND STATEMENT OF REVENUES, EXPENDITURES, AND CHANGES IN FUND BALANCES

**WORKSHEET ENTRIES**

**Debt Service Funds**
**Balance Sheet**
**June 30, 20X1**

| | Senior Citizens' Center Bonds | Easely Street Bridge Bonds | Bland Street Drainage Bonds | West End Recreation Center Bonds | Total |
|---|---|---|---|---|---|
| **ASSETS** | | | | | |
| Cash | $40,000 | $28,000 | $105,000 | $37,000 | $210,000 |
| Temporary investments | 20,000 | 17,000 | 24,000 | 6,000 | 67,000 |
| Total assets | $60,000 | $45,000 | $129,000 | $43,000 | $277,000 |
| **LIABILITIES AND FUND BALANCES** | | | | | |
| Liabilities: | | | | | |
| Accounts payable | $2,000 | $3,000 | $3,000 | $1,000 | $9,000 |
| Total liabilities | 2,000 | 3,000 | 3,000 | 1,000 | 9,000 |
| Fund balances: | | | | | |
| Fund balance—reserved | 58,000 | 42,000 | 126,000 | 42,000 | 268,000 |
| Total liabilities and fund balances | $60,000 | $45,000 | $129,000 | $43,000 | $277,000 |

## WORKSHEET ENTRIES (Continued)

### Debt Service Funds
### Statement of Revenues, Expenditures, and Changes in Fund Balances
### June 30, 20X1

| | Senior Citizens' Center Bonds | Easely Street Bridge Bonds | Bland Street Drainage Bonds | West End Recreation Center Bonds | Total |
|---|---|---|---|---|---|
| **REVENUES** | | | | | |
| Interest | $ 4,000 | $ 1,000 | $ 3,000 | $ 1,000 | $ 9,000 |
| Total revenue | 4,000 | 1,000 | 3,000 | 1,000 | 9,000 |
| **EXPENDITURES** | | | | | |
| General government | 9,000 | 11,000 | 15,000 | 7,000 | 42,000 |
| Principal | 750,000 | — | 700,000 | 500,000 | 1,950,000 |
| Interest | 500,000 | 200,000 | 294,000 | 180,000 | 1,174,000 |
| Total expenditures | 1,259,000 | 211,000 | 1,009,000 | 687,000 | 3,166,000 |
| Excess (deficiency) of revenues over expenditures | (1,255,000) | (210,000) | (1,006,000) | (686,000) | (3,157,000) |
| **OTHER FINANCING SOURCES (USES)** | | | | | |
| Transfers in | 1,300,000 | 220,000 | 1,100,000 | 700,000 | 3,320,000 |
| Total other financing sources and uses | 1,300,000 | 220,000 | 1,100,000 | 700,000 | 3,320,000 |
| Net change in fund balances | 45,000 | 10,000 | 94,000 | 14,000 | 163,000 |
| Fund balances—beginning | 13,000 | 32,000 | 32,000 | 28,000 | 105,000 |
| Fund balances—ending | $ 58,000 | $ 42,000 | $ 126,000 | $ 42,000 | $ 268,000 |

## APPENDIX 5F: DEBT SERVICE FUNDS—WORKSHEET TO CONVERT FROM MODIFIED ACCRUAL TO ACCRUAL BASIS

### WORKSHEET ENTRIES

| | Modified Accrual Basis | | Adjustments | Accrual Basis |
|---|---|---|---|---|
| Cash | 210,000 | | | 210,000 |
| Temporary investments | 67,000 | | | 67,000 |
| Accounts payable | (9,000) | | | (9,000) |
| Interest payable | | JE05.28 | (525,000) | (525,000) |
| Revenue bonds payable | | JE05.25 | (10,000,000) | (9,250,000) |
| | | JE05.26 | 750,000 | |
| Bonds payable | | JE05.25 | (6,964,791) | (5,785,359) |
| | | JE05.27 | 14,169 | |
| | | JE05.28 | (34,737) | |
| | | JE05.29 | 700,000 | |
| | | JE05.30 | 500,000 | |
| Fund balance—reserved | (105,000) | JE05.25 | 16,964,791 | 16,859,791 |
| Interest | (9,000) | | | (9,000) |
| General government | 42,000 | | | 42,000 |
| Principal | 1,950,000 | JE05.26 | (750,000) | |
| | | JE05.29 | (700,000) | |
| | | JE05.30 | (500,000) | |

## WORKSHEET ENTRIES (Continued)

|  | Modified Accrual Basis |  |  | Adjustments | Accrual Basis |
|---|---|---|---|---|---|
| Interest | 1,174,000 | JE05.27 | JE05.28 | (14,169) 559,737 | 1,719,568 0 |
| Transfers in | (3,320,000) |  |  |  | (3,320,000) |
| Total | 0 |  |  | 0 | 0 |

## APPENDIX 5G: DEBT SERVICE FUNDS—ADJUSTED TRIAL BALANCES (ACCRUAL BASIS)

### WORKSHEET ENTRIES

#### Adjusted Trial Balance

| Accounts | Senior Citizens' Center Bonds Debits (Credits) | Easely Street Bridge Bonds Debits (Credits) | Bland Street Drainage Bonds Debits (Credits) | West End Recreation Center Bonds Debits (Credits) | Totals Debits (Credits) |
|---|---|---|---|---|---|
| Cash | $40,000 | $28,000 | $105,000 | $37,000 | $210,000 |
| Temporary investments | 20,000 | 17,000 | 24,000 | 6,000 | 67,000 |
| Accounts payable | (2,000) | (3,000) | (3,000) | (1,000) | (9,000) |
| Interest payable | — | (525,000) | — | — | (525,000) |
| Revenue bonds payable | (9,250,000) | — | — | — | (9,250,000) |
| Bonds payable | — | (2,085,359) | (4,200,000) | 500,000 | (5,785,359) |
| Fund balance | 9,987,000 | 2,032,791 | 4,868,000 | (28,000) | 16,859,791 |
| Interest revenue | (4,000) | (1,000) | (3,000) | (1,000) | (9,000) |
| Expenditures—general government | 9,000 | 11,000 | 15,000 | 7,000 | 42,000 |
| Expenditures—interest | 500,000 | 745,568 | 294,000 | 180,000 | 1,719,568 |
| Transfers in | (1,300,000) | (220,000) | (1,100,000) | (700,000) | (3,320,000) |
| Totals | $ -0- | $ -0- | $ -0- | $ -0- | $ -0- |

# CHAPTER 6
# PERMANENT FUNDS

## CONTENTS

| | |
|---|---|
| Nature of Permanent Funds | 6-1 |
| Measurement Focus and Basis of Accounting | 6-2 |
| Financial Reporting at Fund Level | 6-3 |
| Financial Reporting at Government-Wide Level | 6-4 |
| Illustrative Transactions | 6-4 |
| Fund Financial Statements | 6-7 |
| Government-Wide Financial Statements | 6-9 |
| Appendix 6A: Worksheet for Summarizing Current Transactions—Centerville Cemetery | 6-10 |
| Appendix 6B: Permanent Funds—Balance Sheet and Statement of Revenues, Expenditures, and Changes in Fund Balances | 6-11 |
| Appendix 6C: No Adjustments | 6-13 |

## NATURE OF PERMANENT FUNDS

GASB-34 states that a Permanent Fund "should be used to report resources that are legally restricted to the extent that only earnings, and not principal, may be used for purposes that support the reporting government's programs—that is, for the benefit of the government or its citizenry." For example, a governmental entity may receive resources from other parties, including individuals, private organizations and other governments, whereby the earnings generated from the investment of the resources can only be used in a way specified by the donor and the beneficiary of the use of those resources must be the governmental entity or its citizenry (GASB-34, par. 65).

Permanent Funds are different from Private-Purpose Funds in that the latter fund type is used when resources (either the principal, the earnings, or both) are to be used for the benefit of individuals, private organizations, or other governments. Permanent Funds are classified as a governmental fund type and Private-Purpose Funds are considered fiduciary funds.

▶ **NEW STANDARD:** Prior to the issuance of GASB-34 there was no Permanent Fund category.

## MEASUREMENT FOCUS AND BASIS OF ACCOUNTING

Since Permanent Funds (which are in effect public-purpose trust funds) are governmental funds, the modified accrual basis and flow of current financial resources are used to prepare their financial statements. These concepts are discussed in Chapter 2 ("General Fund").

▶ **NEW STANDARD:** Based on the standards established by GASB-34, public-purpose trust funds, previously presented as Nonexpendable Trust Funds, are now to be presented as Permanent Funds and, therefore, as noted above, reported on a modified accrual basis of accounting. This approach was taken for two reasons. The GASB believes that even though a public-purpose trust fund might initially appear to be appropriately classified in the fiduciary fund category, these funds are created for the benefit of the governmental entity rather than for external parties. Thus, it is more appropriate for them to be considered governmental funds (at the fund financial statement reporting level) and governmental activities (at the government-wide financial statement reporting level). Furthermore, the GASB acknowledges that technically the resources held by a Permanent Fund should be accounted for on the accrual basis (rather than the modified accrual basis); however, based on research it appears that public-purpose trust funds that are nonexpendable predominantly account for financial resources and for this reason "revenue recognition is generally consistent between the accrual and modified accrual bases." If the GASB had not adopted this approach, it would have been necessary to classify public-purpose nonexpendable trust funds as proprietary funds and then require that their activities be presented in the governmental activities of the government-wide financial statements. That reporting strategy would have required another reconciling item between the proprietary fund financial statements and the government-wide financial statements, thus adding one more element of complexity to an already complex reporting model.

▶ **NEW STANDARD:** GASB-34 notes that in some instances net assets may be restricted on a permanent basis (in perpetuity). Under this circumstance, the restricted net assets must be subdivided into expendable and nonexpendable restricted net assets at the government-wide financial reporting level (GASB-34, par. 35).

The resources that flow into a Permanent Fund include contributions from external parties as well as transfers within the governmental entity (usually the General Fund) and earnings generated by the resources once they are invested. Contributions from external parties are considered voluntary nonexchange transactions and are accounted for based on the standards established by GASB-33 (Accounting and Financial Reporting for Nonexchange Transactions). Resources received by a Permanent Fund from another fund are accounted for as transfers as required by GASB-34. Investment income that arises from resources invested by a Permanent Fund is accounted for and reported in the financial statements based on the standards established by GASB-31 (Accounting and Financial Reporting for Certain Investments and for External Investment Pools).

> ▶ **NEW STANDARD:** Under previous governmental GAAP, a transfer from a governmental fund to a fund similar to a Permanent Fund would have been accounted for as a residual equity transfer. GASB-34 eliminates the concepts of operating and residual equity transfers in that all transfers are reported as simply transfers. Furthermore, no transfer can be reported as an adjustment to the beginning balance of the fund (GASB-34, par. 112).

Expenditures of a Permanent Fund are recorded on the modified accrued basis of accounting. These expenditures are limited to the activities specifically identified in the donor agreement, legislative statute, or ordinance that created the fund. These expenditures are reported to conform to the level of detail presented in the governmental entity's operating statement. For example, the expenditures are generally classified as general government, education, public safety, and the like.

## FINANCIAL REPORTING AT FUND LEVEL

The balances and activities of Permanent Funds are presented in the following financial statements at the fund financial statement level:

- Balance Sheet
- Statement of Revenues, Expenditures, and Changes in Fund Balances

> ■ **CONTINUING STANDARD:** Although Permanent Funds are a new creation of GASB-34, the financial statements related to the funds are no different from other governmental funds and are based on standards established by various NCGA/GASB Statements and Interpretations that were outstanding before the issuance of GASB-34.

These two fund financial statements include all of the governmental funds (General Fund, Special Revenue Funds, Capital Projects Funds,

Debt Service Funds, and Permanent Funds), and these funds are reported based on the concept of a major fund as established by GASB-34.

## FINANCIAL REPORTING AT GOVERNMENT-WIDE LEVEL

The fund-based financial statements described above are included in a governmental entity's financial report in order to demonstrate that restrictions imposed by statutes, regulations, or donor contracts have been followed. Balances in these fund financial statements are converted from a modified accrual basis to an accrual basis in order to create the basic information for the government-wide financial statements. For the most part this approach requires that all of the Permanent Funds' combined ending trial balances (which are on a modified accrual basis) be adjusted to reflect accrual balances, if necessary. Because of the nature of Permanent Funds, there may be few, if any, adjustments needed for this conversion.

## ILLUSTRATIVE TRANSACTIONS

In order to illustrate accounting and financial reporting standards that are followed for a Permanent Fund, assume that the City of Centerville has a Cemetery Fund that was created several years ago by a few families that have been part of the community for many generations. Only the investment earnings from the permanent endowment received can be used to help preserve and maintain the Centerville Cemetery, a public cemetery. The trial balance for the beginning of the fiscal year is as follows:

| Accounts | Trial Balance Debits | Credits |
| --- | --- | --- |
| Cash | $ 13,000 | |
| Investment in debt securities | 215,000 | |
| Accounts payable | | $ 6,000 |
| Fund balance | | 222,000 |
| Totals | $228,000 | $228,000 |

This section presents illustrative transactions and entries for the Permanent Fund during the fiscal year ended June 30, 20X1.

> **OBSERVATION:** In the current illustration, the expenditures related to the purpose of the Permanent Fund are recorded directly in the Permanent Fund. Alternatively, the expendable portion of the fund balance could be transferred to another fund

(usually the General Fund or a Special Revenue Fund), in which case that fund would report the expenditures.

***Transaction JE06.01***—Accounts payable of $6,000 from the previous year were paid:

| Accounts | Debit | Credit |
|---|---|---|
| Accounts payables | 6,000 | |
| Cash | | 6,000 |

***Transaction JE06.02***—During the year interest and investment revenue of $30,000 was earned and received:

| Accounts | Debit | Credit |
|---|---|---|
| Cash | 30,000 | |
| Interest and Investment Revenue (program revenue—operating grants and contributions [general government]) | | 30,000 |

The transaction is reported as interest and investment revenue at the fund financial statement level; however, because the earnings are restricted to a particular activity they are reported at the government-wide financial statement level as program revenue related to general government activities.

***Transaction JE06.03***—Maintenance expenditures related to the cemetery of $35,000 were incurred, of which $31,000 was paid:

| Accounts | Debit | Credit |
|---|---|---|
| Expenditures—general government | 35,000 | |
| Cash | | 31,000 |
| Accounts payable | | 4,000 |

■ **CONTINUING STANDARD:** Based on the standards established by GASBI-6 (Recognition and Measurement of Certain Liabilities and Expenditures in Governmental Fund Financial Statements), expenditures for the newly created Permanent Funds should continue to be recorded on an accrual basis except with respect to the expenditures identified in the Interpretation.

***Transaction JE06.04***—Additional contributions of $22,000 to the permanent endowment of the fund were received from private citizens during the year:

| Accounts | Debit | Credit |
|---|---|---|
| Cash | 22,000 | |
|    Revenue—permanent endowment additions | | 22,000 |

▶ **NEW STANDARD:** GASB-34 notes that when a governmental entity receives contributions to its term and permanent endowments or to permanent fund principal, those contributions should be reported as separate items in the lower portion of the statement of activities. These receipts are not considered to be program revenues (such as program-specific grants), because in the case of term endowments there is an uncertainty of the timing of the release of the resources from the term restriction and in the case of permanent contributions the principal can never be expended (GASB-34, par. 53).

▶ **NEW STANDARD:** GASB-34 requires that the following disclosures be made for donor-restricted endowments: (1) the amount of net appreciation on investments related to donor-restricted endowments that are available for expenditure and how that appreciation is reported in net assets, (2) the state law that establishes how net appreciation may be spent by the governmental entity, and (3) the investment-spending policy (that is, the rate of endowment investments that may be authorized for expenditure) (GASB-34, par. 121).

▶ **NEW STANDARD:** GASB-34 requires that when net assets are restricted on a permanent basis (in perpetuity), the restricted net assets section of the statement of net assets (government-wide financial statement) must be subdivided into expendable and nonexpendable amounts.

***Transaction JE06.05***—Additional investments of $25,000 in bonds for the year were made:

| Accounts | Debit | Credit |
|---|---|---|
| Investments in debt securities | 25,000 | |
|    Cash | | 25,000 |

***Transaction JE06.06***—At the end of the year the portfolio of debt securities had increased in value by $4,000:

| Accounts | Debit | Credit |
|---|---|---|
| Investments in debt securities | 4,000 | |
| Interest and Investment Revenue (program revenue—operating grants and contributions [general government]) | | 4,000 |

■ **CONTINUING STANDARD:** Investments and related revenue continue to be accounted for in accordance with the standards established by GASB-31 (Accounting and Financial Reporting for Certain Investments and for External Investment Pools).

After the transactions for the year are posted, the year-end trial balance (June 30, 20X1) for the Cemetery Fund appears as follows:

| Accounts | Adjusted Trial Balance Debit | Credit |
|---|---|---|
| Cash | $ 3,000 | |
| Investment in debt securities | 244,000 | |
| Accounts payable | | $ 4,000 |
| Fund balance | | 222,000 |
| Interest and investment revenue (program revenue—operating grants and contributions [general government]) | | 34,000 |
| Expenditures—general government | 35,000 | |
| Revenue—permanent endowment additions | | 22,000 |
| Totals | $282,000 | $282,000 |

The worksheet that summarizes the foregoing journal entries for the Centerville Cemetery Permanent Fund for the year-end trial balance is presented in Appendix 6A.

## FUND FINANCIAL STATEMENTS

At the fund financial statement level, a governmental fund must prepare a statement of revenues, expenditures, and changes in fund balances and a balance sheet. Based on the adjusted trial balances created above, the following financial statements reflect the balances and activities of the Permanent Fund (see Appendix 6B):

▶ **NEW STANDARD:** NCGA-1 illustrates three distinct formats that can be used to prepare the statement of revenues, expenditures, and changes in fund balances for governmental funds. However, GASB-34 eliminates two of the options; so, only the format illustrated below can now be used (GASB-34, par. 86).

■ **CONTINUING STANDARD:** The formatting of the balance sheet at the fund financial statement level was not changed by GASB-34.

### Permanent Fund
### Balance Sheet
### June 30, 20X1

**ASSETS**

| | |
|---|---|
| Cash | $ 3,000 |
| Investments in debt securities | 244,000 |
| Total Assets | $247,000 |

**LIABILITIES AND FUND BALANCES**

| | |
|---|---|
| Liabilities: | |
| Accounts payable | $ 4,000 |
| Total Liabilities | 4,000 |
| Fund balances: | |
| Fund balance | 243,000 |
| Total Liabilities and Fund Balances | $247,000 |

### Permanent Funds
### Statement of Revenues, Expenditures, and Changes
### in Fund Balances
### June 30, 20X1

**REVENUES**

| | |
|---|---|
| Interest and investment revenue (Program Revenue—Operating Grants and Contributions [General Government]) | $ 34,000 |
| Revenue—permanent endowment additions | 22,000 |
| Total Revenue | 56,000 |

**EXPENDITURES**

| | |
|---|---|
| General government | 35,000 |
| Total Expenditures | 35,000 |
| Excess (deficiency) of revenues over expenditures | 21,000 |
| Fund balances—beginning | 222,000 |
| Fund balances—ending | $243,000 |

The financial statements for the Permanent Fund are not reported separately in the governmental entity's financial report, but they are used in Chapter 12 ("Developing Information for Fund Financial Statements").

## GOVERNMENT-WIDE FINANCIAL STATEMENTS

Government-wide financial statements are reported on the accrual basis of accounting. Generally most governments will work from their governmental fund financial statements (which are on a modified accrual basis) and through the use of worksheet entries convert to accrual based financial statements.

There are no adjustments needed to convert the above Permanent Fund from a modified accrual basis to an accrual basis (see Apppendix 6C).

**6-10** *Governmental Funds*

## APPENDIX 6A
## WORKSHEET FOR SUMMARIZING CURRENT TRANSACTIONS—CENTERVILLE CEMETERY

### WORKSHEET ENTRIES

| Accounts | Trial Balance Debits | Trial Balance Credits | | Adjustments Debits | | Adjustments Credits | Adjusted Trial Balance Debits | Adjusted Trial Balance Credits | Operating Statement Debits | Operating Statement Credits | Balance Sheet Debits | Balance Sheet Credits |
|---|---|---|---|---|---|---|---|---|---|---|---|---|
| Cash | 13,000 | — | JE06.02 | 30,000 | JE06.01 | 6,000 | 3,000 | — | — | — | 3,000 | — |
| | | | JE06.04 | 22,000 | JE06.03 | 31,000 | | | | | | |
| | | | | — | JE06.05 | 25,000 | | | | | | |
| Investment in debt securities | 215,000 | — | JE06.05 | 25,000 | | — | 244,000 | — | — | — | 244,000 | — |
| | | | JE06.06 | 4,000 | | | | | | | | |
| Accounts payable | — | 6,000 | JE06.01 | 6,000 | JE06.03 | 4,000 | — | 4,000 | — | — | — | 4,000 |
| Fund balance | — | 222,000 | | — | | — | — | 222,000 | — | — | — | 222,000 |
| Interest and investment revenue (Program Revenue—Operating Grants and Contributions [General Government]) | — | — | | — | JE06.02 | 30,000 | — | 34,000 | — | 34,000 | — | — |
| | | | | — | JE06.06 | 4,000 | | | | | | |
| Expenditures—general government | — | — | JE06.03 | 35,000 | | — | 35,000 | — | 35,000 | — | — | — |
| Revenue—permanent endowment additions | — | — | | — | JE06.04 | 22,000 | — | 22,000 | — | 22,000 | — | — |
| Totals | 228,000 | 228,000 | | 122,000 | | 122,000 | 282,000 | 282,000 | 35,000 | 56,000 | 247,000 | 226,000 |
| Net increase (decrease) | | | | | | | | | 21,000 | | | 21,000 |
| | | | | | | | | | 56,000 | 56,000 | 247,000 | 247,000 |

# APPENDIX 6B: PERMANENT FUNDS—BALANCE SHEET AND STATEMENT OF REVENUES, EXPENDITURES, AND CHANGES IN FUND BALANCES

## WORKSHEET ENTRIES

**Permanent Fund**
**Balance Sheet**
**June 30, 20X1**

**ASSETS**
| | |
|---|---:|
| Cash | $ 3,000 |
| Investments in debt securities | 244,000 |
| Total Assets | $247,000 |

**LIABILITIES AND FUND BALANCES**
Liabilities:
| | |
|---|---:|
| Accounts payable | $ 4,000 |
| Total Liabilities | 4,000 |
| Fund balances: | |
| Fund balance | 243,000 |
| Total Liabilities and Fund Balances | $247,000 |

**Permanent Funds**
**Statement of Revenues, Expenditures, and Changes in Fund Balances**
**June 30, 20X1**

**REVENUES**
| | |
|---|---:|
| Interest and investment revenue (Program Revenue—Operating Grants and Contributions [General Government]) | $ 34,000 |
| Revenue—permanent endowment additions | 22,000 |
| Total Revenue | 56,000 |

## WORKSHEET ENTRIES (Continued)

**EXPENDITURES**
| | |
|---|---:|
| General government | 35,000 |
| Total Expenditures | 35,000 |
| Excess (deficiency) of revenues over expenditures | 21,000 |
| Fund balances—beginning | 222,000 |
| Fund balances—ending | $243,000 |

## APPENDIX 6C: NO ADJUSTMENTS

There are no adjustments needed to convert Permanent Funds from a modified accrual basis to an accrual basis.

# PART III.
# PROPRIETARY FUNDS

# CHAPTER 7
# ENTERPRISE FUNDS

## CONTENTS

| | |
|---|---|
| Nature of Enterprise Funds | 7-1 |
| Measurement Focus and Basis of Accounting | 7-2 |
| Financial Reporting at Fund Level | 7-3 |
| Financial Reporting at Government-Wide Level | 7-5 |
| Illustrative Transactions | 7-6 |
|     Centerville Toll Bridge | 7-6 |
|     Centerville Utilities Authority | 7-14 |
|     Centerville Parking Authority | 7-21 |
|     Centerville Municipal Airport | 7-28 |
| Fund Financial Statements | 7-35 |
| Converting to Government-Wide Financial Statements | 7-42 |
| Appendix 7A: Worksheet for Summarizing Current Transactions—Centerville Toll Bridge | 7-43 |
| Appendix 7B: Worksheet for Summarizing Current Transactions—Centerville Utilities Authority | 7-47 |
| Appendix 7C: Worksheet for Summarizing Current Transactions—Centerville Parking Authority | 7-51 |
| Appendix 7D: Worksheet for Summarizing Current Transactions—Centerville Municipal Airport | 7-55 |
| Appendix 7E: Enterprise Funds—Statement of Net Assets; Statement of Revenues, Expenses, and Changes in Fund Net Assets; and Statement of Cash Flows | 7-60 |

## NATURE OF ENTERPRISE FUNDS

An Enterprise Fund is a proprietary fund that is generally used to account for governmental activities that are similar to activities that may be performed by a commercial enterprise. For example, an Enterprise Fund can be used to account for transit systems, solid-waste landfills, toll roads, hospitals, and other activities that charge a fee in order to recover operational costs.

More specifically, an Enterprise Fund *may* be used to "report any activity for which a fee is charged to external users for goods or services." However, GASB-34 states that an Enterprise Fund *must* be used to account for an activity if any one of the following criteria is satisfied (GASB-34, paragraph 67):

- The activity is financed with debt that is secured *solely* by a pledge of the net revenues from fees and charges of the activity.
- Laws or regulations require that the activity's costs of providing services, including capital costs (such as depreciation or capital debt service), be recovered with fees and charges, rather than with taxes or similar revenues.
- The pricing policies of the activity establish fees and charges designed to recover its costs, including capital costs (such as depreciation or debt service).

> ▶ **NEW STANDARD:** The criteria established by GASB-34 are different from the standards that were previously used to determine when an Enterprise Fund should be used by a governmental entity. The GASB believes that the establishment of the criteria listed above will reduce the degree of subjectivity that is used by governmental entities in determining when an Enterprise Fund should be used.

> ▶ **NEW STANDARD:** Some financial statement preparers raised the question about whether the criteria listed above apply to activities that are currently accounted for in Internal Service Funds. GASB-34 takes the position that an Enterprise Fund, not an Internal Service Fund, must be used when external users are the predominant participants in the fund. GASB-37 (Basic Financial Statements—and Management's Discussion and Analysis—for State and Local Governments: Omnibus) reemphasizes this point by adding a footnote to paragraph 67 that states, "the focus of these criteria is on fees charged to external users."

## MEASUREMENT FOCUS AND BASIS OF ACCOUNTING

The accrual basis of accounting and the flow of economic resources are used to prepare the financial statements of an Enterprise Fund. Generally, under the flow of economic resources, measurement focus and accrual basis of accounting, revenues are recognized when earned and expenses are recorded when incurred when these activities are related to exchange and exchange-like activities. In addition, long-lived assets (such as buildings and equipment) are capitalized and depreciated, and all debt is reported in the fund (GASB-34, par. 16).

Generally, activities accounted for in Enterprise Funds are characterized as business-type activities. Business-type activities must follow either Alternative 1 or Alternative 2 as described in GASB-20 (Accounting and Financial Reporting for Proprietary Funds and Other Governmental Entities That Use Proprietary Fund Accounting). Under Alternative 1, governmental entities using proprietary fund accounting must follow (1) all GASB pronouncements and (2) FASB Statements and Interpretations, APB Opinions, and Accounting Research Bulletins (ARBs) issued on or before November 30, 1989, except those that conflict with a GASB pronouncement. Under Alternative 2, governmental entities using proprietary fund accounting must follow (1) all GASB pronouncements and (2) all FASB Statements and Interpretations, APB Opinions, and ARBs, no matter when issued, except those that conflict with a GASB pronouncement. Unlike Alternative 1, Alternative 2 has no cutoff date for determining the applicability of FASB pronouncements.

> ▶ **NEW STANDARD:** Prior to the issuance of GASB-34, an Enterprise Fund could account for depreciation expense in the conventional manner or depreciation expense could be closed at the end of the year directly to the fund's contributed capital account that was created when a restricted grant, entitlement, or shared revenue was provided to acquire the related capital asset. GASB-34 prohibits the latter method of accounting for depreciation expense (GASB-34, par. 103).

> ▶ **NEW STANDARD:** NCGA-1 allowed for certain transfers to an Enterprise Fund to be accounted as an equity or fund balance transaction (residual equity transfer). GASB-34 does not allow for residual equity transfer in that all transfers must be reported on an Enterprise Fund's operating statement (GASB-34, par. 112).

## FINANCIAL REPORTING AT FUND LEVEL

The balances and activities of Enterprise funds are presented in the following three financial statements at the fund financial statement level:

1. Statement of net assets (or balance sheet)
2. Statement of Revenues, Expenses, and changes in fund net assets (or fund equity)
3. Statement of cash flows

These three fund financial statements include all of the proprietary funds (Enterprise Funds and Internal Service Funds). The financial statements of Enterprise Funds are presented at the fund financial statement reporting level based on the major fund concept; however, the financial statements of Internal Service Funds (as explained in

Chapter 8) are all combined into a single column and the major fund criteria are not used.

> ▶ **NEW STANDARD:** A significant change in the focus of reporting governmental funds and Enterprise Funds is that major funds are reported for these funds; however, combined financial statements for fund types are not required to be reported (GASB-34, par. 75).

A fund is considered a major fund if both of the following two criteria (GASB-34, pars. 75 and 76) are satisfied:

1. Total assets, liabilities, revenues, or expenditures/expenses of the governmental (enterprise) fund are equal to or greater than 10 percent of the corresponding element total (assets, liability, and so forth) for all funds that are considered governmental funds (enterprise funds).
2. The same element that met the 10 percent criterion in (1) is at least 5 percent of the corresponding element total for all governmental and enterprise funds combined.

> ▶ **NEW STANDARD:** In establishing the above two criteria, the GASB intended that a major fund arises when a particular element (assets, for example) of a fund meets both the 10 percent threshold and the 5 percent threshold. Some preparers read the requirement to mean that a major fund arises when one element (assets, for example) satisfies the 10 percent threshold and another element (revenues, for example) satisfies the 5 percent threshold. GASB-37 (Basic Financial Statements—and Management's Discussion and Analysis—for State and Local Governments: Omnibus) clarifies the GASB's original intent. That is, a single element must satisfy both criteria.

> ▶ **NEW STANDARD:** Proprietary funds must prepare a statement of cash flows based on the guidance established by GASB-9, except the statement of cash flows should be formatted based on the *direct method* in computing cash flows from operating activities. Prior to the issuance of GASB-34, the statement of cash flows could be prepared based on either the direct or indirect method (GASB-34, par. 105).

> ▶ **NEW STANDARD:** GASB-34 requires a reconciliation between the fund financial statements (statement of net assets and statement of changes in net assets) and business-type activities. Often, there is no need for this reconciliation because both sets of financial statements are based on the same

measurement focus and basis of accounting. When there are differences between the two sets of financial statements, the differences must be reconciled on the face of the proprietary fund financial statements. GASB-34 notes that a reconciling item could arise when the transactions and perhaps residual assets and liabilities of an Internal Service Fund are related to business-type activities (GASB-34, par. 104).

## FINANCIAL REPORTING AT GOVERNMENT-WIDE LEVEL

Government-wide financial statements were established by GASB-34 in order to provide a basis for determining (1) the extent to which current services provided by the entity were financed with current revenues and (2) the degree to which a governmental entity's financial position has changed during the fiscal year. In order to achieve these objectives, government-wide financial statements include a statement of net assets and a statement of activities. Government-wide financial statements are based on a flow of all economic resources applied on the accrual basis of accounting. The flow of economic resources refers to all assets available to the governmental unit for the purpose of providing goods and services to the public.

Perhaps the major implementation problem facing those who prepare governmental financial statements based on the standards established by GASB-34 is the development of system procedures that facilitate the presentation of the two levels of financial statements. However, because there are generally no or few reconciling items between totals reported for Enterprise Funds on the proprietary fund financial statements and totals reported in the government-wide financial statements for businesses-type activities, the conversion of the information from a fund financial statement format to a business-type activities format can be relatively straightforward.

For the most part, this approach requires that the Enterprise Funds' ending trial balances (which are already on an accrual basis) be adjusted to reflect Internal Service Fund activities, if any. That is, Internal Service Funds and similar activities related to business-type activities are eliminated to avoid doubling-up expenses and revenues in preparing the business-type activities column of the statement of activities. The effect of this approach is to adjust activities in an Internal Service Fund to a break-even balance. For example, if the Internal Service Fund had a "net profit" for the year, there is a pro rata reduction in the charges made to the funds that used the Internal Service Fund's services for the year. Likewise, a net loss requires a pro rata adjustment that increases the charges made to the various Enterprise Funds. After making these eliminations, any residual balances related to the Internal Service Fund's assets, liabilities, and net assets are reported in the business-type activities column in the statement of net assets (as demonstrated in Chapter 8).

▶ **NEW STANDARD:** GASB-34 requires that business-type activities be separately reported at least by segment on the statement of activities (government-wide financial statement). The GASB's objective for reporting disaggregated information in the business-type activities section of the statement of activities was not to identify segment information but rather to have a separate presentation for activities that are *different*. In order to better achieve this objective, GASB-37 (Basic Financial Statements—and Management's Discussion and Analysis—for State and Local Governments: Omnibus) amends GASB-34 by requiring that the statement of activities present "activities accounted for in Enterprise Funds by different identifiable activities," which is described the following way: "An activity within an Enterprise Fund is identifiable if it has a specific revenue stream and related expenses and gains and losses that are accounted for separately."

## ILLUSTRATIVE TRANSACTIONS

In order to illustrate accounting and financial reporting standards that are observed for Enterprise Funds, assume that the City of Centerville has the following Enterprise Funds:

- Centerville Toll Bridge
- Centerville Parking Authority
- Centerville Utilities Authority
- Centerville Municipal Airport

### Centerville Toll Bridge

The Centerville Toll Bridge (CTB) was constructed several years ago and provides access across the Centerville River from the downtown area to a primarily residential section of the city. The fund's trial balance for the beginning of the fiscal year is as follows:

| Accounts | Trial Balance Debits | Credits |
|---|---|---|
| Cash | $ 220,000 | |
| Interest receivable | 4,500 | |
| Temporary investments | 33,000 | |
| Supplies | 26,000 | |
| Construction in progress | 40,000 | |
| Land and improvements | 100,000 | |
| Superstructure | 1,400,000 | |

|                                    | Trial Balance |             |
| ---------------------------------- | ------------: | ----------: |
| Accounts                           | Debits        | Credits     |
| Accumulated depreciation—superstructure |          | $ 650,000   |
| Buildings                          | 250,000       |             |
| Accumulated depreciation—buildings |               | 120,000     |
| Equipment                          | 40,000        |             |
| Accumulated depreciation—equipment |               | 25,000      |
| Vehicles                           | 800,000       |             |
| Accumulated depreciation—vehicles  |               | 270,000     |
| Accounts payable and accrued expenses |            | 26,000      |
| Due to other funds—Communications and Technology Center |  | 4,000 |
| Compensated absences liability     |               | 7,000       |
| Claims and judgements payable      |               | 25,000      |
| Notes payable                      |               | 40,000      |
| Bonds payable                      |               | 100,000     |
| Net assets                         |               | 1,646,500   |
| Totals                             | $2,913,500    | $2,913,500  |

This section presents illustrative transactions and entries for the CTB during the fiscal year ended June 30, 20X1.

■ **CONTINUING STANDARD:** GASB-34 generally did not change the manner of accounting for transactions that are recorded in Enterprise Funds.

*Transaction JE07.01*—Accounts payable and accrued expenses of $26,000 from the previous year were paid:

| Accounts                              | Debit  | Credit |
| ------------------------------------- | ------ | ------ |
| Accounts payable and accrued expenses | 26,000 |        |
| Cash                                  |        | 26,000 |

*Transaction JE07.02*—Accrued interest receivable from the previous year was received:

| Accounts            | Debit | Credit |
| ------------------- | ----- | ------ |
| Cash                | 4,500 |        |
| Interest receivable |       | 4,500  |

## 7-8 Proprietary Funds

***Transaction JE07.03***—During the year, cash tolls collected from customers totaled $4,750,000:

| Accounts | Debit | Credit |
|---|---|---|
| Cash | 4,750,000 | |
|     Charges for services | | 4,750,000 |

***Transaction JE07.04***—The following operating expenses were incurred during the year, of which $4,150,000 were paid in cash:

| | |
|---|---|
| Personal services | $2,400,000 |
| Contractual services | 1,200,000 |
| Repairs and maintenance | 400,000 |
| Other supplies and expenses | 200,000 |
| Total | $4,200,000 |

| Accounts | Debit | Credit |
|---|---|---|
| Personal services expenses | 2,400,000 | |
| Contractual services expenses | 1,200,000 | |
| Repairs and maintenance expenses | 400,000 | |
| Other supplies and expenses | 200,000 | |
|     Cash | | 4,150,000 |
|     Accounts payable and accrued expenses | | 50,000 |

***Transaction JE07.05***—During the year, interest and investment revenue of $30,000 was earned, of which $27,000 was received in cash:

| Accounts | Debit | Credit |
|---|---|---|
| Cash | 27,000 | |
| Interest receivable | 3,000 | |
|     Interest and investment revenue | | 30,000 |

■ **CONTINUING STANDARD:** The accounting for investments continues to be recorded based on the standards established by GASB-31 (Accounting and Financial Reporting for Certain Investments and for External Investment Pools).

***Transaction JE07.06***—The following capital assets were purchased during the year for cash:

| | |
|---|---|
| Land and improvements | $ 40,000 |
| Equipment | 30,000 |
| Vehicles | 120,000 |
| Total | $190,000 |

| Accounts | Debit | Credit |
|---|---|---|
| Land and improvements | 40,000 | |
| Equipment | 30,000 | |
| Vehicles | 120,000 | |
| Cash | | 190,000 |

*Transaction JE07.07*—During the year, a building under construction (construction in progress) was completed at a total cost of $170,000 (after incurring additional costs of $130,000 for the current year) and new construction costs of $70,000 were incurred on a new unfinished project:

| Accounts | Debit | Credit |
|---|---|---|
| Construction in progress | 130,000 | |
| Cash | | 130,000 |
| | | |
| Building | 170,000 | |
| Construction in progress | | 170,000 |
| | | |
| Construction in progress | 70,000 | |
| Cash | | 70,000 |

*Transaction JE07.08*—The following assets were sold or abandoned during the year. The cash proceeds were $50,000:

| | Original Cost | Accumulated Depreciation |
|---|---|---|
| Buildings | $ 90,000 | $ 70,000 |
| Equipment | 15,000 | 12,000 |
| Vehicles | 85,000 | 65,000 |
| Total | $190,000 | $147,000 |

| Accounts | Debit | Credit |
|---|---|---|
| Cash | 50,000 | |
| Accumulated depreciation—buildings | 70,000 | |
| Accumulated depreciation—equipment | 12,000 | |
| Accumulated depreciation—vehicles | 65,000 | |
| Buildings | | 90,000 |
| Equipment | | 15,000 |
| Vehicles | | 85,000 |
| Miscellaneous revenue—gain on sale of assets | | 7,000 |

*Transaction JE07.09*—During the year, a portion of the notes payable ($10,000), a portion of the bonds payable ($20,000), and interest expense of $6,000 were paid:

## 7-10 Proprietary Funds

| Accounts | Debit | Credit |
|---|---|---|
| Notes payable | 10,000 | |
| Bonds payable | 20,000 | |
| Interest expense | 6,000 | |
| Cash | | 36,000 |

***Transaction JE07.10***—Compensated absences of $1,000 were paid during the year and additional costs of $2,000 were accrued:

| Accounts | Debit | Credit |
|---|---|---|
| Personal services expenses | 2,000 | |
| Compensated absences liability | | 1,000 |
| Cash | | 1,000 |

***Transaction JE07.11***—Claims and judgements of $8,000 were paid during the year and additional costs of $10,000 were accrued:

| Accounts | Debit | Credit |
|---|---|---|
| Insurance claims and expenses | 10,000 | |
| Claims and judgements payable | | 2,000 |
| Cash | | 8,000 |

***Transaction JE07.12***—Depreciation expense recognized during the year was as follows:

| | |
|---|---|
| Superstructure | $ 28,000 |
| Buildings | 25,000 |
| Equipment | 6,000 |
| Vehicles | 280,000 |
| Total | $339,000 |

| Accounts | Debit | Credit |
|---|---|---|
| Depreciation expense | 339,000 | |
| Accumulated depreciation—superstructure | | 28,000 |
| Accumulated depreciation—buildings | | 25,000 |
| Accumulated depreciation—equipment | | 6,000 |
| Accumulated depreciation—vehicles | | 280,000 |

▶ **NEW STANDARD:** GASB-34 does not require that infrastructure assets that are part of a network or subsystem of a network (referred to as "eligible infrastructure assets") be depreciated if certain conditions relating to the asset management system and the documentation of the condition level of the infrastructure are met. The *Miller Governmental GAAP Guide* explains these conditions. Generally, infrastructure assets are related to governmental rather than business-type activities; however, if an Enterprise Fund has eligible infrastructure assets, the fund may choose not to depreciate the assets. The illustration in this book assumes that the governmental entity's Enterprise Funds depreciate all eligible infrastructure assets (GASB-34, par. 23).

*Transaction JE07.13*—An operating grant of $100,000 and a capital grant of $250,000 were received from the state government:

| Accounts | Debit | Credit |
|---|---|---|
| Cash | 350,000 | |
|    Operating grants and contributions | | 100,000 |
|    Capital grants and contributions | | 250,000 |

■ **CONTINUING STANDARD:** The accounting for nonexchange revenues (such as operating and capital grants) continues to be recorded based on the standards established by GASB-33 (Accounting and Financial Reporting for Nonexchange Transactions).

*Transaction JE07.14*—Other operating revenues earned and received during the year amounted to $20,000 and other operating expenses incurred and paid during the year amounted to $30,000:

| Accounts | Debit | Credit |
|---|---|---|
| Cash | 20,000 | |
|    Operating revenues—miscellaneous | | 20,000 |
| | | |
| Operating expenses—miscellaneous | 30,000 | |
|    Cash | | 30,000 |

▶ **NEW STANDARD:** GASB-34 notes that an important element of the statement of revenues, expenses, and changes in fund net assets is that there must be a differentiation between operating revenues and nonoperating revenues, and operating expenses and nonoperating expenses, based on policies established by the governmental entity. Those policies are disclosed in the entity's summary of significant accounting policies and applied consistently from period to period. GASB-34 states that, in general, differentiations between operating and nonoperating transactions should follow the broad guidance established by GASB-9 (Reporting Cash Flows of Proprietary and Nonexpendable Trust Funds and governmental Entities that Use Proprietary Fund Accounting). For example, transactions related to (1) capital and related financing activities, (2) noncapital financing activities, (3) investing activities, and (4) nonexchange revenues, such as tax revenues, would generally be considered nonoperating transactions for purposes of preparing the statement of revenues, expenses, and changes in net assets (GASB-34, par. 102).

***Transaction JE07.15***—Additional temporary investments of $25,000 were purchased during the year:

| Accounts | Debit | Credit |
| --- | --- | --- |
| Temporary investments | 25,000 | |
| Cash | | 25,000 |

***Transaction JE07.16***—An operating grant (transfer) of $50,000 was received from the General Fund:

| Accounts | Debit | Credit |
| --- | --- | --- |
| Cash | 50,000 | |
| Transfers in—General Fund | | 50,000 |

***Transaction JE07.17***—During the year, the Communications and Technology Support Center (Internal Service Fund) billed the CTB $80,000 for services performed. The CTB made payments of $66,000.

| Accounts | Debit | Credit |
| --- | --- | --- |
| Contractual services expenses | 80,000 | |
| Cash | | 66,000 |
| Due to other funds—Internal Service Fund—Communications and Technology Support Center | | 14,000 |

■ **CONTINUING STANDARD:** Interfund receivables/payables may arise from an operating activity (that is the sale of goods and services) between funds rather than in the form of a loan arrangement. If the interfund operating activity is recorded at an amount that approximates the fair value of the goods or services exchanged, the provider/seller fund should record the activity as revenue and the user/purchaser fund should record an expenditure/expense. "Interfund services provided" and "interfund services used" replace the previous term "quasi-external transactions." However, except for changes in terminology, GASB-34 does not change the essential manner by which reciprocal interfund activity is reported (GASB-34, par. 112).

*Transaction JE07.18*—Supplies of $32,000 were on hand at the end of the year:

| Accounts | Debit | Credit |
|---|---|---|
| Inventories | 6,000 | |
|    Other supplies and expenses | | 6,000 |

■ **CONTINUING STANDARD:** Inventories/supplies can only be accounted for in an Enterprise Fund based on the consumption method.

After the transactions for the year are posted, the year-end trial balance (June 30, 20X1) for the Centerville Toll Bridge appears as follows:

| Accounts | Adjusted Trial Balance Debits | Credits |
|---|---|---|
| Cash | $ 739,500 | |
| Interest receivable | 3,000 | |
| Temporary investments | 58,000 | |
| Supplies | 32,000 | |
| Construction in progress | 70,000 | |
| Land and improvements | 140,000 | |
| Superstructure | 1,400,000 | |
| Accumulated depreciation—superstructure | | $ 678,000 |
| Buildings | 330,000 | |
| Accumulated depreciation—buildings | | 75,000 |
| Equipment | 55,000 | |
| Accumulated depreciation—equipment | | 19,000 |
| Vehicles | 835,000 | |
| Accumulated depreciation—vehicles | | 485,000 |
| Accounts payable and accrued expenses | | 50,000 |
| Due to other funds—Communications and Technology Center | | 18,000 |
| Compensated absences liability | | 8,000 |
| Claims and judgements payable | | 27,000 |
| Notes payable | | 30,000 |
| Bonds payable | | 80,000 |
| Net assets | | 1,646,500 |
| Charges for services | | 4,750,000 |
| Interest and investment revenue | | 30,000 |

7-14  *Proprietary Funds*

|  | Adjusted Trial Balance |  |
|---|---|---|
| Accounts | Debits | Credits |
| Miscellaneous revenue—gain on sale of assets |  | 7,000 |
| Operating grants and contributions |  | 100,000 |
| Capital grants and contributions |  | 250,000 |
| Operating revenues—miscellaneous |  | 20,000 |
| Personal services expenses | 2,402,000 |  |
| Contractual services expenses | 1,280,000 |  |
| Repairs and maintenance expenses | 400,000 |  |
| Other supplies and expenses | 194,000 |  |
| Insurance claims and expenses | 10,000 |  |
| Depreciation expense | 339,000 |  |
| Interest expense | 6,000 |  |
| Operating expenses—miscellaneous | 30,000 |  |
| Transfers in—General Fund |  | 50,000 |
| Totals | $8,323,500 | $8,323,500 |

The worksheet that summarizes the foregoing journal entries for the CTB's year-end trial balance is presented in Appendix 7A.

## Centerville Utilities Authority

The Centerville Utilities Authority (CUA) provides sewer services to citizens, businesses, and other institutions of Centerville. The fund's trial balance for the beginning of the fiscal year is as follows:

|  | Adjusted Trial Balance |  |
|---|---|---|
| Accounts | Debits | Credits |
| Cash | $2,970,000 |  |
| Interest receivable | 15,000 |  |
| Accounts receivable | 6,000,000 |  |
| Allowance for doubtful accounts |  | $ 300,000 |
| Temporary investments | 40,000 |  |
| Due from other governments |  |  |
| Supplies | 54,000 |  |
| Construction in progress | 1,500,000 |  |
| Land and improvements | 4,000,000 |  |
| Distribution and collection systems | 45,000,000 |  |
| Accumulated depreciation—distribution and collection systems |  | 41,000,000 |
| Buildings | 13,000,000 |  |

|                                         | Adjusted Trial Balance |              |
|-----------------------------------------|-----------------------:|-------------:|
| Accounts                                | Debits                 | Credits      |
| Accumulated depreciation—buildings      |                        | 10,920,000   |
| Equipment                               | 6,500,000              |              |
| Accumulated depreciation—equipment      |                        | 2,380,000    |
| Vehicles                                | 1,400,000              |              |
| Accumulated depreciation—vehicles       |                        | 800,000      |
| Accounts payable and accrued expenses   |                        | 1,100,000    |
| Due to other funds—Internal Service Fund—Communications and Technology Support Center |  | 15,000 |
| Compensated absences liability          |                        | 75,000       |
| Claims and judgements payable           |                        | 220,000      |
| Notes payable                           |                        | 250,000      |
| Bonds payable                           |                        | 7,400,000    |
| Net assets                              |                        | 16,019,000   |
| Totals                                  | $80,479,000            | $80,479,000  |

This section presents illustrative transactions and entries for the CUA during the fiscal year ended June 30, 20X1.

*Transaction JE07.19*—Accounts payable and accrued expenses of $1,100,000 from the previous year were paid:

| Accounts                              | Debit     | Credit    |
|---------------------------------------|-----------|-----------|
| Accounts payable and accrued expenses | 1,100,000 |           |
| Cash                                  |           | 1,100,000 |

*Transaction JE07.20*—Accrued interest receivable from the previous year was received:

| Accounts            | Debit  | Credit |
|---------------------|--------|--------|
| Cash                | 15,000 |        |
| Interest receivable |        | 15,000 |

*Transaction JE07.21*—During the year, customers were billed $36,000,000 for services provided and cash collections on account amounted to $34,000,000:

| Accounts             | Debit      | Credit     |
|----------------------|------------|------------|
| Cash                 | 34,000,000 |            |
| Accounts receivable  | 2,000,000  |            |
| Charges for services |            | 36,000,000 |

Bad debts expense of $150,000 (classified as other supplies and expenses for the period) was recorded during the year and customer accounts of $80,000 were written off:

| Accounts | Debit | Credit |
|---|---|---|
| Other supplies and expenses | 150,000 | |
| Accounts receivable | | 80,000 |
| Allowance for doubtful accounts | | 70,000 |

***Transaction JE07.22***—The following operating expenses were incurred during the year, of which $30,000,000 was paid in cash:

| | |
|---|---|
| Personal services | $22,000,000 |
| Contractual services | 11,000,000 |
| Repairs and maintenance | 700,000 |
| Other supplies and expenses | 600,000 |
| Total | $34,300,000 |

| Accounts | Debit | Credit |
|---|---|---|
| Personal services expenses | 22,000,000 | |
| Contractual services expenses | 11,000,000 | |
| Repairs and maintenance expenses | 700,000 | |
| Other supplies and expenses | 600,000 | |
| Cash | | 30,000,000 |
| Accounts payable and accrued expenses | | 4,300,000 |

***Transaction JE07.23***—During the year, interest and investment revenue of $400,000 was earned, of which $350,000 was received in cash:

| Accounts | Debit | Credit |
|---|---|---|
| Cash | 350,000 | |
| Interest receivable | 50,000 | |
| Interest and investment revenue | | 400,000 |

***Transaction JE07.24***—The following capital assets were purchased during the year for cash:

| | |
|---|---|
| Land and improvements | $1,200,000 |
| Distribution and collection systems | 1,300,000 |
| Equipment | 1,200,000 |
| Vehicles | 750,000 |
| Total | $4,450,000 |

*Enterprise Funds* 7-17

| Accounts | Debit | Credit |
|---|---|---|
| Land and improvements | 1,200,000 | |
| Distribution and collection systems | 1,300,000 | |
| Equipment | 1,200,000 | |
| Vehicles | 750,000 | |
| Cash | | 4,450,000 |

***Transaction JE07.25***—During the year, a building under construction (construction in progress) was completed at a cost of $2,200,000 (after incurring additional costs of $700,000) and new construction costs of $200,000 were incurred on a new unfinished project:

| Accounts | Debit | Credit |
|---|---|---|
| Construction in progress | 700,000 | |
| Cash | | 700,000 |
| Building | 2,200,000 | |
| Construction in progress | | 2,200,000 |
| Construction in progress | 200,000 | |
| Cash | | 200,000 |

***Transaction JE07.26***—The following assets were sold or abandoned during the year. The cash proceeds were $500,000:

| | Original Cost | Accumulated Depreciation |
|---|---|---|
| Buildings | $750,000 | 600,000 |
| Equipment | 3,100,000 | 2,800,000 |
| Vehicles | 490,000 | 330,000 |
| Total | $4,340,000 | $3,730,000 |

| Accounts | Debit | Credit |
|---|---|---|
| Cash | 500,000 | |
| Miscellaneous expenses (loss on sale of assets) | 110,000 | |
| Accumulated depreciation—buildings | 600,000 | |
| Accumulated depreciation—equipment | 2,800,000 | |
| Accumulated depreciation—vehicles | 330,000 | |
| Buildings | | 750,000 |
| Equipment | | 3,100,000 |
| Vehicles | | 490,000 |

## 7-18 Proprietary Funds

**Transaction JE07.27**—During the year, a portion of the notes payable ($40,000), a portion of the bonds payable ($1,700,000), and interest expense of $450,000 were paid. In addition, bonds of $2,000,000 and notes of $120,000 were issued during the year:

| Accounts | Debit | Credit |
|---|---|---|
| Notes payable | 40,000 | |
| Bonds payable | 1,700,000 | |
| Interest expense | 450,000 | |
|    Cash | | 2,190,000 |

| Accounts | Debit | Credit |
|---|---|---|
| Cash | 2,120,000 | |
|    Bonds payable | | 2,000,000 |
|    Notes payable | | 120,000 |

**Transaction JE07.28**—Compensated absences of $13,000 were paid during the year and additional costs of $22,000 were accrued:

| Accounts | Debit | Credit |
|---|---|---|
| Personal services expenses | 22,000 | |
|    Compensated absences liability | | 9,000 |
|    Cash | | 13,000 |

**Transaction JE07.29**—Claims and judgements of $12,000 were paid during the year and additional costs of $21,000 were accrued:

| Accounts | Debit | Credit |
|---|---|---|
| Insurance claims and expenses | 21,000 | |
|    Claims and judgements payable | | 9,000 |
|    Cash | | 12,000 |

**Transaction JE07.30**—Depreciation expense recognized during the year was as follows:

| | |
|---|---|
| Distribution and collection systems | $1,200,000 |
| Buildings | 625,000 |
| Equipment | 920,000 |
| Vehicles | 280,000 |
| Total | $3,025,000 |

| Accounts | Debit | Credit |
|---|---|---|
| Depreciation expense | 3,025,000 | |
| Accumulated depreciation—distribution and collection systems | | 1,200,000 |
| Accumulated depreciation—buildings | | 625,000 |
| Accumulated depreciation—equipment | | 920,000 |
| Accumulated depreciation—vehicles | | 280,000 |

*Transaction JE07.31*—A capital grant of $1,250,000 was received from the state government:

| Accounts | Debit | Credit |
|---|---|---|
| Cash | 1,250,000 | |
| Capital grants and contributions | | 1,250,000 |

*Transaction JE07.32*—Other operating revenues earned and received during the year amounted to $10,000 and other operating expenses incurred and paid during the year amounted to $5,000:

| Accounts | Debit | Credit |
|---|---|---|
| Cash | 10,000 | |
| Operating revenues—miscellaneous | | 10,000 |
| Operating expenses—miscellaneous | 5,000 | |
| Cash | | 5,000 |

*Transaction JE07.33*—Additional temporary investments of $15,000 were purchased during the year:

| Accounts | Debit | Credit |
|---|---|---|
| Temporary investments | 15,000 | |
| Cash | | 15,000 |

*Transaction JE07.34*—A loan of $2,000,000 was made to the General Fund:

| Accounts | Debit | Credit |
|---|---|---|
| Due from other funds—General Fund | 2,000,000 | |
| Cash | | 2,000,000 |

## 7-20 Proprietary Funds

***Transaction JE07.35***—During the year, the Communications and Technology Support Center (Internal Service Fund) billed the CUA $220,000 for services performed. The CUA made payments of $200,000:

| Accounts | Debit | Credit |
|---|---|---|
| Contractual services expenses | 220,000 | |
| Cash | | 200,000 |
| Due to other funds—Internal Service Fund—Communications and Technology Support Center | | 20,000 |

***Transaction JE07.36***—A loan of $100,000 was made to another government:

| Accounts | Debit | Credit |
|---|---|---|
| Due from other governments | 100,000 | |
| Cash | | 100,000 |

***Transaction JE07.37***—Supplies of $75,000 were on hand at the end of the year:

| Accounts | Debit | Credit |
|---|---|---|
| Inventories | 21,000 | |
| Other supplies and expenses | | 21,000 |

After the transactions for the year are posted, the year-end trial balance (June 30, 20X1) for the CUA appears as follows:

| Accounts | Adjusted Trial Balance Debits | Credits |
|---|---|---|
| Cash | $ 230,000 | |
| Interest receivable | 50,000 | |
| Accounts receivable | 7,920,000 | |
| Allowance for doubtful accounts | | $ 370,000 |
| Temporary investments | 55,000 | |
| Due from other funds—General Fund | 2,000,000 | |
| Due from other governments | 100,000 | |
| Supplies | 75,000 | |
| Construction in progress | 200,000 | |
| Land and improvements | 5,200,000 | |
| Distribution and collection systems | 146,300,000 | |
| Accumulated depreciation—distribution and collection systems | | 142,200,000 |
| Buildings | 14,450,000 | |

|                                      | Adjusted Trial Balance |             |
| ------------------------------------ | ----------: | ----------: |
| Accounts                             | Debits      | Credits     |
| Accumulated depreciation—buildings   |             | 10,945,000  |
| Equipment                            | 4,600,000   |             |
| Accumulated depreciation—equipment   |             | 500,000     |
| Vehicles                             | 1,660,000   |             |
| Accumulated depreciation—vehicles    |             | 750,000     |
| Accounts payable and accrued expenses |            | 4,300,000   |
| Due to other funds—Internal Service Fund—Communications and Technology Support Center | | 35,000 |
| Compensated absences liability       |             | 84,000      |
| Claims and judgements payable        |             | 229,000     |
| Notes payable                        |             | 330,000     |
| Bonds payable                        |             | 7,700,000   |
| Net assets                           |             | 16,019,000  |
| Charges for services                 |             | 36,000,000  |
| Interest and investment revenue      |             | 400,000     |
| Capital grants and contributions     |             | 1,250,000   |
| Operating revenues—miscellaneous     |             | 10,000      |
| Personal services expenses           | 22,022,000  |             |
| Contractual services expenses        | 11,220,000  |             |
| Repairs and maintenance expenses     | 700,000     |             |
| Other supplies and expenses          | 729,000     |             |
| Insurance claims and expenses        | 21,000      |             |
| Depreciation expense                 | 3,025,000   |             |
| Interest expense                     | 450,000     |             |
| Operating expenses—miscellaneous     | 5,000       |             |
| Miscellaneous expenses—loss on sale of assets | 110,000 |          |
| Totals                               | $121,122,000 | $121,122,000 |

The worksheet that summarizes the foregoing journal entries for the CUA's year-end trial balance is presented in Appendix 7B.

## Centerville Parking Authority

The Centerville Parking Authority (CPA) owns and manages parking garages and parking lots in downtown Centerville. Its trial balance for the beginning of the fiscal year is as follows:

## Proprietary Funds

| Accounts | Adjusted Trial Balance Debits | Credits |
|---|---|---|
| Cash | $ 150,000 | |
| Interest receivable | 1,000 | |
| Temporary investments | | |
| Supplies | 20,000 | |
| Construction in progress | 150,000 | |
| Land and improvements | 3,000,000 | |
| Buildings | 2,400,000 | |
| Accumulated depreciation—buildings | | $ 1,300,000 |
| Equipment | 120,000 | |
| Accumulated depreciation—equipment | | 75,000 |
| Vehicles | 90,000 | |
| Accumulated depreciation—vehicles | | 32,000 |
| Accounts payable and accrued expenses | | 4,000 |
| Due to other funds—Communications and Technology Center | | 7,000 |
| Compensated absences liability | | 4,000 |
| Claims and judgements payable | | 5,000 |
| Notes payable | | 10,000 |
| Bonds payable | | 500,000 |
| Net assets | | 3,994,000 |
| Totals | $5,931,000 | $5,931,000 |

This section presents illustrative transactions and entries for the CPA during the fiscal year ended June 30, 20X1.

*Transaction JE07.38*—Accounts payable and accrued expenses of $4,000 from the previous year were paid:

| Accounts | Debit | Credit |
|---|---|---|
| Accounts payable and accrued expenses | 4,000 | |
| Cash | | 4,000 |

*Transaction JE07.39*—Accrued interest receivable from the previous year was received:

| Accounts | Debit | Credit |
|---|---|---|
| Cash | 1,000 | |
| Interest receivable | | 1,000 |

*Transaction JE07.40*—During the year, parking revenue collected from customers totaled $1,500,000:

| Accounts | Debit | Credit |
|---|---|---|
| Cash | 1,500,000 | |
|     Charges for services | | 1,500,000 |

*Transaction JE07.41*—The following operating expenses were incurred during the year, of which $5,700,000 was paid in cash:

| | |
|---|---|
| Personal services | $5,400,000 |
| Contractual services | 300,000 |
| Repairs and maintenance | 50,000 |
| Other supplies and expenses | 40,000 |
| Total | $5,790,000 |

| Accounts | Debit | Credit |
|---|---|---|
| Personal services expenses | 5,400,000 | |
| Contractual services expenses | 300,000 | |
| Repairs and maintenance expenses | 50,000 | |
| Other supplies and expenses | 40,000 | |
|     Cash | | 5,700,000 |
|     Accounts payable and accrued expenses | | 90,000 |

*Transaction JE07.42*—During the year, interest and investment revenue of $10,000 was earned, of which $7,000 was received in cash:

| Accounts | Debit | Credit |
|---|---|---|
| Cash | 7,000 | |
| Interest receivable | 3,000 | |
|     Interest and investment revenue | | 10,000 |

*Transaction JE07.43*—The following capital assets were purchased during the year for cash:

| | |
|---|---|
| Land and improvements | $120,000 |
| Equipment | 30,000 |
| Vehicles | 25,000 |
| Total | $175,000 |

## 7-24 Proprietary Funds

| Accounts | Debit | Credit |
|---|---|---|
| Land and improvements | 120,000 | |
| Equipment | 30,000 | |
| Vehicles | 25,000 | |
| Cash | | 175,000 |

**Transaction JE07.44**—During the year, a parking lot under construction (construction in progress) was completed at a total cost of $160,000 (after incurring additional costs of $10,000 for the current year) and new construction costs of $15,000 were incurred on a new unfinished project:

| Accounts | Debit | Credit |
|---|---|---|
| Construction in progress | 10,000 | |
| Cash | | 10,000 |
| | | |
| Land and land improvements | 160,000 | |
| Construction in progress | | 160,000 |
| | | |
| Construction in progress | 15,000 | |
| Cash | | 15,000 |

**Transaction JE07.45**—The following assets were sold or abandoned during the year. The land and improvements represent a parking lot that was sold for $5,000,000 to a local real estate developer. The other capital assets were sold for $5,000:

| | Original Cost | Accumulated Depreciation |
|---|---|---|
| Land and improvements | $1,500,000 | |
| Equipment | 10,000 | 7,000 |
| Vehicles | 13,000 | 12,000 |
| Total | $ 190,000 | $19,000 |

| Accounts | Debit | Credit |
|---|---|---|
| Cash | 5,005,000 | |
| Accumulated depreciation—equipment | 7,000 | |
| Accumulated depreciation—vehicles | 12,000 | |
|    Land and improvements | | 1,500,000 |
|    Equipment | | 10,000 |
|    Vehicles | | 13,000 |
|    Miscellaneous revenue—gain on sale of assets | | 1,000 |
|    Special item—gain on sale of parking lot | | 3,500,000 |

▶ **NEW STANDARD:** GASB-34 defines a "special item" as "significant transactions or other events within the control of management that are either unusual in nature or infrequent in occurrence." Special items should be reported separately and before extraordinary items. If a significant transaction or other event occurs but is not within the control of management and that item is either unusual or infrequent, the item is not reported as a special item, but the nature of the item must be described in a note to the financial statements (GASB-34, par. 56).

*Transaction JE07.46*—During the year, a portion of the notes payable ($10,000) and interest expense of $27,000 were paid. In addition, notes payable of $30,000 were issued during the year:

| Accounts | Debit | Credit |
|---|---|---|
| Notes Payable | 10,000 | |
| Interest expense | 27,000 | |
| Cash | | 37,000 |

| Accounts | Debit | Credit |
|---|---|---|
| Cash | 30,000 | |
| Notes Payable | | 30,000 |

*Transaction JE07.47*—Compensated absences of $1,000 were paid during the year and additional costs of $2,000 were accrued:

| Accounts | Debit | Credit |
|---|---|---|
| Personal services expenses | 2,000 | |
| Compensated absences liability | | 1,000 |
| Cash | | 1,000 |

*Transaction JE07.48*—Claims and judgements of $1,000 were paid during the year and additional costs of $3,000 were accrued:

| Accounts | Debit | Credit |
|---|---|---|
| Insurance claims and expenses | 3,000 | |
| Claims and judgements payable | | 2,000 |
| Cash | | 1,000 |

*Transaction JE07.49*—Depreciation expense recognized during the year was as follows:

| | |
|---|---|
| Buildings | $90,000 |
| Equipment | 15,000 |
| Vehicles | 12,000 |
| Total | $117,000 |

| Accounts | Debit | Credit |
|---|---|---|
| Depreciation expense | 117,000 | |
|   Accumulated depreciation—buildings | | 90,000 |
|   Accumulated depreciation—equipment | | 15,000 |
|   Accumulated depreciation—vehicles | | 12,000 |

*Transaction JE07.50*—Other operating revenues earned and received during the year amounted to $22,000 and other operating expenses incurred and paid during the year amounted to $3,000:

| Accounts | Debit | Credit |
|---|---|---|
| Cash | 22,000 | |
|   Operating revenues—miscellaneous | | 22,000 |
| Operating expenses—miscellaneous | 3,000 | |
|   Cash | | 3,000 |

*Transaction JE07.51*—Additional temporary investments of $5,000 were purchased during the year:

| Accounts | Debit | Credit |
|---|---|---|
| Temporary investments | 5,000 | |
|   Cash | | 5,000 |

*Transaction JE07.52*—A transfer of $90,000 was received from the General Fund:

| Accounts | Debit | Credit |
|---|---|---|
| Cash | 90,000 | |
|   Transfers in—General Fund | | 90,000 |

*Transaction JE07.53*—During the year, the Communications and Technology Support Center (Internal Service Fund) billed the CPA $100,000 for services performed. The CPA made payments of $90,000:

| Accounts | Debit | Credit |
|---|---|---|
| Contractual services expenses | 100,000 | |
|   Cash | | 90,000 |
|   Due to other funds—Internal Service Fund—Communications and Technology Support Center | | 10,000 |

*Transaction JE07.54*—Supplies of $24,000 were on hand at the end of the year:

| Accounts | Debit | Credit |
|---|---|---|
| Inventories | 4,000 | |
|    Other supplies and expenses | | 4,000 |

After the transactions for the year are posted, the year-end trial balance (June 30, 20X1) for the CPA appears as follows:

| Accounts | Adjusted Trial Balance Debits | Credits |
|---|---|---|
| Cash | $ 764,000 | |
| Interest receivable | 3,000 | |
| Temporary investments | 5,000 | |
| Supplies | 24,000 | |
| Construction in progress | 15,000 | |
| Land and improvements | 1,780,000 | |
| Buildings | 2,400,000 | |
| Accumulated depreciation—buildings | | $1,390,000 |
| Equipment | 140,000 | |
| Accumulated depreciation—equipment | | 83,000 |
| Vehicles | 102,000 | |
| Accumulated depreciation—vehicles | | 32,000 |
| Accounts payable and accrued expenses | | 90,000 |
| Due to other funds—Communications and Technology Center | | 17,000 |
| Compensated absences liability | | 5,000 |
| Claims and judgements payable | | 7,000 |
| Notes payable | | 30,000 |
| Bonds payable | | 500,000 |
| Net assets | | 3,994,000 |
| Charges for services | | 1,500,000 |
| Interest and investment revenue | | 10,000 |
| Miscellaneous revenue—gain on sale of assets | | 1,000 |
| Operating revenues—miscellaneous | | 22,000 |
| Personal services expenses | 5,402,000 | |
| Contractual services expenses | 400,000 | |
| Repairs and maintenance expenses | 50,000 | |
| Other supplies and expenses | 36,000 | |

|  | Adjusted Trial Balance | |
| --- | --- | --- |
| Accounts | Debits | Credits |
| Insurance claims and expenses | 3,000 | |
| Depreciation expense | 117,000 | |
| Interest expense | 27,000 | |
| Operating expenses—miscellaneous | 3,000 | |
| Special item—gain on sale of parking lot | | 3,500,000 |
| Transfers out—General Fund | | 90,000 |
| Totals | $11,271,000 | $11,271,000 |

The worksheet that summarizes the foregoing journal entries for the CPA's year-end trial balance is presented in Appendix 7C.

## Centerville Municipal Airport

The Centerville Municipal Airport (CMA) is a regional airport that serves the City and several smaller communities in the three adjacent counties. The fund's balance for the beginning of the fiscal year is as follows:

|  | Trial Balance | |
| --- | --- | --- |
| Accounts | Debits | Credits |
| Cash | $ 1,150,000 | |
| Interest receivable | 55,000 | |
| Temporary investments | 10,000,000 | |
| Accounts receivable | 5,000,000 | |
| Due from other funds—General Fund | | |
| Due from other governments | | |
| Supplies | 50,000 | |
| Construction in progress | 25,000,000 | |
| Land and improvements | 10,000,000 | |
| Runways and tarmacs | 27,000,000 | |
| Accumulated depreciation—runways and tarmacs | | $ 6,500,000 |
| Buildings | 30,000,000 | |
| Accumulated depreciation—buildings | | 6,500,000 |
| Equipment | 7,000,000 | |
| Accumulated depreciation—equipment | | 4,300,000 |
| Vehicles | 2,300,000 | |
| Accumulated depreciation—vehicles | | 1,900,000 |
| Accounts payable and accrued expenses | | 3,400,000 |

| Accounts | Trial Balance Debits | Trial Balance Credits |
|---|---|---|
| Due to other funds—Communications and Technology Center | | 25,000 |
| Due to other funds—Internal Service Fund—Special Services Support Center | | 77,000 |
| Compensated absences liability | | 125,000 |
| Claims and judgements payable | | 120,000 |
| Notes payable | | 4,500,000 |
| Revenue bonds payable—Terminal A | | 12,000,000 |
| Revenue bonds payable—Terminal B | | 4,500,000 |
| Net assets | | 73,608,000 |
| Totals | $117,555,000 | $117,555,000 |

This section presents illustrative transactions and entries for the CMA during the fiscal year ended June 30, 20X1.

*Transaction JE07.55*—Accounts payable and accrued expenses of $3,400,000 from the previous year were paid:

| Accounts | Debit | Credit |
|---|---|---|
| Accounts payable and accrued expenses | 3,400,000 | |
| Cash | | 3,400,000 |

*Transaction JE07.56*—Accrued interest receivable from the previous year was received:

| Accounts | Debit | Credit |
|---|---|---|
| Cash | 55,000 | |
| Interest receivable | | 55,000 |

*Transaction JE07.57*—During the year, airlines were billed $175,000,000 for services provided and cash collections on account amounted to $165,000,000. In addition, during the year lessees were billed for $52,000,000 and cash collections on account amounted to $49,000,000. These rental revenues are used as security for revenue bonds for Terminal A ($30,000,000) and Terminal B ($22,000,000):

| Accounts | Debit | Credit |
|---|---|---|
| Cash | 165,000,000 | |
| Accounts receivable | 10,000,000 | |
| Charges for services | | 175,000,000 |

## 7-30 Proprietary Funds

| Accounts | Debit | Credit |
|---|---|---|
| Cash | 49,000,000 | |
| Accounts receivable | 3,000,000 | |
|   Charges for services—rental income—security for Terminal A revenue bonds | | 30,000,000 |
|   Charges for services—rental income—security for Terminal B revenue bonds | | 22,000,000 |

***Transaction JE07.58***—The following operating expenses were incurred during the year, of which $191,000,000 were paid in cash:

| | |
|---|---|
| Personal services | $161,000,000 |
| Contractual services | 30,000,000 |
| Repairs and maintenance | 2,100,000 |
| Other supplies and expenses | 1,800,000 |
| Total | $194,900,000 |

| Accounts | Debit | Credit |
|---|---|---|
| Personal services expenses | 161,000,000 | |
| Contractual services expenses | 30,000,000 | |
| Repairs and maintenance expenses | 2,100,000 | |
| Other supplies and expenses | 1,800,000 | |
|   Cash | | 191,000,000 |
|   Accounts payable and accrued expenses | | 3,900,000 |

***Transaction JE07.59***—During the year, interest and investment revenue of $1,200,000 was earned, of which $1,000,000 was received in cash:

| Accounts | Debit | Credit |
|---|---|---|
| Cash | 1,000,000 | |
| Interest receivable | 200,000 | |
|   Interest and investment revenue | | 1,200,000 |

***Transaction JE07.60***—The following capital assets were purchased during the year for cash:

| | |
|---|---|
| Land and improvements | $3,200,000 |
| Runways and tarmac | 500,000 |
| Equipment | 2,300,000 |
| Vehicles | 1,100,000 |
| Total | $7,100,000 |

| Accounts | Debit | Credit |
|---|---|---|
| Land and improvements | 3,200,000 | |
| Runways and tarmac | 500,000 | |
| Equipment | 2,300,000 | |
| Vehicles | 1,100,000 | |
| Cash | | 7,100,000 |

***Transaction JE07.61***—During the year, a building under construction (construction in progress) was completed at a cost of $3,200,000 (after incurring additional costs of $400,000) and new construction costs of $1,300,000 were incurred on a new unfinished project:

| Accounts | Debit | Credit |
|---|---|---|
| Construction in progress | 400,000 | |
| Cash | | 400,000 |
| | | |
| Building | 3,200,0000 | |
| Construction in progress | | 3,200,0000 |
| | | |
| Construction in progress | 1,300,000 | |
| Cash | | 1,300,000 |

***Transaction JE07.62***—The following assets were sold or abandoned during the year. The cash proceeds were $420,000:

| | Original Cost | Accumulated Depreciation |
|---|---|---|
| Equipment | $2,100,000 | $1,600,000 |
| Vehicles | 900,000 | 715,000 |
| Total | $3,000,000 | $2,315,000 |

| Accounts | Debit | Credit |
|---|---|---|
| Cash | 420,000 | |
| Miscellaneous expenses (loss on sale of assets) | 265,000 | |
| Accumulated depreciation—equipment | 1,600,000 | |
| Accumulated depreciation—vehicles | 715,000 | |
| Equipment | | 2,100,000 |
| Vehicles | | 900,000 |

***Transaction JE07.63***—During the year, additional notes payable of $3,200,000 were issued and revenue bonds related to Terminal A ($2,000,000) and Terminal B ($500,000) were paid off. Interest expense of $1,220,000 was paid:

**7-32** *Proprietary Funds*

| Accounts | Debit | Credit |
|---|---|---|
| Cash | 3,200,000 | |
|   Notes payable | | 3,200,000 |
| | | |
| Revenue bonds payable—Terminal A | 2,000,000 | |
| Revenue bonds payable—Terminal B | 500,000 | |
| Interest expense | 1,220,000 | |
|   Cash | | 3,720,000 |

***Transaction JE07.64***—Compensated absences of $17,000 were paid during the year and additional costs of $25,000 were accrued:

| Accounts | Debit | Credit |
|---|---|---|
| Personal services expenses | 25,000 | |
|   Compensated absences liability | | 8,000 |
|   Cash | | 17,000 |

***Transaction JE07.65***—Claims and judgements of $25,000 were paid during the year and additional costs of $100,000 were accrued:

| Accounts | Debit | Credit |
|---|---|---|
| Insurance claims and expenses | 100,000 | |
|   Claims and judgements payable | | 75,000 |
|   Cash | | 25,000 |

***Transaction JE07.66***—Depreciation expense recognized during the year was as follows:

| | |
|---|---|
| Runways and tarmacs | $1,300,000 |
| Buildings | 1,200,000 |
| Equipment | 450,000 |
| Vehicles | 420,000 |
| Total | $3,370,000 |

| Accounts | Debit | Credit |
|---|---|---|
| Depreciation expense | 3,370,000 | |
|   Accumulated depreciation—runways and tarmacs | | 1,300,000 |
|   Accumulated depreciation—buildings | | 1,200,000 |
|   Accumulated depreciation—equipment | | 450,000 |
|   Accumulated depreciation—vehicles | | 420,000 |

*Transaction JE07.67*—A capital grant of $2,000,000 was authorized by the state government. As of the end of the year, $1,700,000 of the amount had been collected:

| Accounts | Debit | Credit |
|---|---|---|
| Cash | 1,700,000 | |
| Due from other governments | 300,000 | |
|     Capital grants and contributions | | 2,000,000 |

*Transaction JE07.68*—Other operating revenues earned and received during the year amounted to $60,000 and other operating expenses incurred and paid during the year amounted to $70,000:

| Accounts | Debit | Credit |
|---|---|---|
| Cash | 60,000 | |
|     Operating revenues—miscellaneous | | 60,000 |
| Operating expenses—miscellaneous | 70,000 | |
|     Cash | | 70,000 |

*Transaction JE07.69*—Additional temporary investments of $50,000 were purchased during the year:

| Accounts | Debit | Credit |
|---|---|---|
| Temporary investments | 50,000 | |
|     Cash | | 50,000 |

*Transaction JE07.70*—A loan of $400,000 was made to the General Fund:

| Accounts | Debit | Credit |
|---|---|---|
| Due from other funds—General Fund | 400,000 | |
|     Cash | | 400,000 |

*Transaction JE07.71*—During the year, the Communications and Technology Support Center (Internal Service Fund) billed the CMA $600,000 for services performed. The CMA made payments of $540,000:

| Accounts | Debit | Credit |
|---|---|---|
| Contractual services expenses | 600,000 | |
|     Cash | | 540,000 |
|     Due to other funds—Internal Service Fund—Communications and Technology Support Center | | 60,000 |

## 7-34  Proprietary Funds

*Transaction JE07.72*—During the year, the Special Services Support Center (Internal Service Fund) billed the CMA $2,950,000 for services performed. The CMA made payments of $2,600,000:

| Accounts | Debit | Credit |
|---|---|---|
| Contractual services expenses | 2,950,000 | |
| Cash | | 2,600,000 |
| Due to other funds—Internal Service Fund—Special Services Support Center | | 350,000 |

*Transaction JE07.73*—Supplies of $55,000 were on hand at the end of the year:

| Accounts | Debit | Credit |
|---|---|---|
| Inventories | 5,000 | |
| Other supplies and expenses | | 5,000 |

After the transactions for the year are posted, the year-end trial balance (June 30, 20X1) for the Centerville Municipal Airport appears as follows:

| Accounts | Adjusted Trial Balance Debits | Credits |
|---|---|---|
| Cash | $10,963,000 | |
| Interest receivable | 200,000 | |
| Temporary investments | 10,050,000 | |
| Accounts receivable | 18,000,000 | |
| Due from other funds—General Fund | 400,000 | |
| Due from other governments | 300,000 | |
| Supplies | 55,000 | |
| Construction in progress | 23,500,000 | |
| Land and improvements | 13,200,000 | |
| Runways and tarmacs | 27,500,000 | |
| Accumulated depreciation—runways and tarmacs | | $ 7,800,000 |
| Buildings | 33,200,000 | |
| Accumulated depreciation—buildings | | 7,700,000 |
| Equipment | 7,200,000 | |
| Accumulated depreciation—equipment | | 3,150,000 |
| Vehicles | 2,500,000 | |
| Accumulated depreciation—vehicles | | 1,605,000 |
| Accounts payable and accrued expenses | | 3,900,000 |

|  | Adjusted Trial Balance | |
| --- | --- | --- |
| Accounts | Debits | Credits |
| Due to other funds—Communications and Technology Center | | 85,000 |
| Due to other funds—Internal Service Fund—Special Services Support Center | | 427,000 |
| Compensated absences liability | | 133,000 |
| Claims and judgements payable | | 195,000 |
| Notes payable | | 7,700,000 |
| Revenue bonds payable—Terminal A | | 10,000,000 |
| Revenue bonds payable—Terminal B | | 4,000,000 |
| Net assets | | 73,608,000 |
| Charges for services | | 175,000,000 |
| Charges for services—rental income—security for Terminal A revenue bonds | | 30,000,000 |
| Charges for services—rental income—security for Terminal B revenue bonds | | 22,000,000 |
| Interest and investment revenue | | 1,200,000 |
| Capital grants and contributions | | 2,000,000 |
| Operating revenues—miscellaneous | | 60,000 |
| Personal services expenses | 161,025,000 | |
| Contractual services expenses | 33,550,000 | |
| Repairs and maintenance expenses | 2,100,000 | |
| Other supplies and expenses | 1,795,000 | |
| Insurance claims and expenses | 100,000 | |
| Depreciation expense | 3,370,000 | |
| Interest expense | 1,220,000 | |
| Operating expenses—miscellaneous | 70,000 | |
| Miscellaneous expenses—loss on sale of assets | 265,000 | |
| Totals | $350,563,000 | $350,563,000 |

The worksheet that summarizes the foregoing journal entries for the CMA's year-end trial balance is presented in Appendix 7D.

## FUND FINANCIAL STATEMENTS

At the fund financial statement level, Enterprise Funds are presented in the proprietary funds along with the Internal Service Funds. Proprietary funds prepare a statement of net assets (or balance sheet), statement of revenues, expenses, and changes in fund net assets (or fund equity) and statement of cash flows. Based on the adjusted trial balances created above, the following financial statements reflect the balances and activities of all the Enterprise Funds.

> ■ **CONTINUING STANDARD:** An Enterprise Fund's statement of net assets can continue to be presented based on the guidance established in Chapter 3 of ARB-43 (Restatement and Revision of Accounting Research Bulletins). The statement of net assets may be presented in either one of the following formats: (1) net assets format, where assets less liabilities equal net assets or (2) balance sheet format, where assets equal liabilities plus net assets (GASB-34, pars. 97 and 98).

In the preparation of the statement of net assets, notes payable were assumed to be associated with the acquisition of capital assets and the current and noncurrent portions of certain liabilities were assumed. Also, certain assumptions were made in determining the amount of restricted net assets. (See Appendix 7E.)

**Enterprise Funds**
**Statement of Net Assets**
**June 30, 20X1**

|  | Centerville Toll Bridge | Centerville Utilities Authority | Centerville Parking Authority | Centerville Municipal Airport | Total |
|---|---|---|---|---|---|
| **ASSETS** | | | | | |
| Current assets: | | | | | |
| Cash | $ 739,500 | $ 230,000 | $ 764,000 | $10,963,000 | $12,696,500 |
| Interest receivable | 3,000 | 50,000 | 3,000 | 200,000 | 256,000 |
| Accounts receivable (net) | — | 7,550,000 | — | 18,000,000 | 25,550,000 |
| Due from other funds | — | 2,000,000 | — | 400,000 | 2,400,000 |
| Due from other governments | — | 100,000 | — | 300,000 | 400,000 |
| Temporary investments | 58,000 | 55,000 | 5,000 | 10,050,000 | 10,168,000 |
| Supplies | 32,000 | 75,000 | 24,000 | 55,000 | 186,000 |
| Total current assets | 832,500 | 10,060,000 | 796,000 | 39,968,000 | 51,656,500 |
| Noncurrent assets: | | | | | |
| Construction in progress | 70,000 | 200,000 | 15,000 | 23,500,000 | 23,785,000 |
| Land and improvements | 140,000 | 5,200,000 | 1,780,000 | 13,200,000 | 20,320,000 |
| Superstructure | 1,400,000 | — | — | — | 1,400,000 |

|  | Centerville Toll Bridge | Centerville Utilities Authority | Centerville Parking Authority | Centerville Municipal Airport | Total |
|---|---|---|---|---|---|
| Distribution and collection systems | — | 46,300,000 | — | — | 46,300,000 |
| Runways and tarmacs | — | — | — | 27,500,000 | 27,500,000 |
| Buildings | 330,000 | 14,450,000 | 2,400,000 | 33,200,000 | 50,380,000 |
| Equipment | 55,000 | 4,600,000 | 140,000 | 7,200,000 | 11,995,000 |
| Vehicles | 835,000 | 1,660,000 | 102,000 | 2,500,000 | 5,097,000 |
| Less accumulated depreciation | (1,257,000) | (54,395,000) | (1,505,000) | (20,255,000) | (77,412,000) |
| Total noncurrent assets | 1,573,000 | 18,015,000 | 2,932,000 | 86,845,000 | 109,365,000 |
| Total assets | $ 2,405,500 | $28,075,000 | $3,728,000 | $126,813,000 | $161,021,500 |

**LIABILITIES**

Current liabilities:

|  | Centerville Toll Bridge | Centerville Utilities Authority | Centerville Parking Authority | Centerville Municipal Airport | Total |
|---|---|---|---|---|---|
| Accounts payable and accrued expenses | $ 50,000 | $ 4,300,000 | $ 90,000 | $ 3,900,000 | $ 8,340,000 |
| Due to other funds | 18,000 | 35,000 | 17,000 | 512,000 | 582,000 |
| Compensated absences | 3,000 | 21,000 | 2,000 | 15,000 | 41,000 |
| Claims and judgements | 5,000 | 17,000 | 4,000 | 25,000 | 51,000 |
| Notes payable | 10,000 | 70,000 | 30,000 |  | 110,000 |
| Revenue bonds—Terminal A | — | — | — | 2,000,000 | 2,000,000 |
| Revenue bonds—Terminal B | — | — | — | 500,000 | 500,000 |
| Bonds payable | 20,000 | 850,000 | — | — | 870,000 |
| Total current liabilities | 106,000 | 5,293,000 | 143,000 | 6,952,000 | 12,494,000 |

Noncurrent liabilities:

|  | Centerville Toll Bridge | Centerville Utilities Authority | Centerville Parking Authority | Centerville Municipal Airport | Total |
|---|---|---|---|---|---|
| Compensated absences | 5,000 | 63,000 | 3,000 | 118,000 | 189,000 |
| Claims and judgments | 22,000 | 212,000 | 3,000 | 170,000 | 407,000 |
| Notes payable | 20,000 | 260,000 | — | 7,700,000 | 7,980,000 |
| Revenue bonds—Terminal A | — | — | — | 8,000,000 | 8,000,000 |
| Revenue bonds—Terminal B | — | — | — | 3,500,000 | 3,500,000 |
| Bonds payable | 60,000 | 6,850,000 | 500,000 | — | 7,410,000 |
| Total noncurrent liabilities | 107,000 | 7,385,000 | 506,000 | 19,488,000 | 27,486,000 |
| Total liabilities | $ 213,000 | $12,678,000 | $ 649,000 | $ 26,440,000 | $ 39,980,000 |

**7-38** *Proprietary Funds*

|  | Centerville Toll Bridge | Centerville Utilities Authority | Centerville Parking Authority | Centerville Municipal Airport | Total |
|---|---|---|---|---|---|
| **NET ASSETS** | | | | | |
| Invested in capital assets, net of related debt | $1,463,000 | $ 9,985,000 | $2,402,000 | $ 69,145,000 | $ 82,995,000 |
| Restricted | 622,000 | 5,250,000 | 595,000 | 30,895,000 | 37,362,000 |
| Unrestricted | 107,500 | 162,000 | 82,000 | 333,000 | 684,500 |
| Total net assets | $2,192,500 | $15,397,000 | $3,079,000 | $100,373,000 | $121,041,500 |

Enterprise Funds
Statement of Revenues, Expenses, and Changes in Fund Net Assets
For the Year Ended June 30, 20X1

|  | Centerville Toll Bridge | Centerville Utilities Authority | Centerville Parking Authority | Centerville Municipal Airport | Total |
|---|---|---|---|---|---|
| **OPERATING REVENUES** | | | | | |
| Charges for services | $4,750,000 | $36,000,000 | $1,500,000 | $175,000,000 | 217,250,000 |
| Charges for services—rental income—security for Terminal A revenue bonds | — | — | — | 30,000,000 | 30,000,000 |
| Charges for services—rental income—security for Terminal B revenue bonds | — | — | — | 22,000,000 | 22,000,000 |
| Miscellaneous | 20,000 | 10,000 | 22,000 | 60,000 | 112,000 |
| Total operating revenues | 4,770,000 | 36,010,000 | 1,522,000 | 227,060,000 | 269,362,000 |
| **OPERATING EXPENSES** | | | | | |
| Personal services | 2,402,000 | 22,022,000 | 5,402,000 | 161,025,000 | 190,851,000 |
| Contractual services | 1,280,000 | 11,220,000 | 400,000 | 33,550,000 | 46,450,000 |
| Repairs and maintenance | 400,000 | 700,000 | 50,000 | 2,100,000 | 3,250,000 |
| Other supplies and expenses | 194,000 | 729,000 | 36,000 | 1,795,000 | 2,754,000 |
| Insurance claims and expenses | 10,000 | 21,000 | 3,000 | 100,000 | 134,000 |
| Depreciation | 339,000 | 3,025,000 | 117,000 | 3,370,000 | 6,851,000 |

|  | Centerville Toll Bridge | Centerville Utilities Authority | Centerville Parking Authority | Centerville Municipal Airport | Total |
|---|---|---|---|---|---|
| Miscellaneous | 30,000 | 5,000 | 3,000 | 70,000 | 108,000 |
| Total operating expenses | 4,655,000 | 37,722,000 | 6,011,000 | 202,010,000 | 250,398,000 |
| Operating income (loss) | 115,000 | (1,712,000) | (4,489,000) | 25,050,000 | 18,964,000 |

**NONOPERATING REVENUES (EXPENSES)**

|  |  |  |  |  |  |
|---|---|---|---|---|---|
| Interest and investment revenue | 30,000 | 400,000 | 10,000 | 1,200,000 | 1,640,000 |
| Interest | (6,000) | (450,000) | (27,000) | (1,220,000) | (1,703,000) |
| Operating grants and contributions | 100,000 | — | — | — | 100,000 |
| Miscellaneous | 7,000 | (110,000) | (1,000) | (265,000) | (367,000) |
| Total nonoperating revenue (expenses) | 131,000 | (160,000) | (16,000) | (285,000) | (330,000) |
| Income (loss) before capital contributions and transfers | 246,000 | (1,872,000) | (4,505,000) | 24,765,000 | 18,634,000 |
| Capital contributions | 250,000 | 1,250,000 | — | 2,000,000 | 3,500,000 |
| Transfers in | 50,000 | — | 90,000 | — | 140,000 |
| Special item—gain on sale of parking lot | — | — | 3,500,000 | — | 3,500,000 |
| Change in net assets | 546,000 | (622,000) | (915,000) | 26,765,000 | 25,774,000 |
| Total net assets—beginning | 1,646,500 | 16,019,000 | 3,994,000 | 73,608,000 | 95,267,500 |
| Total net assets—ending | $2,192,500 | $15,397,000 | $3,079,000 | $100,373,000 | $121,041,500 |

**Enterprise Funds**
**Statement of Cash Flows**
**For The Year Ended June 30, 20X1**

|  | Centerville Toll Bridge | Centerville Utilities Authority | Centerville Parking Authority | Centerville Municipal Airport | Total |
|---|---|---|---|---|---|
| **CASH FLOWS FROM OPERATING ACTIVITIES** |  |  |  |  |  |
| Receipts from customers | $4,750,000 | $34,000,000 | $1,500,000 | $214,000,000 | $254,250,000 |
| Payments to suppliers | (1,806,000) | (12,112,000) | (345,000) | (36,425,000) | (50,688,000) |

**7-40** *Proprietary Funds*

|  | Centerville Toll Bridge | Centerville Utilities Authority | Centerville Parking Authority | Centerville Municipal Airport | Total |
|---|---|---|---|---|---|
| Payments to employees | (2,371,000) | (19,013,000) | (5,361,000) | (158,017,000) | (184,762,000) |
| Internal activity—payments to other funds | (66,000) | (200,000) | (90,000) | (3,140,000) | (3,496,000) |
| Other receipts (payments) | (18,000) | 5,000 | 19,000 | (10,000) | (4,000) |
| Net cash provided by operating activities | 489,000 | 2,680,000 | (4,277,000) | 16,408,000 | 15,300,000 |

**CASH FLOWS FROM NONCAPITAL FINANCING ACTIVITIES**

|  |  |  |  |  |  |
|---|---|---|---|---|---|
| Subsidies and transfers from (to) other funds and state government | 150,000 | — | 90,000 | — | 240,000 |

**CASH FLOWS FROM CAPITAL AND RELATED FINANCING ACTIVITIES**

|  |  |  |  |  |  |
|---|---|---|---|---|---|
| Proceeds from the issuance of capital debt | — | 2,120,000 | — | 3,200,000 | 5,320,000 |
| Capital contributions | 250,000 | 1,250,000 | 30,000 | 1,700,000 | 3,230,000 |
| Acquisitions of capital assets | (390,000) | (5,350,000) | (200,000) | (8,800,000) | (14,740,000) |
| Proceeds from sale of capital assets | 50,000) | 500,000 | 5,005,000 | 420,000 | 5,975,000 |
| Principal paid on capital debt | (30,000) | (1,740,000) | (10,000) | (2,500,000) | (4,280,000) |
| Interest paid on capital debt | (6,000) | (450,000) | (27,000) | (1,220,000) | (1,703,000) |
| Net cash (used) by capital and related financing activities | (126,000) | (3,670,000) | 4,798,000 | (7,200,000) | (6,198,000) |

**CASH FLOWS FROM INVESTING ACTIVITIES**

|  |  |  |  |  |  |
|---|---|---|---|---|---|
| Loans to other funds | — | (2,000,000) | — | (400,000) | (2,400,000) |
| Loans to other governments | — | (100,000) | — | — | (100,000) |

|  | Centerville Toll Bridge | Centerville Utilities Authority | Centerville Parking Authority | Centerville Municipal Airport | Total |
|---|---|---|---|---|---|
| Interest and dividends | 31,500 | 365,000 | 8,000 | 1,055,000 | 1,459,500 |
| Purchase of investments | (25,000) | (15,000) | (5,000) | (50,000) | (95,000) |
| Net cash provided (used) by investing activities | 6,500 | (1,750,000) | 3,000 | 605,000 | (1,135,500) |
| Net increase (decrease) in cash | 519,500 | (2,740,000) | 614,000 | 9,813,000 | 8,206,500 |
| Balances— beginning of year | 220,000 | 2,970,000 | 150,000 | 1,150,000 | 4,490,000 |
| Balances— end of year | $739,500 | $230,000 | $764,000 | $10,963,000 | $12,696,500 |

**Reconciliation of operating income (loss) to net cash provided (used) by operating activities:**

Operating income (loss)

| Adjustments: | $115,000 | $(1,712,000) | $(4,489,000) | $25,050,000 | $18,964,000 |
|---|---|---|---|---|---|
| Depreciation expense | 339,000 | 3,025,000 | 117,000 | 3,370,000 | 6,851,000 |
| Change in assets and liabilities: |  |  |  |  |  |
| Receivables, net |  | (1,850,000) |  | (13,000,000) | (14,850,000) |
| Inventories | (6,000) | (21,000) | (4,000) | (5,000) | (36,000) |
| Accounts and accrued liabilities | 41,000 | 3,238,000 | 99,000 | 993,000 | 4,371,000 |
| Net cash provided (used) by operating activities | $489,000 | $2,680,000 | $(4,277,000) | $16,408,000 | $15,300,000 |

▶ **NEW STANDARD:** As noted earlier in this chapter, an Enterprise Fund must use the direct method in displaying cash flows from operating activities.

The combined financial statements for the Enterprise Funds are used in Chapter 12 ("Developing Information for Fund Financial Statements").

## CONVERTING TO GOVERNMENT-WIDE FINANCIAL STATEMENTS

Government-wide financial statements are reported on the accrual basis of accounting. Generally, most governments will work from their proprietary fund financial statements and through the use of worksheet entries convert to accrual based financial statements. Because proprietary funds are presented on an accrual basis, often there is no need to make worksheet entries to convert the information from a fund basis to a government-wide basis; however, the residual balances and the activities of Internal Service Funds must be analyzed to determine how they are to be merged into the government-wide financial statements. This consolidation process is illustrated in Chapter 13 ("Developing Information for Government-Wide Financial Statements").

## APPENDIX 7A
## WORKSHEET FOR SUMMARIZING CURRENT TRANSACTIONS—CENTERVILLE TOLL BRIDGE

### WORKSHEET ENTRIES

| Accounts | Trial Balance Debits | Trial Balance Credits | Adjustments Debits | | Adjustments Credits | | Adjusted Trial Balance Debits | Adjusted Trial Balance Credits | Operating Statement Debits | Operating Statement Credits | Balance Sheet Debits | Balance Sheet Credits |
|---|---|---|---|---|---|---|---|---|---|---|---|---|
| Cash | 220,000 | — | JE07.02 | 4,500 | JE07.01 | 26,000 | 739,500 | — | — | — | 739,500 | — |
| | | — | JE07.03 | 4,750,000 | JE07.04 | 4,150,000 | | | | | | |
| | | — | JE07.05 | 27,000 | JE07.06 | 190,000 | | | | | | |
| | | — | JE07.08 | 50,000 | JE07.07 | 130,000 | | | | | | |
| | | — | JE07.13 | 350,000 | JE07.07 | 70,000 | | | | | | |
| | | — | JE07.14 | 20,000 | JE07.09 | 36,000 | | | | | | |
| | | — | JE07.16 | 50,000 | JE07.10 | 1,000 | | | | | | |
| | | — | | | JE07.11 | 8,000 | | | | | | |
| | | — | | | JE07.14 | 30,000 | | | | | | |
| | | — | | | JE07.15 | 25,000 | | | | | | |
| | | — | | | JE07.17 | 66,000 | | | | | | |
| Interest receivable | 4,500 | — | JE07.05 | 3,000 | JE07.02 | 4,500 | 3,000 | — | — | — | 3,000 | — |
| Temporary investments | 33,000 | — | JE07.15 | 25,000 | | — | 58,000 | — | — | — | 58,000 | — |
| Supplies | 26,000 | — | JE07.18 | 6,000 | | — | 32,000 | — | — | — | 32,000 | — |
| Construction in progress | 40,000 | — | JE07.07 | 130,000 | JE07.07 | 170,000 | 70,000 | — | — | — | 70,000 | — |
| | — | — | JE07.07 | 70,000 | | — | | | | | | |

Enterprise Funds 7-43

## WORKSHEET ENTRIES (Continued)

| Accounts | Trial Balance Debits | Trial Balance Credits | Adjustments Debits | | Adjustments Credits | | Adjusted Trial Balance Debits | Adjusted Trial Balance Credits | Operating Statement Debits | Operating Statement Credits | Balance Sheet Debits | Balance Sheet Credits |
|---|---|---|---|---|---|---|---|---|---|---|---|---|
| Land and improvements | 100,000 | — | 40,000 | JE07.06 | — | | 140,000 | — | — | — | 140,000 | — |
| Superstructure | 1,400,000 | — | — | | — | | 1,400,000 | — | — | — | 1,400,000 | — |
| Accumulated depreciation—superstructure | — | 650,000 | — | | 28,000 | JE07.12 | — | 678,000 | — | — | — | 678,000 |
| Buildings | 250,000 | — | 170,000 | JE07.07 | 90,000 | JE07.08 | 330,000 | — | — | — | 330,000 | — |
| Accumulated depreciation—buildings | — | 120,000 | 70,000 | JE07.08 | 25,000 | JE07.12 | — | 75,000 | — | — | — | 75,000 |
| Equipment | 40,000 | — | 30,000 | JE07.06 | 15,000 | JE07.08 | 55,000 | — | — | — | 55,000 | — |
| Accumulated depreciation—equipment | — | 25,000 | 12,000 | JE07.08 | 6,000 | JE07.12 | — | 19,000 | — | — | — | 19,000 |
| Vehicles | 800,000 | — | 120,000 | JE07.06 | 85,000 | JE07.08 | 835,000 | — | — | — | 835,000 | — |
| Accumulated depreciation—vehicles | — | 270,000 | 65,000 | JE07.08 | 280,000 | JE07.12 | — | 485,000 | — | — | — | 485,000 |
| Accounts payable and accrued expenses | — | 26,000 | 26,000 | JE07.01 | 50,000 | JE07.04 | — | 50,000 | — | — | — | 50,000 |
| Due to other funds—Communications and Technology Center | — | 4,000 | — | | 14,000 | JE07.17 | — | 18,000 | — | — | — | 18,000 |
| Compensated absences liability | — | 7,000 | — | | 1,000 | JE07.10 | — | 8,000 | — | — | — | 8,000 |

7-44 *Proprietary Funds*

## WORKSHEET ENTRIES (Continued)

| Accounts | Trial Balance Debits | Trial Balance Credits | Adjustments Debits | | Adjustments Credits | | Adjusted Trial Balance Debits | Adjusted Trial Balance Credits | Operating Statement Debits | Operating Statement Credits | Balance Sheet Debits | Balance Sheet Credits |
|---|---|---|---|---|---|---|---|---|---|---|---|---|
| Claims and judgements payable | — | 25,000 | — | | JE07.11 | 2,000 | — | 27,000 | — | — | — | 27,000 |
| Notes payable | — | 40,000 | JE07.09 | 10,000 | — | | — | 30,000 | — | — | — | 30,000 |
| Bonds payable | — | 100,000 | JE07.09 | 20,000 | — | | — | 80,000 | — | — | — | 80,000 |
| Net assets | — | 1,646,500 | — | | — | | — | 1,646,500 | — | — | — | 1,646,500 |
| Charges for services | — | — | — | | JE07.03 | 4,750,000 | — | 4,750,000 | — | 4,750,000 | — | — |
| Interest and investment revenue | — | — | — | | JE07.05 | 30,000 | — | 30,000 | — | 30,000 | — | — |
| Miscellaneous revenue—gain on sale of assets | — | — | — | | JE07.08 | 7,000 | — | 7,000 | — | 7,000 | — | — |
| Operating grants and contributions | — | — | — | | JE07.13 | 100,000 | — | 100,000 | — | 100,000 | — | — |
| Capital grants and contributions | — | — | — | | JE07.13 | 250,000 | — | 250,000 | — | 250,000 | — | — |
| Operating revenues—miscellaneous | — | — | — | | JE07.14 | 20,000 | — | 20,000 | — | 20,000 | — | — |
| Personal services expenses | — | — | JE07.04 | 2,400,000 | — | | 2,402,000 | — | 2,402,000 | — | — | — |
| | | | JE07.10 | 2,000 | | | | | | | | |
| Contractual services expenses | — | — | JE07.04 | 1,200,000 | — | | 1,280,000 | — | 1,280,000 | — | — | — |
| | | | JE07.17 | 80,000 | | | | | | | | |

Enterprise Funds  7-45

**7-46** *Proprietary Funds*

## WORKSHEET ENTRIES (Continued)

| Accounts | Trial Balance Debits | Trial Balance Credits | Adjustments Debits | | Adjustments Credits | | Adjusted Trial Balance Debits | Adjusted Trial Balance Credits | Operating Statement Debits | Operating Statement Credits | Balance Sheet Debits | Balance Sheet Credits |
|---|---|---|---|---|---|---|---|---|---|---|---|---|
| Repairs and maintenance expenses | — | — | JE07.04 | 400,000 | | — | 400,000 | — | 400,000 | — | — | — |
| Other supplies and expenses | — | — | JE07.04 | 200,000 | JE07.18 | 6,000 | 194,000 | — | 194,000 | — | — | — |
| Insurance claims and expenses | — | — | JE07.11 | 10,000 | | — | 10,000 | — | 10,000 | — | — | — |
| Depreciation expense | — | — | JE07.12 | 339,000 | | — | 339,000 | — | 339,000 | — | — | — |
| Interest expense | — | — | JE07.09 | 6,000 | | — | 6,000 | — | 6,000 | — | — | — |
| Operating expenses—miscellaneous | — | — | JE07.14 | 30,000 | | — | 30,000 | — | 30,000 | — | — | — |
| Transfers in—General Fund | — | — | | — | JE07.16 | 50,000 | — | 50,000 | — | 50,000 | — | — |
| Totals | 2,913,500 | 2,913,500 | | 10,715,500 | | 10,715,500 | 8,323,500 | 8,323,500 | 4,661,000 | 5,207,000 | 3,662,500 | 3,116,500 |
| Net increase (decrease) | | | | | | | | | 546,000 | — | — | 546,000 |
| | | | | | | | | | 5,207,000 | 5,207,000 | 3,662,500 | 3,662,500 |

## APPENDIX 7B
## WORKSHEET FOR SUMMARIZING CURRENT TRANSACTIONS—CENTERVILLE UTILITIES AUTHORITY

Enterprise Funds  7-47

### WORKSHEET ENTRIES

| Accounts | Trial Balance Debits | Trial Balance Credits | Adjustments Debits | | Adjustments Credits | | Adjusted Trial Balance Debits | Adjusted Trial Balance Credits | Operating Statement Debits | Operating Statement Credits | Balance Sheet Debits | Balance Sheet Credits |
|---|---|---|---|---|---|---|---|---|---|---|---|---|
| Cash | 2,970,000 | — | JE07.20 | 15,000 | JE07.19 | 1,100,000 | 230,000 | — | — | — | 230,000 | — |
| | | | JE07.21 | 34,000,000 | JE07.16 | 30,000,000 | — | — | — | — | — | — |
| | | | JE07.23 | 350,000 | JE07.24 | 4,450,000 | — | — | — | — | — | — |
| | | | JE07.26 | 500,000 | JE07.25 | 700,000 | — | — | — | — | — | — |
| | | | JE07.27 | 2,120,000 | JE07.25 | 200,000 | — | — | — | — | — | — |
| | | | JE07.31 | 1,250,000 | JE07.27 | 2,190,000 | — | — | — | — | — | — |
| | | | JE07.32 | 10,000 | JE07.28 | 13,000 | — | — | — | — | — | — |
| | | | | | JE07.29 | 12,000 | — | — | — | — | — | — |
| | | | | | JE07.32 | 5,000 | — | — | — | — | — | — |
| | | | | | JE07.33 | 15,000 | — | — | — | — | — | — |
| | | | | | JE07.35 | 200,000 | — | — | — | — | — | — |
| | | | | | JE07.34 | 2,000,000 | — | — | — | — | — | — |
| | | | | | JE07.36 | 100,000 | — | — | — | — | — | — |
| Interest receivable | 15,000 | — | JE07.23 | 50,000 | JE07.20 | 15,000 | 50,000 | — | — | — | 50,000 | — |
| Accounts receivable | 6,000,000 | — | JE07.21 | 2,000,000 | JE07.21 | 80,000 | 7,920,000 | — | — | — | 7,920,000 | — |
| Allowance for doubtful accounts | — | 300,000 | — | | JE07.21 | 70,000 | — | 370,000 | — | — | — | 370,000 |
| Temporary investments | 40,000 | — | JE07.33 | 15,000 | — | | 55,000 | — | — | — | 55,000 | — |

**7-48** *Proprietary Funds*

## WORKSHEET ENTRIES (Continued)

| Accounts | Trial Balance Debits | Trial Balance Credits | Adjustments Debits | | Adjustments Credits | | Adjusted Trial Balance Debits | Adjusted Trial Balance Credits | Operating Statement Debits | Operating Statement Credits | Balance Sheet Debits | Balance Sheet Credits |
|---|---|---|---|---|---|---|---|---|---|---|---|---|
| Due from other funds—General Fund | — | — | 2,000,000 | JE07.34 | | | 2,000,000 | — | — | — | 2,000,000 | — |
| Due from other governments | — | — | 100,000 | JE07.36 | | | 100,000 | — | — | — | 100,000 | — |
| Supplies | 54,000 | — | 21,000 | JE07.37 | | | 75,000 | — | — | — | 75,000 | — |
| Construction in progress | 1,500,000 | — | 700,000 | JE07.25 | 2,200,000 | JE07.25 | 200,000 | — | — | — | 200,000 | — |
| | | | 200,000 | JE07.25 | | | | | | | | |
| Land and improvements | 4,000,000 | — | 1,200,000 | JE07.24 | | | 5,200,000 | — | — | — | 5,200,000 | — |
| Distribution and collection systems | 45,000,000 | — | 1,300,000 | JE07.24 | | | 46,300,000 | — | — | — | 46,300,000 | — |
| Accumulated depreciation—distribution and collection systems | — | 41,000,000 | — | JE07.30 | 1,200,000 | | — | 42,200,000 | — | — | — | 42,200,000 |
| Buildings | 13,000,000 | — | 2,200,000 | JE07.25 | 750,000 | JE07.26 | 14,450,000 | — | — | — | 14,450,000 | — |
| Accumulated depreciation—buildings | — | 10,920,000 | 600,000 | JE07.30 | 625,000 | | — | 10,945,000 | — | — | — | 10,945,000 |
| Equipment | 6,500,000 | — | 1,200,000 | JE07.24 | 3,100,000 | JE07.26 | 4,600,000 | — | — | — | 4,600,000 | — |
| Accumulated depreciation—equipment | — | 2,380,000 | 2,800,000 | JE07.26 | 920,000 | JE07.30 | — | 500,000 | — | — | — | 500,000 |
| Vehicles | 1,400,000 | — | 750,000 | JE07.24 | 490,000 | JE07.26 | 1,660,000 | — | — | — | 1,660,000 | — |
| Accumulated depreciation—vehicles | — | 800,000 | 330,000 | JE07.26 | 280,000 | JE07.30 | — | 750,000 | — | — | — | 750,000 |

## WORKSHEET ENTRIES (Continued)

| Accounts | Trial Balance Debits | Trial Balance Credits | Adjustments Debits | | Adjustments Credits | | Adjusted Trial Balance Debits | Adjusted Trial Balance Credits | Operating Statement Debits | Operating Statement Credits | Balance Sheet Debits | Balance Sheet Credits |
|---|---|---|---|---|---|---|---|---|---|---|---|---|
| Accounts payable and accrued expenses | — | 1,100,000 | JE07.19 1,100,000 | JE07.22 | 4,300,000 | | — | 4,300,000 | — | — | — | 4,300,000 |
| Due to other funds—Internal Service Fund—Communications and Technology Support Center | — | 15,000 | — | JE07.35 | 20,000 | | — | 35,000 | — | — | — | 35,000 |
| Compensated absences liability | — | 75,000 | — | JE07.28 | 9,000 | | — | 84,000 | — | — | — | 84,000 |
| Claims and judgements payable | — | 220,000 | — | JE07.29 | 9,000 | | — | 229,000 | — | — | — | 229,000 |
| Notes payable | — | 250,000 | JE07.27 40,000 | JE07.27 | 120,000 | | — | 330,000 | — | — | — | 330,000 |
| Bonds payable | — | 7,400,000 | JE07.27 1,700,000 | JE07.27 | 2,000,000 | | — | 7,700,000 | — | — | — | 7,700,000 |
| Net assets | — | 16,019,000 | — | | — | | — | 16,019,000 | — | — | — | 16,019,000 |
| Charges for services | — | — | — | JE07.21 | 36,000,000 | | — | 36,000,000 | — | 36,000,000 | — | — |
| Interest and investment revenue | — | — | — | JE07.23 | 400,000 | | — | 400,000 | — | 400,000 | — | — |
| Capital grants and contributions | — | — | — | JE07.31 | 1,250,000 | | — | 1,250,000 | — | 1,250,000 | — | — |
| Operating revenues—miscellaneous | — | — | — | JE07.32 | 10,000 | | — | 10,000 | — | 10,000 | — | — |
| Personal services expenses | — | — | JE07.22 22,000,000 JE07.28 22,000 | | — | | 22,022,000 | — | 22,022,000 | — | — | — |

Enterprise Funds 7-49

## WORKSHEET ENTRIES (Continued)

| Accounts | Trial Balance Debits | Trial Balance Credits | Adjustments Debits | | Adjustments Credits | | Adjusted Trial Balance Debits | Adjusted Trial Balance Credits | Operating Statement Debits | Operating Statement Credits | Balance Sheet Debits | Balance Sheet Credits |
|---|---|---|---|---|---|---|---|---|---|---|---|---|
| Contractual services expenses | — | — | JE07.22 | 11,000,000 | | — | 11,220,000 | — | 11,220,000 | — | — | — |
| | | | JE07.35 | 220,000 | | | | | | | | |
| Repairs and maintenance expenses | — | — | JE07.22 | 700,000 | | — | 700,000 | — | 700,000 | — | — | — |
| Other supplies and expenses | — | — | JE07.22 | 600,000 | JE07.37 | 21,000 | 729,000 | — | 729,000 | — | — | — |
| | | | JE07.21 | 150,000 | | | | | | | | |
| Insurance claims and expenses | — | — | JE07.29 | 21,000 | | — | 21,000 | — | 21,000 | — | — | — |
| Depreciation expense | — | — | JE07.30 | 3,025,000 | | — | 3,025,000 | — | 3,025,000 | — | — | — |
| Interest expense | — | — | JE07.27 | 450,000 | | — | 450,000 | — | 450,000 | — | — | — |
| Operating expenses—miscellaneous | — | — | JE07.32 | 5,000 | | — | 5,000 | — | 5,000 | — | — | — |
| Miscellaneous expenses—loss on sale of assets | — | — | JE07.26 | 110,000 | | — | 110,000 | — | 110,000 | — | — | — |
| Totals | 80,479,000 | 80,479,000 | | 94,854,000 | | 94,854,000 | 121,122,000 | 121,122,000 | 38,282,000 | 37,660,000 | 82,840,000 | 83,462,000 |
| Net increase (decrease) | | | | | | | | | (622,000) | — | — | (622,000) |
| | | | | | | | | | 37,660,000 | 37,660,000 | 82,840,000 | 82,840,000 |

## APPENDIX 7C
## WORKSHEET FOR SUMMARIZING CURRENT TRANSACTIONS—CENTERVILLE PARKING AUTHORITY

### WORKSHEET ENTRIES

| Accounts | Trial Balance Debits | Trial Balance Credits | Adjustments Debits | | Adjustments Credits | | Adjusted Trial Balance Debits | Adjusted Trial Balance Credits | Operating Statement Debits | Operating Statement Credits | Balance Sheet Debits | Balance Sheet Credits |
|---|---|---|---|---|---|---|---|---|---|---|---|---|
| Cash | 150,000 | — | JE07.39 | 1,000 | JE07.38 | 4,000 | 764,000 | — | — | — | 764,000 | — |
| | | — | JE07.40 | 1,500,000 | JE07.41 | 5,700,000 | — | — | — | — | — | — |
| | | — | JE07.42 | 7,000 | JE07.43 | 175,000 | — | — | — | — | — | — |
| | | — | JE07.45 | 5,005,000 | JE07.44 | 10,000 | — | — | — | — | — | — |
| | | — | JE07.46 | 30,000 | JE07.44 | 15,000 | — | — | — | — | — | — |
| | | — | JE07.50 | 22,000 | JE07.46 | 37,000 | — | — | — | — | — | — |
| | | — | JE07.52 | 90,000 | JE07.47 | 1,000 | — | — | — | — | — | — |
| | | — | | — | JE07.48 | 1,000 | — | — | — | — | — | — |
| | | — | | — | JE07.50 | 3,000 | — | — | — | — | — | — |
| | | — | | — | JE07.51 | 5,000 | — | — | — | — | — | — |
| | | — | | — | JE07.53 | 90,000 | — | — | — | — | — | — |
| Interest receivable | 1,000 | — | JE07.42 | 3,000 | JE07.39 | 1,000 | 3,000 | — | — | — | 3,000 | — |
| Temporary investments | — | — | JE07.51 | 5,000 | | — | 5,000 | — | — | — | 5,000 | — |
| Supplies | 20,000 | — | JE07.54 | 4,000 | | — | 24,000 | — | — | — | 24,000 | — |
| Construction in progress | 150,000 | — | JE07.44 | 10,000 | JE07.44 | 160,000 | 15,000 | — | — | — | 15,000 | — |

## 7-52 Proprietary Funds

### WORKSHEET ENTRIES (Continued)

| Accounts | Trial Balance Debits | Trial Balance Credits | Adjustments Debits | | Adjustments Credits | | Adjusted Trial Balance Debits | Adjusted Trial Balance Credits | Operating Statement Debits | Operating Statement Credits | Balance Sheet Debits | Balance Sheet Credits |
|---|---|---|---|---|---|---|---|---|---|---|---|---|
| Land and improvements | 3,000,000 | — | 15,000 | JE07.44 | 1,500,000 | JE07.43 | 1,780,000 | — | — | — | 1,780,000 | — |
| | | | 120,000 | JE07.43 | | | | | | | | |
| | | | 160,000 | JE07.44 | | | | | | | | |
| Buildings | 2,400,000 | — | — | | — | | 2,400,000 | — | — | — | 2,400,000 | — |
| Accumulated depreciation—buildings | — | 1,300,000 | — | | 90,000 | JE07.49 | — | 1,390,000 | — | — | — | 1,390,000 |
| Equipment | 120,000 | — | 30,000 | JE07.43 | 10,000 | JE07.45 | 140,000 | — | — | — | 140,000 | — |
| Accumulated depreciation—equipment | — | 75,000 | 7,000 | JE07.45 | 15,000 | JE07.49 | — | 83,000 | — | — | — | 83,000 |
| Vehicles | 90,000 | — | 25,000 | JE07.43 | 13,000 | JE07.45 | 102,000 | — | — | — | 102,000 | — |
| Accumulated depreciation—vehicles | — | 32,000 | 12,000 | JE07.45 | 12,000 | JE07.49 | — | 32,000 | — | — | — | 32,000 |
| Accounts payable and accrued expenses | — | 4,000 | 4,000 | JE07.38 | 90,000 | JE07.41 | — | 90,000 | — | — | — | 90,000 |
| Due to other funds—Communications and Technology Center | — | 7,000 | — | | 10,000 | JE07.53 | — | 17,000 | — | — | — | 17,000 |
| Compensated absences liability | — | 4,000 | — | | 1,000 | JE07.47 | — | 5,000 | — | — | — | 5,000 |
| Claims and judgments payable | — | 5,000 | — | | 2,000 | JE07.48 | — | 7,000 | — | — | — | 7,000 |

## WORKSHEET ENTRIES (Continued)

| Accounts | Trial Balance Debits | Trial Balance Credits | Adjustments Debits | | Adjustments Credits | | Adjusted Trial Balance Debits | Adjusted Trial Balance Credits | Operating Statement Debits | Operating Statement Credits | Balance Sheet Debits | Balance Sheet Credits |
|---|---|---|---|---|---|---|---|---|---|---|---|---|
| Notes payable | — | 10,000 | JE07.46 | 10,000 | JE07.46 | 30,000 | — | 30,000 | — | — | — | 30,000 |
| Bonds payable | — | 500,000 | | — | | — | — | 500,000 | — | — | — | 500,000 |
| Net assets | — | 3,994,000 | | — | | — | — | 3,994,000 | — | — | — | 3,994,000 |
| Charges for services | — | — | | — | JE07.40 | 1,500,000 | — | 1,500,000 | — | 1,500,000 | — | — |
| Interest and investment revenue | — | — | | — | JE07.42 | 10,000 | — | 10,000 | — | 10,000 | — | — |
| Miscellaneous revenue—gain on sale of assets | — | — | | — | JE07.45 | 1,000 | — | 1,000 | — | 1,000 | — | — |
| Operating revenues— miscellaneous | — | — | | — | JE07.50 | 22,000 | — | 22,000 | — | 22,000 | — | — |
| Personal services expenses | — | — | JE07.41 | 5,400,000 | | — | 5,402,000 | — | 5,402,000 | — | — | — |
| | | | JE07.47 | 2,000 | | — | | | | | | |
| Contractual services expenses | — | — | JE07.41 | 300,000 | | — | 400,000 | — | 400,000 | — | — | — |
| | | | JE07.53 | 100,000 | | — | | | | | | |
| Repairs and maintenance expenses | — | — | JE07.41 | 50,000 | | — | 50,000 | — | 50,000 | — | — | — |
| Other supplies and expenses | — | — | JE07.41 | 40,000 | JE07.54 | 4,000 | 36,000 | — | 36,000 | — | — | — |
| Insurance claims and expenses | — | — | JE07.48 | 3,000 | | — | 3,000 | — | 3,000 | — | — | — |
| Depreciation expense | — | — | JE07.49 | 117,000 | | — | 117,000 | — | 117,000 | — | — | — |
| Interest expense | — | — | JE07.46 | 27,000 | | — | 27,000 | — | 27,000 | — | — | — |

Enterprise Funds 7-53

**7-54** *Proprietary Funds*

## WORKSHEET ENTRIES (Continued)

| Accounts | Trial Balance Debits | Trial Balance Credits | Adjustments Debits | Adjustments Credits | Adjusted Trial Balance Debits | Adjusted Trial Balance Credits | Operating Statement Debits | Operating Statement Credits | Balance Sheet Debits | Balance Sheet Credits |
|---|---|---|---|---|---|---|---|---|---|---|
| Operating expenses—miscellaneous | — | — | JE07.50 3,000 | — | 3,000 | — | 3,000 | — | — | — |
| Special item—gain on sale of parking lot | — | — | — | JE07.45 3,500,000 | — | 3,500,000 | — | 3,500,000 | — | — |
| Transfers in—General Fund | — | — | — | 90,000 | — | 90,000 | — | 90,000 | — | — |
| Totals | 5,931,000 | 5,931,000 | 13,102,000 | 13,102,000 | 11,271,000 | 11,271,000 | 6,038,000 | 5,123,000 | 5,233,000 | 6,148,000 |
| Net increase (decrease) | | | | | | | (915,000) | — | — | (915,000) |
| | | | | | | | 5,123,000 | 5,123,000 | 5,233,000 | 5,233,000 |

## APPENDIX 7D
## WORKSHEET FOR SUMMARIZING CURRENT TRANSACTIONS—CENTERVILLE MUNICIPAL AIRPORT

### WORKSHEET ENTRIES

| Accounts | Trial Balance Debits | Trial Balance Credits | Adjustments Debits | | Adjustments Credits | | Adjusted Trial Balance Debits | Adjusted Trial Balance Credits | Operating Statement Debits | Operating Statement Credits | Balance Sheet Debits | Balance Sheet Credits |
|---|---|---|---|---|---|---|---|---|---|---|---|---|
| Cash | 1,150,000 | — | JE07.56 | 55,000 | JE07.55 | 3,400,000 | 10,963,000 | — | — | — | 10,963,000 | — |
| | | — | JE07.57 | 165,000,000 | JE07.58 | 191,000,000 | — | — | — | — | — | — |
| | | — | JE07.57 | 49,000,000 | JE07.60 | 7,100,000 | — | — | — | — | — | — |
| | | — | JE07.59 | 1,000,000 | JE07.61 | 400,000 | — | — | — | — | — | — |
| | | — | JE07.62 | 420,000 | JE07.61 | 1,300,000 | — | — | — | — | — | — |
| | | — | JE07.63 | 3,200,000 | JE07.63 | 3,720,000 | — | — | — | — | — | — |
| | | — | JE07.67 | 1,700,000 | JE07.64 | 17,000 | — | — | — | — | — | — |
| | | — | JE07.68 | 60,000 | JE07.65 | 25,000 | — | — | — | — | — | — |
| | | — | | | JE07.68 | 70,000 | — | — | — | — | — | — |
| | | — | | | JE07.69 | 50,000 | — | — | — | — | — | — |
| | | — | | | JE07.70 | 400,000 | — | — | — | — | — | — |
| | | — | | | JE07.71 | 540,000 | — | — | — | — | — | — |
| | | — | | | JE07.72 | 2,600,000 | — | — | — | — | — | — |
| Interest receivable | 55,000 | — | JE07.59 | 200,000 | JE07.56 | 55,000 | 200,000 | — | — | — | 200,000 | — |
| Temporary investments | 10,000,000 | — | JE07.69 | 50,000 | | | 10,050,000 | — | — | — | 10,050,000 | — |
| Accounts receivable | 5,000,000 | — | JE07.57 | 10,000,000 | | | 18,000,000 | — | — | — | 18,000,000 | — |

## 7-56 Proprietary Funds

### WORKSHEET ENTRIES (Continued)

| Accounts | Trial Balance Debits | Trial Balance Credits | Adjustments Debits | | Adjustments Credits | | Adjusted Trial Balance Debits | Adjusted Trial Balance Credits | Operating Statement Debits | Operating Statement Credits | Balance Sheet Debits | Balance Sheet Credits |
|---|---|---|---|---|---|---|---|---|---|---|---|---|
| Due from other funds—General Fund | — | — | JE07.57 | 3,000,000 | | — | — | — | — | — | — | — |
| Due from other governments | — | — | JE07.70 | 400,000 | | — | 400,000 | — | — | — | 400,000 | — |
| Supplies | 50,000 | — | JE07.67 | 300,000 | | — | 300,000 | — | — | — | 300,000 | — |
| | | | JE07.73 | 5,000 | | — | 55,000 | — | — | — | 55,000 | — |
| Construction in progress | 25,000,000 | — | JE07.61 | 400,000 | JE07.61 | 3,200,000 | 23,500,000 | — | — | — | 23,500,000 | — |
| | | | JE07.61 | 1,300,000 | | | | | | | | |
| Land and improvements | 10,000,000 | — | JE07.60 | 3,200,000 | | — | 13,200,000 | — | — | — | 13,200,000 | — |
| Runways and tarmacs | 27,000,000 | — | JE07.60 | 500,000 | | — | 27,500,000 | — | — | — | 27,500,000 | — |
| Accumulated depreciation—runways and tarmacs | — | 6,500,000 | — | | JE07.66 | 1,300,000 | — | 7,800,000 | — | — | — | 7,800,000 |
| Buildings | 30,000,000 | — | JE07.61 | 3,200,000 | | — | 33,200,000 | — | — | — | 33,200,000 | — |
| Accumulated depreciation—buildings | — | 6,500,000 | — | | JE07.66 | 1,200,000 | — | 7,700,000 | — | — | — | 7,700,000 |
| Equipment | 7,000,000 | — | JE07.60 | 2,300,000 | JE07.62 | 2,100,000 | 7,200,000 | — | — | — | 7,200,000 | — |
| Accumulated depreciation—equipment | — | 4,300,000 | JE07.62 | 1,600,000 | JE07.66 | 450,000 | — | 3,150,000 | — | — | — | 3,150,000 |
| Vehicles | 2,300,000 | — | JE07.60 | 1,100,000 | JE07.62 | 900,000 | 2,500,000 | — | — | — | 2,500,000 | — |

## Enterprise Funds 7-57

**WORKSHEET ENTRIES (Continued)**

| Accounts | Trial Balance Debits | Trial Balance Credits | Adjustments Debits | | Adjustments Credits | | Adjusted Trial Balance Debits | Adjusted Trial Balance Credits | Operating Statement Debits | Operating Statement Credits | Balance Sheet Debits | Balance Sheet Credits |
|---|---|---|---|---|---|---|---|---|---|---|---|---|
| Accumulated depreciation—vehicles | — | — | — | JE07.57 | — | — | — | — | — | — | — | — |
| Accounts payable and accrued expenses | — | 1,900,000 | JE07.62 | 715,000 | JE07.66 | 420,000 | — | 1,605,000 | — | — | — | 1,605,000 |
| Due to other funds—Communications and Technology Center | — | 3,400,000 | JE07.55 | 3,400,000 | JE07.58 | 3,900,000 | — | 3,900,000 | — | — | — | 3,900,000 |
| Due to other funds—Internal Service Fund—Special Services Support Center | — | 25,000 | — | | JE07.71 | 60,000 | — | 85,000 | — | — | — | 85,000 |
| Compensated absences liability | — | 77,000 | — | | JE07.72 | 350,000 | — | 427,000 | — | — | — | 427,000 |
| Claims and judgements payable | — | 125,000 | — | | JE07.64 | 8,000 | — | 133,000 | — | — | — | 133,000 |
| Notes payable | — | 120,000 | — | | JE07.65 | 75,000 | — | 195,000 | — | — | — | 195,000 |
| Revenue bonds payable—Terminal A | — | 4,500,000 | — | | JE07.63 | 3,200,000 | — | 7,700,000 | — | — | — | 7,700,000 |
| Revenue bonds payable—Terminal B | — | 12,000,000 | JE07.63 | 2,000,000 | — | — | — | 10,000,000 | — | — | — | 10,000,000 |
| | — | 4,500,000 | JE07.66 | 500,000 | — | — | — | 4,000,000 | — | — | — | 4,000,000 |

**7-58** *Proprietary Funds*

## WORKSHEET ENTRIES (Continued)

| Accounts | Trial Balance Debits | Trial Balance Credits | Adjustments Debits | Adjustments Credits | Adjusted Trial Balance Debits | Adjusted Trial Balance Credits | Operating Statement Debits | Operating Statement Credits | Balance Sheet Debits | Balance Sheet Credits |
|---|---|---|---|---|---|---|---|---|---|---|
| Net assets | — | 73,608,000 | JE07.57 3,000,000 | — | — | 73,608,000 | — | — | — | 73,608,000 |
| Charges for services | — | — | — | JE07.57 175,000,000 | — | 175,000,000 | — | 175,000,000 | — | — |
| Charges for services—rental income—security for Terminal A revenue bonds | — | — | — | JE07.57 30,000,000 | — | 30,000,000 | — | 30,000,000 | — | — |
| Charges for services—rental income—security for Terminal B revenue bonds | — | — | — | JE07.57 22,000,000 | — | 22,000,000 | — | 22,000,000 | — | — |
| Interest and investment revenue | — | — | — | JE07.59 1,200,000 | — | 1,200,000 | — | 1,200,000 | — | — |
| Capital grants and contributions | — | — | — | JE07.67 2,000,000 | — | 2,000,000 | — | 2,000,000 | — | — |
| Operating revenues—miscellaneous | — | — | — | JE07.68 60,000 | — | 60,000 | — | 60,000 | — | — |
| Personal services expenses | — | — | JE07.58 161,000,000 JE07.64 25,000 | — | 161,025,000 | — | 161,025,000 | — | — | — |
| Contractual services expenses | — | — | JE07.58 30,000,000 JE07.71 600,000 JE07.72 2,950,000 | — | 33,550,000 | — | 33,550,000 | — | — | — |

## WORKSHEET ENTRIES (Continued)

| Accounts | Trial Balance Debits | Trial Balance Credits | Adjustments Debits | | Adjustments Credits | Adjusted Trial Balance Debits | Adjusted Trial Balance Credits | Operating Statement Debits | Operating Statement Credits | Balance Sheet Debits | Balance Sheet Credits |
|---|---|---|---|---|---|---|---|---|---|---|---|
| Repairs and maintenance expenses | — | — | JE07.57 | | — | — | — | — | — | — | — |
| Other supplies and expenses | — | — | JE07.58 | 2,100,000 | — | 2,100,000 | — | 2,100,000 | — | — | — |
| Insurance claims and expenses | — | — | JE07.58 | 1,800,000 JE07.73 | 5,000 | 1,795,000 | — | 1,795,000 | — | — | — |
| Depreciation expense | — | — | JE07.65 | 100,000 | — | 100,000 | — | 100,000 | — | — | — |
| Interest expense | — | — | JE07.66 | 3,370,000 | — | 3,370,000 | — | 3,370,000 | — | — | — |
| Operating expenses—miscellaneous | — | — | JE07.63 | 1,220,000 | — | 1,220,000 | — | 1,220,000 | — | — | — |
| Miscellaneous expenses—loss on sale of assets | — | — | JE07.68 | 70,000 | — | 70,000 | — | 70,000 | — | — | — |
| | — | — | JE07.62 | 265,000 | — | 265,000 | — | 265,000 | — | — | — |
| Totals | 117,555,000 | 117,555,000 | 458,105,000 | | 458,105,000 | 350,563,000 | 350,563,000 | 203,495,000 | 230,260,000 | 147,068,000 | 120,303,000 |
| Net increase (decrease) | | | | | | | | 26,765,000 | — | — | 26,765,000 |
| | | | | | | | | 230,260,000 | 230,260,000 | 147,068,000 | 147,068,000 |

# APPENDIX 7E: ENTERPRISE FUNDS—STATEMENT OF NET ASSETS; STATEMENT OF REVENUES, EXPENSES, AND CHANGES IN FUND NET ASSETS; AND STATEMENT OF CASH FLOWS

**WORKSHEET ENTRIES**

**Enterprise Funds**
**Statement of Net Assets**
**June 30, 20X1**

| | Centerville Toll Bridge | Centerville Utilities Authority | Centerville Parking Authority | Centerville Municipal Airport | Total |
|---|---|---|---|---|---|
| **ASSETS** | | | | | |
| Current assets: | | | | | |
| Cash | $ 739,500 | $ 230,000 | $ 764,000 | $10,963,000 | $12,696,500 |
| Interest receivable | 3,000 | 50,000 | 3,000 | 200,000 | 256,000 |
| Accounts receivable (net) | — | 7,550,000 | — | 18,000,000 | 25,550,000 |
| Due from other funds | — | 2,000,000 | — | 400,000 | 2,400,000 |
| Due from other governments | — | 100,000 | — | 300,000 | 400,000 |
| Temporary investments | 58,000 | 55,000 | 5,000 | 10,050,000 | 10,168,000 |
| Supplies | 32,000 | 75,000 | 24,000 | 55,000 | 186,000 |
| Total current assets | 832,500 | 10,060,000 | 796,000 | 39,968,000 | 51,656,500 |
| Noncurrent assets: | | | | | |
| Construction in progress | 70,000 | 200,000 | 15,000 | 23,500,000 | 23,785,000 |
| Land and improvements | 140,000 | 5,200,000 | 1,780,000 | 13,200,000 | 20,320,000 |
| Superstructure | 1,400,000 | — | — | — | 1,400,000 |

## WORKSHEET ENTRIES (Continued)

| | Centerville Toll Bridge | Centerville Utilities Authority | Centerville Parking Authority | Centerville Municipal Airport | Total |
|---|---|---|---|---|---|
| Distribution and collection systems | — | 46,300,000 | — | — | 46,300,000 |
| Runways and tarmacs | — | — | — | 27,500,000 | 27,500,000 |
| Buildings | 330,000 | 14,450,000 | 2,400,000 | 33,200,000 | 50,380,000 |
| Equipment | 55,000 | 4,600,000 | 140,000 | 7,200,000 | 11,995,000 |
| Vehicles | 835,000 | 1,660,000 | 102,000 | 2,500,000 | 5,097,000 |
| Less accumulated depreciation | (1,257,000) | (54,395,000) | (1,505,000) | (20,255,000) | (77,412,000) |
| Total noncurrent assets | 1,573,000 | 18,015,000 | 2,932,000 | 86,845,000 | 109,365,000 |
| Total assets | $2,405,500 | $28,075,000 | $3,728,000 | $126,813,000 | $161,021,500 |
| **LIABILITIES** | | | | | |
| Current liabilities: | | | | | |
| Accounts payable and accrued expenses | $ 50,000 | $ 4,300,000 | $ 90,000 | $ 3,900,000 | $ 8,340,000 |
| Due to other funds | 18,000 | 35,000 | 17,000 | 512,000 | 582,000 |
| Compensated absences | 3,000 | 21,000 | 2,000 | 15,000 | 41,000 |
| Claims and judgements | 5,000 | 17,000 | 4,000 | 25,000 | 51,000 |
| Notes payable | 10,000 | 70,000 | 30,000 | | 110,000 |
| Revenue bonds—Terminal A | — | — | — | 2,000,000 | 2,000,000 |
| Revenue bonds—Terminal B | — | — | — | 500,000 | 500,000 |
| Bonds payable | 20,000 | 850,000 | | | 870,000 |
| Total current liabilities | 106,000 | 5,293,000 | 143,000 | 6,952,000 | 12,494,000 |
| Noncurrent liabilities: | | | | | |
| Compensated absences | 5,000 | 63,000 | 3,000 | 118,000 | 189,000 |
| Claims and judgements | 22,000 | 212,000 | 3,000 | 170,000 | 407,000 |
| Notes payable | 20,000 | 260,000 | — | 7,700,000 | 7,980,000 |

## WORKSHEET ENTRIES (Continued)

|  | Centerville Toll Bridge | Centerville Utilities Authority | Centerville Parking Authority | Centerville Municipal Airport | Total |
|---|---|---|---|---|---|
| Revenue bonds—Terminal A | — | — | — | 8,000,000 | 8,000,000 |
| Revenue bonds—Terminal B | — | — | — | 3,500,000 | 3,500,000 |
| Bonds payable | 60,000 | 6,850,000 | 500,000 | — | 7,410,000 |
| Total noncurrent liabilities | 107,000 | 7,385,000 | 506,000 | 19,488,000 | 27,486,000 |
| Total liabilities | $ 213,000 | $12,678,000 | $ 649,000 | $ 26,440,000 | $ 39,980,000 |
| **NET ASSETS** | | | | | |
| Invested in capital assets, net of related debt | $1,463,000 | $ 9,985,000 | $2,402,000 | $ 69,145,000 | $ 82,995,000 |
| Restricted | 622,000 | 5,250,000 | 595,000 | 30,895,000 | 37,362,000 |
| Unrestricted | 107,500 | 162,000 | 82,000 | 333,000 | 684,500 |
| Total net assets | $2,192,500 | $15,397,000 | $3,079,000 | $100,373,000 | $121,041,500 |

### Enterprise Funds
### Statement of Revenues, Expenses, and Changes in Fund Net Assets
### For the Year Ended June 30, 20X1

|  | Centerville Toll Bridge | Centerville Utilities Authority | Centerville Parking Authority | Centerville Municipal Airport | Total |
|---|---|---|---|---|---|
| **OPERATING REVENUES** | | | | | |
| Charges for services | $4,750,000 | $36,000,000 | $1,500,000 | $175,000,000 | $217,250,000 |
| Charges for services—rental income—security for Terminal A revenue bonds | — | — | — | 30,000,000 | 30,000,000 |

## WORKSHEET ENTRIES (Continued)

| | Centerville Toll Bridge | Centerville Utilities Authority | Centerville Parking Authority | Centerville Municipal Airport | Total |
|---|---|---|---|---|---|
| Charges for services—rental income—security for Terminal B revenue bonds | — | — | — | 22,000,000 | 22,000,000 |
| Miscellaneous | 20,000 | 10,000 | 22,000 | 60,000 | 112,000 |
| Total operating revenues | 4,770,000 | 36,010,000 | 1,522,000 | 227,060,000 | 269,362,000 |
| **OPERATING EXPENSES** | | | | | |
| Personal services | 2,402,000 | 22,022,000 | 5,402,000 | 161,025,000 | 190,851,000 |
| Contractual services | 1,280,000 | 11,220,000 | 400,000 | 33,550,000 | 46,450,000 |
| Repairs and maintenance | 400,000 | 700,000 | 50,000 | 2,100,000 | 3,250,000 |
| Other supplies and expenses | 194,000 | 729,000 | 36,000 | 1,795,000 | 2,754,000 |
| Insurance claims and expenses | 10,000 | 21,000 | 3,000 | 100,000 | 134,000 |
| Depreciation | 339,000 | 3,025,000 | 117,000 | 3,370,000 | 6,851,000 |
| Miscellaneous | 30,000 | 5,000 | 3,000 | 70,000 | 108,000 |
| Total operating expenses | 4,655,000 | 37,722,000 | 6,011,000 | 202,010,000 | 250,398,000 |
| Operating income (loss) | 115,000 | (1,712,000) | (4,489,000) | 25,050,000 | 18,964,000 |
| **NONOPERATING REVENUES (EXPENSES)** | | | | | |
| Interest and investment revenue | 30,000 | 400,000 | 10,000 | 1,200,000 | 1,640,000 |
| Interest | (6,000) | (450,000) | (27,000) | (1,220,000) | (1,703,000) |
| Operating grants and contributions | 100,000 | — | — | — | 100,000 |
| Miscellaneous | 7,000 | (110,000) | (1,000) | (265,000) | (367,000) |
| Total nonoperating revenue (expenses) | 131,000 | (160,000) | (16,000) | (285,000) | (330,000) |
| Income (loss) before capital contributions and transfers | 246,000 | (1,872,000) | (4,505,000) | 24,765,000 | 18,634,000 |

**7-64** Proprietary Funds

## WORKSHEET ENTRIES (Continued)

| | Centerville Toll Bridge | Centerville Utilities Authority | Centerville Parking Authority | Centerville Municipal Airport | Total |
|---|---|---|---|---|---|
| Capital contributions | 250,000 | 1,250,000 | — | 2,000,000 | 3,500,000 |
| Transfers in | 50,000 | — | 90,000 | — | 140,000 |
| Special item—gain on sale of parking lot | — | — | 3,500,000 | — | 3,500,000 |
| Change in net assets | 546,000 | (622,000) | (915,000) | 26,765,000 | 25,774,000 |
| Total net assets—beginning | 1,646,500 | 16,019,000 | 3,994,000 | 73,608,000 | 95,267,500 |
| Total net assets—ending | $2,192,500 | $15,397,000 | $3,079,000 | $100,373,000 | $121,041,500 |

### Enterprise Funds
### Statement of Cash Flows
### For The Year Ended June 30, 20X1

| | Centerville Toll Bridge | Centerville Utilities Authority | Centerville Parking Authority | Centerville Municipal Airport | Total |
|---|---|---|---|---|---|
| **CASH FLOWS FROM OPERATING ACTIVITIES** | | | | | |
| Receipts from customers | $4,750,000 | $34,000,000 | $1,500,000 | $214,000,000 | $254,250,000 |
| Payments to suppliers | (1,806,000) | (12,112,000) | (345,000) | (36,425,000) | (50,688,000) |
| Payments to employees | (2,371,000) | (19,013,000) | (5,361,000) | (158,017,000) | (184,762,000) |
| Internal activity—payments to other funds | (66,000) | (200,000) | (90,000) | (3,140,000) | (3,496,000) |
| Other receipts (payments) | (18,000) | 5,000 | 19,000 | (10,000) | (4,000) |
| Net cash provided by operating activities | 489,000 | 2,680,000 | (4,277,000) | 16,408,000 | 15,300,000 |

## WORKSHEET ENTRIES (Continued)

| | Centerville Toll Bridge | Centerville Utilities Authority | Centerville Parking Authority | Centerville Municipal Airport | Total |
|---|---:|---:|---:|---:|---:|
| **CASH FLOWS FROM NONCAPITAL FINANCING ACTIVITIES** | | | | | |
| Subsidies and transfers from (to) other funds and state government | 150,000 | — | 90,000 | — | 240,000 |
| **CASH FLOWS FROM CAPITAL AND RELATED FINANCING ACTIVITIES** | | | | | |
| Proceeds from the issuance of capital debt | — | 2,120,000 | — | 3,200,000 | 5,320,000 |
| Capital contributions | 250,000 | 1,250,000 | 30,000 | 1,700,000 | 3,230,000 |
| Acquisitions of capital assets | (390,000) | (5,350,000) | (200,000) | (8,800,000) | (14,740,000) |
| Proceeds from sale of capital assets | 50,000 | 500,000 | 5,005,000 | 420,000 | 5,975,000 |
| Principal paid on capital debt | (30,000) | (1,740,000) | (10,000) | (2,500,000) | (4,280,000) |
| Interest paid on capital debt | (6,000) | (450,000) | (27,000) | (1,220,000) | (1,703,000) |
| Net cash (used) by capital and related financing activities | (126,000) | (3,670,000) | 4,798,000 | (7,200,000) | (6,198,000) |
| **CASH FLOWS FROM INVESTING ACTIVITIES** | | | | | |
| Loans to other funds | — | (2,000,000) | — | (400,000) | (2,400,000) |
| Loans to other governments | — | (100,000) | — | — | (100,000) |
| Interest and dividends | 31,500 | 365,000 | 8,000 | 1,055,000 | 1,459,500 |
| Purchase of investments | (25,000) | (15,000) | (5,000) | (50,000) | (95,000) |
| Net cash provided (used) by investing activities | 6,500 | (1,750,000) | 3,000 | 605,000 | (1,135,500) |
| Net increase (decrease) in cash | 519,500 | (2,740,000) | 614,000 | 9,813,000 | 8,206,500 |

## 7-66 Proprietary Funds

### WORKSHEET ENTRIES (Continued)

| | Centerville Toll Bridge | Centerville Utilities Authority | Centerville Parking Authority | Centerville Municipal Airport | Total |
|---|---|---|---|---|---|
| **CASH FLOWS FROM NONCAPITAL FINANCING ACTIVITIES** | | | | | |
| Balances—beginning of year | 220,000 | 2,970,000 | 150,000 | 1,150,000 | 4,490,000 |
| Balances—end of year | $739,500 | $ 230,000 | $ 764,000 | $10,963,000 | $12,696,500 |
| Reconciliation of operating income (loss) to net cash provided (used) by operating activities: | | | | | |
| Operating income (loss) | $115,000 | $(1,712,000) | $(4,489,000) | $25,050,000 | $18,964,000 |
| Adjustments: | | | | | |
| Depreciation expense | 339,000 | 3,025,000 | 117,000 | 3,370,000 | 6,851,000 |
| Change in assets and liabilities: | | | | | |
| Receivables, net | | (1,850,000) | | (13,000,000) | (14,850,000) |
| Inventories | (6,000) | (21,000) | (4,000) | (5,000) | (36,000) |
| Accounts and accrued liabilities | 41,000 | 3,238,000 | 99,000 | 993,000 | 4,371,000 |
| Net cash provided (used) by operating activities | $489,000 | $ 2,680,000 | $(4,277,000) | $16,408,000 | $15,300,000 |

# CHAPTER 8
# INTERNAL SERVICE FUNDS

## CONTENTS

| | |
|---|---|
| Nature of Internal Service Funds | 8-2 |
| Measurement Focus and Basis of Accounting | 8-2 |
| Financial Reporting at Fund Level | 8-3 |
| Financial Reporting at Government-Wide Level | 8-4 |
| Illustrative Transactions | 8-4 |
|     Communications and Technology Support Center | 8-5 |
|     Fleet Management Unit | 8-11 |
|     Special Services Support Center | 8-17 |
| Fund Financial Statements | 8-23 |
| Converting to Government-Wide Financial Statements | 8-28 |
|     Determining the Allocation Base | 8-29 |
|         Interest and Investment Revenue | 8-29 |
|         Interest Expense | 8-30 |
|         Transfers In/Out | 8-30 |
|         Billings to External Parties | 8-30 |
|     Communications and Technology Support Center | 8-31 |
|     Fleet Management | 8-34 |
|     Special Services Support Center | 8-35 |
| Appendix 8A: Worksheet for Summarizing Current Transactions—Communications and Technology Support Center | 8-37 |
| Appendix 8B: Worksheet for Summarizing Current Transactions—Fleet Management | 8-41 |
| Appendix 8C: Worksheet for Summarizing Current Transactions—Special Services Support Center | 8-45 |
| Appendix 8D: Internal Service Funds—Statement of Net Assets; Statement of Revenues, Expenses, and Changes in Fund Net Assets; and Statement of Cash Flows | 8-48 |
| Appendix 8E: Merging Internal Service Funds into the Government-Wide Financial Statements | 8-54 |

## NATURE OF INTERNAL SERVICE FUNDS

GASB-34 states that Internal Service Funds may be used to report "any activity that provides goods or services to other funds, departments, or agencies of the primary government and its component units, or to other governments, on a cost reimbursement basis." An Internal Service Fund should be used only when the reporting government itself is the *predominant participant* in the fund. When the transactions with the other governmental entities represent the predominant portion of the activity, an Enterprise Fund is used (GASB-34, par. 68).

> ▶ **NEW STANDARD:** The criteria established by GASB-34 are different from the standards that were previously used to determine when an Internal Service Fund should be used by a governmental entity.

> ■ **CONTINUING STANDARD:** Prior to the issuance of GASB-34, there was no circumstance under which an Internal Service Fund *must* be used. GASB-34 continues with that philosophy.

## MEASUREMENT FOCUS AND BASIS OF ACCOUNTING

The accrual basis of accounting and the flow of economic resources are used to prepare the financial statements of an Internal Service Fund. Under the flow of economic resources measurement focus and accrual basis of accounting, revenues are recognized when earned and expenses are recorded when incurred when these activities are related to exchange and exchange-like activities. In addition, long-lived assets (such as buildings and equipment) are capitalized and depreciated, and all debt is reported in the fund (GASB-34, par. 16).

> ▶ **NEW STANDARD:** As discussed in Chapter 7 ("Enterprise Funds"), the Enterprise fund type can follow either Alternative 1 or Alternative 2 as described in GASB-20 (Accounting and Financial Reporting for Proprietary Funds and Other Governmental Entities That Use Proprietary Fund Accounting). Prior to the issuance of GASB-34, there was some confusion about whether Internal Service Funds were subject to the two alternatives established by GASB-20. The GASB clarified the issue by stating that "the option should not apply to Internal Service Funds" (GASB-34, par. 423).

> ■ **CONTINUING STANDARD:** As part of a self-insurance strategy, a state or local government may establish a separate Internal Service Fund (Self-Insurance Fund) to account for the payment of claims and judgements. The recognition of a

loss contingency in a Self-Insurance Internal Service Fund arising from claims and judgements is governed by accounting and reporting standards established by FAS-5 (Accounting for Contingencies). GASB-34 does change the option of using a Self-Insurance Internal Service Fund.

## FINANCIAL REPORTING AT FUND LEVEL

The balances and activities of Internal Service Funds are presented in the following three financial statements at the fund financial statement level:

1. Statement of net assets (or balance sheet)
2. Statement of revenues, expenses, and changes in fund net assets (or fund equity)
3. Statement of cash flows

> ■ **CONTINUING STANDARD:** An Internal Service Fund's statement of net assets can continue to be presented based on the guidance established in Chapter 3 of ARB-43 (Restatement and Revision of Accounting Research Bulletins). The statement of net assets may be presented in either one of the following formats: (1) net assets format, where assets less liabilities equal net assets, or (2) balance sheet format, where assets equal liabilities plus net assets (GASB-34, pars. 97 and 98).

These three fund financial statements include all of the proprietary funds (Internal Service Funds and Enterprise Funds). The financial statements of all Internal Service Funds are combined into a single column and are presented to the right of the Enterprise Funds. The Internal Service Funds column and the Enterprise Funds total column should not be added together in the proprietary fund financial statements.

> ▶ **NEW STANDARD:** A significant change in the focus of reporting governmental funds and proprietary funds is that major funds are reported for these funds; however, the major fund concept does not apply to Internal Service Funds (GASB-34, par. 75).

> ▶ **NEW STANDARD:** Proprietary funds must prepare a statement of cash flows based on the guidance established by GASB-9, except the statement of cash flows should be formatted based on the *direct method* in computing cash flows from operating activities. Prior to the issuance of GASB-34, the statement of cash flows could be prepared based on either the direct or indirect method (GASB-34, par. 105).

▶ **NEW STANDARD:** GASB-34 requires a reconciliation between the government-wide financial statements (statement of net assets and statement of changes in net assets) and the governmental fund activities; however, no reconciliation is needed for the Internal Service Fund column, because the Internal Service Fund financial statements are merged with governmental activities and/or business-type activities for presentation on the government-wide financial statements (GASB-34, par. 104).

## FINANCIAL REPORTING AT GOVERNMENT-WIDE LEVEL

Government-wide financial statements are divided into governmental activities and business-type activities. Generally, the activities conducted by an Internal Service Fund are related to government activities, and therefore the residual amounts of the Internal Service Funds are consolidated with other governmental funds and presented in the governmental activities column of the government-wide financial statements. However, the activities of an Internal Service Fund must be analyzed to determine whether they are governmental or business-type in nature or both. If the activities are business-type in nature, the residual amounts are consolidated with the business-type activities in the government-wide financial statements.

Internal Service Funds are eliminated to avoid doubling-up expenses and revenues in preparing the government activities column of the statement of activities. The effect of this approach is to adjust activities in an Internal Service Fund to a break-even balance. That is, if the Internal Service Fund had a "net profit" for the year, there should be a pro rata reduction in the charges made to the funds that used the Internal Service Fund's services for the year. Likewise, a net loss would require a pro rata adjustment that would increase the charges made to the various participating funds.

## ILLUSTRATIVE TRANSACTIONS

In order to illustrate accounting and financial reporting standards that should be observed for Internal Service Funds, assume that the City of Centerville has the following three Internal Service Funds:

1. Communications and Technology Support Center
2. Fleet Management Unit
3. Special Services Support Center

## Communications and Technology Support Center

The Communications and Technology Support Center (CTSC) provides a variety of communication and computer support services to all of the City's governmental and proprietary funds. The fund's trial balance for the beginning of the fiscal year is as follows:

| Accounts | Trial Balance Debits | Trial Balance Credits |
|---|---|---|
| Cash | $ 260,000 | |
| Interest receivable | 3,000 | |
| Due from other funds—General Fund | 70,000 | |
| Due from other funds—Centerville Municipal Airport | 25,000 | |
| Due from other funds—Centerville Utilities Authority | 15,000 | |
| Due from other funds—Centerville Parking Authority | 7,000 | |
| Due from other funds—Centerville Toll Bridge | 4,000 | |
| Temporary investments | 15,000 | |
| Inventories | 7,000 | |
| Land and improvements | 2,300,000 | |
| Buildings | 1,400,000 | |
| Accumulated depreciation—buildings | | $ 350,000 |
| Equipment | 5,500,000 | |
| Accumulated depreciation—equipment | | 1,200,000 |
| Vehicles | 120,000 | |
| Accumulated depreciation—vehicles | | 55,000 |
| Accounts payable and accrued expenses | | 15,000 |
| Compensated absences liability | | 4,000 |
| Claims and judgements payable | | 12,000 |
| Notes payable | | 1,500,000 |
| Net assets | | 6,590,000 |
| Totals | $ 9,726,000 | $9,726,000 |

This section presents illustrative transactions and entries for the CTSC during the fiscal year ended June 30, 20X1.

> ■ **CONTINUING STANDARD:** GASB-34 generally did not change the manner of accounting for transactions that are recorded in Internal Service Funds.

## 8-6 Proprietary Funds

***Transaction JE08.01***—Accounts payable and accrued expenses of $15,000 from the previous year were paid:

| Accounts | Debits | Credits |
|---|---|---|
| Accounts payable and accrued expenses | 15,000 | |
| Cash | | 15,000 |

***Transaction JE08.02***—Accrued interest receivable from the previous year was received:

| Accounts | Debits | Credits |
|---|---|---|
| Cash | 3,000 | |
| Interest receivable | | 3,000 |

***Transaction JE08.03***—During the year, the following billings and cash collections were made from the various funds serviced by the CTSC:

| Fund Name | Billings | Cash Collections |
|---|---|---|
| General Fund | $4,500,000 | $4,400,000 |
| Centerville Municipal Airport | 600,000 | 540,000 |
| Centerville Utilities Authority | 220,000 | 200,000 |
| Centerville Parking Authority | 100,000 | 90,000 |
| Centerville Toll Bridge | 80,000 | 66,000 |
| Total | $5,500,000 | $5,296,000 |

| Accounts | Debits | Credits |
|---|---|---|
| Cash | 5,296,000 | |
| Due from other funds—General Fund | 100,000 | |
| Due from other funds—Centerville Municipal Airport | 60,000 | |
| Due from other funds—Centerville Utilities Authority | 20,000 | |
| Due from other funds—Centerville Parking Authority | 10,000 | |
| Due from other funds—Centerville Toll Bridge | 14,000 | |
| Charges for services | | 5,500,000 |

***Transaction JE08.04***—The following operating expenses were incurred during the year, of which $7,200,000 was paid in cash:

| | | |
|---|---:|---:|
| Personal services | $4,800,000 | |
| Contractual services | 1,300,000 | |
| Repairs and maintenance | 1,100,000 | |
| Other supplies and expenses | 50,000 | |
| Total | $7,250,000 | |

| Accounts | Debits | Credits |
|---|---:|---:|
| Personal services expenses | 4,800,000 | |
| Contractual services expenses | 1,300,000 | |
| Repairs and maintenance expenses | 1,100,000 | |
| Other supplies and expenses | 50,000 | |
| Cash | | 7,200,000 |
| Accounts payable and accrued expenses | | 50,000 |

*Transaction JE08.05*—During the year, interest and investment revenue of $5,000 was earned, of which $4,000 was received in cash:

| Accounts | Debits | Credits |
|---|---:|---:|
| Cash | 4,000 | |
| Interest receivable | 1,000 | |
| Interest and investment revenue | | 5,000 |

■ **CONTINUING STANDARD:** The accounting for investments continues to be recorded based on the standards established by GASB-31 (Accounting and Financial Reporting for Certain Investments and for External Investment Pools).

*Transaction JE08.06*—The following capital assets were purchased during the year for cash:

| | |
|---|---:|
| Land and improvements | $ 400,000 |
| Equipment | 1,100,000 |
| Vehicles | 35,000 |
| Total | $1,535,000 |

| Accounts | Debits | Credits |
|---|---:|---:|
| Land and Improvements | 400,000 | |
| Equipment | 1,100,000 | |
| Vehicles | 35,000 | |
| Cash | | 1,535,000 |

*Transaction JE08.07*—The following assets were sold or abandoned during the year. The cash proceeds were $340,000:

## 8-8 Proprietary Funds

|  | Original Cost | Accumulated Depreciation |
|---|---|---|
| Equipment | 730,000 | 420,000 |
| Vehicles | 12,000 | 9,000 |
| Total | $742,000 | $429,000 |

| Accounts | Debits | Credits |
|---|---|---|
| Cash | 340,000 |  |
| Accumulated depreciation—equipment | 420,000 |  |
| Accumulated depreciation—vehicles | 9,000 |  |
| Equipment |  | 730,000 |
| Vehicles |  | 12,000 |
| Miscellaneous revenue—gain on sale of assets |  | 27,000 |

*Transaction JE08.08*—During the year, additional notes of $3,200,000 were issued and interest expense of $97,000 was paid. All notes are related to capital-asset transactions:

| Accounts | Debits | Credits |
|---|---|---|
| Cash | 3,103,000 |  |
| Interest expense | 97,000 |  |
| Notes payable |  | 3,200,000 |

*Transaction JE08.09*—Compensated absences of $2,000 were paid during the year and additional costs of $5,000 were accrued:

| Accounts | Debits | Credits |
|---|---|---|
| Personal services expenses | 5,000 |  |
| Compensated absences liability |  | 3,000 |
| Cash |  | 2,000 |

*Transaction JE08.10*—Claims and judgements of $3,000 were paid during the year and additional costs of $10,000 were accrued:

| Accounts | Debits | Credits |
|---|---|---|
| Insurance claims and expenses | 10,000 |  |
| Claims and judgements payable |  | 7,000 |
| Cash |  | 3,000 |

*Transaction JE08.11*—Depreciation expense recognized during the year was as follows:

| | | |
|---|---:|---:|
| Buildings | $ 220,000 | |
| Equipment | 1,700,000 | |
| Vehicles | 7,000 | |
| Total | $1,927,000 | |

| Accounts | Debits | Credits |
|---|---:|---:|
| Depreciation expense | 1,927,000 | |
| Accumulated depreciation—buildings | | 220,000 |
| Accumulated depreciation—equipment | | 1,700,000 |
| Accumulated depreciation—vehicles | | 7,000 |

*Transaction JE08.12*—An operating grant of $200,000 and a capital grant of $450,000 were received from the state government:

| Accounts | Debits | Credits |
|---|---:|---:|
| Cash | 650,000 | |
| Operating grants and contributions | | 200,000 |
| Capital grants and contributions | | 450,000 |

*Transaction JE08.13*—Other operating revenues earned and received during the year amounted to $10,000 and other operating expenses incurred and paid during the year amounted to $5,000:

| Accounts | Debits | Credits |
|---|---:|---:|
| Cash | 10,000 | |
| Operating revenues—miscellaneous | | 10,000 |
| Operating expenses—miscellaneous | 5,000 | |
| Cash | | 5,000 |

▶ **NEW STANDARD:** GASB-34 notes that an important element of the statement of revenues, expenses, and changes in fund net assets is that there must be a differentiation between operating revenues and nonoperating revenues, and operating expenses and nonoperating expenses based on policies established by the governmental entity. Those policies should be disclosed in the entity's summary of significant accounting policies and must be applied consistently from period to period. GASB-34 states that, in general, differentiations between operating and nonoperating transactions should follow the broad guidance established by GASB-9 (Reporting Cash Flows of Proprietary and Nonexpendable Trust Funds and Governmental Entities that Use Proprietary Fund Accounting). For example, transactions related to (1) capital and related financing activities, (2) noncapital financing activities, (3) investing activities, and

(4) nonexchange revenues, such as tax revenues, generally are to be considered nonoperating transactions for purposes of preparing the statement of revenues, expenses, and changes in net assets (GASB-34, par. 102).

***Transaction JE08.14***—A transfer of $40,000 was received from the General Fund:

| Accounts | Debits | Credits |
|---|---|---|
| Cash | 40,000 | |
|    Transfers in—General Fund | | 40,000 |

***Transaction JE08.15***—Inventories of $9,000 were on hand at the end of the year:

| Accounts | Debits | Credits |
|---|---|---|
| Inventories | 2,000 | |
|    Other supplies and expenses | | 2,000 |

After the transactions for the year are posted, the year-end trial balance (June 30, 20X1) for the CTSC appears as follows:

| Accounts | Adjusted Trial Balance Debits | Credits |
|---|---|---|
| Cash | $ 946,000 | |
| Interest receivable | 1,000 | |
| Due from other funds—General Fund | 170,000 | |
| Due from other funds—Centerville Municipal Airport | 85,000 | |
| Due from other funds—Centerville Utilities Authority | 35,000 | |
| Due from other funds—Centerville Parking Authority | 17,000 | |
| Due from other funds—Centerville Toll Bridge | 18,000 | |
| Temporary investments | 15,000 | |
| Inventories | 9,000 | |
| Land and improvements | 2,700,000 | |
| Buildings | 1,400,000 | |
| Accumulated depreciation—buildings | | $ 570,000 |
| Equipment | 5,870,000 | |

|  | Adjusted Trial Balance | |
| --- | --- | --- |
| Accounts | Debits | Credits |
| Accumulated depreciation—equipment |  | 2,480,000 |
| Vehicles | 143,000 |  |
| Accumulated depreciation—vehicles |  | 53,000 |
| Accounts payable and accrued expenses |  | 50,000 |
| Compensated absences liability |  | 7,000 |
| Claims and judgements payable |  | 19,000 |
| Notes payable |  | 4,700,000 |
| Net assets |  | 6,590,000 |
| Charges for services |  | 5,500,000 |
| Interest and investment revenue |  | 5,000 |
| Miscellaneous revenue—gain on sale of assets |  | 27,000 |
| Operating grants and contributions |  | 200,000 |
| Capital grants and contributions |  | 450,000 |
| Operating revenues—miscellaneous |  | 10,000 |
| Personal services expenses | 4,805,000 |  |
| Contractual services expenses | 1,300,000 |  |
| Repairs and maintenance expenses | 1,100,000 |  |
| Other supplies and expenses | 48,000 |  |
| Insurance claims and expenses | 10,000 |  |
| Depreciation expense | 1,927,000 |  |
| Interest expense | 97,000 |  |
| Operating expenses—miscellaneous | 5,000 |  |
| Transfers in—General Fund |  | 40,000 |
| Totals | $20,701,000 | $20,701,000 |

The worksheet that summarizes the journal entries for the CTSC Internal Service Fund for the year-end trial balance is presented in Appendix 8A.

## Fleet Management Unit

The Fleet Management Unit (FMU) provides a motor pool to all of the City's governmental funds and to some other governmental units that are not part of the City's reporting entity. The FMU provides no services to Enterprise Funds. The fund's trial balance for the beginning of the fiscal year is as follows:

## 8-12 Proprietary Funds

| Accounts | Trial Balance Debits | Credits |
|---|---|---|
| Cash | $ 805,000 | |
| Interest receivable | 4,500 | |
| Due from other funds—General Fund | 22,000 | |
| Due from other governments—County Fire District | 7,000 | |
| Due from other governments—Regional Pollution Control District | 3,000 | |
| Temporary investments | 19,000 | |
| Inventories | 4,000 | |
| Land and improvements | 50,000 | |
| Buildings | 1,600,000 | |
| Accumulated depreciation—buildings | | $ 450,000 |
| Equipment | 1,200,000 | |
| Accumulated depreciation—equipment | | 770,000 |
| Vehicles | 7,400,000 | |
| Accumulated depreciation—vehicles | | 4,300,000 |
| Accounts payable and accrued expenses | | 90,000 |
| Compensated absences liability | | 5,000 |
| Claims and judgements payable | | 10,000 |
| Notes payable | | 4,000,000 |
| Net assets | | 1,489,500 |
| Totals | $11,114,500 | $11,114,500 |

This section presents illustrative transactions and entries for the FMU during the fiscal year ended June 30, 20X1.

***Transaction JE08.16***—Accounts payable and accrued expenses of $90,000 from the previous year were paid:

| Accounts | Debits | Credits |
|---|---|---|
| Accounts payable and accrued expenses | 90,000 | |
| Cash | | 90,000 |

***Transaction JE08.17***—Accrued interest receivable from the previous year was received:

| Accounts | Debits | Credits |
|---|---|---|
| Cash | 4,500 | |
| Interest receivable | | 4,500 |

*Internal Service Funds* 8-13

***Transaction JE08.18***—During the year, the following billings and cash collections were made from the various funds serviced by the FMU:

| Fund Name | Billings | Cash Collections |
|---|---|---|
| General Fund | $4,700,000 | $4,650,000 |
| County Fire District | 200,000 | 190,000 |
| Regional Pollution Control District | 100,000 | 75,000 |
| Total | $5,000,000 | $4,915,000 |

| Accounts | Debits | Credits |
|---|---|---|
| Cash | 4,915,000 | |
| Due from other funds—General Fund | 50,000 | |
| Due from other governments—County Fire District | 10,000 | |
| Due from other governments—Regional Pollution Control District | 25,000 | |
|     Charges for services | | 5,000,000 |

***Transaction JE08.19***—The following operating expenses were incurred during the year, of which $1,825,000 was paid in cash:

| | |
|---|---|
| Personal services | $1,200,000 |
| Contractual services | 400,000 |
| Repairs and maintenance | 200,000 |
| Other supplies and expenses | 150,000 |
| Total | $1,950,000 |

| Accounts | Debits | Credits |
|---|---|---|
| Personal services expenses | 1,200,000 | |
| Contractual services expenses | 400,000 | |
| Repairs and maintenance expenses | 200,000 | |
| Other supplies and expenses | 150,000 | |
|     Cash | | 1,825,000 |
|     Accounts payable and accrued expenses | | 125,000 |

***Transaction JE08.20***—During the year, interest and investment revenue of $5,000 was earned, of which $3,000 was received in cash:

| Accounts | Debits | Credits |
|---|---|---|
| Cash | 3,000 | |
| Interest receivable | 2,000 | |
|     Interest and investment revenue | | 5,000 |

## 8-14 Proprietary Funds

**Transaction JE08.21**—The following capital assets were purchased during the year for cash:

| | | |
|---|---|---|
| Equipment | $ 350,000 | |
| Vehicles | 2,600,000 | |
| Total | $2,950,000 | |

| Accounts | Debits | Credits |
|---|---|---|
| Equipment | 350,000 | |
| Vehicles | 2,600,000 | |
| Cash | | 2,950,000 |

**Transaction JE08.22**—The following assets were sold or abandoned during the year. The cash proceeds were $410,000:

| | Original Cost | Accumulated Depreciation |
|---|---|---|
| Equipment | $ 220,000 | $ 195,000 |
| Vehicles | 1,800,000 | 1,350,000 |
| Total | $2,020,000 | $1,545,000 |

| Accounts | Debits | Credits |
|---|---|---|
| Cash | 410,000 | |
| Accumulated depreciation—equipment | 195,000 | |
| Accumulated depreciation—vehicles | 1,350,000 | |
| Miscellaneous expenses—loss on sale of assets | 65,000 | |
| Equipment | | 220,000 |
| Vehicles | | 1,800,000 |

**Transaction JE08.23**—During the year, notes of $1,000,000 were paid along with interest expense of $180,000. All notes are related to capital-asset transactions:

| Accounts | Debits | Credits |
|---|---|---|
| Notes payable | 1,000,000 | |
| Interest expense | 180,000 | |
| Cash | | 1,180,000 |

**Transaction JE08.24**—Compensated absences of $3,000 were paid during the year and additional costs of $6,000 were accrued:

| Accounts | Debits | Credits |
|---|---|---|
| Personal services expenses | 6,000 | |
|     Compensated absences liability | | 3,000 |
|     Cash | | 3,000 |

*Transaction JE08.25*—Claims and judgements of $4,000 were paid during the year and additional costs of $7,000 were accrued:

| Accounts | Debits | Credits |
|---|---|---|
| Insurance claims and expenses | 7,000 | |
|     Claims and judgements payable | | 3,000 |
|     Cash | | 4,000 |

*Transaction JE08.26*—Depreciation expense recognized during the year was as follows:

| | |
|---|---|
| Buildings | $ 370,000 |
| Equipment | 310,000 |
| Vehicles | 1,850,000 |
| Total | $2,530,000 |

| Accounts | Debits | Credits |
|---|---|---|
| Depreciation expense | 2,530,000 | |
|     Accumulated depreciation—buildings | | 370,000 |
|     Accumulated depreciation—equipment | | 310,000 |
|     Accumulated depreciation—vehicles | | 1,850,000 |

*Transaction JE08.27*—An operating grant of $100,000 was received from the state government:

| Accounts | Debits | Credits |
|---|---|---|
| Cash | 100,000 | |
|     Operating grants and contributions | | 100,000 |

*Transaction JE08.28*—Other operating revenues earned and received during the year amounted to $4,000 and other operating expenses incurred and paid during the year amounted to $2,000:

| Accounts | Debits | Credits |
|---|---|---|
| Cash | 4,000 | |
|     Operating revenues—miscellaneous | | 4,000 |

| Accounts | Debits | Credits |
|---|---|---|
| Operating expenses—miscellaneous | 2,000 | |
| Cash | | 2,000 |

***Transaction JE08.29***—A transfer of $50,000 was made from the FMU to the General Fund:

| Accounts | Debits | Credits |
|---|---|---|
| Transfers out—General Fund | 50,000 | |
| Cash | | 50,000 |

***Transaction JE08.30***—Inventories of $7,000 were on hand at the end of the year:

| Accounts | Debits | Credits |
|---|---|---|
| Inventories | 3,000 | |
| Other supplies and expenses | | 3,000 |

After the transactions for the year are posted, the year-end trial balance (June 30, 20X1) for the FMU appears as follows:

| Accounts | Adjusted Trial Balance Debits | Credits |
|---|---|---|
| Cash | $ 137,500 | |
| Interest receivable | 2,000 | |
| Due from other funds—General Fund | 72,000 | |
| Due from other governments—County Fire District | 17,000 | |
| Due from other governments—Regional Pollution Control District | 28,000 | |
| Temporary investments | 19,000 | |
| Inventories | 7,000 | |
| Land and improvements | 50,000 | |
| Buildings | 1,600,000 | |
| Accumulated depreciation—buildings | | $ 820,000 |
| Equipment | 1,330,000 | |
| Accumulated depreciation—equipment | | 885,000 |
| Vehicles | 8,200,000 | |
| Accumulated depreciation—vehicles | | 4,800,000 |
| Accounts payable and accrued expenses | | 125,000 |
| Compensated absences liability | | 8,000 |
| Claims and judgements payable | | 13,000 |

|  | Adjusted Trial Balance |  |
| --- | --- | --- |
| Accounts | Debits | Credits |
| Notes payable |  | 3,000,000 |
| Net assets |  | 1,489,500 |
| Charges for services |  | 5,000,000 |
| Interest and investment revenue |  | 5,000 |
| Operating grants and contributions |  | 100,000 |
| Operating revenues—miscellaneous |  | 4,000 |
| Personal services expenses | 1,206,000 |  |
| Contractual services expenses | 400,000 |  |
| Repairs and maintenance expenses | 200,000 |  |
| Other supplies and expenses | 147,000 |  |
| Insurance claims and expenses | 7,000 |  |
| Depreciation expense | 2,530,000 |  |
| Interest expense | 180,000 |  |
| Operating expenses—miscellaneous | 2,000 |  |
| Miscellaneous expenses—loss on sale of assets | 65,000 |  |
| Transfers out—General Fund | 50,000 |  |
| Totals | $16,249,500 | $16,249,500 |

The worksheet that summarizes the journal entries for the FMU for the year-end trial balance is presented in Appendix 8B.

## Special Services Support Center

The Special Services Support Center (SSSC) provides services exclusively for the Centerville Municipal Airport. The fund's trial balance for the beginning of the fiscal year is as follows:

|  | Trial Balance |  |
| --- | --- | --- |
| Accounts | Debits | Credits |
| Cash | $ 503,000 |  |
| Interest receivable | 9,000 |  |
| Due from other funds—Centerville Municipal Airport | 77,000 |  |
| Temporary investments | 12,000 |  |
| Inventories | 16,000 |  |
| Land and improvements | 1,400,000 |  |
| Buildings | 1,600,000 |  |
| Accumulated depreciation—buildings |  | $450,000 |

8-18  *Proprietary Funds*

|  | Trial Balance | |
| --- | --- | --- |
| Accounts | Debits | Credits |
| Equipment | 2,300,000 | |
| Accumulated depreciation—equipment | | 1,300,000 |
| Vehicles | 1,800,000 | |
| Accumulated depreciation—vehicles | | 650,000 |
| Accounts payable and accrued expenses | | 35,000 |
| Compensated absences liability | | 14,000 |
| Claims and judgements payable | | 22,000 |
| Notes payable | | 450,000 |
| Net assets | | 4,796,000 |
| Totals | $7,717,000 | $7,717,000 |

This section presents illustrative transactions and entries for the SSSC during the fiscal year ended June 30, 20X1.

***Transaction JE08.31***—Accounts payable and accrued expenses of $35,000 from the previous year were paid:

| Accounts | Debits | Credits |
| --- | --- | --- |
| Accounts payable and accrued expenses | 35,000 | |
| Cash | | 35,000 |

***Transaction JE08.32***—Accrued interest receivable from the previous year was received:

| Accounts | Debits | Credits |
| --- | --- | --- |
| Cash | 9,000 | |
| Interest receivable | | 9,000 |

***Transaction JE08.33***—During the year, billings of $2,950,000 and cash collections of $2,600,000 were made by the CTSC:

| Accounts | Debits | Credits |
| --- | --- | --- |
| Cash | 2,600,000 | |
| Due from other funds— Centerville Municipal Airport | 350,000 | |
| Charges for services | | 2,950,000 |

***Transaction JE08.34***—The following operating expenses were incurred during the year, of which $1,750,000 was paid in cash:

| Personal services | $ 900,000 |
| --- | --- |
| Contractual services | 400,000 |
| Repairs and maintenance | 350,000 |
| Other supplies and expenses | 175,000 |
| Total | $1,825,000 |

| Accounts | Debits | Credits |
| --- | --- | --- |
| Personal services expenses | 900,000 | |
| Contractual services expenses | 400,000 | |
| Repairs and maintenance expenses | 350,000 | |
| Other supplies and expenses | 175,000 | |
| Cash | | 1,750,000 |
| Accounts payable and accrued expenses | | 75,000 |

*Transaction JE08.35*—During the year, interest and investment revenue of $15,000 was earned, of which $14,000 was received in cash:

| Accounts | Debits | Credits |
| --- | --- | --- |
| Cash | 14,000 | |
| Interest receivable | 1,000 | |
| Interest and investment revenue | | 15,000 |

*Transaction JE08.36*—The following capital assets were purchased during the year for cash:

| Land and improvements | $ 350,000 |
| --- | --- |
| Equipment | 780,000 |
| Vehicles | 425,000 |
| Total | $1,555,000 |

| Accounts | Debits | Credits |
| --- | --- | --- |
| Land and improvements | 350,000 | |
| Equipment | 780,000 | |
| Vehicles | 425,000 | |
| Cash | | 1,555,000 |

*Transaction JE08.37*—The following assets were sold or abandoned during the year. The cash proceeds were $95,000:

8-20  *Proprietary Funds*

|  | Original Cost | Accumulated Depreciation |
|---|---|---|
| Equipment | $120,000 | $ 90,000 |
| Vehicles | 230,000 | 195,000 |
| Total | $350,000 | $285,000 |

| Accounts | Debits | Credits |
|---|---|---|
| Cash | 95,000 |  |
| Accumulated depreciation—equipment | 90,000 |  |
| Accumulated depreciation—vehicles | 195,000 |  |
|    Equipment |  | 120,000 |
|    Vehicles |  | 230,000 |
|    Miscellaneous revenue—gain on sale of assets |  | 30,000 |

*Transaction JE08.38*—During the year, additional notes of $200,000 were issued and interest expense of $32,000 was paid. Also, notes of $100,000 were paid off. All notes are related to capital-asset transactions:

| Accounts | Debits | Credits |
|---|---|---|
| Cash | 168,000 |  |
| Interest expense | 32,000 |  |
|    Notes payable |  | 200,000 |
|  |  |  |
| Notes payable | 100,000 |  |
|    Cash |  | 100,000 |

*Transaction JE08.39*—Compensated absences of $12,000 were paid during the year and additional costs of $15,000 were accrued:

| Accounts | Debits | Credits |
|---|---|---|
| Personal services expenses | 15,000 |  |
|    Compensated absences liability |  | 3,000 |
|    Cash |  | 12,000 |

*Transaction JE08.40*—Claims and judgements of $13,000 were paid during the year and additional costs of $12,000 were accrued:

| Accounts | Debits | Credits |
|---|---|---|
| Insurance claims and expenses | 12,000 |  |
| Claims and judgements payable | 1,000 |  |
|    Cash |  | 13,000 |

*Transaction JE08.41*—Depreciation expense recognized during the year was as follows:

| | |
|---|---:|
| Buildings | $ 375,000 |
| Equipment | 175,000 |
| Vehicles | 575,000 |
| Total | $1,125,000 |

| Accounts | Debits | Credits |
|---|---:|---:|
| Depreciation expense | 1,125,000 | |
|   Accumulated depreciation—buildings | | 375,000 |
|   Accumulated depreciation—equipment | | 175,000 |
|   Accumulated depreciation—vehicles | | 575,000 |

*Transaction JE08.42*—An operating grant of $70,000 and a capital grant of $40,000 were received from the state government:

| Accounts | Debits | Credits |
|---|---:|---:|
| Cash | 110,000 | |
|   Operating grants and contributions | | 70,000 |
|   Capital grants and contributions | | 40,000 |

*Transaction JE08.43*—Other operating revenues earned and received during the year amounted to $3,000 and other operating expenses incurred and paid during the year amounted to $15,000:

| Accounts | Debits | Credits |
|---|---:|---:|
| Cash | 3,000 | |
|   Operating revenues—miscellaneous | | 3,000 |
| Operating expenses—miscellaneous | 15,000 | |
|   Cash | | 15,000 |

*Transaction JE08.44*—Inventories of $20,000 were on hand at the end of the year:

| Accounts | Debits | Credits |
|---|---:|---:|
| Inventories | 4,000 | |
|   Other supplies and expenses | | 4,000 |

**8-22** *Proprietary Funds*

After the transactions for the year are posted, the year-end trial balance (June 30, 20X1) for the SSSC appears as follows:

| Accounts | Adjusted Trial Balance Debits | Credits |
|---|---|---|
| Cash | $ 22,000 | |
| Interest receivable | 1,000 | |
| Due from other funds—Centerville Municipal Airport | 427,000 | |
| Temporary investments | 12,000 | |
| Inventories | 20,000 | |
| Land and improvements | 1,750,000 | |
| Buildings | 1,600,000 | |
| Accumulated depreciation—buildings | | $ 825,000 |
| Equipment | 2,960,000 | |
| Accumulated depreciation—equipment | | 1,385,000 |
| Vehicles | 1,995,000 | |
| Accumulated depreciation—vehicles | | 1,030,000 |
| Accounts payable and accrued expenses | | 75,000 |
| Compensated absences liability | | 17,000 |
| Claims and judgements payable | | 21,000 |
| Notes payable | | 550,000 |
| Net assets | | 4,796,000 |
| Charges for services | | 2,950,000 |
| Interest and investment revenue | | 15,000 |
| Miscellaneous revenue—gain on sale of assets | | 30,000 |
| Operating grants and contributions | | 70,000 |
| Capital grants and contributions | | 40,000 |
| Operating revenues—miscellaneous | | 3,000 |
| Personal services expenses | 915,000 | |
| Contractual services expenses | 400,000 | |
| Repairs and maintenance expenses | 350,000 | |
| Other supplies and expenses | 171,000 | |
| Insurance claims and expenses | 12,000 | |
| Depreciation expense | 1,125,000 | |
| Interest expense | 32,000 | |
| Operating expenses—miscellaneous | 15,000 | |
| Totals | $11,807,000 | $11,807,000 |

The worksheet that summarizes the journal entries for the SSSC for the year-end trial balance is presented in Appendix 8C.

## FUND FINANCIAL STATEMENTS

At the fund financial statement level, Internal Service Fund balances and activities are combined into a single column and placed on the proprietary fund financial statements to the right of the financial statements of Enterprise Funds. Proprietary funds must prepare a statement of net assets (or balance sheet), statement of revenues, expenses, and changes in fund net assets or fund equity and statement of cash flows. Based on the adjusted trial balances created above, the following financial statements reflect the balances and activities of the three Internal Service Funds (see Appendix 8D).

In the preparation of the statement of net assets, notes payable were assumed to be associated with the acquisition of capital assets and the current and noncurrent portions of certain liabilities were assumed.

**Internal Service Funds**
**Statement of Net Assets**
**June 30, 20X1**

|  | Communications and Technology Support Center | Fleet Management | Special Services Support Center | Total |
|---|---|---|---|---|
| **ASSETS** | | | | |
| Current assets: | | | | |
| Cash | $ 946,000 | $ 137,500 | $ 22,000 | $1,105,500 |
| Interest receivable | 1,000 | 2,000 | 1,000 | 4,000 |
| Due from other funds | 325,000 | 72,000 | 427,000 | 824,000 |
| Due from other governments |  | 45,000 |  | 45,000 |
| Temporary investments | 15,000 | 19,000 | 12,000 | 46,000 |
| Inventories | 9,000 | 7,000 | 20,000 | 36,000 |
| Total current assets | 1,296,000 | 282,500 | 482,000 | 2,060,500 |
| Noncurrent assets: | | | | |
| Land and improvements | 2,700,000 | 50,000 | 1,750,000 | 4,500,000 |
| Buildings | 1,400,000 | 1,600,000 | 1,600,000 | 4,600,000 |

8-24  *Proprietary Funds*

|  | Communications and Technology Support Center | Fleet Management | Special Services Support Center | Total |
|---|---|---|---|---|
| Equipment | 5,870,000 | 1,330,000 | 2,960,000 | 10,160,000 |
| Vehicles | 143,000 | 8,200,000 | 1,995,000 | 10,338,000 |
| Less accumulated depreciation | (3,103,000) | (6,505,000) | (3,240,000) | (12,848,000) |
| Total non-current assets | 7,010,000 | 4,675,000 | 5,065,000 | 16,750,000 |
| Total assets | $8,306,000 | $4,957,500 | $5,547,000 | $18,810,500 |

**LIABILITIES**
Current liabilities:

|  |  |  |  |  |
|---|---|---|---|---|
| Accounts payable and accrued expenses | 50,000 | 125,000 | 75,000 | 250,000 |
| Compensated absences | 3,000 | 2,000 | 5,000 | 10,000 |
| Claims and judgements | 4,000 | 2,000 | 7,000 | 13,000 |
| Notes payable |  | 1,500,000 | 200,000 | 1,700,000 |
| Total current liabilities | 57,000 | 1,629,000 | 287,000 | 1,973,000 |

Noncurrent liabilities:

|  |  |  |  |  |
|---|---|---|---|---|
| Compensated absences | 4,000 | 6,000 | 12,000 | 22,000 |
| Claims and judgements | 15,000 | 11,000 | 14,000 | 40,000 |
| Notes payable | 4,700,000 | 1,500,000 | 350,000 | 6,550,000 |
| Total non-current liabilities | 4,719,000 | 1,517,000 | 376,000 | 6,612,000 |
| Total liabilities | $4,776,000 | $3,146,000 | $663,000 | $8,585,000 |

**NET ASSETS**

|  |  |  |  |  |
|---|---|---|---|---|
| Invested in capital assets, net of related debt | 2,310,000 | 1,675,000 | 4,515,000 | 8,500,000 |
| Unrestricted | 1,220,000 | 136,500 | 369,000 | 1,725,500 |
| Total net assets | $3,530,000 | $1,811,500 | $4,884,000 | $10,225,500 |

## Internal Service Funds
## Statement of Revenues, Expenses, and Changes in Fund Net Assets
## For the Year Ended June 30, 20X1

|  | Communications and Technology Support Center | Fleet Management | Special Services Support Center | Total |
|---|---|---|---|---|
| **OPERATING REVENUES** | | | | |
| Charges for services | $5,500,000 | $5,000,000 | $2,950,000 | $13,450,000 |
| Miscellaneous | 10,000 | 4,000 | 3,000 | 17,000 |
| Total operating revenues | 5,510,000 | 5,004,000 | 2,953,000 | 13,467,000 |
| **OPERATING EXPENSES** | | | | |
| Personal services | 4,805,000 | 1,206,000 | 915,000 | 6,926,000 |
| Contractual services | 1,300,000 | 400,000 | 400,000 | 2,100,000 |
| Repairs and maintenance | 1,100,000 | 200,000 | 350,000 | 1,650,000 |
| Other supplies and expenses | 48,000 | 147,000 | 171,000 | 366,000 |
| Insurance claims and expenses | 10,000 | 7,000 | 12,000 | 29,000 |
| Depreciation | 1,927,000 | 2,530,000 | 1,125,000 | 5,582,000 |
| Miscellaneous | 5,000 | 2,000 | 15,000 | 22,000 |
| Total operating expenses | 9,195,000 | 4,492,000 | 2,988,000 | 16,675,000 |
| Operating income (loss) | (3,685,000) | 512,000 | (35,000) | (3,208,000) |
| **NONOPERATING REVENUES (EXPENSES)** | | | | |
| Interest and investment revenue | 5,000 | 5,000 | 15,000 | 25,000 |
| Interest | (97,000) | (180,000) | (32,000) | (309,000) |
| Operating grants and contributions | 200,000 | 100,000 | 70,000 | 370,000 |
| Miscellaneous | 27,000 | (65,000) | 30,000 | (8,000) |
| Total nonoperating revenue (expenses) | 135,000 | (140,000) | 83,000 | 78,000 |

|  | Communications and Technology Support Center | Fleet Management | Special Services Support Center | Total |
|---|---|---|---|---|
| Income (loss) before capital contributions and transfers | (3,550,000) | 372,000 | 48,000 | (3,130,000) |
| Capital contributions | 450,000 |  | 40,000 | 490,000 |
| Transfers in | 40,000 |  |  | 40,000 |
| Transfers out |  | (50,000) |  | (50,000) |
| Change in net assets | (3,060,000) | 322,000 | 88,000 | (2,650,000) |
| Total net assets—beginning | 6,590,000 | 1,489,500 | 4,796,000 | 12,875,500 |
| Total net assets—ending | $3,530,000 | $1,811,500 | $4,884,000 | $10,225,500 |

## Internal Service Funds
## Statement of Cash Flows
## For the Year Ended June 30, 20X1

|  | Communications and Technology Support Center | Fleet Management | Special Services Support Center | Total |
|---|---|---|---|---|
| **CASH FLOWS FROM OPERATING ACTIVITIES** |  |  |  |  |
| Receipts from customers | $ 5,296,000 | $ 4,915,000 | $2,600,000 | $12,811,000 |
| Payments to suppliers | (2,435,000) | (815,000) | (935,000) | (4,185,000) |
| Payments to employees | (4,782,000) | (1,103,000) | (862,000) | (6,747,000) |
| Other receipts (payments) | 2,000 | (2,000) | (25,000) | (25,000) |
| Net cash provided by operating activities | (1,919,000) | 2,995,000 | 778,000 | 1,854,000 |

|  | Communications and Technology Support Center | Fleet Management | Special Services Support Center | Total |
|---|---|---|---|---|
| **CASH FLOWS FROM NONCAPITAL FINANCING ACTIVITIES** | | | | |
| Operating subsidies and transfers from (to) other funds | 240,000 | 50,000 | 70,000 | 360,000 |
| **CASH FLOWS FROM CAPITAL AND RELATED FINANCING ACTIVITIES** | | | | |
| Proceeds from the issuance of capital debt | 3,200,000 | | 200,000 | 3,400,000 |
| Capital contributions | 450,000 | | 40,000 | 490,000 |
| Acquisitions of capital assets | (1,535,000) | (2,950,000) | (1,555,000) | (6,040,000) |
| Proceeds from sale of capital assets | 340,000 | 410,000 | 95,000 | 845,000 |
| Principal paid on capital debt | | (1,000,000) | (100,000) | (1,100,000) |
| Interest paid on capital debt | (97,000) | (180,000) | (32,000) | (309,000 |
| Net cash (used) by capital and related financing activities | 2,358,000 | (3,720,000) | (1,352,000) | (2,714,000) |
| **CASH FLOWS FROM INVESTING ACTIVITIES** | | | | |
| Interest and dividends | 7,000 | 7,500 | 23,000 | 37,500 |
| Net increase (decrease) in cash | 686,000 | (667,500) | (481,000) | (462,500) |
| Balances— beginning of year | 260,000 | 805,000 | 503,000 | 1,568,000 |
| Balances— end of year | $946,000 | $137,500 | $22,000 | $1,105,500 |

|  | Communications and Technology Support Center | Fleet Management | Special Services Support Center | Total |
|---|---|---|---|---|
| **Reconciliation of operating income (loss) to net cash provided (used) by operating activities:** | | | | |
| Operating income (loss) | $(3,685,000) | 512,000 | $(35,000) | $(3,208,000) |
| Adjustments: | | | | |
| Depreciation expense | 1,927,000 | 2,530,000 | 1,125,000 | 5,582,000 |
| Change in assets and liabilities: | | | | |
| Receivables, net | $(204,000) | $(85,000) | $(350,000) | $(639,000) |
| Inventories | (2,000) | (3,000) | (4,000) | (9,000) |
| Accounts and accrued liabilities | 45,000 | 41,000 | 42,000 | 128,000 |
| Net cash provided (used) by operating activities | $(1,919,000) | 2,995,000 | 778,000 | 1,854,000 |

The combined financial statements for the Internal Service Funds are used later, in Chapter 12 ("Developing Information for Fund Financial Statements").

## CONVERTING TO GOVERNMENT-WIDE FINANCIAL STATEMENTS

Government-wide financial statements are reported on the accrual basis of accounting. Generally, most governments will work from their proprietary fund financial statements and through the use of worksheet entries convert to accrual based financial statements. Proprietary funds are presented on an accrual basis. Therefore, there often is no need to make worksheet entries to convert the information from a fund basis to a government-wide basis; however, the residual balances and the activities of Internal Service Funds must be analyzed to determine how they are to be merged into the government-wide financial statements (see Appendix 8E).

## Determining the Allocation Base

As noted earlier in this chapter, any profit or loss from an Internal Service Fund must be allocated to governmental and/or business-type activities in order to reduce or increase the operating activities of the fund to break-even amounts. However, the following items are generally not used to determine the allocation of operating results of an Internal Service Fund:

- Interest and investment revenue
- Interest expense
- Transfers in/out
- Billings to external parties

*Interest and Investment Revenue*

A fundamental concept in the formatting of the statement of activities is the identification of resource inflows to the governmental entities that are related to specific programs and those that are general in nature. GASB-34 notes that governmental activities are generally financed from the following sources of resource inflows:

- Parties who purchase, use, or directly benefit from goods and services provided through the program (for example, fees for public transportation and licenses)
- Outside parties (other governments and nongovernmental entities or individuals) who provide goods and services to the governmental entity (for example, a grant to a local government from a state government)
- The reporting government's constituencies (for example, property taxes)
- The governmental entity (for example, investment income)

The first source of resources is always program revenue. The second source is program revenue if it is restricted to a specific program; otherwise the item is considered general revenue. The third source is always general revenue, even when restricted. The fourth source of resources, which includes investment income, is usually general revenue.

Based on the nature of an Internal Service Fund, investment income will usually be considered general revenue and reported in the lower section of the statement of activities. Therefore, when an Internal Service

Fund has investment income, only the *net profit or loss before investment income* should be allocated to the operating programs. Because none of the interest and investment income is restricted, the amount should be combined with other unrestricted income and presented as a separate line item in the statement of activities for both governmental activities and business-type activities.

*Interest Expense*

Generally, interest expense on debt issued by an Internal Service Fund is considered an indirect expense and should not be allocated as a direct expense to specific functional categories that appear on the statement of activities but rather should be presented as a single line item, appropriately labeled. For this reason, when an Internal Service Fund has interest expense, only the *profit or loss before interest charges* should be allocated to the governmental operating programs. The interest expense should be combined with other interest expense related to governmental activities and the single amount should be presented on the statement of activities.

When interest expense is incurred by an Internal Service Fund that services only Enterprise Funds, the interest is directly related to business-type activities. That is, the funds could have been borrowed by the Internal Service Fund or directly by the Enterprise Funds. For this reason, interest expense under this circumstance should be used in determining the amount of net profit or loss incurred by the Internal Service Fund that should be allocated to business-type activities.

*Transfers In/Out*

GASB-34 states that transfers in/out are nonreciprocal transactions and represent interfund activities whereby the two parties to the events do not receive equivalent cash, goods, or services. Governmental funds should report transfers of this nature in their fund operating statements as other financing uses and other financial sources of funds. Proprietary funds should report this type of transfer in their activity statements after nonoperating revenues and nonoperating expenses. Based on the nature of transfers in/out as defined in GASB-34, these transfers should not be considered when determining the amount of net profit or loss that must be allocated back to the various programs reported on the statement of activities.

*Billings to External Parties*

A governmental entity may establish an Internal Service Fund that has its predominant activities with other units of the reporting entity but for simplicity purposes also makes sales (of a nonpredominant amount) to external parties. Under this circumstance, the external sales and related cost of sales should not be used to determine the net profit or loss amount that is the basis for adjusting the expenses incurred in the governmental column of the statement of activities

Based on the guidance provided above, the basis used to allocate the results of operations of the three Internal Service Funds is computed as follows:

|  | Communications and Technology Support Center | Fleet Management Unit | Special Services Support Center |
|---|---|---|---|
| Change in net assets as reported in the statement of revenues, expenses, and changes in fund net assets | $(3,060,000) | $322,000 | $ 88,000 |
| Less interest and investment revenue | (5,000) | (5,000) | (15,000) |
| Add interest expense | 97,000 | 180,000 |  |
| Less transfers in | (40,000) |  |  |
| Add transfers out |  | 50,000 |  |
| Less profit on external sales* |  | (30,000) |  |
| Net amount to be allocated to governmental/ business-type activities | $(3,008,000) | $517,000 | $73,000 |

* The Fleet Management Unit provides services to two external governments (County Fire District and Regional Pollution Control District). The billings for the year to these external parties totaled $300,000 and the estimated cost of providing these services was $270,000. Thus, the profit on external sales was $30,000 ($300,000–$270,000). As shown later in this chapter (based on the assumed nature of the activities), the external sales are reported as "program revenues—charges for services (general government)" and the related expenses are reported as "expenses—general government" in the statement of activities (a government-wide financial statement).

## Communications and Technology Support Center

The CTSC supports all of the City's governmental and proprietary funds. The billings to each of these activities were as follows during the year:

## 8-32  Proprietary Funds

| Fund Name | Billings | Percentage of Total Billings | Amount of operating loss ($3,008,000) allocated |
|---|---|---|---|
| General Fund | $4,500,000 | 81.8% | $2,460,544 |
| Centerville Municipal Airport | 600,000 | 10.9 | 327,872 |
| Centerville Utilities Authority | 220,000 | 4.0 | 120,320 |
| Centerville Parking Authority | 100,000 | 1.8 | 54,144 |
| Centerville Toll Bridge | 80,000 | 1.5 | 45,120 |
| Total | $5,500,000 | 100.0% | $3,008,000 |

Based on the above analysis, the following worksheet entries are made in order to adjust the expenses reported on the statement of activities and allocate the net assets of the Internal Service Fund to the governmental activities column of the statement of net assets:

| | Accounts | Debit | Credit |
|---|---|---|---|
| JE08.45 | Cash | 946,000 | |
| | Interest receivable | 1,000 | |
| | Due from other funds | 325,000 | |
| | Temporary investments | 15,000 | |
| | Inventories | 9,000 | |
| | Land and improvements | 2,700,000 | |
| | Buildings | 1,400,000 | |
| | Equipment | 5,870,000 | |
| | Vehicles | 143,000 | |
| | Expenses—general government ($2,460,544 × 60%)* | 1,476,326 | |
| | Expenses—public safety ($2,460,544 × 20%)* | 492,109 | |
| | Expenses—streets ($2,460,544 × 10%)* | 246,055 | |
| | Expenses—recreation and parks ($2,460,544 × 5%)* | 123,027 | |
| | Expenses—health and welfare ($2,460,544 × 5%)* | 123,027 | |
| | Internal balances | 547,456 | |
| | Interest expense | 97,000 | |
| | Accumulated depreciation | | 3,103,000 |

| Accounts | Debit | Credit |
|---|---|---|
| Accounts payable and accrued expenses | | 50,000 |
| Compensated absences—current | | 3,000 |
| Claims and judgements—current | | 4,000 |
| Compensated absences—noncurrent | | 4,000 |
| Claims and judgements—noncurrent | | 15,000 |
| Notes payable—noncurrent | | 4,700,000 |
| Interest and investment revenue | | 5,000 |
| Transfers in | | 40,000 |
| Net assets | | 6,590,000 |
| (To merge balances of the Communications and Technology Support Center Internal Service Fund with governmental activities) | | |

---

* The allocation to the General Fund is distributed to the various program activities based on the following assumption:

| | |
|---|---|
| General government | 60% |
| Public safety | 20% |
| Streets | 10% |
| Recreation and Parks | 5% |
| Health and Welfare | 5% |
| Total | 100% |

In addition, the following worksheet entry is made in order to adjust the expenses reported on the statement of activities and to allocate the net assets of the Internal Service Fund to the business-type activities column of the statement of net assets:

| | Accounts | Debit | Credit |
|---|---|---|---|
| JE08.46 | Expenses—Centerville Municipal Airport | 327,872 | |
| | Expenses—Centerville Utilities Authority | 120,320 | |
| | Expenses—Centerville Parking Authority | 54,144 | |

| Accounts | Debit | Credit |
|---|---|---|
| Expenses—Centerville Toll Bridge | 45,120 | |
| Internal balances | | 547,456 |
| (To merge balances of the Communications and Technology Support Center Internal Service Fund with business-type activities) | | |

The two entries made above are taken forward to Chapter 13 ("Developing Information For Government-Wide Financial Statements").

## Fleet Management

The FMU provides a motor pool to all of the City's governmental funds and to some other governmental units that are not part of the City's reporting entity. The FMU provides no services to other proprietary funds.

Based on the above analysis, the following worksheet entry is made in order to adjust the expenses reported on the statement of activities and allocate the net assets of the Internal Service Fund to the governmental activities column of the statement of net assets.

| | Accounts | Debit | Credit |
|---|---|---|---|
| JE08.47 | Cash | 137,500 | |
| | Interest receivable | 2,000 | |
| | Due from other funds | 72,000 | |
| | Due from other governments | 45,000 | |
| | Temporary investments | 19,000 | |
| | Inventories | 7,000 | |
| | Land and improvements | 50,000 | |
| | Buildings | 1,600,000 | |
| | Equipment | 1,330,000 | |
| | Vehicles | 8,200,000 | |
| | Interest expense | 180,000 | |
| | Transfers out | 50,000 | |
| | Expenses—general government [($517,000 × 60%) - $270,000] | | 40,200 |
| | Expenses—public safety ($517,000 × 20%) | | 103,400 |
| | Expenses—streets ($517,000 × 10%) | | 51,700 |

*Internal Service Funds* 8-35

| Accounts | Debit | Credit |
|---|---|---|
| Expenses—recreation and parks ($517,000 × 5%) | | 25,850 |
| Expenses—health and welfare ($517,000 × 5%) | | 25,850 |
| Accumulated depreciation | | 6,505,000 |
| Accounts payable and accrued expenses | | 125,000 |
| Compensated absences—current | | 2,000 |
| Claims and judgements—current | | 2,000 |
| Notes payable—durrent | | 1,500,000 |
| Compensated absences—noncurrent | | 6,000 |
| Claims and judgements—noncurrent | | 11,000 |
| Notes payable—noncurrent | | 1,500,000 |
| Interest and investment revenue | | 5,000 |
| Program revenues—charges for services (general government) | | 300,000 |
| Net assets | | 1,489,500 |
| (To merge balances of the Fleet Management Unit Internal Service Fund with governmental activities) | | |

The entry made above is taken forward to Chapter 13 ("Developing Information For Government-Wide Financial Statements").

## Special Services Support Center

The SSSC provides services exclusively for the Centerville Municipal Airport; therefore, all of the residual balances and the adjustment for the operating profit for the year are allocated to the airport (business-type activities) in the following worksheet entry:

| | Accounts | Debit | Credit |
|---|---|---|---|
| JE08.48 | Cash | 22,000 | |
| | Interest receivable | 1,000 | |
| | Due from other funds | 427,000 | |
| | Temporary investments | 12,000 | |

## 8-36  Proprietary Funds

| Accounts | Debit | Credit |
|---|---|---|
| Inventories | 20,000 | |
| Land and improvements | 1,750,000 | |
| Buildings | 1,600,000 | |
| Equipment | 2,960,000 | |
| Vehicles | 1,995,000 | |
| Expenses—Centerville Municipal Airport | | 73,000 |
| Accumulated depreciation | | 3,240,000 |
| Accounts payable and accrued expenses | | 75,000 |
| Compensated absences—current | | 5,000 |
| Claims and judgements—current | | 7,000 |
| Notes payable—current | | 200,000 |
| Compensated absences—noncurrent | | 12,000 |
| Claims and judgements—noncurrent | | 14,000 |
| Notes payable—noncurrent | | 350,000 |
| Interest and investment revenue | | 15,000 |
| Net assets | | 4,796,000 |
| (To merge balances of the Special Services Support Center Internal Service Fund with business-type activities) | | |

The above entry is taken forward to Chapter 13 ("Developing Information For Government-Wide Financial Statements").

## APPENDIX 8A: WORKSHEET FOR SUMMARIZING CURRENT TRANSACTIONS—COMMUNICATIONS AND TECHNOLOGY SUPPORT CENTER

**WORKSHEET ENTRIES**

| Accounts | Trial Balance Debits | Trial Balance Credits | Adjustments Debits | | Adjustments Credits | | Adjusted Trial Balance Debits | Adjusted Trial Balance Credits | Operating Statement Debits | Operating Statement Credits | Balance Sheet Debits | Balance Sheet Credits |
|---|---|---|---|---|---|---|---|---|---|---|---|---|
| Cash | 260,000 | | JE08.02 3,000 | JE08.01 15,000 | | | 946,000 | | | | 946,000 | |
| | | | JE08.03 5,296,000 | JE08.04 7,200,000 | | | | | | | | |
| | | | JE08.05 4,000 | JE08.06 1,535,000 | | | | | | | | |
| | | | JE08.07 340,000 | | | | | | | | | |
| | | | JE08.12 650,000 | JE08.09 2,000 | | | | | | | | |
| | | | JE08.13 10,000 | JE08.10 3,000 | | | | | | | | |
| | | | JE08.14 40,000 | JE08.13 5,000 | | | | | | | | |
| | | | JE08.08 3,103,000 | | | | | | | | | |
| Interest receivable | 3,000 | | JE08.05 1,000 | JE08.02 3,000 | | | 1,000 | | | | 1,000 | |
| Due from other funds—Centerville General Fund | 70,000 | | JE08.03 100,000 | | | | 170,000 | | | | 170,000 | |
| Due from other funds—Centerville Municipal Airport | 25,000 | | JE08.03 60,000 | | | | 85,000 | | | | 85,000 | |
| Due from other funds—Centerville Utilities Authority | 15,000 | | JE08.03 20,000 | | | | 35,000 | | | | 35,000 | |

Internal Service Funds  8-37

8-38  Proprietary Funds

## WORKSHEET ENTRIES (Continued)

| Accounts | Trial Balance Debits | Trial Balance Credits | Adjustments Debits | | Adjustments Credits | | Adjusted Trial Balance Debits | Adjusted Trial Balance Credits | Operating Statement Debits | Operating Statement Credits | Balance Sheet Debits | Balance Sheet Credits |
|---|---|---|---|---|---|---|---|---|---|---|---|---|
| Due from other funds—Centerville Parking Authority | 7,000 | | JE08.03 | 10,000 | | | 17,000 | | | | 17,000 | |
| Due from other funds—Centerville Toll Bridge | 4,000 | | JE08.03 | 14,000 | | | 18,000 | | | | 18,000 | |
| Temporary investments | 15,000 | | | | | | 15,000 | | | | 15,000 | |
| Inventories | 7,000 | | JE08.15 | 2,000 | | | 9,000 | | | | 9,000 | |
| Land and improvements | 2,300,000 | | JE08.06 | 400,000 | | | 2,700,000 | | | | 2,700,000 | |
| Buildings | 1,400,000 | | | | | | 1,400,000 | | | | 1,400,000 | |
| Accumulated depreciation—buildings | | 350,000 | | | JE08.11 | 220,000 | | 570,000 | | | | 570,000 |
| Equipment | 5,500,000 | | JE08.06 | 1,100,000 | JE08.07 | 730,000 | 5,870,000 | | | | 5,870,000 | |
| Accumulated depreciation—equipment | | 1,200,000 | JE08.07 | 420,000 | JE08.11 | 1,700,000 | | 2,480,000 | | | | 2,480,000 |
| Vehicles | 120,000 | | JE08.06 | 35,000 | JE08.07 | 12,000 | 143,000 | | | | 143,000 | |
| Accumulated depreciation—vehicles | | 55,000 | JE08.07 | 9,000 | JE08.11 | 7,000 | | 53,000 | | | | 53,000 |
| Accounts payable and accrued expenses | | 15,000 | JE08.01 | 15,000 | JE08.04 | 50,000 | | 50,000 | | | | 50,000 |
| Compensated absences liability | | 4,000 | | | JE08.09 | 3,000 | | 7,000 | | | | 7,000 |

Internal Service Funds 8-39

## WORKSHEET ENTRIES (Continued)

| Accounts | Trial Balance Debits | Trial Balance Credits | Adjustments Debits | | Adjustments Credits | | Adjusted Trial Balance Debits | Adjusted Trial Balance Credits | Operating Statement Debits | Operating Statement Credits | Balance Sheet Debits | Balance Sheet Credits |
|---|---|---|---|---|---|---|---|---|---|---|---|---|
| Claims and judgements payable | | 12,000 | | | JE08.10 | 7,000 | | 19,000 | | | | 19,000 |
| Notes payable | | 1,500,000 | | | JE08.08 | 3,200,000 | | 4,700,000 | | | | 4,700,000 |
| Net assets | | 6,590,000 | | | | | | 6,590,000 | | | | 6,590,000 |
| Charges for services | | | | | JE08.03 | 5,500,000 | | 5,500,000 | | 5,500,000 | | |
| Interest and investment revenue | | | | | JE08.05 | 5,000 | | 5,000 | | 5,000 | | |
| Miscellaneous revenue—gain on sale of assets | | | | | JE08.07 | 27,000 | | 27,000 | | 27,000 | | |
| Operating grants and contributions | | | | | JE08.12 | 200,000 | | 200,000 | | 200,000 | | |
| Capital grants and contributions | | | | | JE08.12 | 450,000 | | 450,000 | | 450,000 | | |
| Operating revenues— miscellaneous | | | | | JE08.13 | 10,000 | | 10,000 | | 10,000 | | |
| Personal services expenses | | | JE08.04 JE08.09 | 4,800,000 5,000 | | | 4,805,000 | | 4,805,000 | | | |
| Contractual services expenses | | | JE08.04 | 1,300,000 | | | 1,300,000 | | 1,300,000 | | | |
| Repairs and maintenance expenses | | | JE08.04 | 1,100,000 | | | 1,100,000 | | 1,100,000 | | | |

## WORKSHEET ENTRIES (Continued)

| Accounts | Trial Balance Debits | Trial Balance Credits | Adjustments Debits | | Adjustments Credits | | Adjusted Trial Balance Debits | Adjusted Trial Balance Credits | Operating Statement Debits | Operating Statement Credits | Balance Sheet Debits | Balance Sheet Credits |
|---|---|---|---|---|---|---|---|---|---|---|---|---|
| Other supplies and expenses | | | JE08.04 | 50,000 | JE08.15 | 2,000 | 48,000 | | 48,000 | | | |
| Insurance claims and expenses | | | JE08.10 | 10,000 | | | 10,000 | | 10,000 | | | |
| Depreciation expense | | | JE08.11 | 1,927,000 | | | 1,927,000 | | 1,927,000 | | | |
| Interest expense | | | JE08.08 | 97,000 | | | 97,000 | | 97,000 | | | |
| Operating expenses—miscellaneous | | | JE08.13 | 5,000 | | | 5,000 | | 5,000 | | | |
| Transfers in—General Fund | | | | | JE08.14 | 40,000 | | 40,000 | | 40,000 | | |
| Totals | 9,726,000 | 9,726,000 | | 20,926,000 | | 20,926,000 | 20,701,000 | 20,701,000 | 9,292,000 | 6,232,000 | 11,409,000 | 14,469,000 |
| Net increase (decrease) | | | | | | | | | (3,060,000) | | | (3,060,000) |
| | | | | | | | | | 6,232,000 | 6,232,000 | 11,409,000 | 11,409,000 |

## APPENDIX 8B: WORKSHEET FOR SUMMARIZING CURRENT TRANSACTIONS—FLEET MANAGEMENT

### WORKSHEET ENTRIES

| Accounts | Trial Balance Debits | Trial Balance Credits | Adjustments Debits | | Adjustments Credits | | Adjusted Trial Balance Debits | Adjusted Trial Balance Credits | Operating Statement Debits | Operating Statement Credits | Balance Sheet Debits | Balance Sheet Credits |
|---|---|---|---|---|---|---|---|---|---|---|---|---|
| Cash | 805,000 | | JE08.17 | 4,500 | JE08.16 | 90,000 | 137,500 | | | | 137,500 | |
| | | | JE08.18 | 4,915,000 | JE08.19 | 1,825,000 | | | | | | |
| | | | JE08.20 | 3,000 | JE08.21 | 2,950,000 | | | | | | |
| | | | JE08.22 | 410,000 | JE08.23 | 1,180,000 | | | | | | |
| | | | JE08.27 | 100,000 | JE08.24 | 3,000 | | | | | | |
| | | | JE08.28 | 4,000 | JE08.25 | 4,000 | | | | | | |
| | | | | | JE08.28 | 2,000 | | | | | | |
| | | | | | JE08.29 | 50,000 | | | | | | |
| Interest receivable | 4,500 | | JE08.20 | 2,000 | JE08.17 | 4,500 | 2,000 | | | | 2,000 | |
| Due from other funds—General Fund | 22,000 | | JE08.18 | 50,000 | | | 72,000 | | | | 72,000 | |
| Due from other governments—County Fire District | 7,000 | | JE08.18 | 10,000 | | | 17,000 | | | | 17,000 | |
| Due from other governments—Regional Pollution Control District | 3,000 | | 3 | 25,000 | | | 28,000 | | | | 28,000 | |

## 8-42 Proprietary Funds

### WORKSHEET ENTRIES (Continued)

| Accounts | Trial Balance Debits | Trial Balance Credits | Adjustments Debits | | Adjustments Credits | | Adjusted Trial Balance Debits | Adjusted Trial Balance Credits | Operating Statement Debits | Operating Statement Credits | Balance Sheet Debits | Balance Sheet Credits |
|---|---|---|---|---|---|---|---|---|---|---|---|---|
| Temporary investments | 19,000 | | | | | | 19,000 | | | | 19,000 | |
| Inventories | 4,000 | | 3,000 | JE08.30 | | | 7,000 | | | | 7,000 | |
| Land and improvements | 50,000 | | | | | | 50,000 | | | | 50,000 | |
| Buildings | 1,600,000 | | | | | | 1,650,000 | | | | 1,600,000 | |
| Accumulated depreciation—buildings | | 450,000 | | | 370,000 | JE08.26 | | 820,000 | | | | 820,000 |
| Equipment | 1,200,000 | | 350,000 | JE08.21 | 220,000 | JE08.22 | 1,330,000 | | | | 1,330,000 | |
| Accumulated depreciation—equipment | | 770,000 | 195,000 | JE08.22 | 310,000 | JE08.26 | | 885,000 | | | | 885,000 |
| Vehicles | 7,400,000 | | 2,600,000 | JE08.21 | 1,800,000 | JE08.22 | 8,200,000 | | | | 8,200,000 | |
| Accumulated depreciation—vehicles | | 4,300,000 | 1,350,000 | JE08.22 | 1,850,000 | JE08.26 | | 4,800,000 | | | | 4,800,000 |
| Accounts payable and accrued expenses | | 90,000 | 90,000 | JE08.16 | 125,000 | JE08.19 | | 125,000 | | | | 125,000 |
| Compensated absences liability | | 5,000 | | | 3,000 | JE08.24 | | 8,000 | | | | 8,000 |
| Claims and judgements payable | | 10,000 | | | 3,000 | JE08.25 | | 13,000 | | | | 13,000 |
| Notes payable | | 4,000,000 | 1,000,000 | JE08.23 | | | | 3,000,000 | | | | 3,000,000 |
| Net assets | | 1,489,500 | | | | | | 1,489,500 | | | | 1,489,500 |
| Charges for services | | | | | | JE08.18 | | 5,000,000 | | 5,000,000 | | |

Internal Service Funds 8-43

## WORKSHEET ENTRIES (Continued)

| Accounts | Trial Balance Debits | Trial Balance Credits | Adjustments Debits | | Adjustments Credits | | Adjusted Trial Balance Debits | Adjusted Trial Balance Credits | Operating Statement Debits | Operating Statement Credits | Balance Sheet Debits | Balance Sheet Credits |
|---|---|---|---|---|---|---|---|---|---|---|---|---|
| Interest and investment revenue | | | | | JE08.20 | 5,000 | | 5,000 | | 5,000 | | |
| Operating grants and contributions | | | | | JE08.27 | 100,000 | | 100,000 | | 100,000 | | |
| Operating revenues—miscellaneous | | | | | JE08.28 | 4,000 | | 4,000 | | 4,000 | | |
| Personal services expenses | | | JE08.19 JE08.24 | 1,200,000 6,000 | | | 1,206,000 | | 1,206,000 | | | |
| Contractual services expenses | | | JE08.19 | 400,000 | | | 400,000 | | 400,000 | | | |
| Repairs and maintenance expenses | | | JE08.19 | 200,000 | | | 200,000 | | 200,000 | | | |
| Other supplies and expenses | | | JE08.19 | 150,000 | JE08.30 | 3,000 | 147,000 | | 147,000 | | | |
| Insurance claims and expenses | | | JE08.25 | 7,000 | | | 7,000 | | 7,000 | | | |
| Depreciation expense | | | JE08.26 | 2,530,000 | | | 2,530,000 | | 2,530,000 | | | |
| Interest expense | | | JE08.23 | 180,000 | | | 180,000 | | 180,000 | | | |
| Operating expenses—miscellaneous | | | JE08.28 | 2,000 | | | 2,000 | | 2,000 | | | |

## WORKSHEET ENTRIES (Continued)

| Accounts | Trial Balance Debits | Trial Balance Credits | | Adjustments Debits | Adjustments Credits | Adjusted Trial Balance Debits | Adjusted Trial Balance Credits | Operating Statement Debits | Operating Statement Credits | Balance Sheet Debits | Balance Sheet Credits |
|---|---|---|---|---|---|---|---|---|---|---|---|
| Miscellaneous expenses—loss on sale of assets | | | JE08.22 | 65,000 | | 65,000 | | 65,000 | | | |
| Transfers out— General Fund | | | JE08.29 | 50,000 | | 50,000 | | 50,000 | | | |
| Totals | 11,114,500 | 11,114,500 | | 15,901,500 | 15,901,500 | 16,249,500 | 16,249,500 | 4,787,000 | 5,109,000 | 11,462,500 | 11,140,500 |
| Net increase (decrease) | | | | | | | | 322,000 | | | 322,000 |
| | | | | | | | | 5,109,000 | 5,109,000 | 11,462,500 | 11,462,500 |

## APPENDIX 8C: WORKSHEET FOR SUMMARIZING CURRENT TRANSACTIONS—SPECIAL SERVICES SUPPORT CENTER

### WORKSHEET ENTRIES

| Accounts | Trial Balance Debits | Trial Balance Credits | Adjustments Debits | | Adjustments Credits | | Adjusted Trial Balance Debits | Adjusted Trial Balance Credits | Operating Statement Debits | Operating Statement Credits | Balance Sheet Debits | Balance Sheet Credits |
|---|---|---|---|---|---|---|---|---|---|---|---|---|
| Cash | 503,000 | | JE08.32 | 9,000 | JE08.31 | 35,000 | 22,000 | | | | 22,000 | |
| | | | JE08.33 | 2,600,000 | JE08.34 | 1,750,000 | | | | | | |
| | | | JE08.35 | 14,000 | JE08.36 | 1,555,000 | | | | | | |
| | | | JE08.37 | 95,000 | JE08.38 | 100,000 | | | | | | |
| | | | JE08.38 | 168,000 | JE08.39 | 12,000 | | | | | | |
| | | | JE08.42 | 110,000 | JE08.40 | 13,000 | | | | | | |
| | | | JE08.43 | 3,000 | JE08.43 | 15,000 | | | | | | |
| Interest receivable | 9,000 | | JE08.35 | 1,000 | JE08.32 | 9,000 | 1,000 | | | | 1,000 | |
| Due from other funds—Centerville Municipal Airport | 77,000 | | JE08.33 | 350,000 | | | 427,000 | | | | 427,000 | |
| Temporary investments | 12,000 | | | | | | 12,000 | | | | 12,000 | |
| inventories | 16,000 | | JE08.44 | 4,000 | | | 20,000 | | | | 20,000 | |
| Land and improvements | 1,400,000 | | JE08.36 | 350,000 | | | 1,750,000 | | | | 1,750,000 | |
| Buildings | 1,600,000 | | | | | | 1,600,000 | | | | 1,600,000 | |
| Accumulated depreciation—buildings | | 450,000 | | | JE08.41 | 375,000 | | 825,000 | | | | 825,000 |

*Internal Service Funds* 8-45

**8-46** Proprietary Funds

## WORKSHEET ENTRIES (Continued)

| Accounts | Trial Balance Debits | Trial Balance Credits | Adjustments Debits | | Adjustments Credits | | Adjusted Trial Balance Debits | Adjusted Trial Balance Credits | Operating Statement Debits | Operating Statement Credits | Balance Sheet Debits | Balance Sheet Credits |
|---|---|---|---|---|---|---|---|---|---|---|---|---|
| Equipment | 2,300,000 | | 780,000 | JE08.36 | 120,000 | JE08.37 | 2,960,000 | | | | 2,960,000 | |
| Accumulated depreciation—equipment | | 1,300,000 | 90,000 | JE08.37 | 175,000 | JE08.41 | | 1,385,000 | | | | 1,385,000 |
| Vehicles | 1,800,000 | | 425,000 | JE08.36 | 230,000 | JE08.37 | 1,995,000 | | | | 1,995,000 | |
| Accumulated depreciation—vehicles | | 650,000 | 195,000 | JE08.37 | 575,000 | JE08.41 | | 1,030,000 | | | | 1,030,000 |
| Accounts payable and accrued expenses | | 35,000 | 35,000 | JE08.31 | 75,000 | JE08.34 | | 75,000 | | | | 75,000 |
| Compensated absences liability | | 14,000 | | | 3,000 | JE08.39 | | 17,000 | | | | 17,000 |
| Claims and judgements payable | | 22,000 | 1,000 | JE08.40 | | | | 21,000 | | | | 21,000 |
| Notes payable | | 450,000 | 100,000 | JE08.38 | 200,000 | JE08.38 | | 550,000 | | | | 550,000 |
| Net assets | | 4,796,000 | | | | | | 4,796,000 | | | | 4,796,000 |
| Charges for services | | | | | 2,950,000 | JE08.33 | | 2,950,000 | | 2,950,000 | | |
| Interest and investment revenue | | | | | 15,000 | JE08.35 | | 15,000 | | 15,000 | | |
| Miscellaneous revenue—gain on sale of assets | | | | | 30,000 | JE08.37 | | 30,000 | | 30,000 | | |

Internal Service Funds 8-47

## WORKSHEET ENTRIES (Continued)

| Accounts | Trial Balance Debits | Trial Balance Credits | Adjustments Debits | | Adjustments Credits | | Adjusted Trial Balance Debits | Adjusted Trial Balance Credits | Operating Statement Debits | Operating Statement Credits | Balance Sheet Debits | Balance Sheet Credits |
|---|---|---|---|---|---|---|---|---|---|---|---|---|
| Operating grants and contributions | | | | | JE08.42 | 70,000 | | 70,000 | | 70,000 | | |
| Capital grants and contributions | | | | | JE08.42 | 40,000 | | 40,000 | | 40,000 | | |
| Operating revenues—miscellaneous | | | | | JE08.43 | 3,000 | | 3,000 | | 3,000 | | |
| Personal services expenses | | | JE08.34 JE08.39 | 900,000 15,000 | | | 915,000 | | 915,000 | | | |
| Contractual services expenses | | | JE08.34 | 400,000 | | | 400,000 | | 400,000 | | | |
| Repairs and maintenance expenses | | | JE08.34 | 350,000 | | | 350,000 | | 350,000 | | | |
| Other supplies and expenses | | | JE08.34 | 175,000 | JE08.44 | 4,000 | 171,000 | | 171,000 | | | |
| Insurance claims and expenses | | | JE08.40 | 12,000 | | | 12,000 | | 12,000 | | | |
| Depreciation expense | | | JE08.41 | 1,125,000 | | | 1,125,000 | | 1,125,000 | | | |
| Interest expense | | | JE08.38 | 32,000 | | | 32,000 | | 32,000 | | | |
| Operating expenses—miscellaneous | | | JE08.43 | 15,000 | | | 15,000 | | 15,000 | | | |
| Totals | 7,717,000 | 7,717,000 | | 8,354,000 | | 8,354,000 | 11,807,000 | 11,807,000 | 3,020,000 | 3,108,000 | 8,787,000 | 8,699,000 |
| Net increase (decrease) | | | | | | | | | 88,000 | | | 88,000 |
| | | | | | | | | | 3,108,000 | 3,108,000 | 8,787,000 | 8,787,000 |

# APPENDIX 8D: INTERNAL SERVICE FUNDS—STATEMENT OF NET ASSETS; STATEMENT OF REVENUES, EXPENSES, AND CHANGES IN FUND NET ASSETS; AND STATEMENT OF CASH FLOW

**WORKSHEET ENTRIES**

**Internal Service Funds**
**Statement of Net Assets**
**June 30, 20X1**

| | Communications and Technology Support Center | Fleet Management | Special Services Support Center | Total |
|---|---|---|---|---|
| **ASSETS** | | | | |
| Current assets: | | | | |
| Cash | $ 946,000 | $ 137,500 | $ 22,000 | $1,105,500 |
| Interest receivable | 1,000 | 2,000 | 1,000 | 4,000 |
| Due from other funds | 325,000 | 72,000 | 427,000 | 824,000 |
| Due from other governments | | 45,000 | | 45,000 |
| Temporary investments | 15,000 | 19,000 | 12,000 | 46,000 |
| Inventories | 9,000 | 7,000 | 20,000 | 36,000 |
| Total current assets | 1,296,000 | 282,500 | 482,000 | 2,060,500 |
| Noncurrent assets: | | | | |
| Land and improvements | 2,700,000 | | 1,750,000 | 4,450,000 |
| Buildings | 1,400,000 | 1,650,000 | 1,600,000 | 4,650,000 |
| Equipment | 5,870,000 | 1,330,000 | 2,960,000 | 10,160,000 |

## WORKSHEET ENTRIES (Continued)

| | Communications and Technology Support Center | Fleet Management | Special Services Support Center | Total |
|---|---|---|---|---|
| Vehicles | 143,000 | 8,200,000 | 1,995,000 | 10,338,000 |
| Less accumulated depreciation | (3,103,000) | (6,505,000) | (3,240,000) | (12,848,000) |
| Total noncurrent assets | 7,010,000 | 4,675,000 | 5,065,000 | 16,750,000 |
| Total assets | $8,306,000 | $4,957,500 | $5,547,000 | $18,810,500 |
| **LIABILITIES** | | | | |
| Current liabilities: | | | | |
| Accounts payable and accrued expenses | 50,000 | 125,000 | 75,000 | 250,000 |
| Compensated absences | 3,000 | 2,000 | 5,000 | 10,000 |
| Claims and judgements | 4,000 | 2,000 | 7,000 | 13,000 |
| Notes payable | | 1,500,000 | 200,000 | 1,700,000 |
| Total current liabilities | 57,000 | 1,629,000 | 287,000 | 1,973,000 |
| Noncurrent liabilities: | | | | |
| Compensated absences | 4,000 | 6,000 | 12,000 | 22,000 |
| Claims and judgements | 15,000 | 11,000 | 14,000 | 40,000 |
| Notes payable | 4,700,000 | 1,500,000 | 350,000 | 6,550,000 |
| Total noncurrent liabilities | 4,719,000 | 1,517,000 | 376,000 | 6,612,000 |
| Total liabilities | $4,776,000 | $3,146,000 | $663,000 | $8,585,000 |
| **NET ASSETS** | | | | |
| Invested in capital assets, net of related debt | 2,310,000 | 1,675,000 | 4,515,000 | 8,500,000 |
| Unrestricted | 1,220,000 | 136,500 | 369,000 | 1,725,500 |
| Total net assets | $3,530,000 | $1,811,500 | $4,884,000 | $10,225,500 |

## WORKSHEET ENTRIES (Continued)

### Internal Service Funds
### Statement of Revenues, Expenses, and Changes in Fund Net Assets
### For the Year Ended June 30, 20X1

| | Communications and Technology Support Center | Fleet Management | Special Services Support Center | Total |
|---|---:|---:|---:|---:|
| **OPERATING REVENUES** | | | | |
| Charges for services | $5,500,000 | $5,000,000 | $2,950,000 | $13,450,000 |
| Miscellaneous | 10,000 | 4,000 | 3,000 | 17,000 |
| Total operating revenues | 5,510,000 | 5,004,000 | 2,953,000 | 13,467,000 |
| **OPERATING EXPENSES** | | | | |
| Personal services | 4,805,000 | 1,206,000 | 915,000 | 6,926,000 |
| Contractual services | 1,300,000 | 400,000 | 400,000 | 2,100,000 |
| Repairs and maintenance | 1,100,000 | 200,000 | 350,000 | 1,650,000 |
| Other supplies and expenses | 48,000 | 147,000 | 171,000 | 366,000 |
| Insurance claims and expenses | 10,000 | 7,000 | 12,000 | 29,000 |
| Depreciation | 1,927,000 | 2,530,000 | 1,125,000 | 5,582,000 |
| Miscellaneous | 5,000 | 2,000 | 15,000 | 22,000 |
| Total operating expenses | 9,195,000 | 4,492,000 | 2,988,000 | 16,675,000 |
| Operating income (loss) | (3,685,000) | 512,000 | (35,000) | (3,208,000) |
| **NONOPERATING REVENUES (EXPENSES)** | | | | |
| Interest and investment revenue | 5,000 | 5,000 | 15,000 | 25,000 |
| Interest | (97,000) | (180,000) | (32,000) | (309,000) |

## WORKSHEET ENTRIES (Continued)

| | Communications and Technology Support Center | Fleet Management | Special Services Support Center | Total |
|---|---|---|---|---|
| Operating grants and contributions | 200,000 | 100,000 | 70,000 | 370,000 |
| Miscellaneous | 27,000 | (65,000) | 30,000 | (8,000) |
| Total nonoperating revenue (expenses) | 135,000 | (140,000) | 83,000 | 78,000 |
| Income (loss) before capital contributions and transfers | (3,550,000) | 372,000 | 48,000 | (3,130,000) |
| Capital contributions | 450,000 | | 40,000 | 490,000 |
| Transfers in | 40,000 | | | 40,000 |
| Transfers out | | (50,000) | | (50,000) |
| Change in net assets | (3,060,000) | 322,000 | 88,000 | (2,650,000) |
| Total net assets—beginning | 6,590,000 | 1,489,500 | 4,796,000 | 12,875,500 |
| Total net assets—ending | $3,530,000 | $1,811,500 | $4,884,000 | $10,225,500 |

## Internal Service Funds
## Statement of Cash Flows
## For the Year Ended June 30, 20X1

| | Communications and Technology Support Center | Fleet Management | Special Services Support Center | Total |
|---|---|---|---|---|
| **CASH FLOWS FROM OPERATING ACTIVITIES** | | | | |
| Receipts from customers | $ 5,296,000 | $ 4,915,000 | $2,600,000 | $12,811,000 |
| Payments to suppliers | (2,435,000) | (815,000) | (935,000) | (4,185,000) |

**8-52** Proprietary Funds

## WORKSHEET ENTRIES (Continued)

| | Communications and Technology Support Center | Fleet Management | Special Services Support Center | Total |
|---|---|---|---|---|
| Payments to employees | (4,782,000) | (1,103,000) | (862,000) | (6,747,000) |
| Other receipts (payments) | 2,000 | (2,000) | (25,000) | (25,000) |
| Net cash provided by operating activities | (1,919,000) | 2,995,000 | 778,000 | 1,854,000 |
| **CASH FLOWS FROM NONCAPITAL FINANCING ACTIVITIES** | | | | |
| Operating subsidies and transfers from (to) other funds | 240,000 | 50,000 | 70,000 | 360,000 |
| **CASH FLOWS FROM CAPITAL AND RELATED FINANCING ACTIVITIES** | | | | |
| Proceeds from the issuance of capital debt | 3,200,000 | | 200,000 | 3,400,000 |
| Capital contributions | 450,000 | | 40,000 | 490,000 |
| Acquisitions of capital assets | (1,535,000) | (2,950,000) | (1,555,000) | (6,040,000) |
| Proceeds from sale of capital assets | 340,000 | 410,000 | 95,000 | 845,000 |
| Principal paid on capital debt | | (1,000,000) | (100,000) | (1,100,000) |
| Interest paid on capital debt | (97,000) | (180,000) | (32,000) | (309,000) |
| Net cash (used) by capital and related financing activities | 2,358,000 | (3,720,000) | (1,352,000) | (2,714,000) |
| **CASH FLOWS FROM INVESTING ACTIVITIES** | | | | |
| Interest and dividends | 7,000 | 7,500 | 23,000 | 37,500 |
| Net increase (decrease) in cash | 686,000 | (667,500) | (481,000) | (462,500) |
| Balances—beginning of year | 260,000 | 805,000 | 503,000 | 1,568,000 |
| Balances—end of year | $946,000 | $137,500 | $22,000 | $1,105,500 |

## WORKSHEET ENTRIES (Continued)

| | Communications and Technology Support Center | Fleet Management | Special Services Support Center | Total |
|---|---|---|---|---|
| **Reconciliation of operating income (loss) to net cash provided (used) by operating activities:** | | | | |
| Operating income (loss) | $(3,685,000) | 512,000 | $(35,000) | $(3,208,000) |
| Adjustments: | | | | |
| Depreciation expense | 1,927,000 | 2,530,000 | 1,125,000 | 5,582,000 |
| Change in assets and liabilities: | | | | |
| Receivables, net | $(204,000) | $(85,000) | $(350,000) | $(639,000) |
| Inventories | (2,000) | (3,000) | (4,000) | (9,000) |
| Accounts and accrued liabilities | 45,000 | 41,000 | 42,000 | 128,000 |
| Net cash provided (used) by operating activities | $(1,919,000) | 2,995,000 | 778,000 | 1,854,000 |

## APPENDIX 8E: MERGING INTERNAL SERVICE FUNDS INTO THE GOVERNMENT-WIDE FINANCIAL STATEMENTS

Proprietary funds are presented on an accrual basis. Therefore, there often is no need to make worksheet entries to convert the information from a fund basis to a government-wide basis; however, the residual balances and the activities of Internal Service Funds must be analyzed to determine how they are to be merged into the government-wide financial statements.

# PART IV.
# FIDUCIARY FUNDS

# PART IV.
# FIDUCIARY FUNDS

# CHAPTER 9
# PENSION TRUST FUNDS

## CONTENTS

| | |
|---|---|
| Nature of Pension Trust Funds | 9-1 |
| Measurement Focus and Basis of Accounting | 9-2 |
| Financial Reporting at Fund Level | 9-2 |
| Financial Reporting at Government-Wide Level | 9-3 |
| Illustrative Transactions | 9-3 |
| Fund Financial Statements | 9-6 |
| Government-Wide Financial Statements | 9-8 |
| Appendix 9A: Worksheet for Summarizing Current Transactions—State Public Employees Retirement Fund | 9-9 |
| Appendix 9B: Pension Trust Funds—Statement of Fiduciary New Assets and Changes in Fiduciary Net Assets | 9-11 |
| Appendix 9C: Pension Trust Funds—Government-Wide Financial Statements | 9-13 |

## NATURE OF PENSION TRUST FUNDS

GASB-25 (Financial Reporting for Defined Benefit Pension Plans and Notes Disclosures for Defined Contribution Plans) characterizes *defined pension benefit plans* as "having terms that specify the amount of pension benefits to be provided at a future date or after a certain period of time; the amount specified usually is a function of one or more factors such as age, years of service, and compensation." A public employee retirement system (PERS) may be established to hold assets and pay benefits earned by governmental employees and their beneficiaries under a defined pension benefit plan; however, GASB-25 notes that the term "public employee retirement system" refers to "a state or local governmental fiduciary entity entrusted with administering a plan (or plans) and not to the plan itself."

The standards established by GASB-25 apply to a particular pension plan and not to the PERS that administers the plan. However, when a PERS presents separate financial statements of a defined pension plan in its financial report, the standards established by GASB-25 must be observed. If the financial statements of more than one defined benefits pension plan is included in the PERS report, the standards must be applied separately to each plan. The financial statements for each plan should be presented separately in the combining financial statements of the PERS, along with the appropriate schedules and other disclosures required by GASB-25. This chapter illustrates a Pension Trust Fund that is part of a PERS but that is also reported in the financial statements of the plan sponsor (The City of Centerville).

## MEASUREMENT FOCUS AND BASIS OF ACCOUNTING

For the most part, a Pension Trust Fund accounts for its assets on an accrual basis; however, liabilities are generally reported on essentially a modified accrual basis. A pension plan invests in a variety of instruments, including equity securities, debt securities, various types of mutual funds, and perhaps derivatives. Most investments held by a pension plan are reported at fair value rather than historical cost. Operating assets, such as buildings, equipment, and leasehold improvements used in the operations of a pension plan, are reported at historical cost. The specific accounting and reporting standards that are followed by a pension plan are established by GASB-31 (Accounting and Financial Reporting for Certain Investments and for External Investment Pools).

No single accounting basis is applicable to the measurement of a pension plan's liabilities. Liabilities related to administrative and investment activities should be reported on an accrual basis, but liabilities related to the plan's obligation for employee benefits should be reported when due and payable as required by the terms of the pension plan.

## FINANCIAL REPORTING AT FUND LEVEL

Unlike governmental funds and proprietary funds, the *major fund* reporting concept does not apply to Pension Trust Funds. GASB-34 requires that fiduciary funds be reported in an entity's financial statements by fund type (Pension [and Other Employee Benefit] Trust Funds, Investment Trust Funds, Private-Purpose Trust Funds, and Agency Funds). If there is more than one pension plan, individual pension plans are presented in the notes to the financial statements unless separate financial statements have been issued. In the latter case, the notes should include information as to how the separate reports may be obtained.

The balances and activities of Pension Trust Funds are presented in the following financial statements at the fund financial statement level:

- Statement of plan net assets
- Statement of changes in plan net assets

The statement of plan net assets reports the pension plan's assets and liabilities; however, there is no need to divide net assets into the three categories (invested in capital assets (net of related debt), restricted net assets, and unrestricted net assets) that must be used in the government-wide financial statements. The equity section of the statement of plan net assets is simply identified as "net assets held in trust for pension benefits."

A pension plan's statement of changes in plan net assets is formatted in a manner to identify (1) additions in net assets, (2) deductions from net assets, and (3) the net increase or decrease in the plan's net assets for the year.

## FINANCIAL REPORTING AT GOVERNMENT-WIDE LEVEL

Financial statements of fiduciary funds are not presented in the government-wide financial statements, because resources of these funds cannot be used to finance a governmental entity's activities. The financial statements are included in the fund financial statements because a governmental entity is financially accountable for those resources even though they belong to other parties (GASB-34, par. 13).

## ILLUSTRATIVE TRANSACTIONS

In order to illustrate accounting and financial reporting standards that are observed for Pension Trust Funds, assume that the City's defined benefits pension agreement is administered by the State Public Employees Retirement Fund (SPERF). The trust fund's trial balance for the beginning of the fiscal year is as follows:

| Accounts | Trial Balance Debits | Trial Balance Credits |
|---|---|---|
| Cash | $ 1,200,000 | |
| Investment in debt securities | 9,000,000 | |
| Investment in marketable equity securities | 22,000,000 | |
| Accrued interest receivable | 19,000 | |
| Accounts payable | | $ 21,000 |
| Refunds payable and other liabilities | | 29,000 |
| Fund balance | | 32,169,000 |
| Totals | $32,219,000 | $32,219,000 |

This section presents illustrative transactions and entries for the SPERF during the fiscal year ended June 30, 20X1.

*Transaction JE09.01*—Refunds payable of $27,000 and accounts payable of $21,000 from the previous year were paid:

**9-4** *Fiduciary Funds*

| Accounts | Debits | Credits |
|---|---|---|
| Refunds payable and other liabilities | 27,000 | |
| Accounts payable | 21,000 | |
| Cash | | 48,000 |

*Transaction JE09.02*—Accrued interest receivable of $19,000 from the previous year was collected:

| Accounts | Debits | Credits |
|---|---|---|
| Cash | 19,000 | |
| Accrued interest receivable | | 19,000 |

*Transaction JE09.03*—During the year, contributions of $7,000,000 and $2,700,000 were received from the City of Centerville and employees, respectively:

| Accounts | Debits | Credits |
|---|---|---|
| Cash | 9,700,000 | |
| Contributions—City of Centerville | | 7,000,000 |
| Contributions—plan members | | 2,700,000 |

*Transaction JE09.04*—During the year, interest and investment revenue of $320,000 was earned and received:

| Accounts | Debits | Credits |
|---|---|---|
| Cash | 320,000 | |
| Interest and investment revenue | | 320,000 |

*Transaction JE09.05*—The following expenditures were paid during the year:

| | |
|---|---|
| Benefits to retirees and beneficiaries | $4,200,000 |
| Administrative expenses | 320,000 |
| Total | $4,520,000 |

| Accounts | Debits | Credits |
|---|---|---|
| Benefits paid | 4,200,000 | |
| Administrative expenses | 320,000 | |
| Cash | | 4,520,000 |

*Transaction JE09.06*—Refunds of $77,000 were made to employees who were terminated and were not vested in the plan:

Pension Trust Funds 9-5

| Accounts | Debits | Credits |
|---|---|---|
| Refunds | 77,000 | |
| Cash | | 77,000 |

*Transaction JE09.07*—Additional investments in the marketable equity securities portfolio of $2,000,000 were made:

| Accounts | Debits | Credits |
|---|---|---|
| Investment in marketable equity securities | 2,000,000 | |
| Cash | | 2,000,000 |

*Transaction JE09.08*—Additional investments in the debt securities portfolio of $750,000 were made:

| Accounts | Debits | Credits |
|---|---|---|
| Investment in debt securities | 750,000 | |
| Cash | | 750,000 |

*Transaction JE09.09*—An investment in the marketable equity securities portfolio that had a carrying value of $330,000 was sold for $400,000:

| Accounts | Debits | Credits |
|---|---|---|
| Cash | 400,000 | |
| Investment in marketable equity securities | | 330,000 |
| Interest and investment revenue | | 70,000 |

*Transaction JE09.010*—Administrative expenses of $29,000 and refunds due to terminated employees of $23,000 were accrued at the end of the year:

| Accounts | Debits | Credits |
|---|---|---|
| Administrative expenses | 29,000 | |
| Refunds | 23,000 | |
| Accounts payable | | 29,000 |
| Refunds payable and other liabilities | | 23,000 |

*Transaction JE09.11*—Accrued interest at the end of the year was $31,000:

| Accounts | Debits | Credits |
|---|---|---|
| Accrued interest receivable | 31,000 | |
| Interest and investment revenue | | 31,000 |

*Transaction JE09.12*—The net appreciation in the fair value of the marketable equities portfolio was $43,000 and the marketable debt portfolio was $22,000 at the end of the year:

**9-6** *Fiduciary Funds*

| Accounts | Debits | Credits |
|---|---|---|
| Investment in marketable equity securities | 43,000 | |
| Investment in debt securities | 22,000 | |
| Interest and investment revenue | | 65,000 |

After the transactions for the year are posted, the year-end trial balance (June 30, 20X1) for the SPERF appears as follows:

| Accounts | Adjusted Trial Balance Debits | Credits |
|---|---|---|
| Cash | $ 4,244,000 | |
| Investment in debt securities | 11,022,000 | |
| Investment in marketable equity securities | 22,463,000 | |
| Accrued interest receivable | 31,000 | |
| Accounts payable | | $ 29,000 |
| Refunds payable and other liabilities | | 25,000 |
| Fund balance | | 32,169,000 |
| Interest and investment revenue | | 486,000 |
| Contributions—City of Centerville | | 7,000,000 |
| Contributions—plan members | | 2,700,000 |
| Administrative expenses | 349,000 | |
| Refunds | 100,000 | |
| Benefits paid | 4,200,000 | |
| Totals | $42,409,000 | $42,409,000 |

The worksheet that summarizes the journal entries for the SPERF for the year-end trial balance is presented in Appendix 9A.

## FUND FINANCIAL STATEMENTS

Based on the adjusted trial balances created above, the following financial statements are prepared for the Centerville Public Employee Retirement Fund (see Appendix 9B):

**City of Centerville**
**Statement of Fiduciary Net Assets**
**June 30, 20X1**

| | Employee Retirement Fund |
|---|---|
| **ASSETS** | |
| Cash | $ 4,244,000 |
| Accrued interest receivable | 31,000 |

|  | Employee Retirement Fund |
|---|---|
| Investments in debt securities | 11,022,000 |
| Investment in marketable equity securities | 22,463,000 |
| Total assets | $37,760,000 |
| **LIABILITIES** | |
| Accounts payable and accrued expenses | $ 29,000 |
| Refunds payable and other liabilities | 25,000 |
| Total liabilities | $ 54,000 |
| **NET ASSETS** | |
| Held in trust for pension benefits | $37,706,000 |

City of Centerville
Statement of Changes in Fiduciary Net Assets
For the Year Ended June 30, 20X1

|  | Employee Retirement Fund |
|---|---|
| **ADDITIONS** | |
| Contributions by: | |
| City of Centerville | $ 7,000,000 |
| Plan members | 2,700,000 |
| Total Contributions | 9,700,000 |
| Interest and investment revenue | 486,000 |
| Total additions | 10,186,000 |
| **DEDUCTIONS** | |
| Benefits paid | 4,200,000 |
| Refunds of contributions | 100,000 |
| Administrative expenses | 349,000 |
| Total deductions | 4,649,000 |
| Change in net assets | 5,537,000 |
| Net assets—beginning of the year | 32,169,000 |
| Net assets—end of the year | $37,706,000 |

The financial statements for the Pension Trust Fund are not reported separately in the governmental entity's financial report, but they are used later in Chapter 12 ("Developing Information for Fund Financial Statements").

## GOVERNMENT-WIDE FINANCIAL STATEMENTS

Fiduciary financial statements are presented only at the fund financial statement level (see Appendix 9C).

## APPENDIX 9A: WORKSHEET FOR SUMMARIZING CURRENT TRANSACTIONS—STATE PUBLIC EMPLOYEES RETIREMENT FUND

### WORKSHEET ENTRIES

| Accounts | Trial Balance Debits | Trial Balance Credits | Adjustments Debits | | Adjustments Credits | | Adjusted Trial Balance Debits | Adjusted Trial Balance Credits | Operating Statement Debits | Operating Statement Credits | Balance Sheet Debits | Balance Sheet Credits |
|---|---|---|---|---|---|---|---|---|---|---|---|---|
| Cash | 1,200,000 | | JE09.02 | 19,000 | JE09.01 | 48,000 | 4,244,000 | | | | 4,244,000 | |
| | | | JE09.03 | 9,700,000 | JE09.05 | 4,520,000 | | | | | | |
| | | | JE09.04 | 320,000 | JE09.06 | 77,000 | | | | | | |
| | | | JE09.09 | 400,000 | JE09.07 | 2,000,000 | | | | | | |
| | | | | | JE09.08 | 750,000 | | | | | | |
| Investment in debt securities | 9,000,000 | | JE09.07 | 2,000,000 | | | 11,022,000 | | | | 11,022,000 | |
| | | | JE09.12 | 22,000 | | | | | | | | |
| Investment in marketable equity securities | 22,000,000 | | JE09.08 | 750,000 | JE09.09 | 330,000 | 22,463,000 | | | | 22,463,000 | |
| | | | | | JE09.12 | 43,000 | | | | | | |
| Accrued interest receivable | 19,000 | | JE09.11 | 31,000 | JE09.02 | 19,000 | 31,000 | | | | 31,000 | |
| Accounts payable | | 21,000 | JE09.01 | 21,000 | JE09.10 | 29,000 | | 29,000 | | | | 29,000 |

## 9-10 Fiduciary Funds

### WORKSHEET ENTRIES (Continued)

| Accounts | Trial Balance Debits | Trial Balance Credits | Adjustments Debits | | Adjustments Credits | | Adjusted Trial Balance Debits | Adjusted Trial Balance Credits | Operating Statement Debits | Operating Statement Credits | Balance Sheet Debits | Balance Sheet Credits |
|---|---|---|---|---|---|---|---|---|---|---|---|---|
| Refunds payable and other liabilities | | 29,000 | JE09.01 | 27,000 | JE09.10 | 23,000 | | 25,000 | | | | 25,000 |
| Fund balance | 32,169,000 | | | | | | 32,169,000 | | | | 32,169,000 | |
| Interest and investment revenue | | | | | JE09.04 | 320,000 | | 486,000 | | 486,000 | | |
| | | | | | JE09.09 | 70,000 | | | | | | |
| | | | | | JE09.011 | 31,000 | | | | | | |
| | | | | | JE09.12 | 65,000 | | | | | | |
| Contributions—City of Centerville | | | | | JE09.03 | 7,000,000 | | 7,000,000 | | 7,000,000 | | |
| Contributions—plan members | | | | | JE09.03 | 2,700,000 | | 2,700,000 | | 2,700,000 | | |
| Administrative expenses | | | JE09.10 | 29,000 | | | 349,000 | | 349,000 | | | |
| | | | JE09.05 | 320,000 | | | | | | | | |
| Refunds | | | JE09.06 | 77,000 | | | 100,000 | | 100,000 | | | |
| | | | JE09.10 | 23,000 | | | | | | | | |
| Benefits paid | | | JE09.05 | 4,200,000 | | | 4,200,000 | | 4,200,000 | | | |
| Totals | 32,219,000 | 32,219,000 | | 17,982,000 | | 17,982,000 | 42,409,000 | 42,409,000 | 4,649,000 | 10,186,000 | 37,760,000 | 32,223,000 |
| Net increase (decrease) | | | | | | | | | 5,537,000 | | | 5,537,000 |
| | | | | | | | | | 10,186,000 | 10,186,000 | 37,760,000 | 37,760,000 |

# APPENDIX 9B: PENSION TRUST FUNDS—STATEMENT OF FIDUCIARY NET ASSETS AND CHANGES IN FIDUCIARY NET ASSETS

**WORKSHEET ENTRIES**

City of Centerville
Statement of Fiduciary Net Assets
June 30, 20X1

| | Employee Retirement Fund |
|---|---|
| **ASSETS** | |
| Cash | $ 4,244,000 |
| Accrued interest receivable | 31,000 |
| Investments in debt securities | 11,022,000 |
| Investment in marketable equity securities | 22,463,000 |
| Total Assets | $37,760,000 |
| **LIABILITIES** | |
| Accounts payable and accrued expenses | $ 29,000 |
| Refunds payable and other liabilities | 25,000 |
| Total liabilities | $ 54,000 |
| **NET ASSETS** | |
| Held in trust for pension benefits | $37,706,000 |

## WORKSHEET ENTRIES (Continued)

### City of Centerville
### Statement of Changes in Fiduciary Net Assets
### For the Year Ended June 30, 20X1

| | Employee Retirement Fund |
|---|---:|
| **ADDITIONS** | |
| Contributions by: | |
|   City of Centerville | $ 7,000,000 |
|   Plan members | 2,700,000 |
| Total Contributions | 9,700,000 |
| Interest and investment revenue | 486,000 |
| Total additions | 10,186,000 |
| **DEDUCTIONS** | |
| Benefits paid | 4,200,000 |
| Refunds of contributions | 100,000 |
| Administrative expenses | 349,000 |
| Total deductions | 4,649,000 |
| Change in net assets | 5,537,000 |
| Net assets—beginning of the year | 32,169,000 |
| Net assets—end of the year | $37,706,000 |

# APPENDIX 9C: PENSION TRUST FUNDS—GOVERNMENT-WIDE FINANCIAL STATEMENTS

Fiduciary financial statements are presented only at the fund financial statement level.

# CHAPTER 10
# PRIVATE-PURPOSE TRUST FUNDS

## CONTENTS

| | |
|---|---|
| Nature of Private-Purpose Trust Funds | 10-1 |
| Measurement Focus and Basis of Accounting | 10-2 |
| Financial Reporting at Fund Level | 10-2 |
| Financial Reporting at Government-Wide Level | 10-3 |
| Illustrative Transactions | 10-3 |
| Fund Financial Statements | 10-5 |
| Government-Wide Financial Statements | 10-6 |
| Appendix 10A: Worksheet for Summarizing Current Transactions—Private-Purpose Trust Fund (Scholarship Fund) | 10-7 |
| Appendix 10B: Private-Purpose Trust Funds—Statement of Fiduciary Net Assets and Changes in Fiduciary Net Assets | 10-8 |
| Appendix 10C: Private-Purpose Trust Funds—Government-Wide Financial Statements | 10-10 |

## NATURE OF PRIVATE-PURPOSE TRUST FUNDS

Governmental entities often establish fiduciary relationships between themselves and other parties. Transactions and balances that arise from these relationships are accounted for in fiduciary funds. There are four types of fiduciary funds: (1) Pension Trust Funds (or similar funds), (2) Investment Trust Funds, (3) Private-Purpose Trust Funds, and (4) Agency Funds. In general, these fund types are used to report activities related to resources held and administered (except for an Agency Fund) by a governmental entity when it is acting in a fiduciary capacity for individuals, private organizations, or other governments. GASB-34 notes that if it is not appropriate to account for the resources related to a fiduciary relationship in a Pension Trust Fund, Investment Trust Fund, or Agency Fund, then a Private-Purpose Trust Fund should be used to account for "all other trust arrangements under which principal and income benefit individuals, private organizations, or other governments."

## MEASUREMENT FOCUS AND BASIS OF ACCOUNTING

The accrual basis of accounting and the flow of economic resources are used to prepare the financial statements of Private-Purpose Trust Funds. Under the flow of economic resources measurement focus and accrual basis of accounting, revenues are recognized when earned and expenses are recorded when incurred if these activities are related to exchange and exchange-like activities. In addition, long-lived assets (such as buildings and equipment), if held by the fund, are capitalized and depreciated over their estimated economic lives (GASB-34, par.16).

> ▶ **NEW STANDARD:** As discussed in Chapter 7 ("Enterprise Funds"), Enterprise Funds can follow either Alternative 1 or Alternative 2 as described in GASB-20 (Accounting and Financial Reporting for Proprietary Funds and Other Governmental Entities That Use Proprietary Fund Accounting). Even though fiduciary funds—including Private-Purpose Trust Funds—use the same accounting basis as Enterprise Funds, they are not allowed to use the two-alternative approach established in GASB-20 (GASB-34, par. 423).

## FINANCIAL REPORTING AT FUND LEVEL

Unlike governmental funds and proprietary funds, the *major fund* reporting concept does not apply to Private-Purpose Trust Funds. GASB-34 requires that fiduciary funds be reported in an entity's financial statements by fund type (Pension [and Other Employee Benefit] Trust Funds, Investment Trust Funds, Private-Purpose Trust Funds, and Agency Funds). If there is more than one Private-Purpose Trust Fund, there is no requirement to report the individual funds in combining financial statements.

The balances and activities of Private-Purpose Trust Funds are presented in the following financial statements at the fund financial statement level:

- Statement of net assets
- Statement of changes in net assets

The statement of net assets reports the trust fund's assets and liabilities; however, there is no need to divide net assets into the three categories (invested in capital assets [net of related debt], restricted net assets, and unrestricted net assets) that must be used in the government-wide financial statements. The equity section of the statement of net assets is simply identified as "net assets held in trust for" an identified third party.

A Private-Purpose Trust Fund's statement of changes in net assets is formatted in a manner to identify (1) additions in net assets, (2) deductions from net assets, and (3) the net increase or decrease in the fund's net assets for the year.

▶ **NEW STANDARD:** GASB-37 (Basic Financial Statements—and Management's Discussion and Analysis—for State and Local Governments: Omnibus) requires generally that escheat property be reported in the governmental or proprietary fund that ultimately will receive the escheat property. Escheat property that is held for individuals, private organizations, or another government is reported in either (1) a Private-Purpose Trust Fund, (2) an Agency Fund, or (3) the governmental or proprietary fund that reports escheat property. An Agency Fund rather than a Private-Purpose Trust Fund is used when the property holding period is expected to be brief. Escheat property that is reported in a Private-Purpose Trust Fund is reported as an *addition* in the statement of changes in fiduciary net assets and any balance remaining at the end of the accounting period is reported as *held in trust for trust beneficiaries* in the statement of fiduciary net assets. When the escheat property is reported in an Agency Fund, only a statement of fiduciary net assets is prepared. Consistent with the basic standards established by GASB-34, escheat property reported in a Private-Purpose Trust Fund or an Agency Fund is not reported in the entity's government-wide financial statements.

## FINANCIAL REPORTING AT GOVERNMENT-WIDE LEVEL

Financial statements of fiduciary funds are not presented in the government-wide financial statements, because resources of these funds cannot be used to finance a governmental entity's activities. The financial statements are included in the fund financial statements because a governmental entity is financially accountable for those resources even though they belong to other parties (GASB-34, par. 13).

## ILLUSTRATIVE TRANSACTIONS

In order to illustrate accounting and financial reporting standards that are observed for a Private-Purpose Trust Fund, assume that the City of Centerville agreed to administer a Scholarship Trust Fund that was created several years ago by a group of local educators. Only the investment earnings from the permanent endowment can be used to finance scholarships awarded to deserving students. The fund's trial balance for the beginning of the fiscal year is as follows:

| Accounts | Debits | Credits |
|---|---|---|
| Cash | $ 4,000 | |
| Investment in debt securities | 450,000 | |
| Accounts payable and accrued expenses | | $ 5,000 |
| Net assets | | 449,000 |
| Totals | $454,000 | $454,000 |

## 10-4  Fiduciary Funds

This section presents illustrative transactions and entries for the Private-Purpose Trust Fund during the fiscal year ended June 30, 20X1.

***Transaction JE10.01***—Accounts payable of $5,000 from the previous year were paid:

| Accounts | Debits | Credits |
|---|---|---|
| Accounts Payable and Accrued Expenses | 5,000 | |
| Cash | | 5,000 |

***Transaction JE10.02***—During the year, interest and investment revenue of $40,000 was earned and received:

| Accounts | Debits | Credits |
|---|---|---|
| Cash | 40,000 | |
| Interest and Investment Revenue | | 40,000 |

***Transaction JE10.03***—Scholarships of $52,000 were paid during the year. Approved tuition payments due at the end of the year but unpaid were $5,000:

| Accounts | Debits | Credits |
|---|---|---|
| Scholarships Paid | 57,000 | |
| Cash | | 52,000 |
| Accounts Payable and Accrued Expenses | | 5,000 |

***Transaction JE10.04***—Additional contributions of $40,000 to the permanent endowment of the fund were received from local educators ($30,000) and the City of Centerville (through its General Fund) ($10,000) during the year:

| Accounts | Debits | Credits |
|---|---|---|
| Cash | 40,000 | |
| Contributions—Individuals | | 30,000 |
| Contributions—City of Centerville | | 10,000 |

***Transaction JE10.05***—Additional investments of $25,000 in bonds for the year were made:

| Accounts | Debits | Credits |
|---|---|---|
| Investments in Debt Securities | 25,000 | |
| Cash | | 25,000 |

***Transaction JE10.06***—At the end of the year, the portfolio of debt securities had increased in value by $9,000:

*Private-Purpose Trust Funds* **10-5**

| Accounts | Debits | Credits |
|---|---|---|
| Investments in debt securities | 9,000 | |
| Interest and Investment Revenue | | 9,000 |

After the transactions for the year are posted, the year-end trial balance (June 30, 20X1) for the Scholarship Trust Fund appears as follows:

| Accounts | Adjusted Trial Balance Debits | Credits |
|---|---|---|
| Cash | $ 27,000 | |
| Investment in debt securities | 459,000 | |
| Accounts payable and accrued expenses | | $ 5,000 |
| Net assets | | 449,000 |
| Interest and investment revenue | | 49,000 |
| Scholarships paid | 57,000 | |
| Contributions—individuals | | 30,000 |
| Contributions—City of Centerville | | 10,000 |
| Totals | $543,000 | $543,000 |

The worksheet that summarizes the journal entries for the Private-Purpose Trust Fund for the year-end trial balance is presented in Appendix 10A.

## FUND FINANCIAL STATEMENTS

Based on the adjusted trial balance created above, the following financial statements are prepared for the Scholarship Trust Fund (see Appendix 10B):

**City of Centerville**
**Statement of Fiduciary Net Assets**
**June 30, 20X1**

| | Scholarship Fund |
|---|---|
| **ASSETS** | |
| Cash | $ 27,000 |
| Investments in debt securities | 459,000 |
| Total Assets | $486,000 |
| **LIABILTIES** | |
| Accounts payable and accrued expenses | $ 5,000 |
| Total Liabilities | $ 5,000 |
| **NET ASSETS** | |
| Held in trust for scholarships | $481,000 |

**10-6** *Fiduciary Funds*

**City of Centerville**
**Statement of Changes in Fiduciary Net Assets**
**For the Year Ended June 30, 20X1**

|  | Scholarship Fund |
|---|---:|
| **ADDITIONS** | |
| Contributions by: | |
| Private individuals | $ 30,000 |
| City of Centerville | 10,000 |
| Total Contributions | 40,000 |
| Interest and investment revenue | 49,000 |
| Total additions | 89,000 |
| **DEDUCTIONS** | |
| Scholarships paid | 57,000 |
| Change in net assets | 32,000 |
| Net assets—beginning of the year | 449,000 |
| Net assets—end of the year | $481,000 |

The financial statements for the Private-Purpose Trust Fund are used later, in Chapter 12 ("Developing Information for Fund Financial Statements").

## GOVERNMENT-WIDE FINANCIAL STATEMENTS

Fiduciary financial statements are presented only at the fund financial statement level (see Appendix 10C).

# APPENDIX 10A: WORKSHEET FOR SUMMARIZING CURRENT TRANSACTIONS—PRIVATE-PURPOSE TRUST FUND (SCHOLARSHIP FUND)

## WORKSHEET ENTRIES

| Accounts | Trial Balance Debits | Trial Balance Credits | Adjustments Debits | | Adjustments Credits | | Trial Balance Debits | Trial Balance Credits | Operating Statement Debits | Operating Statement Credits | Balance Sheet Debits | Balance Sheet Credits |
|---|---|---|---|---|---|---|---|---|---|---|---|---|
| Cash | 4,000 | | 40,000 | JE10.02 | 5,000 | JE10.01 | 27,000 | | | | 27,000 | |
| | | | 40,000 | JE10.04 | 52,000 | JE10.03 | | | | | | |
| Investment in debt securities | 450,000 | | 9,000 | JE10.05 | | | 459,000 | | | | 459,000 | |
| Accounts payable and accrued expenses | | 5,000 | 5,000 | JE10.01 | 5,000 | JE10.03 | | 5,000 | | | | 5,000 |
| Net assets | | 449,000 | | | | | | 449,000 | | | | 449,000 |
| Interest and investment revenue | | | | | 40,000 | JE10.02 | | 49,000 | | 49,000 | | |
| | | | | | 9,000 | JE10.05 | | | | | | |
| Scholarships paid | | | 57,000 | JE0.03 | | | 57,000 | | 57,000 | | | |
| Contribution—individuals | | | | | 30,000 | JE10.04 | | 30,000 | | 30,000 | | |
| Contributions—City of Centerville | | | | | 10,000 | JE10.04 | | 10,000 | | 10,000 | | |
| Totals | 454,000 | 454,000 | 151,000 | | 151,000 | | 543,000 | 543,000 | 57,000 | 89,000 | 486,000 | 454,000 |
| Net increase (decrease) | | | | | | | | | 32,000 | | | 32,000 |
| | | | | | | | | | 89,000 | 89,000 | 486,000 | 486,000 |

## APPENDIX 10B: PRIVATE-PURPOSE TRUST FUNDS—STATEMENT OF FIDUCIARY NET ASSETS AND CHANGES IN FIDUCIARY NET ASSETS

**WORKSHEET ENTRIES**

City of Centerville
Statement of Fiduciary Net Assets
June 30, 20X1

| | Scholarship Fund |
|---|---|
| **ASSETS** | |
| Cash | $ 27,000 |
| Investments in debt securities | 459,000 |
| Total Assets | $486,000 |
| **LIABILITIES** | |
| Accounts payable and accrued expenses | $ 5,000 |
| Total Liabilities | $ 5,000 |
| **NET ASSETS** | |
| Held in trust for scholarships | $481,000 |

**WORKSHEET ENTRIES (Continued)**

**City of Centerville**
**Statement of Changes in Fiduciary Net Assets**
**For the Year Ended June 30, 20X1**

|  | Scholarship Fund |
|---|---|
| **ADDITIONS** |  |
| Contributions by: |  |
| Private individuals | $ 30,000 |
| City of Centerville | 10,000 |
| Total Contributions | 40,000 |
| Interest and investment revenue | 49,000 |
| Total additions | 89,000 |
| **DEDUCTIONS** |  |
| Scholarships paid | 57,000 |
| Change in net assets | 32,000 |
| Net assets—beginning of the year | 449,000 |
| Net assets—end of the year | $481,000 |

*Private-Purpose Trust Funds* **10-9**

## APPENDIX 10C: PRIVATE-PURPOSE TRUST FUNDS—GOVERNMENT-WIDE FINANCIAL STATEMENTS

Fiduciary financial statements are presented only at the fund financial statement level.

# CHAPTER 11
# AGENCY FUNDS

## CONTENTS

| | |
|---|---|
| Nature of Agency Funds | 11-1 |
| Measurement Focus and Basis of Accounting | 11-1 |
| Financial Reporting at Fund Level | 11-2 |
| Financial Reporting at Government-Wide Level | 11-2 |
| Illustrative Transactions | 11-3 |
| Fund Financial Statements | 11-5 |
| Government-Wide Financial Statements | 11-5 |
| Appendix 11A: Worksheet for Summarizing Current Transactions—Agency Fund | 11-6 |
| Appendix 11B: Agency Funds—Statement of Fiduciary Net Assets | 11-7 |
| Appendix 11C: Agency Funds—Government-Wide Financial Statements | 11-8 |

## NATURE OF AGENCY FUNDS

Generally, an Agency Fund is created to act as a custodian for private entities or other governmental units. Assets are recorded by the Agency Fund, held for a period of time as determined by legal contract or circumstances, and then returned to their owners or to some other party that is entitled to receive the resources.

## MEASUREMENT FOCUS AND BASIS OF ACCOUNTING

The accrual basis of accounting and the flow of economic resources are used to prepare the financial statements of an Agency Fund. Under the flow of economic resources measurement focus and the accrual basis of accounting as applied to an Agency Fund, resources are recognized when they are required to be provided to the governmental entity and reductions to resources are recorded when resources are actually distributed to the appropriate party under agency agreement (GASB-34, par. 16).

▶ **NEW STANDARD:** GASB-37 (Basic Financial Statements—and Management's Discussion and Analysis—for State and Local Governments: Omnibus) requires generally that escheat property be reported in the governmental or proprietary fund that ultimately will receive the escheat property. Escheat property that is held for individuals, private organizations, or another government is reported in either (1) a Private-Purpose Trust Fund, (2) an Agency Fund, or (3) the governmental or proprietary fund that reports escheat property. An Agency Fund rather than a Private-Purpose Trust Fund is used when the property-holding period is expected to be brief. Escheat property that is reported in a Private-Purpose Trust Fund is reported as an *addition* in the statement of changes in fiduciary net assets and any balance remaining at the end of the accounting period is reported as *held in trust for trust beneficiaries* in the statement of fiduciary net assets. When the escheat property is reported in an Agency Fund, only a statement of fiduciary net assets is prepared. Consistent with the basic standards established by GASB-34, escheat property reported in a Private-Purpose Trust Fund or an Agency Fund is not reported in the entity's government-wide financial statements.

## FINANCIAL REPORTING AT FUND LEVEL

Unlike governmental funds and proprietary funds, the *major fund* reporting concept does not apply to Agency Funds. GASB-34 requires that fiduciary funds be reported in an entity's financial statements by fund type (Pension [and Other Employee Benefit] Trust Funds, Investment Trust Funds, Private-Purpose Trust Funds, and Agency Funds). If there is more than one Agency Fund, there is no requirement to report the individual funds in combining financial statements.

The balances of an Agency Fund are presented in a statement of net assets. An Agency Fund is not required to prepare a statement of changes in net assets like other fiduciary funds are.

The statement of net assets reports the Agency Fund's assets and liabilities; however, there is no net asset balance (equity balance) in an Agency Fund since all of the assets are distributable to third parties.

## FINANCIAL REPORTING AT GOVERNMENT-WIDE LEVEL

Financial statements of fiduciary funds are not presented in the government-wide financial statements, because resources of these funds cannot be used to finance a governmental entity's activities. The financial statements are included in the fund financial statement, because a governmental entity is financially accountable for those resources even though they belong to other parties (GASB-34, par. 13).

## ILLUSTRATIVE TRANSACTIONS

In order to illustrate accounting and financial reporting standards that are observed for an Agency Fund, assume that the City of Centerville uses a fund (Community Support Fund) to distribute certain state grants to various not-for-profit organizations. The state grants are transferred to the City for the convenience of the not-for-profit organizations. Currently, the not-for-profit organizations that are eligible for state funding are Reading Is Fundamental, Inc., Food For All, Inc., and Basic Heating Program, Inc. All of the state grants are accounted for in a single fund. The fund's trial balance for the beginning of the fiscal year is as follows:

| Accounts | Trial Balance Debits | Credits |
|---|---|---|
| Cash | $31,000 | |
| Accounts payable | | $31,000 |
| Totals | $31,000 | $31,000 |

This section presents illustrative transactions and entries for the Agency Fund during the fiscal year ended June 30, 20X1.

*Transaction JE11.01*—The following amounts due to not-for-profit organizations from the previous year were paid:

| | |
|---|---|
| Reading Is Fundamental, Inc. | $20,000 |
| Food For All, Inc. | 4,000 |
| Basic Heating Program, Inc. | 9,000 |
| Total | $31,000 |

| Accounts | Debits | Credits |
|---|---|---|
| Accounts payable—Reading Is Fundamental, Inc. | 20,000 | |
| Accounts payable—Food For All, Inc. | 4,000 | |
| Accounts payable—Basic Heating Program, Inc. | 9,000 | |
| Cash | | 31,000 |

*Transaction JE11.02*—During the year, the following state grants were received in the name of the not-for-profit organizations:

## 11-4 Fiduciary Funds

| | |
|---|---:|
| Reading Is Fundamental, Inc. | $230,000 |
| Food For All, Inc. | 120,000 |
| Basic Heating Program, Inc. | 90,000 |
| Total | $440,000 |

| Accounts | Debits | Credits |
|---|---:|---:|
| Cash | 440,000 | |
| Accounts payable—Reading Is Fundamental, Inc. | | 230,000 |
| Accounts payable—Food For All, Inc. | | 120,000 |
| Accounts payable—Basic Heating Program, Inc. | | 90,000 |

***Transaction JE11.03***—During the year, the following amounts from the current-year grants were distributed to the not-for-profit organizations:

| | |
|---|---:|
| Reading Is Fundamental, Inc. | $225,000 |
| Food For All, Inc. | 100,000 |
| Basic Heating Program, Inc. | 80,000 |
| Total | $405,000 |

| Accounts | Debits | Credits |
|---|---:|---:|
| Accounts payable—Reading Is Fundamental, Inc. | 225,000 | |
| Accounts payable—Food For All, Inc. | 100,000 | |
| Accounts payable—Basic Heating Program, Inc. | 80,000 | |
| Cash | | 405,000 |

After the transactions for the year are posted, the year-end trial balance (June 30, 20X1) for the Agency Fund appears as follows:

| Accounts | Adjusted Debits | Adjusted Trial Balance Credits |
|---|---:|---:|
| Cash | $35,000 | |
| Accounts payable | | $35,000 |
| Totals | $35,000 | $35,000 |

The worksheet that summarizes the journal entries for the Agency Fund for the year-end trial balance is presented in Appendix 11A.

# FUND FINANCIAL STATEMENTS

Based on the adjusted trial balances created above, the following financial statement is prepared for the Agency Trust Fund (see Appendix 11B):

City of Centerville
Statement of Fiduciary Net Assets
June 30, 20X1

|  | Agency Trust Fund |
|---|---|
| **ASSETS** |  |
| Cash | $ 35,000 |
| Total assets | $35,000 |
| **LIABILTIES** |  |
| Accounts payable | $ 35,000 |
| Total liabilities | $35,000 |

The financial statement for the Agency Fund is used later, in Chapter 12 ("Developing Information for Fund Financial Statements").

# GOVERNMENT-WIDE FINANCIAL STATEMENTS

Fiduciary financial statements are presented only at the fund financial statement level (see Appendix 11C).

**11-6** *Fiduciary Funds*

## APPENDIX 11A: WORKSHEET FOR SUMMARIZING CURRENT TRANSACTIONS—AGENCY FUND

### WORKSHEET ENTRIES

| Accounts | Trial Balance Debits | Trial Balance Credits | Adjustments Debits | | Adjustments Credits | | Adjusted Trial Balance Debits | Adjusted Trial Balance Credits | Balance Sheet Debits | Balance Sheet Credits |
|---|---|---|---|---|---|---|---|---|---|---|
| Cash | 31,000 | | JE11.02 | 440,000 | JE11.01 | 31,000 | 35,000 | | 35,000 | |
| | | | | | JE11.03 | 405,000 | | | | |
| Accounts payable | | 31,000 | JE11.01 | 31,000 | JE11.02 | 440,000 | | 35,000 | | 35,000 |
| | | | JE11.03 | 405,000 | | | | | | |
| Totals | 31,000 | 31,000 | | 876,000 | | 876,000 | 35,000 | 35,000 | | |
| Net increase (decrease) | | | | | | | | | 0 | 0 |
| Totals | | | | | | | | | 35,000 | 35,000 |

# APPENDIX 11B: AGENCY FUNDS—STATEMENT OF FIDUCIARY NET ASSETS

**WORKSHEET ENTRIES**

City of Centerville
Statement of Fiduciary Net Assets
June 30, 20X1

|  | Agency Trust Fund |
|---|---|
| **ASSETS** |  |
| Cash | $ 35,000 |
| Total assets | $35,000 |
| **LIABILITIES** |  |
| Accounts payable | $ 35,000 |
| Total liabilities | $35,000 |

## APPENDIX 11C: AGENCY FUNDS—GOVERNMENT-WIDE FINANCIAL STATEMENTS

Fiduciary financial statements are presented only at the fund financial statement level.

# PART V.
# THE CONSOLIDATION AND CONVERSION PROCESS

# CHAPTER 12
# DEVELOPING INFORMATION FOR FUND FINANCIAL STATEMENTS

## CONTENTS

| | |
|---|---|
| Introduction | 12-1 |
| Identifying a Major Fund | 12-2 |
|    10% Threshold | 12-3 |
|    5% Threshold | 12-4 |
| Governmental Funds Financial Statements | 12-5 |
|    Combining Trial Balances for Nonmajor Funds | 12-6 |
|    Combining Trial Balances for All Governmental Funds | 12-10 |
|    Identification of Reservations | 12-13 |
|    Governmental Fund Financial Statements | 12-15 |
|    Reconciliations | 12-17 |
| Proprietary Funds Financial Statements | 12-17 |
|    Combining Trial Balances for Nonmajor Enterprise Funds | 12-18 |
|    Combining Trial Balances for All Proprietary Funds | 12-19 |
|    Proprietary Fund Financial Statements | 12-21 |
|    Reconciliations | 12-26 |
| Fiduciary Fund Financial Statements | 12-27 |
|    Statement of Fiduciary Net Assets | 12-27 |
|    Statement of Changes in Fiduciary Net Assets | 12-28 |

## INTRODUCTION

Fund-based financial statements are included in a governmental entity's financial statements in order to demonstrate that restrictions imposed by statutes, regulations, or contracts have been followed. The fund financial statements are built around (1) governmental funds (General Fund, Special Revenue Funds, Capital Projects Funds, Debt Service Funds, and Permanent Funds), (2) proprietary funds (Enterprise Funds and Internal Service Funds), and (3) fiduciary funds (Pension Trust Funds [and similar benefit funds], Investment Trust Funds, Private-Purpose Trust Funds, and Agency Funds). Governmental funds and Enterprise Funds are reported based on the *major fund concept*. The major fund concept does not apply to Internal Service Funds and fiduciary funds. All Internal Service Funds are combined into a single column and presented on the proprietary fund financial statements (to the right of Enterprise Funds). Fiduciary funds are presented by fund-type. These concepts are illustrated in this chapter.

## IDENTIFYING A MAJOR FUND

GASB-34 requires that a governmental fund or Enterprise Fund be presented in a separate column in the fund financial statements if the fund is considered a major fund. A major fund is one that satisfies *both* of the following criteria: (GASB-34, pars. 75 and 76, as amended by GASB-37, par. 15)

> A. 10% Threshold—Total assets, liabilities, revenues, or expenditures/expenses of the governmental (enterprise) fund are equal to or greater 10 percent of the corresponding element total (assets, liability, and so forth) for all funds that are considered governmental funds (enterprise funds)

> B. 5% Threshold—The same element that met the 10 percent criterion in (A) is at least 5 percent of the corresponding element total for all governmental and Enterprise Funds combined.

> ▶ **NEW STANDARD:** In establishing major fund criteria, the GASB intended that a major fund arises when a particular element (assets, for example) of a fund meets both the 10% threshold and the 5% threshold. Some preparers read the requirement as originally stated in GASB-34 to mean that a major fund arises when one element (assets, for example) satisfies the 10% threshold and another element (revenues, for example) satisfies the 5% threshold. GASB-37 (Basic Financial Statements—and Management's Discussion and Analysis—for State and Local Governments: Omnibus) clarifies the GASB's original intent. That is, a single element of a particular fund must satisfy both criteria in order for that fund to be considered a major fund.

> **OBSERVATION:** Total revenues and expenditures/expenses, extraordinary items are be excluded in determining a major fund.

The General Fund is always considered a major fund and, therefore, must be presented in a separate column. If a fund does not satisfy the conditions described above, it can still be presented as a major fund if the governmental entity believes it is important to do so. All other funds that are not considered major funds must be combined in a separate column and labeled as nonmajor funds.

## 10% Threshold

The following summarization is used to determine which individual funds (governmental and Enterprise Funds) discussed in previous chapters pass the 10% threshold:

| 10% Threshold Governmental Funds | Total Assets | % | Total Liabilities | % | Total Revenues | % | Total Expenditures/ Expenses | % |
|---|---|---|---|---|---|---|---|---|
| General Fund | 15,937,600 | 77.4 | 3,607,000 | 94.1 | 115,020,600 | 92.2 | 110,471,213 | 81.7 |
| Special Revenue Fund—Center City Special Services District | 89,500 | 0.4 | 60,000 | 1.6 | 2,688,000 | 2.2 | 2,750,000 | 2.0 |
| Special Revenue Fund—Local Fuel Tax Fund | 44,000 | 0.2 | 25,000 | 0.7 | 4,506,000 | 3.6 | 4,200,000 | 3.1 |
| Capital Projects Fund—Easely Street Bridge Project | 824,956 | 4.0 | 95,000 | 2.5 | 1,280,000 | 1.0 | 11,595,000 | 8.6 |
| Capital Projects Fund—Bland Street Drainage Project | 220,000 | 1.1 | 27,000 | 0.7 | 754,000 | 0.6 | 1,597,000 | 1.2 |
| Capital Projects Fund—West End Recreation Center | 2,941,000 | 14.3 | 5,000 | 0.1 | 452,000 | 0.4 | 1,325,000 | 1.0 |
| Debt Service Fund—Senior Citizens' Center Bonds | 60,000 | 0.3 | 2,000 | 0.1 | 4,000 | 0.0 | 1,259,000 | 0.9 |
| Debt Service Fund—Easely Street Bridge Bonds | 45,000 | 0.2 | 3,000 | 0.1 | 1,000 | 0.0 | 211,000 | 0.2 |
| Debt Service Fund—Bland Bonds | 129,000 | 0.6 | 3,000 | 0.1 | 3,000 | 0.0 | 1,009,000 | 0.7 |
| Debt Service Fund—West End Recreation Center Bonds | 43,000 | 0.2 | 1,000 | 0.0 | 1,000 | 0.0 | 687,000 | 0.5 |
| Permanent Fund— Centerville Cemetery | 247,000 | 1.2 | 4,000 | 0.1 | 56,000 | 0.0 | 35,000 | 0.0 |
| Total | 20,581,056 | 1.000 | 3,832,000 | 1.000 | 124,765,600 | 1.000 | 135,139,213 | 1.000 |

**12-4** *The Consolidation and Conversion Process*

| 10% Threshold Governmental Funds | Total Assets | % | Total Liabilities | % | Total Revenues | % | Total Expenditures/ Expenses | % |
|---|---|---|---|---|---|---|---|---|
| Centerville Toll Bridge | 2,405,500 | 1.5 | 213,000 | 0.5 | 5,157,000 | 1.9 | 4,661,000 | 1.8 |
| Centerville Utilities Authority | 28,075,000 | 17.4 | 12,678,000 | 31.7 | 37,660,000 | 13.7 | 38,282,000 | 15.2 |
| Centerville Parking Authority | 3,728,000 | 2.3 | 649,000 | 1.6 | 1,533,000 | 0.6 | 6,038,000 | 2.4 |
| Centerville Municipal Airport | 126,813,000 | 78.8 | 26,440,000 | 66.1 | 230,260,000 | 83.8 | 203,495,000 | 80.6 |
| Total | 161,021,500 | 1.000 | 39,980,000 | 1.000 | 274,610,000 | 1.000 | 252,476,000 | 1.000 |

Based on the above analysis, the following funds pass the 10% threshold test:

- Governmental Fund—Capital Projects Fund—West End Recreation Center (14% of total assets)
- Enterprise Fund—Centerville Utilities Authority (17% of total assets, 32% of total liabilities, 14% of total revenues and 15% of total expenses)
- Enterprise Fund—Centerville Municipal Airport (79% of total assets, 66% of total liabilities, 84% of total revenues, and 81% of total expenses)

## 5% Threshold

The following summarization is used to determine which of the three funds that passed the 10% threshold also pass the 5% threshold:

| 5% Threshold Governmental Funds | Total Assets | % | Total Liabilities | % | Total Revenues | % | Total Expenditures/ Expenses | % |
|---|---|---|---|---|---|---|---|---|
| Capital Projects Fund— West End Recreation Center | 2,941,000 | 2 | 5,000 | n/a | 452,000 | n/a | 1,325,000 | n/a |
| Centerville Utilities Authority | 28,075,000 | 15 | 12,678,000 | 29 | 37,660,000 | 9 | 38,282,000 | 10 |
| Centerville Municipal Airport | 126,813,000 | 70 | 26,440,000 | 60 | 230,360,000 | 58 | 203,495,000 | 52 |
| Total for governmental funds | 20,581,056 | | 3,832,000 | | 124,765,600 | | 135,139,213 | |

| 5% Threshold Governmental Funds | Total Assets | % | Total Liabilities | % | Total Revenues | % | Total Expenditures/ Expenses | % |
|---|---|---|---|---|---|---|---|---|
| Total for enterprise funds | 161,021,500 | | 39,980,000 | | 274,610,000 | | 252,476,000 | |
| Total | 181,602,556 | | 43,812,000 | | 399,375,600 | | 387,615,213 | |

n/a - These computations are not applicable, because the element did not pass the 10% threshold.

The Capital Projects Fund (West End Recreation Center) does not pass the 5% threshold. The two Enterprise Funds (Centerville Utilities and Centerville Municipal Airport) pass all four of the criteria thresholds and, therefore, must be reported as major funds.

As noted earlier, a government may consider a fund to be a major fund, even if it does not satisfy the 10% and 5% thresholds. For presentation purposes, it is assumed that the City of Centerville believes that the Special Revenue Fund—Local Fuel Tax Fund (for consistency reasons) and Capital Projects Fund—West End Recreation Center (for public interest reasons) are major funds, even though they do not satisfy the 10% and 5% thresholds. Thus, the following five funds are considered to be major funds:

1. General Fund (always considered a major fund)
2. Special Revenue Fund—Local Fuel Tax Fund (does not pass both of the threshold criteria but for consistency is considered a major fund)
3. Capital Projects Fund—West End Recreation Center (does not pass both of the threshold criteria but for public interest reasons is considered a major fund)
4. Enterprise Fund—Centerville Utilities Authority (passes both of the threshold criteria)
5. Enterprise Fund—Centerville Municipal Airport (passes both of the threshold criteria)

## GOVERMENTAL FUNDS FINANCIAL STATEMENTS

At the fund financial statement level, a statement of revenues, expenditures, and changes in fund balances and a balance sheet are prepared for governmental funds. Based on the adjusted trial balances (modified accrual basis) created in previous chapters, this chapter illustrates how the previously created information is used to prepare the fund financial statements for governmental funds.

## Combining Trial Balances for Nonmajor Funds

The governmental funds in Exhibit 12-1 were illustrated in previous chapters and constitute the City of Centerville's nonmajor governmental funds.

### EXHIBIT 12-1—CITY OF CENTERVILLE'S NONMAJOR GOVERNMENTAL FUNDS

| Nonmajor Governmental Funds | Chapter Reference |
|---|---|
| Center City Special Services District | 3: Special Revenue Funds |
| Easely Street Bridge Project | 4: Capital Projects Funds |
| Bland Street Drainage Project | 4: Capital Projects Funds |
| Senior Citizens' Center Bonds | 5: Debt Service Funds |
| Easely Street Bridge Bonds | 5: Debt Service Funds |
| Bland Street Drainage Bonds | 5: Debt Service Funds |
| West End Recreation Center Bonds | 5: Debt Service Funds |
| Centerville Cemetery | 6: Permanent Funds |

Based on the information developed in the previous chapters, the following combining trial balance (modified accrual basis) is prepared for the nonmajor funds:

| | Special Services District (SRF) (Chapter 3) Debits (Credits) | Easely Street Bridge Project (CPF) (Chapter 4) Debits (Credits) | Bland Street Bridge Project (CPF) (Chapter 4) Debits (Credits) | Debt Service Funds (See Note) (Chapter 5) Debits (Credits) | Centerville Cemetery Fund (PF) (Chapter 6) Debits (Credits) | Nonmajor Funds Total Debits (Credits) |
|---|---|---|---|---|---|---|
| Cash | 26,500 | 129,956 | 158,000 | 210,000 | 3,000 | 527,456 |
| Interest receivable | | | | | | |
| Temporary investments | | 695,000 | 62,000 | 67,000 | | 824,000 |
| Property taxes receivable | 108,000 | | | | | 108,000 |
| Allowance for uncollectible property taxes | (60,000) | | | | | (60,000) |

*Developing Information for Fund Financial Statements* **12-7**

|  | Special Services District (SRF) (Chapter 3) Debits (Credits) | Easely Street Bridge Project (CPF) (Chapter 4) Debits (Credits) | Bland Street Bridge Project (CPF) (Chapter 4) Debits (Credits) | Debt Service Funds (See Note) (Chapter 5) Debits (Credits) | Centerville Cemetery Fund (PF) (Chapter 6) Debits (Credits) | Nonmajor Funds Total Debits (Credits) |
|---|---|---|---|---|---|---|
| Other receivables | 15,000 |  |  |  |  | 15,000 |
| Intergovernmental grants receivable |  |  |  |  |  |  |
| Investments in marketable debt securities |  |  |  |  | 244,000 | 244,000 |
| Investments in marketable equity securities |  |  |  |  |  |  |
| Inventories |  |  |  |  |  |  |
| Accounts payable | (50,000) | (95,000) | (27,000) | (9,000) | (4,000) | (185,000) |
| Deferred revenue— property taxes | (10,000) |  |  |  |  | (10,000) |
| Due to other funds—Internal Service Fund— Communications and Technology Support Center |  |  |  |  |  |  |
| Due to other funds—Internal Service Fund—Fleet Management Unit |  |  |  |  |  |  |
| Due to other funds—Enterprise Fund—Centerville Utilities Authority |  |  |  |  |  |  |
| Due to other funds—Enterprise Fund—Centerville Municipal Airport |  |  |  |  |  |  |
| Reserve for encumbrances |  |  |  |  |  |  |
| Fund balance— reserved for inventories |  |  |  |  |  |  |
| Fund balance— reserved for encumbrances |  |  |  |  |  |  |
| Fund balance | (16,500) | (716,000) | (136,000) | (105,000) | (222,000) | (1,195,500) |
| Program revenues— charges for services (general government) |  |  |  |  |  |  |

## 12-8 The Consolidation and Conversion Process

|  | Special Services District (SRF) (Chapter 3) Debits (Credits) | Easely Street Bridge Project (CPF) (Chapter 4) Debits (Credits) | Bland Street Bridge Project (CPF) (Chapter 4) Debits (Credits) | Debt Service Funds (See Note) (Chapter 5) Debits (Credits) | Centerville Cemetery Fund (PF) (Chapter 6) Debits (Credits) | Nonmajor Funds Total Debits (Credits) |
|---|---|---|---|---|---|---|
| Program revenues—operating grants (recreation and parks) | | | | | | |
| Program revenues—charges for services (recreation and parks) | | | | | | |
| Program revenues—charges for services (health and welfare) | | | | | | |
| Program revenues—operating contributions (health and welfare) | | | | | | |
| Program revenues—charges for services (streets) | | | | | | |
| Program revenues—capital grants (streets) | | (1,250,000) | (750,000) | | | (2,000,000) |
| Program revenues—capital grants (public safety) | | | | | | |
| Program revenues—charges for services (public safety) | | | | | | |
| General revenues—property taxes | (2,670,000) | | | | | (2,670,000) |
| General revenues—franchise taxes | | | | | | |
| General revenues—unrestricted grants | | | | | | |
| Miscellaneous revenue | (18,000) | | | | | (18,000) |

*Developing Information for Fund Financial Statements* **12-9**

| | Special Services District (SRF) (Chapter 3) Debits (Credits) | Easely Street Bridge Project (CPF) (Chapter 4) Debits (Credits) | Bland Street Bridge Project (CPF) (Chapter 4) Debits (Credits) | Debt Service Funds (See Note) (Chapter 5) Debits (Credits) | Centerville Cemetery Fund (PF) (Chapter 6) Debits (Credits) | Nonmajor Funds Total Debits (Credits) |
|---|---|---|---|---|---|---|
| Interest and investment revenue | | (30,000) | (4,000) | (9,000) | | (43,000) |
| Revenue— change in fair value of investments | | | | | | |
| Interest and investment revenue (program revenue— operating grants and contributions [general government]) | | | | | (34,000) | (34,000) |
| Expenditures— general government | 550,000 | 495,000 | 97,000 | 42,000 | 35,000 | 1,219,000 |
| Expenditures— public safety | | | | | | |
| Expenditures— streets | 2,200,000 | | | | | 2,200,000 |
| Expenditures— recreation and parks | | | | | | |
| Expenditures— health and welfare | | | | | | |
| Encumbrances | | | | | | |
| Expenditures— education (component unit) | | | | | | |
| Expenditures— capital outlays | | 11,100,000 | 1,500,000 | | | 12,600,000 |
| Expenditures— principal | | | | 1,950,000 | | 1,950,000 |
| Expenditures— interest | | | | 1,174,000 | | 1,174,000 |
| Revenue— permanent endowment additions | | | | | (22,000) | (22,000) |
| Other financing sources—long-term debt issued | | (10,000,000) | | | | (10,000,000) |
| Other financing uses—discount on long-term debt issued | | 671,044 | | | | 671,044 |
| Other financing sources— capitalized leases | | | | | | |

**12-10**  The Consolidation and Conversion Process

|  | Special Services District (SRF) (Chapter 3) Debits (Credits) | Easely Street Bridge Project (CPF) (Chapter 4) Debits (Credits) | Bland Street Bridge Project (CPF) (Chapter 4) Debits (Credits) | Debt Service Funds (See Note) (Chapter 5) Debits (Credits) | Centerville Cemetery Fund (PF) (Chapter 6) Debits (Credits) | Nonmajor Funds Total Debits (Credits) |
|---|---|---|---|---|---|---|
| Transfers in | (75,000) | (1,000,000) | (900,000) | (3,320,000) |  | (5,295,000) |
| Transfers out |  |  |  |  |  |  |
| Total | 0 | 0 | 0 | 0 | 0 | 0 |

**NOTE:** For the details of the four Debt Service Funds see Chapter 5 ("Debt Service Funds").

## Combining Trial Balances for All Governmental Funds

After the trial balance for the nonmajor funds is prepared, that information can be combined with the trial balances for the General Fund, and the two other major governmental funds (Special Revenue Fund—Local Fuel Tax Fund and Capital Projects Fund—West End Recreation Center) in order to create a combined trial balance for all governmental funds as follows:

|  | General Fund (Chapter 2) Debits (Credits) | Local Fuel Tax Fund (SRF) (Chapter 3) Debits (Credits) | West End Recreation Center Fund (CPF) (Chapter 4) Debits (Credits) | Nonmajor Funds Debits (Credits) | Total Governmental Funds Debits (Credits) |
|---|---|---|---|---|---|
| Cash | 9,440,000 | 42,000 | 19,000 | 527,456 | 10,028,456 |
| Interest receivable |  |  |  |  | — |
| Temporary investments |  |  | 2,922,000 | 824,000 | 3,746,000 |
| Property taxes receivable | 2,355,000 |  |  | 108,000 | 2,463,000 |
| Allowance for uncollectible property taxes | (2,000,000) |  |  | (60,000) | (2,060,000) |
| Other receivables | 35,600 | 2,000 |  | 15,000 | 52,600 |
| Intergovernmental grants receivable |  |  |  |  | — |
| Investments in marketable debt securities | 2,150,000 |  |  | 244,000 | 2,394,000 |
| Investments in marketable equity securities | 3,940,000 |  |  |  | 3,940,000 |
| Inventories | 17,000 |  |  |  | 17,000 |
| Accounts payable | (665,000) | (25,000) | (5,000) | (185,000) | (880,000) |
| Deferred revenue— property taxes | (300,000) |  |  | (10,000) | (310,000) |

Developing Information for Fund Financial Statements  12-11

| | General Fund (Chapter 2) Debits (Credits) | Local Fuel Tax Fund (SRF) (Chapter 3) Debits (Credits) | West End Recreation Center Fund (CPF) (Chapter 4) Debits (Credits) | Nonmajor Funds Debits (Credits) | Total Governmental Funds Debits (Credits) |
|---|---|---|---|---|---|
| Due to other funds | (2,642,000) | | | | (2,642,000) |
| Fund balance | (12,775,000) | (13,000) | (509,000) | (1,195,500) | (14,492,500) |
| Program revenues—charges for services (general government) | | | | | — |
| Program revenues—operating grants (Recreation and parks) | | | | | — |
| Program revenues—charges for services (recreation and parks) | | | | | — |
| Program revenues—charges for services (health and welfare) | | | | | — |
| Program revenues—operating contributions (health and welfare) | | | | | — |
| Program revenues—charges for services (streets) | | | | | — |
| Program revenues—capital grants (streets) | | | | (2,000,000) | (2,000,000) |
| Program revenues—operating grants (street) | | (4,500,000) | | | (4,500,000) |
| Program revenues—capital grants (public safety) | | | | | — |
| Program revenues—charges for services (public safety) | | | | | — |
| Program revenues—capital grants and contributions (recreations and parks) | | | (450,000) | | (450,000) |
| General revenues—property taxes | (87,600,000) | | | (2,670,000) | (90,270,000) |
| General revenues—franchise taxes | (1,300,000) | | | | (1,300,000) |
| General revenues—unrestricted grants | | | | | — |
| Intergovernmental grants | (20,500,000) | | | | (20,500,000) |
| Charges for services | (537,600) | | | | (537,600) |
| Contributions | (50,000) | | | | (50,000) |

**12-12** *The Consolidation and Conversion Process*

| | General Fund (Chapter 2) Debits (Credits) | Local Fuel Tax Fund (SRF) (Chapter 3) Debits (Credits) | West End Recreation Center Fund (CPF) (Chapter 4) Debits (Credits) | Nonmajor Funds Debits (Credits) | Total Governmental Funds Debits (Credits) |
|---|---|---|---|---|---|
| Miscellaneous revenue | (4,800,000) | | | (18,000) | (4,818,000) |
| Interest and investment revenue | (93,000) | (6,000) | (2,000) | (43,000) | (144,000) |
| Change in fair value of investments | (140,000) | | | | (140,000) |
| Interest and investment revenue (program revenue—operating grants and contributions [general government]) | | | | (34,000) | (34,000) |
| Expenditures—general government | 33,701,098 | 210,000 | 25,000 | 1,219,000 | 35,155,098 |
| Expenditures—public safety | 18,036,628 | | | | 18,036,628 |
| Expenditures—streets | 11,863,314 | 3,990,000 | | 2,200,000 | 18,053,314 |
| Expenditures—recreation and parks | 6,481,657 | | | | 6,481,657 |
| Expenditures—health and welfare | 8,076,657 | | | | 8,076,657 |
| Encumbrances | | | | | — |
| Expenditures—education (component unit) | 32,000,000 | | | | 32,000,000 |
| Expenditures—capital outlays | | | 1,300,000 | 12,600,000 | 13,900,000 |
| Expenditures—principal | | | | 1,950,000 | 1,950,000 |
| Expenditures-interest | 311,859 | | | 1,174,000 | 1,485,859 |
| Revenues—permanent endowment additions | | | | (22,000) | (22,000) |
| Other financing sources—long-term debt issued | | | (3,000,000) | (10,000,000) | (13,000,000) |
| Other financing uses—discount on long-term debt issued | | | | 671,044 | 671,044 |

|  | General Fund (Chapter 2) Debits (Credits) | Local Fuel Tax Fund (SRF) (Chapter 3) Debits (Credits) | West End Recreation Center Fund (CPF) (Chapter 4) Debits (Credits) | Nonmajor Funds Debits (Credits) | Total Governmental Funds Debits (Credits) |
|---|---|---|---|---|---|
| Other financing source— capitalized leases | (431,213) |  |  |  | (431,213) |
| Transfers in | (50,000) |  | (300,000) | (5,295,000) | (5,645,000) |
| Transfers out | 5,475,000 | 300,000 |  |  | 5,775,000 |
| Totals | 0 | 0 | 0 | 0 | 0 |

The information for the General Fund, the Local Fuel Tax Fund (Special Revenue Fund), and the West End Recreation Center Fund (Capital Projects Fund) is taken from previous chapters.

## Identification of Reservations

The equity of a governmental fund (total assets minus total liabilities) should be identified as reserved amounts and unreserved amounts, based on the standards established in paragraphs 118 through 121 of NCGA-1. The reserved fund balances of the combined nonmajor funds must be presented in appropriate detail to inform the reader of the nature of the reservation and to identify the amount of net unreserved current financial resources that are available for future appropriation. For example, the fund balance for nonmajor Debt Service Funds may be described as reserved for debt service. In addition, unreserved fund balances for nonmajor funds must be identified by fund type on the face of the balance sheet (GASB-34, par. 84).

The following is an analysis of unreserved and reserved fund balances (many of the reservations are assumed) for the City of Centerville's governmental funds:

**12-14** *The Consolidation and Conversion Process*

| | Total Fund Balance | Reserved for Inventories | Reserved for Enc. | Reserved for Debt Service | Reserved for Endow. | Reserved for Other Purposes | Unreserved Major Funds | Unreserved Nonmajor Funds |
|---|---|---|---|---|---|---|---|---|
| **MAJOR FUNDS:** | | | | | | | | |
| General Fund | 12,330,600 | 17,000 | 25,000 | | | | 12,288,600 | |
| Special Revenue Fund—Local Fuel Tax Fund | 19,000 | | | | | | 19,000 | |
| Capital Projects Fund—West End Recreation Center | 2,936,000 | | | | | | 2,936,000 | |
| **NONMAJOR FUNDS:** | | | | | | | | |
| Special Revenue Fund—Center City Special Services District | 29,500 | | | | | 3,000 | | 26,500 |
| Capital Projects Fund—Easely Street Bridge Project | 729,956 | | | | | 4,000 | | 725,956 |
| Capital Projects Fund—Bland Street Drainage Project | 193,000 | | | | | 9,000 | | 184,000 |
| Debt Service Fund—Senior Citizens' Center Bonds | 58,000 | | | 58,000 | | | | |
| Debt Service Fund—Easely Street Bridge Bonds | 42,000 | | | 42,000 | | | | |
| Debt Service Fund—Bland Street Drainage Bonds | 126,000 | | | 126,000 | | | | |
| Debt Service Fund—West End Recreation Center Bonds | 42,000 | | | 42,000 | | | | |
| Permanent Fund—Centerville Cemetery | 243,000 | | | | 243,000 | | | |
| | 16,749,056 | 17,000 | 25,000 | 268,000 | 243,000 | 16,000 | 15,243,600 | 936,456 |

## Governmental Fund Financial Statements

The governmental fund financial statements includes the following:
- Balance sheet
- Statement of revenues, expenditures, and changes in fund balances

Based on the trial balance presented above, the balance sheet and the statement of revenues, expenditures, and changes in fund balances for the City of Centerville are as follows:

Governmental Funds
Balance Sheet
June 30, 20X1

|  | General Fund (Chapter 2) | Local Fuel Tax Fund (Chapter 3) | West End Recreation Center Fund (Chapter 5) | Other Governmental Funds | Total Governmental Funds |
|---|---|---|---|---|---|
| **ASSETS** | | | | | |
| Cash | 9,440,000 | 42,000 | 19,000 | 527,456 | 10,028,456 |
| Temporary investments | | | 2,922,000 | 824,000 | 3,746,000 |
| Property taxes receivable (net) | 355,000 | | | 48,000 | 403,000 |
| Other receivables | 35,600 | 2,000 | | 15,000 | 52,600 |
| Investments | 6,090,000 | | | 244,000 | 6,334,000 |
| Inventories | 17,000 | | | | 17,000 |
| Total Assets | 15,937,600 | 44,000 | 2,941,000 | 1,658,456 | 20,581,056 |
| **LIABILITIES AND FUND BALANCES** | | | | | |
| Liabilities: | | | | | |
| Accounts payable | 665,000 | 25,000 | 5,000 | 185,000 | 880,000 |
| Due to other funds | 2,642,000 | | | | 2,642,000 |
| Deferred revenue | 300,000 | | | 10,000 | 310,000 |
| Total Liabilities | 3,607,000 | 25,000 | 5,000 | 195,000 | 3,832,000 |
| Fund balances: | | | | | |
| Reserved for: | | | | | |
| Inventories | 17,000 | | | | 17,000 |
| Encumbrances | 25,000 | | | | 25,000 |
| Debt service | | | | 268,000 | 268,000 |
| Other purposes | | | | 16,000 | 16,000 |
| Permanent endowment | | | | 243,000 | 243,000 |

## 12-16 The Consolidation and Conversion Process

|  | General Fund (Chapter 2) | Local Fuel Tax Fund (Chapter 3) | West End Recreation Center Fund (Chapter 5) | Other Governmental Funds | Total Governmental Funds |
|---|---|---|---|---|---|
| Unreserved | 12,288,600 | 19,000 | 2,936,000 | 936,456 | 16,180,056 |
| Unreserved, reported in nonmajor: |  |  |  |  |  |
| Capital projects funds |  |  |  | 16,000 | 16,000 |
| Total Fund Balances | 12,330,600 | 19,000 | 2,936,000 | 1,463,456 | 16,749,056 |
| Total Liabilities and Fund Balances | 15,937,600 | 44,000 | 2,941,000 | 1,658,456 | 20,581,056 |

### Governmental Funds
### Statement of Revenues, Expenditures, and Changes in Fund Balances
### June 30, 20X1

|  | General Fund (Chapter 2) | Local Fuel Tax Fund (Chapter 3) | West End Recreation Center Fund (Chapter 5) | Other Governmental Funds | Total Governmental Funds |
|---|---|---|---|---|---|
| **REVENUES** |  |  |  |  |  |
| Property taxes | 87,600,000 |  |  | 2,670,000 | 90,270,000 |
| Franchise taxes | 1,300,000 |  |  |  | 1,300,000 |
| Intergovernmental grants | 20,500,000 | 4,500,000 | 450,000 | 2,000,000 | 27,450,000 |
| Charges for services | 537,600 |  |  |  | 537,600 |
| Contributions | 50,000 |  |  |  | 50,000 |
| Interest and investment revenue | 233,000 | 6,000 | 2,000 | 77,000 | 318,000 |
| Miscellaneous revenue | 4,800,000 |  |  | 40,000 | 4,840,000 |
| Total Revenue | 115,020,600 | 4,506,000 | 452,000 | 4,787,000 | 124,765,600 |
| **EXPENDITURES** |  |  |  |  |  |
| Current: |  |  |  |  |  |
| General government | 33,701,098 | 210,000 | 25,000 | 1,219,000 | 35,155,098 |
| Public safety | 18,036,628 |  |  |  | 18,036,628 |
| Streets | 11,863,314 | 3,990,000 |  | 2,200,000 | 18,053,314 |
| Recreation and parks | 6,481,657 |  |  |  | 6,481,657 |
| Health and welfare | 8,076,657 |  |  |  | 8,076,657 |
| Education (component unit) | 32,000,000 |  |  |  | 32,000,000 |

|  | General Fund (Chapter 2) | Local Fuel Tax Fund (Chapter 3) | West End Recreation Center Fund (Chapter 5) | Other Governmental Funds | Total Governmental Funds |
|---|---|---|---|---|---|
| Debt service: | | | | | |
| Principal | | | | 1,950,000 | 1,950,000 |
| Interest | 311,859 | | | 1,174,000 | 1,485,859 |
| Capital outlays | | | 1,300,000 | 12,600,000 | 13,900,000 |
| Total Expenditures | 110,471,213 | 4,200,000 | 1,325,000 | 19,143,000 | 135,139,213 |
| Excess (deficiency) of revenues over expenditures | 4,549,387 | 306,000 | (873,000) | (14,356,000) | (10,373,613) |
| OTHER FINANCING SOURCES (USES): | | | | | |
| Long-term debt issued | | | 3,000,000 | 10,000,000 | 13,000,000 |
| Discount on long-term debt issued | | | | (671,044) | (671,044) |
| Execution of capital leases | 431,213 | | | | 431,213 |
| Transfers in | 50,000 | | 300,000 | 5,295,000 | 5,645,000 |
| Transfers out | (5,475,000) | (300,000) | | | (5,775,000) |
| Total other financing sources and uses | (4,993,787) | (300,000) | 3,300,000 | 14,623,956 | 12,630,169 |
| Net change in fund balances | (444,400) | 6,000 | 2,427,000 | 267,956 | 2,256,556 |
| Fund balances—beginning | 12,775,000 | 13,000 | 509,000 | 1,195,500 | 14,492,500 |
| Fund balances—ending | 12,330,600 | 19,000 | 2,936,000 | 1,463,456 | 16,749,056 |

## Reconciliations

GASB-34 requires a summary reconciliation between the governmental fund financial statements and the governmental activities column of the government-wide financial statements. These reconciliations are illustrated in Chapter 14 ("Basic Financial Statements").

## PROPRIETARY FUNDS FINANCIAL STATEMENTS

At the fund financial statement level, a statement of net assets (or balance sheet), statement of revenues, expenses, and changes in fund net assets or fund equity, and a statement of cash flows are prepared for proprietary funds. Based on the adjusted trial balances created in previous chapters, this chapter illustrates how the previously created information is used to prepare the fund financial statements for proprietary funds.

## Combining Trial Balances for Nonmajor Enterprise Funds

The following governmental funds are illustrated in Chapter 7 ("Enterprise Funds") and constitute the City of Centerville's nonmajor Enterprise Funds:

- Centerville Toll Bridge
- Centerville Parking Authority

Based on the information developed in Chapter 13, the following combining trial balance (accrual basis) is prepared for the nonmajor Enterprise Funds:

|  | Centerville Toll Bridge (Chapter 7) Debits (Credits) | Centerville Parking Authority (Chapter 7) Debits (Credits) | Nonmajor Funds Total Debits (Credits) |
|---|---|---|---|
| Cash | 739,500 | 764,000 | 1,503,500 |
| Interest receivable | 3,000 | 3,000 | 6,000 |
| Temporary investments | 58,000 | 5,000 | 63,000 |
| Inventories | 32,000 | 24,000 | 56,000 |
| Construction in progress | 70,000 | 15,000 | 85,000 |
| Land and improvements | 140,000 | 1,780,000 | 1,920,000 |
| Superstructure | 1,400,000 |  | 1,400,000 |
| Buildings | 330,000 | 2,400,000 | 2,730,000 |
| Equipment | 55,000 | 140,000 | 195,000 |
| Vehicles | 835,000 | 102,000 | 937,000 |
| Accumulated depreciation | (1,257,000) | (1,505,000) | (2,762,000) |
| Accounts payable and accrued expenses | (50,000) | (90,000) | (140,000) |
| Due to other funds | (18,000) | (17,000) | (35,000) |
| Compensated absences | (8,000) | (5,000) | (13,000) |
| Claims and judgements | (27,000) | (7,000) | (34,000) |
| Notes payable | (30,000) | (30,000) | (60,000) |
| Bonds payable | (80,000) | (500,000) | (580,000) |

|  | Centerville Toll Bridge (Chapter 7) Debits (Credits) | Centerville Parking Authority (Chapter 7) Debits (Credits) | Nonmajor Funds Total Debits (Credits) |
|---|---|---|---|
| Net assets | (1,646,500) | (3,994,000) | (5,640,500) |
| Charges for services | (4,750,000) | (1,500,000) | (6,250,000) |
| Miscellaneous revenues | (20,000) | (22,000) | (42,000) |
| Expenses—personal services | 2,402,000 | 5,402,000 | 7,804,000 |
| Expenses—contractual services | 1,280,000 | 400,000 | 1,680,000 |
| Expenses—repairs and maintenance | 400,000 | 50,000 | 450,000 |
| Expenses—other supplies and expenses | 194,000 | 36,000 | 230,000 |
| Expenses—insurance claims and expenses | 10,000 | 3,000 | 13,000 |
| Expenses—depreciation | 339,000 | 117,000 | 456,000 |
| Expenses—miscellaneous | 30,000 | 3,000 | 33,000 |
| Interest and investment revenue | (30,000) | (10,000) | (40,000) |
| Interest expense | 6,000 | 27,000 | 33,000 |
| Operating grants and contributions | (100,000) |  | (100,000) |
| Nonoperating miscellaneous expenses (revenues) | (7,000) | (1,000) | (8,000) |
| Capital contributions | (250,000) |  | (250,000) |
| Transfers in | (50,000) | (90,000) | (140,000) |
| Special item—gain on sale of parking lot |  | (3,500,000) | (3,500,000) |
| Total | 0 | 0 | 0 |

## Combining Trial Balances for All Proprietary Funds

After the trial balance for the nonmajor Enterprise Funds is prepared, that information is presented with the trial balances for the two major Enterprise Funds (Centerville Utilities Authority and Centerville Municipal Airport) and all Internal Service Funds in order to create a combined trial balance for all Enterprise Funds as shown below. (The information for the Internal Service Fund column was created in Chapter 8 ["Internal Service Funds"].)

**12-20** *The Consolidation and Conversion Process*

|  | Centerville Utilities Authority (Chapter 7) Debit (Credit) | Centerville Municipal Airport (Chapter 7) Debit (Credit) | Other Enterprise Funds (Chapter 7) Debit (Credit) | Total Debit (Credit) | Internal Service Funds (Chapter 8) Debit (Credit) |
|---|---|---|---|---|---|
| Cash | 230,000 | 10,963,000 | 1,503,500 | 12,696,500 | 1,105,500 |
| Interest receivable | 50,000 | 200,000 | 6,000 | 256,000 | 4,000 |
| Accounts receivable (net) | 7,550,000 | 18,000,000 |  | 25,550,000 |  |
| Due from other funds | 2,000,000 | 400,000 |  | 2,400,000 | 824,000 |
| Due from other governments | 100,000 | 300,000 |  | 400,000 | 45,000 |
| Temporary investments | 55,000 | 10,050,000 | 63,000 | 10,168,000 | 46,000 |
| Inventories | 75,000 | 55,000 | 56,000 | 186,000 | 36,000 |
| Construction in progress | 200,000 | 23,500,000 | 85,000 | 23,785,000 |  |
| Land and improvements | 5,200,000 | 13,200,000 | 1,920,000 | 20,320,000 | 4,450,000 |
| Superstructure |  |  | 1,400,000 | 1,400,000 |  |
| Distribution and collection systems | 46,300,000 |  |  | 46,300,000 |  |
| Runways and tarmacs |  | 27,500,000 |  | 27,500,000 |  |
| Buildings | 14,450,000 | 33,200,000 | 2,730,000 | 50,380,000 | 4,650,000 |
| Equipment | 4,600,000 | 7,200,000 | 195,000 | 11,995,000 | 10,160,000 |
| Vehicles | 1,660,000 | 2,500,000 | 937,000 | 5,097,000 | 10,338,000 |
| Accumulated depreciation | (54,395,000) | (20,255,000) | (2,762,000) | (77,412,000) | (12,848,000) |
| Accounts payable and accrued expenses | (4,300,000) | (3,900,000) | (140,000) | (8,340,000) | (250,000) |
| Due to other funds | (35,000) | (512,000) | (35,000) | (582,000) |  |
| Compensated absences | (84,000) | (133,000) | (13,000) | (230,000) | (32,000) |
| Claims and judgements | (229,000) | (195,000) | (34,000) | (458,000) | (53,000) |
| Notes payable | (330,000) | (7,700,000) | (60,000) | (8,090,000) | (8,250,000) |
| Revenue bonds—Terminal A |  | (10,000,000) |  | (10,000,000) |  |
| Revenue bonds—Terminal B |  | (4,000,000) |  | (4,000,000) |  |
| Bonds payable | (7,700,000) |  | (580,000) | (8,280,000) |  |
| Net assets | (16,019,000) | (73,608,000) | (5,640,500) | (95,267,500) | (12,875,500) |
| Charges for services | (36,000,000) | (175,000,000) | (6,250,000) | (217,250,000) | (13,450,000) |
| Charges for services—rental income—security for Terminal A revenue bonds |  | (30,000,000) |  | (30,000,000) |  |
| Charges for services—rental income—security for Terminal B revenue bonds |  | (22,000,000) |  | (22,000,000) |  |
| Miscellaneous revenues | (10,000) | (60,000) | (42,000) | (112,000) | (17,000) |

*Developing Information for Fund Financial Statements* **12-21**

|  | Centerville Utilities Authority (Chapter 7) Debit (Credit) | Centerville Municipal Airport (Chapter 7) Debit (Credit) | Other Enterprise Funds (Chapter 7) Debit (Credit) | Total Debit (Credit) | Internal Service Funds (Chapter 8) Debit (Credit) |
|---|---|---|---|---|---|
| Expenses—personal services | 22,022,000 | 161,025,000 | 7,804,000 | 190,851,000 | 6,926,000 |
| Expenses—contractual services | 11,220,000 | 33,550,000 | 1,680,000 | 46,450,000 | 2,100,000 |
| Expenses—repairs and maintenance | 700,000 | 2,100,000 | 450,000 | 3,250,000 | 1,650,000 |
| Expenses—other supplies and expenses | 729,000 | 1,795,000 | 230,000 | 2,754,000 | 366,000 |
| Expenses—insurance claims and expenses | 21,000 | 100,000 | 13,000 | 134,000 | 29,000 |
| Expenses—depreciation | 3,025,000 | 3,370,000 | 456,000 | 6,851,000 | 5,582,000 |
| Expenses—miscellaneous | 5,000 | 70,000 | 33,000 | 108,000 | 22,000 |
| Interest and investment revenue | (400,000) | (1,200,000) | (40,000) | (1,640,000) | (25,000) |
| Interest expense | 450,000 | 1,220,000 | 33,000 | 1,703,000 | 309,000 |
| Operating grants and contributions |  |  | (100,000) | (100,000) | (370,000) |
| Nonoperating miscellaneous expenses (revenues) | 110,000 | 265,000 | (8,000) | 367,000 | 8,000 |
| Capital contributions | (1,250,000) | (2,000,000) | (250,000) | (3,500,000) | (490,000) |
| Transfers in |  |  | (140,000) | (140,000) | (40,000) |
| Transfers out |  |  |  | 0 | 50,000 |
| Special item—gain on sale of parking lot |  |  | (3,500,000) | (3,500,000) |  |
| Total | 0 | 0 | 0 | 0 | 0 |

## Proprietary Fund Financial Statements

The proprietary fund financial statements includes the following:

- Statement of net assets (or balance sheet)
- Statement of revenues, expenses, and changes in fund net assets or fund equity
- Statement of cash flows

Based on the trial balance presented above, the statement of net assets (or balance sheet), statement of revenues, expenses, and changes in fund net assets or fund equity and statement of cash flows for the City of Centerville's proprietary funds are as follows:

**12-22** *The Consolidation and Conversion Process*

## Proprietary Funds
## Statement of Net Assets
## June 30, 20X1

| | Centerville Utilities Authority (Chapter 7) | Centerville Municipal Airport (Chapter 7) | Other Enterprise Funds (Chapter 7) | Total | Internal Service Funds (Chapter 8) |
|---|---|---|---|---|---|
| **ASSETS** | | | | | |
| Current assets: | | | | | |
| Cash | 230,000 | 10,963,000 | 1,503,500 | 12,696,500 | 1,105,500 |
| Interest receivable | 50,000 | 200,000 | 6,000 | 256,000 | 4,000 |
| Accounts receivable (net) | 7,550,000 | 18,000,000 | | 25,550,000 | |
| Due from other funds | 2,000,000 | 400,000 | | 2,400,000 | 824,000 |
| Due from other governments | 100,000 | 300,000 | | 400,000 | 45,000 |
| Temporary investments | 55,000 | 10,050,000 | 63,000 | 10,168,000 | 46,000 |
| Inventories | 75,000 | 55,000 | 56,000 | 186,000 | 36,000 |
| Total current assets | 10,060,000 | 39,968,000 | 1,628,500 | 51,656,500 | 2,060,500 |
| Noncurrent assets: | | | | | |
| Construction in progress | 200,000 | 23,500,000 | 85,000 | 23,785,000 | |
| Land and improvements | 5,200,000 | 13,200,000 | 1,920,000 | 20,320,000 | 4,450,000 |
| Superstructure | | | 1,400,000 | 1,400,000 | |
| Distribution and collection systems | 46,300,000 | | | 46,300,000 | |
| Runways and tarmacs | | 27,500,000 | | 27,500,000 | |
| Buildings | 14,450,000 | 33,200,000 | 2,730,000 | 50,380,000 | 4,650,000 |
| Equipment | 4,600,000 | 7,200,000 | 195,000 | 11,995,000 | 10,160,000 |
| Vehicles | 1,660,000 | 2,500,000 | 937,000 | 5,097,000 | 10,338,000 |
| Less accumulated depreciation | (54,395,000) | (20,255,000) | (2,762,000) | (77,412,000) | (12,848,000) |
| Total noncurrent assets | 18,015,000 | 86,845,000 | 4,505,000 | 109,365,000 | 16,750,000 |
| Total assets | 28,075,000 | 126,813,000 | 6,133,500 | 161,021,500 | 18,810,500 |
| **LIABILITIES** | | | | | |
| Current liabilities: | | | | | |
| Accounts payable and accrued expenses | 4,300,000 | 3,900,000 | 140,000 | 8,340,000 | 250,000 |
| Due to other funds | 35,000 | 512,000 | 35,000 | 582,000 | |
| Compensated absences | 21,000 | 15,000 | 5,000 | 41,000 | 10,000 |
| Claims and judgements | 17,000 | 25,000 | 9,000 | 51,000 | 13,000 |
| Notes payable | 70,000 | | 40,000 | 110,000 | 1,700,000 |

*Developing Information for Fund Financial Statements* **12-23**

|  | Centerville Utilities Authority (Chapter 7) | Centerville Municipal Airport (Chapter 7) | Other Enterprise Funds (Chapter 7) | Total | Internal Service Funds (Chapter 8) |
|---|---|---|---|---|---|
| Revenue bonds—Terminal A |  | 2,000,000 |  | 2,000,000 |  |
| Revenue bonds—Terminal B |  | 500,000 |  | 500,000 |  |
| Bonds payable | 850,000 |  | 20,000 | 870,000 |  |
| Total current liabilities | 5,293,000 | 6,952,000 | 249,000 | 12,494,000 | 1,973,000 |
| Noncurrent liabilities: |  |  |  |  |  |
| Compensated absences | 63,000 | 118,000 | 8,000 | 189,000 | 22,000 |
| Claims and judgements | 212,000 | 170,000 | 25,000 | 407,000 | 40,000 |
| Notes payable | 260,000 | 7,700,000 | 20,000 | 7,980,000 | 6,550,000 |
| Revenue bonds—Terminal A |  | 8,000,000 |  | 8,000,000 |  |
| Revenue bonds—Terminal B |  | 3,500,000 |  | 3,500,000 |  |
| Bonds payable | 6,850,000 |  | 560,000 | 7,410,000 |  |
| Total noncurrent liabilities | 7,385,000 | 19,488,000 | 613,000 | 27,486,000 | 6,612,000 |
| Total liabilities | 12,678,000 | 26,440,000 | 862,000 | 39,980,000 | 8,585,000 |
| **NET ASSETS** |  |  |  |  |  |
| Invested in capital assets, net of related debt | 9,985,000 | 69,145,000 | 3,865,000 | 82,995,000 | 8,500,000 |
| Restricted: |  |  |  |  |  |
| Capital projects | 2,000,000 | 17,000,000 | 1,000,000 | 20,000,000 |  |
| Debt service | 500,000 | 1,450,000 | 50,000 | 2,000,000 |  |
| Other | 2,750,000 | 12,445,000 | 167,000 | 15,362,000 |  |
| Unrestricted | 162,000 | 333,000 | 189,500 | 684,500 | 1,725,500 |
| Total net assets | 15,397,000 | 100,373,000 | 5,271,500 | 121,041,500 | 10,225,500 |

**Proprietary Funds**
**Statement of Revenues, Expenses, and**
**Changes in Fund Net Assets**
**For the Year Ended June 30, 20X1**

|  | Centerville Utilities Authority (Chapter 7) | Centerville Municipal Airport (Chapter 7) | Other Enterprise Funds (Chapter 7) | Total | Internal Service Funds (Chapter 8) |
|---|---|---|---|---|---|
| **OPERATING REVENUES** |  |  |  |  |  |
| Charges for services | 36,000,000 | 175,000,000 | 6,250,000 | 217,250,000 | 13,450,000 |
| Charges for services—rental income—security for Terminal A revenue bonds |  | 30,000,000 |  | 30,000,000 |  |

**12-24** *The Consolidation and Conversion Process*

|  | Centerville Utilities Authority (Chapter 7) | Centerville Municipal Airport (Chapter 7) | Other Enterprise Funds (Chapter 7) | Total | Internal Service Funds (Chapter 8) |
|---|---|---|---|---|---|
| Charges for services—rental income—security for Terminal B revenue bonds | | 22,000,000 | | 22,000,000 | |
| Miscellaneous | 10,000 | 60,000 | 42,000 | 112,000 | 17,000 |
| Total operating revenues | 36,010,000 | 227,060,000 | 6,292,000 | 269,362,000 | 13,467,000 |
| **OPERATING EXPENSES** | | | | | |
| Personal services | 22,022,000 | 161,025,000 | 7,804,000 | 190,851,000 | 6,926,000 |
| Contractual services | 11,220,000 | 33,550,000 | 1,680,000 | 46,450,000 | 2,100,000 |
| Repairs and maintenance | 700,000 | 2,100,000 | 450,000 | 3,250,000 | 1,650,000 |
| Other supplies and expenses | 729,000 | 1,795,000 | 230,000 | 2,754,000 | 366,000 |
| Insurance claims and expenses | 21,000 | 100,000 | 13,000 | 134,000 | 29,000 |
| Depreciation | 3,025,000 | 3,370,000 | 456,000 | 6,851,000 | 5,582,000 |
| Miscellaneous | 5,000 | 70,000 | 33,000 | 108,000 | 22,000 |
| Total operating expenses | 37,722,000 | 202,010,000 | 10,666,000 | 250,398,000 | 16,675,000 |
| Operating income (loss) | (1,712,000) | 25,050,000 | (4,374,000) | 18,964,000 | (3,208,000) |
| **NONOPERATING REVENUES (EXPENSES)** | | | | | |
| Interest and investment revenue | 400,000 | 1,200,000 | 40,000 | 1,640,000 | 25,000 |
| Interest | (450,000) | (1,220,000) | (33,000) | (1,703,000) | (309,000) |
| Operating grants and contributions | | 100,000 | 100,000 | 370,000 | |
| Miscellaneous | (110,000) | (265,000) | 8,000 | (367,000) | (8,000) |
| Total nonoperating revenue (expenses) | (160,000) | (285,000) | 115,000 | (330,000) | 78,000 |
| Income (loss) before capital contributions and transfers | (1,872,000) | 24,765,000 | (4,259,000) | 18,634,000 | (3,130,000) |
| Capital contributions | 1,250,000 | 2,000,000 | 250,000 | 3,500,000 | 490,000 |
| Transfers in | | | 140,000 | 140,000 | 40,000 |
| Transfers out | | | | | (50,000) |
| Special item—gain on sale of parking lot | | | 3,500,000 | 3,500,000 | |
| Change in net assets | (622,000) | 26,765,000 | (369,000) | 25,774,000 | (2,650,000) |
| Total net assets—beginning | 16,019,000 | 73,608,000 | 5,640,500 | 95,267,500 | 12,875,500 |
| Total net assets—ending | 15,397,000 | 100,373,000 | 5,271,500 | 121,041,500 | 10,225,500 |

**Proprietary Funds**
**Statement of Cash Flows**
**For the Year Ended June 30, 20X1**

|  | Centerville Utilities Authority (Chapter 7) | Centerville Municipal Airport (Chapter 7) | Other Enterprise Funds (Chapter 7) | Total | Internal Service Funds (Chapter 8) |
|---|---|---|---|---|---|
| **CASH FLOWS FROM OPERATING ACTIVITIES** | | | | | |
| Receipts from customers | 34,000,000 | 214,000,000 | 6,250,000 | 254,250,000 | 12,811,000 |
| Payments to suppliers | (12,112,000) | (36,425,000) | (2,151,000) | (50,688,000) | (4,185,000) |
| Payments to employees | (19,013,000) | (158,017,000) | (7,732,000) | (184,762,000) | (6,747,000) |
| Internal activity—payments to other funds | (200,000) | (3,140,000) | (156,000) | (3,496,000) | |
| Other receipts (payments) | 5,000 | (10,000) | 1,000 | (4,000) | (25,000) |
| Net cash provided by operating activities | 2,680,000 | 16,408,000 | (3,788,000) | 15,300,000 | 1,854,000 |
| **CASH FLOWS FROM NONCAPITAL FINANCING ACTIVITIES** | | | | | |
| Subsidies and transfers from (to) other funds and state government | | | 240,000 | 240,000 | 360,000 |
| **CASH FLOWS FROM CAPITAL AND RELATED FINANCING ACTIVITIES** | | | | | |
| Proceeds from the issuance of capital debt | 2,120,000 | 3,200,000 | | 5,320,000 | 3,400,000 |
| Capital contributions | 1,250,000 | 1,700,000 | 280,000 | 3,230,000 | 490,000 |
| Acquisitions of capital assets | (5,350,000) | (8,800,000) | (590,000) | (14,740,000) | (6,040,000) |
| Proceeds from sale of capital assets | 500,000 | 420,000 | 5,055,000 | 5,975,000 | 845,000 |
| Principal paid on capital debt | (1,740,000) | (2,500,000) | (40,000) | (4,280,000) | (1,100,000) |
| Interest paid on capital debt | (450,000) | (1,220,000) | (33,000) | (1,703,000) | (309,000) |
| Net cash (used) by capital and related financing activities | (3,670,000) | (7,200,000) | 4,672,000 | (6,198,000) | (2,714,000) |

**12-26** *The Consolidation and Conversion Process*

|  | Centerville Utilities Authority (Chapter 7) | Centerville Municipal Airport (Chapter 7) | Other Enterprise Funds (Chapter 7) | Total | Internal Service Funds (Chapter 8) |
|---|---|---|---|---|---|
| **CASH FLOWS FROM INVESTING ACTIVITIES** |  |  |  |  |  |
| Loans to other funds | (2,000,000) | (400,000) |  | (2,400,000) |  |
| Loans to other governments | (100,000) |  |  | (100,000) |  |
| Interest and dividends | 365,000 | 1,055,000 | 39,500 | 1,459,500 | 37,500 |
| Purchase of investments | (15,000) | (50,000) | (30,000) | (95,000) |  |
| Net cash provided (used) by investing activities | (1,750,000) | 605,000 | 9,500 | (1,135,500) | 37,500 |
| Net increase (decrease) in cash | (2,740,000) | 9,813,000 | 1,133,500 | 8,206,500 | (462,500) |
| Balances— beginning of year | 2,970,000 | 1,150,000 | 370,000 | 4,490,000 | 1,568,000 |
| Balances— end of year | 230,000 | 10,963,000 | 1,503,500 | 12,696,500 | 1,105,500 |
| **Reconciliation of operating income (loss) to net cash provided (used) by operating activities:** |  |  |  |  |  |
| Operating income (loss) | (1,712,000) | 25,050,000 | (4,374,000) | 18,964,000 | (3,208,000) |
| Adjustments: |  |  |  |  |  |
| Depreciation expense | 3,025,000 | 3,370,000 | 456,000 | 6,851,000 | 5,582,000 |
| Change in assets and liabilities: |  |  |  |  |  |
| Receivables, net | (1,850,000) | (13,000,000) |  | (14,850,000) | (639,000) |
| Inventories | (21,000) | (5,000) | (10,000) | (36,000) | (9,000) |
| Accounts and accrued liabilities | 3,238,000 | 993,000 | 140,000 | 4,371,000 | 128,000 |
| Net cash provided (used) by operating activities | 2,680,000 | 16,408,000 | (3,788,000) | 15,300,000 | 1,854,000 |

# Reconciliations

GASB-34 requires a summary reconciliation between the columns for the total Enterprise Fund balances and the business-type activities column of the government-wide financial statements. These reconciliations are illustrated in Chapter 14 ("Basic Financial Statements").

## FIDUCIARY FUND FINANCIAL STATEMENTS

Assets held by a governmental entity for other parties (either as a trustee or as an agent) and that cannot be used to finance the governmental entity's own operating programs are reported in the entity's fiduciary fund financial statement category. The financial statements for fiduciary funds are based on the flow of economic resources measurement focus and the accrual basis of accounting (with the exception of certain liabilities of defined benefit pension plans and certain postemployment health-care plans). Fiduciary fund financial statements are not reported by major fund (which is required for governmental funds and proprietary funds as illustrated earlier in this chapter) but must be reported based on the following fund types (GASB-34, pars. 106 and 107):

- Pension (and other employee benefit) Trust Funds
- Private-Purpose Trusts
- Investment Trust Funds
- Agency Funds
- Component Units (that are fiduciary in nature)

The following financial statements should be included for fiduciary funds:

- Statement of fiduciary net assets
- Statement of changes in fiduciary net assets

**OBSERVATION:** Only a statement of fiduciary net assets is prepared for an Agency Fund.

### Statement of Fiduciary Net Assets

The assets, liabilities, and net assets of fiduciary funds are presented in the statement of fiduciary net assets. There is no need to divide net assets into the three categories (invested in capital assets [net of related debt], restricted net assets, and unrestricted net assets) that must be used in the government-wide financial statements.

The following statement of fiduciary net assets reflects the fiduciary funds illustrated in previous chapters:

## City of Centerville
### Statement of Fiduciary Net Assets
### Fiduciary Funds
### June 30, 20X1

|  | Employee Retirement Fund (Chapter 9) | Private-Purpose Trust Fund (Chapter 10) | Agency Fund (Chapter 11) |
|---|---|---|---|
| **ASSETS** |  |  |  |
| Cash | $ 4,244,000 | $ 27,000 | $ 35,000 |
| Accrued interest receivable | 31,000 |  |  |
| Investments in debt securities | 11,022,000 | 459,000 |  |
| Investment in marketable equity securities | 22,463,000 |  |  |
| Total Assets | $37,760,000 | $486,000 | $ 35,000 |
| **LIABILTIES** |  |  |  |
| Accounts payable and accrued expenses | $ 29,000 | $ 5,000 | $ 35,000 |
| Refunds payable and other liabilities | 25,000 |  |  |
| Total Liabilities | $ 54,000 | $ 5,000 | $ 35,000 |
| **NET ASSETS** |  |  |  |
| Held in trust for pension benefits and other purposes | $37,706,000 | $481,000 |  |

## Statement of Changes in Fiduciary Net Assets

The statement of changes in fiduciary net asset summarizes the additions to, deductions from, and net increase or decrease in net assets for the year. In addition, GASB-34 requires that the statement provide information "about significant year-to-year changes in net assets":

## City of Centerville
## Statement of Changes in Fiduciary Net Assets
## Fiduciary Funds
## For the Year Ended June 30, 20X1

|  | Employee Retirement Fund (Chapter 9) | Private- Purpose Trust Fund (Chapter 10) |
|---|---|---|
| **ADDITIONS** |  |  |
| Contributions by: |  |  |
|   City of Centerville | $ 7,000,000 | $ 10,000 |
|   Plan members/individuals | 2,700,000 | 30,000 |
| Total Contributions | 9,700,000 | 40,000 |
| Interest and investment revenue | 486,000 | 49,000 |
| Total additions | 10,186,000 | 89,000 |
| **DEDUCTIONS** |  |  |
| Benefits paid | 4,200,000 | 57,000 |
| Refunds of contributions | 100,000 |  |
| Administrative expenses | 349,000 |  |
| Total deductions | 4,649,000 | 57,000 |
| Change in net assets | 5,537,000 | 32,000 |
| Net assets—beginning of the year | 32,169,000 | 449,000 |
| Net assets—end of the year | $37,706,000 | $481,000 |

# CHAPTER 13
# DEVELOPING INFORMATION FOR GOVERNMENT-WIDE FINANCIAL STATEMENTS

## CONTENTS

| | |
|---|---|
| Introduction | 13-1 |
| Governmental Activities | 13-2 |
|     Merging Internal Service Funds into Governmental Activities | 13-5 |
|     Reclassification of Account Balances | 13-8 |
| Business-Type Activities | 13-16 |
|     Merging Internal Service Funds into Business-Type Activities | 13-19 |
|     Reclassification of Account Balances | 13-20 |
|     Components of Net Assets | 13-30 |

## INTRODUCTION

The flow of economic resources measurement focus and accrual accounting (which are the concepts upon which commercial enterprises prepare their financial statements) are the basis upon which government-wide financial statements are prepared. Generally, under the flow of economic resources measurement focus and accrual basis of accounting, revenues are recognized when earned and expenses are recorded when incurred when these activities are related to exchange and exchange-like activities. In addition, long-lived assets (such as buildings and equipment) are capitalized and depreciated, and all debt is reported in the fund (GASB-34, par. 16).

Government-wide financial statements are formatted to identify a separate column for governmental activities and business-type activities.

## GOVERNMENTAL ACTIVITIES

GASB-34 notes that governmental activities "generally are financed through taxes, intergovernmental revenues, and other nonexchange revenues (and) are usually reported in governmental funds and Internal Service Funds." The information presented in governmental funds is accounted for under the modified accrual basis of accounting and must be converted to an accrual basis. Internal Service Fund information is prepared on an accrual basis, but must be merged into governmental fund financial information that has been converted to an accrual basis. The conversion process was begun in previous chapters, and the accrual balances created in those chapters for governmental funds and Internal Service Funds are consolidated in this chapter.

The following worksheet consolidates all of the *accrual trial balances* for governmental funds that were developed in previous chapters:

|  | General Fund (Ch. 2) (Accrual Based) Debits (Credits) | Special Revenue Funds (Ch. 3) (Accrual Based) Debits (Credits) | Capital Projects Funds (Ch. 4) (Accrual Based) Debits (Credits) | Debt Service Funds (Ch. 5) (Accrual Based) Debits (Credits) | Permanent Fund (Ch. 6) (Accrual Based) Debits (Credits) | Governmental Funds Accrual Basis Total |
|---|---|---|---|---|---|---|
| Cash | $ 9,440,000 | $ 68,500 | $ 306,956 | $210,000 | $ 3,000 | $ 10,028,456 |
| Temporary investments |  |  | 3,679,000 | 67,000 |  | 3,746,000 |
| Property taxes receivable (net) | 1,755,000 | 48,000 |  |  |  | 1,803,000 |
| Other receivables | 44,000 | 17,000 |  |  |  | 61,000 |
| Investments | 6,090,000 |  |  |  | 244,000 | 6,334,000 |
| Inventories | 17,000 |  |  |  |  | 17,000 |
| Intergovernmental grants receivable | 6,000,000 | 70,000 |  |  |  | 6,070,000 |
| Land and improvements | 125,000,000 |  |  |  |  | 125,000,000 |
| Construction in progress | 2,050,000 |  | 13,900,000 |  |  | 15,950,000 |
| Buildings | 213,000,000 |  |  |  |  | 213,000,000 |
| Equipment | 22,300,000 |  |  |  |  | 22,300,000 |
| Vehicles | 73,220,000 |  |  |  |  | 73,220,000 |
| Leased capital assets | 8,249,753 |  |  |  |  | 8,249,753 |
| Infrastructure assets | 20,000,000 |  |  |  |  | 20,000,000 |
| Accumulated depreciation | (163,619,947) |  |  |  |  | (163,619,947) |
| Accounts payable | (665,000) | (75,000) | (127,000) | (9,000) | (4,000) | (880,000) |
| Interest payable | (24,290) |  |  | (525,000) |  | (549,290) |
| Due to other funds | (2,642,000) |  |  |  |  | (2,642,000) |

Developing Information for Government-Wide Financial Statements  13-3

| | General Fund (Ch. 2) (Accrual Based) Debits (Credits) | Special Revenue Funds (Ch. 3) (Accrual Based) Debits (Credits) | Capital Projects Funds (Ch. 4) (Accrual Based) Debits (Credits) | Debt Service Funds (Ch. 5) (Accrual Based) Debits (Credits) | Permanent Fund (Ch. 6) (Accrual Based) Debits (Credits) | Governmental Funds Accrual Basis Total |
|---|---|---|---|---|---|---|
| Deferred revenue | (300,000) | (10,000) | | | | (310,000) |
| Claims payable | (1,900,000) | | | | | (1,900,000) |
| Compensated absences payable | (4,660,000) | | | | | (4,660,000) |
| Lease obligation payable | (4,340,724) | | | | | (4,340,724) |
| Revenue bonds payable | | | | (9,250,000) | | (9,250,000) |
| Bonds payable | | | (12,328,956) | (5,785,359) | | (18,114,315) |
| Fund balance/net assets | (314,445,888) | (29,500) | (1,361,000) | 16,859,791 | (222,000) | (299,198,597) |
| General revenue—property taxes | (89,000,000) | (2,670,000) | | | | (91,670,000) |
| Franchise taxes | (1,300,000) | | | | | (1,300,000) |
| Intergovernmental grants—General revenues—unrestricted grants | (26,500,000) | | | | | (26,500,000) |
| Program revenues/charges for services (general government) | (55,000) | | | | | (55,000) |
| Program revenues—operating grants and contributions (general government) | | | | | (34,000) | (34,000) |
| Program revenues/charges for services (recreations and parks) | (135,000) | | | | | (135,000) |
| Program revenues—capital grants and contributions (recreation and parks) | | | (450,000) | | | (450,000) |
| Program revenues/charges for services (public safety) | (202,000) | | | | | (202,000) |
| Program revenues/charges for services (health and welfare) | (4,000) | | | | | (4,000) |
| Program revenues/charges for services (streets) | (150,000) | | | | | (150,000) |

**13-4** *The Consolidation and Conversion Process*

| | General Fund (Ch. 2) (Accrual Based) Debits (Credits) | Special Revenue Funds (Ch. 3) (Accrual Based) Debits (Credits) | Capital Projects Funds (Ch. 4) (Accrual Based) Debits (Credits) | Debt Service Funds (Ch. 5) (Accrual Based) Debits (Credits) | Permanent Fund (Ch. 6) (Accrual Based) Debits (Credits) | Governmental Funds Accrual Basis Total |
|---|---|---|---|---|---|---|
| Program revenues—operating grants (Streets) | | (4,570,000) | | | | (4,570,000) |
| Program revenues—capital grants (Streets) | | | (2,000,000) | | | (2,000,000) |
| Contributions | (50,000) | | | | | (50,0000) |
| Interest and investment revenue | (93,000) | (6,000) | (36,000) | (9,000) | | (144,0000 |
| Miscellaneous revenue | | (18,000) | | | | (18,000) |
| Investment revenue—change in fair value of investments | (140,000) | | | | | (140,000) |
| General government expenditures/expenses | 51,041,503 | 760,000 | 617,000 | 42,000 | 35,000 | 52,495,503 |
| Public safety expenditures/expenses | 22,448,222 | | | | | 22,448,222 |
| Streets expenditures/expenses | 14,803,278 | 6,190,000 | | | | 20,993,278 |
| Recreation and parks expenditures/expenses | 7,524,694 | | | | | 7,524,694 |
| Health and welfare expenditures/expenses | 9,482,250 | | | | | 9,482,250 |
| Interest expense | 336,149 | | | 1,719,568 | | 2,055,717 |
| Education (component unit) | 32,000,000 | | | | | 32,000,000 |
| Revenues—permanent endowment additions | | | | | (22,000) | (22,0000) |
| Extraordinary item—donation of land by the state | (20,000,000) | | | | | (20,000,0000) |
| Transfers in | (50,000) | (75,000) | (2,200,000) | (3,320,000) | | (5,645,000) |
| Transfers out | 5,475,000 | 300,000 | | | | 5,775,000 |
| Total | $ 0 | $ 0 | $ 0 | $ 0 | $ 0 | $ 0 |

In order to convert the combined totals for all governmental funds restated on an accrual basis presented in the above consolidated trial balance to the trial balance for governmental activities, the following items are considered:

- Integration of Internal Service Fund account balances
- Reclassification of account balances

## Merging Internal Service Funds into Governmental Activities

As described in Chapter 8 ("Internal Service Funds"), at the government-wide financial statement level, activities related to Internal Service Funds are eliminated to avoid doubling-up expenses and revenues in the presentation of the governmental activities and business-type activities columns in the statement of activities. The effect of this approach is to adjust activities in an Internal Service Fund to a break-even balance. That is, if the Internal Service Fund had a "net profit" for the year, there is a pro rata reduction in the charges made to the funds that used the Internal Service Fund's services for the year. Likewise, a net loss requires a pro rata adjustment that increases the charges made to the various participating funds. After making these eliminations, any residual balances related to the Internal Service Fund's assets and liabilities are reported in either the government activities column or the business-type activities column.

The City of Centerville has the following Internal Service Funds:

- Communications and Technology Support Center (provides a variety of communication and computer support services to all of the City's governmental and proprietary funds)
- Fleet Management (provides a motor pool to all of the City's governmental funds and to some other governmental units that are not part of the City's reporting entity; it provides no service to Enterprise Funds)
- Special Services Support Center (provides services exclusively for the Centerville Municipal Airport)

Based on the nature of each Internal Service Fund, the Communications and Technology Support Center balances are allocated to both governmental activities and business-type activities, the Fleet Management Fund is allocated exclusively to governmental activities, and the Special Services Support Center is allocated exclusively to business-type activities.

## 13-6 The Consolidation and Conversion Process

The previous consolidated trial balance of all governmental funds reported on an accrual basis is adjusted in the following to reflect the first two Internal Service Funds:

▶ **NEW STANDARD:** Prior to the issuance of GASB-34, Internal Service Funds were presented by fund type and were not merged into governmental funds or Enterprise Funds.

|  | Governmental Funds Accrual Basis Total | Communications And Technology Support Center* (Chapter 8) | Preliminary Fleet Management Unit** (Chapter 8) | Governmental Activities Total |
|---|---|---|---|---|
| Cash | 10,028,456 | 946,000 | 137,500 | 11,111,956 |
| Temporary investments | 3,746,000 | 15,000 | 19,000 | 3,780,000 |
| Property taxes receivable (net) | 1,803,000 |  |  | 1,803,000 |
| Other receivables | 61,000 | 1,000 | 2,000 | 64,000 |
| Due from other funds |  | 325,000 | 72,000 | 397,000 |
| Investments | 6,334,000 |  |  | 6,334,000 |
| Inventories | 17,000 | 9,000 | 7,000 | 33,000 |
| Due from other governments |  |  | 45,000 | 45,000 |
| Intergovernmental grants receivable | 6,070,000 |  |  | 6,070,000 |
| Internal balances |  | 547,456 |  | 547,456 |
| Land and improvements | 125,000,000 | 2,700,000 | 50.000 | 127,750,000 |
| Construction in progress | 15,950,000 |  |  | 15,950,000 |
| Buildings | 213,000,000 | 1,400,000 | 1,600,000 | 216,050,000 |
| Equipment | 22,300,000 | 5,870,000 | 1,330,000 | 29,500,000 |
| Vehicles | 73,220,000 | 143,000 | 8,200,000 | 81,563,000 |
| Leased capital assets | 8,249,753 |  |  | 8,249,753 |
| Infrastructure assets | 20,000,000 |  |  | 20,000,000 |
| Accumulated depreciation | (163,619,947) | (3,103,000) | (6,505,000) | (173,227,947) |
| Accounts payable | (880,000) | (50,000) | (125,000) | (1,055,000) |
| Interest payable | (549,290) |  |  | (549,290) |
| Due to other funds | (2,642,000) |  |  | (2,642,000) |
| Deferred revenue | (310,000) |  |  | (310,000) |
| Claims payable | (1,900,000) | (19,000) | (13,000) | (1,932,000) |
| Compensated absences payable | (4,660,000) | (7,000) | (8,000) | (4,675,000) |
| Notes payable |  | (4,700,000) | (3,000,000) | (7,700,000) |
| Lease obligation payable | (4,340,724) |  |  | (4,340,724) |
| Revenue bonds payable | (9,250,000) |  |  | (9,250,000) |
| Bonds payable | (18,114,315) |  |  | (18,114,315) |

*Developing Information for Government-Wide Financial Statements* 13-7

|  | Governmental Funds Accrual Basis Total | Communications And Technology Support Center* (Chapter 8) | Preliminary Fleet Management Unit** (Chapter 8) | Governmental Activities Total |
|---|---|---|---|---|
| Fund balance/net assets | (299,198,597) | (6,590,000) | (1,489,500) | (307,278,097) |
| General revenue— property taxes | (91,670,000) |  |  | (91,670,000) |
| Franchise taxes | (1,300,000) |  |  | (1,300,000) |
| Intergovernmental grants—general revenues— unrestricted grants | (26,500,000) |  |  | (26,500,000) |
| Program revenues/ charges for services (general government) | (55,000) |  | (300,000) | (355,000) |
| Program revenues— operating grants and contributions (general government) | (34,000) |  |  | (34,000) |
| Program revenues/ charges for services (recreations and parks) | (135,000) |  |  | (135,000) |
| Program revenues— capital grants and contributions (recreation and parks) | (450,000) |  |  | (450,000) |
| Program revenues/ charges for services (public safety) | (202,000) |  |  | (202,000) |
| Program revenues/ charges for services (health and welfare) | (4,000) |  |  | (4,000) |
| Program revenues/ charges for services (streets) | (150,000) |  |  | (150,000) |
| Program revenues— operating grants (Streets) | (4,570,000) |  |  | (4,570,000) |
| Program revenues— capital grants (Streets) | (2,000,000) |  |  | (2,000,000) |
| Contributions | (50,000) |  |  | (50,000) |
| Interest and investment revenue | (144,000) | (5,000) | (5,000) | (154,000) |
| Miscellaneous revenue | (18,000) |  |  | (18,000) |
| Investment revenue— change in fair value of investments | (140,000) |  |  | (140,000) |
| General government expenditures/ expenses | 52,495,503 | 1,476,326 | (40,200) | 53,931,629 |
| Public safety expenditures/ expenses | 22,448,222 | 492,109 | (103,400) | 22,836,931 |
| Streets expenditures/ expenses | 20,993,278 | 246,055 | (51,700) | 21,187,633 |

**13-8**  The Consolidation and Conversion Process

|  | Governmental Funds Accrual Basis Total | Communications And Technology Support Center* (Chapter 8) | Preliminary Fleet Management Unit** (Chapter 8) | Governmental Activities Total |
|---|---|---|---|---|
| Recreation and parks expenditures/ expenses | 7,524,694 | 123,027 | (25,850) | 7,621,871 |
| Health and welfare expenditures/ expenses | 9,482,250 | 123,027 | (25,850) | 9,579,427 |
| Interest expense | 2,055,717 | 97,000 | 180,000 | 2,332,717 |
| Education (component unit) | 32,000,000 |  |  | 32,000,000 |
| Revenues—permanent endowment additions | (22,000) |  |  | (22,000) |
| Extraordinary item— donation of land by the state | (20,000,000) |  |  | (20,000,000) |
| Transfers in | (5,645,000) | (40,000) |  | (5,685,000) |
| Transfers out | 5,775,000 |  | 50,000 | 5,825,000 |
| Total | $ 0 | $ 0 | $ 0 | $ 0 |

\* This column is based on worksheet entry JE08.45 that was made in Chapter 8 ("Internal Service Funds").

\*\* This column is based on worksheet entry JE08.47 that was made in Chapter 8 ("Internal Service Funds").

## Reclassification of Account Balances

In order to reclassify a variety of accounts that appear in the consolidated totals for governmental activities as presented in the above trial balance, the following reclassification entries are made:

|  | Accounts | Debit | Credit |
|---|---|---|---|
| JE13.01 | Investments | 3,780,000 |  |
|  | Temporary investments |  | 3,780,000 |
|  | (To reclassify temporary investments) |  |  |
| JE13.02 | Receivables (net) | 7,982,000 |  |
|  | Intergovernmental grants receivable |  | 6,070,000 |
|  | Property taxes receivable (net) |  | 1,803,000 |
|  | Due from other governments |  | 45,000 |
|  | Other receivables |  | 64,000 |
|  | (To reclassify various receivables) |  |  |

|  | Accounts | Debit | Credit |
|---|---|---|---|
| **JE13.03** | Due to other funds | 242,000 | |
| | Internal balances | 155,000 | |
| |     Due from other funds | | 397,000 |

(To eliminate amounts due to and due funds that make up governmental activities (amounts due from the General Fund to Communications and Technology Support Center ($170,000) and Fleet Management ($72,000) and to reclassify the amounts due to the Enterprise Funds ($155,000) as an internal balance)

|  | Accounts | Debit | Credit |
|---|---|---|---|
| **JE13.04** | Due to other funds | 2,400,000 | |
| |     Internal balances | | 2,400,000 |

(To reclassify amounts due from the General Fund to Enterprise Funds [Utilities Authority {$2,000,000} and Municipal Airport {$400,000}] as an Internal Balance)

|  | Accounts | Debit | Credit |
|---|---|---|---|
| **JE13.05** | Land, improvements, and construction in progress | 143,700,000 | |
| |     Construction in progress | | 15,950,000 |
| |     Land and improvements | | 127,750,000 |

(To reclassify capital assets not subject to depreciation)

|  | Accounts | Debit | Credit |
|---|---|---|---|
| **JE13.06** | Other capital assets (net) | 182,084,806 | |
| | Accumulated depreciation | 173,227,947 | |
| |     Buildings | | 216,000,000 |
| |     Equipment | | 29,500,000 |
| |     Vehicles | | 81,563,000 |
| |     Leased capital assets | | 8,249,753 |
| |     Infrastructure assets | | 20,000,000 |

(To reclassify accumulated depreciation and capital assets subject to depreciation)

|  | Accounts | Debit | Credit |
|---|---|---|---|
| **JE13.07** | Accounts payable | 1,055,000 | |
| | Interest payable | 549,290 | |
| |     Accounts payable and accrued expenses | | 1,604,290 |

(To reclassify various payables)

|  | Accounts | Debit | Credit |
|---|---|---|---|
| JE13.08 | Compensated absences payable | 4,675,000 | |
|  | Claims and judgements payable | 1,932,000 | |
|  | Notes payable | 7,700,000 | |
|  | Lease obligation payable | 4,340,724 | |
|  | Revenue bonds payable | 9,250,000 | |
|  | Bonds payable | 18,114,315 | |
|  |   Long-term liabilities—due within one year | | 4,658,932 |
|  |   Long-term liabilities—due in more than one year | | 41,353,107 |
|  | (To reclassify debt into due within one year and beyond one year) | | |
| JE13.09 | Contributions | 50,000 | |
|  |   Program revenues—operating grants and contributions (health and welfare) | | 50,000 |
|  | (To reclassify corporate contributions) | | |
| JE13.10 | Interest and investment revenue | 154,000 | |
|  | Investment revenue—change in fair value of investments | 140,000 | |
|  |   Unrestricted investment earnings | | 294,000 |
|  | (To reclassify interest and investment revenue as unrestricted investment earnings) | | |
| JE13.11 | Interest on long-term debt | 2,332,717 | |
|  | Payments to school district | 32,000,000 | |
|  |   Interest expense | | 2,332,717 |
|  |   Education (component unit) | | 32,000,000 |
|  | (To reclassify various expenses) | | |
| JE13.12 | Revenue—permanent endowment additions | 22,000 | |
|  |   Contributions to permanent funds | | 22,000 |
|  | (To reclassify addition to endowment) | | |
| JE13.13 | Transfers in | 5,685,000 | |
|  |   Transfers out | | 5,685,000 |
|  | (To eliminate transfers within governmental activities) | | |

Developing Information for Government-Wide Financial Statements 13-11

After posting the entries for reclassifying various accounts, the trial balance for governmental activities appears as follows:

|  | Preliminary Governmental Activities Total Debit (Credit) | Reclassifications and Adjustments Debit (Credit) |  | Government-Wide Financial Statements Debit (Credit) |
|---|---|---|---|---|
| Cash | $ 11,111,956 |  |  | $ 11,111,956 |
| Internal Balances | 547,456 | JE13.04 | $ (2,400,000) | (1,697,544) |
|  |  | JE13.03 | 155,000 |  |
| Temporary investments | 3,780,000 | JE13.01 | (3,780,000) | 0 |
| Receivables (net) |  | JE13.02 | 7,982,000 | 7,982,000 |
| Property taxes receivable (net) | 1,803,000 | JE13.02 | (1,803,000) | 0 |
| Other receivables | 64,000 | JE13.02 | (64,000) | 0 |
| Due from other funds | 397,000 | JE13.03 | (397,000) | 0 |
| Investments | 6,334,000 | JE13.01 | 3,780,000 | 10,114,000 |
| Inventories | 33,000 |  |  | 33,000 |
| Due from other governments | 45,000 | JE13.02 | (45,000) | 0 |
| Intergovernmental grants receivable | 6,070,000 | JE13.02 | (6,070,000) | 0 |
| Land, improvements, and construction in progress |  | JE13.05 | 143,700,000 | 143,700,000 |
| Land and improvements | 127,750,000 | JE13.05 | (127,750,000) | 0 |
| Construction in progress | 15,950,000 | JE13.05 | (15,950,000) | 0 |
| Other capital assets (net) |  | JE13.06 | 182,084,806 | 182,084,806 |
| Buildings | 216,000,000 | JE13.06 | (216,000,000) | 0 |
| Equipment | 29,500,000 | JE13.06 | (29,500,000) | 0 |
| Vehicles | 81,563,000 | JE13.06 | (81,563,000) | 0 |
| Leased capital assets | 8,249,753 | JE13.06 | (8,249,753) | 0 |
| Infrastructure assets | 20,000,000 | JE13.06 | (20,000,000) | 0 |

## 13-12 The Consolidation and Conversion Process

|  | Preliminary Governmental Activities Total Debit (Credit) |  | Reclassifications and Adjustments Debit (Credit) | Government-Wide Financial Statements Debit (Credit) |
|---|---|---|---|---|
| Accumulated depreciation | (173,227,947) | JE13.06 | 173,227,947 | 0 |
| Interest payable and accrued expenses |  | JE13.07 | (1,604,290) | (1,604,290) |
| Accounts payable | (1,055,000) | JE13.07 | 1,055,000 | 0 |
| Interest payable | (549,290) | JE13.07 | 549,290 | 0 |
| Due to other funds | (2,642,000) | JE13.03 | 242,000 | 0 |
|  |  | JE13.04 | 2,400,000 |  |
| Deferred revenue | (310,000) |  |  | (310,000) |
| Long-term liabilities—due within one year |  | JE13.08 | (4,658,932) | (4,658,932) |
| Long-term liabilities—due in more than one year |  | JE13.08 | (41,353,107) | (41,353,107) |
| Claims payable | (1,932,000) | JE13.08 | 1,932,000 | 0 |
| Compensated absences payable | (4,675,000) | JE13.08 | 4,675,000 | 0 |
| Notes payable | (7,700,000) | JE13.08 | 7,700,000 | 0 |
| Lease obligation payable | (4,340,724) | JE13.08 | 4,340,724 | 0 |
| Revenue bonds payable | (9,250,000) | JE13.08 | 9,250,000 | 0 |
| Bonds payable | (18,114,315) | JE13.08 | 18,114,315 | 0 |
| Fund balance/ net assets | (307,278,097) |  |  | (307,278,097) |
| General revenue— property taxes | (91,670,000) |  |  | (91,670,000) |
| Franchise taxes | (1,300,000) |  |  | (1,300,000) |
| Intergovernmental grants—general revenues— unrestricted grants | (26,500,000) |  |  | (26,500,000) |

*Developing Information for Government-Wide Financial Statements* 13-13

| | Preliminary Governmental Activities Total Debit (Credit) | Reclassifications and Adjustments Debit (Credit) | | Government-Wide Financial Statements Debit (Credit) |
|---|---|---|---|---|
| Program revenues/ charges for services (general government) | (355,000) | | | (355,000) |
| Program revenues— operating grants and contributions (general government) | (34,000) | | | (34,000) |
| Program revenues/ charges for services (recreations and parks) | (135,000) | | | (135,000) |
| Program revenues— capital grants and contributions (recreation and parks) | (450,000) | | | (450,000) |
| Program revenues/ charges for services (public safety) | (202,000) | | | (202,000) |
| Program revenues/ charges for services (health and welfare) | (4,000) | | | (4,000) |
| Program revenues— operating grants and contributions (health and welfare) | | **JE13.09** | (50,000) | (50,000) |
| Program revenues/ charges for services (streets) | (150,000) | | | (150,000) |
| Program revenues— operating grants and contributions (streets) | (4,570,000) | | | (4,570,000) |
| Program revenues— capital grants and contributions (streets) | (2,000,000) | | | (2,000,000) |
| Contributions | (50,000) | **JE13.09** | 50,000 | 0 |

| | Preliminary Governmental Activities Total Debit (Credit) | Reclassifications and Adjustments Debit (Credit) | | Government-Wide Financial Statements Debit (Credit) |
|---|---|---|---|---|
| Unrestricted investment earnings | | JE13.10 | (294,000) | (294,000) |
| Interest and investment revenue | (154,000) | JE13.10 | 154,000 | 0 |
| Miscellaneous revenue | (18,000) | | | (18,000) |
| Investment revenue—change in fair value of investments | (140,000) | JE13.10 | 140,000 | 0 |
| General government expenses | 53,931,629 | | | 53,931,629 |
| Public safety expenses | 22,836,931 | | | 22,836,931 |
| Streets expenditures/expenses | 21,187,633 | | | 21,187,633 |
| Recreation and parks expenses | 7,621,871 | | | 7,621,871 |
| Health and welfare expenses | 9,579,427 | | | 9,579,427 |
| Interest on long-term debt | | JE13.11 | 2,332,717 | 2,332,717 |
| Payments to school district | | JE13.11 | 32,000,000 | 32,000,000 |
| Interest expense | 2,332,717 | JE13.11 | (2,332,717) | 0 |
| Contributions to permanent funds | | JE13.12 | (22,000) | (22,000) |
| Education (component unit) | 32,000,000 | JE13.11 | (32,000,000) | 0 |
| Revenues—permanent endowment additions | (22,000) | JE13.12 | 22,000 | 0 |

|  | Preliminary Governmental Activities Total Debit (Credit) | | Reclassifications and Adjustments Debit (Credit) | Government-Wide Financial Statements Debit (Credit) |
|---|---|---|---|---|
| Extraordinary item—donation of land by the state | (20,000,000) | | | (20,000,000) |
| Transfers in | (5,685,000) | JE13.13 | 5,685,000 | 0 |
| Transfers out | 5,825,000 | JE13.13 | (5,685,000) | 140,000 |
| Total | $ 0 | | $ 0 | $ 0 |

The last column in the above worksheet is the basis for preparing the governmental activities column in the government-wide financial statements.

▶ **NEW STANDARD:** GASB-34 introduced the concept of an "internal balance" between governmental funds and proprietary funds. Internal balances are presented on the face of the statement of net assets for both the governmental activities and the business-type activities, but they offset (net to zero) when totals are extended to the "reporting entity column" on the statement.

▶ **NEW STANDARD:** GASB-34 requires that program revenues be classified and reported as (1) charges for services, (2) operating grants and contributions, and (3) capital grants and contributions. During the implementation process for GASB-34, questions arose about how revenues raised by one function/activity but used by another function/activity should be classified in the statement of activities. For example, if revenue generated by a state lottery (a separately reported function/activity) must be used to finance education (another function/activity), should the proceeds from the lottery be reported as revenue for the lottery or for education? GASB-37 (Basic Financial Statements—and Management's Discussion and Analysis—for State and Local Governments: Omnibus) concludes that the following factors are to be used to determine which revenue should be related to a program: (1) for charges for services the determining factor is which function generates the revenue and (2) for grants and contributions the determining factor is the function the revenue is restricted to. Thus, in the lottery example, the proceeds from the lottery are reported as charges for services of the lottery activity because the educational activity used the resources but did not create the proceeds from lottery activities.

▶ **NEW STANDARD:** The language used in GASB-34 strongly implied that only three categories could be used to identify program revenues, namely: (1) charges for services, (2) operating grants and contributions, and (3) capital grants and contributions. GASB-37 states that the formatting of the statement of activities is more flexible than originally conveyed in GASB-34. For example, more than one column could be included under one of the three program revenue columns. Furthermore, the columnar heading may be modified to be more descriptive. For example, a program revenue column could be labeled "operating grants, contributions, and restricted interest."

▶ **NEW STANDARD:** With the issuance of GASB-34, some financial statement preparers were unsure about how revenues related to fines and forfeitures should be classified in the statement of activities. GASB-37 modifies GASB-34 by specifically stating that fines and forfeitures are to be classified as charges for services because "they result from direct charges to those who are otherwise directly affected by a program or service, even though they receive no benefit." However, GASB-37 recognizes that there is an element of confusion and arbitrariness in classifying fines and forfeitures as charges for services by noting that the statement of activities could be formatted (1) in order to present a separate column labeled Fines and Forfeitures" under the "Charges for Services" column or (2) by retitling the column "Charges for Services, Fees, Fines, and Forfeitures."

▶ **NEW STANDARD:** GASB-38 (Certain Financial Statement Note Disclosures) requires that a governmental entity present in the notes to its financial statements the details of receivables and payables reported on the statements of net assts and balance sheets "when significant components have been obscured by aggregation." In addition, significant receivable balances that are not expected to be collected within one year of the date of the financial statements should be disclosed.

## BUSINESS-TYPE ACTIVITIES

GASB-34 notes that business-type activities "are financed in whole or in part by fees charged to external parties for goods or services [and] these activities are usually reported in Enterprise Funds." The information presented in Enterprise Funds is accounted for using the accrual basis of accounting and, therefore, the balances that appeared on the fund financial statements for Enterprise Funds do not have to be adjusted before they are reported in the business-type activities column of the government-wide financial statements. However, because of the unique format of the government-wide financial statements, it is

*Developing Information for Government-Wide Financial Statements* **13-17**

necessary to combine and reclassify some of the accounts that were reported in the Enterprise Funds at the fund financial statement level. In some instances, it may also be necessary to merge Internal Service Fund balances with Enterprise Funds. To begin this process, the following consolidating trial balance for all Enterprise Funds is presented below and is based on the information developed in Chapter 7 ("Enterprise Funds").

|  | Centerville Toll Bridge (Chapter 7) Debit (Credit) | Centerville Utilities Authority (Chapter 7) Debit (Credit) | Centerville Parking Authority (Chapter 7) Debit (Credit) | Centerville Municipal Airport (Chapter 7) Debit (Credit) | Combined Totals For Enterprise Funds Debit (Credit) |
|---|---|---|---|---|---|
| Cash | 739,500 | 230,000 | 764,000 | 10,963,000 | 12,696,500 |
| Interest receivable | 3,000 | 50,000 | 3,000 | 200,000 | 256,000 |
| Accounts receivable (net) |  | 7,550,000 |  | 18,000,000 | 25,550,000 |
| Due from other funds |  | 2,000,000 |  | 400,000 | 2,400,000 |
| Due from other governments |  | 100,000 |  | 300,000 | 400,000 |
| Temporary investments | 58,000 | 55,000 | 5,000 | 10,050,000 | 10,168,000 |
| Inventories | 32,000 | 75,000 | 24,000 | 55,000 | 186,000 |
| Construction in progress | 70,000 | 200,000 | 15,000 | 23,500,000 | 23,785,000 |
| Land and improvements | 140,000 | 5,200,000 | 1,780,000 | 13,200,000 | 20,320,000 |
| Superstructure | 1,400,000 |  |  |  | 1,400,000 |
| Distribution and collection systems |  | 46,300,000 |  |  | 46,300,000 |
| Runways and tarmacs |  |  |  | 27,500,000 | 27,500,000 |
| Buildings | 330,000 | 14,450,000 | 2,400,000 | 33,200,000 | 50,380,000 |
| Equipment | 55,000 | 4,600,000 | 140,000 | 7,200,000 | 11,995,000 |
| Vehicles | 835,000 | 1,660,000 | 102,000 | 2,500,000 | 5,097,000 |
| Accumulated depreciation | (1,257,000) | (54,395,000) | (1,505,000) | (20,255,000) | (77,412,000) |
| Accounts payable and accrued expenses | (50,000) | (4,300,000) | (90,000) | (3,900,000) | (8,340,000) |
| Due to other funds | (18,000) | (35,000) | (17,000) | (512,000) | (582,000) |
| Compensated absences | (8,000) | (84,000) | (5,000) | (133,000) | (230,000) |
| Claims and judgements | (27,000) | (229,000) | (7,000) | (195,000) | (458,000) |
| Notes payable | (30,000) | (30,000) | (330,000) | (7,700,000) | (8,090,000) |
| Revenue bonds—Terminal A |  |  |  | (10,000,000) | (10,000,000) |
| Revenue bonds—Terminal B |  |  |  | (4,000,000) | (4,000,000) |

**13-18**  *The Consolidation and Conversion Process*

| | Centerville Toll Bridge (Chapter 7) Debit (Credit) | Centerville Utilities Authority (Chapter 7) Debit (Credit) | Centerville Parking Authority (Chapter 7) Debit (Credit) | Centerville Municipal Airport (Chapter 7) Debit (Credit) | Combined Totals For Enterprise Funds Debit (Credit) |
|---|---|---|---|---|---|
| Bonds payable | (80,000) | (7,700,000) | (500,000) | | (8,280,000) |
| Net assets | (1,646,500) | (16,019,000) | (3,994,000) | (73,608,000) | (95,267,500) |
| Charges for services | (4,750,000) | (36,000,000) | (1,500,000) | (175,000,000) | (217,250,000) |
| Charges for services—rental income—security for Terminal A revenue bonds | | | | (30,000,000) | (30,000,000) |
| Charges for services—rental income—security for Terminal B revenue bonds | | | | (22,000,000) | (22,000,000) |
| Miscellaneous revenues | (20,000) | (10,000) | (22,000) | (60,000) | (112,000) |
| Expenses—personal services | 2,402,000 | 22,022,000 | 5,402,000 | 161,025,000 | 190,851,000 |
| Expenses—contractual services | 1,280,000 | 11,220,000 | 400,000 | 33,550,000 | 46,450,000 |
| Expenses—repairs and maintenance | 400,000 | 700,000 | 50,000 | 2,100,000 | 3,250,000 |
| Expenses—other supplies and expenses | 194,000 | 729,000 | 36,000 | 1,795,000 | 2,754,000 |
| Expenses—insurance claims and expenses | 10,000 | 21,000 | 3,000 | 100,000 | 134,000 |
| Expenses—depreciation | 339,000 | 3,025,000 | 117,000 | 3,370,000 | 6,851,000 |
| Expenses—miscellaneous | 30,000 | 5,000 | 3,000 | 70,000 | 108,000 |
| Interest and investment revenue | (30,000) | (400,000) | (10,000) | (1,200,000) | (1,640,000) |
| Interest expense | 6,000 | 450,000 | 27,000 | 1,220,000 | 1,703,000 |
| Operating grants and contributions | (100,000) | | | | (100,000) |
| Nonoperating miscellaneous expenses (revenues) | (7,000) | 110,000 | (1,000) | 265,000 | 367,000 |
| Capital contributions | (250,000) | (1,250,000) | | (2,000,000) | (3,500,000) |
| Transfers in | (50,000) | | (90,000) | | (140,000) |
| Transfers out | | | | | 0 |
| Special item—gain on sale of parking lot | | | (3,500,000) | | (3,500,000) |
| Total | $ 0 | $ 0 | $ 0 | $ 0 | $ 0 |

In order to convert the combined totals for all Enterprise Funds as presented in the above trial balance to the trial balance for business-type activities, the following items are considered:

- Integration of Internal Service Fund account balances
- Reclassification of account balances

## Merging Internal Service Funds into Business-Type Activities

Based on the nature of each Internal Service Fund, the Communications and Technology Support Center balances are allocated to both governmental activities (which was done earlier) and business-type activities, and the Special Services Support Center balances are allocated exclusively to business-type activities. This analysis was made in Chapter 8 ("Internal Service Funds") and resulted in the following entries:

| | Accounts | Debit | Credit |
|---|---|---|---|
| JE08.46 | Expenses—Centerville Municipal Airport | 327,872 | |
| | Expenses—Centerville Utilities Authority | 120,320 | |
| | Expenses—Centerville Parking Authority | 54,144 | |
| | Expenses—Centerville Toll Bridge | 45,120 | |
| | Internal balances | | 547,456 |

| | Accounts | Debit | Credit |
|---|---|---|---|
| JE08.48 | Cash | 22,000 | |
| | Interest receivable | 1,000 | |
| | Due from other funds | 427,000 | |
| | Temporary investments | 12,000 | |
| | Inventories | 20,000 | |
| | Land and improvements | 1,750,000 | |
| | Buildings | 1,600,000 | |
| | Equipment | 2,960,000 | |
| | Vehicles | 1,995,000 | |
| | Expenses—Centerville Municipal Airport | | 73,000 |
| | Accumulated depreciation | | 3,240,000 |
| | Accounts payable and accrued expenses | | 75,000 |
| | Compensated absences | | 17,000 |
| | Claims and judgements | | 21,000 |
| | Notes payable | | 550,000 |
| | Interest and investment revenue | | 15,000 |
| | Net assets | | 4,796,000 |

Entry JE08.46 merges the appropriate balances from the Communications and Technology Support Center and Entry JE08.48 merges the balances from the Special Services Support Center. These entries are combined with the reclassification entries in the following section.

## Reclassification of Account Balances

On the statement of net assets, only totals for business activities are presented. That is, a single balance for cash (for business-type activities) is presented rather than cash for each Enterprise Fund. In this illustration, the following account titles are used to prepare the statement of net assets:

- Cash
- Interest receivable
- Temporary investments
- Internal balances
- Receivables (net)
- Inventories
- Land, improvements, and construction in progress
- Other capital assets (net)
- Accounts payable and accrued expenses
- Long-term liabilities—due in one year
- Long-term liabilities—due in more than one year
- Net assets (the three components of net assets are added later in the chapter)

On the statement of activities, generally only the following nominal accounts are presented for business-type activities (not all of these accounts are used in this illustration):

- Charges for services—Centerville Toll Bridge
- Charges for services—Centerville Parking Authority
- Charges for services—Centerville Utilities Authority
- Charges for services—Centerville Municipal Airport
- Operating grants and contributions—Centerville Toll Bridge
- Operating grants and contributions—Centerville Parking Authority
- Operating grants and contributions—Centerville Utilities Authority

- Operating grants and contributions—Centerville Municipal Airport
- Capital grants and contributions—Centerville Toll Bridge
- Capital grants and contributions—Centerville Parking Authority
- Capital grants and contributions—Centerville Utilities Authority
- Capital grants and contributions—Centerville Municipal Airport
- Expenses—Centerville Toll Bridge
- Expenses—Centerville Utilities Authority
- Expenses—Centerville Parking Authority
- Expenses—Centerville Municipal Airport
- Unrestricted investment earnings
- Miscellaneous revenue
- Extraordinary items
- Special items

> ▶ **NEW STANDARD:** The format for the government-wide statement of activities as established by GASB-34 is significantly different from any operating statement currently used in governmental financial reporting. The focus of the statement of activities is on the *net cost* of various activities provided by the governmental entity. The statement begins with a column that identifies the cost of each governmental activity. Another column identifies the revenues that are specifically related to the classified governmental activities. The difference between the expenses and revenues related to specific activities computes the net cost or benefits of the activities, which "identifies the extent to which each function of the government draws from the general revenues of the government or is self-financing through fees and intergovernmental aid" (GASB-34, pars. 38–40).

In order to reclassify a variety of accounts that appear in the consolidated totals for Enterprise Funds as presented in the above trial balance, the following reclassification entries are made. (The amounts that are reclassified reflect the consolidated amounts in the trial balance for all Enterprise Funds and the two entries made to integrate Internal Service Fund balances [represented by amounts in parentheses].)

| | Accounts | Debit | Credit |
|---|---|---|---|
| JE13.14 | Investments | 10,180,000 | |
| | Temporary investments ($28,168,000 + $12,000) | | 10,180,000 |
| | (To reclassify temporary investments) | | |

**13-22** *The Consolidation and Conversion Process*

| | Accounts | Debit | Credit |
|---|---|---|---|
| **JE13.15** | Receivable (net) | 26,207,000 | |
| | Interest receivable ($256,000 + $1,000) | | 257,000 |
| | Accounts receivable (net) | | 25,550,000 |
| | Due from other governments | | 400,000 |
| | (To reclassify various receivables) | | |
| **JE13.16** | Internal balances | 2,400,000 | |
| | Due from other funds | | 2,400,000 |
| | (To reclassify amounts due from the General Fund as an internal balance) | | |
| **JE13.17** | Land, improvements, and construction in progress | 45,855,000 | |
| | Construction in progress | | 23,785,000 |
| | Land and improvements ($20,320,000 + $1,750,000) | | 22,070,000 |
| | (To reclassify capital assets not subject to depreciation) | | |
| **JE13.18** | Other capital assets (net) | 68,575,000 | |
| | Accumulated depreciation ($77,412,000 + $3,240,000) | 80,652,000 | |
| | Superstructure | | 1,400,000 |
| | Distribution and collection systems | | 46,300,000 |
| | Runways and tarmacs | | 27,500,000 |
| | Buildings ($50,380,000 + $1,600,000) | | 51,980,000 |
| | Equipment ($11,995,000 + $2,960,000) | | 14,955,000 |
| | Vehicles ($5,097,000 + $1,995,000) | | 7,092,000 |
| | (To reclassify accumulated depreciation and capital assets subject to depreciation) | | |
| **JE13.19** | Due to other funds | 582,000 | |
| | Internal balances | | 155,000 |
| | Due from other funds | | 427,000 |
| | (To eliminate the intrafund receivable/payable ($427,000) and to reclassify the amount due to the Communication and Technology Support Center— Internal Service Fund that was merged with the governmental activities [$155,000]) | | |

|  | Accounts | Debit | Credit |
|---|---|---|---|
| JE13.20 | Compensated absences | 247,000 | |
| | Claims and judgements | 479,000 | |
| | Notes payable | 8,640,000 | |
| | Revenue bonds—Terminal A | 10,000,000 | |
| | Revenue bonds—Terminal B | 4,000,000 | |
| | Bonds payable | 8,280,000 | |
| | Long-term liabilities—due within one year | | 3,784,000 |
| | Long-term liabilities—due in more than one year | | 27,862,000 |
| | (To reclassify debt into due within one year and beyond one year) | | |
| JE13.21 | Charges for services | 217,250,000 | |
| | Charges for services—rental income—security for Terminal A revenue bonds | 30,000,000 | |
| | Charges for services—rental income—security for Terminal B revenue bonds | 22,000,000 | |
| | Miscellaneous revenue | 112,000 | |
| | Charges for services—Centerville Toll Bridge | | 4,770,000 |
| | Charges for services—Centerville Parking Authority | | 1,522,000 |
| | Charges for services—Centerville Utilities Authority | | 36,010,000 |
| | Charges for services—Centerville Municipal Airport | | 227,060,000 |
| | (To reclassify charges for services to specific activities) | | |
| JE13.22 | Operating grants and contributions | 100,000 | |
| | Capital contributions | 3,500,000 | |
| | Operating grants and contributions—Centerville Toll Bridge | | 100,000 |
| | Capital grants and contributions—Centerville Toll Bridge | | 250,000 |
| | Capital grants and contributions—Centerville Utilities Authority | | 1,250,000 |
| | Capital grants and contributions—Centerville Municipal Airport | | 2,000,000 |
| | (To reclassify grants and contributions to specific activities) | | |

|  | Accounts | Debit | Credit |
|---|---|---|---|
| JE13.23 | Expenses—Centerville Municipal Airport | 202,010,000 |  |
|  | Expenses—Centerville Utilities Authority | 37,722,000 |  |
|  | Expenses—Centerville Parking Authority | 6,011,000 |  |
|  | Expenses—Centerville Toll Bridge | 4,655,000 |  |
|  | Expenses—personal services |  | 190,851,000 |
|  | Expenses—contractual services |  | 46,450,000 |
|  | Expenses—repairs and maintenance |  | 3,250,000 |
|  | Expenses—other supplies and expenses |  | 2,754,000 |
|  | Expenses—insurance claims and expenses |  | 134,000 |
|  | Expenses—depreciation |  | 6,851,000 |
|  | Expenses—miscellaneous |  | 108,000 |
|  | (To reclassify operating expenses to specific activities) |  |  |
| JE13.24 | Expenses—Centerville Municipal Airport | 1,220,000 |  |
|  | Expenses—Centerville Utilities Authority | 450,000 |  |
|  | Expenses—Centerville Parking Authority | 27,000 |  |
|  | Expenses—Centerville Toll Bridge | 6,000 |  |
|  | Interest expense |  | 1,703,000 |
|  | (To reclassify interest expense to specific activities) |  |  |
| JE13.25 | Expenses—Centerville Municipal Airport | 110,000 |  |
|  | Expenses—Centerville Utilities Authority | 265,000 |  |
|  | Expenses—Centerville Parking Authority |  | 1,000 |
|  | Expenses—Centerville Toll Bridge |  | 7,000 |
|  | Nonoperating miscellaneous expenses (revenues) |  | 367,000 |
|  | (To reclassify gains and losses on the sale of assets to specific activities) |  |  |

|  | Accounts | Debit | Credit |
|---|---|---|---|
| JE13.26 | Interest and Investment Revenue ($1,640,000 + $15,000) | 1,655,000 | |
|  | Unrestricted Investment Earnings | | 1,655,000 |
|  | (To reclassify interest and investment revenue as unrestricted investment earnings) | | |

After posting the entries to merge the balances of the Internal Service Fund and to reclassify various accounts, the trial balance for business-type activities appears below is as follows:

|  | Combined Totals For Enterprise Funds Debit (Credit) | Reclassifications and Adjustments Debit (Credit) |  | Government-Wide Financial Statements Debit (Credit) |
|---|---|---|---|---|
| Cash | 12,696,500 | JE08.48 | 22,000 | 12,718,500 |
| Internal Balances |  | JE08.46 | (547,456) | 1,697,544 |
|  |  | JE13.16 | 2,400,000 |  |
|  |  | JE13.19 | (155,000) |  |
| Receivables (net) |  | JE13.15 | 26,207,000 | 26,207,000 |
| Interest receivable | 256,000 | JE08.48 | 1,000 | 0 |
|  |  | JE13.15 | (257,000) |  |
| Accounts receivable (net) | 25,550,000 | JE13.15 | (25,550,000) | 0 |
| Due from other funds | 2,400,000 | JE08.48 | 427,000 | 0 |
|  |  | JE13.16 | (2,400,000) |  |
|  |  | JE13.19 | (427,000) |  |
| Due from other governments | 400,000 | JE13.15 | (400,000) | 0 |
| Temporary investments | 10,168,000 | JE08.48 | 12,000 | 0 |
|  |  | JE13.14 | (10,180,000) |  |
| Investments |  | JE13.14 | 10,180,000 | 10,180,000 |
| Inventories | 186,000 | JE08.48 | 20,000 | 206,000 |

**13-26** *The Consolidation and Conversion Process*

|  | Combined Totals For Enterprise Funds Debit (Credit) | Reclassifications and Adjustments Debit (Credit) |  | Government-Wide Financial Statements Debit (Credit) |
|---|---|---|---|---|
| Land, improvements, and construction in progress |  | JE13.17 | 45,855,000 | 45,855,000 |
| Construction in progress | 23,785,000 | JE13.17 | (23,785,000) | 0 |
| Land and improvements | 20,320,000 | JE08.48 | 1,750,000 | 0 |
|  |  | JE13.17 | (22,070,000) |  |
| Other capital assets (net) |  | JE13.18 | 68,575,000 | 68,575,000 |
| Superstructure | 1,400,000 | JE13.18 | (1,400,000) | 0 |
| Distribution and collection systems | 46,300,000 | JE13.18 | (46,300,000) | 0 |
| Runways and tarmacs | 27,500,000 | JE13.18 | (27,500,000) | 0 |
| Buildings | 50,380,000 | JE08.48 | 1,600,000 | 0 |
|  |  | JE13.18 | (51,980,000) |  |
| Equipment | 11,995,000 | JE08.48 | 2,960,000 | 0 |
|  |  | JE13.18 | (14,955,000) |  |
| Vehicles | 5,097,000 | JE08.48 | 1,995,000 | 0 |
|  |  | JE13.18 | (7,092,000) |  |
| Accumulated depreciation | (77,412,000) | JE08.48 | (3,240,000) | 0 |
|  |  | JE13.18 | 80,652,000 |  |
| Accounts payable and accrued expenses | (8,340,000) | JE08.48 | (75,000) | (8,415,000) |
| Due to other funds | (582,000) | JE13.19 | 582,000 | 0 |
| Long-Term Liabilities—Due within one year |  | JE13.20 | (3,784,000) | (3,784,000) |
| Long-Term Liabilities—Due in more than one year |  | JE13.20 | (27,862,000) | (27,862,000) |

*Developing Information for Government-Wide Financial Statements* **13-27**

|  | Combined Totals For Enterprise Funds Debit (Credit) |  | Reclassifications and Adjustments Debit (Credit) | Government-Wide Financial Statements Debit (Credit) |
|---|---|---|---|---|
| Compensated absences | (230,000) | JE08.48 | (17,000) | 0 |
|  |  | JE13.20 | 247,000 |  |
| Claims and judgements | (458,000) | JE08.48 | (21,000) | 0 |
|  |  | JE13.20 | 479,000 |  |
| Notes payable | (8,090,000) | JE08.48 | (550,000) | 0 |
|  |  | JE13.20 | 8,640,000 |  |
| Revenue bonds—Terminal A | (10,000,000) | JE13.20 | 10,000,000 | 0 |
| Revenue bonds—Terminal B | (4,000,000) | JE13.20 | 4,000,000 | 0 |
| Bonds payable | (8,280,000) | JE13.20 | 8,280,000 | 0 |
| Net assets | (95,267,500) | JE08.48 | (4,796,000) | (100,063,500) |
| Charges for services—Centerville Toll Bridge |  | JE13.21 | (4,770,000) | (4,770,000) |
| Charges for services—Centerville Parking Authority |  | JE13.21 | (1,522,000) | (1,522,000) |
| Charges for services—Centerville Utilities Authority |  | JE13.21 | (36,010,000) | (36,010,000) |
| Charges for services—Centerville Municipal Airport |  | JE13.21 | (227,060,000) | (227,060,000) |
| Charges for services | (217,250,000) | JE13.21 | 217,250,000 | 0 |
| Charges for services—rental income—security for Terminal A revenue bonds | (30,000,000) | JE13.21 | 30,000,000 | 0 |

**13-28** *The Consolidation and Conversion Process*

|  | Combined Totals For Enterprise Funds Debit (Credit) | | Reclassifications and Adjustments Debit (Credit) | Government-Wide Financial Statements Debit (Credit) |
|---|---:|---|---:|---:|
| Charges for services—rental income—security for Terminal B revenue bonds | (22,000,000) | JE13.21 | 22,000,000 | 0 |
| Miscellaneous revenues | (112,000) | JE13.21 | 112,000 | 0 |
| Expenses—personal services | 190,851,000 | JE13.23 | (190,851,000) | 0 |
| Expenses—contractual services | 46,450,000 | JE13.23 | (46,450,000) | 0 |
| Expenses—repairs and maintenance | 3,250,000 | JE13.23 | (3,250,000) | 0 |
| Expenses—other supplies and expenses | 2,754,000 | JE13.23 | (2,754,000) | 0 |
| Expenses—insurance claims and expenses | 134,000 | JE13.23 | (134,000) | 0 |
| Expenses—depreciation | 6,851,000 | JE13.23 | (6,851,000) | 0 |
| Expenses—miscellaneous | 108,000 | JE13.23 | (108,000) | 0 |
| Expenses—Centerville Municipal Airport | | JE08.46 | 327,872 | 203,594,872 |
|  | | JE08.48 | (73,000) | |
|  | | JE13.23 | 202,010,000 | |
|  | | JE13.24 | 1,220,000 | |
|  | | JE13.25 | 110,000 | |
| Expenses—Centerville Utilities Authority | | JE08.46 | 120,320 | 38,557,320 |

|  | Combined Totals For Enterprise Funds Debit (Credit) |  | Reclassifications and Adjustments Debit (Credit) | Government-Wide Financial Statements Debit (Credit) |
|---|---|---|---|---|
|  |  | JE13.23 | 37,722,000 |  |
|  |  | JE13.24 | 450,000 |  |
|  |  | JE13.25 | 265,000 |  |
| Expenses—Centerville Parking Authority |  | JE08.46 | 54,144 | 6,091,144 |
|  |  | JE13.23 | 6,011,000 |  |
|  |  | JE13.24 | 27,000 |  |
|  |  | JE13.25 | (1,000) |  |
| Expenses—Centerville Toll Bridge |  | JE08.46 | 45,120 | 4,699,120 |
|  |  | JE13.23 | 4,655,000 |  |
|  |  | JE13.24 | 6,000 |  |
|  |  | JE13.25 | (7,000) |  |
| Unrestricted investment earnings |  | JE13.26 | (1,655,000) | (1,655,000) |
| Interest and investment revenue | (1,640,000) | JE08.48 | (15,000) | 0 |
|  |  | JE13.26 | 1,655,000 |  |
| Interest expense | 1,703,000 | JE13.24 | (1,703,000) | 0 |
| Operating grants and contributions—Centerville Toll Bridge |  | JE13.22 | (100,000) | (100,000) |
| Capital grants and contributions—Centerville Toll Bridge |  | JE13.22 | (250,000) | (250,000) |
| Capital grants and contributions—Centerville Utilities Authority |  | JE13.22 | (1,250,000) | (1,250,000) |

|  | Combined Totals For Enterprise Funds Debit (Credit) |  | Reclassifications and Adjustments Debit (Credit) | Government-Wide Financial Statements Debit (Credit) |
|---|---|---|---|---|
| Capital grants and contributions—Centerville Municipal Airport |  | JE13.22 | (2,000,000) 0 | (2,000,000) |
| Operating grants and contributions | (100,000) | JE13.22 | 100,000 | 0 |
| Nonoperating miscellaneous expenses (revenues) | 367,000 | JE13.25 | (367,000) | 0 |
| Capital contributions | (3,500,000) | JE13.22 | 3,500,000 | 0 |
| Transfers in | (140,000) |  |  | (140,000) |
| Transfers out |  |  |  |  |
| Special item—gain on sale of parking lot | (3,500,000) |  |  | (3,500,000) |
| Total | $ 0 |  | $ 0 | $ 0 |

The information on the foregoing worksheet is brought forward to Chapter 14 ("Basic Financial Statements").

## Components of Net Assets

The above illustrations present only a single amount for net assets. GASB-34 requires that the statement of net assets identify the components of net assets, namely (1) invested in capital assets, net of related debt, (2) restricted net assets, and (3) unrestricted net assets. The method used to identify these three components is illustrated in Chapter 14 ("Basic Financial Statements").

> ▶ **NEW STANDARD:** GASB-34 introduces the concept of *net assets*, which represents the difference between a governmental entity's total assets and its total liabilities.

# PART VI.
# THE FINANCIAL STATEMENTS AND RELATED DISCLOSURES

# CHAPTER 14
# BASIC FINANCIAL STATEMENTS

## CONTENTS

| | |
|---|---|
| Introduction | 14-2 |
|   Reconciliations for Governmental Activities | 14-2 |
|     Exhibit 14-1: Categorization Scheme | 14-16 |
|     Exhibit 14-2: Categorization Scheme | 14-16 |
|   Reconciliations for Business-Type Activities | 14-19 |
|   Components of Net Assets—Governmental Activities | 14-22 |
|   Components of Net Assets—Business-Type Activities | 14-24 |
| Financial Statements | 14-24 |
|   Exhibit 14-3: Statement of Net Assets | 14-25 |
|   Exhibit 14-4: Statement of Activities | 14-27 |
|   Exhibit 14-5: Balance Sheet—Governmental Funds | 14-29 |
|   Exhibit 14-6: Reconciliation of the Balance Sheet of Governmental Funds to the Statement of Net Assets | 14-30 |
|   Exhibit 14-7: Statement of Revenues, Expenditures, and Changes in Fund Balances—Governmental Funds | 14-31 |
|   Exhibit 14-8: Reconciliation of the Statement of Revenues, Expenditures, and Changes in Fund Balances of Governmental Funds to the Statement of Activities | 14-32 |
|   Exhibit 14-9: Statement of Net Assets—Proprietary Funds | 14-33 |
|   Exhibit 14-10: Statement of Revenues, Expenses, and Changes in Fund Net Assets—Proprietary Funds | 14-35 |
|   Exhibit 14-11: Statement of Cash Flows—Proprietary Funds | 14-37 |
|   Exhibit 14-12: Statement of Fiduciary Net Assets | 14-39 |
|   Exhibit 14-13: Statement of Changes in Fiduciary Net Assets | 14-40 |

## INTRODUCTION

The basic financial statements include two financial statement components: (1) fund financial statements and (2) government-wide financial statements. This type of reporting model may lead financial statements readers to wonder which set is *correct*. In order to help readers understand the relationship between the two sets of financial statements, GASB-34 requires summary reconciliations between the fund financial statements and the government-wide financial statements. The nature of the reconciliations can be divided into the following categories:

- Reconciliations for governmental activities
- Reconciliations for business-type activities

### Reconciliations for Governmental Activities

The totals in the fund financial statements for governmental funds will not equal totals in the governmental activities columns of the government-wide financial statements, because different measurement focuses and bases of accounting are used to prepare the two different sets of financial statements. (The totals may not equal because of the merging of balances from Internal Service Funds.) For this reason, the GASB requires that at the bottom of the fund financial statements or in a separate schedule there be a summary reconciliation between the fund financial statements and the government-wide financial statements. That is, the amount shown as the "total fund balances" in the "total governmental funds" column on the fund balance sheets is reconciled to the "net assets" for governmental activities presented on the statement of net assets. Also, the amount shown as "net changes in fund balance" in the "total governmental funds" column on the statement of revenues, expenditures, and change in fund balances is reconciled to the "change in net assets" for governmental activities presented on the statement of activities.

Based on the illustration developed in previous chapters of this book, the balances to be reconciled are as follows:

|  | Fund Balances/<br>Net Assets | Change in<br>Fund Balances/<br>Net Assets |
|---|---|---|
| Total balances for governmental funds* | $ 16,749,056 | $2,256,556 |
| Total balances for governmental activities** | $305,401,889 | $(1,876,208) |

\* These balances are from the governmental fund financial statements presented later in this chapter.

\*\* These balances are from the government-wide financial statements (governmental activities) presented later in this chapter.

Basic Financial Statements  14-3

In order to explain the differences between the two sets of financial statements' balances, the worksheet entries—made to convert from a modified accrual basis to an accrual basis and to merge the balances of Internal Service Funds—are as follows:

|  | Debits | Credits | Effects on Balances Fund Balances/ Net Assets | Change in Fund Balances/ Net Assets |
|---|---|---|---|---|
| Per Governmental Fund Financial Statements | — | — | $16,749,056 | $2,256,556 |
| General Fund: | — | — | | |
| **JE02.51A** | | | | |
| Other financing sources— capitalized leases | 431,213 | | | (431,213) |
| Expenditures— general government | | 431,213 | | 431,213 |
| Leased capital assets | 431,213 | | 431,213 | |
| Lease obligation payable | | 431,213 | (431,213) | |
| Lease obligation payable | 100,000 | | 100,000 | |
| Expenditures— general government | | 100,000 | | 100,000 |
| Expenses— general government | 79,058 | | (79,058) | (79,058) |
| Accumulated depreciation— leased capital assets | | 79,058 | | |
| Interest expenses | 24,290 | | (24,290) | (24,290) |
| Interest payable | | 24,290 | | |

**14-4** *The Financial Statements and Related Disclosures*

|  | Debits | Credits | Effects on Balances Fund Balances/ Net Assets | Change in Fund Balances/ Net Assets |
|---|---|---|---|---|
| **JE02.51B** | | | | |
| Lease obligation payable | 1,188,141 | | 1,188,141 | 1,188,141 |
| Expenditures—general government | | 712,885 | | |
| Expenditures—public safety | | 237,628 | | |
| Expenditures—streets | | 118,814 | | |
| Expenditures—recreation and parks | | 59,407 | | |
| Expenditures—health and welfare | | 59,407 | | |
| **JE02.52** | | | | |
| Intergovernmental grants receivable | 6,000,000 | | 6,000,000 | |
| General revenues—unrestricted grants | | 6,000,000 | | 6,000,000 |
| **JE02.53** | | | | |
| Vehicles | 900,000 | | 900,000 | 900,000 |
| Expenditures—general government | | 100,000 | | |
| Expenditures—public safety | | 300,000 | | |
| Expenditures—streets | | 400,000 | | |
| Expenditures—recreation and parks | | 100,000 | | |

## Basic Financial Statements 14-5

|  | Debits | Credits | Effects on Balances — Fund Balances/ Net Assets | Change in Fund Balances/ Net Assets |
|---|---|---|---|---|
| Expenses—general government | 19,445 |  | (175,000) | (175,000) |
| Expenses—public safety | 58,333 |  |  |  |
| Expenses—streets | 77,778 |  |  |  |
| Expenses—recreation and parks | 19,444 |  |  |  |
| Accumulated depreciation—vehicles |  | 175,000 |  |  |
| Vehicles | 520,000 |  | 520,000 | 520,000 |
| Expenditures—public safety |  | 520,000 |  |  |
| Expenses—public safety | 28,889 |  | (28,889) | (28,889) |
| Accumulated depreciation—vehicles |  | 28,889 |  |  |
| Equipment | 4,700,000 |  | 4,700,000 | 4,700,000 |
| Expenditures—general government |  | 2,000,000 |  |  |
| Expenditures—public safety |  | 1,300,000 |  |  |
| Expenditures—streets |  | 700,000 |  |  |
| Expenditures—recreation and parks |  | 500,000 |  |  |
| Expenditures—health and welfare |  | 200,000 |  |  |

**14-6** *The Financial Statements and Related Disclosures*

|  | Debits | Credits | Effects on Balances Fund Balances/ Net Assets | Change in Fund Balances/ Net Assets |
|---|---|---|---|---|
| Expenses—general government | 170,000 |  | (437,000) | (437,000) |
| Expenses—public safety | 110,000 |  |  |  |
| Expenses—streets | 95,000 |  |  |  |
| Expenses—recreation and parks | 40,000 |  |  |  |
| Expenses—health and welfare | 22,000 |  |  |  |
| Accumulated depreciation—equipment |  | 437,000 |  |  |
| **JE02.54** |  |  |  |  |
| Accumulated depreciation—buildings | 2,000,000 |  | (5,600,000) | (5,600,000) |
| Accumulated depreciation—equipment | 1,000,000 |  |  |  |
| Accumulated depreciation—vehicles | 3,000,000 |  |  |  |
| Miscellaneous revenue | 4,800,000 |  |  |  |
| Expenses—general government | 700,000 |  |  |  |
| Expenses—public safety | 100,000 |  |  |  |
| Buildings |  | 7,000,000 |  |  |
| Equipment |  | 1,400,000 |  |  |
| Vehicles |  | 3,200,000 |  |  |
| **JE02.55** |  |  |  |  |
| Expenses—general government | 19,620,000 |  | (33,400,000) | (33,400,000) |
| Expenses—public safety | 6,540,000 |  |  |  |

*Basic Financial Statements* **14-7**

|  | Debits | Credits | Effects on Balances Fund Balances/ Net Assets | Change in Fund Balances/ Net Assets |
|---|---|---|---|---|
| Expenses—streets | 3,970,000 | | | |
| Expenses—recreation and parks | 1,635,000 | | | |
| Expenses—health and welfare | 1,635,000 | | | |
| Accumulated depreciation—buildings | | 8,000,000 | | |
| Accumulated depreciation—equipment | | 1,500,000 | | |
| Accumulated depreciation—vehicles | | 22,000,000 | | |
| Accumulated depreciation—leased capital assets | | 1,200,000 | | |
| Accumulated depreciation—infrastructure assets | | 700,000 | | |
| **JE02.56** | | | | |
| Land | 20,000,000 | | 20,000,000 | 20,000,000 |
| Extraordinary item—donation of land by the state | | 20,000,000 | | |
| **JE02.57A** | | | | |
| Expenses—public safety | 300,000 | | (300,000) | (300,000) |
| Claims payable | | 300,000 | | |
| Expenses—general government | 132,000 | | (220,000) | (220,000) |
| Expenses—public safety | 44,000 | | | |
| Expenses—streets | 22,000 | | | |

**14-8** *The Financial Statements and Related Disclosures*

|  | Debits | Credits | Effects on Balances Fund Balances/ Net Assets | Change in Fund Balances/ Net Assets |
|---|---|---|---|---|
| Expenses— recreation and parks | 11,000 | | | |
| Expenses— health and welfare | 11,000 | | | |
|     Compensated absences payable | | 220,000 | | |
| **JE02.57B** | | | | |
| Claims payable | 400,000 | | 400,000 | 400,000 |
|     Expenditures— public safety | | 400,000 | | |
| **JE02.57C** | | | | |
| Compensated absences payable | 60,000 | | 60,000 | 60,000 |
|     Expenditures— general government | | 36,000 | | |
|     Expenditures— public safety | | 12,000 | | |
|     Expenditures— streets | | 6,000 | | |
|     Expenditures— recreation and parks | | 3,000 | | |
|     Expenditures— health and welfare | | 3,000 | | |
| **JE02.58** | | | | |
| Property taxes receivable | 1,400,000 | | 1,400,000 | 1,400,000 |
|     General revenues— property taxes | | 1,400,000 | | |

Basic Financial Statements **14-9**

|  | Debits | Credits | Effects on Balances Fund Balances/ Net Assets | Change in Fund Balances/ Net Assets |
|---|---|---|---|---|
| **JE02.59** | | | | |
| Other receivables | 8,400 | | 8,400 | 8,400 |
| Program revenues—charges for services (recreation and parks) | | 4,000 | | |
| Program revenues—charges for services (public safety) | | 800 | | |
| Program revenues—charges for services (health and welfare) | | 1,600 | | |
| Program revenues—charges for services (general government) | | 2,000 | | |
| **JE02.60** | | | | |
| Land and improvements | 105,000,000 | | 313,368,540 | |
| Construction in progress | 2,050,000 | | | |
| Buildings | 220,000,000 | | | |
| Equipment | 19,000,000 | | | |
| Vehicles | 75,000,000 | | | |
| Leased capital assets | 7,818,540 | | | |
| Infrastructure assets | 20,000,000 | | | |
| Accumulated depreciation—buildings | | 75,000,000 | | |

**14-10** *The Financial Statements and Related Disclosures*

|  | Debits | Credits | Effects on Balances Fund Balances/ Net Assets | Change in Fund Balances/ Net Assets |
|---|---:|---:|---:|---:|
| Accumulated depreciation—equipment |  | 7,000,000 |  |  |
| Accumulated depreciation—vehicles |  | 39,000,000 |  |  |
| Accumulated depreciation—leased capital assets |  | 2,500,000 |  |  |
| Accumulated depreciation—infrastructure assets |  | 12,000,000 |  |  |
| Net assets |  | 313,368,540 |  |  |
| **JE02.61** |  |  |  |  |
| Net assets | 5,197,652 |  | (5,197,652) |  |
| Lease obligations payable |  | 5,197,652 |  |  |
| **JE02.62** |  |  |  |  |
| Net assets | 6,500,000 |  | (6,500,000) |  |
| Compensated absences payable |  | 4,500,000 |  |  |
| Claims and judgements payable |  | 2,000,000 |  |  |
| **Special Revenue Funds:** |  |  |  |  |
| **JE03.19** |  |  |  |  |
| Intergovernmental receivables | 50,000 |  | 50,000 | 50,000 |
| General revenues—unrestricted grants |  | 50,000 |  |  |
| **JE03.20** |  |  |  |  |
| Intergovernmental receivables | 20,000 |  | 20,000 | 20,000 |
| General revenues—unrestricted grants |  | 20,000 |  |  |

Basic Financial Statements **14-11**

|  | Debits | Credits | Effects on Balances Fund Balances/ Net Assets | Change in Fund Balances/ Net Assets |
|---|---|---|---|---|
| **Capital Projects Funds:** | | | | |
| **JE04.25** | | | | |
| Construction-in-progress | 11,100,000 | | 11,100,000 | 11,100,000 |
|     Expenditures—capital outlays (streets) | | 11,100,000 | | |
| **JE04.26** | | | | |
| Long-term debt issued (other sources of financial resources) | 10,000,000 | | (9,328,956) | (9,328,956) |
| Discount on long-term debt issued (other uses of financial resources) | | 671,044 | | |
|     Bonds payable | | 9,328,956 | | |
| **JE04.27** | | | | |
| Construction-in-progress | 1,500,000 | | 1,500,000 | 1,500,000 |
|     Expenditures—capital outlays (streets) | | 1,500,000 | | |
| **JE04.28** | | | | |
| Construction-in-progress | 1,300,000 | | 1,300,000 | 1,300,000 |
|     Expenditures—capital outlays (recreation and parks) | | 1,300,000 | | |
| **JE04.29** | | | | |
| Long-term debt issued (other sources of financial resources) | 3,000,000 | | (3,000,000) | (3,000,000) |
|     Bonds payable | | 3,000,000 | | |

**14-12** *The Financial Statements and Related Disclosures*

|  | Debits | Credits | Effects on Balances Fund Balances/ Net Assets | Change in Fund Balances/ Net Assets |
|---|---|---|---|---|
| **Debt Service Funds:** | | | | |
| **JE05.25** | | | | |
| Fund balance—Senior Citizens' Center bonds | 10,000,000 | | (16,964,791) | |
| Fund balance—Easely Street Bridge bonds | 2,064,791 | | | |
| Fund balance—Bland Street Drainage bonds | 4,900,000 | | | |
| Revenue bonds payable (Senior Citizens' Center bonds) | | 10,000,000 | | |
| Bonds payable (Easely Street Bridge bonds) | | 2,064,791 | | |
| Bonds payable (Bland Street Drainage bonds) | | 4,900,000 | | |
| **JE05.26** | | | | |
| Revenue bonds payable | 750,000 | | 750,000 | 750,000 |
| Expenditures—principal | | 750,000 | | |
| **JE05.27** | | | | |
| Bonds payable | 14,169 | | 14,169 | 14,169 |
| Interest expense | | 14,169 | | |
| **JE05.28** | | | | |
| Interest expense | 559,737 | | (559,737) | (559,737) |
| Interest payable | | 525,000 | | |
| Bonds payable | | 34,737 | | |
| **JE05.29** | | | | |
| Bonds payable | 700,000 | | 700,000 | 700,000 |
| Expenditures—principal | | 700,000 | | |

Basic Financial Statements  14-13

|  | Debits | Credits | Fund Balances/ Net Assets | Change in Fund Balances/ Net Assets |
|---|---|---|---|---|
| **JE05.30** | | | | |
| Bonds payable | 500,000 | | 500,000 | 500,000 |
| Expenditures—principal | | 500,000 | | |
| **Internal Service Funds:** | | | | |
| **JE08.45** | | | | |
| Cash | 946,000 | | 6,590,000 | (2,512,544) |
| Interest receivable | 1,000 | | (2,512,544) | |
| Due from other funds | 325,000 | | | |
| Temporary investments | 15,000 | | | |
| Inventories | 9,000 | | | |
| Land and improvements | 2,700,000 | | | |
| Buildings | 1,400,000 | | | |
| Equipment | 5,870,000 | | | |
| Vehicles | 143,000 | | | |
| Expenses—general government | 1,476,326 | | | |
| Expenses—public safety | 492,109 | | | |
| Expenses—streets | 246,055 | | | |
| Expenses—recreation and parks | 123,027 | | | |
| Expenses—health and welfare | 123,027 | | | |
| Internal balances | 547,456 | | | |
| Interest expense | 97,000 | | | |
| Accumulated depreciation | | 3,103,000 | | |
| Accounts payable and accrued expenses | | 50,000 | | |
| Compensated absences—current | | 3,000 | | |

Effects on Balances

**14-14** *The Financial Statements and Related Disclosures*

|  | Debits | Credits | Effects on Balances Fund Balances/ Net Assets | Change in Fund Balances/ Net Assets |
|---|---|---|---|---|
| Claims and judgements — current |  | 4,000 |  |  |
| Compensated absences—noncurrent |  | 4,000 |  |  |
| Claims and judgements—noncurrent |  | 15,000 |  |  |
| Notes payable—noncurrent |  | 4,700,000 |  |  |
| Interest and investment revenue |  | 5,000 |  |  |
| Transfers in |  | 40,000 |  |  |
| Net assets |  | 6,590,000 |  |  |
| **JE08.47** |  |  |  |  |
| Cash | 137,500 |  | 1,489,500 | 322,000 |
| Interest receivable | 2,000 |  | 322,000 |  |
| Due from other funds | 72,000 |  |  |  |
| Due from other governments | 45,000 |  |  |  |
| Temporary investments | 19,000 |  |  |  |
| Inventories | 7,000 |  |  |  |
| Land and improvements | 50,000 |  |  |  |
| Buildings | 1,600,000 |  |  |  |
| Equipment | 1,330,000 |  |  |  |
| Vehicles | 8,200,000 |  |  |  |
| Interest expense | 180,000 |  |  |  |
| Transfers out | 50,000 |  |  |  |
| Expenses—general government |  | 40,200 |  |  |
| Expenses—public safety |  | 103,400 |  |  |
| Expenses—streets |  | 51,700 |  |  |
| Expenses—recreation and parks |  | 25,850 |  |  |

|  | Debits | Credits | Effects on Balances Fund Balances/ Net Assets | Change in Fund Balances/ Net Assets |
|---|---|---|---|---|
| Expenses—health and welfare |  | 25,850 |  |  |
| Accumulated depreciation |  | 6,505,000 |  |  |
| Accounts payable and accrued expenses |  | 125,000 |  |  |
| Compensated absences—current |  | 2,000 |  |  |
| Claims and judgements—current |  | 2,000 |  |  |
| Notes payable—current |  | 1,500,000 |  |  |
| Compensated absences–noncurrent |  | 6,000 |  |  |
| Claims and judgement—noncurrent |  | 11,000 |  |  |
| Notes payable—noncurrent |  | 1,500,000 |  |  |
| Interest and investment revenue |  | 5,000 |  |  |
| Program revenues—charges for services (general government) |  | 300,000 |  |  |
| Net assets |  | 1,489,500 |  |  |
| **Per Government-Wide Financial Statement** |  |  | $305,401,889 | $(1,876,208) |

Each of the foregoing worksheet entries is taken from a previous chapter. For example, JE02.51A refers to a worksheet entry ("51A") discussed in Chapter 2 ("General Fund").

It is also necessary to categorize each reconciling item so that the items can be presented in the reconciliation in a manageable way.

The categorization scheme shown in Exhibits 14-1 and 14-2 is used for the balance sheet and the statement of changes in revenues, expenditures, and changes in fund balances. (The focus of the explanations in Exhibits 14-1 and 14-2 is from the fund financial statements to the government-wide financial statements.)

### EXHIBIT 14-1—CATEGORIZATION SCHEME

| Categories For Balance Sheet | Type of Reconciling Item |
|---|---|
| A | Capital assets are not reported in this fund financial statement because they are not current financial resources, but they are reported in the statement of net assets. |
| B | Certain long-term assets are not reported in this fund financial statement because they are not available to pay current-period expenditures, but they are reported as assets in the statement of net assets. |
| C | Certain liabilities (such as bonds payable and accrued expenses) are not reported in this fund financial statement because they are not due and payable, but they are presented as liabilities in the statement of net assets. |
| D | Assets and liabilities of certain Internal Service Funds related to governmental programs are not reported in this fund financial statement because they are presented on a different accounting basis, but they are presented as assets and liabilities in the statement of net assets. |

### EXHIBIT 14-2—CATEGORIZATION SCHEME

| Categories For Statements of Revenues, Expenditures, and Changes in Fund Balances | Type of Reconciling Item |
|---|---|
| AA | Capital outlays are reported as expenditures in this fund financial statement because they use current financial resources, but they are presented as assets in the statement of activities and depreciated |

Basic Financial Statements  14-17

|  | |
|---|---|
|  | over their estimated economic lives. The amount by which capital outlays ($20,019,000), which is made up of capital outlays reported in Capital Projects Funds of $13,900,000 and $6,120,000 of capital outlays reported in the General Fund, exceeds depreciation ($33,419,947) for the year. |
| BB | Revenues that are not available to pay current obligations are not reported in this fund financial statement, but they are presented as revenues in the statement of activities. |
| CC | The proceeds from the issuance of bonds provide current financial resources and are reported in this fund financial statement, but they are presented as liabilities in the statement of net assets. |
| DD | The net revenues (expenses) of certain Internal Service Funds related to governmental programs are not reported in this fund financial statement because they are presented on a different accounting basis (in the proprietary fund financial statements), but they are presented in the statement of activities. |
| EE | Generally expenditures recognized in this fund's financial statements are limited to only those that use current financial resources but expenses are recognized in the statement of activities when they are incurred. |
| FF | Gains and losses are not presented in this financial statement because they do not provided or use current financial resources, but they are presented in the statement of activities. |

Using the classification scheme in Exhibits 14-1 and 14-2, the specific worksheet entries presented earlier in this chapter are classified for the fund balance sheet reconciliation disclosure as follows:

| Fund balances per governmental funds financial statements | | | | | |
|---|---|---|---|---|---|
| | — | — | — | — | $16,749,056 |
| Entries | A | B | C | D | |
| JE02.51A | $ 352,155 | | (355,503) | | (3,348) |
| JE02.51B | | | 1,188,141 | | 1,188,141 |
| JE02.52 | | 6,000,000 | | | 6,000,000 |
| JE02.53 | 5,479,111 | | | | 5,479,111 |
| JE02.54 | (5,600,000) | | | | (5,600,000) |
| JE02.55 | (33,400,000) | | | | (33,400,000) |
| JE02.56 | 20,000,000 | | | | 20,000,000 |

**14-18** *The Financial Statements and Related Disclosures*

| Entries | A | B | C | D |
|---|---|---|---|---|
| JE02.57A | | | (520,000) | (520,000) |
| JE02.57B | | | 400,000 | 400,000 |
| JE02.57C | | | 60,000 | 60,000 |
| JE02.58 | | 1,400,000 | | 1,400,000 |
| JE02.59 | | 8,400 | | 8,400 |
| JE02.60 | 313,368,540 | | | 313,368,540) |
| JE02.61 | | | (5,197,652) | (5,197,652) |
| JE02.62 | | | (6,500,000) | (6,500,000) |
| JE03.19 | | 50,000 | | 50,000 |
| JE03.20 | | 20,000 | | 20,000 |
| JE04.25 | 11,100,000 | | | 11,100,000 |
| JE04.26 | | | (9,328,956) | (9,328,956) |
| JE04.27 | 1,500,000 | | | 1,500,000 |
| JE04.28 | 1,300,000 | | | 1,300,000 |
| JE04.29 | | | (3,000,000) | (3,000,000) |
| JE05.25 | | | (16,964,791) | (16,964,791) |
| JE05.26 | | | 750,000 | 750,000 |
| JE05.27 | | | 14,169 | 14,169 |
| JE05.28 | | | (559,737) | (559,737) |
| JE05.29 | | | 700,000 | 700,000 |
| JE05.30 | | | 500,000 | 500,000 |
| JE08.45 | | | | 4,077,456 | 4,077,456 |
| JE08.47 | | | | 1,811,500 | 1,811,500 |
| Net difference | $314,099,806 | $7,478,400 | $(38,814,329) | $5,888,956 | $288,652,833 |
| Net assets per government-wide financial statements | | | | | $305,401,889 |

The specific worksheet entries presented earlier in this chapter are classified for the statement of revenues, expenditures, and changes in fund balances classifications as follows:

| | | | | | | |
|---|---|---|---|---|---|---|
| Change in fund balances per statement of revenues, expenditures and changes in fund balances | | | | | | $2,256,556 |

| Entries | AA | BB | CC | DD | EE | FF |
|---|---|---|---|---|---|---|
| JE02.51A | (79,058) | | | 75,710 | | (3,348) |
| JE02.51B | | | | 1,188,141 | | 1,188,141 |
| JE02.52 | | 6,000,000 | | | | 6,000,000 |
| JE02.53 | 5,479,111 | | | | | 5,479,111 |
| JE02.54 | | | | | (5,600,000) | (5,600,000) |
| JE02.55 | (33,400,000) | | | | | (33,400,000) |
| JE02.56 | | | | | 20,000,000 | 20,000,000 |

| Entries | AA | BB | CC | DD | EE | FF |
|---|---|---|---|---|---|---|
| JE02.57A | | | | (520,000) | | (520,000) |
| JE02.57B | | | | 400,000 | | 400,000 |
| JE02.57C | | | 60,000 | | 60,000 | |
| JE02.58 | 1,400,000 | | | | 1,400,000 | |
| JE02.59 | 8,400 | | | | 8,400 | |
| JE02.60 | | | | | 0 | |
| JE02.61 | | | | | 0 | |
| JE02.62 | | | | | 0 | |
| JE03.19 | 50,000 | | | | 50,000 | |
| JE03.20 | 20,000 | | | | 20,000 | |
| JE04.25 | 11,100,000 | | | | | 11,100,000 |
| JE04.26 | | (9,328,956) | | | (9,328,956) | |
| JE04.27 | 1,500,000 | | | | | 1,500,000 |
| JE04.28 | 1,300,000 | | | | | 1,300,000 |
| JE04.29 | | (3,000,000) | | | (3,000,000) | |
| JE05.25 | | | | | 0 | |
| JE05.26 | | | | 750,000 | 750,000 | |
| JE05.27 | | | | 14,169 | 14,169 | |
| JE05.28 | | | | (559,737) | (559,737) | |
| JE05.29 | | | | 700,000 | 700,000 | |
| JE05.30 | | | | 500,000 | 500,000 | |
| JE08.45 | | | (2,512,544) | | (2,512,544) | |
| JE08.47 | | | 322,000 | | 322,000 | |
| Net difference | (14,099,947) | 7,478,400 | (12,328,956) | (2,190,544) | 2,608,283 | 14,400,000 | (4,132,764) |
| Change in net assets per statement of activities | | | | | | $(1,876,208) |

These foregoing balances by categories are used in the presentation of the fund financial statements presented later in this chapter.

## Reconciliations for Business-Type Activities

Often the totals in the business-type activities columns of the government-wide financial statements will be equal to the totals in the fund financial statements for Enterprise Funds, because the accrual basis of accounting is used to prepare the two different sets of financial statements. However, if balances related to an Internal Service Fund(s) are reflected in the government-wide financial statements, there must be a summary reconciliation between the fund financial statements and the government-wide financial statements. That is, the amount shown as the "total net assets" in the "total for Enterprise Funds" column on the fund balance sheets are reconciled to the "net assets" for business-type activities presented on the statement of net assets. Also, the amount shown as "change in net assets" in the total column for Enterprise Funds on the statement of revenues, expenses, and changes in fund net assets is reconciled to the "change in net assets" for business-type activities presented on the statement of activities.

Based on the continuing illustration used in this book, the balances to be reconciled are as follows:

|  | Net Assets | Change in Net Assets |
|---|---|---|
| Total balances for Enterprise Funds* | $121,041,500 | $25,774,000 |
| Total balances for business-type activities** | $125,378,044 | $25,314,544 |

\* These balances are from the proprietary fund financial statements presented later in this chapter.

\*\* These balances are from the government-wide financial statements (business-type activities) presented later in this chapter.

In order to explain the differences between the two sets of financial statements balances, the worksheet entries made to merge the balances of Internal Service Funds are as follows:

|  | Debits | Credits | Effects on Balances Net Assets | Change in Net Assets |
|---|---|---|---|---|
| Net asset balance per Enterprise Fund financial statements |  |  | $121,041,500 | $25,774,000 |
| **JE08.46** |  |  |  |  |
| Expenses—Centerville Municipal Airport | 327,872 |  |  |  |
| Expenses—Centerville Utilities Authority | 120,320 |  |  |  |
| Expenses—Centerville Parking Authority | 54,144 |  |  |  |
| Expenses—Centerville Toll Bridge | 45,120 |  |  |  |
| Internal balances |  | 547,456 | (547,456) | (547,456) |

|  | Debits | Credits | Effects on Balances Net Assets | Change in Net Assets |
|---|---|---|---|---|
| **JE08.48** | | | | |
| Cash | 22,000 | | | |
| Interest receivable | 1,000 | | | |
| Due from other funds | 427,000 | | | |
| Temporary investments | 12,000 | | | |
| Inventories | 20,000 | | | |
| Land and improvements | 1,750,000 | | | |
| Buildings | 1,600,000 | | | |
| Equipment | 2,960,000 | | | |
| Vehicles | 1,995,000 | | | |
| Expenses—Centerville Municipal Airport | | 73,000 | 73,000 | 73,000 |
| Accumulated depreciation | | 3,240,000 | | |
| Accounts payable and accrued expenses | | 75,000 | | |
| Compensated absences | | 17,000 | | |
| Claims and judgements | | 21,000 | | |
| Notes payable | | 550,000 | | |
| Interest and investment revenue | | 15,000 | 15,000 | 15,000 |
| Net assets | | 4,796,000 | 4,796,000 | |
| Net adjustment to reconcile | | | 4,336,544 | (459,456) |
| **Net asset balance per government-wide financial statements** | | | **$125,378,044** | **$25,314,544** |

Each of the above worksheet entries is taken from Chapter 8 ("Internal Service Funds"). In addition, each of the worksheet entries is classified to identify the nature of the worksheet entry based on the classification scheme discussed earlier in this chapter for governmental activities. The reconciling items for the Enterprise Funds are all related to Internal Service Fund categories (D and DD).

These balances by categories are used in the presentation of the fund financial statements presented later in this chapter.

## Components of Net Assets—Governmental Activities

Net assets represent the difference between a governmental entity's total assets and its total liabilities. The statement of net assets must identify the components of net assets, namely (1) invested in capital assets, net of related debt, (2) restricted net assets, and (3) unrestricted net assets.

Invested in capital assets (net of related debt) is the difference between (1) capital assets, net of accumulated depreciation, and (2) liabilities "attributable to the acquisition, construction, or improvement of those assets." Restricted net assets arise if either of the following conditions exists:

- Externally imposed by creditor (such as through debt covenants), grantors, contributors, or laws or regulations of other governments; or
- Imposed by law through constitutional provisions or enabling legislation.

Restricted net assets should be identified based on major categories that make up the restricted balance. These categories could include items such as net assets restricted for capital projects and for debt service. In some instances, net assets may be restricted on a permanent basis (in perpetuity). Under this circumstance, the restricted net assets are subdivided into expendable and nonexpendable restricted net assets.

Assets that are not classified as invested in capital assets (net of related debt) or restricted are included in the category unrestricted net assets. Portions of the entity's net assets may be identified by management to reflect tentative plans or commitments of governmental resources. The *tentative* plans or commitments may be related to items, such as plans to retire debt at some future date or to replace infrastructure or specified capital assets. Designated amounts are not the same as restricted amounts because designations represent planned actions, not actual commitments. For this reason, designated amounts should not be classified with restricted net assets, but rather should be reported as part of the unrestricted net asset component. In addition, designations cannot be disclosed as such on the face of the statement of net assets.

The components for net assets for the City of Centerville for governmental activities are determined in the following analysis:

Basic Financial Statements **14-23**

| Fund Balances | Capital Projects | Restricted for Debt Service | Other Purposes | Unrestricted | Invested in Capital Assets Net of Related Debt | Total |
|---|---|---|---|---|---|---|
| General Fund | | | | $12,330,600 | | $12,330,600 |
| Major funds: | | | | | | |
| Local Fuel Tax | | | $ 19,000 | | | 19,000 |
| West End Recreation Center | $2,936,000 | | | | | 2,936,000 |
| Nonmajor funds: | | | | | | |
| Special Services District | | | 29,500 | | | 29,500 |
| Easely Street Bridge Project | 729,956 | | | | | 729,956 |
| Bland Street Drainage Project | 193,000 | | | | | 193,000 |
| All Debt Service Funds | | $268,000 | | | | 268,000 |
| Cemetery Fund | - | - | 243,000 | - | - | 243,000 |
| Total fund balances | 3,858,956 | 268,000 | 291,500 | 12,330,600 | - | 16,749,056 |
| Accrual adjustments: | | | | | | |
| JE02.51A | | | | (24,290) | 20,942 | (3,348) |
| JE02.51B | | | | | 1,188,141 | 1,188,141 |
| JE02.52 | | | | 6,000,000 | | 6,000,000 |
| JE02.53 | | | | | 5,479,111 | 5,479,111 |
| JE02.54 | | | | | (5,600,000) | (5,600,000) |
| JE02.55 | | | | | (33,400,000) | (33,400,000) |
| JE02.56 | | | | | 20,000,000 | 20,000,000 |
| JE02.57A | | | | (520,000) | | (520,000) |
| JE02.57B | | | | 400,000 | | 400,000 |
| JE02.57C | | | | 60,000 | | 60,000 |
| JE02.58 | | | | 1,400,000 | | 1,400,000 |
| JE02.59 | | | | 8,400 | | 8,400 |
| JE02.60 | | | | | 313,368,540 | 313,368,540 |
| JE02.61 | | | | | (5,197,652) | (5,197,652) |
| JE02.62 | | | | (6,500,000) | | (6,500,000) |
| JE03.19 | | | 50,000 | | | 50,000 |
| JE03.20 | | | 20,000 | | | 20,000 |
| JE04.25 | | | | | 11,100,000 | 11,100,000 |
| JE04.26 | | | | | (9,328,956) | (9,328,956) |
| JE04.27 | | | | | 1,500,000 | 1,500,000 |
| JE04.28 | | | | | 1,300,000 | 1,300,000 |
| JE04.29 | | | | | (3,000,000) | (3,000,000) |
| JE05.25 | | | | | (16,964,791) | (16,964,791) |

**14-24**  The Financial Statements and Related Disclosures

| Fund Balances | Restricted for Capital Projects | Debt Service | Other Purposes | Unrestricted | Invested in Capital Assets Net of Related Debt | Total |
|---|---|---|---|---|---|---|
| JE05.26 | | | | | 750,000 | 750,000 |
| JE05.27 | | | | 14,169 | | 14,169 |
| JE05.28 | | | | (559,737) | | (559,737) |
| JE05.29 | | | | | 700,000 | 700,000 |
| JE05.30 | | | | | 500,000 | 500,000 |
| JE08.45 | | | | 1,767,456 | 2,310,000 | 4,077,456 |
| JE08.47 | | | | 136,500 | 1,675,000 | 1,811,500 |
| Net assets | $3,858,956 | $268,000 | $361,500 | $14,513,098 | $286,400,335 | $305,401,889 |

In the above analysis, interest accrued on capital debt and the amortization of discount and premium (see JE02.51A, JE05.17, and JE05.28) are not related to "net assets invested in capital assets, net of related debt." Also, part of the balance identified as "restricted for other purposes" includes the net assets of the Cemetery Fund (Permanent Fund), which are nonexpendable. The statement of net asset must identify any restricted net assets that are nonexpendable.

## Components of Net Assets—Business-Type Activities

The components of net assets for Enterprise Funds (as reported on the fund financial statements) are generally equal to the same components as reported on the statement of net assets. However, in the current illustration, the effects of merging an Internal Service Fund (Special Services Support Center) must be taken into consideration. The component for net assets for the City of Centerville for business-type activities is determined in the following analysis:

| NET ASSETS | Total Enterprise Fund | Internal Service Fund | Total |
|---|---|---|---|
| Invested in capital assets, net of related debt | $82,995,000 | $4,515,000 | $ 87,510,000 |
| Restricted | 37,362,000 | | 37,362,000 |
| Unrestricted | 684,500 | (178,456) | 506,044 |
| Total net assets | $121,041,500 | $4,336,544 | $125,378,044 |

## FINANCIAL STATEMENTS

Using the illustrations developed in this and in previous chapters, the City of Centerville presents the following financial statements:

- Statement of Net Assets (Exhibit 14-3)
- Statement of Activities (Exhibit 14-4)
- Balance Sheet—Governmental Funds (Exhibit 14-5)
- Reconciliation of the Balance Sheet of Governmental Funds to the Statement of Net Assets (Exhibit 14-6)
- Statement of Revenues, Expenditures, and Changes in Fund Balances—Governmental Funds (Exhibit 14-7)
- Reconciliation of the Statement of Revenues, Expenditures, and Changes in Fund Balances of Governmental Funds to the Statement of Activities (Exhibit 14-8)
- Statement of Net Assets-Proprietary Funds (Exhibit 14-9)
- Statement of Revenues, Expenses, and Changes in Fund Net Assets—Proprietary Funds (Exhibit 14-10)
- Statement of Cash Flows (Exhibit 14-11)
- Statement of Fiduciary Net Assets (Exhibit 14-12)
- Statement of Changes in Fiduciary Net Assets (Exhibit 14-13)

### EXHIBIT 14-3—STATEMENT OF NET ASSETS

**City of Centerville**
**Statement of Net Assets**
**June 30, 20X1**

|  | Primary Government |  |  |  |
|---|---|---|---|---|
|  | Governmental Activities | Business-Type Activities | Total | Component Units |
| **ASSETS** |  |  |  |  |
| Cash | $11,111,956 | $12,718,500 | $23,830,456 | $2,345,000 |
| Internal balances | (1,697,544) | 1,697,544 |  |  |
| Receivables (net) | 7,982,000 | 26,207,000 | 34,189,000 | 777,000 |
| Investments | 10,114,000 | 10,180,000 | 20,294,000 | 235,000 |
| Inventories | 33,000 | 206,000 | 239,000 | 122,000 |
| Capital assets: |  |  |  |  |
|   Land, improvements, and construction in progress | 143,700,000 | 45,855,000 | 189,555,000 | 17,500,000 |

## 14-26 The Financial Statements and Related Disclosures

|  | Primary Government |  |  |  |
|---|---|---|---|---|
|  | Governmental Activities | Business-Type Activities | Total | Component Units |
| Other capital assets, net of depreciation | 182,084,806 | 68,575,000 | 250,709,806 | 33,900,000 |
| Total assets | $353,328,218 | $165,439,044 | $518,767,262 | $54,879,000 |

**LIABILITIES**

| | | | | |
|---|---|---|---|---|
| Accounts payable and accrued expenses | $1,604,290 | $8,415,000 | $10,019,290 | $1,200,000 |
| Deferred revenue | 310,000 | | 310,000 | |
| Long-term liabilities: | | | | |
| Due within one year | 4,658,932 | 3,784,000 | 8,442,932 | 3,400,000 |
| Due in more than one year | 41,353,107 | 27,862,000 | 69,215,107 | 8,350,000 |
| Total liabilities | $47,926,329 | $40,061,000 | $87,987,329 | $20,179,000 |

**NET ASSETS**

| | | | | |
|---|---|---|---|---|
| Invested in capital assets, net of related debt | $285,830,477 | $87,510,000 | $373,340,477 | |
| Restricted for: | | | | |
| Capital projects | 3,858,956 | 20,000,000 | 23,858,956 | 3,500,000 |
| Debt service | 268,000 | 2,000,000 | 2,268,000 | — |
| Other purposes | 118,500 | 15,362,000 | 15,480,500 | 212,000 |
| Other purposes (non-expendable) | 243,000 | — | 243,000 | — |
| Unrestricted (deficit) | 15,082,956 | 506,044 | 15,589,000 | 30,988,000 |
| Total net assets | $305,401,889 | $125,378,044 | $430,779,933 | $34,700,000 |

# EXHIBIT 14-4—STATEMENT OF ACTIVITIES

**CITY OF CENTERVILLE**
**STATEMENT OF ACTIVITIES**
**FOR THE YEAR ENDED JUNE 30, 20X1**

| Functions: | Expenses | Program Revenues: Charges For Services | Program Revenues: Operating Grants and Contributions | Program Revenues: Capital Grants and Contributions | Net (Expense) Revenue and Chain Net Assets Primary Government: Governmental Activities | Net (Expense) Revenue and Chain Net Assets Primary Government: Business-Type Activities | Total | Component Units |
|---|---|---|---|---|---|---|---|---|
| **Primary government:** | | | | | | | | |
| **Governmental activities:** | | | | | | | | |
| General government | $53,931,629 | $355,000 | $34,000 | | $(53,542,629) | | $(53,542,629) | |
| Public safety | 22,836,931 | 202,000 | | | (22,634,931) | | (22,634,931) | |
| Streets | 21,187,633 | 150,000 | 4,570,000 | 2,000,000 | (14,467,633) | | (14,467,633) | |
| Recreation and parks | 7,621,871 | 135,000 | | 450,000 | (7,036,871) | | (7,036,871) | |
| Health and welfare | 9,579,427 | 4,000 | 50,000 | | (9,525,427) | | (9,525,427) | |
| Payment to school district | 32,000,000 | | | | (32,000,000) | | (32,000,000) | |
| Interest on long-term debt | 2,332,717 | | | | (2,332,717) | | (2,332,717) | |
| Total governmental activities | 149,490,208 | 846,000 | 4,654,000 | 2,450,000 | (141,540,208) | | (141,540,208) | |
| **Business-type activities:** | | | | | | | | |
| Airport | 203,594,872 | 227,060,000 | | 2,000,000 | | 25,465,128 | 25,465,128 | |
| Utilities | 38,557,320 | 36,010,000 | | 1,250,000 | | (1,297,320) | (1,297,320) | |
| Parking | 6,091,144 | 1,522,000 | | | | (4,569,144) | (4,569,144) | |
| Toll Bridge | 4,699,120 | 4,770,000 | 100,000 | 250,000 | | 420,880 | 420,880 | |
| Total business-type activities | 252,942,456 | 269,362,000 | 100,000 | 3,500,000 | | 20,019,544 | 20,019,544 | |
| Total primary government | $402,432,664 | $270,208,000 | $4,754,000 | $5,945,000,000 | (141,540,208) | 20,019,544 | (121,520,664) | |

## EXHIBIT 14-4 (Continued)

### NET (EXPENSE) REVENUE AND CHAIN NET ASSETS

|  | | PROGRAM REVENUES | | | PRIMARY GOVERNMENT | | | |
|---|---:|---:|---:|---:|---:|---:|---:|---:|
|  | Expenses | Charges For Services | Operating Grants and Contributions | Capital Grants and Contributions | Governmental Activities | Business-Type Activities | Total | Component Units |
| **Component units:** | | | | | | | | |
| Public school system | 45,700,000 | 1,200,000 | 6,200,000 | 3,800,000 | | | | $(34,500,000) |
| Municipal transit system | 9,300,000 | 6,700,000 | 1,200,000 | 750,000 | | | | (650,000) |
| Total component units | 55,000,000 | 7,900,000 | 7,400,000 | 4,550,000 | | | | (35,150,000) |
| **General revenues:** | | | | | | | | |
| Taxes: | | | | | | | | |
| Property taxes | | | | | 91,670,000 | | 91,670,000 | |
| Franchise taxes | | | | | 1,300,000 | | 1,300,000 | |
| Contributions to permanent funds | | | | | 22,000 | | 22,000 | |
| Payment to school district | | | | | | | | 32,000,000 |
| Grants and contributions not restricted to specific programs | | | | | 26,500,000 | | 26,500,000 | 1,950,000 |
| Unrestricted investment earnings | | | | | 294,000 | 1,655,000 | 1,949,000 | 125,000 |
| Miscellaneous | | | | | 18,000 | | 18,000 | 95,000 |
| Special item—gain on sale of parking lot | | | | | 20,000,000 | | 20,000,000 | |
| Extraordinary gain—donation of land from state | | | | | | 3,500,000 | 3,500,000 | |
| Transfers | | | | | (140,000) | 140,000 | | |
| Total general revenues, special items, extraordinary items and transfers | | | | | 139,664,000 | 5,295,000 | 144,959,000 | 34,170,000 |
| Change in net assets | | | | | (1,876,208) | 25,314,544 | 23,438,336 | (980,000) |
| Net assets—beginning | | | | | 307,278,097 | 100,063,500 | 407,341,597 | 35,750,000 |
| Net assets—ending | | | | | 305,401,889 | 125,378,044 | $430,779,933 | $34,770,000 |

## EXHIBIT 14-5—BALANCE-SHEET—GOVERNMENTAL FUNDS

Governmental Funds
Balance Sheet
June 30, 20X1

|  | General Fund | Local Fuel Tax Fund | West End Recreation Center Fund | Other Governmental Funds | Total Governmental Funds |
|---|---|---|---|---|---|
| **ASSETS** | | | | | |
| Cash | $ 9,440,000 | $42,000 | $ 19,000 | $ 527,456 | $10,028,456 |
| Temporary investments | | | 2,922,000 | 824,000 | 3,746,000 |
| Property taxes receivable (net) | 355,000 | | | 48,000 | 403,000 |
| Other receivables | 35,600 | 2,000 | | 15,000 | 52,600 |
| Investments | 6,090,000 | | | 244,000 | 6,334,000 |
| Inventories | 17,000 | | | | 17,000 |
| Total assets | $ 15,937,600 | $44,000 | $2,941,000 | $1,658,456 | $20,581,056 |
| **LIABILITIES AND FUND BALANCES** | | | | | |
| Liabilities: | | | | | |
| Accounts payable | 665,000 | 25,000 | 5,000 | 185,000 | 880,000 |
| Due to other funds | 2,642,000 | | | | 2,642,000 |
| Deferred revenue | 300,000 | | | 10,000 | 310,000 |
| Total liabilities | 3,607,000 | 25,000 | 5,000 | 195,000 | 3,832,000 |
| Fund balances: | | | | | |
| Reserved for: | | | | | |
| Inventories | 17,000 | | | | 17,000 |
| Encumbrances | 25,000 | | | | 25,000 |
| Debt service | | | | 268,000 | 268,000 |
| Other purposes | | | | 16,000 | 16,000 |
| Permanent endowment | | | | 243,000 | 243,000 |
| Unreserved | 12,288,600 | 19,000 | 2,936,000 | 936,456 | 16,180,056 |
| Unreserved, reported in nonmajor: | | | | | |
| Capital projects funds | | | | 16,000 | 16,000 |
| Total fund balances | 12,330,600 | 19,000 | 2,936,000 | 1,463,456 | 16,749,056 |
| Total liabilities and fund balances | $15,937,600 | $44,000 | $2,941,000 | $1,658,456 | $20,581,056 |

## EXHIBIT 14-6—RECONCILIATION OF THE BALANCE SHEET OF GOVERNMENTAL FUNDS TO THE STATEMENT OF NET ASSETS

**City of Centerville**
**Reconciliation of the Balance Sheet**
**of Governmental Funds**
**To the Statement of Net Assets**
**June 30, 20X1**

| | |
|---|---:|
| Total fund balances per fund financial statements | $ 16,749,056 |
| Amounts reported for governmental activities in the statement of net assets are different because: | |
| Capital assets are not reported in this fund financial statement because they are not current financial resources, but they are reported in the statement of net assets. | 314,099,806 |
| Certain long-term assets are not reported in this fund financial statement because they are not available to pay current-period expenditures, but they are reported in the statement of net assets. | 7,478,400 |
| Certain liabilities (such as bonds payable and accrued expenses) are not reported in this fund financial statement because they are not due and payable, but they are presented in the statement of net assets. | (38,814,329) |
| Assets and liabilities of certain Internal Service Funds related to governmental programs are not reported in this fund financial statement because they are presented on a different accounting basis, but they are presented in the statement of net assets. | 5,888,956 |
| Net assets for governmental activities | $305,401,889 |

## EXHIBIT 14-7—STATEMENT OF REVENUES, EXPENDITURES, AND CHANGES IN FUND BALANCES—GOVERNMENTAL FUNDS

### Governmental Funds
### Statement of Revenues, Expenditures, and Changes in Fund Balances
### June 30, 20X1

| | General Fund | Local Fuel Tax Fund | West End Recreation Center Fund | Other Governmental Funds | Total Governmental Funds |
|---|---|---|---|---|---|
| **REVENUES** | | | | | |
| Property taxes | $ 87,600,000 | | | $ 2,670,000 | $ 90,270,000 |
| Franchise taxes | 1,300,000 | | | | 1,300,000 |
| Intergovernmental grants | 20,500,000 | $4,500,000 | $450,000 | 2,000,000 | 27,450,000 |
| Charges for services | 537,600 | | | | 537,600 |
| Contributions | 50,000 | | | | 50,000 |
| Interest and investment revenue | 233,000 | 6,000 | 2,000 | 77,000 | 318,000 |
| Miscellaneous revenue | 4,800,000 | | | 40,000 | 4,840,000 |
| Total revenue | 115,020,600 | 4,506,000 | 452,000 | 4,787,000 | 124,765,600 |
| **EXPENDITURES** | | | | | |
| Current: | | | | | |
| General government | 33,888,213 | 210,000 | 25,000 | 1,219,000 | 35,342,213 |
| Public safety | 18,099,000 | | | | 18,099,000 |
| Streets | 11,894,500 | 3,990,000 | | 2,200,000 | 18,084,500 |
| Recreation and parks | 6,497,250 | | | | 6,497,250 |
| Health and welfare | 8,092,250 | | | | 8,092,250 |
| Education (component unit) | 32,000,000 | | | | 32,000,000 |
| Debt service: | | | | | |
| Principal | | | | 1,950,000 | 1,950,000 |
| Interest | | | | 1,174,000 | 1,174,000 |
| Capital outlays | | | 1,300,000 | 12,600,000 | 13,900,000 |
| Total expenditures | 110,471,213 | 4,200,000 | 1,325,000 | 19,143,000 | 135,139,213 |
| Excess (deficiency) of revenues over expenditures | 4,549,387 | 306,000 | (873,000) | (14,356,000) | (10,373,613) |

**14-32** *The Financial Statements and Related Disclosures*

| | General Fund | Local Fuel Tax Fund | West End Recreation Center Fund | Other Governmental Funds | Total Governmental Funds |
|---|---|---|---|---|---|
| **OTHER FINANCING SOURCES (USES):** | | | | | |
| Long-term debt issued | | | 3,000,000 | 10,000,000 | 13,000,000 |
| Discount on long-term debt issued | | | | (671,044) | (671,044) |
| Execution of capital leases | 431,213 | | | | 431,213 |
| Transfers in | 50,000 | | 300,000 | 5,295,000 | 5,645,000 |
| Transfers out | (5,475,000) | (300,000) | | | (5,775,000) |
| Total other financing sources and uses | (4,993,787) | (300,000) | 3,300,000 | 14,623,956 | 12,630,169 |
| Net change in fund balances | (444,400) | 6,000 | 2,427,000 | 267,956 | 2,256,556 |
| Fund balances—beginning | 12,775,000 | 13,000 | 509,000 | 1,195,500 | 14,492,500 |
| Fund balances—ending | $12,330,600 | $19,000 | $2,936,000 | $1,463,456 | $16,749,056 |

---

**EXHIBIT 14-8—RECONCILIATION OF THE STATEMENT OF REVENUES, EXPENDITURES, AND CHANGES IN FUND BALANCES OF GOVERNMENTAL FUNDS TO THE STATEMENT OF ACTIVITIES**

**City of Centerville**
**Reconciliation of the Statement of Revenues, Expenditures, and Changes in Fund Balances of Governmental Funds**
**To the Statement of Activities**
**For the Year Ended June 30, 20X1**

Net change in total fund balances per fund financial statements $ 2,256,556

Amounts reported for governmental activities in the statement of activities are different because:

Capital outlays are reported as expenditures in this fund financial statement because they use current financial resources, but they are presented as assets in the statement of activities and depreciated over their estimated economic lives. The amount by which capital outlays ($20,019,000), which is made up of capital outlays reported in Capital Projects Funds of $13,900,000 and $6,120,000 of capital outlays reported in the General

| | | |
|---|---|---|
| Fund exceeds depreciation ($33,419,947) for the year. | | (14,099,947) |
| Revenues that are not available to pay current obligations are not reported in this fund financial statement, but they are presented in the statement of activities. | | 7,478,400 |
| The proceeds from the issuance of bonds provide current financial resources and are reported in this fund financial statement, but they are presented as liabilities in the statement of net assets. | | (12,328,956) |
| The net revenues (expenses) of certain Internal Service Funds related to governmental programs are not reported in this fund financial statement because they are presented on a different accounting basis, but they are presented in the statement of activities. | | (2,190,544) |
| Generally expenditures recognized in this fund's financial statements are limited to only those that use current financial resources, but expenses are recognized in the statement of activities when they are incurred. | | 2,608,283 |
| Gains or losses are not presented in this financial statement because they do not provided or use current financial resources, but they are presented in the statement of activities. | | 14,400,000 |
| Change in net assets of governmental activities | | $ (1,876,208) |

### EXHBIT 14-9—STATEMENT OF NET ASSETS—PROPRIETARY FUNDS

**Proprietary Funds**
**Statement of Net Assets**
**June 30, 20X1**

| | Centerville Utilities Authority | Centerville Municipal Airport | Other Enterprise Funds | Total | Internal Service Funds |
|---|---|---|---|---|---|
| **ASSETS** | | | | | |
| Current assets: | | | | | |
| Cash | $ 230,000 | $10,963,000 | $1,503,500 | $12,696,500 | $1,105,500 |
| Interest receivable | 50,000 | 200,000 | 6,000 | 256,000 | 4,000 |
| Accounts receivable (net) | 7,550,000 | 18,000,000 | | 25,550,000 | |

**14-34** *The Financial Statements and Related Disclosures*

|  | Centerville Utilities Authority | Centerville Municipal Airport | Other Enterprise Funds | Total | Internal Service Funds |
|---|---|---|---|---|---|
| Due from other funds | 2,000,000 | 400,000 |  | 2,400,000 | 824,000 |
| Due from other governments | 100,000 | 300,000 |  | 400,000 | 45,000 |
| Temporary investments | 55,000 | 10,050,000 | 63,000 | 10,168,000 | 46,000 |
| Inventories | 75,000 | 55,000 | 56,000 | 186,000 | 36,000 |
| Total current assets | 10,060,000 | 39,968,000 | 1,628,500 | 51,656,500 | 2,060,500 |
| Noncurrent assets: |  |  |  |  |  |
| Construction in progress | 200,000 | 23,500,000 | 85,000 | 23,785,000 |  |
| Land and improvements | 5,200,000 | 13,200,000 | 1,920,000 | 20,320,000 | 4,500,000 |
| Superstructure |  |  | 1,400,000 | 1,400,000 |  |
| Distribution and collection systems | 46,300,000 |  |  | 46,300,000 |  |
| Runways and tarmacs |  | 27,500,000 |  | 27,500,000 |  |
| Buildings | 14,450,000 | 33,200,000 | 2,730,000 | 50,380,000 | 4,600,000 |
| Equipment | 4,600,000 | 7,200,000 | 195,000 | 11,995,000 | 10,160,000 |
| Vehicles | 1,660,000 | 2,500,000 | 937,000 | 5,097,000 | 10,338,000 |
| Less accumulated depreciation | (54,395,000) | (20,255,000) | (2,762,000) | (77,412,000) | (12,848,000) |
| Total noncurrent assets | 18,015,000 | 86,845,000 | 4,505,000 | 109,365,000 | 16,750,000 |
| Total assets | $28,075,000 | $126,813,000 | $6,133,500 | $161,021,500 | $18,810,500 |
| **LIABILITIES** |  |  |  |  |  |
| Current liabilities: |  |  |  |  |  |
| Accounts payable and accrued expenses | $ 4,300,000 | $ 3,900,000 | $ 140,000 | $ 8,340,000 | $ 250,000 |
| Due to other funds | 35,000 | 512,000 | 35,000 | 582,000 |  |
| Compensated absences | 21,000 | 15,000 | 5,000 | 41,000 | 10,000 |
| Claims and judgements | 17,000 | 25,000 | 9,000 | 51,000 | 13,000 |
| Notes payable | 70,000 |  | 40,000 | 110,000 | 1,700,000 |
| Revenue bonds— Terminal A |  | 2,000,000 |  | 2,000,000 |  |
| Revenue bonds— Terminal B |  | 500,000 |  | 500,000 |  |
| Bonds payable | 850,000 |  | 20,000 | 870,000 |  |
| Total current liabilities | 5,293,000 | 6,952,000 | 249,000 | 12,494,000 | 1,973,000 |
| Noncurrent liabilities: |  |  |  |  |  |
| Compensated absences | 63,000 | 118,000 | 8,000 | 189,000 | 22,000 |

|  | Centerville Utilities Authority | Centerville Municipal Airport | Other Enterprise Funds | Total | Internal Service Funds |
|---|---|---|---|---|---|
| Claims and judgements | 212,000 | 170,000 | 25,000 | 407,000 | 40,000 |
| Notes payable | 260,000 | 7,700,000 | 20,000 | 7,980,000 | 6,550,000 |
| Revenue bonds—Terminal A |  | 8,000,000 |  | 8,000,000 |  |
| Revenue bonds—Terminal B |  | 3,500,000 |  | 3,500,000 |  |
| Bonds payable | 6,850,000 |  | 560,000 | 7,410,000 |  |
| Total noncurrent liabilities | 7,385,000 | 19,488,000 | 613,000 | 27,486,000 | 6,612,000 |
| Total liabilities | 12,678,000 | 26,440,000 | 862,000 | 39,980,000 | 8,585,000 |
| **NET ASSETS** |  |  |  |  |  |
| Invested in capital assets, net of related debt | 9,985,000 | 69,145,000 | 3,865,000 | 82,995,000 | 8,500,000 |
| Restricted: |  |  |  |  |  |
| Capital projects | 2,000,000 | 17,000,000 | 1,000,000 | 20,000,000 |  |
| Debt service | 500,000 | 1,450,000 | 50,000 | 2,000,000 |  |
| Other | 2,750,000 | 12,445,000 | 167,000 | 15,362,000 |  |
| Unrestricted | 162,000 | 333,000 | 189,500 | 684,500 | 1,725,500 |
| Total net assets | $ 15,397,000 | $100,373,000 | $5,271,500 | $121,041,500 | $10,225,500 |

| | |
|---|---|
| Some amounts reported for business-type activities in the statement of net assts are different because certain Internal Service Fund assets and liabilities are included with business-type activities | 4,336,544 |
| Net assets of business-type activities | $125,378,044 |

## EXHIBIT 14-10—STATEMENT OF REVENUES, EXPENSES, AND CHANGES IN FUND NET ASSETS—PROPRIETARY FUNDS

### Proprietary Funds Statement of Revenues, Expenses, and Changes in Fund Net Assets
### For the Year Ended June 30, 20X1

|  | Centerville Utilities Authority | Centerville Municipal Airport | Other Enterprise Funds | Total | Internal Service Funds |
|---|---|---|---|---|---|
| **OPERATING REVENUES** |  |  |  |  |  |
| Charges for services | $36,000,000 | $175,000,000 | $6,250,000 | $217,250,000 | $13,450,000 |
| Charges for services—rental income—security for Terminal A revenue bonds |  | 30,000,000 |  | 30,000,000 |  |

|  | Centerville Utilities Authority | Centerville Municipal Airport | Other Enterprise Funds | Total | Internal Service Funds |
|---|---|---|---|---|---|
| Charges for services—rental income—security for Terminal B revenue bonds | | 22,000,000 | | 22,000,000 | |
| Miscellaneous | 10,000 | 60,000 | 42,000 | 112,000 | 17,000 |
| Total operating revenues | 36,010,000 | 227,060,000 | 6,292,000 | 269,362,000 | 13,467,000 |
| **OPERATING EXPENSES** | | | | | |
| Personal services | 22,022,000 | 161,025,000 | 7,804,000 | 190,851,000 | 6,926,000 |
| Contractual services | 11,220,000 | 33,550,000 | 1,680,000 | 46,450,000 | 2,100,000 |
| Repairs and maintenance | 700,000 | 2,100,000 | 450,000 | 3,250,000 | 1,650,000 |
| Other supplies and expenses | 729,000 | 1,795,000 | 230,000 | 2,754,000 | 366,000 |
| Insurance claims and expenses | 21,000 | 100,000 | 13,000 | 134,000 | 29,000 |
| Depreciation | 3,025,000 | 3,370,000 | 456,000 | 6,851,000 | 5,582,000 |
| Miscellaneous | 5,000 | 70,000 | 33,000 | 108,000 | 22,000 |
| Total operating expenses | 37,722,000 | 202,010,000 | 10,666,000 | 250,398,000 | 16,675,000 |
| Operating income (loss) | (1,712,000) | 25,050,000 | (4,374,000) | 18,964,000 | (3,208,000) |
| **NONOPERATING REVENUES (EXPENSES)** | | | | | |
| Interest and investment revenue | 400,000 | 1,200,000 | 40,000 | 1,640,000 | 25,000 |
| Interest | (450,000) | (1,220,000) | -33,000 | (1,703,000) | (309,000) |
| Operating grants and contributions | | 100,000 | 100,000 | 370,000 | |
| Miscellaneous | (110,000) | (265,000) | 8,000 | (367,000) | (8,000) |
| Total nonoperating revenue (expenses) | (160,000) | (285,000) | 115,000 | (330,000) | 78,000 |
| Income (loss) before capital contributions and transfers | (1,872,000) | 24,765,000 | (4,259,000) | 18,634,000 | (3,130,000) |
| Capital contributions | 1,250,000 | 2,000,000 | 250,000 | 3,500,000 | 490,000 |
| Transfers in | | | 140,000 | 140,000 | 40,000 |
| Transfers out | | | | | (50,000) |

|  | Centerville Utilities Authority | Centerville Municipal Airport | Other Enterprise Funds | Total | Internal Service Funds |
|---|---|---|---|---|---|
| Special item—gain on sale of parking lot | | | 3,500,000 | 3,500,000 | |
| Change in net assets | (622,000) | 26,765,000 | (369,000) | 25,774,000 | (2,650,000) |
| Total net assets—beginning | 16,019,000 | 73,608,000 | 5,640,500 | 95,267,500 | 12,875,500 |
| Total net assets—ending | $15,397,000 | $100,373,000 | $5,271,500 | $121,041,500 | $10,225,500 |

Some amounts reported for business-type activities in the statement of activities are different because the net revenue (expense) of certain Internal Service Funds is reported with business-type activities. (459,456)

Change in net assets of business-type activities $ 25,314,544

## EXHIBIT 14-11—STATEMENT OF CASH FLOWS—PROPRIETARY FUNDS

### Proprietary Funds
### Statement of Cash Flows
### For the Year Ended June 30, 20X1

|  | Centerville Utilities Authority | Centerville Municipal Airport | Other Enterprise Funds | Total | Internal Service Funds |
|---|---|---|---|---|---|
| **CASH FLOWS FROM OPERATING ACTIVITIES** | | | | | |
| Receipts from customers | $34,000,000 | $214,000,000 | $6,250,000 | $254,250,000 | $12,811,000 |
| Payments to suppliers | (12,112,000) | (36,425,000) | (2,151,000) | (50,688,000) | (4,185,000) |
| Payments to employees | (19,013,000) | (158,017,000) | (7,732,000) | (184,762,000) | (6,747,000) |
| Internal activity-payments to other funds | (200,0000) | (3,140,000) | (156,000) | (3,496,000) | |
| Other receipts (payments) | 5,000 | (10,0000) | 1,000 | (4,000) | (25,000) |
| Net cash provided by operating activities | 2,680,000 | 16,408,000 | (3,788,000) | 15,300,000 | 1,854,000 |
| **CASH FLOWS FROM NONCAPITAL FINANCING ACTIVITIES** | | | | | |
| Subsidies and transfers from (to) other funds and state government | | | 240,000 | 240,000 | 360,000 |

## 14-38 The Financial Statements and Related Disclosures

| | Centerville Utilities Authority | Centerville Municipal Airport | Other Enterprise Funds | Total | Internal Service Funds |
|---|---|---|---|---|---|
| **CASH FLOWS FROM CAPITAL AND RELATED FINANCING ACTIVITIES** | | | | | |
| Proceeds from the issuance of capital debt | 2,120,000 | 3,200,000 | | 5,320,000 | 3,400,000 |
| Capital contributions | 1,250,000 | 1,700,000 | 280,000 | 3,230,000 | 490,000 |
| Acquisitions of capital assets | (5,350,000) | (8,800,000) | (590,000) | (14,740,000) | (6,040,000) |
| Proceeds from sale of capital assets | 500,000 | 420,000 | 5,055,000 | 5,975,000 | 845,000 |
| Principal paid on capital debt | (1,740,000) | (2,500,000) | (40,000) | (4,280,000) | (1,100,000) |
| Interest paid on capital debt | (450,000) | (1,220,000) | (33,000) | (1,703,000) | (309,000) |
| Net cash (used) by capital and related financing activities | (3,670,000) | (7,200,000) | 4,672,000 | (6,198,000) | (2,714,000) |
| **CASH FLOWS FROM INVESTING ACTIVITIES** | | | | | |
| Loans to other funds | (2,000,000) | (400,000) | | (2,400,000) | |
| Loans to other governments | (100,000) | | | (100,000) | |
| Interest and dividends | 365,000 | 1,055,000 | 39,500 | 1,459,500 | 37,500 |
| Purchase of investments | (15,000) | (50,000) | (30,000) | (95,000) | |
| Net cash provided (used) by investing activities | (1,750,000) | 605,000 | 9,500 | (1,135,500) | 37,500 |
| Net increase (decrease) in cash | (2,740,000) | 9,813,000 | 1,133,500 | 8,206,500 | (462,500) |
| Balances— beginning of year | 2,970,000 | 1,150,000 | 370,000 | 4,490,000 | 1,568,000 |
| Balances— end of year | 230,000 | 10,963,000 | 1,503,500 | 12,696,500 | 1,105,500 |
| **Reconciliation of operating income (loss) to net cash provided (used) by operating activities:** | | | | | |
| Operating income (loss) | $(1,712,000) | $25,050,000 | $(4,374,000) | $18,964,000 | $(3,208,000) |

|  | Centerville Utilities Authority | Centerville Municipal Airport | Other Enterprise Funds | Total | Internal Service Funds |
|---|---|---|---|---|---|
| Adjustments: | | | | | |
| Depreciation expense | 3,025,000 | 3,370,000 | 456,000 | 6,851,000 | 5,582,000 |
| Change in assets and liabilities: | | | | | |
| Receivables, net | (1,850,000) | (13,000,000) | | (14,850,000) | (639,000) |
| Inventories | (21,000) | (5,000) | (10,000) | (36,000) | (9,000) |
| Accounts and accrued liabilities | 3,238,000 | 993,000 | 140,000 | 4,371,000 | 128,000 |
| Net cash provided (used) by operating activities | $ 2,680,000 | $ 16,408,000 | $(3,788,000) | $ 15,300,000 | $ 1,854,000 |

## EXHIBIT 14-12—STATEMENT OF FIDUCIARY NET ASSETS

### City of Centerville
### Statement of Fiduciary Net Assets
### Fiduciary Funds
### June 30, 20X1

|  | Employee Retirement Fund | Private-Purpose Trust Fund | Agency Fund |
|---|---|---|---|
| **ASSETS** | | | |
| Cash | $ 4,244,000 | $ 27,000 | $ 35,000 |
| Accrued interest receivable | 31,000 | | |
| Investments in debt securities | 11,022,000 | 459,000 | |
| Investment in marketable equity securities | 22,463,000 | | |
| Total Assets | $37,760,000 | $486,000 | $ 35,000 |
| **LIABILTIES** | | | |
| Accounts payable and accrued expenses | $ 29,000 | $ 5,000 | $ 35,000 |
| Refunds payable and other liabilities | 25,000 | | |
| Total Liabilities | $ 54,000 | 5,000 | $ 35,000 |

|  | Employee Retirement Fund | Private-Purpose Trust Fund | Agency Fund |
|---|---|---|---|
| **NET ASSETS** |  |  |  |
| Held in trust for pension benefits and other purposes | $37,706,000 | $481,000 |  |

## EXHIBIT 14-13—STATEMENT OF CHANGES IN FIDUCIARY NET ASSETS

**City of Centerville**
**Statement of Changes in Fiduciary Net Assets**
**Fiduciary Funds**
**For the Year Ended June 30, 20X1**

|  | Employee Retirement Fund | Private-Purpose Trust Fund |
|---|---|---|
| **ADDITIONS** |  |  |
| Contributions by: |  |  |
| City of Centerville | $ 7,000,000 | $ 10,000 |
| Plan members/individuals | 2,700,000 | 30,000 |
| Total Contributions | 9,700,000 | 40,000 |
| Interest and investment revenue | 486,000 | 49,000 |
| Total additions | 10,186,000 | 89,000 |
| **DEDUCTIONS** |  |  |
| Benefits paid | 4,200,000 | 57,000 |
| Refunds of contributions | 100,000 |  |
| Administrative expenses | 349,000 |  |
| Total deductions | 4,649,000 | 57,000 |
| Change in net assets | 5,537,000 | 32,000 |
| Net assets—beginning of the year | 32,169,000 | 449,000 |
| Net assets—end of the year | $37,706,000 | $481,000 |

The disclosures and required supplementary information established by GASB-34 are developed in Chapter 15.

# CHAPTER 15
# MANAGEMENT'S DISCUSSION AND ANALYSIS, OTHER REQUIRED SUPPLEMENTARY INFORMATION, AND NOTES

## CONTENTS

| | |
|---|---|
| Introduction | 15-2 |
| Management's Discussion and Analysis | 15-2 |
| Nature and Structure of MD&A | 15-2 |
| Budgetary Comparison Schedules | 15-4 |
| Certain Note Disclosures—Capital Assets and Long-Term Liabilities | 15-8 |
| Capital Asset Disclosures | 15-8 |
| Long-Term Liabilities Disclosures | 15-12 |
| Appendix 15: MD&A—City of Centerville | 15-15 |
| Basic Financial Statements | 15-15 |
| Government-Wide Statements | 15-15 |
| Fund Financial Statements | 15-16 |
| Governmental Funds | 15-17 |
| Proprietary Funds | 15-17 |
| Fiduciary Funds | 15-18 |
| Overview of the City's Financial Position and Operations | 15-20 |
| Governmental Activities | 15-22 |
| Business-Type Activities | 15-26 |
| Analysis of Balances and Transactions of Individual Funds | 15-26 |
| General Budgetary Funds Highlights | 15-27 |
| Capital Asset and Debt Administration | 15-30 |
| Capital Assets | 15-30 |
| Long-Term Obligations | 15-31 |

Relevant Current Economic Factors,
　　Decisions, and Conditions　　　　　　　　　　　　**15-32**
Request for Information　　　　　　　　　　　　　　**15-33**

# INTRODUCTION

GASB-34 requires that the following information be presented in a governmental entity's financial statements:

- Management's Discussion and Analysis Information (pars. 8–11)
- Budgetary Comparison Schedules (pars. 130–131)
- Certain notes to the financial statements related to capital assets and long-term debt (pars. 116–117)

## MANAGEMENT'S DISCUSSION AND ANALYSIS

GASB-34 significantly changes how governmental entities present information in their financial statements. One of the new requirements established by GASB-34 is the introduction of management's discussion and analysis (MD&A) as an integral part of an entity's financial report. The purpose of this section is to discuss and illustrate the MD&A requirements established by the GASB.

> ▶ **NEW STANDARD:** Although the SEC has required public companies to present MD&A for many years, the GASB's requirement for a similar presentation is new to governmental financial reporting.

### Nature and Structure of MD&A

GASB-34 requires that a governmental entity's basic financial statements be preceded by MD&A, which the GASB identifies as required supplementary information (RSI). The purpose of MD&A is to "provide an objective and easily readable analysis of the government's financial activities based on currently known facts, decisions, or conditions." "Currently known facts" are "information that management is aware of as of the date of the auditor's report."

MD&A should portray a broad analysis of a governmental entity's short-term and long-term activities, based on information presented in the financial report and fiscal policies that have been adopted by the governmental entity. Although the analysis provided by management should be directed to current-year results in comparison with the previous year's results, the emphasis should be on the current year. In an attempt to make the information understandable to constituents, the governmental entities should consider using graphs, multicolor presentations, or other presentation strategies.

The MD&A should focus on the primary government's activities (both governmental and business-type activities) and distinguish between its activities and its discretely presented component units. The GASB emphasizes that management of the governmental entity should see the MD&A section of the financial report as an opportunity to communicate with interested parties and warns against preparing boilerplate material that adds little insight into the financial position and activity of the government.

GASB-34 requires that MD&A include relevant information about the following categories:

- Brief discussion of the basic financial statements
- Presentation of condensed financial information
- Analysis of the overall financial position and results of operations
- Analysis of balances and transactions of individual funds
- Analysis of significant budget variations
- Discussion of significant capital assets and long-term debt activity
- Description of currently known facts

> ▶ **NEW STANDARD:** In order to achieve the objectives of MD&A, GASB-34 requires that "at a minimum, MD&A should include" information about the above broad components. Some readers interpreted this requirement to mean that MD&A had to include at least these eight components but that a financial statement preparer was free to add other components. GASB-37 (Basic Financial Statements—and Management's Discussion and Analysis—for State and Local Governments: Omnibus) points out that the language in paragraph 11 should have been interpreted to mean that "the information presented should be confined to the topics discussed in a through h."

The MD&A illustration in Appendix 15 is based on the example developed in the previous chapters.

> **OBSERVATION:** GASB-34 also requires that MD&A include a discussion of the modified depreciation approach if that approach is employed by a governmental entity. This illustration assumes that a governmental entity does not use the modified depreciation approach, but rather records depreciation expense on all infrastructure assets.

## BUDGETARY COMPARISON SCHEDULES

GASB-34 requires that a budgetary comparison schedules for the General Fund and each major Special Revenue Fund that has a legally adopted annual budget be presented as RSI. The schedule should include columns for the following:

- The original budget
- The final appropriated budget
- Actual results (presented on the government's budgetary basis as defined in NCGA-1, paragraph 154)

> ▶ **NEW STANDARD:** Prior to the issuance of GASB-34, NCGA-1 (Governmental Accounting and Financial Reporting Principles) required that a governmental entity present a "combined statement of revenues, expenditures and changes in fund balances—budget and actual" for each governmental fund type that had an annual appropriated budget.

The following budgetary descriptions are established by the GASB-34:

- *Original budget*—The first complete appropriated budget. The original budget may be adjusted by reserves, transfers, allocations, supplemental appropriations, and other legally authorized legislative and executive changes before the beginning of the fiscal year. The original budget should also include the actual appropriation amount automatically carried over from prior years by law.
- *Final budget*—The original budget adjusted by all reserves, transfers, allocations, supplemental appropriations and other legally authorized legislative and executive changes applicable to the fiscal year, whenever signed into law or otherwise legally authorized.
- *Appropriated budget*—The expenditure authority created by the appropriation bills or ordinances that are signed into law and related estimated revenues.

The GASB encourages (but does not require) governmental entities to present an additional column that reflects the differences between the final budget and the actual amounts. An additional column may present the differences between the original budget and the final budget.

> **OBSERVATION:** The comparative budgetary information described above can be presented as a basic financial statement rather than as RSI (schedule presentation).

The comparative budgetary information may be presented "using the same format, terminology, and classifications as the budget document, or using the format, terminology, and classifications in a statement of revenues, expenditures, and changes in fund balances." In either case, there must be a reconciliation (presented in a separate schedule or in notes to the RSI) between the budgetary information and the GAAP information (as discussed in NCGAI-10). Any excess of expenditures over appropriations in an individual fund must be disclosed in a note to the RSI as required by NCGAI- 6, paragraph 4. If the governmental entity presents the comparative budgetary information as a basic financial statement, the note related to the excess of expenditures over appropriations must be reported as a note to the financial statements rather than as a note to RSI.

The following is an illustration of a budgetary comparison schedule for the General Fund and a reconciliation between the budgetary basis and the GAAP basis:

**OBSERVATION:** It is assumed that the major Special Revenue Fund (Local Fuel Tax Fund) is not required to have a legally adopted annual budget.

Required Supplementary Information
City of Centerville
Budgetary Comparison Schedule—General Fund
For the Year Ended June 30, 20X1

|  | Budgetary Amounts Original | Final | Actual Amounts (See Note A) | Variance with Final Budget Positive (Negative) |
|---|---|---|---|---|
| Budgetary fund balance beginning of year | $13,478,000 | $12,748,000 | $12,748,000 | |
| **Resources (inflows):** | | | | |
| Property taxes | 87,000,000 | 87,100,000 | 87,600,000 | $ 500,000 |
| Franchise taxes | 1,300,000 | 1,400,000 | 1,300,000 | (100,000) |
| Intergovernmental grants | 19,000,000 | 21,000,000 | 20,500,000 | (500,000) |
| Charges for services | 500,000 | 550,000 | 537,600 | (12,400) |
| Contributions | | | 50,000 | 50,000 |
| Interest and investment revenue | 240,000 | 250,000 | 233,000 | (17,000) |

|  | Budgetary Amounts Original | Budgetary Amounts Final | Actual Amounts (See Note A) | Variance with Final Budget Positive (Negative) |
|---|---|---|---|---|
| Miscellaneous revenue | 4,800,000 | 5,000,000 | 4,800,000 | (200,000) |
| Transfers from other funds |  |  | 50,000 | 50,000 |
| Amounts available for appropriation | 126,318,000 | 128,048,000 | 127,818,600 | (229,400) |
| **Charges to appropriations (outflows):** |  |  |  |  |
| General government | 33,500,000 | 33,302,885 | 33,289,885 | 13,000 |
| Public safety | 18,000,000 | 18,137,628 | 18,036,628 | 101,000 |
| Streets | 11,200,000 | 11,868,814 | 11,863,314 | 5,500 |
| Recreation and parks | 6,500,000 | 6,584,407 | 6,481,657 | 102,750 |
| Health and welfare | 8,000,000 | 8,084,407 | 8,076,657 | 7,750 |
| Interest | 311,859 | 311,859 | 311,859 | 0 |
| Education (component unit) | 30,000,000 | 32,000,000 | 32,000,000 | 0 |
| Transfers to other funds | 5,300,000 | 5,500,000 | 5,475,000 | 25,000 |
| Total charges to appropriations | 112,811,859 | 115,790,000 | 115,535,000 | 255,000 |
| **Budgetary fund balance, end of year** | $ 13,506,141 | $ 12,258,000 | $ 12,283,600 | $ 25,600 |

Requires Supplementary Information
Budgetary Comparison Schedule
Note to Required Supplementary Information

General Fund

**NOTE A: Explanation of Differences Between Budgetary Inflows and Outflows and GAAP Revenues and Expenditures**

**Sources/Inflow of Resources:**

Actual amounts (budgetary basis) "available for appropriation" from the budgetary comparison schedule         $127,818,600

|  | General Fund |
|---|---:|
| Differences—Budget to GAAP | |
| The fund balance at the beginning of the year is a budgetary resource but is not a current-year revenue for financial reporting purposes. | (12,748,000) |
| Transfers from other funds are inflows of budgetary resources but are not revenues for financial reporting purposes. | (50,000) |
| Total revenues as reported on the statement of revenues, expenditures, and changes in fund balances—governmental funds | 115,020,600 |
| **Uses/Outflows of Resources** | |
| Actual amounts (budgetary basis) "total charges to appropriations": from the budgetary comparison schedule | 115,535,000 |
| Differences—budget to GAAP: | |
| The city budgets for purchases of inventories on the cash basis, rather than on the modified accrual basis. | (5,000) |
| Encumbrances for certain contract expenditures ordered but not received are reported in the year the order is placed for budgetary purposes and in the year the resources are received for financial reporting purposes. | (15,000) |
| Capital leases executed during a year are not reported as expenditures for budgetary purposes, but are reported as program expenditures for financial reporting purposes. | 431,213 |
| Transfers to other funds are outflows of budgetary resources but are not expenditures for financial reporting purposes. | (5,475,000) |
| Total expenditures as reported on the statement of revenues, expenditures, and changes in fund balances—governmental funds | $110,471,213 |

■ **CONTINUING STANDARD:** GASB-34 continued the requirement that there be reconciliation between the budgetary information and the GAAP-based information.

▶ **NEW STANDARD:** Paragraph 131 of GASB-34 establishes disclosure requirements for budgetary comparison schedules, which are required supplementary information. One of the requirements states that any excess of expenditures over appropriations in an individual fund must be disclosed. The question has arisen as to whether the required disclosure applies to only those funds that are presented in the budgetary comparison schedule. GASB-37 (Basic Financial Statements—and Management's Discussion and Analysis—for State and Local Governments: Omnibus) clarifies the standards established by GASB-34 by limiting the disclosures related to budgetary comparison schedules to the funds that are part of the required supplementary information.

▶ **NEW STANDARD:** The appendix to NCGAI-6 recommends that the financial statements include a description of general budgetary policies. To comply with this recommendation, some governmental entities disclose their budgetary calendar and the legal level of budgetary control. GASB-38 (Certain Financial Statement Note Disclosures) concludes that general budget policies not be included as part of the appendix to NCGAI-6. The GASB believes that sufficient presentation of budgetary information is achieved by the requirements established by previously NCGA pronouncements and GASB-34. These presentation requirements include (1) budgetary comparison schedules, (2) reconciliation of budgetary information to GAAP information, (3) disclosure of the budgetary basis of accounting, and (4) disclosure of violations of legal provisions.

## CERTAIN NOTE DISCLOSURES— CAPITAL ASSETS AND LONG-TERM LIABILITIES

In order to support information included in a governmental entity's statement of net assets prepared on a government-wide basis, disclosures related to capital assets and long-term liabilities are included in the governmental entity's notes. The disclosures should observe the following guidance:

- The presentations should be based on major classes of capital assets and long-term liabilities
- Capital assets and long-term liabilities should be segregated into governmental activities and business-type activities
- Nondepreciable capital assets, such as land, must be presented separately from depreciable capital assets

▶ **NEW STANDARD:** The standards established by GASB-34 with respect to capital assets and long-term debt replaces the disclosures related to the presentations of General Fixed Assets Account Group and General Long-Term Debt Account Group.

### Capital Asset Disclosures

Disclosures that relate to capital assets should include the following information:

- Beginning and year-end balances (regardless of whether prior-year data are presented on the face of the government-wide financial statements), with accumulated depreciation separately identified
- Capital acquisitions for the period
- Sales or other dispositions for the period
- Current-period depreciation expense, supported with identification of amounts allocated to each functional expense presented in the statement of activities

If a governmental entity chooses not to capitalize collection items, the following disclosures should be made (GASB-34, par. 118):

- A description of the capitalized assets not capitalized
- The reason the assets are not capitalized

**OBSERVATION:** If collections are capitalized, the disclosures that apply to all other capital assets must be observed.

The following illustration incorporates the disclosure requirements for capital assets established GASB-34:

|  | Beginning Balances | Increases | Decreases | Ending Balances |
|---|---|---|---|---|
| **Analysis of Capital Assets** | | | | |
| Capital assets not being depreciated: | | | | |
| Land and improvements | $107,300,000 | $20,400,000 | | $127,700,000 |
| Construction in progress | 2,050,000 | 13,900,000 | | 15,950,000 |
| Total capital assets not being depreciated | 109,400,000 | 34,300,000 | | 143,700,000 |
| Other capital assets: | | | | |
| Buildings | 223,000,000 | | | 223,000,000 |
| Equipment | 25,700,000 | 6,150,000 | 7,000,000 | 24,850,000 |
| Vehicles | 82,520,000 | 4,055,000 | 2,350,000 | 84,225,000 |
| Leased capital assets | 7,818,540 | 431,213 | 5,012,000 | 3,237,753 |

|  | Beginning Balances | Increases | Decreases | Ending Balances |
|---|---|---|---|---|
| Infrastructure assets | 20,000,000 | | | 20,000,000 |
| Total other capital assets | 359,038,540 | 10,636,213 | 14,362,000 | 355,312,753 |
| Less accumulated depreciation for: | | | | |
| Buildings | 75,800,000 | 8,590,000 | 2,000,000 | 82,390,000 |
| Equipment | 8,970,000 | 3,947,000 | 1,615,000 | 11,302,000 |
| Vehicles | 43,355,000 | 24,060,889 | 4,359,000 | 63,056,889 |
| Leased capital assets | 2,500,000 | 1,279,058 | | 3,779,058 |
| Infrastructure assets | 12,000,000 | 700,000 | | 12,700,000 |
| Total accumulated depreciation | 142,625,000 | 38,576,947 | 7,974,000 | 173,227,947 |
| Other capital assets, net | 216,413,540 | (27,940,734) | 6,388,000 | 182,084,806 |
| Governmental activities capital assets, net | $325,813,540 | $ 6,359,266 | $6,388,000 | $325,784,806 |

**Depreciation expense was charged to functions as follows:**

Governmental activities:

| | |
|---|---|
| General government | $ 19,888,503 |
| Public safety | 6,737,222 |
| Streets | 4,142,778 |
| Recreation and parks | 1,694,444 |
| Health and welfare | 1,657,000 |
| In addition, depreciation on capital assets held by the City's Internal Service Funds that are predominantly related to governmental activities is charged to various functions based on their usage of the assets. | 4,457,000 |
| Total depreciation expense—governmental activities | $ 38,576,947 |

## Management's Discussion and Analysis

| Analysis of Capital Assets | Beginning Balances | Increases | Decreases | Ending Balances |
|---|---|---|---|---|
| Capital assets not being depreciated: | | | | |
| Land and improvements | $ 18,500,000 | $ 5,070,000 | $1,500,000 | $ 22,070,000 |
| Construction in progress | 26,690,000 | 2,825,000 | 5,730,000 | 23,785,000 |
| Total capital assets not being depreciated | 45,190,000 | 7,895,000 | 7,230,000 | 45,855,000 |
| Other capital assets: | | | | |
| Superstructure | 1,400,000 | | | 1,400,000 |
| Distribution and collection systems | 45,000,000 | 1,300,000 | | 46,300,000 |
| Runways and tarmacs | 27,000,000 | 500,000 | | 27,500,000 |
| Buildings | 47,250,000 | 5,570,000 | 840,000 | 51,980,000 |
| Equipment | 15,960,000 | 4,340,000 | 5,345,000 | 14,955,000 |
| Vehicles | 6,390,000 | 2,420,000 | 1,718,000 | 7,092,000 |
| Total other capital assets | 143,000,000 | 14,130,000 | 7,903,000 | 149,227,000 |
| Less accumulated depreciation for: | | | | |
| Superstructure | 650,000 | 28,000 | | 678,000 |
| Distribution and collection systems | 27,000,000 | 1,200,000 | | 28,200,000 |
| Runways and tarmacs | 6,500,000 | 1,300,000 | | 7,800,000 |
| Buildings | 12,670,000 | 2,315,000 | 670,000 | 14,315,000 |
| Equipment | 28,700,000 | 1,566,000 | 4,509,000 | 25,757,000 |
| Vehicles | 3,652,000 | 1,567,000 | 1,317,000 | 3,902,000 |
| Total accumulated depreciation | 78,522,000 | 7,976,000 | 6,496,000 | 80,652,000 |
| Other capital assets, net | 64,478,000 | 6,154,000 | 1,407,000 | 68,575,000 |
| Business-type activities capital assets, net | $109,668,000 | $14,049,000 | $8,637,000 | $114,430,000 |

Depreciation expense was charged to activities as follows:

Business-type activities:

Toll Bridge      $     339,000

| Analysis of Capital Assets | Beginning Balances | Increases | Decreases | Ending Balances |
|---|---|---|---|---|
| Parking | 117,000 | | | |
| Utilities | 3,025,000 | | | |
| Airport | 3,370,000 | | | |
| In addition, depreciation on capital assets held by the City's Internal Service Funds that are predominantly related to business-type activities is charged to various activities based on their usage of the assets. | 1,125,000 | | | |
| Total depreciation expense—business-type activities | $ 7,976,000 | | | |

## Long-Term Liabilities Disclosures

The disclosures related to long-term debt should encompass both long-term debt instruments (such as bonds, loans, and capitalized leases), and other long-term liabilities (such as estimated liabilities related to compensated absences and claims and judgements). These disclosures should include the following information:

- Beginning and year-end balances (regardless of whether prior-year data are presented on the face of the government-wide perspective financial statements)
- Increases and decreases (separately presented) for the period
- The part of each liability that is due within one year
- The governmental fund that has been generally used to pay other long-term liabilities (that is, such items as compensated absences and claims and judgements)

The following is an illustration that incorporates the disclosure requirements for capital assets established GASB-34:

| Analysis of Long-Term Liabilities Beginning Governmental Activities | Balances | Additions | Decreases | Ending Balances | Amounts Due Within One Year |
|---|---|---|---|---|---|
| Bonds, notes and capital leases: | | | | | |
| Capital leases | $5,197,652 | $ 431,213 | $1,288,141 | $4,340,724 | $1,332,932 |
| Notes payable | 5,500,000 | 3,200,000 | 1,000,000 | 7,700,000 | 1,500,000 |

## Analysis of Long-Term Liabilities
### Governmental Activities

| | Beginning Balances | Additions | Decreases | Ending Balances | Amounts Due Within One Year |
|---|---|---|---|---|---|
| General obligation bonds | 6,964,791 | 12,363,693 | 1,214,169 | 18,114,315 | 700,000 |
| Revenue bonds | 10,000,000 | | 750,000 | 9,250,000 | 750,000 |
| Total bonds, notes and capital leases | 27,662,443 | 15,994,906 | 4,252,310 | 39,405,039 | 4,282,932 |
| Other Liabilities: | | | | | |
| Compensated absences | 4,509,000 | 231,000 | 65,000 | 4,675,000 | 70,000 |
| Claims and judgements | 2,022,000 | 317,000 | 407,000 | 1,932,000 | 306,000 |
| Total other liabilities | 6,531,000 | 548,000 | 472,000 | 6,607,000 | 376,000 |
| Governmental activities long-term liabilities | $34,193,443 | $16,542,906 | $4,724,310 | $46,012,039 | $4,658,932 |

### Business-Type Activities Analysis of Long-Term Liabilities

| | Beginning Balances | Increases | Decreases | Ending Balances | Amounts Due Within One Year |
|---|---|---|---|---|---|
| Notes payable | $ 5,250,000 | $3,550,000 | $ 160,000 | $ 8,640,000 | $2,310,000 |
| Bonds payable | 24,500,000 | 2,000,000 | 4,220,000 | 22,280,000 | 1,370,000 |
| Compensated absences | 225,000 | 66,000 | 44,000 | 247,000 | 46,000 |
| Claims and judgements | 392,000 | 146,000 | 59,000 | 479,000 | 58,000 |
| Business-type activities long-term liabilities | $30,367,000 | $5,762,000 | $4,483,000 | $31,646,000 | $3,784,000 |

▶ **NEW STANDARD:** NCGAI-6 requires that a governmental entity disclose debt service requirements to maturity but does not specify the detail information that should be included in the disclosure. GASB-38 (Certain Financial Statement Note Disclosures) requires that the disclosure be continued but with separate presentations for each of the five years following the date of the balance sheet and in five-year increments thereafter through the year of maturity. The disclosure must identify the principal and interest components of debt service. The disclosure requirement also applies to the minimum lease payments for capital leases and noncancelable operating leases.

▶ **NEW STANDARD:** GASB-34 requires that the activity in long-term debt presented in the statement of net assets be summarized in a note to the financial statements, but there is no similar requirement for short-term debt. GASB-38 (Certain Financial Statement Note Disclosures) extends the analysis to the statement of net assets and balance sheet for short-term debt outstanding during the year, "even if no short-term debt is outstanding at year-end." GASB-38 does define short-term debt but notes that it "results from borrowings characterized by anticipation notes, use of lines of credit, and similar loans." The schedule of changes in short-term debt is presented in a note to the financial statements and includes the following components: (1) beginning balance,

(2) increases for the year, (3) decreases for the year and (4) ending balance. In addition, the disclosure should include the reason the short-term debt was issued during the year. In the current illustration, the City of Centerville had no short-term borrowing during the year.

# APPENDIX 15
# MD&A—CITY OF CENTERVILLE

## Basic Financial Statements

In general, the purpose of financial reporting is to provide external parties that read financial statements with information that will help them to make decisions or draw conclusions about an entity. There are many external parties that read the City of Centerville's financial statements; however, these parties do not always have the same specific objectives. In order to address the needs of as many parties as reasonably possible, the City, in accordance with required reporting standards, presents (1) government-wide financial statements and (2) fund financial statements.

*Government-Wide Financial Statements*

The focus of government-wide financial statements is on the overall financial position and activities of the City of Centerville. These financial statements are constructed around the concept of a primary government, the City, and its component units, except for fiduciary funds. As described below, the financial statements of the City's fiduciary funds are not included in the government-wide financial statements, because resources of these funds cannot be used to finance the City's activities. However, the financial statements of fiduciary funds are included in the City's financial statements because the City is financially accountable for those resources, even though they belong to other parties.

The City's government-wide financial statements include the statement of net assets and statement of activities, which are prepared using accounting principles that are similar to commercial enterprises. The purpose of the statement of net assets is to attempt to report all of the assets held and liabilities owed by the City. The City reports all of its assets when it acquires ownership over the assets and reports all of its liabilities when they are incurred. For example, the City reports buildings and infrastructure as assets, even though they are not available to pay the obligations incurred by the City. On the other hand, the City reports liabilities, such as litigation claims, even though these liabilities might not be paid until several years into the future.

The difference between the City's total assets and total liabilities is labeled as *net assets* and this difference is similar to the total owners' equity presented by a commercial enterprise. Although the purpose of the City is not to accumulate net assets, in general, as this amount increases it indicates that the financial position of the City is improving over time.

The purpose of the statement of activities is to present the revenues and expenses of the City. Again, the items presented on the statement of activities are measured in a manner similar to the approach used by a commercial enterprise in that revenues are recognized when earned or established criteria are satisfied and expenses are reported when incurred by the City. Thus, revenues are reported even when they may not be collected for several months after the end of the accounting period and expenses are recorded even though they may not have used cash during the current period.

Although the statement of activities looks different from a commercial enterprise's income statement, the financial statements is different only in format, not substance. Whereas the bottom line in a commercial enterprise is its net income, the City reports an amount described as *change in net assets*, essentially the same thing.

The focus of the statement of activities is on the *net cost* of various activities provided by the City. The statement begins with a column that identifies the cost of each of the City's major functions. Another column identifies the revenues that are specifically related to the classified governmental functions. The difference between the expenses and revenues related to specific program/activities computes the net cost or benefits of the program/activities, which identifies the extent to which each function of the City draws from general revenues or is self-financing through fees, intergovernmental aid, and other sources of resources.

The City's government-wide financial statements are divided into the primary government and its component units. The primary government is further divided into governmental activities and business-type activities. Governmental activities are generally financed through taxes, intergovernmental revenues, and other nonexchange revenues, while business-type activities are financed to some degree by charging external parties for the goods or services they acquire from the City. Governmental activities include programs/activities such as general government, public safety, streets, and health and welfare. Business-type activities, an integral part of the City's activities and responsibilities, include the City's Toll Bridge, Utilities Authority, Parking Authority, and airport. Component units are legally separate from the City, but because the City is financially accountable for them, they are reported in the City's financial statements. The City's component units include the Centerville Public School System and the Municipal Transit System.

The City's government-wide financial statements are presented on pages XX-XXX.

*Fund Financial Statements*

Unlike government-wide financial statements, the focus of fund financial statements is directed to specific activities of the City rather than the city as a whole. Except for the General Fund, a specific fund is established to satisfy managerial control over resources or to satisfy finance-related legal requirements established by external parties or governmental statutes or regulations. The City's fund financial statements are divided into three broad categories, namely, (1) governmental funds, (2) proprietary funds, and (3) fiduciary funds.

**Governmental funds** Governmental fund financial statements consist of a balance sheet and statement of revenues, expenditures, and change in fund balances and are prepared on an accounting basis that is significantly different from that used to prepare the government-wide financial statements.

In general, these financial statements have a short-term emphasis and, for the most part, measure and account for cash and other assets that can easily be converted to cash. For example, amounts reported on the balance sheet include items such as cash and receivables collectible within a very short period of time, but do not include capital assets such as land and buildings. Fund liabilities include amounts that are to be paid within a very short period after the end of the fiscal year. The difference between a fund's total assets and total liabilities is labeled as the fund balance, and generally indicates the amount that can be used to finance the next fiscal year's activities. Likewise, the operating statement for governmental funds reports only those revenues and expenditures that were collected in cash or paid with cash, respectively, during the current period or very shortly after the end of the year.

For the most part, the balances and activities accounted for in governmental funds are also reported in the governmental activities columns of the government-wide financial statements; however, because different accounting bases are used to prepare fund financial statements and government-wide financial statements, there are often significant differences between the totals presented in these financial statements. For this reason, there is an analysis at the bottom of the balance sheet that reconciles the total fund balances to the amount of net assets presented in the governmental activities column on the statement of net assets. Also, there is an analysis at the bottom of the statement of revenues, expenditures, and changes in fund balances that reconciles the total change in fund balances for all governmental funds to the change in net assets as reported in the governmental activities column in the statement of activities.

The City presents in separate columns funds that are most significant to the City (major funds) and all other governmental funds are aggregated and reported in a single column (nonmajor funds).

The City's governmental fund financial statements are presented on pages XX-XXX.

**Proprietary funds** Proprietary fund financial statements consist of a statement of net assets, statement of revenues, expenses, and changes in fund net assets and statement of cash flows, and are prepared on an accounting basis that is similar to the basis used to prepare the government-wide financial statements. For financial reporting purposes, proprietary funds are grouped into Enterprise Funds and Internal Service Funds.

The City uses Enterprise Funds to account for business-type activities that charge fees to customers for the use of specific goods or services. For the most part, the balances and activities accounted for in the City's Enterprise Funds are also reported in the business-type activities columns of the government-wide financial statements; however, because of the nature of Internal Service Funds, as described below, there are some differences between the totals presented in these financial statements. These differences are presented as reconciling items on the bottom part of the Enterprise Funds' statement of net assets, and statement of revenues, expenses, and changes in fund net assets.

The City uses Internal Service Funds to account for services provided and billed on an internal basis. These services may be billed to either governmental funds or an Enterprise Fund. The balances and activities of Internal Service Funds are presented in the proprietary funds (along with Enterprise Funds), but they are integrated into the government-wide financial statements, depending upon whether a particular Internal Service Fund services a governmental fund or an Enterprise Fund.

The City presents in separate columns Enterprise Funds that are most significant to the City and all other Enterprise Funds are aggregated and reported in a single column. Internal Service Funds are all aggregated and presented in a single column. A statement of cash flows is presented at the fund financial statement level for proprietary funds, but no equivalent statement is presented in the government-wide financial statements for either governmental activities or business-type activities.

The City's proprietary fund financial statements are presented on pages XX-XXX.

**Fiduciary funds** Fiduciary fund financial statements consist of a statement of fiduciary net assets and a statement of changes in fiduciary net assets. Assets held by the City for other parties (either as a trustee or as an agent) and that cannot be used to finance the City's own operating programs are reported in the fiduciary funds. The City is responsible for ensuring that the activities reported in fiduciary funds are based on their intended purposes.

As noted earlier, fiduciary funds are presented in the fund financial statements but are not reported in the government-wide financial statements.

The City's fiduciary fund financial statements are presented on page XX-XXX.

The relationships between the fund financial statements and the government-wide financial statements are summarized in Exhibit I.

## Exhibit I: Summary of Government-Wide Financial Statements

**FUND FINANCIAL STATEMENTS**

**GOVERNMENTAL FUNDS**
- Balance Sheet
- Statement of Revenues, Expenditures, and Changes in Fund Balances

**PROPRIETARY FUNDS**

Internal Service Funds
- Statement of Net Assets
- Statement of Revenues, Expenses, and Changes in Fund Net Assets
- Statement of Cash Flows

Enterprise Funds
- Statement of Net Assets
- Statement of Revenues, Expenses, and Changes in Fund Net Assets
- Statement of Cash Flows

**FIDUCIARY FUNDS**
- Statement of Changes in Fiduciary Net Assets
- Statement of Fiduciary Net Assets

*Information is not presented at the government-wide level*

**GOVERNMENT-WIDE FINANCIAL STATEMENTS**

Statement of Net Assets
- Governmental Activities Column
- Business-Type Activities Column

Statement of Activities
- Governmental Activities Column
- Business-Type Activities Column

NOTES:
- [A] = Information is converted to the accounting basis used by business enterprises.
- [B] = Internal Service Fund balances and activities related to governmental activities.
- [C] = Internal Service Fund balances and activities related to business-type activities.

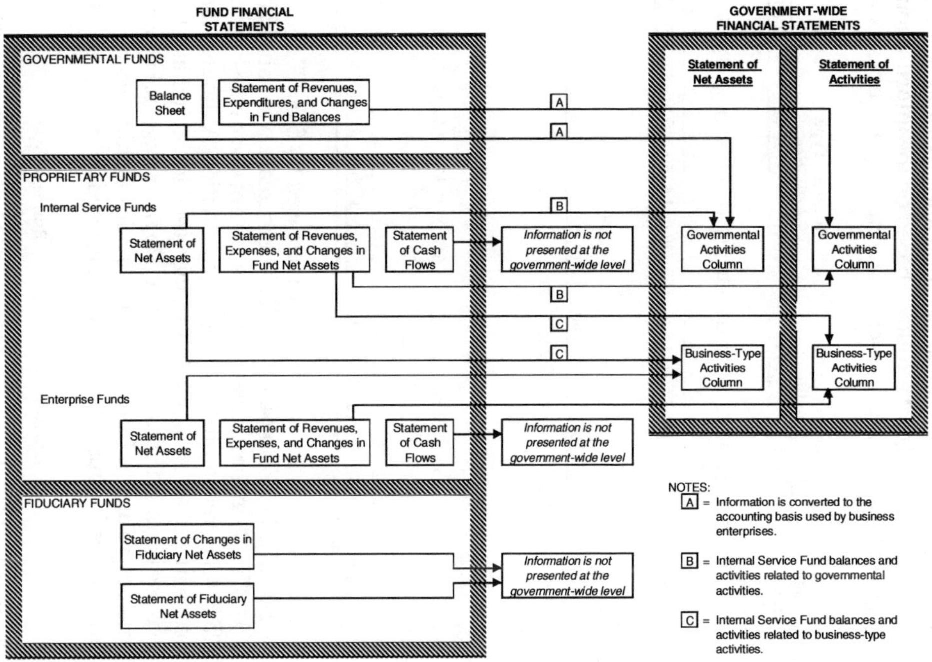

**OBSERVATION:** The presentation of condensed financial information is illustrated in the following section along with the analysis of the information.

## Overview of the City's Financial Position and Operations

The City's overall financial position and operations for the past two years are summarized as follows based on the information included in the government-wide financial statements (see pages xx-xxx):

| Financial Position | Governmental Activities 20X1 | Governmental Activities 20X0 | Business-Type Activities 20X1 | Business-Type Activities 20X0 | Total 20X1 | Total 20X0 |
|---|---|---|---|---|---|---|
| Current and other assets | $ 27,543,412 | $ 26,722,350 | $51,009,044 | $49,822,616 | $78,552,456 | $76,544,966 |
| Capital assets | 325,784,806 | 325,813,540 | 114,430,000 | 109,668,000 | 440,214,806 | 435,481,540 |
| Total assets | $353,328,218 | $352,535,890 | $165,439,044 | $159,490,616 | $518,767,262 | $512,026,506 |
| Long-term liabilities | $41,353,107 | $29,469,133 | $27,862,000 | $25,884,000 | $69,215,107 | $55,353,133 |
| Other liabilities | 6,573,222 | 15,788,660 | 12,199,000 | 33,543,116 | 18,772,222 | 49,331,776 |
| Total liabilities | $47,926,329 | $45,257,793 | $40,061,000 | $59,427,116 | $87,987,329 | $104,684,909 |
| Net assets: | | | | | | |
| Invested in capital assets, net of related debt | $285,830,477 | $298,151,097 | $87,510,000 | $79,918,000 | $373,340,477 | $378,069,097 |
| Restricted | 4,488,456 | 3,412,600 | 37,362,000 | 19,745,000 | 41,850,456 | 23,157,600 |
| Unrestricted | 15,082,956 | 5,714,400 | 506,044 | 400,500 | 15,589,000 | 6,114,900 |
| Total net assets | $305,401,889 | $307,278,097 | $125,378,044 | $100,063,500 | $430,779,933 | $407,341,597 |

The total net assets of the City increased by $23,438,336 (about 5.8%), from $407,341,597 to $430,779,933. The increase was caused by a decrease of $1,876,208 in the net assets of governmental activities and an increase of $25,314,544 related to business-type activities. Although some of the increase in net assets is related to increases in capital assets, most of the increase is liquid in that it is unrelated to capital assets. However, few of the net assets related to business-type activities are transferable to governmental activities, because of restrictions imposed by statutes or contracts.

| Operations | Governmental Activities 20X1 | Governmental Activities 20X0 | Business-Type Activities 20X1 | Business-Type Activities 20X0 | Total 20X1 | Total 20X0 |
|---|---|---|---|---|---|---|
| Revenues | | | | | | |
| Program revenues: | | | | | | |
| Charges for services | $ 846,000 | $ 805,000 | $ 269,362,000 | $245,550,000 | $270,208,000 | $246,355,000 |
| Operating grants and contributions | 4,584,000 | 9,505,000 | 100,000 | 250,000 | 4,684,000 | 9,755,000 |
| Capital grants and contributions | 2,450,000 | 3,500,000 | 3,500,000 | 4,000,000 | 5,950,000 | 7,500,000 |

## Management's Discussion and Analysis 15-21

| Operations | Governmental Activities 20X1 | Governmental Activities 20X0 | Business-Type Activities 20X1 | Business-Type Activities 20X0 | Total 20X1 | Total 20X0 |
|---|---|---|---|---|---|---|
| General revenues: | | | | | | |
| Property taxes | 91,670,000 | 89,340,000 | | | 91,670,000 | 89,340,000 |
| Franchise taxes | 1,300,000 | 1,050,000 | | | 1,300,000 | 1,050,000 |
| Unrestricted grants and contributions | 26,570,000 | 29,505,000 | | | 26,570,000 | 29,505,000 |
| Other general revenues | 334,000 | 220,000 | 1,655,000 | 1,855,000 | 1,989,000 | 2,075,000 |
| Total revenues | 127,754,000 | 133,925,000 | 274,617,000 | 251,655,000 | 402,371,000 | 385,580,000 |
| Program expenses: | | | | | | |
| General | 53,931,629 | 49,220,000 | | | 53,931,629 | 49,220,000 |
| Public safety | 22,836,931 | 21,003,000 | | | 22,836,931 | 21,003,000 |
| Streets | 21,187,633 | 19,200,000 | | | 21,187,633 | 19,200,000 |
| Recreation and parks | 7,621,871 | 5,400,000 | | | 7,621,871 | 5,400,000 |
| Health and welfare | 9,579,427 | 8,100,000 | | | 9,579,427 | 8,100,000 |
| School district | 32,000,000 | 29,500,000 | | | 32,000,000 | 29,500,000 |
| Interest | 2,332,717 | 1,856,000 | | | 2,332,717 | 1,856,000 |
| Airport | | | 203,594,872 | 189,770,000 | 203,594,872 | 189,770,000 |
| Utilities | | | 38,557,320 | 35,333,000 | 38,557,320 | 35,333,000 |
| Parking | | | 6,091,144 | 5,400,000 | 6,091,144 | 5,400,000 |
| Toll Bridge | | | 4,699,120 | 4,100,000 | 4,699,120 | 4,100,000 |
| Total expenses | 149,490,208 | 134,279,000 | 252,942,456 | 234,603,000 | 402,432,664 | 368,882,000 |
| Change in net assets before other items | (21,736,208) | (354,000) | 21,674,544 | 17,052,000 | (61,664) | 16,698,000 |
| Special item—gain on sale of parking lot | | 3,500,000 | | | | 3,500,000 |
| Extraordinary item—donation of land from state | 20,000,000 | | | | 20,000,000 | |
| Transfers | -140,000 | -220,000 | 140,000 | 220,000 | | |
| Increase (decrease) in net assets | $(1,876,208) | $ (574,000) | $25,314,544 | $17,272,000 | $23,438,336 | $16,698,000 |

There was a significant decrease ($16,759,664) in the change in *net assets before other items* for the City as a whole, when operations for the current year are compared to those of the previous year. This occurred because even though total revenue during the year increased by $16,791,000, that increase was not sufficient to offset the increase in total expenses of $33,550,664. However, due to two irregular items that occurred during the year, the overall increase in net assets rose from $16,698,000 to $23,438,336. These changes are more fully explained below.

## Governmental Activities

Last year there was a decrease in net assets related to governmental activities of $574,000; however, this year, there was a decrease of $1,876,208. If irregular items are excluded from operating activities, there was a decrease in net assets of $21,736,208 during the year ended June 30, 20X1. Last year, there was a decrease of $354,000 for the change in net assets before irregular items. The reason for the significant deterioration in operations during the current year and related fiscal policies that the City has implemented to address these issues are summarized as follows:

- The current year's total revenues decreased by $6,171,000, a 4.6% decline. Most of this decrease arose because intergovernmental operating and capital grants fell $8,906,000, because both the state and federal governments reduced certain types of grants to governmental entities. In order to address the revenue shortfall, property tax rates have been increased by 8% for the year 20X2 and property tax ratables for the same year have increased by 5%. The 20X2 budget reflects these changes and budgeted property tax revenues are projected to increase accordingly.
- During the current year, expenses related to overtime pay increased by approximately $4,200,000; however, the City recently signed new agreements with all of its unions. New provisions in the contracts will significantly reduce the cost of overtime pay. These new work rules are consistent with rules implemented by most municipalities that are of a size similar to the City and the financial implication of these revised rules have been reflected in the 20X2 city budget.
- A hiring freeze and other cost containment strategies have been adopted and a $7,000,000 reduction for operating expenses is reflected in the 20X2 City budget.
- Based on new legislation adopted by the state, the state will begin a program to help fund public education. The statue is applicable to the 20X2 budgetary period and the state has authorized a payment of $6,000,000 to the City to help fund the public school system.

A comparison of revenue sources related to governmental activities for the two-year period is summarized in Exhibit 15-1, "Governmental Activities Revenue Sources—20X1 vs. 20X0."

## Exhibit 15-1—Governmental Activities Revenue Sources—20X1 vs. 20X0

| | 20X1 | 20X0 |
|---|---|---|
| Operating grants and contributions | $ 4,584,000 | $ 9,505,000 |
| Capital grants and contributions | 2,450,000 | 3,500,000 |
| Property taxes | 91,670,000 | 89,340,000 |
| Unrestricted grants and contributions | 26,570,000 | 29,505,000 |
| Charges, franchise taxes and other revenues | 2,480,000 | 2,075,000 |

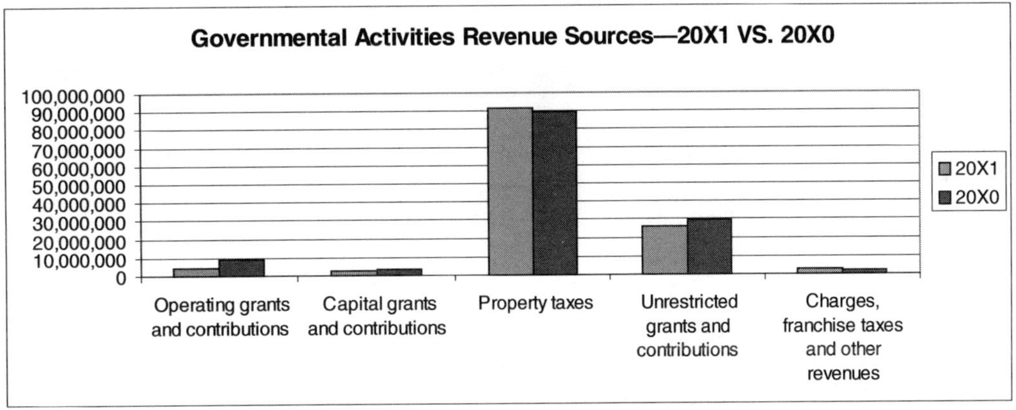

Governmental Activities Revenue Sources—20X1 VS. 20X0

A comparison of expenses related to governmental activities for the two-year period is summarized in Exhibit 15-2, "Governmental Activities Expenses—20X1 vs. 20X0."

## Exhibit 15-2—Governmental Activities Expenses - 20X1 vs. 20X0

|  | 20X1 | 20X0 |
|---|---|---|
| General | $53,931,629 | $49,220,000 |
| Public safety | 22,836,931 | 21,003,000 |
| Streets | 21,187,633 | 18,500,000 |
| Recreation and parks | 7,621,871 | 5,400,000 |
| Health and welfare | 9,579,427 | 8,100,000 |
| School district | 32,000,000 | 29,500,000 |
| Interest | 2,332,717 | 1,856,000 |

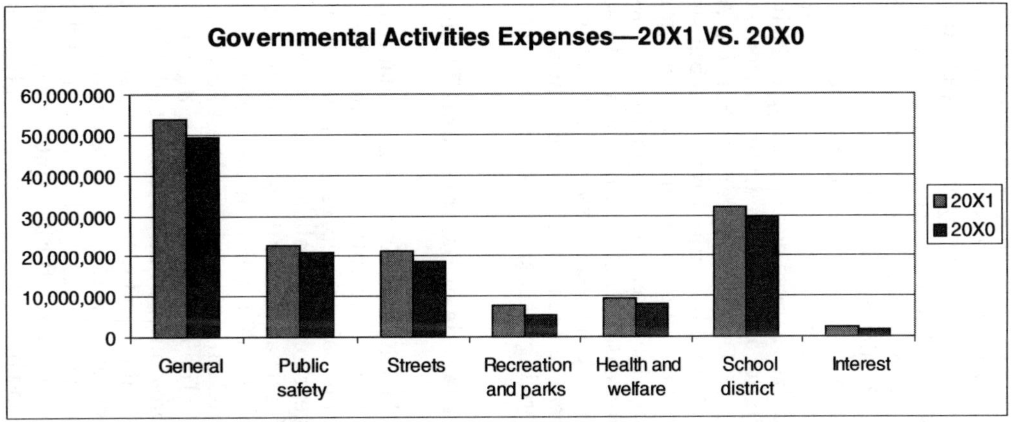

**Governmental Activities Expenses—20X1 VS. 20X0**

## Business-Type Activities

The combined change in net assets before irregular items for business-type activities increased by 27% ($4,622,544) from the previous year. Most of that change was due to the activities of the City airport. Recent runway additions and the expansion of retail shops at the airport have resulted in significant growth in revenues and a general consensus that the facility is becoming an attractive regional alternative to the two major airports that are within a 60-mile radius.

While the airport growth had a positive impact on overall business-type activities, the combined numbers somewhat obscure the poorer operating results for the Parking Authority and Utility Authority. These two operating units had a 7% and 5% drop in changes in net assets before irregular items when compared to the previous year. During the year, the Parking Authority sold one of its parking lots that had minor revenues but significant fixed costs. The sale of the parking lot generated a one-time gain of $3,500,000. Also, parking fees were increased by 25% as of July 1, 20X1, the first rate increased in almost five years. In addition, The State Utility Board has approved a new method for determining utility rates that better reflects the market cost of natural gas and other fossil fuels. This new pricing mechanism goes into effect on January 1, 20X2.

## Analysis of Balances and Transactions of Individual Funds

The City's combined fund balances as of the end of the current year for governmental funds, presented on page xx, were $16.7 million. This balance represent an increase of $2.3 million (16%) over last year's ending balance. Although this was a significant increase in the fund balance for the year, that net amount for the most part comprised a $444,000 deficit in the General Fund, which was offset by a $2.4 million increase in the West End Recreation Center Capital Project.

The primary reasons for the General Fund deficit were discussed previously in the section titled "An Overview of the City's Financial Position and Operations." In addition, approximately $2.1 million of resources were transferred from the General Fund for the construction of capital assets ($1.9 million), and to support activities included in other funds. While capital assets expenditures do reduce the overall fund balance for governmental funds, those expenditures create long-term assets that will benefit the community for many years to come. Total transfers from the General Fund amounted to $5.5 million.

On the other hand, the increase in the fund balance for the West End Recreation Center Capital Project was mainly due to the issuance of $3,300,000 of serial bonds for the year. The bond proceeds at the end of the year were placed in temporary investments, but they will be used during the next fiscal year to finish construction on the Center. The proceeds represent a liability of the City, and the bonds will have to be paid off over the next six years.

Also during the year, significant resources were received and expended by the Easely Street Bridge Project. Bond proceeds and capital grants amounted to $10.6 million and capital expenditures on the bridge totaled $11.1 million. When completed, the bridge will relieve much of the downtown congestion for the foreseeable future. The bonds will be paid off over a 10-year period.

## General Fund Budgetary Highlights

The original budget passed by the City Council anticipated an increase in the budgetary fund balance during the year of $340,000; however, the final budgetary amounts expected a decrease of $490,000, a net unfavorable change of $730,000. The change from the original budget to the final budget was mainly due to the expected position of the budgetary fund balance that was brought forward from the 20X0 fiscal year. It was anticipated that budgetary resources of $13.5 million dollars would be brought forward from the previous year but this amount was subsequently changed to $12.7 million.

There were minor differences between the final budgetary amounts and the actual budgetary figures. The anticipated budgetary fund balance as of June 30, 20X1 was expected to be $12.3 million and the actual results were $25,600 more than the anticipated amount. Exhibit 15-3 compares final budgetary figures and the actual budgetary figures for revenues.

**Exhibit 15-3—Comparison of Final Budgetary Resources and Actual Budgetary Resources – 20X1**

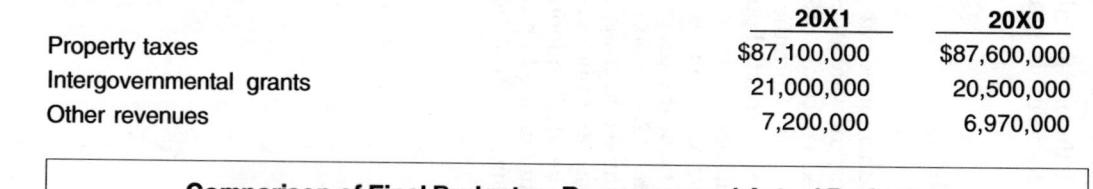

|  | 20X1 | 20X0 |
|---|---|---|
| Property taxes | $87,100,000 | $87,600,000 |
| Intergovernmental grants | 21,000,000 | 20,500,000 |
| Other revenues | 7,200,000 | 6,970,000 |

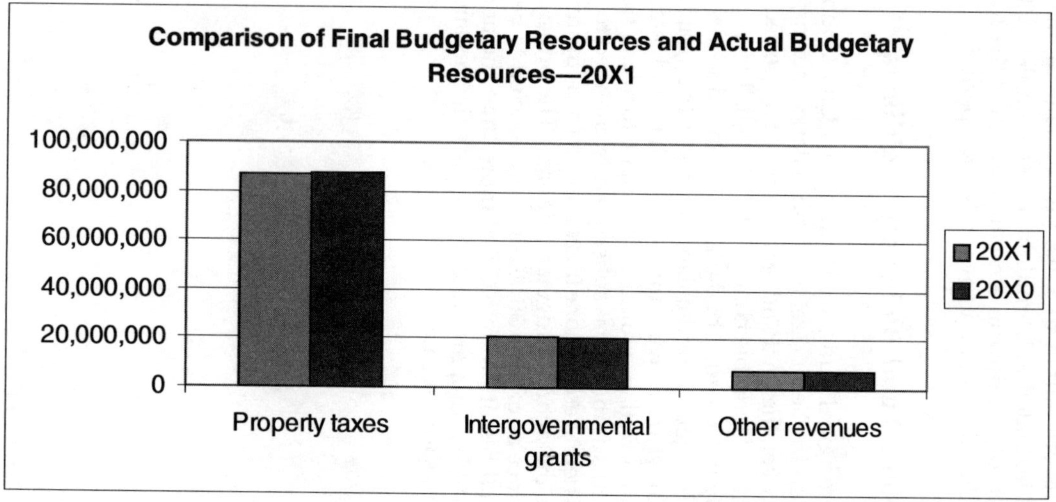

**Comparison of Final Budgetary Resources and Actual Budgetary Resources—20X1**

The budgetary figures and actual budgetary amounts for expenditures are compared in Exhibit 15-4.

### Exhibit 15-4—Comparison of Final Budgetary Appropriations and Actual Budgetary Appropriations – 20X1

|  | 20X1 | 20X0 |
|---|---|---|
| General government | $33,490,000 | 33,477,000 |
| Public safety | 18,200,000 | 18,099,000 |
| Streets | 11,900,000 | 11,894,500 |
| Recreation and parks | 6,600,000 | 6,497,250 |
| Health and welfare | 8,100,000 | 8,092,250 |
| Education (component unit) | 32,000,000 | 32,000,000 |
| Transfers to other funds | 5,000,000 | 5,475,000 |

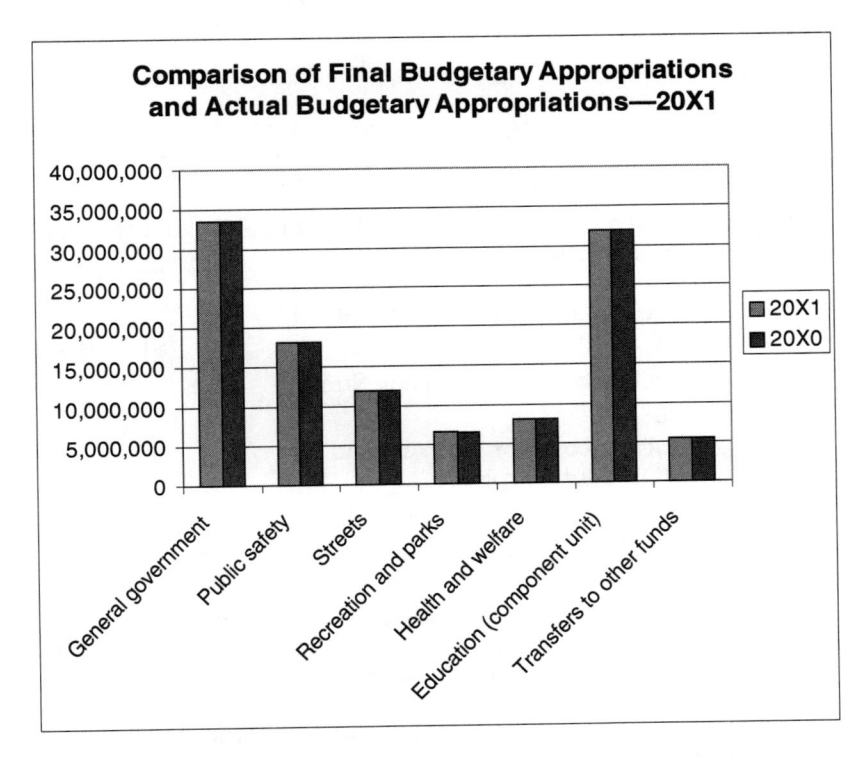

## Capital Asset and Debt Administration

*Capital Assets*

The City has invested $440 million in capital assets (net of depreciation). Approximately 81% of this investment is related to governmental activities and includes infrastructure, buildings, equipment, and land. Governmental capital assets have declined slightly from the previous year, while capital assets held for business-type activities have increased by about 5%. Capital assets held by the City at the end of the current and previous year are summarized as follows:

| | Governmental Activities 20X1 | Governmental Activities 20X0 | Business-Type Activities 20X1 | Business-Type Activities 20X0 | Total 20X1 | Total 20X0 |
|---|---|---|---|---|---|---|
| Land, improvements and construction in progress | $143,700,000 | $109,400,000 | $45,855,000 | $ 45,190,000 | $189,555,000 | $154,590,000 |
| Buildings | 140,610,000 | 147,200,000 | 31,045,000 | 27,960,000 | 171,655,000 | 175,160,000 |
| Equipment and vehicles | 34,174,806 | 61,213,540 | 13,008,000 | 10,618,000 | 47,182,806 | 71,831,540 |
| Infrastructure assets | 7,300,000 | 8,000,000 | 24,522,000 | 25,250,000 | 31,822,000 | 33,250,000 |
| Totals | $325,784,806 | $325,813,540 | $114,430,000 | $109,018,000 | $440,214,806 | $434,831,540 |

During the current year, major capital additions for governmental activities were as follows:

- Construction costs for the Easely Street Bridge Project     $11,100,000
- Construction costs for the Bland Street Drainage Project     1,500,000
- Construction costs for the West End Recreation Center Project     1,300,000
- Acquisitions of equipment and vehicles     6,551,213
- Gift of land from the state     20,000,000

The overall amount of capital assets related to governmental activities remained about the same, because assets with a net cost basis of about $6 million were sold and depreciation expense for the year was $38.5 million.

In addition, the following major acquisitions were made by for business-type activities:

- Construction costs for distribution and collection systems (Centerville Utilities Authority)     $ 1,500,000

- Construction costs for runways and tarmacs (Centerville Municipal Airport)     500,000
- Investments in buildings, equipment and vehicles     12,330,000

Additional information about the City's capital assets is presented in Note XX (page xx) of the financial statements.

*Long-Term Obligations*

At the end of the current year, the City had long-term debt related to governmental activities of $39.4 million, which was an increase from the previous year of $11.7 million. Of the amount of debt outstanding as of the end of 20X1, about 77% was backed by the full faith and credit of the government and the balance was secured by various revenue sources. The total amount of debt related to business-type activities remained stable from the end of 20X0 to 20X1. Approximately 55% of this debt was backed by the full faith and credit of the government.

The debt position of the City is summarized below and is more fully analyzed in Note XX on page xx of the financial statements.

|  | Governmental Activities |  | Business-Type Activities |  | Total |  |
| --- | --- | --- | --- | --- | --- | --- |
|  | 20X1 | 20X0 | 20X1 | 20X0 | 20X1 | 20X0 |
| General obligation debt backed by the City | $30,155,039 | $17,662,443 | $16,920,000 | $13,250,000 | $47,075,039 | $30,912,443 |
| Revenue bonds backed by specific sources of revenues | 9,250,000 | 10,000,000 | 14,000,000 | 16,500,000 | 23,250,000 | 26,500,000 |
| Totals | $39,405,039 | $27,662,443 | $30,920,000 | $29,750,000 | $70,325,039 | $57,412,443 |

During the current year, major debt changes for governmental activities were as follows:

- Bonds issued to support construction of Easely Street Bridge     $9,363,693
- Bonds issued to support construction of West End Recreation Center     3,000,000
- Execution of capital leases for general government purposes     431,213

Also during the year, approximately $3.3 million was paid to reduce the City's debt position.

In addition, the following major debt changes for business-type activities were as follows:

- Debt issued to finance the construction of assets for the Centerville Municipal Airport    $3,200,000
- Debt issued to finance the construction of assets for the Utilities Authority    2,100,000

Also during the year, approximately $4.5 million was paid to reduce the debt outstanding related to business-type activities.

The City also has long-term liabilities related to compensated absences and claims and judgements. These liabilities, for both governmental activities and business-type activities, increased by less than $200,000 during the current year.

The credit rating for the City's general obligation bonds is the third highest rating possible. That rate has not changed over the last several years.

*Relevant Current Economic Factors, Decisions, and Conditions*

Regional economic trends that affect the financial conditions of the City are generally favorable. The unemployment rate for the second quarter of 20X1 in the Centerville Metropolitan Area is approximately 2.1%, which is significantly lower than either the rate for the state (2.9%) or the nation (3.1%). The metropolitan region's retail sales and new construction continue to grow at a rate that is significantly greater than that experience by the United States as a whole. During the last several years, the region's higher growth rate has tended to increase the inflation rate (as measured by the Consumer Price Index) slightly higher than either the state or the nation. For example, the inflation rate for the year ended December 31, 20X0 in the metropolitan area (3.9%) was slightly higher than the rate for either the state (3.7%) or the nation (3.6%). Recent estimates of current inflation trends reconfirm the region's experience for the past few years.

All of these factors, as well as others referred to elsewhere in this MD&A, were taken into consideration in preparing the budget for the General Fund for the year ended June 30, 20X2. The City's property tax base has increased by approximately 5% because of the continued new construction in both the downtown and residential areas. Over the past few years, property tax rates have essentially remained stable but the 20X2 budget reflects a rate increase of 8%. Even with this rate increase, the overall tax rate for the City is approximately 20–25% less than the tax rate assessed by other cities of the approximate same size within a 25-mile radius. These budgetary changes are expected to offset declines in certain grants that have been traditionally made by the state and federal governments. However, one important development during the past year was the state's legislative action to begin to increase its commitment to public education. During the 20X2 budgetary year, the state has pledged to fund approximately 15% of total public education expenditures and over the next three years that percentage will grow to 33%.

In addition to increases in revenue sources, the City has implemented a plan to better control operating expenditures for the next budgetary period. These strategies, which were discussed earlier, include a hiring freeze, cost reduction strategies for most departments, and new provisions in all of the union contracts that are expected to significantly reduce the cost of overtime pay.

If the strategies and estimates described above are realized, the City's budgetary fund balance for the General Fund is expected to increase by approximately 3% by the end of the 20X2 fiscal year.

Overall, the business-type activities conducted by the City are expected to continue to improve. Most of these favorable results are expected to be related to the operations of the Municipal Airport. Toward the end of the 20X1 fiscal year, the management of the airport signed several new contracts with retail stores located in the airport concourses. The new rental rates, which will take effect on January 1, 20X2, represent an overall increase of approximately 21% in rental rates spread evenly over a three-year period. The activities of the Centerville Toll Bridge are expected to increase modestly and its financial position is not expected to change significantly by the end of the 20X2 fiscal year. The other two business-type activities (parking and utilities) are expected to reverse a downward trend that has been experienced for the past three years. As explained earlier, parking fees have been increased significantly and a new method for determining utility rates will take effect during the next budgetary period.

*Request for Information*

This financial report is designed to provide various interested parties with a general overview of the City's finances and to show the City's accountability for the money it receives. If you have questions about this report or need additional financial information, contact the City Controller's Office at 856-555-5555, or you may request a copy of the Comprehensive Annual Financial Report at our Web site (http://www.centervillenj.gov).

# APPENDIX
# GASB STATEMENT NO. 34

Excerpts from GASB Statement No. 34, Basic Financial Statements—and Management's Discussion and Analysis—for State and Local Governments, copyright by Governmental Accounting Standards Board, 401 Merritt 7, Norwalk, Connecticut, 06856 USA, is reproduced by permission. All rights reserved. No part of these excerpts may be reproduced, stored in a retrieval system, or transmitted in any form or by any means, electronic, mechanical, photocopying, recording, or otherwise, without the prior written permission of the Governmental Accounting Standards Board.

# Statement No. 34 of the Governmental Accounting Standards Board

## Basic Financial Statements—and Management's Discussion and Analysis—for State and Local Governments

### June 1999

## CONTENTS

|  | Paragraph Numbers |
|---|---|
| Introduction | 1–2 |
| Standards of Governmental Accounting and Financial Reporting | 3–141 |
|   Scope and Applicability | 3–5 |
|   Minimum Requirements for Basic Financial Statements and Required Supplementary Information | 6–7 |
|   Management's Discussion and Analysis (MD&A) | 8–11 |
|   Government-wide Financial Statements | 12–62 |
|     Focus of the Government-wide Financial Statements | 13–15 |
|     Measurement Focus and Basis of Accounting | 16–29 |
|       Reporting Capital Assets | 18–29 |
|         Modified Approach | 23–26 |
|         Reporting Works of Art and Historical Treasures | 27–29 |
|     Required Financial Statements—Statement of Net Assets | 30–37 |
|       Invested in Capital Assets, Net of Related Debt | 33 |
|       Restricted Net Assets | 34–35 |
|       Unrestricted Net Assets | 36–37 |
|     Required Financial Statements—Statement of Activities | 38–62 |

Copyright © 1999 by Governmental Accounting Standards Board. All rights reserved. No part of this publication may be reproduced, stored in a retrieval system, or transmitted, in any form or by any means, electronic, mechanical, photocopying, recording, or otherwise, without the prior written permission of the Governmental Accounting Standards Board.

Expenses ....................................................................... 41–46
Revenues ...................................................................... 47–53
    Program Revenues ............................................. 48–51
    General Revenues ...................................................... 52
    Reporting Contributions to Term and Permanent Endowments, Contributions to Permanent Fund Principal, Special and Extraordinary Items, and Transfers ...................... 53
Statement of Activities Format ........................................ 54
Special and Extraordinary Items .............................. 55–56
Eliminations and Reclassifications ........................... 57–61
    Internal Balances—Statement of Net Assets ......... 58
    Internal Activities—Statement of Activities ......................................................... 59–60
    Intra-entity Activity ................................................... 61
Reporting Internal Service Fund Balances .................... 62
Fund Financial Statements ................................................... 63–112
    Funds—Overview and Definitions .............................. 63–73
        Governmental Funds ................................................ 64–65
        Proprietary Funds .................................................... 66–68
        Fiduciary Funds ........................................................ 69–73
    Governmental and Proprietary Fund Financial Statements ...................................................................... 74–105
        Focus on Major Funds ............................................... 75–76
        Required Reconciliation to Government-wide Statements ..................................................................... 77
        Required Financial Statements—Governmental Funds ............................................. 78–90
            Measurement Focus and Basis of Accounting ...... 79
            Reporting General Capital Assets .......................... 80
            Reporting General Long-term Liabilities ......... 81–82
            Balance Sheet ......................................................... 83–84
                Separate Display of Reserved and Unreserved Fund Balance ............................ 84
            Required Reconciliation ......................................... 85
            Statement of Revenues, Expenditures, and Changes in Fund Balances ................................. 86–90
                Classification of Revenues and Expenditures ............................................. 87
                Other Financing Sources and Uses .................. 88
                Special and Extraordinary Items ..................... 89
                Required Reconciliation ..................................... 90

Required Financial Statements—
Proprietary Funds .................................................. 91–105
   Measurement Focus and Basis
   of Accounting ...................................................... 92–95
   Separate Presentation of Internal
   Service Funds .............................................................. 96
   Statement of Net Assets ..................................... 97–99
      Reporting Restrictions on Asset Use ............... 99
   Statement of Revenues, Expenses, and
   Changes in Fund Net Assets ....................... 100–104
      Defining Operating Revenues
      and Expenses .............................................. 102
      Reporting Capital Contributions
      and Additions to Permanent and
      Term Endowments ........................................ 103
      Required Reconciliations ............................... 104
   Statement of Cash Flows ........................................ 105
Required Financial Statements—Fiduciary Funds
and Similar Component Units ................................... 106–111
   Measurement Focus and Basis of Accounting ........... 107
   Statement of Fiduciary Net Assets ............................. 108
   Statement of Changes in Fiduciary Net Assets .......... 109
   Reporting Agency Funds ....................................... 110–111
Reporting Interfund Activity ............................................. 112
Basic Financial Statements—Notes to the Financial
Statements ....................................................................... 113–123
   General Disclosure Requirements ............................. 114–115
   Required Note Disclosures about Capital
   Assets and Long-term Liabilities .............................. 116–120
   Disclosures about Donor-restricted Endowments ............ 121
   Segment Information ................................................. 122–123
Reporting Component Units .............................................. 124–128
Required Supplementary Information Other
Than MD&A .................................................................. 129–133
   Budgetary Comparison Schedules ............................. 130–131
   Modified Approach for Reporting Infrastructure .... 132–133
Basic Financial Statements Required for Special-purpose
Governments ................................................................ 134–141
   Reporting by Special-purpose Governments
   Engaged in Governmental Activities ....................... 135–137
   Reporting by Special-purpose Governments
   Engaged Only in Business-type Activities ...................... 138

Reporting by Special-purpose Governments
Engaged Only in Fiduciary Activities ...................... 139–141
Effective Date and Transition ....................................................... 142–160
Governmental Entities That Use the AICPA
Not-for-Profit Model ...................................................................... 147
Reporting General Infrastructure Assets
at Transition ......................................................................... 148–151
Modified Approach for Reporting
Infrastructure Assets .......................................................... 152–153
Initial Capitalization of General Infrastructure
Assets ..................................................................................... 154–160
Determining Major General Infrastructure
Assets ............................................................................. 154–156
Establishing Capitalization at Transition .................... 157–160
Estimated Historical Cost—Current
Replacement Cost ................................................. 158–159
Estimated Historical Cost from Existing
Information .................................................................. 160
Methods for Calculating Depreciation ....................................... 161–166
Composite Methods ............................................................. 163–166

---

**Statement No. 34 of the Governmental Accounting Standards Board**

**Basic Financial Statements—and Management's Discussion and Analysis—for State and Local Governments**

**June 1999**

## INTRODUCTION

1. The objective of this Statement is to enhance the understandability and usefulness of the general purpose external financial reports of state and local governments to the citizenry, legislative and oversight bodies, and investors and creditors. GASB Concepts Statement No. 1, *Objectives of Financial Reporting,* recognizes these groups as the primary intended users of governmental financial reports and establishes financial reporting objectives to meet their information needs. Those objectives are the foundation for the standards in this Statement.

2. Accountability is the paramount objective of governmental financial reporting—the objective from which all other financial reporting objectives flow.[1] Governments' duty to be accountable includes providing financial information that is useful for economic, social, and political decisions. Financial reports that contribute to these decisions include information useful for (a) comparing actual financial results with the legally adopted budget, (b) assessing financial condition and results of operations, (c) assisting in determining compliance with finance-related laws, rules, and regulations, and (d) assisting in evaluating efficiency and effectiveness.[2]

## STANDARDS OF GOVERNMENTAL ACCOUNTING AND FINANCIAL REPORTING

### Scope and Applicability

3. This Statement establishes accounting and financial reporting standards for general purpose external financial reporting by state and local governments.[3] It is written from the perspective of *general purpose* governments—states, cities, counties, towns, and villages. Specific financial reporting standards for *special-purpose* governments are established in paragraphs 134 through 141.

4. This Statement establishes specific standards for the basic financial statements, management's discussion and analysis (MD&A), and certain required supplementary information (RSI) other than MD&A.

5. This Statement supersedes NCGA Statement 1, *Governmental Accounting and Financial Reporting Principles,* Summary Statement of Principles nos. 3, 6, and 7, paragraphs 19, 20, 34–41, 47–56, 60, 71, 74, 101–106, 122, 131, 136, 137, 140–142, 144, 146–154, 162–164, and 166–171, and footnote 4; NCGA Statement 2, *Grant, Entitlement, and Shared Revenue Accounting by State and Local Governments,* paragraphs 15, 16, and 18; NCGA Statement 4, *Accounting and Financial Reporting Principles for Claims and Judgments and Compensated Absences,* paragraphs 5–7 and 32–42; NCGA Statement 5, *Accounting and Financial Reporting Principles for Lease Agreements of State and Local Governments,* paragraphs 7–9; NCGA Interpretation 2, *Segment Information for Enterprise Funds;* NCGA Interpretation 5, *Authoritative Status of Governmental Accounting, Auditing, and Financial*

---

[1] Concepts Statement 1, paragraphs 56 and 76.
[2] Concepts Statement 1, paragraph 32.
[3] The scope of this Statement excludes public colleges and universities. A revised Exposure Draft, *Basic Financial Statements—and Management's Discussion and Analysis—for Public Colleges and Universities,* issued June 30, 1999, proposes standards for public colleges and universities.

*Reporting (1968);* NCGA Interpretation 6, *Notes to the Financial Statements Disclosure,* paragraph 3; NCGA Interpretation 10, *State and Local Government Budgetary Reporting,* paragraph 12; AICPA Statement of Position 77-2, *Accounting for Interfund Transfers of State and Local Governments;* AICPA Statement of Position 78-7, *Financial Accounting and Reporting by Hospitals Operated by a Governmental Unit;* GASB Statement No. 7, *Advance Refundings Resulting in Defeasance of Debt,* paragraph 9 and footnote 1; GASB Statement No. 11, *Measurement Focus and Basis of Accounting—Governmental Fund Operating Statements,* paragraphs 1–39, 62–76, and 81–99; GASB Statement No. 14, *The Financial Reporting Entity,* paragraphs 45–47, 49, 56, and 57; GASB Statement No. 17, *Measurement Focus and Basis of Accounting—Governmental Fund Operating Statements: Amendment of the Effective Dates of GASB Statement No. 11 and Related Statements,* paragraphs 1–3 and 5; GASB Statement No. 20, *Accounting and Financial Reporting for Proprietary Funds and Other Governmental Entities That Use Proprietary Fund Accounting,* footnote 1; GASB Statement No. 21, *Accounting for Escheat Property,* paragraph 6; and GASB Statement No. 29, *The Use of Not-for-Profit Accounting and Financial Reporting Principles by Governmental Entities,* paragraphs 1, 3, 4, and 6. In addition, this Statement amends NCGA Statement 1, Summary Statement of Principles nos. 1, 2, 5, 8–10, and 12 and paragraphs 2–4, 16–18, 22, 25–27, 30, 32, 33, 42–44, 46, 57, 59, 61, 72, 99, 100, 107, 128, 129, 135, 138, 139, 145, 155–159, 173, and 175; NCGA Statement 4, paragraphs 6, 13, 16, and 17; NCGA Statement 5, paragraphs 5, 6, 10, 11, and 14–17; NCGA Interpretation 3, *Revenue Recognition—Property Taxes,* paragraph 3; NCGA Interpretation 6, paragraphs 2, 4, 5, and 8; NCGA Interpretation 8, *Certain Pension Matters,* paragraph 12; NCGA Interpretation 9, *Certain Fund Classifications and Balance Sheet Accounts,* paragraphs 9 and 12; NCGA Interpretation 10, paragraphs 11, 14, 15, and 25; GASB Statement No. 1, *Authoritative Status of NCGA Pronouncements and AICPA Industry Audit Guide,* paragraph 8; GASB Statement No. 3, *Deposits with Financial Institutions, Investments (including Repurchase Agreements), and Reverse Repurchase Agreements,* paragraphs 64 and 65; GASB Statement No. 6, *Accounting and Financial Reporting for Special Assessments,* paragraphs 13, 15, 17, 19, and 23; GASB Statement 7, paragraphs 1, 3, 7, 8, 10, 11, and 14; GASB Statement No. 8, *Applicability of FASB Statement No. 93, "Recognition of Depreciation by Not-for-Profit Organizations," to Certain State and Local Governmental Entities,* paragraphs 10 and 11 and footnote 3; GASB Statement No. 9, *Reporting Cash Flows of Proprietary and Nonexpendable Trust Funds and Governmental Entities That Use Proprietary Fund Accounting,* paragraphs 1, 5, 17, 18, 21, 22, and 31–34; GASB Statement No. 10, *Accounting and Financial Reporting for Risk Financing and Related Insurance Issues,* paragraphs 52, 53, 61, 63–65, 67–69, and 78 and footnote 12; GASB Statement No. 12, *Disclosure of Information on Postemployment Benefits Other Than Pension Benefits by State and Local Governmental Employers,* paragraph 12; GASB Statement No. 13, *Accounting for Operating Leases with Scheduled Rent Increases,* paragraphs 1, 4, 7, and 9; GASB Statement 14, paragraphs 9, 11, 12, 19, 42, 44, 50–52, 54, 58, 63, 73, 74, and 131; GASB Statement No. 16, *Accounting for Compensated Absences,* paragraph 13; GASB Statement 17, paragraphs 4 and 6; GASB Statement No. 18, *Accounting for Municipal Solid Waste Landfill Closure and Postclosure Care Costs*, paragraphs 3, 7, 10, 11, and 16 and footnote 2; GASB Statement 20, paragraphs 7–9; GASB Statement 21, paragraphs 3–5; GASB Statement No. 23, *Accounting and Financial Reporting for Refundings of Debt Reported by Proprietary Activities*, paragraphs 1, 3, 4, and 6; GASB Statement No. 25, *Financial Reporting for Defined Benefit Pension Plans and Note Disclosures for Defined Contribution Plans*, paragraph 13 and footnote 9; GASB Statement No. 26, *Financial Reporting for Postemployment Healthcare Plans Administered by Defined Benefit Pension Plans*, paragraph 4 and footnote 4; GASB Statement No. 27, *Accounting for Pensions by State and Local Governmental Employers*, paragraphs 15–17, 19, 23, and 25 and footnote 14; GASB Statement No. 28, *Accounting and Financial Reporting for Securities Lending Transactions*, paragraphs 3, 4, and 10 and footnotes 3, 6, and 9; GASB Statement 29, paragraph 7; GASB Statement No. 31, *Accounting and Financial Reporting for Certain Investments and for External Investment Pools*, paragraphs 7, 14, 18, and 19; GASB Statement No. 32, *Accounting and Financial Reporting for Internal Revenue Code Section 457 Deferred Compensation Plans*, paragraph 4; GASB Statement No. 33, *Accounting and Financial Reporting for Nonexchange Transactions*, paragraph 11; GASB Interpretation No. 1, *Demand Bonds Issued by State and Local Governmental Entities*, paragraphs 6, 10, and 13 and footnote 2; and GASB Interpretation No. 4, *Accounting and Financial Reporting for Capitalization Contributions to Public Entity Risk Pools*, paragraph 6.

## Minimum Requirements for Basic Financial Statements and Required Supplementary Information

6.  The minimum requirements for management's discussion and analysis (MD&A), basic financial statements, and required supplementary information other than MD&A are:

a.  *Management's discussion and analysis.* MD&A, a component of RSI, should introduce the basic financial statements and provide an analytical overview of the government's financial activities. (See paragraphs 8–11.)

b.  *Basic financial statements.* The basic financial statements should include:

(1) *Government-wide financial statements.* The government-wide statements should display information about the reporting government as a whole, except for its fiduciary activities. The statements should include separate columns for the governmental and business-type activities of the primary government[4] as well as for its component units. Government-wide financial statements should be prepared

---

[4] Unless otherwise noted, the term *primary government* includes the primary government and its blended component units, as defined in Statement 14.

using the economic resources measurement focus and the accrual basis of accounting. (See paragraphs 12–62.)

(2) *Fund financial statements.* Fund financial statements for the primary government's governmental, proprietary, and fiduciary funds should be presented after the government-wide statements. These statements display information about major funds individually and nonmajor funds in the aggregate for governmental and enterprise funds. Fiduciary statements should include financial information for fiduciary funds and similar component units. Each of the three fund categories should be reported using the measurement focus and basis of accounting required for that category. (See paragraphs 63–112.)

(3) *Notes to the financial statements.* (See paragraphs 113–123.)

c. *Required supplementary information other than MD&A.* Except for MD&A, required supplementary information, including the required budgetary comparison information, should be presented immediately following the notes to the financial statements.[5] (See paragraphs 129–133.)

7. The following diagram illustrates the minimum requirements for general purpose external financial statements.

```
         ┌─────────────────────────┐
         │ Management's discussion │
         │      and analysis       │
         └─────────────────────────┘
                     │
┌──────────────────────┬──────────────────────┐
│   Government-wide    │   Fund financial     │
│ financial statements │     statements       │
├──────────────────────┴──────────────────────┤
│      Notes to the financial statements      │
└─────────────────────────────────────────────┘
                     │
         ┌─────────────────────────┐
         │ Required supplementary  │
         │      information        │
         │   (other than MD&A)     │
         └─────────────────────────┘
```

---

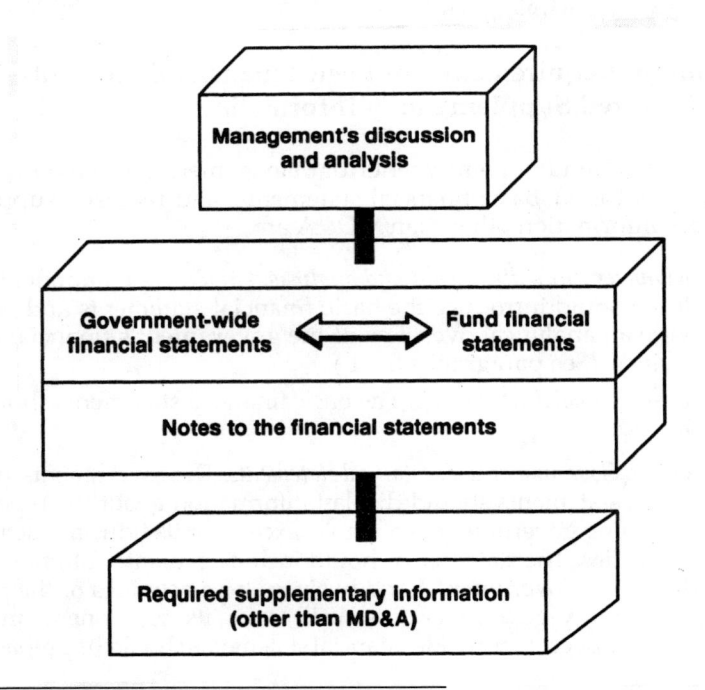

[5] This paragraph does not modify the provisions of GASB Statement No. 30, *Risk Financing Omnibus,* paragraph 7.

## Management's Discussion and Analysis (MD&A)

8. The basic financial statements should be preceded by MD&A, which is required supplementary information (RSI). MD&A should provide an objective and easily readable analysis of the government's financial activities based on currently known[6] facts, decisions, or conditions. The financial managers of governments are knowledgeable about the transactions, events, and conditions that are reflected in the government's financial report and of the fiscal policies that govern its operations. MD&A provides financial managers with the opportunity to present both a short- and a long-term analysis of the government's activities.[7]

9. MD&A should discuss the current-year results in comparison with the prior year, with emphasis on the current year. This fact-based analysis should discuss the positive and negative aspects of the comparison with the prior year. The use of charts, graphs, and tables is encouraged to enhance the understandability of the information.

10. MD&A should focus on the primary government. Comments in MD&A should distinguish between information pertaining to the primary government and that of its component units. Determining whether to discuss matters related to a component unit is a matter of professional judgment and should be based on the individual component unit's significance to the total of all discretely presented component units and that component unit's relationship with the primary government. When appropriate, the reporting entity's MD&A should refer readers to the component unit's separately issued financial statements.

11. MD&A requirements established by this Statement are general rather than specific to encourage financial managers to effectively report only the most relevant information and avoid "boilerplate" discussion. At a minimum, MD&A should include:

a. A brief discussion of the basic financial statements, including the relationships of the statements to each other, and the significant differences in the information they provide. This discussion should include analyses that assist readers in understanding why measurements and results reported in fund financial statements either reinforce information in government-wide statements or provide additional information.

---

[6] For purposes of MD&A, *currently known facts* are information that management is aware of as of the date of the auditor's report.

[7] If a letter of transmittal is presented in the introductory section of a comprehensive annual financial report (CAFR), governments are encouraged not to duplicate information contained in MD&A.

b. Condensed financial information derived from government-wide financial statements comparing the current year to the prior year. At a minimum, governments should present the information needed to support their analysis of financial position and results of operations required in c, below, including these elements:
   (1) Total assets, distinguishing between capital and other assets
   (2) Total liabilities, distinguishing between long-term liabilities and other liabilities
   (3) Total net assets, distinguishing among amounts invested in capital assets, net of related debt; restricted amounts; and unrestricted amounts
   (4) Program revenues, by major source
   (5) General revenues, by major source
   (6) Total revenues
   (7) Program expenses, at a minimum by function
   (8) Total expenses
   (9) Excess (deficiency) before contributions to term and permanent endowments or permanent fund principal, special and extraordinary items, and transfers
   (10) Contributions
   (11) Special and extraordinary items
   (12) Transfers
   (13) Change in net assets
   (14) Ending net assets
c. An analysis of the government's overall financial position and results of operations to assist users in assessing whether financial position has improved or deteriorated as a result of the year's operations. The analysis should address both governmental and business-type activities as reported in the government-wide financial statements and should include *reasons* for significant changes from the prior year, not simply the amounts or percentages of change. In addition, important economic factors, such as changes in the tax or employment bases, that significantly affected operating results for the year should be discussed.
d. An analysis of balances and transactions of individual funds. The analysis should address the reasons for significant changes in fund balances or fund net assets and whether restrictions, commitments, or other limitations significantly affect the availability of fund resources for future use.
e. An analysis of significant variations between original and final budget amounts and between final budget amounts and actual budget results for the general fund (or its equivalent). The

analysis should include any currently known reasons for those variations that are expected to have a significant effect on future services or liquidity.

f.  A description of significant capital asset and long-term debt activity[8] during the year, including a discussion of commitments made for capital expenditures, changes in credit ratings, and debt limitations that may affect the financing of planned facilities or services.

g.  A discussion by governments that use the modified approach (paragraphs 23–25) to report some or all of their infrastructure assets including:

   (1) Significant changes in the assessed condition of eligible infrastructure assets from previous condition assessments

   (2) How the current assessed condition compares with the condition level the government has established

   (3) Any significant differences from the estimated annual amount to maintain/preserve eligible infrastructure assets compared with the actual amounts spent during the current period.

h.  A description of currently known facts,[9] decisions, or conditions that are expected to have a significant effect on financial position (net assets) or results of operations (revenues, expenses, and other changes in net assets).

## Government-wide Financial Statements

12. The government-wide financial statements consist of a statement of net assets and a statement of activities. Those statements should:

a.  Report information about the overall government without displaying individual funds or fund types

b.  Exclude information about fiduciary activities, including component units that are fiduciary in nature (such as certain public employee retirement systems)

c.  Distinguish between the primary government and its discretely presented component units

d.  Distinguish between governmental activities and business-type activities of the primary government

---

[8] Paragraphs 116 through 120 require certain disclosures about capital assets and long-term debt. It is sufficient for purposes of this discussion in MD&A to summarize that information and refer to it for additional details.

[9] See footnote 6.

e.   Measure and report all assets (both financial and capital), liabilities, revenues, expenses, gains, and losses using the economic resources measurement focus and accrual basis of accounting.

### Focus of the Government-wide Financial Statements

13. The statement of net assets and the statement of activities should display information about the reporting government as a whole. The statements should include the primary government and its component units, except for the fiduciary funds of the primary government and component units that are fiduciary in nature. Those funds and component units should be reported only in the statements of fiduciary net assets and changes in fiduciary net assets. (See paragraphs 106–111.)

14. The focus of the government-wide financial statements should be on the primary government, as defined in Statement 14. Separate rows and columns should be used to distinguish between the total primary government and its discretely presented component units. A total column should be presented for the primary government. A total column for the entity as a whole may be presented but is not required. Prior-year data may be presented in the government-wide statements but also are not required.

15. Separate rows and columns also should be used to distinguish between the governmental and business-type activities[10] of the primary government. Governmental activities generally are financed through taxes, intergovernmental revenues, and other nonexchange revenues. These activities are usually reported in governmental funds and internal service funds. Business-type activities are financed in whole or in part by fees charged to external parties for goods or services. These activities are usually reported in enterprise funds.

### Measurement Focus and Basis of Accounting

16. The statement of net assets and the statement of activities should be prepared using the economic resources measurement focus and the accrual basis of accounting. Revenues, expenses, gains, losses, assets, and liabilities resulting from exchange and exchange-like transactions should be recognized when the exchange

---

[10] This paragraph is not intended to require segregation of activities into governmental and proprietary funds beyond what is currently reported by management of the government unless the activity is required to be reported as an enterprise fund, as discussed in paragraph 67.

takes place.[11] Revenues, expenses, gains, losses, assets, and liabilities resulting from nonexchange transactions should be recognized in accordance with the requirements of Statement 33. (Additional guidance on reporting capital assets is discussed in paragraphs 18 through 29, below.)

17. Reporting for governmental and business-type activities should be based on all applicable GASB pronouncements as well as the following pronouncements issued on or before November 30, 1989, *unless* those pronouncements conflict with or contradict GASB pronouncements:

a. Financial Accounting Standards Board (FASB) Statements[12] and Interpretations
b. Accounting Principles Board (APB) Opinions[13]
c. Accounting Research Bulletins (ARBs) of the Committee on Accounting Procedure.

Business-type activities may also apply FASB pronouncements issued after November 30, 1989, as provided in paragraph 7 of GASB Statement 20, as amended by this Statement.

*Reporting Capital Assets*

18. Capital assets should be reported at historical cost. The cost of a capital asset should include capitalized interest and ancillary charges necessary to place the asset into its intended location and condition for use. Ancillary charges include costs that are directly attributable to asset acquisition—such as freight and transportation charges, site preparation costs, and professional fees. Donated capital assets should be reported at their estimated fair value at the time of acquisition plus ancillary charges, if any.

---

[11] In this Statement, the terms *transaction* and *transactions* refer only to *external* events in which something of value (benefit) passes between two or more parties. The difference between exchange and exchange-like transactions is a matter of degree. In contrast to a "pure" exchange transaction, an exchange-like transaction is one in which the values exchanged, though related, may not be quite equal or in which the direct benefits may not be exclusively for the parties to the transaction. Nevertheless, the exchange characteristics of the transaction are strong enough to justify treating the transaction as an exchange for accounting recognition.

[12] The provisions of FASB Statement No. 71, *Accounting for the Effects of Certain Types of Regulation,* only apply to governments that have *qualifying* enterprise funds.

[13] Changes in accounting principles, addressed in APB Opinion No. 20, *Accounting Changes,* as amended, should be reported as restatements of beginning net assets/fund equity, not as a separately identified cumulative effect in the current-period statement of activities or proprietary fund statement of revenues, expenses, and changes in fund net assets.

19. As used in this Statement, the term *capital assets* includes land, improvements to land, easements, buildings, building improvements, vehicles, machinery, equipment, works of art and historical treasures, infrastructure, and all other tangible or intangible assets that are used in operations and that have initial useful lives extending beyond a single reporting period. *Infrastructure assets* are long-lived capital assets that normally are stationary in nature and normally can be preserved for a significantly greater number of years than most capital assets. Examples of infrastructure assets include roads, bridges, tunnels, drainage systems, water and sewer systems, dams, and lighting systems. Buildings, except those that are an ancillary part of a network of infrastructure assets, should not be considered infrastructure assets for purposes of this Statement.

20. Capital assets that are being or have been depreciated (paragraph 22) should be reported net of accumulated depreciation in the statement of net assets. (Accumulated depreciation may be reported on the face of the statement or disclosed in the notes.) Capital assets that are not being depreciated, such as land or infrastructure assets reported using the modified approach (paragraphs 23 through 25), should be reported separately if the government has a significant amount of these assets. Capital assets also may be reported in greater detail, such as by major class of asset (for example, infrastructure, buildings and improvements, vehicles, machinery and equipment). Required disclosures are discussed in paragraphs 116 and 117.

21. Capital assets should be depreciated over their estimated useful lives unless they are either inexhaustible or are infrastructure assets reported using the modified approach in paragraphs 23 through 25. Inexhaustible capital assets such as land and land improvements should not be depreciated.

22. Depreciation expense should be reported in the statement of activities as discussed in paragraphs 44 and 45. Depreciation expense should be measured by allocating the net cost of depreciable assets (historical cost less estimated salvage value) over their estimated useful lives in a systematic and rational manner. It may be calculated for (a) a class of assets, (b) a network of assets,[14] (c) a subsystem of a network,[15] or (d) individual assets. (Composite methods may be used to calculate

---

[14] A network of assets is composed of all assets that provide a particular type of service for a government. A network of infrastructure assets may be only one infrastructure *asset* that is composed of many *components*. For example, a network of infrastructure assets may be a dam composed of a concrete dam, a concrete spillway, and a series of locks.

[15] A subsystem of a network of assets is composed of all assets that make up a similar portion or segment of a network of assets. For example, all the roads of a government could be considered a network of infrastructure assets. Interstate highways, state highways, and rural roads could each be considered a subsystem of that network.

depreciation expense. See paragraphs 161 through 166 for a more complete discussion of depreciation.)

Modified approach

23. Infrastructure assets that are part of a network or subsystem of a network[16] (hereafter, eligible infrastructure assets) are not required to be depreciated as long as two requirements are met. First, the government manages the eligible infrastructure assets using an asset management system that has the characteristics set forth below; second, the government documents that the eligible infrastructure assets are being preserved approximately at (or above) a condition level established and disclosed by the government.[17] To meet the first requirement, the asset management system should:

a. Have an up-to-date inventory of eligible infrastructure assets

b. Perform condition assessments[18] of the eligible infrastructure assets and summarize the results using a measurement scale

c. Estimate each year the annual amount to maintain and preserve the eligible infrastructure assets at the condition level established and disclosed by the government.

24. Determining what constitutes adequate documentary evidence to meet the second requirement in paragraph 23 for using the modified approach requires professional judgment because of variations among governments' asset management systems and condition assessment methods. These factors also may vary within governments for different eligible infrastructure assets. However, governments should document that:

a. Complete condition assessments of eligible infrastructure assets are performed in a consistent manner at least every three years.[19]

---

[16] If a government chooses not to depreciate a subsystem of infrastructure assets based on the provisions of this paragraph, the characteristics of the asset management system required by this paragraph and the documentary evidence required by paragraph 24 should be for that *subsystem* of infrastructure assets.

[17] The condition level should be established and documented by administrative or executive policy, or by legislative action.

[18] Condition assessments should be documented in such a manner that they can be replicated. Replicable condition assessments are those that are based on sufficiently understandable and complete measurement methods such that different measurers using the same methods would reach substantially similar results. Condition assessments may be performed by the government itself or by contract.

[19] Condition assessments may be performed using statistical samples that are representative of the eligible infrastructure assets being preserved. Governments may choose to assess their eligible infrastructure assets on a cyclical basis. For example, one-third may be assessed each year. If a cyclical basis is used, a condition assessment is considered *complete* for a network or subsystem only when condition assessments have been performed for all (or statistical samples of) eligible infrastructure assets in that network or subsystem.

APP-18   *Appendix*

b.   The results of the three most recent complete condition assessments provide reasonable assurance that the eligible infrastructure assets are being preserved approximately at (or above) the condition level[20] established and disclosed by the government.

25.   If eligible infrastructure assets meet the requirements of paragraphs 23 and 24 and are not depreciated, all expenditures made for those assets (except for additions and improvements) should be expensed in the period incurred. Additions and improvements to eligible infrastructure assets should be capitalized. Additions or improvements increase the capacity or efficiency of infrastructure assets rather than preserve the useful life of the assets.

26.   If the requirements of paragraphs 23 and 24 are no longer met, the depreciation requirements of paragraphs 21 and 22 should be applied for subsequent reporting periods.[21]

**Reporting works of art and historical treasures**

27.   Except as discussed in this paragraph, governments should capitalize works of art, historical treasures, and similar assets at their historical cost or fair value at date of donation (estimated if necessary) whether they are held as individual items or in a collection. Governments are encouraged, but not required, to capitalize a collection (and all additions to that collection) whether donated or purchased that meets all of the following conditions.[22] The collection is:

a.   Held for public exhibition, education, or research in furtherance of public service, rather than financial gain
b.   Protected, kept unencumbered, cared for, and preserved
c.   Subject to an organizational policy that requires the proceeds from sales of collection items to be used to acquire other items for collections.

Governments should disclose information about their works of art and historical collections as required by paragraph 118.

28.   Recipient governments should recognize as revenues donations of works of art, historical treasures, and similar assets, in accordance with Statement 33. When donated collection items are added

---

[20] For example, condition could be measured either by a condition index or as the percentage of a network of infrastructure assets in good or poor condition.
[21] This change should be reported as a change in accounting estimate.
[22] Collections already capitalized at June 30, 1999, should remain capitalized and all additions to those collections should be capitalized, even if they meet the conditions for exemption from capitalization.

to *noncapitalized* collections, governments should recognize program expense equal to the amount of revenues recognized.

29. Capitalized collections or individual items that are exhaustible, such as exhibits whose useful lives are diminished by display or educational or research applications, should be depreciated over their estimated useful lives. Depreciation is not required for collections or individual items that are inexhaustible.

### Required Financial Statements—Statement of Net Assets

30. The statement of net assets should report all financial and capital resources. Governments are encouraged to present the statement in a format that displays *assets less liabilities equal net assets*, although the traditional balance sheet format (assets equal liabilities plus net assets) may be used. Regardless of the format used, however, the statement of net assets should report the difference between assets and liabilities as *net assets*, not fund balances or equity.

31. Governments are encouraged to present assets and liabilities in order of their relative liquidity.[23] An asset's liquidity should be determined by how readily it is expected to be converted to cash and whether restrictions limit the government's ability to use the resources. A liability's liquidity is based on its maturity, or when cash is expected to be used to liquidate it. The liquidity of an asset or liability may be determined by assessing the average liquidity of the class of assets or liabilities to which it belongs, even though individual balances may be significantly more or less liquid than others in the same class and some items may have both current and long-term elements. Liabilities whose average maturities are greater than one year should be reported in two components—the amount due within one year and the amount due in more than one year. Additional disclosures concerning long-term liabilities are discussed in paragraph 119.

32. The difference between a government's assets and its liabilities is its *net assets*. Net assets should be displayed in three components—*invested in capital assets, net of related debt; restricted* (distinguishing between major categories of restrictions); and *unrestricted*.

### Invested in Capital Assets, Net of Related Debt

33. This component of net assets consists of capital assets (see paragraph 19), including *restricted* capital assets, net of accumulated

---

[23] Use of a *classified* statement of net assets, which distinguishes between all current and long-term assets and liabilities, is also acceptable. (Paragraphs 97 through 99 provide guidance on presenting classified balance sheets, including reporting on restricted assets.)

depreciation and reduced by the outstanding balances of any bonds, mortgages, notes, or other borrowings that are attributable to the acquisition, construction, or improvement of those assets. If there are significant unspent related debt proceeds at year-end, the portion of the debt attributable to the unspent proceeds should *not* be included in the calculation of *invested in capital assets, net of related debt*. Rather, that portion of the debt should be included in the same net assets component as the unspent proceeds—for example, *restricted for capital projects*.

### Restricted Net Assets

34. Net assets should be reported as restricted when constraints placed on net asset use are either:[24]

a. Externally imposed by creditors (such as through debt covenants), grantors, contributors, or laws or regulations of other governments

b. Imposed by law through constitutional provisions or enabling legislation.

*Enabling legislation*,[25] as the term is used in this Statement, authorizes the government to assess, levy, charge, or otherwise mandate payment of resources (from external resource providers) *and* includes a legally enforceable requirement that those resources be used only for the specific purposes stipulated in the legislation.

35. When permanent endowments or permanent fund principal amounts are included, "restricted net assets" should be displayed in two additional components—expendable and nonexpendable. Nonexpendable net assets are those that are required to be retained in perpetuity.

### Unrestricted Net Assets

36. Unrestricted net assets consist of net assets that do not meet the definition of "restricted" or "invested in capital assets, net of related debt."

37. In the governmental environment, net assets often are *designated* to indicate that management does not consider them to be

---

[24] Because different measurement focuses and bases of accounting are used in the statement of net assets than in governmental fund statements, and because the definition of *reserved* includes more than resources that are *restricted* (as discussed in this paragraph), amounts reported as *reserved fund balances* in governmental funds will generally be different from amounts reported as *restricted net assets* in the statement of net assets.

[25] Enabling legislation also includes restrictions on asset use established by a governmental utility's own governing board when that utility reports based on FASB Statement 71.

available for general operations. In contrast to *restricted* net assets, these types of constraints on resources are *internal* and management can remove or modify them. As described in paragraph 34, however, *enabling legislation* established by the reporting government should not be construed as an *internal constraint*. Designations of net assets should not be reported on the face of the statement of net assets.

### Required Financial Statements—Statement of Activities

38. The operations of the reporting government should be presented in a format that reports the *net (expense) revenue* of its individual functions. An objective of using the net (expense) revenue format is to report the relative financial burden of each of the reporting government's functions on its taxpayers. This format identifies the extent to which each function of the government draws from the general revenues of the government or is self-financing through fees and intergovernmental aid. As discussed in paragraph 47, this notion of burden on the reporting government's taxpayers is important in determining what is program or general revenue. General revenues, contributions to term and permanent endowments, contributions to permanent fund principal, special and extraordinary items, and transfers should be reported separately after the total net expenses of the government's functions, ultimately arriving at the "change in net assets" for the period. An example of a format that meets these requirements is illustrated in paragraph 54.[26]

39. The statement of activities should present *governmental* activities at least at the level of detail required in the governmental fund statement of revenues, expenditures, and changes in fund balances—at a minimum by *function*,[27] as discussed in NCGA Statement 1, paragraphs 111 through 116. Governments should present *business-type* activities at least by *segment*, as discussed in paragraph 122.

40. Governments are encouraged to provide data in the statement of activities at a more detailed level if the additional detail provides more useful information without significantly reducing readers' ability to understand the statement. No specific level of detail is appropriate for all governments; some have hundreds of programs and others have only a few. Therefore, reporting in greater detail than the minimum requirements in paragraph 39 may be practical for some governments but not for others.

---

[26] Some governments may modify the standard format of the statement of activities or use an alternative format. See paragraph 136.

[27] The term *function* is used in this Statement to refer to the minimum level of detail for *both* governmental *and* business-type activities required to be presented in the statement of activities.

## Expenses

41. Governments should report all expenses by function except for those that meet the definitions of special or extraordinary items, discussed in paragraphs 55 and 56. As a minimum, governments should report direct expenses for each function. *Direct* expenses are those that are specifically associated with a service, program, or department and, thus, are clearly identifiable to a particular function.

42. Some functions, such as general government, support services, or administration, include expenses that are, in essence, *indirect* expenses of other functions. Governments are not required to allocate those indirect expenses to other functions. However, some governments may prefer to allocate some indirect expenses or use a full-cost allocation approach[28] among functions. If indirect expenses are allocated, direct and indirect expenses should be presented in separate columns to enhance comparability of direct expenses between governments that allocate indirect expenses and those that do not. A column totaling direct and indirect expenses may be presented but is not required.

43. Some governments charge funds or programs (through internal service funds or the general fund) for "centralized" expenses, which may include an administrative overhead component. Governments are not required to identify and eliminate these administrative overhead charges, but the summary of significant accounting policies should disclose that they are included in direct expenses.

44. Depreciation expense for capital assets that can specifically be identified with a function should be included in its direct expenses. Depreciation expense for "shared" capital assets (for example, a facility that houses the police department, the building inspection office, and the water utility office) should be ratably included in the direct expenses of the appropriate functions. Depreciation expense for capital assets such as a city hall or a state office building that essentially serves all functions is not required to be included in the *direct* expenses of the various functions. This depreciation expense may be included as a separate line in the statement of activities or as part of the "general government" (or its counterpart) function (and in either case, may be allocated to other functions as discussed in paragraph 42). If a government uses a separate line in the statement of activities to report *unallocated* depreciation expense, it should clearly indicate on the face of the statement that this line item excludes *direct* depreciation expenses of the various programs. Required disclosures about depreciation expense are discussed in paragraph 117.

---

[28] As used in this Statement, a *full-cost allocation approach* means allocating indirect expenses among functions with the objective of allocating *all* expenses, including certain general government expenses.

45. Depreciation expense for general infrastructure assets should not be allocated to the various functions. It should be reported as a direct expense of the function (for example, public works or transportation) that the reporting government normally associates with capital outlays for, and maintenance of, infrastructure assets or as a separate line in the statement of activities.

46. *Interest on general long-term liabilities* generally should be considered an indirect expense. However, interest on long-term debt should be *included* in direct expenses in those limited instances when borrowing is essential to the creation or continuing existence of a program and it would be misleading to exclude the interest from direct expenses of that program (for example, a new program that is highly leveraged in its early stages). Excluding the cost of the borrowing when it is necessary to establish or maintain the program would significantly understate its direct program expenses. Most interest on general long-term liabilities, however, does not qualify as a direct expense and should be reported in the statement of activities as a separate line that clearly indicates that it excludes direct interest expenses, if any, reported in other functions. The amount excluded should be disclosed in the notes or presented on the face of the statement.

*Revenues*

47. Programs are financed from essentially four sources:

a. Those who purchase, use, or directly benefit from the goods or services of the program (This group may extend beyond the boundaries of the reporting government's taxpayers or citizenry or be a subset of it.)

b. Parties outside the reporting government's citizenry (This group includes other governments and nongovernmental entities or individuals.)

c. The reporting government's taxpayers (This is all taxpayers, regardless of whether they benefit from a particular program.)

d. The governmental institution itself (for example, through investing).

For the purposes of the statement of activities:

- Type a is always a program revenue.
- Type b is a program revenue, if restricted to a specific program or programs. If unrestricted, type b is a general revenue.
- Type c is always a general revenue, even if restricted to a specific program.
- Type d is usually a general revenue.

**Program revenues**

48. Program revenues derive directly from the program itself or from parties outside the reporting government's taxpayers or citizenry, as a whole; they reduce the net cost of the function to be financed from the government's general revenues. The statement of activities should separately report three categories of program revenues: (a) charges for services, (b) program-specific *operating* grants and contributions, and (c) program-specific *capital* grants and contributions.

49. *Charges for services* include revenues based on exchange or exchange-like transactions. These revenues arise from charges to customers or applicants who purchase, use, or directly benefit from the goods, services, or privileges provided. Revenues in this category include fees charged for specific services, such as water use or garbage collection; licenses and permits, such as dog licenses, liquor licenses, and building permits; operating special assessments, such as for street cleaning or special street lighting; and any other amounts charged to service recipients. Payments from other governments that are exchange transactions—for example, when County A reimburses County B for boarding County A's prisoners—also should be reported as charges for services.

50. *Program-specific grants and contributions (operating and capital)* include revenues arising from mandatory and voluntary nonexchange transactions with other governments, organizations, or individuals that are restricted[29] for use in a particular program. Some grants and contributions consist of capital assets or resources that are restricted for capital purposes—to purchase, construct, or renovate capital assets associated with a specific program. These should be reported separately from grants and contributions that may be used *either* for operating expenses or for capital expenditures of the program at the discretion of the reporting government. These categories of program revenue are specifically attributable to a program and reduce the net expense of that program to the reporting government. For example, a state may provide an operating grant to a county sheriff's department for a drug-awareness-and-enforcement program or a capital grant to finance construction of a new jail. Multipurpose grants (those that provide financing for more than one program) should be reported as program revenue if the amounts restricted to each program are specifically identified in either the grant award or the grant application.[30] Multipurpose grants that do not provide for specific identification of the programs and amounts should be reported as general revenues.

---

[29] Paragraph 34 discusses the meaning of the term *restricted*.
[30] The grant application should be used for this purpose only if the grant award was based on that application.

51. Earnings on endowments or permanent fund investments should be reported as program revenues if restricted to a program or programs specifically identified in the endowment or permanent fund agreement or contract. Earnings from endowments or permanent funds that finance "general fund programs" or "general operating expenses," for example, should not be reported as program revenue. Similarly, earnings on investments not held by permanent funds also may be legally restricted to specific functions or programs. For example, interest earnings on state grants may be required to be used to support a specific program. When earnings on the *invested accumulated resources* of a program are *legally restricted* to be used for that program, the net cost to be financed by the government's general revenues is reduced, and those investment earnings should be reported as program revenues.

**General revenues**

52. All revenues are *general revenues* unless they are required to be reported as program revenues, as discussed in paragraphs 48 through 51. All taxes, even those that are levied for a specific purpose, are general revenues and should be reported by type of tax—for example, sales tax, property tax, franchise tax, income tax. All other nontax revenues (including interest, grants, and contributions) that do not meet the criteria to be reported as program revenues should also be reported as general revenues. General revenues should be reported after total net expense of the government's functions.

**Reporting contributions to term and permanent endowments, contributions to permanent fund principal, special and extraordinary items, and transfers**

53. Contributions to term and permanent endowments, contributions to permanent fund principal, special and extraordinary items (defined in paragraphs 55 and 56), and transfers (defined in paragraph 112) between governmental and business-type activities should each be reported separately from, but in the same manner as, general revenues. That is, these sources of financing the net cost of the government's programs should be reported at the bottom of the statement of activities to arrive at the all-inclusive change in net assets for the period.

## *Statement of Activities Format*

54. For most governments, the following format provides the most appropriate method[31] for displaying the information required to be reported in the statement of activities:

---

[31] See paragraph 136.

| Functions | Expenses | Program Revenues ||| Net (Expense) Revenue and Changes in Net Assets ||||
| | | Charges for Services | Operating Grants and Contributions | Capital Grants and Contributions | Primary Government ||| Component Units |
| | | | | | Governmental Activities | Business-type Activities | Total | |
|---|---|---|---|---|---|---|---|---|
| **Primary government** | | | | | | | | |
| Governmental activities | | | | | | | | |
| Function # 1 | XX | XX | X | X | (XX) | — | (XX) | — |
| Function # 2 | XX | XX | X | — | (XX) | — | (XX) | — |
| Function # 3 | XX | XX | X | X | (X) | — | (X) | — |
| Total governmental activities | XXXX | XXX | XX | XX | (XX) | — | (XX) | — |
| Business-type activities | | | | | | | | |
| BTA # 1 | XXXX | XXXX | — | X | — | XX | XX | — |
| BTA # 2 | XXXXX | XXXX | — | XX | — | XXX | XXX | — |
| Total business-type activities | XXXXX | XXXX | XX | XX | (XXX) | XXX | XXX | — |
| Total primary government | XXXXXX | XXXXX | XX | XX | — | XXX | XX | — |
| **Component units** | | | | | | | | |
| CU # 1 | XXXX | XXXX | XX | XX | | | XX | XX |
| | | General revenues—detailed | | | XXX | X | XXX | XX |
| | | Contributions to permanent funds | | | XX | — | XX | — |
| | | Special items | | | X | X | X | — |
| | | Transfers | | | XX | (XX) | — | — |
| | | Total general revenues, contributions, special items, and transfers | | | XXX | X | XXX | XX |
| | | Change in net assets | | | X | XX | XX | XX |
| | | Net assets—beginning | | | XXXXX | XXXXX | XXXX | XXXXX |
| | | Net assets—ending | | | XXXXX | XXXXX | XXXX | XXXXX |

## Special and Extraordinary Items

55. *Extraordinary items* are transactions or other events that are both unusual in nature and infrequent in occurrence. APB Opinion No. 30, *Reporting the Results of Operations—Reporting the Effects of Disposal of a Segment of a Business, and Extraordinary, Unusual and Infrequently Occurring Events and Transactions,* as amended and interpreted, defines the terms *unusual in nature* and *infrequency of occurrence.* As discussed in paragraph 53, extraordinary items should be reported separately at the bottom of the statement of activities.

56. Significant transactions or other events *within the control of management* that are *either* unusual in nature *or* infrequent in occurrence are *special items.* Special items should also be reported separately in the statement of activities, before extraordinary items, if any. In addition, governments should disclose in the notes to financial statements any significant transactions or other events that are either unusual or infrequent but not within the control of management.

## Eliminations and Reclassifications

57. In the process of aggregating data for the statement of net assets and the statement of activities, some amounts reported as interfund activity and balances in the funds should be eliminated or reclassified.

### Internal balances—statement of net assets

58. Eliminations should be made in the statement of net assets to minimize the "grossing-up" effect on assets and liabilities within the governmental and business-type activities columns of the primary government. As a result, amounts reported in the funds as interfund receivables and payables should be eliminated in the governmental and business-type activities columns of the statement of net assets, except for the net residual amounts due between governmental and business-type activities, which should be presented as internal balances. Amounts reported in the funds as receivable from or payable to fiduciary funds should be included in the statement of net assets as receivable from and payable to external parties (consistent with the nature of fiduciary funds), rather than as internal balances. All internal balances should be eliminated in the total primary government column.

### Internal activities—statement of activities

59. Eliminations should be made in the statement of activities to remove the "doubling-up" effect of internal service fund activity. The effect of similar internal events (such as allocations of accounting staff salaries) *that are, in effect, allocations of overhead expenses* from one

function to another or within the same function also should be eliminated, so that the allocated expenses are reported only by the function to which they were allocated.

60. The effect of interfund services provided and used (see paragraph 112) between functions—for example, the sale of water or electricity from a utility to the general government—should not be eliminated in the statement of activities. To do so would misstate both the expenses of the purchasing function and the program revenues of the selling function.

**Intra-entity activity**

61. Resource flows between the primary government and *blended* component units should be reclassified in accordance with the provisions of paragraph 112 as internal activity in the financial statements of the reporting entity. Resource flows (except those that affect the balance sheet only, such as loans and repayments) between a primary government and its discretely presented component units should be reported as if they were external transactions—that is, as revenues and expenses. However, amounts payable and receivable between the primary government and its discretely presented component units or between those components should be reported on a separate line.

*Reporting Internal Service Fund Balances*

62. Internal service fund asset and liability balances that are not eliminated in the statement of net assets should normally be reported in the *governmental* activities column. Although internal service funds are reported as proprietary funds, the activities accounted for in them (the financing of goods and services for other funds of the government) are usually more governmental than business-type in nature. If enterprise funds are the predominant or only participants in an internal service fund, however, the government should report that internal service fund's residual assets and liabilities within the business-type activities column in the statement of net assets.

# Fund Financial Statements

## Funds—Overview and Definitions

63. Fund financial statements should be used to report additional and detailed information about the primary government. Governments should report governmental, proprietary, and fiduciary funds to the extent that they have activities that meet the criteria for using those funds. (See paragraphs 64–73.)

a. Governmental funds (emphasizing major funds)
   (1) The general fund
   (2) Special revenue funds
   (3) Capital projects funds
   (4) Debt service funds
   (5) Permanent funds
b. Proprietary funds
   (6) Enterprise funds (emphasizing major funds)
   (7) Internal service funds
c. Fiduciary funds and similar component units
   (8) Pension (and other employee benefit) trust funds
   (9) Investment trust funds
   (10) Private-purpose trust funds
   (11) Agency funds.

*Governmental Funds*

64. Governmental fund reporting focuses primarily on the sources, uses, and balances of current financial resources and often has a budgetary orientation. The governmental fund category includes the general fund, special revenue funds, capital projects funds, debt service funds, and permanent funds. With the exception of permanent funds, those governmental funds are defined in NCGA Statement 1, as amended.

65. *Permanent funds* should be used to report resources that are legally restricted to the extent that only earnings, and not principal, may be used for purposes that support the reporting government's programs—that is, for the benefit of the government or its citizenry.[32] (Permanent funds do not include *private-purpose trust funds*, defined in paragraph 72, which should be used to report situations in which the government is required to use the principal or earnings for the benefit of *individuals, private organizations, or other governments*.)

*Proprietary Funds*

66. Proprietary fund reporting focuses on the determination of operating income, changes in net assets (or cost recovery), financial position, and cash flows. The proprietary fund category includes enterprise and internal service funds.

---

[32] An example is a cemetery perpetual-care fund, which provides resources for the ongoing maintenance of a public cemetery.

67. *Enterprise funds* may be used to report any activity for which a fee is charged to external users for goods or services. Activities are *required* to be reported as enterprise funds if any one of the following criteria is met. Governments should apply each of these criteria in the context of the activity's *principal revenue sources*.[33]

    a. The activity is financed with debt that is secured solely by a pledge of the net revenues from fees and charges of the activity. Debt that is secured by a pledge of net revenues from fees and charges *and* the full faith and credit of a related primary government or component unit—even if that government is not expected to make any payments—is not payable solely from fees and charges of the activity. (Some debt may be secured, in part, by a portion of its own proceeds but should be considered as payable "solely" from the revenues of the activity.)

    b. Laws or regulations require that the activity's costs of providing services, including capital costs (such as depreciation or debt service), be recovered with fees and charges, rather than with taxes or similar revenues.[34]

    c. The pricing policies of the activity establish fees and charges designed to recover its costs, including capital costs (such as depreciation or debt service).

68. *Internal service funds* may be used to report any activity that provides goods or services to other funds, departments, or agencies of the primary government and its component units, or to other governments, on a cost-reimbursement basis. Internal service funds should be used only if the reporting government is the predominant participant in the activity. Otherwise, the activity should be reported as an enterprise fund.

---

[33] These criteria do not require insignificant activities of governments to be reported as enterprise funds. For example, state law may require a county's small claims court to assess plaintiffs a fee to cover the cost of frivolous claims. However, taxes, not fees, are the principal revenue source of the county's court system, and the fees in question cover only the cost of frivolous small claims court cases. In this case, the county would not be required to remove its court system or the small claims court activity from its general fund and report it in an enterprise fund. Conversely, a state department of environmental protection regulation may require a water utility to recover the costs of operating its water plant, including debt service costs, through charges to its customers—the utility's principal revenue source. Because these charges are the activity's principal revenue source and because the water utility is required to recover its costs, the utility should be reported as an enterprise fund.

[34] Based on this criterion, state unemployment compensation funds should be reported in enterprise funds.

## Fiduciary Funds

69. Fiduciary fund reporting focuses on net assets and changes in net assets. Fiduciary funds should be used to report assets held in a trustee or agency capacity for others and therefore cannot be used to support the government's own programs. The fiduciary fund category includes pension (and other employee benefit) trust funds, investment trust funds, private-purpose trust funds, and agency funds. The three types of trust funds should be used to report resources held and administered by the reporting government when it is acting in a fiduciary capacity for individuals, private organizations, or other governments. These funds are distinguished from agency funds generally by the existence of a trust agreement that affects the degree of management involvement and the length of time that the resources are held.

70. *Pension (and other employee benefit) trust funds* should be used to report resources that are required to be held in trust for the members and beneficiaries of defined benefit pension plans, defined contribution plans, other postemployment benefit plans, or other employee benefit plans.

71. *Investment trust funds* should be used to report the external portion of investment pools reported by the sponsoring government, as required by Statement 31, paragraph 18.

72. *Private-purpose trust funds*, such as a fund used to report escheat property, should be used to report all other trust arrangements under which principal and income benefit individuals, private organizations, or other governments.

73. *Agency funds* should be used to report resources held by the reporting government in a purely custodial capacity (assets equal liabilities). Agency funds typically involve only the receipt, temporary investment, and remittance of fiduciary resources to individuals, private organizations, or other governments.

## Governmental and Proprietary Fund Financial Statements

74. Separate financial statements should be presented for the primary government's governmental and proprietary funds.

### Focus on Major Funds

75. The focus of governmental and proprietary fund financial statements is on *major* funds.[35] Fund statements should present the financial

---

[35] Major fund reporting requirements do not apply to internal service funds.

information of each major fund in a separate column. Nonmajor funds should be aggregated and displayed in a single column.[36]

76. The reporting government's main operating fund (the general fund or its equivalent) should always be reported as a major fund. Other individual governmental and enterprise funds should be reported in separate columns as major funds based on these criteria:

a. Total assets, liabilities, revenues, or expenditures/expenses[37] of that individual governmental or enterprise fund are at least 10 percent of the corresponding total (assets, liabilities, and so forth) for all funds of that category or type (that is, total governmental or total enterprise funds), *and*

b. Total assets, liabilities, revenues, or expenditures/expenses of the individual governmental fund or enterprise fund are at least 5 percent of the corresponding total for all governmental and enterprise funds combined.

In addition to funds that meet the major fund criteria, any other governmental or enterprise fund that the government's officials believe is particularly important to financial statement users (for example, because of public interest or consistency) may be reported as a major fund.

### Required Reconciliation to Government-wide Statements

77. Governments should present a summary reconciliation to the government-wide financial statements at the bottom of the fund financial statements or in an accompanying schedule. In many cases, brief explanations presented on the face of the statements will be sufficient to allow users to assess the relationship between the statements. However, if aggregated information in the summary reconciliation obscures the nature of the individual elements of a particular reconciling item, governments should provide a more detailed explanation in the notes to financial statements. (See paragraphs 85, 90, and 104.)

### Required Financial Statements—Governmental Funds

78. The financial statements required for governmental funds are:

a. Balance sheet
b. Statement of revenues, expenditures, and changes in fund balances.

---

[36] Combining statements for nonmajor funds are not required but may be presented as supplementary information.

[37] Excluding revenues and expenditures/expenses reported as extraordinary items.

### Measurement focus and basis of accounting

79. Financial statements for governmental funds should be presented using the *current financial resources measurement focus* and the *modified accrual basis of accounting,* as the terms are discussed in NCGA Statement 1, as amended.

### Reporting general capital assets

80. General capital assets are capital assets of the government that are not specifically related to activities reported in proprietary or fiduciary funds. General capital assets are associated with and generally arise from governmental activities. Most often, they result from the expenditure of governmental fund financial resources. They should not be reported as assets in governmental funds but should be reported in the governmental activities column in the government-wide statement of net assets.

### Reporting general-long term liabilities

81. NCGA Statement 1, paragraph 32, provides that "a clear distinction should be made between . . . fund long-term liabilities and general long-term debt." That Statement, as amended, requires recognition of *governmental fund liabilities* using the modified accrual basis of accounting. Paragraph 43 of that Statement states that "general long-term debt is the *unmatured principal* of bonds, warrants, notes, or other forms of noncurrent or long-term *general obligation* indebtedness. . . . General long-term debt is not limited to liabilities arising from debt issuances *per se,* but may also include noncurrent liabilities on lease-purchase agreements and other commitments that are not current liabilities properly recorded in governmental funds." Subsequent NCGA and GASB pronouncements also define the noncurrent portion of capital leases, operating leases with scheduled rent increases, compensated absences, claims and judgments, pensions, special termination benefits, and landfill closure and postclosure care liabilities as general long-term liabilities. Liabilities arising from interfund activities (see paragraph 112) do not constitute general long-term liabilities and therefore should be reported in governmental funds.

82. General long-term liabilities should not be reported as liabilities in governmental funds but should be reported in the governmental activities column in the government-wide statement of net assets.

### Balance sheet

83. The balance sheet should report information about the current financial resources (assets, liabilities, and fund balances) of each

major governmental fund and for nonmajor governmental funds in the aggregate. A total column should be presented. Assets, liabilities, and fund balances of governmental funds should be displayed in a balance sheet format (assets equal liabilities plus fund balances).

*Separate display of reserved and unreserved fund balance*

84.  Governmental fund balances should be segregated into *reserved* and *unreserved* amounts. (See paragraphs 118–121 of NCGA Statement 1.) Reserved fund balances of the combined nonmajor funds should be displayed in sufficient detail to disclose the purposes of the reservations (for example, reserved for debt service or reserved for encumbrances). Unreserved fund balances of nonmajor funds should be displayed by fund type on the face of the balance sheet.

**Required reconciliation**

85.  Paragraph 77 requires governments to present a summary reconciliation at the bottom of the fund financial statements or in an accompanying schedule. Items that typically will be required to reconcile total governmental fund balances to net assets of governmental activities in the statement of net assets include, but are not limited to, the effects of:

- Reporting capital assets at their historical cost and depreciating them instead of reporting capital acquisitions as expenditures when incurred
- Adding general long-term liabilities not due and payable in the current period
- Reducing deferred revenue for those amounts that were not available to pay current-period expenditures
- Adding internal service fund net asset balances (see paragraph 62).

**Statement of revenues, expenditures, and changes in fund balances**

86.  The statement of revenues, expenditures, and changes in fund balances should report information about the inflows, outflows, and balances of current financial resources of each major governmental fund and for the nonmajor governmental funds in the aggregate. A total column should be presented. The statement should present the following information, in the format and sequence indicated:

Revenues (detailed)
Expenditures (detailed)
  Excess (deficiency) of revenues over expenditures

Other financing sources and uses, including transfers (detailed)
Special and extraordinary items (detailed)
> Net change in fund balances
> Fund balances[38]—beginning of period
> Fund balances—end of period

*Classification of revenues and expenditures*

87. Governmental fund revenues should be classified in the statement of revenues, expenditures, and changes in fund balances by major revenue source as discussed in NCGA Statement 1, paragraph 110. Governmental fund expenditures should be classified at a minimum by function, as discussed in paragraphs 111 through 116 of that Statement. Debt issue costs paid out of debt proceeds, such as underwriter fees, should be reported as expenditures. Issue costs, such as attorney and rating agency fees or bond insurance, paid from existing resources should be reported as expenditures when the related liability is incurred.

*Other financing sources and uses*

88. Items that should be reported as other financing sources and uses include proceeds of long-term debt, issuance premium or discount, certain payments to escrow agents for bond refundings, transfers, and sales of capital assets (unless the sale meets the criteria, as defined in paragraph 56, for reporting as a special item).

*Special and extraordinary items*

89. Special and extraordinary items, defined in paragraphs 55 and 56, should be reported separately after "other financing sources and uses." If both occur during the same period, special and extraordinary items should be reported separately within a "special and extraordinary items" classification. Significant transactions or other events that are either unusual or infrequent but are not within the control of management should be separately identified within the appropriate revenue or expenditure category in the statement of revenues, expenditures, and changes in fund balances or be disclosed in the notes to financial statements. (Because other financing sources and uses, rather than *gains* or *losses*, are reported for debt refundings in governmental funds, these transactions should not be reported as extraordinary items.)

*Required reconciliation*

90. Paragraph 77 requires governments to present a summary reconciliation at the bottom of the fund financial statements or in an

---

[38] Fund balances should consist of both reserved and unreserved amounts as described in paragraph 84.

APP-36  *Appendix*

accompanying schedule. Items that typically will be required to reconcile the total change in governmental fund balances to the change in net assets of governmental activities in the statement of activities include, but are not limited to, the effects of:

- Reporting revenues on the accrual basis
- Reporting annual depreciation expense instead of expenditures for capital outlays
- Reporting long-term debt proceeds in the statement of net assets as liabilities instead of other financing sources; also, reporting debt principal payments in the statement of net assets as reductions of liabilities instead of expenditures
- Reporting other expenses on the accrual basis
- Adding the net revenue (expense) of internal service funds, as discussed in paragraph 62.

*Required Financial Statements—Proprietary Funds*

91. Required financial statements for proprietary funds are:

a. Statement of net assets or balance sheet[39]
b. Statement of revenues, expenses, and changes in fund net assets or fund equity[40]
c. Statement of cash flows.

**Measurement focus and basis of accounting**

92. Proprietary fund statements of net assets and revenues, expenses, and changes in fund net assets should be presented using the economic resources measurement focus and the accrual basis of accounting.

93. Based on the provisions of Statement 20, paragraph 6, proprietary funds should be reported based on all applicable GASB pronouncements as well as applicable FASB Statements and Interpretations, APB Opinions, and ARBs of the Committee on Accounting Procedure issued on or before November 30, 1989, *unless* those pronouncements conflict with or contradict GASB pronouncements.

94. For *enterprise* funds, governments may elect to apply *all* FASB Statements and Interpretations issued after November 30, 1989, *except for* those that conflict with or contradict GASB pronouncements,

---

[39] Either a *balance sheet* or a *net assets* format may be used. For convenience, *only* the statement of net assets is referred to in this Statement.

[40] Either *fund net assets* or *fund equity* may be used as the label for the difference between proprietary fund assets and liabilities; for convenience, only the term *fund net assets* is used in this Statement.

based on the provisions of paragraph 7 of Statement 20, as amended by this Statement. Governments are encouraged to use the same application of FASB pronouncements for all enterprise funds.

95. FASB Statement 71 and related pronouncements issued on or before November 30, 1989, may be applied to qualifying *enterprise* funds as discussed in paragraph 9 of Statement 20, as amended by this Statement.

**Separate presentation of internal service funds**

96. As discussed in paragraph 75, proprietary fund statements should present the financial information for each major enterprise fund in a separate column. Nonmajor enterprise funds should be aggregated and displayed in a single column, and a combined total column should be presented for all enterprise funds. Major fund reporting requirements do not apply to internal service funds. The combined totals for all internal service funds should be reported in separate columns on the face of the proprietary fund financial statements to the right of the total enterprise funds column.

**Statement of net assets**

97. Assets and liabilities of proprietary funds should be presented in a *classified* format to distinguish between current and long-term assets and liabilities as discussed in Chapter 3 of ARB 43, *Restatement and Revision of Accounting Research Bulletins*.

98. Governments may use either a net assets format—*assets less liabilities equal net assets*—or a balance sheet format—*assets equal liabilities plus net assets*—to report their proprietary funds. Net assets should be displayed in three broad components—*invested in capital assets, net of related debt; restricted* (distinguishing between major categories of restrictions); and *unrestricted*. Paragraphs 33 through 37 define these terms for purposes of determining the amount to be reported in the various components of net assets. Capital contributions should not be displayed as a separate component of net assets. Designations of net assets should not be reported on the face of the financial statements. (See paragraph 37.)

*Reporting restrictions on asset use*

99. Restricted assets should be reported when restrictions (as defined in paragraph 34) on asset use change the nature or normal understanding of the availability of the asset. For example, cash and investments normally are classified as current assets, and a normal understanding of these assets presumes that restrictions do not limit the government's ability to use the resources to pay current liabilities. But cash and

investments held in a separate account that can be used to pay debt principal and interest only (as required by the debt covenant) and that cannot be used to pay other current liabilities should be reported as restricted assets. Because restricted assets may include temporarily invested debt proceeds or other resources that are not generated through operations (such as customer deposits), the amount reported as restricted assets will not necessarily equal restricted net assets.

**Statement of revenues, expenses, and changes in fund net assets**

100. The operating statement for proprietary funds is the statement of revenues, expenses, and changes in fund net assets. Revenues should be reported by major source[41] and should identify revenues used as security for revenue bonds. This statement also should distinguish between operating and nonoperating revenues and expenses (as discussed in paragraph 102) and should present a separate subtotal for *operating revenues, operating expenses,* and *operating income.* Nonoperating revenues and expenses should be reported after operating income. Revenues from capital contributions and additions to the principal of permanent and term endowments, special and extraordinary items, and transfers should be reported separately, after nonoperating revenues and expenses as illustrated below.

101. The statement of revenues, expenses, and changes in fund net assets should be presented in the following sequence using the all-inclusive format:

Operating revenues (detailed)
    Total operating revenues
Operating expenses (detailed)
    Total operating expenses
        Operating income (loss)
Nonoperating revenues and expenses (detailed)
    Income before other revenues, expenses, gains, losses, and transfers
Capital contributions (grant, developer, and other), additions to permanent and term endowments, special and extraordinary items (detailed), and transfers
    Increase (decrease) in net assets
Net assets—beginning of period
Net assets—end of period

---

[41] Revenues should be reported net of discounts and allowances with the discount or allowance amount parenthetically disclosed on the face of the statement or in a note to the financial statements. Alternatively, revenues may be reported gross with the related discounts and allowances reported directly beneath the revenue amount.

*Defining operating revenues and expenses*

102. Governments should establish a policy that defines operating revenues and expenses that is appropriate to the nature of the activity being reported, disclose it in the summary of significant accounting policies, and use it consistently from period to period. A consideration for defining a proprietary fund's operating revenues and expenses is how individual transactions would be categorized for purposes of preparing a statement of cash flows using Statement 9. Transactions for which cash flows are reported as capital and related financing activities, noncapital financing activities, or investing activities normally would *not* be reported as components of operating income.[42] This includes most revenues considered to be nonexchange and exchange-like, such as tax revenues and, in some cases, fees and charges (such as passenger facilities charges).

*Reporting capital contributions and additions to permanent and term endowments*

103. All proprietary fund revenues, including capital contributions and additions to permanent and term endowments, should be reported in the statement of revenues, expenses, and changes in fund net assets. As discussed in paragraphs 100 and 101, capital contributions and additions to permanent and term endowments should be reported after nonoperating revenues and expenses. Revenue recognition for these and all other nonexchange revenues should be based on the requirements of Statement 33. Net assets resulting from certain capital contributions may be required to be reported as invested in capital assets net of related debt, as discussed in paragraph 33. Paragraph 35 provides that restricted net assets should be separated into expendable and nonexpendable subcategories when net assets arise from additions to permanent endowments.

*Required reconciliations*

104. Generally, the amounts reported as net assets and changes in net assets in the proprietary fund financial statements for total enterprise funds will be the same as net assets and changes in net assets of business-type activities in the government-wide statement of activities. However, if there are differences (for example, if reclassification of internal service fund transactions, as discussed in paragraph 62, affects enterprise funds), they should be explained on the face of the fund statement (or in an accompanying schedule) as discussed in paragraph 77.

---

[42] Revenue and expense transactions normally classified as other than operating cash flows from operations in most proprietary funds may be classified as operating revenues and expenses if those transactions constitute the reporting proprietary fund's principal ongoing operations. For example, interest revenue and expense transactions should be reported as operating revenue and expense by a proprietary fund established to provide loans to first-time homeowners.

**Statement of cash flows**

105. Governments should present a statement of cash flows for proprietary funds based on the provisions of Statement 9, as amended by this Statement. The direct method of presenting cash flows from operating activities (including a reconciliation of operating cash flows to operating income) should be used.

### Required Financial Statements—Fiduciary Funds and Similar Component Units

106. Required financial statements for fiduciary funds are the statement of fiduciary net assets and the statement of changes in fiduciary net assets.[43] Fiduciary fund financial statements should include information about all fiduciary funds of the primary government, as well as component units that are fiduciary in nature. The statements should provide a separate column for each fund type—pension (and other employee benefit) trust funds, investment trust funds, private-purpose trusts, agency funds. Financial statements for individual pension plans and postemployment healthcare plans[44] should be presented in the notes to the financial statements of the primary government if separate, GAAP financial reports have not been issued. If separate, GAAP financial reports have been issued, the notes should include information about how to obtain those separate reports.

*Measurement Focus and Basis of Accounting*

107. Financial statements of fiduciary funds should be reported using the *economic resources measurement focus* and the *accrual basis of accounting*, except for the recognition of certain liabilities of defined benefit pension plans and certain postemployment healthcare plans. Paragraph 26 of Statement 25 and paragraph 7 of Statement 26 provide guidance on recognition of these liabilities.

*Statement of Fiduciary Net Assets*

108. The statement of fiduciary net assets should include information about the assets, liabilities, and net assets for each fiduciary fund type. The detailed display requirements of Statements 25 and 26 apply to the statements of plan net assets of pension and other employee benefit trust funds. Statement 31 provides detailed guidance for investment trust

---

[43] For defined benefit pension plans, the statement of fiduciary net assets and statement of changes in fiduciary net assets required by this Statement are equivalent to the statement of *plan* net assets and statement of changes in *plan* net assets, respectively, required by Statement 25.

[44] See paragraph 19 of Statement 25 and paragraph 7 of Statement 26, respectively.

funds. The components of net assets, discussed in paragraphs 32 through 37, are not required to be presented in the statement of fiduciary net assets.

## Statement of Changes in Fiduciary Net Assets

109. The statement of changes in fiduciary net assets should include information about the additions to, deductions from, and net increase (or decrease) for the year in net assets for each fiduciary fund type. The statement should provide information about significant year-to-year changes in net assets. The detailed display requirements of Statements 25 and 26 apply to the statements of changes in plan net assets for pension and other employee benefit trust funds.

## Reporting Agency Funds

110. In the statement of net assets, agency fund assets should equal liabilities. Agency funds should not be reported in the statement of changes in fiduciary net assets.

111. Sometimes an agency fund is used as a *clearing account* to distribute financial resources to other funds of the government, as well as other entities. For example, county property tax collectors customarily collect and distribute property taxes to the county's funds as well as to other governments within the county. When this occurs, the portion of the clearing account balance that pertains to other funds of the county should not be reported in agency funds. Rather, it should be reported as assets in the appropriate funds.

## Reporting Interfund Activity

112. Interfund activity within and among the three fund categories (governmental, proprietary, and fiduciary) should be classified and reported as follows:

a. *Reciprocal interfund activity* is the internal counterpart to exchange and exchange-like transactions. It includes:

(1) *Interfund loans*—amounts provided with a requirement for repayment. Interfund loans should be reported as interfund receivables in lender funds and interfund payables in borrower funds. This activity should not be reported as other financing sources or uses in the fund financial statements. If repayment is not expected within a reasonable time, the interfund balances should be reduced and the amount that is not expected to be repaid

should be reported as a transfer from the fund that made the loan to the fund that received the loan.

    (2) *Interfund services provided and used*—sales and purchases of goods and services between funds for a price approximating their external exchange value. Interfund services provided and used should be reported as revenues in seller funds and expenditures or expenses in purchaser funds.[45] Unpaid amounts should be reported as interfund receivables and payables in the fund balance sheets or fund statements of net assets.

b.   *Nonreciprocal interfund activity* is the internal counterpart to nonexchange transactions. It includes:

    (1) *Interfund transfers*—flows of assets (such as cash or goods) without equivalent flows of assets in return and without a requirement for repayment. This category includes payments in lieu of taxes that are not payments for, and are not reasonably equivalent in value to, services provided. In governmental funds, transfers should be reported as other financing uses in the funds making transfers and as other financing sources in the funds receiving transfers. In proprietary funds, transfers should be reported after nonoperating revenues and expenses as discussed in paragraphs 100 and 101.

    (2) *Interfund reimbursements*—repayments from the funds responsible for particular expenditures or expenses to the funds that initially paid for them. Reimbursements should not be displayed in the financial statements.

## Basic Financial Statements—Notes to the Financial Statements

113. The notes to the financial statements should communicate information essential for fair presentation of the financial statements that is not displayed on the face of the financial statements. As such, the notes are an integral part of the basic financial statements. The notes should focus on the primary government—specifically, its governmental activities, business-type activities, major funds, and nonmajor funds in the aggregate. Information about the government's discretely presented component units should be presented as discussed in Statement 14, paragraph 63, as amended by this Statement.

---

[45] However, Statement 10, paragraph 64, requires that when the general fund is used to account for risk-financing activity, interfund charges to other funds should be accounted for as reimbursements.

## General Disclosure Requirements

114. Guidance pertaining to existing note disclosures is found in NCGA Interpretation 6, as amended.[46]

115. Governments should provide these additional disclosures (if applicable) in their summary of significant accounting policies based on the requirements of this Statement:

a. A description of the government-wide financial statements, noting that neither fiduciary funds nor component units that are fiduciary in nature are included. (See paragraph 13.)
b. The measurement focus and basis of accounting used in the government-wide statements. (See paragraph 16.)
c. The policy for eliminating internal activity in the statement of activities. (See paragraphs 57–61.)
d. The policy for applying FASB pronouncements issued after November 30, 1989, to business-type activities and to enterprise funds of the primary government. (See paragraphs 17 and 94.)
e. The policy for capitalizing assets and for estimating the useful lives of those assets (used to calculate depreciation expense). (See paragraphs 20 and 23.) Governments that choose to use the modified approach for reporting eligible infrastructure assets should describe that approach.
f. A description of the types of transactions included in program revenues (see paragraph 48) and the policy for allocating indirect expenses to functions in the statement of activities. (See paragraphs 41–46.)
g. The government's policy for defining operating and nonoperating revenues of proprietary funds. (See paragraph 102.)
h. The government's policy regarding whether to first apply restricted or unrestricted resources when an expense is incurred for purposes for which both restricted and unrestricted net assets are available. (See paragraph 34.)

## Required Note Disclosures about Capital Assets and Long-term Liabilities

116. Governments should provide detail in the notes to the financial statements about capital assets and long-term liabilities of the primary

---

[46] The GASB has a project on its agenda to review the appropriateness of existing note disclosure requirements. The disclosures in paragraphs 115 through 123 are those most directly related to the new requirements of this Statement. Other changes in note disclosure requirements may be proposed or required before implementation of this Statement is required.

government reported in the statement of net assets. The information disclosed should be divided into major classes of capital assets and long-term liabilities as well as between those associated with governmental activities and those associated with business-type activities. Capital assets that are not being depreciated should be disclosed separately from those that are being depreciated. (See paragraph 20.)

117. Information presented about major classes of capital assets should include:

a. Beginning- and end-of-year balances (regardless of whether beginning-of-year balances are presented on the face of the government-wide financial statements), with accumulated depreciation presented separately from historical cost
b. Capital acquisitions
c. Sales or other dispositions
d. Current-period depreciation expense, with disclosure of the amounts charged to each of the functions in the statement of activities.

118. For collections not capitalized (see paragraphs 27–29), disclosures should provide a description of the collection and the reasons these assets are not capitalized. For collections that are capitalized, governments should make the disclosures required by paragraphs 116 and 117.

119. Information about long-term liabilities should include both long-term debt (such as bonds, notes, loans, and leases payable) and other long-term liabilities[47] (such as compensated absences, and claims and judgments). Information presented about long-term liabilities should include:

a. Beginning- and end-of-year balances (regardless of whether prior-year data are presented on the face of the government-wide financial statements)
b. Increases and decreases (separately presented)
c. The portions of each item that are due within one year of the statement date
d. Which governmental funds typically have been used to liquidate other long-term liabilities (such as compensated absences and pension liabilities) in prior years.

120. Determining whether to provide similar disclosures about capital assets and long-term liabilities of discretely presented component

---

[47] Information about net pension obligations should be reported in a separate pension note, as required by Statement 27.

units is a matter of professional judgment. The decision to disclose should be based on the individual component unit's significance to the total of all discretely presented component units and that component unit's relationship with the primary government.

### Disclosures about Donor-restricted Endowments

121.  Note disclosures should include the following information about donor-restricted endowments:

a.  The amounts of net appreciation on investments of donor-restricted endowments that are available for authorization for expenditure by the governing board, and how those amounts are reported in net assets
b.  The state law regarding the ability to spend net appreciation
c.  The policy for authorizing and spending investment income, such as a spending-rate or total-return policy.

### Segment Information

122.  Governments that report enterprise funds or that use enterprise fund accounting and reporting standards to report their activities are required to present segment information for those activities in the notes to the financial statements. For purposes of this disclosure, a segment is an identifiable activity reported as or within an enterprise fund or an other stand-alone entity for which one or more revenue bonds or other revenue-backed debt instruments (such as certificates of participation) are outstanding.[48] A segment has a specific identifiable revenue stream pledged in support of revenue bonds or other revenue-backed debt and has related expenses, gains and losses, assets, and liabilities that can be identified. Segment disclosure requirements should by met by providing condensed financial statements in the notes:

a.  Type of goods or services provided by the segment.
b.  Condensed statement of net assets:

   (1)  Total assets—distinguishing between current assets, capital assets, and other assets. Amounts receivable from other funds or component units should be reported separately.
   (2)  Total liabilities—distinguishing between current and long-term amounts. Amounts payable to other funds or component units should be reported separately.

---

[48] Segment disclosures are not required for an activity whose only outstanding debt is conduit debt for which the government has no obligation beyond the resources provided by related leases or loans. In addition, segment reporting is not required when an individual fund both is a segment and is reported as a major fund.

(3) Total net assets—distinguishing among restricted (separately reporting expendable and nonexpendable components); unrestricted; and amounts invested in capital assets, net of related debt.

c. Condensed statement of revenues, expenses, and changes in net assets:

(1) Operating revenues (by major source).

(2) Operating expenses. Depreciation (including any amortization) should be identified separately.

(3) Operating income (loss).

(4) Nonoperating revenues (expenses)—with separate reporting of major revenues and expenses.

(5) Capital contributions and additions to permanent and term endowments.

(6) Special and extraordinary items.

(7) Transfers.

(8) Change in net assets.

(9) Beginning net assets.

(10) Ending net assets.

d. Condensed statement of cash flows:

(1) Net cash provided (used) by:

(a) Operating activities.

(b) Noncapital financing activities.

(c) Capital and related financing activities.

(d) Investing activities.

(2) Beginning cash and cash equivalent balances.

(3) Ending cash and cash equivalent balances.

Determining whether to provide segment disclosures about component units that use enterprise fund accounting and reporting standards is a matter of professional judgment. The decision to disclose should be based on the individual component unit's significance to the total of all discretely presented component units and that component unit's relationship with the primary government.

123. Governments that want to present disaggregated data for their multiple-function enterprise funds beyond what is required for segment reporting (for example, net program cost information) are encouraged to present (as supplementary information) a statement of activities (as discussed in paragraphs 38–60). Special-purpose governments engaged only in business-type activities (paragraph 138) also are encouraged to present this information.

## Reporting Component Units

124. Paragraph 42 of Statement 14 requires that "financial statements of the reporting entity should provide an overview of the entity based on financial accountability, yet allow users to distinguish between the primary government and its component units." Paragraph 11 states that ". . . the reporting entity's financial statements should . . . provide an overview of the discretely presented component units."

125. These financial reporting requirements are met by discrete presentation of component unit financial data in the statement of net assets and the statement of activities. Component units that are fiduciary in nature, however, should be included only in the fund financial statements with the primary government's fiduciary funds. Blended component units should be reported in accordance with Statement 14, paragraphs 52 through 54.

126. Paragraph 51 of Statement 14, as amended by this Statement, requires information about each major component unit to be provided in the basic financial statements of the reporting entity. Governments can satisfy that requirement by (a) presenting each major component unit[49] in a separate column in the reporting entity's statements of net assets and activities, (b) including combining statements of major component units[50] in the reporting entity's basic statements after the fund financial statements, or (c) presenting condensed financial statements in the notes to the reporting entity's financial statements. If the combining statement approach is used, the "aggregated total" component unit information, as discussed in Statement 14, should be taken from the total columns in the component units' statements of net assets and activities[51] so that the details support the totals reported in the reporting entity's government-wide statements.

127. If governments choose to present component unit information in the notes, these details should be presented, at a minimum:

a. Condensed statement of net assets:

---

[49] Major component unit information is not required for component units that are fiduciary in nature.

[50] Nonmajor component units should be aggregated in a single column. A combining statement for the nonmajor component units is not required but may be presented as supplementary information.

[51] Because component units that are engaged only in business-type activities are not required to prepare a statement of activities, this disclosure should be taken from the information provided in the component unit's combined statement of revenues, expenses, and changes in fund net assets.

(1) Total assets—distinguishing between capital assets and other assets. Amounts receivable from the primary government or from other component units should be reported separately.

(2) Total liabilities—distinguishing between long-term debt outstanding and other liabilities. Amounts payable to the primary government or to other component units should be reported separately.

(3) Total net assets—distinguishing between restricted, unrestricted, and amounts invested in capital assets, net of related debt.

b. Condensed statement of activities:[52]

(1) Expenses (by major functions and for depreciation expense, if separately reported).

(2) Program revenues (by type).

(3) Net program (expense) revenue.

(4) Tax revenues.

(5) Other nontax general revenues.

(6) Contributions to endowments and permanent fund principal.

(7) Special and extraordinary items.

(8) Change in net assets.

(9) Beginning net assets.

(10) Ending net assets.

128. In addition to the financial statement information required by paragraph 126, the notes to the financial statements should disclose, for each major component unit, the nature and amount of significant transactions with the primary government and other component units.

## Required Supplementary Information Other Than MD&A

129. Statement 10, as amended, and Statements 25 and 27 require governments to present certain data as RSI. In addition to those presentations, this Statement requires governments to present as RSI MD&A (paragraphs 8–11), budgetary comparison schedules for governmental funds (discussed below) and information about infrastructure assets reported using the modified approach (paragraphs 23–25).

---

[52] See footnote 51.

## Budgetary Comparison Schedules

130. Budgetary comparison schedules should be presented as RSI[53] for the general fund and for each major special revenue fund that has a legally adopted annual budget. The budgetary comparison schedule should present both (a) the original and (b) the final appropriated budgets for the reporting period as well as (c) actual inflows, outflows, and balances, stated on the government's budgetary basis.[54] A separate column to report the variance between the final budget and actual amounts is encouraged but not required. Governments may also report the variance between original and final budget amounts.

a. The *original budget* is the first complete appropriated budget.[55] The original budget may be adjusted by reserves, transfers, allocations, supplemental appropriations, and other legally authorized legislative and executive changes *before* the beginning of the fiscal year. The original budget should also include actual appropriation amounts automatically carried over from prior years by law. For example, a legal provision may require the automatic rolling forward of appropriations to cover prior-year encumbrances.

b. The *final budget* is the original budget adjusted by all reserves, transfers, allocations, supplemental appropriations, and other legally authorized legislative and executive changes applicable to the fiscal year, whenever signed into law or otherwise legally authorized.

131. Governments may present the budgetary comparison schedule using the same format, terminology, and classifications as the budget document, or using the format, terminology, and classifications in a statement of revenues, expenditures, and changes in fund balances. Regardless of the format used, the schedule should be accompanied by information (either in a separate schedule or in notes to RSI) that reconciles budgetary information to GAAP information, as discussed in NCGA Interpretation 10, as amended by this Statement. Notes to RSI should disclose any excess of expenditures

---

[53] Governments may elect to report the budgetary comparison information in a budgetary comparison *statement* as part of the basic financial statements, rather than as RSI. If presented, the additional statement should include the same items of information that paragraphs 130 and 131 require to be displayed or disclosed.

[54] The budgetary basis of accounting is discussed in NCGA Statement 1, paragraph 154.

[55] NCGA Interpretation 10, paragraph 11, as amended by this Statement, defines *appropriated budget* as "the expenditure authority created by the appropriation bills or ordinances which are signed into law and related estimated revenues."

APP-50  *Appendix*

over appropriations in individual funds, as discussed in NCGA Interpretation 6, paragraph 4, as amended by this Statement.[56]

**Modified Approach for Reporting Infrastructure**

132. Governments should present the following schedules, derived from asset management systems, as RSI for all eligible infrastructure assets[57] that are reported using the modified approach:

a. The assessed condition, performed at least every three years, for at least the three most recent complete condition assessments, indicating the dates of the assessments

b. The estimated annual amount calculated at the beginning of the fiscal year to maintain and preserve at (or above) the condition level established and disclosed by the government compared with the amounts actually expensed (as discussed in paragraph 25) for each of the past five reporting periods.

133. The following disclosures[58] should accompany the schedules required by paragraph 132:

a. The basis for the condition measurement and the measurement scale used to assess and report condition. For example, a basis for *condition measurement* could be distresses found in pavement surfaces. A *scale* used to assess and report condition could range from zero for a failed pavement to 100 for a pavement in perfect condition.

b. The condition level at which the government intends to preserve its eligible infrastructure assets reported using the modified approach.

c. Factors that significantly affect trends in the information reported in the required schedules, including any changes in the measurement scale, the basis for the condition measurement, or the condition assessment methods used during the periods covered by the schedules. If there is a change in the condition level at which the government intends to preserve eligible infrastructure assets, an estimate of the effect of the change on the estimated annual amount to maintain and preserve those assets for the current period also should be disclosed.

---

[56] If the budgetary comparison information is included in the basic statements, as described in footnote 53, these disclosures should be in the notes to the financial statements, rather than as notes to RSI.

[57] If a government applies the provisions of paragraphs 23 and 24 to a subsystem of infrastructure assets (for example, interstate highways), then the RSI disclosures required by this paragraph should be for that *subsystem*.

[58] Governments with asset management systems for infrastructure assets that gather the information required by paragraphs 132 and 133 and that do not use the modified approach are encouraged to provide the information as supplementary information.

# Basic Financial Statements Required for Special-purpose Governments

134. This Statement is written from the perspective of general purpose governments—states, cities, counties, towns, and villages. However, many governments are *special-purpose* governments. Those governments are legally separate entities, as discussed in Statement 14, and may be component units[59] or other stand-alone governments.[60] Paragraphs 135 through 141 describe the effects of this Statement on GAAP reporting by special-purpose governments.

## Reporting by Special-purpose Governments Engaged in Governmental Activities

135. Special-purpose governments engaged in more than one governmental program or that have both governmental and business-type activities[61] should provide both fund financial statements and government-wide financial statements. For these governments, all the requirements for basic financial statements and RSI in paragraphs 8 through 131 apply.

136. For special-purpose governments engaged in a single governmental program (for example, some cemetery districts, levee districts, assessment districts, drainage districts), the fund financial statements and the government-wide statements may be combined using a columnar format that reconciles individual line items of fund financial data to government-wide data in a separate column on the face of the financial statements rather than at the bottom of the statements or in an accompanying schedule.[62] Or the single-program government may present separate government-wide and fund financial statements and may present its government-wide statement of activities using a different format. For example, the statement of activities may be presented in a single column

---

[59] As defined in Statement 14, *component units* are legally separate organizations for which the elected officials of the primary government are financially accountable. In addition, a component unit can be another organization for which the nature and significance of its relationship with a primary government are such that exclusion would cause the reporting entity's financial statements to be misleading or incomplete.

[60] As defined in Statement 14, an *other stand-alone government* is a legally separate governmental organization that (a) does not have a separately elected governing body and (b) does not meet the definition of a component unit. Other stand-alone governments include some special-purpose governments, joint ventures, jointly governed organizations, and pools.

[61] See paragraph 15 for a discussion of governmental and business-type activities.

[62] If a columnar format is used, single-program governments should provide the reconciliation information required by paragraphs 85 and 90 between the fund financial data and the government-wide data. Descriptions of the reconciling items should be presented either on the face of the financial statements, in an accompanying schedule, or in the notes to the financial statements, as discussed in paragraph 77.

that reports expenses first followed by revenues (by major sources). The difference between these amounts is net revenue (expense) and should be followed by contributions to permanent and term endowments, special and extraordinary items, transfers, and beginning and ending net assets.

137. For the purpose of applying the provisions of paragraph 136, a government should not be considered "single-program" if it budgets, manages, or accounts for its activities as multiple programs. For example, "programs" within the *education* functional category for a typical school district might include regular instruction, special instruction, vocational education, and adult education.

### Reporting by Special-purpose Governments Engaged Only in Business-type Activities

138. Governments engaged only in business-type activities should present only the financial statements required for enterprise funds. (See paragraphs 91–105.) For these governments, basic financial statements and RSI consist of:

a. MD&A (paragraphs 8–11, as appropriate)
b. Enterprise fund financial statements (paragraphs 91–105), consisting of:
   (1) Statement of net assets or balance sheet
   (2) Statement of revenues, expenses, and changes in fund net assets
   (3) Statement of cash flows
c. Notes to financial statements (paragraphs 113–123)
d. RSI other than MD&A, if applicable (paragraphs 132–133).

### Reporting by Special-purpose Governments Engaged Only in Fiduciary Activities

139. A special-purpose government engaged only in fiduciary activities should present only the financial statements required for fiduciary funds. For those governments, basic financial statements and RSI consist of:

a. MD&A (paragraphs 8–11, as appropriate)
b. Statement of fiduciary net assets (paragraph 108)
c. Statement of changes in fiduciary net assets (paragraph 109)
d. Notes to financial statements (paragraphs 113 through 123).

140. A *public employee retirement system (PERS)* is a special-purpose government that administers one or more defined benefit pension

plans and sometimes other types of employee benefit plans, including defined contribution, deferred compensation, and postemployment healthcare plans.[63] Statements 25 and 26 require a PERS that administers more than one defined benefit pension plan or postemployment healthcare plan to present in its financial report combining financial statements for all plans administered by the system and, if applicable, required schedules for each plan.[64] A PERS should meet this financial statement requirement by (a) presenting a separate column for each plan administered on the statement of fiduciary net assets and the statement of changes in fiduciary net assets or (b) presenting combining statements for those plans as part of the basic financial statements.

141. For all plans *other than* defined benefit pension plans and postemployment healthcare plans, a PERS should apply the requirements of this Statement for measurement focus, basis of accounting, and display. Combining financial statements are encouraged, but not required, for those plans.

## EFFECTIVE DATE AND TRANSITION

142. The requirements of this Statement are effective in three phases based on total annual revenues, as discussed in paragraph 143, below. Earlier application is encouraged. Governments that elect early implementation of this Statement for periods beginning before June 15, 2000, also should implement Statement 33 at the same time. If a primary government chooses early implementation of this Statement, all of its component units also should implement this standard early to provide the financial information required for the government-wide financial statements.

143. The requirements of this Statement are effective in three phases based on a government's total annual revenues in the first fiscal year ending after June 15, 1999:

- Phase 1 governments—with total annual revenues of $100 million or more—should apply the requirements of this Statement in financial statements for periods beginning after June 15, 2001.

---

[63] See Statement 25, paragraphs 14 and 44.
[64] As stated in paragraph 15 of Statement 25, if a PERS administers one or more agent multiple-employer plans, the requirements of that Statement apply at the aggregate plan level; the PERS is not required to present financial statements and schedules for the individual plans of the participating employers.

- Phase 2 governments—with total annual revenues of $10 million or more but less than $100 million—should apply the requirements of this Statement in financial statements for periods beginning after June 15, 2002.
- Phase 3 governments—with total annual revenues of less than $10 million—should apply the requirements of this Statement in financial statements for periods beginning after June 15, 2003.

For purposes of identifying the appropriate implementation phase, *revenues* includes all revenues (not other financing sources) of the primary government's governmental and enterprise funds, except for extraordinary items as defined in paragraph 55. Special-purpose governments engaged only in fiduciary activities should use total annual *additions*, rather than *revenues*, to determine the appropriate implementation phase. All component units should implement the requirements of this Statement no later than the same year as their primary government, regardless of the amount of each component unit's total revenues. Paragraphs 148 through 153 provide additional phase-in provisions for reporting general infrastructure assets.

144. Adjustments to governmental, proprietary, and fiduciary funds resulting from a change to comply with this Statement should be treated as adjustments of prior periods, and financial statements presented for the periods affected should be restated. If restatement of the financial statements for prior periods is not practical, the cumulative effect of applying this Statement should be reported as a restatement of beginning fund balance or fund net assets, as appropriate, for the earliest period restated (generally, the current period). In the first period that this Statement is applied, the financial statements should disclose the nature of the restatement and its effect.

145. In the first period that this Statement is applied, governments are not required to restate prior periods for purposes of providing the comparative data for MD&A as required in paragraph 11. However, governments are encouraged to provide comparative analyses of key elements of total governmental funds and total enterprise funds in MD&A for that period. Also, in the first year of implementation, MD&A should include a statement that, in future years, when prior-year information is available, a comparative analysis of government-wide data will be presented.

146. The requirements of APB Opinions No. 12, *Omnibus Opinion—1967*, and No. 21, *Interest on Receivables and Payables*, as amended, require deferral and amortization of debt issue premium or discount. These Opinions may be applied prospectively to governmental activities in the statement of net assets and the statement of activities, except

for governmental activity debt that is deep-discount or zero-coupon debt.[65] Similarly, FASB Statement No. 34, *Capitalization of Interest Cost*, as amended, which requires capitalization of interest cost as a component of the historical cost of capital assets, also may be applied prospectively by governmental activities. Finally, Statement 23, which requires deferral and amortization of the difference between the reacquisition price and the net carrying amount of old debt in debt-refunding transactions, may be applied prospectively by governmental activities. The retroactive effect of applying those standards is not required to be considered in determining beginning net assets for governmental activities.

## Governmental Entities That Use the AICPA Not-for-Profit Model

147. Governmental entities that report as of the date of this Statement using the AICPA Not-for-Profit model, as defined in Statement 29, but that do not meet the criteria in paragraph 67 may use enterprise fund accounting and financial reporting.

## Reporting General Infrastructure Assets at Transition

148. Prospective reporting of general infrastructure assets in the statement of net assets is required beginning at the effective dates of this Statement. Retroactive reporting of all *major* general infrastructure assets[66] is encouraged at that date. Phase 1 governments as described in paragraph 143 should retroactively report all major general infrastructure assets for fiscal years beginning after June 15, 2005. Phase 2 governments should retroactively report all major general infrastructure assets for fiscal years beginning after June 15, 2006. Phase 3 governments are encouraged but are not required to report major general infrastructure assets retroactively.

149. If determining the actual historical cost of general infrastructure assets is not practical because of inadequate records, governments should report the estimated historical cost for major general infrastructure assets that were acquired or significantly reconstructed, or that received significant improvements, in fiscal years ending after June 30, 1980. (See

---

[65] For purposes of this Statement, deep-discount debt is debt that is sold at a discount of 20 percent or more from its face or par value at the time it is issued. Zero-coupon debt is originally sold at far below par value and pays no interest until it matures.

[66] *Major* general infrastructure assets are assets that (a) meet the definition of a major asset as described in paragraph 156, (b) are associated with and generally arise from governmental activities, and (c) are long-lived capital assets that normally are stationary in nature and normally can be preserved for a significantly greater number of years than most capital assets, as described in paragraph 19. The transition period does not apply to proprietary funds and special-purpose governments engaged in business-type activities.

paragraphs 155 through 166 for a more complete discussion of methods of estimating the cost of infrastructure assets and, if appropriate, accumulated depreciation on infrastructure assets.)

150. If, during the transition period, information is not available for all networks of infrastructure assets, those networks for which information is available may be reported.

151. While governments are applying the transition provisions, they should make these disclosures:

a. A description of the infrastructure assets being reported and of those that are not
b. A description of any eligible infrastructure assets that the government has decided to report using the modified approach (paragraphs 23–25).

## Modified Approach for Reporting Infrastructure Assets

152. Governments may begin to use the modified approach for reporting eligible infrastructure assets (as described in paragraphs 23–25) as long as at least one complete condition assessment is available and the government documents that the eligible infrastructure assets are being preserved approximately at (or above) the condition level the government has established and disclosed.

153. The three most recent complete condition assessments and the estimated and actual amounts to maintain and preserve the infrastructure assets for the previous five reporting periods required by paragraph 132 may not be available initially. In these cases, the information required by that paragraph should be presented for as many complete condition assessments and years of estimated and actual expenses as are available.

## Initial Capitalization of General Infrastructure Assets

### Determining Major General Infrastructure Assets

154. At the applicable general infrastructure transition date, phase 1 and 2 governments are required to capitalize and report major general infrastructure assets that were acquired (purchased, constructed, or donated)[67] in fiscal years ending after June 30, 1980, or that received major renovations, restorations, or improvements during that period.

---

[67] For purposes of this Statement, governments that have the primary responsibility for managing an infrastructure asset should report the asset. A government should report an asset even if it has contracted with a third party to maintain the asset.

155. The approaches in paragraphs 158 through 160 may be used to estimate the costs of existing general infrastructure assets when actual historical cost data are not available. These approaches are examples only; governments may use any approach that complies with the intent of this Statement. General infrastructure assets acquired after the effective dates of this Statement should be reported using historical costs.

156. The determination of major general infrastructure assets should be at the network or subsystem level and should be based on these criteria:

a.  The cost or estimated cost of the subsystem is expected to be at least 5 percent of the total cost of all general capital assets reported in the first fiscal year ending after June 15, 1999, *or*
b.  The cost or estimated cost of the network is expected to be at least 10 percent of the total cost of all general capital assets reported in the first fiscal year ending after June 15, 1999.

Reporting of nonmajor networks is encouraged but not required.

**Establishing Capitalization at Transition**

157. The initial capitalization amount should be based on historical cost. If determining historical cost is not practical because of inadequate records, estimated historical cost may be used.

*Estimated Historical Cost—Current Replacement Cost*

158. A government may estimate the historical cost of general infrastructure assets by calculating the current replacement cost of a similar asset and deflating this cost through the use of price-level indexes to the acquisition year (or estimated acquisition year if the actual year is unknown). There are a number of price-level indexes that may be used, both private- and public-sector, to remove the effects of price-level changes from current prices. Accumulated depreciation would be calculated based on the deflated amount, except for general infrastructure assets reported according to the modified approach.

159. The following example illustrates the calculation of estimated historical cost. In 1998, a government has sixty-five lane-miles of roads in a secondary road subsystem, and the current construction cost of similar roads is $1 million per lane-mile. The estimated total current replacement cost of the secondary road subsystem of a highway network, therefore, is $65 million ($1 million x 65). The roads have an estimated weighted-average age of fifteen years; therefore, 1983 is considered to be the acquisition year. Based on the U.S. Department of Transportation, Federal Highway Administration's

*Price Trend Information for Federal-Aid Highway Construction* (publication number FHWA-IF-99-001) for 1983 and 1998, 1983 construction costs were 69.03 percent of 1998 costs. The estimated historical cost of the subsystem, therefore, is $44,869,500 ($65 million x 0.6903). In 1998, the government would have reported the subsystem in its financial statements at an estimated historical cost of $44,869,500 less accumulated depreciation for fifteen years based on that deflated amount.

### Estimated Historical Cost from Existing Information

160. Other information may provide sufficient support for establishing initial capitalization. This information includes bond documents used to obtain financing for construction or acquisition of infrastructure assets, expenditures reported in capital project funds or capital outlays in governmental funds, and engineering documents.

## Methods for Calculating Depreciation

161. Governments may use any established depreciation method. Depreciation may be based on the estimated useful life of a class of assets, a network of assets, a subsystem of a network, or individual assets. For estimated useful lives, governments can use (a) general guidelines obtained from professional or industry organizations, (b) information for comparable assets of other governments, or (c) internal information. In determining estimated useful life, a government also should consider an asset's present condition and how long it is expected to meet service demands.

162. Continuing the example from paragraph 159, assume that, in 1998, the road subsystem had a total estimated useful life of twenty-five years from 1983 and therefore has an estimated remaining useful life of ten years. Assuming no residual value at the end of that time, straight-line depreciation expense would be $1,794,780 per year ($44,869,500 ₃ 25), and accumulated depreciation in 1998 would be $26,921,700 ($1,794,780 ´ 15).

### Composite Methods

163. Governments also may use composite methods to calculate depreciation expense. Composite methods refer to depreciating a grouping of similar assets (for example, interstate highways in a state) or dissimilar assets of the same class (for example, all the roads and bridges of a state) using the same depreciation rate. Initially, a depreciation rate for the composite is determined. Annually, the determined rate is multiplied by the cost of the grouping of assets to calculate depreciation expense.

164. A composite depreciation rate can be calculated in different ways. The rate could be calculated based on a weighted average or on an unweighted-average estimate of useful lives of assets in the composite. For example, the composite depreciation rate of three interstate highways with estimated remaining useful lives of sixteen, twenty, and twenty-four years could be calculated using an unweighted average estimated as follows:

$$\frac{1}{(16 + 20 + 24)/3} = 5\% \text{ annual depreciation rate}$$

A composite depreciation rate may also be calculated based on an assessment of the useful lives of the grouping of assets. This assessment could be based on condition assessments or experience with the useful lives of the grouping of assets. For example, based on experience, engineers may determine that interstate highways generally have estimated remaining useful lives of approximately twenty years. In this case, the annual depreciation rate would be 5 percent.

165. The composite depreciation rate is generally used throughout the life of the grouping of assets. However, it should be recalculated if the composition of the assets or the estimate of average useful lives changes significantly. The average useful lives of assets may change as assets are capitalized or taken out of service.

166. The annual depreciation expense is calculated by multiplying the annual depreciation rate by the cost of the assets. For example, if the interstate highway subsystem cost $100 million and the annual depreciation rate was 10 percent, then the annual depreciation charge would be $10 million. Accumulated depreciation should not exceed the reported cost of the assets.

**The provisions of this Statement need
not be applied to immaterial items.**

*This Statement was adopted by unanimous vote of the seven members of
the Governmental Accounting Standards Board:*

> Tom L. Allen, *Chairman*
> Robert J. Freeman, *Vice-chairman*
> Cynthia B. Green
> Barbara A. Henderson
> Edward M. Klasny
> Edward J. Mazur
> Paul R. Reilly

# Accounting Resources on the Web

Presented here are World Wide Web URLs of interest to governmental accountants. Because of the constantly changing nature of the Internet, addresses change and new resources become available every day. To find additional resources, use search engines such as HotBot (http://www.hotbot.lycos.com/), the Open Directory Project (http://www.dmoz.org/), and Yahoo! (http://www.yahoo.com).

**AICPA** http://www.aicpa.org

**American Accounting Association** http://accounting.rutgers.edu/raw/aaa/

**American Center for Continuing Professional Education** http://www.ACCPE.com/

**Aspen Publishers, Inc.** http://www.aspenpublishers.com/

**Aspen Law & Business** http://www.aspenlawdirect.com/

**Aspen Miller Series** http://www.millerseries.com/

**Code of Federal Regulations** http://www.access.gpo.gpv/nara/cfr/index.html

**ePace! Software** http://www.epacesoftware.com

**FASB** http://accounting.rutgers.edu/raw/fasb/

**Federal Register** http://www.access.gpo.gov/su_dpcs/aces/aces140.html

**Federal Tax Code Search** http://www.tns.lcs.mit.edu/uscode/

**Fedworld** http://www.fedworld.gov/

**FinanceNet** http://www.financenet.gov/financenet/state/cafr.htm

**GASB** http://accounting.rutgers.edu/raw/fasb/

**General Accounting Office** http://www.gao.gov/

**IRS Digital Daily** http://www.irs.gov/

**Library of Congress** http://www.loc.gov

**Loislaw** http://www.loislaw.com

**National Archives and Records Administration Code of Federal Regulations** http://www.access.gpo.gov/nara/cfr/index.html

**Office of Management and Budget** http://www.whitehouse.gov/omb

**Thomas Legislative Research** http://thomas.loc.gov/

**U.S. House of Representatives** http://www.house.gov/

**U.S. Senate** http://www.senate.gov/

**The White House** http://www.whitehouse.gov

# Index

## A

Accountability, 1-3—1-4
Accounting and Financial Reporting for Certain Investments and for External Investment Pools (GASB-31). *See* GASB-31
Accounting changes. *See* Changes in accounting estimates; Changes in accounting principles
Accounting Principles Board (APB) Opinions. *See* APB Opinions
Accounting Research Bulletins (ARBs) of the Committee on Accounting Procedure
  Enterprise Funds, 7-3
  proprietary fund accounting, 1-10—1-11
Accrual basis of accounting, 1-8. *See also* Converting from modified accrual to accrual basis
  government-wide financial statements, 1-6, 1-8
  unrestricted operating grant revenue, 2-36
Accrual for Claims/Assessments and Compensated Absences
  General Fund, worksheet conversion entry, 2-40—2-42
Accrual of expenses
  current period transactions, 1-44—1-45
  previous year's balances, 1-45—1-46
  worksheet conversion entries, 1-45—1-46
  worksheet conversion entry checklist, 1-13
Accrual of revenues
  current period transactions, 1-46—1-47
  previous year's balances, 1-47—1-48
  worksheet conversion entries, 1-47—1-48
  worksheet conversion entry checklist, 1-13

Accrual trial balances
  governmental activities, 13-2—13-4
Advance refundings of debt, 1-21—1-22
  worksheet conversion entry checklist, 1-12
Agency Funds
  basis of accounting, 11-1—11-2
  new standard, 11-2
  financial statements for fund types, 1-9
  fund financial statements, 11-5
  fund level financial reporting, 11-2
  government-wide financial statements, 11-5
  government-wide level financial reporting, 11-2—11-3
  illustration, 1-61
  illustrative transactions, 11-3—11-4
  measurement focus, 11-1—11-2
  new standard, 11-2
  nature of fund, 11-1
  statement of fiduciary net assets, 11-5, 11-7
  worksheet for summarizing transactions, 11-6
Allocation of operating results of Internal Service Fund, 8-29—8-31
Alternative 1 for proprietary fund accounting. *See* GASB-20, Alternative 1; GASB-20, Alternative 2
Amortization of discount/premium, 1-17
  discount bonds, 1-19—1-20
  exceptions, 1-18—1-19
Analysis of year ended June 30, 20X1, 1-14—1-15
APB Opinion 12 (Omnibus Opinion—1967)
  debt discounts, 1-18
APB Opinion 20 (Accounting Changes), 1-38
APB Opinion 21 (Interest on Receivables and Payables), 1-40, 1-41

APB Opinion 27 (Interest on Receivables and Payables)
debt discounts, 1-18
APB Opinion 29 (Accounting for Nonmonetary Transactions), 1-29, 1-33
APB Opinion 30 (Reporting the Results of Operations—Reporting the Effects of Disposal of a Segment of a Business, and Extraordinary, Unusual and Infrequently Occurring Events and Transactions), 1-48
APB Opinions
  Enterprise Funds, 7-3
  government-wide financial statements, new standard, 1-10
  proprietary fund accounting, 1-10—1-11
Appropriated budget requirement, 15-4
ARBs
  Enterprise Funds, 7-3
  proprietary fund accounting, 1-10—1-11
Assessment of accountability, 1-3—1-4

# B

Balances and transactions analysis
  management's discussion and analysis, 15-26—15-27
Balance sheets
  Capital Projects Funds, 4-3, 4-14, 4-25
  Debt Service Funds, 5-3, 5-13, 5-24
  exhibit, 14-29
  General Fund, 2-6, 2-32—2-33
  governmental funds. *See* Governmental fund financial statements
  Permanent Funds, 6-8, 6-11
  reconciliation to statement of net assets (exhibit), 14-30
  Special Revenue Funds, 3-2, 3-10, 3-16—3-19
Basic financial statements, 14-1
  balance sheet, governmental funds (exhibit), 14-29
  components of net assets, business-type activities, 14-24
  components of net assets, governmental activities, 14-22
  exhibits, 14-24—14-40
  introduction, 14-2
  management's discussion and analysis (Appendix 15), 15-15—15-26
  Reconciliation of Statement of Revenues, Expenditures, and Changes in Fund Balances of Governmental Funds to the Statement of Activities, 14-32
  Reconciliation of the Balance Sheet of Governmental Funds to the Statement of Net Assets, 14-30
  reconciliations for business-type activities, 14-19—14-22
  reconciliations for governmental activities, 14-2—14-19
  Statement of Activities, 14-27
  Statement of Cash Flows—Proprietary Funds, 14-37
  Statement of Changes in Fiduciary Net Assets, 14-40
  Statement of Fiduciary Net Assets, 14-39
  Statement of Net Assets, 14-25
  Statement of Net Assets—Proprietary Funds, 14-33
  Statement of Revenues, Expenditures, and Changes in Fund Balances—Governmental Funds, 14-31
  Statement of Revenues, Expenditures, and Changes in Fund Balances—Proprietary Funds, 14-35
Basic Financial Statements—and Management's Discussion and Analysis—for Public Colleges and Universities. *See* GASB-35
Basic Financial Statements—and Management's Discussion and Analysis—for State and Local Governments. *See* GASB-34
Billings, interfund, 2-5—2-6
Billings to external parties, 8-30—8-31
Bonds
  amortization, 1-17
  Debt Service Funds, 5-4—5-19
  required supplementary information, 15-12—15-14

Budget, 1-4
Budgetary comparison schedules,
　15-4—15-8
　illustration, 15-5—15-7
　management's discussion and
　　analysis, 15-27—15-29
　new standard, 15-4, 15-7—15-8
　Special Revenue Funds, new
　　standard, 3-3
Budgetary highlights
　management's discussion and
　　analysis, 15-27
Budgetary information, journalizing
　General Fund, 2-10
Business-type activities
　components of net assets, 13-30,
　　14-24
　Enterprise Funds, 7-2—7-3, 7-5
　new standard, 7-6
　government-wide financial
　　statements, 13-16—13-30
　Internal Service Funds, 8-4, 13-19—
　　13-20
　management's discussion and
　　analysis, 15-26
　proprietary fund accounting, 1-10—
　　1-11
　reclassification of account
　　balances, 13-20—13-30
　reconciliations for, 14-19—14-22

## C

Capital assets
　changes in accounting estimates,
　　1-39—1-40
　cost of construction, new standard,
　　4-6
　donations of capital assets from
　　outside parties, 1-33—1-34
　donations of capital assets to
　　outside parties, 1-34
　gains and losses related to capital
　　asset dispositions, 1-28—1-29,
　　1-34—1-35
　General Fund, beginning of year
　　balances, 2-43—2-44
　General Fund, current period
　　transactions, 2-37—2-39
　illustration of disclosure require-
　　ments, 15-9—15-12
　invested in, 14-22
　involuntary conversions, 1-35—1-36
　management's discussion and
　　analysis, 15-30—15-31
　nonmonetary exchanges. *See*
　　Nonmonetary exchanges
　previous year's balances, 1-24—1-25
　required supplementary informa-
　　tion, 15-8—15-12
　statement of net assets, new
　　standard, 1-24
　worksheet conversion entry
　　checklist, 1-13
Capital expenditures
　worksheet conversion entries for
　　current period transactions,
　　1-23—1-24
　worksheet conversion entry
　　checklist, 1-13
Capital leases
　current period transactions, 1-25—
　　1-26, 2-34—2-36
　General Fund, 2-34—2-36
　previous year's balances, 1-26—1-28
　required supplementary informa-
　　tion (RSI), 15-12
　worksheet conversion entries,
　　1-26—1-28, 2-34—2-36
　worksheet conversion entry
　　checklist, 1-13
Capital Projects Funds
　adjusted trial balances (Appendix
　　4F), 4-30
　balance sheet, 4-3, 4-14, 4-25
　basis of accounting, 4-2—4-3
　Bland Street Drainage Project, 4-8—
　　4-10
　Bland Street Drainage Project,
　　worksheet conversion entries,
　　4-16—4-17
　Bland Street Drainage Project,
　　worksheet conversion entries
　　(Appendix 4B), 4-21—4-22
　converting to accrual based
　　financial statements, 4-15
　Easely Street Bridge Project, 4-5—
　　4-8
　Easely Street Bridge Project, work-
　　sheet conversion entries, 4-16
　Easely Street Bridge Project, work-
　　sheet for summarizing current
　　transactions (Appendix 4A),
　　4-19—4-20

Capital Projects Funds, *(cont.)*
  expenditures, recording of, 4-3
  financial statements for fund types, 1-8
  fund financial statements, 4-13
  fund level financial reporting, 4-3—4-4
  government-wide financial reporting, 4-4
  illustration, 1-59—1-60
  illustrative transactions, 4-4—4-15
  interfund transfers, 1-54
  major funds, new standard for reporting, 4-4
  measurement focus, 4-2—4-3
  nature of fund, 4-1—4-2
  statement of revenues, expenditures, and changes, 4-3, 4-4-26—4-27, 4-14—4-15
  West End Center Recreation Project, worksheet conversion entries (Appendix 4C), 4-23—4-24
  West End Recreation Center Project, 4-11—4-13
  West End Recreation Center Project, worksheet conversion entries, 4-17—4-18
  worksheets for summarizing current transactions (Appendix 4A, 4B, 4C), 4-19—4-24
  worksheet to convert to accrual basis (Appendix 4E), 4-19—4-24
Certain financial note disclosures. *See* Disclosures; GASB-38
Changes in accounting estimates, 1-39—1-40
  worksheet conversion entry checklist, 1-13
Changes in accounting principles
  new standard, 1-38
  worksheet conversion entries, 1-37—1-38
  worksheet conversion entry checklist, 1-13
Claims/Assessments and Compensated Absences
  General Fund, worksheet conversion entry, 2-40—2-42
Claims/judgments
  General Fund, 2-45
  required supplementary information, 15-12
Colleges and universities. *See* Public colleges and universities
Committee on Accounting Procedures
  government-wide financial statements, new standard, 1-10
Compensated absences
  General Fund, worksheet conversion entries, 2-40—2-42, 2-45
  required supplementary information, 15-12
Components of net assets. *See* Net assets
Component units funds
  financial statements for fund types, 1-9
Component units of primary government
  fund financial statements, 1-10
Converting from modified accrual to accrual basis
  Capital Projects Funds, 4-15, 4-28—4-29
  Debt Service Funds, 5-14
  Enterprise Funds, 7-42
  General Fund. *See* General Fund
  Internal Service Funds, 8-28
  methodology, 1-11—1-12
  Special Revenue Funds, 3-11—3-13
  worksheet conversion entry checklist, 1-12—1-14

# D

Debt
  advance refundings, 1-21—1-22
  early extinguishments, 1-22—1-23
  issuance of, 1-14—1-15
  long-term debt. *See* Long-term debt
Debt discounts
  amortization of discount/premium, 1-17
  deep-discount debt, 1-18
Debt funds
  illustration, 1-60
Debt Service Funds
  adjusted trial balances (accrual basis), 5-28
  balance sheet, 5-3, 5-13, 5-24
  basis of accounting, 5-2—5-3
  Bland Street Drainage Bonds, 5-8—5-10

Bland Street Drainage Bonds, worksheet conversion entries, 5-17—5-18
Bland Street Drainage Bonds, worksheet for summarizing (Appendix 5C), 5-22
converting to government-wide financial statements, 5-14—5-19, 5-26—5-27
debt outstanding at beginning of the year, 5-15
Easely Street Bridge Bonds, 5-7—5-8
Easely Street Bridge Bonds, worksheet conversion entries, 5-16—5-17
Easely Street Bridge Bonds, worksheet for summarizing (Appendix 5B), 5-21
expenditures, recording of, 5-3
financial statements for fund types, 1-8
fund financial statements, 5-12—5-14
fund level financial reporting, 5-3—5-4
government-wide financial reporting, 5-4
illustrative transactions, 5-4—5-12
measurement focus, 5-2—5-3
nature of fund, 5-2
Senior Citizens' Center Bonds, 5-4—5-6
Senior Citizens' Center Bonds, worksheet conversion entries, 5-15—5-16
Senior Citizens' Center Bonds, worksheet for summarizing (Appendix 5A), 5-20
statement of revenues, expenditures, and changes, 5-3, 5-13—5-14, 5-25
transfers, new standard, 5-2—5-3
West End Recreation Center Bonds, 5-10—5-12
West End Recreation Center Bonds, worksheet conversion entries, 5-18—5-19
West End Recreation Center Bonds, worksheet for summarizing (Appendix 5D), 5-23
worksheets for summarizing current transactions (Appendix 5A—5D), 5-20—5-23
worksheet to convert to accrual method (Appendix 5F), 5-26—5-27
Debt service requirements disclosure, new standard, 15-13
Debt service transactions, 1-15—1-16
amortization of discount/premium, 1-17
interest paid during the year, 1-16
principal repaid during the year, 1-16—1-17
worksheet conversion entry checklist, 1-12
Deep-discount debt
defined, 1-18
worksheet conversion entry checklist, 1-12
Deferred revenue account
General Fund, 2-11
Defined benefit pension plans
public employee retirement system and, 9-1
Depreciable assets
changes in accounting estimates, 1-39—1-40
Depreciation expense
Enterprise Funds accounting, new standard, 7-3
Enterprise Funds infrastructure assets, new standard, 7-10—7-11
General Fund, worksheet conversion entries, 2-39—2-40
General Fund infrastructure assets, new standard, 2-39—2-40
Direct financing lease, 1-43
Disclosures. *See also* GASB-38; Required Supplementary Information
capital asset disclosures, 15-8—15-12
certain note disclosures, 15-8—15-14
long-term liabilities, 15-12—15-14
Discount bonds
amortization, 1-19—1-21
worksheet conversion entries, 1-20—1-21
worksheet conversion entry checklist, 1-12
Discount/premium amortization. *See* Amortization of discount/premium

Donations of capital assets
  from outside parties, 1-33—1-34
  to outside parties, 1-34
  worksheet conversion entries, 1-33—1-34
  worksheet conversion entry checklist, 1-13

# E

Early extinguishments of debt, 1-22—1-23
  worksheet conversion entry checklist, 1-12
Economic factors, relevant management's discussion and analysis, 15-32—15-33
Effective dates, 1-58—1-59
Eliminations of transfers, 1-52—1-55
  worksheet reclassification entries, 1-13
Encumbrances
  disclosure requirements, new standard, 2-10
Enterprise Funds
  basis of accounting, 7-2—7-3
  business-type activities, 7-2—7-3, 7-5, 13-16
    new standard, 7-6
  Centerville Municipal Airport, 7-28—7-35
  Centerville Municipal Airport (Appendix 7D), 7-55—7-59
  Centerville Parking Authority, 7-21—7-28
  Centerville Parking Authority (Appendix 7C), 7-51—7-54
  Centerville Toll Bridge, 7-6—7-14
  Centerville Toll Bridge (Appendix 7A), 7-43—7-46
  Centerville Utilities Authority, 7-14—7-21
  Centerville Utilities Authority (Appendix 7B), 7-47—7-50
  combining and reclassifying accounts, 13-16—13-30
  combining trial balances for nonmajor Enterprise Funds, 12-18—12-19
  converting to government-wide financial statements, 7-42
  criteria established by GASB-34, new standard, 7-2
  depreciation expense, new standard, 7-3
  depreciation of infrastructure assets, new standard, 7-10—7-11
  external users, new standard, 7-2
  financial statements for fund types, 1-8
  fund financial statements, 7-35—7-41, 12-2—12-5, 15-18
  fund level financial reporting, 7-3—7-5
  government-wide financial reporting, 2-8, 7-5—7-6
  government-wide financial statements, 13-16—13-30
  illustration, 1-60
  illustrative transactions, 7-6—7-35
  interfund loans, 1-52—1-53
  interfund transfers and reimbursements, 1-54—1-55
  major funds, identifying, 12-2—12-5
  major funds, new standard, 7-4
  management's discussion and analysis (Appendix 15), 15-18
  measurement focus, 7-2—7-3
  nature of fund, 7-1—7-2
  Proprietary Fund financial statements, 12-18—12-19
  special items, new standard, 7-25
  statement of cash flows, 7-3, 7-39—7-41, 7-64—7-66
  statement of cash flows, new standard, 7-4, 7-41
  statement of net assets, 7-3, 7-35—7-38, 7-60—7-62
  statement of net assets, new standard, 7-4—7-5
  statement of revenues, expenses, and changes in fund net assets, 7-3, 7-38—7-39, 7-62—7-64
    new standard, 7-11—7-12
  transfers, new standard, 7-3
  worksheets for summarizing current transactions (Appendix 7A, 7B, 7C, 7D), 7-43—7-59
Escheat property
  new standard, 10-3, 11-2
Exchange transactions
  accrual basis of accounting, 1-8
  General Fund, 2-2, 2-3
  nonmonetary exchanges. *See* Nonmonetary exchanges
  revenue recognition, 2-2, 2-3

Expendable Trust Fund
  new standard, 3-2
Expenditure recognition, 2-4. See also GASBI-6
Extraordinary items
  General Fund, new standard, 2-18
  General Fund, worksheet conversion entry, 2-40
  worksheet conversion entries, 1-48
  worksheet conversion entry checklist, 1-13

# F

FAS-5 (Accounting for Contingencies), 1-45
FAS-13 (Accounting for Leases), 1-25, 1-41
FAS-34 (Capitalization of Interest Cost)
  construction of capital asset, new standard, 4-6
FASB Statements and Interpretations
  deep-discount debt, 1-18
  Enterprise Funds, 7-3
  government-wide financial statements, new standard, 1-10
  Interpretation 30 (Accounting for Involuntary Conversions of Nonmonetary Assets to Monetary Assets), 1-35—1-36
  proprietary fund accounting, 1-10—1-11
Fiduciary fund financial statements
  developing information for, 12-27—12-29
  management's discussion and analysis, 15-18
  statement of changes in fiduciary net assets, 12-28, 14-40
  statement of fiduciary net assets, 12-27—12-28, 14-39—14-40
Fiduciary funds
  Agency Funds. See Agency Funds
  comprehensive illustration, 1-61
  financial statements for fund types, 1-9
  fund financial statements. See Fiduciary fund financial statements
  government-wide financial statements, 1-9, 1-11
  Pension Trust Funds. See Pension Trust Funds
  Private-Purpose Trust Funds. See Private-Purpose Trust Funds
Final budget requirement, 15-4
Financial Accounting Standards Board. See FASB Statements and Interpretations
Financial position and operations overview
  management's discussion and analysis, 15-20—15-22
Financial reporting for Defined Benefit Pension Plans and Notes Disclosures for Defined Contribution Plans (GASB-25). See GASB-25
Financial statements. See Basic financial statements; Fund financial statements; Government-wide financial statements
Fines and forfeitures, classification of revenues
  new standard, 13-16
Flow of current financial resources, 1-4, 1-6
Fuel taxes, local. See Local Fuel Tax Fund
Fund balances and transactions analysis
  management's discussion and analysis, 15-26—15-27
Fund financial statements
  accrual of liabilities, 1-6—1-7
  Agency Funds, 11-5
  Capital Projects Funds, 4-13—4-15
  converting information from modified accrual to accrual basis, 1-11, 1-12
  Debt Service Funds, 5-12—5-14
  developing information for. See Fund financial statements, developing information for
  Enterprise Funds, 7-35—7-41, 12-2—12-5
  fiduciary fund financial statements. See Fiduciary fund financial statements
  fiduciary fund information, 1-11
  fund types, 1-8—1-9
  General Fund, 2-31—2-33, 12-2—12-3
  governmental funds. See Governmental funds

Fund financial statements, *(cont.)*
  implementation of GASB-34 standards, 1-5
  Internal Service Funds, 8-23—8-28, 15-18
  major funds, identifying, 12-2—12-5
  management's discussion and analysis, 15-16—15-18
  modified accrual basis of accounting, 1-4 , 1-5
  pension trust funds, 9-2—9-3, 9-6—9-7
  Permanent Funds, 6-7—6-8
  Private-Purpose Trust Funds, 10-5—10-6, 10-8—10-9
  Proprietary Funds. *See* Proprietary Fund financial statements
  reconciliations, 14-2—14-22
  Special Revenue Funds, 3-9—3-11
  statement of net assets, new standard, 7-4—7-5
Fund financial statements, developing information for, 12-1—12-29
  fiduciary fund financial statements, 12-27—12-29
  governmental fund financial statements, 12-5—12-17
  identifying a major fund, 12-2—12-5
  introduction, 12-1—12-2
  Proprietary Funds financial statements, 12-17—12-27
Fund level financial reporting
  Agency Funds, 11-2
  Capital Projects Funds, 4-3—4-4
  Debt Service Funds, 5-3—5-4
  Enterprise Funds, 7-3—7-5
  establishment of GASB-34 standards, 1-5
  General Fund, 2-6—2-7
  Internal Service Funds, 8-3—8-4
  Permanent Funds, 6-3—6-4
  Private-Purpose Trust Funds, 10-2—10-3
  Special Revenue Funds, 3-2—3-3
Fund types, 1-8—1-9

# G

Gains and losses related to capital asset dispositions
  worksheet conversion entries, 1-28—1-29 , 1-34—1-35
  worksheet conversion entry checklist, 1-13
GASB-9 (Reporting Cash Flows of Proprietary and Nonexpendable Trust Funds and Governmental Entities that Use Proprietary Fund Accounting)
  Enterprise Funds, new standard, 7-4, 7-11—7-12
  Internal Service Funds, new standard, 8-9
GASB-14 (The Financial Reporting Entity)
  concept of primary government, 1-9
  General Fund financial statements, new standard, 2-34
GASB-20 (Accounting and Financial Reporting for Proprietary Funds and Other Governmental Entities That Use Proprietary Fund Accounting), 7-3
  Alternative 1, 1-10
  Alternative 2, 1-10—1-11
  Enterprise Funds, Alternative 1, 7-2—7-3
  Enterprise Funds, Alternative 2, 7-2—7-3
  Internal Service Funds, Alternative 1, 8-2
  Internal Service Funds, Alternative 2, 8-2
  Private-Purpose Trust Funds, 10-2
GASB-24 (Accounting and Financial Reporting for Certain Grants and Other Financial Assistance), 3-2
GASB-25 (Financial reporting for Defined Benefit Pension Plans and Notes Disclosures for Defined Contribution Plans)
  public employee retirement system, applicable to, 9-1—9-2
GASB-31 (Accounting and Financial Reporting for Certain Investments and for External Investment Pools)
  Pension Trust Funds, 9-2
GASB-33 (Accounting and Financial Reporting for Nonexchange Transactions)
  accrual basis of accounting, 1-8
  accrual basis of accounting, revenue recognition, 2-36

accrual of revenues—current period transactions, 1-46—1-47
availability of accrued revenue, new standard, 2-3
Capital Projects Fund, 4-2
General Fund, operating grant revenue, 2-36
General Fund, revenue recognition, 2-3
GASB-34 (Basic Financial Statements—and Management's Discussion and Analysis—for State and Local Governments), 1-3—1-5
application of standards, 1-4
colleges and universities, 1-4
effective implementation dates, 1-58—1-59
financial statements for fund types, 1-8—1-9
formatting guidelines for government-wide financial statements, 1-9—1-10, 1-11
Guide to Implementation of GASB Statement 34, 1-36
implementation issue, 1-5—1-6
text of statement, APP-1
GASB-35 (Basic Financial Statements—and Management's Discussion and Analysis—for Public Colleges and Universities), 1-4
GASB-37 (Basic Financial Statements—and Management's Discussion and Analysis—for State and Local Governments)
budgetary comparison schedules, 15-7—15-8
classification of revenues, 13-16
cost of construction of capital asset, new standard, 4-6
Enterprise Funds business-type activities, new standard, 7-6
escheat property, new standard, 10-3, 11-2
major funds, identifying, 12-2
major funds, new standard, 7-4
relevant information, new standard, 15-3
revenues related to programs, new standard, 13-15
sale of long-term debt, new standard, 4-7

GASB-38 (Certain Financial Statement Note Disclosures)
availability criterion for recognized revenue, new standard, 2-3, 2-14
encumbrances disclosure requirement, new standard, 2-10
interfund transfers disclosure requirement, new standard, 2-28
receivables and payables, 13-16
short-term debt, new standard, 15-13—15-14
GASB Concept Statement No. 1. See GASB:CS-1
GASB:CS-1 (Objectives of Financial Reporting), 1-3
GASBI-6 (Recognition and Measurement of Certain Liabilities and Expenditures in Governmental Fund Financial Statements)
accrual of expenses, 1-44
accrual of liabilities, 1-6—1-7, 2-41
debt service payments, 5-5
debt service payments, new standard, 5-3
General Fund liabilities and expenditures, 2-4, 2-41
GASB pronouncements
deep-discount debt, 1-18
Enterprise Funds, 7-3
government-wide financial statements, new standard, 1-10
proprietary fund accounting, 1-10
General Fund
accrual for claims/assessments, 2-40—2-42
adjusted trial balance, 2-45—2-47, 2-65—2-67
balance sheet, 2-6, 2-32—2-33, 2-59—2-60
basis of accounting, 2-2—2-6
beginning of year balances, 2-43—2-47
budgetary comparison schedule, 15-4—15-8, 15-27—15-29
budgetary comparison schedule, new standard, 2-7
budgetary highlights, MD&A, 15-27
capital assets, beginning of year balances, 2-43—2-44
capital assets, current period transactions, 2-37—2-39

General Fund *(cont.)*
  capital leases, current period transactions, 2-34—2-36
  claims/judgments, 2-45
  compensated absences, 2-40—2-42, 2-45
  converting to accrual based financial statements, new standard, 2-34
  converting to accrual basis worksheet (Appendix 2C), 2-61—2-64
  converting to government-wide financial statements, 2-33
  current transactions, 2-34—2-43
  current transactions, worksheet for summarizing (Appendix 2A), 2-48—2-57
  deferred revenue account, 2-11
  depreciation expense, 2-39—2-40
  elimination of interfund transfers, 1-53—1-55
  encumbrances, 2-10
  exchange transactions, 2-2, 2-3
  expenditure recognition, 2-4
  expenditure reimbursement, 1-54, 2-6
  extraordinary items, 2-40
  extraordinary items, new standard, 2-18
  financial statements, 2-6, 2-31—2-33, 12-2—12-3
  financial statements for fund types, 1-8
  fund balance reservations, 2-6
  fund level financial reporting, 2-6—2-7
  government-wide financial reporting, 2-7—2-8
  illustrative transactions, 2-8—2-31
  infrastructure assets, new standard, 2-39—2-40
  interfund billings and activities, 2-5—2-6
  interfund loans, 1-52—1-53, 2-5
  interfund transfers, 1-54
  interfund transfers, new standard, 2-28
  journalizing budgetary information, 2-10
  liabilities and expenditures, 2-4
  long-term debt, 2-44—2-45
  major funds, 1-5, 2-6—2-7
  major funds, identifying, 12-2—12-3
  measurement focus, 2-2—2-6
  nature of fund, 2-2
  nonexchange transactions, 2-2—2-3
  nonmajor funds, 1-5
  other financing uses and sources, 2-5
  program revenue accruals, 2-43
  property tax revenue accrual, 2-42—2-43
  revenue recognition, 2-2—2-3
  revenue recognition disclosure requirements, new standard, 2-3, 2-14
  special items, new standard, 2-18
  statement of revenues, expenditures, and changes, 2-6, 2-31—2-33, 2-58—2-60
  new standard, 2-31
  unrestricted operating grants, 2-36
  worksheet conversion entries, 2-33—2-47
  worksheet for summarizing current transactions and adjustments (Appendix 2A), 2-48—2-57
  worksheet to convert to accrual basis (Appendix 2C), 2-61—2-64
General long-term liabilities government-wide financial statements, 1-7
General-purpose governments, 1-4
Governmental Accounting and Financial Reporting Principles (NCGA-1). *See* NCGA-1
Governmental activities
  accrual trial balances, 13-2—13-4
  categorization scheme, 14-16—14-17
  components of net assets, 14-22—14-24
  government-wide financial statements, 13-2—13-16
  management's discussion and analysis, 15-22—15-25
  merging Internal Service Funds, 13-5—13-8
  new standard, 13-6
  reclassification of account balances, 13-8—13-16
  new standards, 13-15—13-16
  reconciliations, 12-17, 14-2—14-19

Governmental fund financial
    statements
  balance sheet, 2-6, 12-15
  balance sheet (exhibit), 14-29
  balance sheet reconciliation
    (exhibit), 14-30
  combining trial balances for all
    governmental funds, 12-10—
    12-13
  combining trial balances for
    nonmajor funds, 12-6—12-10
  developing information, 12-5—
    12-17
  format, new standard, 1-56
  fund financial statements, 12-5—
    12-17
  fund level financial reporting, 2-
    6, 3-2—3-3
  fund types, 1-8
  issuance of debt, 1-14—1-15
  major funds, identifying, 12-2—
    12-5
  major funds, new standard, 1-9
  management's discussion and
    analysis, 15-17
  new standard for reporting major
    funds, 4-4
  reconciliations, 12-17, 14-30
  reservations, identifying, 12-13—
    12-14
  statement of revenues, expendi-
    tures, and changes in fund
    balances, 12-16—12-17
  terminology and format, 1-55—1-56
Governmental funds
  accrued liabilities, 1-6—1-7
  Capital Projects Funds. See
    Capital Projects Funds
  comprehensive illustration, 1-59—
    1-60
  converting information from
    modified accrual to accrual
    basis, 1-11
  Debt Service Funds. See Debt
    Service Funds
  fund financial statements. See
    Governmental fund financial
    statements
  General Fund. See General Fund
  issuance of debt, 1-14—1-15
  liabilities and expenditures, 2-4
  major funds, 1-8
    new standard, 2-6—2-7
  modified accrual basis of
    accounting, 1-6—1-7
  new standard for financial
    reporting, 4-4
  Permanent Funds. See Permanent
    Funds
  Special Revenue Funds. See
    Special Revenue Funds
  statement of revenues, expendi-
    tures, and changes in fund
    balances (exhibit), 14-31
Government-wide financial
    statements
  accrual basis of accounting, 1-6, 1-8
  accrual trial balances worksheet,
    13-2—13-4
  Agency Funds, 11-2—11-3, 11-5
  business-type activities, 13-16—
    13-30
    new standard, 13-21
  Capital Projects Funds, 4-4
  Capital Projects Funds,
    worksheet conversion entries,
    4-15—4-18
  City of Centerville MD&A (Appen-
    dix 15), 15-15—15-16, 15-19
  converting information from
    modified accrual to accrual
    basis, 1-11, 2-33
  Debt Service Funds, 5-4
  Debt Service Funds, worksheet
    conversion entries, 5-14—5-19
  developing information for. See
    Government-wide financial
    statements, developing
    information for
  Enterprise Funds, 7-5—7-6, 7-42
  General Fund, 2-7—2-8
  General Fund, worksheet conver-
    sion entries, 2-33—2-47
  general long-term liabilities, 1-7
  governmental activities, 13-2—
    13-16
    new standards, 13-15—13-16
  Internal Service Funds, 8-4, 8-28—
    8-36
  internal service funds, merging. See
    Merging internal service funds
  issuance of long-term debt, 1-15
  management's discussion and
    analysis (Appendix 15), 15-15—
    15-16
  overview, 1-5—1-6, 1-9—1-11

**IND-12** *Index*

Government-wide financial statements, *(cont.)*
  pension trust funds, 9-3, 9-8
  Permanent Funds, 6-4, 6-9
  Private-Purpose Trust Funds, 10-3, 10-6, 10-10
  pronouncements applied, new standard, 1-10
  reconciliations with fund financial statements, 12-17, 14-2—14-22
  Special Revenue Funds, 3-3
  Special Revenue Funds worksheet conversion entries, 3-11—3-13
  terminology and format, 1-56—1-58
  worksheet conversion entries for year ended June 30, 20X1, 1-14—1-55
  worksheet conversion entry checklist, 1-12—1-14
Government-wide financial statements, developing information for
  business-type activities, 13-16—13-30
  governmental activities, 13-2—13-16
  introduction, 13-1

# I

Interest and investment income
  Internal Service Fund, 8-29—8-30
Interest expense
  capital asset construction, new standard, 4-6
  on debt service, 1-16
  Internal Service Funds, 8-30
Interfund activities
  disclosure requirements, new standard, 2-28
  General Fund, 2-5—2-6, 2-28
  loans, 1-52—1-53, 2-5
  receivables/payables, 1-53, 2-5
  reimbursements, 1-54—1-55
  reporting interfund activities, new standard, 2-5, 2-6
  transfers, 1-53—1-54
Interfund service provided and used, 1-53
  new standard, 2-6
Internal balances, 1-52—1-55

  new standard, 13-15
  worksheet reclassification entries, 1-13
Internal Service Funds
  allocation of operating results, 8-29—8-31
  basis of accounting, 8-2—8-3
    new standard, 8-2
  billings to external parties, 8-30—8-31
  business-type activities, 8-4
  Communications and Technology Support Center, 8-5—8-11, 8-31—8-34, 8-37—8-40
  converting to government-wide financial statements, 8-28—8-36
  criteria established by GASB-34, new standard, 8-2
  Enterprise Fund vs., new standard, 7-2
  external users, new standard, 7-2
  financial statements for fund types, 1-8
  Fleet Management Unit, 8-11—8-17, 8-34—8-35, 8-41—8-44
  fund financial statements, 8-23—8-28, 15-18
  fund level financial reporting, 8-3—8-4
  general revenue, 8-29
  government-wide financial reporting, 8-4
  illustration, 1-60—1-61
  illustrative transactions, 8-4—8-23
  interest and investment income, 8-29—8-30
  interest expense, 8-30
  management's discussion and analysis (Appendix 15), 15-18
  measurement focus, 8-2—8-3
  merging into government-wide financial statements. *See* Merging Internal Service Funds
  nature of fund, 8-2
  program revenue, 8-29
  sales to external parties, 8-30—8-31
  Self-Insurance Fund, 8-2—8-3
  Special Services Support Center, 8-17—8-23, 8-35—8-36, 8-45—8-47
  statement of cash flows, 8-51—8-52
    new standard, 8-3, 8-26—8-28

statement of net assets, 8-23—8-24, 8-48—8-49
   new standard, 8-4
statement of revenues, expenses, and changes in fund net assets, 8-25—8-26, 8-50—8-51
   new standard, 8-9—8-10
transfers in/out, 8-30
worksheets for summarizing current transactions (Appendix 8A, 8B, 8C), 8-37—8-47
Interperiod equity, 1-3
Investment income of Internal Service Fund, 8-29—8-30
Investment trust funds
   financial statements for fund types, 1-9
Involuntary conversions of capital assets
   worksheet conversion entries, 1-35—1-36
   worksheet conversion entry checklist, 1-13
Issuance of debt
   worksheet conversion entry, 1-14—1-15

## L

Leasehold improvements
   worksheet conversion entries, 1-28
   worksheet conversion entry checklist, 1-13
Lease payments receivable
   direct financing lease, 1-43
   sales-type lease, 1-41—1-42
   worksheet conversion entries, 1-41—1-43
   worksheet conversion entry checklist, 1-13
Leases, capital. *See* Capital leases
Liabilities. *See also* Debt; Long-term debt
   accrual of, 1-6—1-7
   governmental funds, 2-4
Loans
   General Fund, 2-5
   interfund activities, 1-52—1-53, 2-5
Local Fuel Tax Fund
   Special Revenue Funds, 3-7—3-9
   worksheet conversion entry, 3-12
   worksheet for summarizing current transactions (Appendix 3C), 3-18—3-19
Long-term debt
   Capital Project Funds, new standard for sale of long-term debt, 4-7
   disclosures, 15-12—15-14
   new standards, 15-13
   General Fund, beginning of year balances, 2-45
   General Fund, worksheet conversion entries, 2-44—2-45
   management's discussion and analysis, 15-31—15-32
   previous year's balances, 1-15
   worksheet conversion entries, 1-15
   worksheet conversion entry checklist, 1-12
Long-term noninterest bearing notes receivable
   new standard, 1-41
   worksheet conversion entries, 1-40—1-41
   worksheet conversion entry checklist, 1-13
Losses. *See* Gains and losses related to capital asset dispositions

## M

Maintenance and preservation costs
   worksheet conversion entries, 1-36—1-37
   worksheet conversion entry checklist, 1-13
Major funds
   Capital Projects Funds, 4-4
   Enterprise Funds, new standard, 7-4
   5-percent threshold, 12-2, 12-4—12-5
   fund financial statements, 1-8—1-9
   new standard, 1-9, 4-4
   GASB-34 requirements, 1-5
   General Fund, 2-6—2-7, 12-2—12-3
   identifying, 12-2—12-5
   new standard, 12-2
   10-percent threshold, 12-2, 12-3—12-4

Management's discussion and
analysis (MD&A), 15-2—15-3
  basic financial statements
    (Appendix 15), 15-15—15-26
  business-type activities, 15-26
  capital assets, 15-30—15-31
  City of Centerville MD&A
    (Appendix 15), 15-15
  fund balances and transactions
    analysis, 15-26—15-27
  fund financial statements, 15-16—15-18
  general fund budgetary highlights,
    15-27—15-29
  governmental activities, 15-22—15-25
  governmental financial reporting,
    new standard for, 15-2
  government-wide financial
    statements (Appendix 15),
    15-15—15-16
  long-term obligations, 15-31—15-32
  nature and structure of MD&A,
    15-2—15-3
  overview of city financial position
    and operations, 15-20—15-22
  relevant economic factors,
    decisions, and conditions,
    15-32—15-33
  relevant information, new
    standard, 15-3
  request for information, 15-33
MD&A. *See* Management's
  discussion and analysis
Merging Internal Service Funds,
  1-49—1-52, 8-28—8-29, 8-54
  business-type activities, 13-19—13-20
  General Fund, 2-8
  governmental activities, 13-5—13-8
  new standard, 13-6
  proprietary fund accounting, 1-11
  worksheet reclassification entries,
    1-13
Modified accrual basis of accounting, 1-6—1-8. *See also* Converting from modified accrual to
  accrual basis
  current governmental accounting
    standards, 1-4
  fund financial statements, 1-4,
    1-5

# N

NCGA-1 (Governmental Accounting and Financial Reporting
  Principles), 1-7—1-8
  accrual of expenditure/liability,
    1-44, 2-40—2-41
  accrual of revenues—current
    period transactions, 1-46, 1-47
  budgetary information require-
    ment, 15-4
  Capital Projects Fund, 4-2
  Debt Service Fund, 5-2
  debt service transactions, 1-15
  encumbrances disclosure require-
    ment, new standard, 2-10
  Enterprise Funds, 7-3
  fund financial statements format,
    new standard, 2-31
  General Fund expenditure/
    liabilities, 2-40—2-41
  General Fund expenditure
    recognition, 2-4
  General Fund financial state-
    ments, 2-31
  governmental funds financial
    statements format, new
    standard, 1-56
  Permanent Fund, new standard,
    6-7
  Special Revenue Funds, 3-1—3-2
  statement of revenues, expendi-
    tures and changes, new
    standard, 6-7
NCGA-5 (Accounting and Finan-
  cial Reporting Principles for
  Lease Agreements of State and
  Local Governments), 1-25, 1-41
  capitalized lease, 2-34
NCGAI-6
  budgetary comparison schedule,
    15-5, 15-8
  debt service requirements disclo-
    sure, new standard, 15-13
NCGAI-10
  budgetary comparison schedule,
    15-5
NCGA pronouncements
  deep-discount debt, 1-18
  government-wide financial
    statements, 1-10
Net asset balance, 1-15

Net assets, components of
  business-type activities, 13-30, 14-24
  new standard, 13-30
  governmental activities, 14-22—14-24
Noncurrent monetary assets
  worksheet conversion entry checklist, 1-13
Nonexchange transactions. *See also* GASB-33
  accrual basis of accounting, 1-8
  GASB-33 standard, 2-11
  period of collectibility, new standard, 2-3
  unrestricted operating grants, 2-36
Nonexpendable trust funds
  new standard, 1-9, 6-2
Nonmajor funds
  Enterprise Funds, combining trial balances, 12-18—12-19
  GASB-34 requirements, 1-5
  governmental funds, combining trial balances, 12-6—12-10
Nonmonetary exchanges
  exchange of dissimilar capital assets, 1-29—1-30
  exchange of similar capital assets with a gain, 1-31—1-33
  exchange of similar capital assets with a loss, 1-30—1-31
  exchange of similar capital assets with boot involved, 1-32—1-33
  exchange of similar capital assets with no boot involved, 1-31
  worksheet conversion entries, 1-29—1-33
  worksheet conversion entry checklist, 1-13
Nonreciprocal interfund activity
  interfund reimbursements, 1-54—1-55
  interfund transfers, 1-53—1-54

# O

Objectives of Financial Reporting. *See* GASB:CS-1
Operating and other transactions, 1-13
Operating grants, unrestricted
  General Fund, 2-36

Operating statement vs. statement of activities
  new standard, 13-21
Operations and financial position overview
  management's discussion and analysis, 15-20—15-22
Original budget requirement, 15-4

# P

Pension Trust Funds
  basis of accounting, 9-2
  financial statements for fund types, 1-9
  fund financial statements, 9-2—9-3, 9-6—9-7
  fund level financial reporting, 9-2—9-3
  government-wide financial statements, 9-8
  government-wide level financial reporting, 9-3
  illustration, 1-61
  illustrative transactions, 9-3—9-6
  measurement focus, 9-2
  nature of fund, 9-1—9-2
  public employee retirement system (PERS) requirements, 9-1—9-2
  statement of changes in fiduciary net assets, 9-7
  statement of changes in plan net assets, 9-3
  statement of fiduciary net assets, 9-6—9-7
  statement of plan net assets, 9-2—9-3
  state public employees retirement fund, statement of fiduciary net assets and changes (Appendix 9B), 9-11
  state public employees retirement fund, worksheet for summarizing current transactions (Appendix 9A), 9-9
  worksheet for summarizing current transactions (Appendix 9A), 9-9
Permanent Funds
  adjustments not needed, 6-13
  balance sheet, 6-8, 6-11
  basis of accounting, 6-2—6-3

IND-16  *Index*

Permanent Funds, *(cont.)*
  contributions, new standard, 6-6
  converting to accrual based financial statements, 6-9
  donor-restricted endowments disclosure requirements, new standard, 6-6
  financial statements for fund types, 1-8
  fund financial statements, 6-7—6-8
  fund level financial reporting, 6-3—6-4
  fund types, new standard, 1-9
  government-wide financial reporting, 6-4
  government-wide financial statements, 6-9
  illustration, 1-60
  illustrative transactions, 6-4—6-8
  measurement focus, 6-2—6-3
  nature of fund, 6-1
  new standard, 6-2
  Nonexpendable Trust Funds, new standard, 6-2
  Private-Purpose Funds compared, 6-1
  restricted net assets, new standard, 6-2, 6-6
  statement of revenues, expenditures, and changes, 6-8, 6-11 to 6-12
    new standard, 6-7
  transfers, new standard, 6-3
  trial balance, year-end, 6-7
  trial balance for beginning of fiscal year, 6-4
  worksheet for summarizing current transactions (Appendix 6A), 6-10
Primary government
  government-wide financial statements, 1-9—1-10
Principal repaid on debt service, 1-16—1-17
Private-Purpose Trust Funds
  basis of accounting, 10-2
  new standard, 10-2
  fund financial statements, 10-5—10-6
  fund level financial reporting, 10-2—10-3
    new standard, 10-3
  fund types, new standard, 1-9
  government-wide financial statements, 10-6, 10-10
  government-wide level financial reporting, 10-3
  illustration, 1-61
  illustrative transactions, 10-3—10-5
  measurement focus, 10-2
  nature of fund, 10-1
  Permanent Funds compared, 6-1
  scholarship fund, worksheet for summarizing current transactions (Appendix 10A), 10-7
  statement of changes in fiduciary net assets, 10-6
  statement of changes in net assets, 10-2—10-3
  statement of fiduciary net assets, 10-5
  statement of net assets, 10-2—10-3
    new standard, 10-3
  worksheet for summarizing current transactions (Appendix 10A), 10-7
Program revenues
  General Fund, worksheet conversion entries, 2-43
  revenues related to programs, new standard, 13-15
Property tax revenue accrual
  General Fund, worksheet conversion entries, 2-42—2-43
Proprietary Fund financial statements
  combining trial balances for all Proprietary Funds, 12-19—12-21
  combining trial balances for nonmajor Enterprise Funds, 12-18—12-19
  developing information for, 12-17—12-27
  fund financial statements, 12-21—12-26
  management's discussion and analysis, 15-17—15-18
  reconciliations, 12-26—12-27
  statement of cash flows, 12-25—12-26, 14-37—14-39
  statement of net assets, 12-22—12-23, 14-33—14-34

statement of revenues, expenses, and changes in fund net assets, 12-23—12-24, 14-35
Proprietary Funds
  accounting alternatives. *See* GASB-20, Alternative 1; GASB-20, Alternative 2
  accrual basis, 1-11
  business-type activities, 1-11
  comprehensive illustration, 1-60—1-61
  Enterprise Funds. *See* Enterprise Funds
  financial statements for fund types, 1-8—1-9
  fund financial statements. *See* Proprietary Fund financial statements
  Internal Service Funds. *See* Internal Service Funds
  new standard for financial reporting, 4-4
  statement of cash flows, new standard, 7-4
Public colleges and universities
  new standard, 1-4
Public employee retirement system (PERS)
  GASB-25 requirements, 9-1—9-2

# R

Reciprocal interfund activity
  interfund loans, 1-52—1-53
  interfund receivables and payables, 1-53
Reclassifications in financial statements
  business-type activities, 13-20—13-30
  eliminations of transfers, 1-13
  governmental activities, 13-8—13-16
  new standards, 13-15—13-16
Reimbursements
  Enterprise Fund, 1-54
  General Fund, 1-54, 2-6
  nonreciprocal interfund activity, 1-54—1-55
Reporting entity
  primary government, 1-10

Request for information
  management's discussion and analysis, 15-33
Required Supplementary Information (RSI)
  budgetary comparison schedule, 15-4—15-8
  management's discussion and analysis, 15-2—15-3
Reservations
  General Fund, 2-6
  identification of, 12-13—12-14
Restricted net assets
  governmental activities, 14-22
Revenue recognition
  availability criterion, new standard, 2-3, 2-14
  exchange and nonexchange transactions, 2-2—2-3
  General Fund, 2-2—2-3
  period of collectibility, new standard, 2-3, 2-14
Revenue sources
  management's discussion and analysis, 15-23
RSI. *See* Required Supplementary Information

# S

Sales to external parties
  Internal Service Funds, 8-30—8-31
Sales-type lease, 1-41—1-42
Scholarship fund
  worksheet for summarizing current transactions (Appendix 10A), 10-7
Self-Insurance Internal Service Fund, 8-2—8-3
Services. *See* Debt Service Funds; Internal Service Funds; Special Services Fund
Short-term debt
  statement of net assets, new standard, 15-13—15-14
Special items
  Enterprise Funds, new standard, 7-25
  General Fund, new standard, 2-18
  worksheet conversion entries, 1-49
  worksheet conversion entry checklist, 1-13

**IND-18** *Index*

Special-purpose government
 implementation date, 1-59
Special Revenue Funds
 adjusted trial balances, 3-12—3-13,
  3-19
 balance sheet, 3-2, 3-10, 3-16
 basis of accounting, 3-2
 budgetary comparison schedule,
  15-4—15-8
 budgetary comparison schedule,
  new standard, 3-3
 converting to accrual based
  financial statements, 3-11—3-13
 Expendable Trust Fund, new
  standard, 3-2
 financial statements for fund
  types, 1-8
 fund financial statements, 3-9—3-11
 fund level financial reporting, 3-2—
  3-3
 government-wide financial
  reporting, 3-3
 illustration, 1-59
 illustrative transactions, 3-3—3-9
 interfund loans, 1-52
 Local Fuel Tax Fund, 3-7—3-9
 Local Fuel Tax Fund worksheet
  (Appendix 3C), 3-18—3-19
 Local Fuel Tax Fund worksheet
  conversion entry, 3-12
 measurement focus, 3-2
 nature of fund, 3-1—3-2
 Special Services Fund, 3-3—3-7
 Special Services Fund worksheet
  conversion entry, 3-12
 statement of revenues, expenditures, and changes in fund
  balances, 3-2, 3-10—3-11, 3-17
 new standard, 3-9—3-10
 worksheets for summarizing
  current transactions (Appendix 3A, Appendix 3C), 3-14—
  3-16, 3-18—3-19
Special Services Fund
 Special Revenue Funds, 3-3—3-7
 worksheet conversion entry,
  3-12
 worksheets for summarizing
  current transactions (Appendix 3A), 3-14—3-16
State and local governments,
 financial reporting by, 1-3—
 1-4

Statement of activities
 exhibit, 14-27—14-28
 government-wide financial
  statements, 13-20—13-21
 new standard, 13-21
 reclassification of account
  balances, 13-20—13-21
 reconciliation, statement of
  revenues, expenditures, and
  changes in fund balances, 14-32
Statement of cash flows
 Enterprise Funds, 7-3, 7-39—7-41,
  7-64—7-66
 new standard, 7-4, 7-41
 Internal Service Funds, 8-26—8-28,
  8-51—8-52
 new standard, 8-3
 Proprietary Funds, 12-25—12-26,
  14-37—14-39
Statement of changes in fiduciary
 net assets, 12-28—12-29, 14-40
 Pension Trust Funds, 9-7
 Private-Purpose Trust Funds, 10-6
Statement of changes in net assets
 Pension Trust Funds, 9-3
 Private-Purpose Trust Funds,
  10-2—10-3
Statement of fiduciary net assets,
 14-39—14-40
 Agency Funds, 11-5, 11-7
 developing information for fund
  financial statements, 12-27—
  12-28
 Pension Trust Funds, 9-6—9-7
 Private-Purpose Trust Funds, 10-
  5
Statement of net assets
 balance sheet reconciliation
  (exhibit), 14-30
 basic financial statement (exhibit), 14-25—14-26
 business-type activities, 13-30, 14-
  24
 capital assets, new standard, 1-24
 Enterprise Funds, 7-3, 7-35—7-38,
  7-60—7-62
 new standard, 7-4—7-5
 governmental activities, 14-22—
  14-24
 government-wide financial
  statements, 13-20, 13-30
 Internal Service Funds, 8-23—8-24,
  8-48—8-49

Index **IND-19**

new standard, 8-4
Pension Trust Funds, 9-2—9-3
Private-Purpose Trust Funds, 10-2—10-3
Proprietary Funds, 12-22—12-23, 14-33—14-34
short-term debt, new standard, 15-13—15-14
Statement of revenues, expenditures, and changes in fund balances
Capital Projects Funds, 4-3, 4-14—4-15, 4-26—4-27
new standard, 4-13
Debt Service Funds, 5-13—5-14
new standard, 5-12
format, new standard, 1-56
General Fund, 2-6, 2-31—2-33
new standard, 2-31
governmental funds, 12-16—12-17
governmental funds (exhibit) exhibit, 14-31
Permanent Funds, 6-8, 6-11—6-12
Permanent Funds, new standard, 6-7
Special Revenue Funds, 3-10—3-11, 3-17
new standard, 3-9—3-10
statement of activities, reconciliation, 14-32
Statement of revenues, expenses, and changes in fund net assets
Enterprise Funds, 7-38—7-39, 7-62—7-64
new standard, 7-11—7-12
Internal Service Funds, 8-25—8-26, 8-50—8-51
new standard, 8-9—8-10
Proprietary Funds, 12-23—12-24, 14-35

## T

Terminology and format
governmental funds financial statements, 1-55—1-56
government-wide financial statements, 1-56—1-58
worksheet reclassification entries, 1-13
Trade-ins. *See* Nonmonetary exchanges
Transfers
Internal Service Fund transfers in/out, 8-30
nonreciprocal interfund activity, 1-53—1-54

## U

Unmatured long-term indebtedness, 1-7
Unrestricted net assets
governmental activities, 14-22
Unrestricted operating grants
General Fund, 2-36

## W

Worksheet conversion entry checklist, 1-12—1-14

## Z

Zero-coupon bonds
worksheet conversion entries, 1-18—1-19
worksheet conversion entry checklist, 1-12
Zero-coupon debt
defined, 1-18